DURHAM PALS

DURHAM PALS

18th, 19th, & 22nd (Service) Battalions of
The Durham Light Infantry

A HISTORY OF THREE BATTALIONS RAISED BY LOCAL COMMITTEE IN COUNTY DURHAM

John Sheen

Pen & Sword
MILITARY

This book is dedicated to the memory of the Officers, Warrant Officers, Non Commissioned Officers and men of the

18th (Service) Battalion Durham Light Infantry (1st County) (Pals)
19th (Service) Battalion Durham Light Infantry (2nd County) (Bantams)
22nd (Service) Battalion Durham Light Infantry (3rd County) (Pioneers

First published in Great Britain in 2007 by
Pen & Sword Military
an imprint of
Pen & Sword Books Ltd
47 Church Street
Barnsley
South Yorkshire
S70 2AS

A CIP catalogue record for this book is
available from the British Library

Typeset in Palatino 9pt

Printed and bound in the United Kingdom by CPI

Pen & Sword Books Ltd incorporates the Imprints of Pen & Sword Aviation, Pen & Sword
Maritime, Pen & Sword Military, Wharncliffe Local History, Pen and Sword Select, Pen and
Sword Military Classics and Leo Cooper.
For a complete list of Pen & Sword titles, please contact
Pen & Sword Books Limited
47 Church Street, Barnsley, South Yorkshire, S70 2AS, England
E-mail: enquiries@pen-and-sword.co.uk
Website: www.pen-and-sword.co.uk

CONTENTS

FOREWORD

In 1998, after years of detailed and painstaking research, John Sheen's pioneering study of 'Tyneside Irish' was published to widespread acclaim. He then co-authored 'Tyneside Scottish' before turning his attention to a subject close to my own heart – The Durham Pals.

Having worked at the DLI Museum for thirty years, I had long been familiar with the superb collection of photographs taken of the 18th Battalion DLI – the original Durham Pals – in the first few months of the War, and of the extensive collection of official documents and private accounts and diaries of the DLI's Kitchener-raised battalions that were kept in the Regimental Archive. All these records needed, was someone with the skill and dedication to turn them into a coherent story. John Sheen has now succeeded in doing this and has produced a book that will be of value not simply to military and family historians but also to anyone interested in the history of County Durham.

In fact what was originally planned as one book has become two. The more John researched the book, the more it grew, as descendants of DLI soldiers sent him copies of letters, diaries and photographs all of which would be used to flesh out the bare bones of the official War Diaries and give the story the human dimension that is so often lacking in many military history books.

So now there are two books. This volume deals with the three battalions of the DLI raised by the Durham County Recruiting Committee, Pals, Bantams and Pioneers and here readers will follow these Pals from the first heady days of volunteering in the early autumn of 1914, to the German bombardment of Hartlepool at the end of that year, to the bloody fields of the Somme on 1st of July 1916, and on to the final victory of 1918. The story of the Wearsiders – the 20th Battalion DLI, raised by The Sunderland Recruiting Committee – will then have its own volume. Both will, I know, ensure that we do not ever forget the real sacrifices made by so many thousands of men who served in Durham Pals ninety years ago.

Steve Shannon
DLI MUSEUM & DURHAM ART GALLERY
January 2007

Sergeant Warwick and his section at Ripon, 1915.

The Pals in training whilst stationed at Cocken Hall, near Durham, autumn 1914.

7

ACKNOWLEDGEMENTS

Thanks are due to many people, and this work could not have been completed without the support of the Trustees of The Durham Light Infantry Museum and the advice and help of Steve Shannon and the late George Fraser at The Durham Light Infantry Museum. Indeed if not for Major Davidson's memoirs the story of the 22nd Battalion would have been hard to tell.

The staff at Durham City Library, Darlington Library, Hartlepool Library, Gateshead Library. The staff at Durham County Record Office in particular Gill Parkes for her assistance with photographs

Dr Alan Pearson Principal of The College of St Hild and St Bede Durham for permission to use the letters in *The Bede Magazine*.

The Librarian at Durham University Library for permission to use Colonel Lowe's papers.

The late Mr Malcolm MacGregor for assistance with Honours and Gallantry Awards to members of the 18th, 19th and 22nd Battalions.

Graham Stewart, Clive Dunn, Andrew Brookes, Fred Bromilow Simon Jervis, Stewart Couper, Michael Richardson all who loaned material from their collections.

I am very indebted to Julian Putowski for his assistance with the events at King Crater on 26 November 1916 and the subsequent Court-martials of Sergeant Stones and Lance Corporals Goggins and Macdonald.

My son, James, assisted with the research in the early stages, now a serving 'Tommy' or 'Squaddie' as they say today, in the Royal Electrical & Mechanical Engineers , I owe him thanks for his work at the National Archives.

Last but not least those relative's who loaned photographs of the soldiers:

Linda & Colin Barker	Sergeant Wilf Barker DCM 18th Bn
Mr A S Borrell	Captain Arthur Borrell 18th Bn
Simon Collins	Private G W Duthie 18th Bn
	Private H F Duthie 21st & 14th Bns
Michael Conroy	Private William Conroy 22nd Bn
Mr G H Dodsworth	Corporal W J J Dodsworh 18th Bn
Mrs Jane Easter	Private John Peacock 19th Bn
Mrs Gaynor Greenwood	Private Joseph Tombling 18th Bn
Kath Heywood	Corporal Henry W Pine 19th Bn
Mr Hanlon	Sergeant Jack Hanlon 20th Bn
Mrs F Kirby,	Private Henry Colwell MM 18th, 14th & 2nd Bns
	Private Mark Colwell 18th Bn
Mr R B Leake	Private Harold Leake 18th Bn
Mrs P McElhill	Private George Layfield 18th Bn
Mr A Merriweather	Lance Corporal A Merriweather. 18th Bn
Mr C Mitchell	CSM W Pearson 18th Bn
Mr Dean Moss	Lance Corporal Charles Moss 18th Bn.
Brian Scollen	Private Hugh Scollen 22nd Bn
Mr & Mrs R Sinclair	Lieutenant Braidford 19th Bn
	Private Jack Wilson 18th Bn
Mr G Storey	Private Ralph Storey 18th Bn
Mrs Nora Kerns	Sergeant Robert Wallis MM 19th Bn
Mr R F Wardle	Private J H Wardell 23rd & 19th Bns
Helen Zdrenka	Private Richard Hawksley 19th Bn

Chapter One

DURHAM, THE LAND OF THE PRINCE BISHOPS

'Half Church of God – half castle 'gainst the Scot!'
SIR WALTER SCOTT

DURHAM IN 1914. The County of Durham lies on the north east coast of England, bordered to the north by the County of Northumberland and south by the North Riding of Yorkshire. To the east lies the North Sea with the Pennines and the counties of Westmorland and Cumberland, now known as Cumbria to the west. Durham is roughly triangular in shape approximately 45 miles long and 35 broad. The River Tyne forms the northern boundary from just above Blaydon until the river reaches the North Sea and separates North and South Shields at the river mouth. The river is navigable beyond Newcastle and many ships came in empty and left loaded with coal from Durham's coalfield from Dunston near Blaydon, where huge staithes ran coal drops out into the river, where the grimy rust stained colliers tied up for loading. For it was coal that made the county famous, from all corners of the county men were employed in their thousands in the mines. By 1912 there were 335 working collieries in the county employing men not only underground, but on the surface also. Many of the villages in the county owed their existence to a nearby mine or in some cases several nearby mines, as they were built as the dormitories for the work force and were built as close to the pit as possible. When a boy left school at the age of eleven, he would start work at the pit, possibly as a trapper – opening and closing trap doors as tubs of coal went by, then as he grew older he would progress to become a putter – filling the tubs with coal, or a driver leading a pit pony pulling the tub to the shaft and sending it to the surface. Then as time went on they became a hewer, actually cutting the coal at

The view of Durham City from North Road Railway Station, 'Half Church of God, half Castle gainst the Scot,' but in truth the Normans built the castle to subdue the local population.

Looking down Northgate, Darlington towards the town clock, a view well known to those 'Pals' from Darlington.

the face with a pick. This work, hard and dangerous was often done in a three foot seam with the floor inches deep in water.

Relations between the coal owners and their miners were not good; many strikes took place, while in some mines the owners locked the miners out. To break these strikes the coal owners recruited far and wide for men. The Irish, originally brought in by Lord Londonderry, who had extensive land and mineral rights in the county, were perhaps the largest immigrant community, but there were Welsh miners, Staffordshire potters Cumbrian lead miners as well as Cornish tin miners and East Anglian farm labourers to be found in many pit villages. In the dangerous conditions of the mines accidents and fatalities were never far away. Danger was ever present, a run away tub or a snapped rope could, and often did, end a miners life suddenly. An explosion, ignited by a careless spark, would rip through the mine destroying the workings and bring the roof crashing down on the miners heads. On 16 February 1909, at West Stanley, the Townley, Tilley and Busty seams were destroyed in this way, only thirty men came out alive and 168 men and boys were killed. This then was the daily risk for those employed in the mines, if they survived they would trudge home to the 'back to back' colliery row, where if they were lucky they could bathe in a tin tub in front of a roaring fire, that's if there was enough water, for many there was only one tap for the whole street. The county was home to the railways too, the earliest of which were simple tracks built to carry the coal to where it could be loaded on to ships. Eventually every colliery was linked by a railway taking the coal away to be sold. Much of the coal produced made its way to the iron and steel works, of which there was a number in County Durham, for Durham coal made exceptional coke, ideal for making steel. Many of the gentleman that owned collieries also had investments in the iron and steel industry. In Gateshead in 1747 Hawk's Iron Works opened and by the early 1800's coal was moved by chauldron wagon on metal rails, in other parts of the county, at Consett, Washington, Felling, Seaham and Witton Park blast furnaces were built, and the Weardale Iron and Coal Company had a large works at Spennymoor, whilst on the edge of Durham City there was the Grange Foundry near Belmont. Perhaps the biggest works was that of Palmers at Jarrow, where the steel works was beside the shipyard. 'Ore and coal went in at one end and a battleship came out of the other', was the boast of the town. Along the south bank of the Tyne, on the Durham side of the river were a number of shipyards with more on the Wear at Sunderland, where other industries were the manufacture of glass and rope. Sail-making was also to be found, as would be expected in a town with many maritime connections.

But for those who were better off, Durham had its University where many trained as teachers and as a part time hobby joined The University Officer Training Corps or the local territorial battalion 8/Durham LI. When war broke out in 1914, Bede College, which already had a company serving with 8/Durham LI, a number of whom would be killed or taken prisoner at Ypres in 1915. But when recruiting started for the 'Pals' in September 1914, a Bede Company was quickly formed, drawing a lot of well educated young men, many of them from the teaching profession, into the battalion, many of whom were eventually commissioned.

THE FAITHFUL DURHAMS – THE COUNTY REGIMENT

The County of Durham has produced for the British Army some of the finest soldiers ever to set foot on a battlefield not only the county regiment, The Durham Light Infantry, but many other regiments have drawn large numbers of Durham men to their colours. The Northumberland Fusiliers, The East Yorkshire Regiment, The West Yorkshire Regiment and The Green Howards all had large contingents of Durham men in their ranks during the First World War. The Durham Pitman, small stocky and hard, used to hard work and danger, had all the attributes needed by the frontline infantryman, but even in peacetime many men escaped the drudgery of the mine by joining the army, regular meals, a bed, a uniform and fresh air to breathe would seem quite attractive during a prolonged dispute with the colliery owners.

The Durham Light Infantry first came in to being, on 29 September 1756 as the second battalion of Lieutenant General Huske's Regiment or the 23rd Regiment of Foot, later the Royal Welch Fusiliers. At that time fifteen regiments of infantry were authorised to raise second battalions. In 1758 these second battalions became separate regiments and were numbered between 61 and 75, thus the second battalion of the 23rd Regiment, Lieutenant General Huske's, became the 68th Regiment. The battalion was raised in the Leicester area where it remained until the end of April 1757, when a move was made to Berkshire, followed by moves made to Chatham, and Dover. Then both battalions of the 23rd marched to the Isle of Wight in 1758, and it was here that the two regiments separated and the 2nd Battalion 23rd Regiment became the 68th Regiment of Foot.

It was on the 13 May 1758 that Lieutenant Colonel John Lambton, of The Coldstream Guards was authorised to raise recruits, 'by beat of drum or otherwise in any county or part of our kingdom'. In 1782, Lambton had the 68th linked to his home county of Durham, although not many of the men were recruited from the county at that time, indeed there were probably more Irishmen than English. The Regiment saw its first action in a raid on the French coast, at Cancale on the coast of Brittany. A few days were spent ashore, before withdrawing to the ships and sailing back to the Isle of Wight. In July another successful raid took place but in September a third raid went wrong and the Grenadier Company of the 68th along with the grenadiers of the other regiments involved, suffered casualties when covering the retreat to the ships.

The next posting for the regiment was to the West Indies, in 1764 the regiment sailed to the

General John Lambton 1710 - 1794
The founder of the regiment.

island of Antigua. Here they lost 150 men to fever and still more were lost to disease in St Vincent before returning to Britain. They were posted back to the West Indies in 1794, to St Lucia and then to Grenada, where fever took its toll of all ranks. By the middle of 1796 there was only sixty men fit for duty. After being sent back to England and reformed they returned to St Lucia for a number of years and again lost many men to disease. Returning to England again the regiment was selected to train as light infantry, skirmishers who used their initiative, using the tactics of fire and manoeuvre and carrying out orders by bugle call. Armed with an improved musket, with better sights and a dull or browned barrel, the regiment was soon called to action. Its first action as a regiment of light infantry was as part of the invasion of the island of Walcheren on the Dutch coast. After taking part in the capture of Flushing the 68th joined the garrison of South Beveland. For six months they remained here losing men daily to the 'Walcheren Fever', a kind of malaria that even after the regiment returned to England was rife among the ranks. Refitted and reorganised the regiment's next posting was to General Wellington's army in Spain. Here they took part in the battles of Salamanca and Vittoria and the fighting in the Pyrenees. They didn't play any part in the final defeat of Napoleon at Waterloo and over the next forty years in postings to Canada, Jamaica and Gibraltar established a reputation as a smart regiment. The year 1854 was the next time the regiment would see action, from their base in Malta the 68th joined the 4th Division and sailed for the

Crimea to fight the Russsians. Although they were present at the Battle of The Alma on 20 September, the regiment saw little action, however on 5 November at The Battle of Inkerman, Private John Byrne won the regiments first Victoria Cross, when he rescued a wounded man under enemy fire. A second Victoria Cross was awarded to the regiment in May 1855 to Captain T de C Hamilton for action at Sebastopol. The force he commanded was attacked by the Russians, at midnight, in a howling gale they managed to enter the trench held by the 68th and spike one of the regiment's guns. Captain Hamilton immediately led a counter attack and recovered the weapon, during which time they killed two Russian officers and a number of their men. The conditions in the Crimea were miserable but the regiment remained until the end. This was the first war to have a photographer with the army in the field and the outstanding thing to emerge was the bravery of the soldiers and the conditions that they endured, whilst the Generals displayed a total mismanagement and indifference to their suffering. It is largely due to the war correspondents that changes to the army were brought about.

There followed a few pleasant years in stations around the Mediterranean, before the regiment finally arrived back in England in 1857. However the Government didn't keep the 68th sitting about at home, within three months the regiment was on its way to Burma and afterwards in 1863 to New Zealand. In one of Queen Victoria's little wars a fierce conflict took place in those South

Sea Islands, where the Maoris, the native people of New Zealand resented the fact their lands were being stolen. The Maori, a brave and resourceful warrior, fought hard and was a difficult opponent. The 68th had to take them on hand to hand and on 21 June 1864; Sergeant John Murray won the regiment's third Victoria Cross leading a bayonet charge, in which he saved the life of Private Byrne VC, by killing a Maori who was just about to kill Byrne. The war ended and by 1866 the regiment was back in England. After six years at home the regiment was posted to India.

In 1881, Cardwell, the Secretary of State for War in the Liberal Government, brought in some sweeping changes to the army. He linked all infantry regiments to a county and for all those without a second battalion he linked them to another regiment. The 68th already with Durham in its title became linked with the 106th Bombay Light Infantry.

The 106th started life in 1839 as the 2nd Bombay Europeans in the Honourable East India Company's forces. They saw action in Persia, at the battles of Reshire and Bushire in 1856 and when taken on to the British Army establishment became the 106th Bombay European Light Infantry. From 1881 the two regiments became 1st and 2nd Battalions of The Durham Light Infantry. One of the other ideas of the reforms was that a regiment would always have one battalion overseas and one battalion stationed in the United Kingdom, the home battalion supplying drafts of men to the overseas battalion. The regiment next saw action in 1885 in the Soudan, where 2/Durham LI fought at the Battle of Ginnis against the wild Dervisher's of the Mahdi's Forces who had taken Khartoum and killed General Gordon and the Garrison.

Throughout the 1890's 2/Durham LI served in India, where they excelled on the Polo field, training their own ponies, they won many cups, beating and upsetting many rich cavalry regiments along the way.

The next time the regiment went into action was in South Africa during the Boer War. Ordered

Officers of the 68th Light Infantry in the Crimea standing second right is Captain Thomas Hamilton who had won the VC a week earlier.

The Band and Colours of the 106th Light Infantry at Umballa about 1869 in 1881 this Regiment became 2/Durham Light Infantry.

out in October 1899 as part of the Army Corps under the command of Sir Redvers Buller, 1/Durham LI won fame on 5 February 1900, when they stormed the hill at Vaal-krantz. With 3/King's Royal Rifle Corps on their right, in extended line the two battalions advanced, taking casualties from enfilading rifle fire from a hill known as Doorn Kloof. They pressed on up Vaal-krantz and took the crest at bayonet point, as they advanced up the steep hill, the regiment left a large number of dead and wounded along the way, from the rifle fire of the Boer marksmen, armed with their Mauser rifles. On 6 February the Boers launched a counter attack which retook some of the ground they had lost the previous day, however, the British troops were rallied and a brilliant bayonet charge by the Durham's and KRRC regained all the ground that the Boer had recaptured. After the Relief of Ladymith the regiment was employed guarding blockhouses along the railway and patrolling the countryside. They were joined by the Volunteer Company formed from the Volunteer Battalions of the Durham Light Infantry, the Territorials of their day.

In 1908, Lord Haldane brought about changes to the Volunteer movement and created the Territorial Force, all the Rifle Volunteer Battalions were renumbered and became battalions in the new force, thus the 5th Stockton, 6th Bishop Auckland, 7th Sunderland, 8th Durham City and 9th Gateshead battalions of the regiment came into being, the 3rd (Reserve) and 4th (Extra Reserve) Battalions being draft finding units for the two regular battalions.

By 1914 1/Durham LI was back in India, on the North West Frontier, 2/Durham LI was stationed at Litchfield in Staffordshire, with one company detached at South Shields. The Territorials were well up to strength, in some cases over strength.

As war clouds drew nearer the Durham Brigade and their supporting arms went away to their annual camp in Conway, North Wales at the end of July, but on 3 August orders came that mobilisation was expected and they hurriedly returned to their home drill halls, where at around 1700 hours on 4 August the telegram ordering mobilisation arrived.

THE OUTBREAK OF WAR – THE CALL TO ARMS

On the bright sunny morning of Sunday 28 June 1914, the visit of the Archduke Franz Ferdinand and his wife, the Duchess Sophie, to Sarajevo, the capital of the Austrian province of Bosnia-

The 1st Battalion march through the small town of Estcourt, in Natal, on their way towards the Tugela River in December 1899.
Men of A Company, 3rd (Militia) Battalion, Durham LI, in South Africa 1900.

Herzegovnia was to set Europe alight. It was a National Fete Day and the streets were decked with flags and thronged with people as the Royal train arrived at the station. Security arrangements began to go wrong almost immediately, when the royal cars left the railway station, the security detectives were left behind and only three local policemen were present with the Royal party. The Archduke with the Military Governor, General Oskar Piotorek, travelled in an open top sports car, which, at the Archduke's request, travelled slowly so he could have a good look at the town.

As the car drove along the Appel Quay, near the Central Police Station a tall young man named Cabrinovic threw a hand grenade at the car. The grenade bounced off the folded roof and exploded under the following car wounding several officers. Despite the threat Archduke Ferdinand ordered a halt to find out who had been injured and it was now that it was discovered that a grenade fragment had grazed the Duchess. Archduke Franz Ferdinand arrived at the town hall in an outrage and decided to visit one of the wounded officers who had been taken to a nearby military hospital, he would then continue with the visit to a local museum as arranged. The cars left the town hall and back along the Appel Quay this time at high speed, but the drivers had not been told of the unplanned visit to the military hospital. The first two cars turned right at the corner of Appel Quay and Franz Josef Street but General Potiorek shouted at the driver of the third car that he was making a mistake. The driver, obviously confused, braked sharply and brought the car to a halt, in the worst possible place. Standing right at the spot was a young Bosnian, Gavrilo Princip, who emerged from the crowd only some three or four paces from the Archdukes vehicle. Drawing a pistol he fired two shots into the car, the first mortally wounded the Archduke and the second struck the Duchess Sophie in the abdomen. The car raced to the Governor's official residence but the bumpy ride only made matters worse and the Royal couple were pronounced dead shortly after arrival. If Austria-Hungary was to continue as a world power this outrage could not go unchallenged.

If Austria-Hungary declared war on Serbia, this would bring in the Russians, but Austria was allied to Germany and as early as the beginning of July the Kaiser, who was a personal friend of the Archduke, is reported to have said 'The Serbs must be disposed of.' Then on 23 July the Austrian Government send a strong memorandum to the Serbs listing ten demands. The strongest of which was that Serbia allow Austria to suppress local agitation and subversion directed against Austria. Although the Serbs accepted most of Austria's conditions Austria deemed it inadequate and declared war. The nations of Europe rushed to mobilise, the Tsar, Nicholas II of Russia tried to maintain peace but the Russian Army mobilised on 31 July. To counter this Germany declared war on Russia, having first offered France the chance to stay out of the conflict and remain neutral. The French however remained true to their treaties and refused the German offer, the Germans therefore declared war on France. Having declared war on France, on 3 August the Imperial German Army crossed the border into Luxembourg and threatened to move into Belgium. Belgium had mobilised on 2 August and the Germans sent an ultimatum on the pretext that the French had crossed the border into Belgium. The French in fact had retired so that they could not give any cause for such an accusation. The note said that if the Belgian Army could not stop the French the Germans would and if the Belgian's resisted then it would be considered an act of war. The Belgian border with Germany was covered by a line of forts and the key to these was the fort at Leige on the river Meuse. The main invasion of Belgium began on 4 August although a cavalry patrol had crossed on 3 August. The German Cavalry moved quickly through the frontier towns and villages, their task to capture the bridges over the Meuse before the defenders could blow them up. They also had the task of providing a screen in front of the advancing infantry and carrying out advance reconnaissance.

Meanwhile in England mobilisation had been ordered On 30 July, more by luck than planning the majority of the Territorial Army were on their annual camp and were quickly moved to their war stations guarding vulnerable points on the coast and along railway lines and docks. The Belgian's had a treaty with England and when the German Army crossed the frontier, Britain sent an ultimatum to Berlin. No reply was received so the British Empire declared war on Germany on 4 August 1914. The British Army at home in England and Ireland had been organised as an Expeditionary Force of six infantry and one cavalry divisions and at a meeting of the principal Ministers, including Lord Kitchener, who became Secretary of State for War on 6 August, the decision was taken to send four infantry divisions and the cavalry division to France on 9 August. The other decision taken by Kitchener was to raise New Armies, each army of six more divisions of civilian volunteers and on 7 August, he appealed for the first hundred thousand. He launched his poster 'Your Country Needs You', the recruiting offices were packed with recruits, over 10,000 men enlisting in five days.

Territorials at camp 1913 Men of 6/Durham LI.

But meanwhile the war was to be fought by the regular army. In the barracks and depots throughout the country, reservists rejoined their battalions, batteries and squadrons, for although the British Expeditionary Force is always described as a Regular Army, the majority of the men had left the Regular Army and when

An artist's impression of the incident that started the war.

mobilisation was ordered they were recalled to the colours. They were hastily issued with their equipment, cap, tunic, trousers, boots, puttees, webbing and rifle and a hundred other small items like boot brushes and mess tins, and before long they were moving to their war station.

In Litchfield 2/Durham LI were part of 18 Brigade of the 6th Division, the Brigade was ordered north to Edinburgh to the Forth Defences, for 6th Division was not to go out to France immediately. But in other barracks the men were made ready and marched, in newly fitted army boots, down to railway sidings, where trains were waiting to take them to unknown destinations. The programme was worked out to the minute and in five days of hectic preparation 1,800 special trains ran in Great Britain and Ireland. At Southampton

Men of Bavarian Reserve Regiment No 7 wait to entrain, note the young boy in uniform wearing a picklehaulbe.

A British Cavalry Trooper taken prior to going overseas.

Docks almost the equivalent of a division a day was arriving at the docks. Up to thirteen ships daily carried the BEF across the channel to the French ports of Boulogne and Le Havre. On 12 August General Headquarters of the BEF left London for Southampton and crossed to Havre, having landed they moved by rail and by the night of 16 August had reached Le Cateau. All arms moved quickly across the channel and inland to the concentration area, between Maubeuge and Le Cateau, the task of the BEF was to move northward and form the left flank of the French Army. On 20 August GHQ issued orders for a general movement northward and the various Corps and Divisions began moving. The British Cavalry screen moved northwards early and patrols of both 9/Lancers and 4/Dragoon Guards sited German Cavalry but had no contact. Then at dawn on 22 August, 4/Dragoon Guards sent out two officers patrols from their C Squadron. One of these came across a German piquet and opened fire on the enemy who made off. Later in the morning a troop from the same squadron came across a German Cavalry unit moving south, they immediately attacked the enemy and then chased them until checked by fire from enemy infantry. Further east the Scots Greys of 5 Cavalry Brigade, were holding two bridges over the River Samme, they came under fire from enemy artillery, but the enemy infantry kept up rifle fire it had little effect on the Greys who only had one officer wounded, in return they inflicted some thirty to forty casualties on the enemy. A troop from 16/Lancers was sent up to support the Scots Greys, as they rode up

July 1914 6/Durham LI at Conway before returning home to mobilise.

they came across an enemy patrol, these they chased and as they followed them they came very suddenly upon some German 'Jager', the Lancers formed line and charged, riding straight over the enemy, turning round they again went straight through the enemy, with only three horses killed and one man wounded.

The British cavalry commanders were now able to report to Headquarters that German infantry in great force was in front of the BEF. Both I and II British Corps were still advancing northwards and eventually they were in the positions worked out for them in GHQ's order of 20 August holding a line along the Mons canal. However the Germans were unsure of the actual location of the British troops and were advancing towards the British. Eventually the Germans met the British Regular Army, trained to fire ten rounds a minute; they thought every man was

A German supply column following the advance on Brussels passes wrecked houses in the Belgian village of Visé.

armed with a machine gun. Even though the British inflicted heavy casualties on the enemy they were forced to fall back from Mons. Then in turn from Le Cateau, they fell back and fought their way to the Aisne where the BEF turned and drove the enemy back. By now 6th Division with 2/Durham LI under command had arrived in France in time to join in the Aisne battle. The next battalions of the regiment to arrive in the theatre of war were the Territorials of the Northumbrian Division; arriving in France in April 1915 they were rushed up to Ypres, where the Germans had just launched the first gas attack against French Territorial troops. With the casualty lists getting longer by the day more men were urgently needed and it would be soon time for the volunteers of Lord Kitchener's New Armies to take the field.

As the front settled down to trench warfare the hand-thrown bomb became an important weapon for both sides. Here Royal Engineers make bombs from jam tins.

Chapter Two

Raising and Training

'The fashions all for khaki now'
RUDYARD KIPLING

IN COUNTY DURHAM recruiting for the 'New Army' was quick to gather pace, as recruits flocked to local recruiting offices the *Durham Chronicle*, reported that in Durham City there was a 'Splendid Response', stating,

> *'Those who are in charge of the recruiting office at the Assize Courts have had few spare moments, so splendid has been the response from young men who are anxious to serve their King and country; From Brandon, Spennymoor, Bishop Auckland, Sacriston, Edmondsley, Langley Park and other mining districts healthy looking men have volunteered their services, desiring chiefly to be enlisted in the Durham Light Infantry. Others have shown a preference for the Hussars, the Dragoons and the Lancers, but the local regiment has received the most recruits and they are essential to see that the new battalions are formed.'*

But what was happening in Durham? Headlines were appearing in local newspapers asking, 'Kitcheners New Army! What is Durham Doing?' At this time it was estimated that between 75 and 100 men per day were enlisting in the city. The men were sworn in for general service for all corps and regiments but by far the greatest number were joining the infantry and of those the majority were joining the Durhams.

Among the many who walked into the city from outlying pit villages, to the recruiting office at the Assize Courts, were Ralph and Jimmy Frater, the brothers, both miners, at Sacriston Colliery, stood side by side in two lines moving slowly to the head of the queue. Ralph didn't know his queue was for the Border Regiment and he became separated from his younger brother. Jimmy on the other hand was in a queue for the Durham's but when he reached the table, the recruiting officer took one look at him and told the 5 feet 2 inch 15 year old and to go away. He did, but kept going back until the formation of the 'Bantams' at last gave him the chance to enlist.

Chairman of the County Durham Parliamentary Recruiting Committee, Earl Durham.

But all over the County similar scenes were being played out; recruiting offices in all the major towns were sending hundreds to join the battalions of the Durham's, being formed. Joining the Regimental Depot at Fenham Barracks in Newcastle the men were formed into parties and sent off to training areas in the south where the Service Battalions of the Durham Light Infantry were being formed. The 10th and 11th Battalions at Woking, the 12th and 13th Battalions went to Bullswater, the 14th to

G.   R.

18th (Service) Battalion Durham Light Infantry (County).

Lord Durham's Regiment
— FOR —

Commercial and Business Men.

Men of Durham, join your own County Regiment and train at Cocken Hall, near Durham.

Newspaper advert for the Durham Comrades Battalion.

DARLINGTON "PALS" COMPANY

Arrangements have been made for "Pals" to serve together as a Special Company of Durham Light Infantry.

Applications are especially invited from Shop Assistants, Clerks, &c., who desire to serve their country.

Telephone 161.   E. W. ORMSTON.

Look out for Parade on Saturday.

PARTICULARS TO-MORROW.

Newspaper advert for the Darlington Pals Company.

Aylesbury and the recruits for the 15th Battalion went to Halton Park. The 16th Battalion formed in Durham City and for a time was billeted in local schools; likewise the 17th was raised in Barnard Castle. The last two named became 2nd Reserve Battalions and did not serve overseas.

While all this recruiting was taking place in County Durham, in the City of London, Major, The Honourable Robert White was raising the 10th (Service) Battalion the Royal Fusiliers, this battalion was also known as the 'Stockbrokers Battalion' and was authorised by the War Office on 21 August 1914. At the same time in Liverpool, Lord Derby began raising his 'City' Battalions for the King's Liverpool Regiment, which were officially sanctioned on the 29 August, however these battalions brought a new word into the British Army Order of Battle, 'PALS'. Lord Derby's idea that groups of workmates, friends and pals could enlist and serve together quickly caught on, and mainly across the industrial counties of the north, civic heads and notable individuals commenced the task of recruiting local battalions. Accrington, Barnsley, Bradford, Hull, Leeds, Liverpool, Manchester and Salford all had Pals Battalions. Sheffield had its 'City' Battalion and Newcastle upon Tyne, recruiting throughout Northumberland and Durham would eventually raise a Commercial Battalion, two Tyneside Pioneer Battalions and four Tyneside Scottish and four Tyneside Irish Battalions for the Northumberland Fusiliers. Further north in Scotland the cities of Glasgow and Edinburgh were also raising their battalions, whilst Wales would have a 'Pals' battalion raised in Cardiff.

Recruits parade on the racecourse in Durham City, The Earl of Durham inspects the men.

It was around the end of August 1914 Major F T Tristram wrote to Colonel Rowland Burdon and suggested that a unit on these lines should be raised for the county regiment, a committee of gentlemen from the county was brought together under the chairmanship of His Lordship the Earl of Durham, consisting of Colonel R Burdon VD MP, Sir William Gray, Bart, and H Pike Pease MP. The idea was put forward of raising a battalion by subscription and presenting it entirely free to the nation. But, while the committee were meeting in Durham, a Darlington man, Mr Ernest Ormston, of the Haughton Bridge Wagon Works set himself the task of raising a 'PALS' unit in that town. On Tuesday 1 September the *Northern Echo* reported that,

'Mr Ormston is convinced that the hesitancy apparent amongst certain sections of young men is largely due to a natural shyness at having to associate with men with whom they are unfamiliar. Acting on advice he has communicated with Lord Robertson the matter, and on receiving the sanction of the authorities he will immediately enter upon an active crusade to raise the necessary recruits. Indeed he has already begun his self-imposed task and has received considerable encouragement from some of the local employers of labour. He hopes during the week to visit most of the engineering works in the town and make a personal appeal to the men working there to volunteer in the nations service'.

Whilst the rival newspaper *The North Star* was reporting that,

In the adjoining villages Mr G G Plant has done excellent work on his own initiative, but from a tour round the villages it is evident there is a need for posters, literature and speakers who can properly enlighten people as to the causes of the war and the crisis it has created.

The following day the *Northern Echo* reported that Mr Ormston was meeting with considerable encouragement to form a 'Darlington Pals Company' and employers were affording him ever opportunity to speak to their workmen. Two companies, Messer's Sanderson's and The Railway Plant Company both let it be known that they would guarantee that any of their employee's who volunteered to join the colours would on their return be given preference in employment to those who stayed at home. The article also stated that,

Young men who are eager to join a 'Pals Corps' composed of Darlington men should at once communicate with Mr Ormston at Messers McLachlan and Co Ltd, Haughton Bridge Wagon Works. Telephone number 161, Mr Ormston will be only too delighted to answer any inquiries.

Meanwhile the committee in Durham were concerned with the costs of raising the battalion and an appeal for subscriptions was made, three members of the committee, Lord Durham, Sir William Gray and Colonel Rowland Burdon each gave £1,000, other donations came in from Mrs Matthew Gray £500, Viscount Boyne £500, Mr Frank Stobbart £100, Mr A F Pease £100, Mr C E Hunter £100, the late Sir Stephen Furness, Bart, £200 and H Pike Pease £50.

Having achieved the task of finding sufficient funds to start the recruiting campaign application was made at once to the War Office for official permission to raise the battalion. Meanwhile it was felt that the enrolment of possible recruits could take place and the committee put out an appeal to all the areas of the county for recruits, writing to the Lord Mayors, of the Towns, Cities and County Boroughs asking for support. It was felt that if Bishop Auckland, Stockton, the Hartlepool's, Durham, Sunderland, Gateshead and other towns in the county were to raise enough recruits the battalion could be together within a week. The forthcoming battalion gained a name at this time, 'Lord Durham's 'Comrades' Battalion', this name stuck for some time.

In the south east of the county, at Hartlepool, permission was granted to raise their own Kitchener battalion, many men from this locality had already enlisted, the King's Own Scottish Borderers and the Gordon Highlanders as well as The Green Howards and the West Yorkshire Regiment recruiting very well from the town. The *Northern Daily Mail* reported that,

At the present time recruits are being enlisted and sent home until called for a retaining fee of 3s

per day is being paid in the meantime. Permission has been given to raise a local battalion but instead of this it has been decided to form local companies to join The Earl of Durham's 'Comrades' Battalion, The latter is being raised by private subscription and more than half the required amount has been obtained.

Recruiting opened for the battalion in the Hartlepools on Monday 7 September and it was hoped that the battalion would be largely recruited from the professional and commercial classes including clerks and artisans.

In Darlington the idea had caught on and Mr Ormiston was inundated with requests and offers to serve, most of them coming from men with good positions, clerks, draughtsmen and others and men were coming forward in batches of four, five or six and even more.

In Darlington and the surrounding villages the interest being shown in the Darlington Pals company was growing by the day and the raisers received a letter from Lord Roberts expressing his best wishes for the success of the movement and intimating that Lord Kitchener approved of young men joining in batches so as to be trained amongst their friends. Not only were men from the town enrolling but also Darlington men, resident in Sunderland and Middlesborough had communicated with requests to be included. It was proposed to hold a parade of all would be members of the company at the Drill Hall in Larchfield Street at 3.00 p.m. on Saturday 5 September. It was intended that the men should assemble at the Drill Hall then march to the Town Hall where enrolment and medical inspection would take place.

That morning *The Northern Echo* recorded that,

It is hoped the response will be so overwhelming as to compel the authorities to take in hand still another 'pals' company for Darlington. It can be done if every group of young fellows who deem it their duty to join the colours turn up at the Drill Hall this afternoon.

The country has responded splendidly to Kitcheners call. Darlington is doing its part well and a great muster of 'pals' today will put the finishing touch to the finest recruiting week that the old Quaker borough has ever seen.'

But a few inadvertent sentences in the rival *North Star* on the same day would throw the whole movement in Darlington back. This newspaper reported in the following way,

The 'Pals' Company which is getting plenty of support will be attached to the 5th Durham's forming an additional company in the ordinary way .The members are to be sworn in this afternoon. A point that struck observers yesterday was the superior type of recruit that came forward – neatly dressed young men of the skilled mechanic and clerical classes. They will make excellent soldiers in a short time.

This rumour was also mentioned in an article in *The Stockton and Darlington Times* which took the rumour a stage further, saying that the men would be distributed amongst the companies of 5/DLI or perhaps be sent to some other regiment.

The thought of joining the Territorial's was against the will of most of those who were enrolling for the Darlington 'Pals' Company as it was rumoured that 5/DLI was earmarked for garrison duty in Egypt or the Colonies for the duration of the war. It was also common knowledge and widely reported in the press that the battalion was short of around 200 men since about that number had not volunteered for overseas service. So it was that when the parade took place at 3.00 p.m. that Saturday afternoon a large number of men who had said they would volunteer were missing from the ranks. The organisers quickly tried to find out the reason why so few were present and things stood in abeyance for a while until things could be sorted out.

The Mayor of Darlington Councillor J G Harbottle now had a letter published in the *Northern Echo*, referring to the letter he had received from Colonel Burdon about the raising of a battalion

Recruits parade on the racecourse in Durham City waiting to march to Cocken Hall.

by private subscription, and he, the Mayor, immediately opened an office in Darlington stating that those who enlisted would be kept together as comrades and that they would be housed, drilled and clothed, under War Office approval in The County of Durham until such times as they were wanted abroad or elsewhere. Furthermore they would be discharged as soon as possible at the end of hostilities

As all this was taking place in Darlington the other towns and villages were not being neglected, Lord Durham, and his brother the Hon F W Lambton, along with the High Sheriff, Mr F Priestman and Mr Grattan Doyle among others were touring the county speaking at recruiting meetings urging young men to enlist.

It was at one of these meetings, in South Hetton Miner's Hall, that the Hon F W Lambton gave out the news that on that day he had spoke to some wounded soldiers in Newcastle and among them were some men from the Coldstream Guards, one of whom had seen his son Lieutenant Geoffery Lambton shot and killed on 1 September, He then completely broke down and received sympathetic cheers from the crowd. However bad he felt about losing his son he did not let it stop his recruiting work and almost every village in the County had a visit from him.

The *North Star* now said that the it was now wisdom not to have attached the 'Pals to the Territorials as it was almost certain that Colonel Burdon would receive the sanction from The War

Office to raise the 'Pals' Battalion for Lord Kitchener's Army.

On 9 September the news now came through that the War Office had given approval for the offer to raise and equip the battalion and permission was granted for recruiting to begin at once, it was also agreed that as Darlington had taken the lead in recruiting they would have the honour of being the first or Grenadier Company of the new battalion. From what was written at the time it can be gathered that the raisers were still talking in terms of an eight-company battalion, each company consisting of 100 men.

In Durham the Mayor, Councillor C Caldecleugh, had the following inserted in the *Durham Chronicle*,

> The proposal to raise and equip by voluntary subscription a Kitchener Regiment in the County of Durham has been approved by the War Office. The new battalion is to be formed on similar lines to Lord Derby's 'PALS' Battalion at Liverpool. The eligible young men of the City who wish to join are requested to hand in their names at once to the Mayor, Councillor C Caldecleugh or to Councillor CW Thwaites at 88 Elvet Bridge.

It was reported that initially there had been some twenty names put forward from the city and that Bede College was to raise a company, likewise the North Eastern County School at Barnard Castle had also offered a company of old boys.

It was now that Mr J Morley Longden of The Cottage, Castle Eden and Somerford Buildings, Sunderland was asked to be the recruiting agent for the battalion. Mr Longden issued a circular in which it stated that the classes particularly desired to recruit are the clerks, artisans and upper middle classes and gentlemen who have been unable to secure a commission up to the present time. The enrolment and registration of names proceeded satisfactorily and there was every indication that the required numbers would soon be attained. Word came from the War Office that the battalion was to be officially known as 'The County Battalion' Durham Light Infantry and the Headquarters would be at 53 Old Elvet, Durham City.

Recruiting in Darlington now had another setback, the North East Railway Company announced that it was going to raise a battalion from among its employees a number of whom lived in the town, and some had already enrolled in the 'Pals' company. With Darlington at the front of recruiting for the battalion the papers were reporting that the town had the honour of raising the 'Grenadier Company' for the new unit and began referring to them as 'The Pals Own',

Thing's were moving a little slower in Hartlepool, the local recruiting officer complained that he had not had as much success men as he would have liked. Locally around sixty men had initially enlisted and it was hoped that orders would soon arrive to commence training.

On 11 September the Durham City volunteers assembled in the Market Place and marched to the Assize Courts for medical examination, many of the men were members of The Durham National Emergency League who had decided to enlist with the 'Pals'. The *Durham Chronicle* published a long list of the names of these volunteers, the first four being, ex regular soldiers, Ex Sergeant Major Hornsby, Ex Sergeant Instructor Chaplin, Ex Sergeant Major Hayes and Ex Sergeant Watts, the experience these men brought with them was to prove valuable to the new unit, indeed, Ex Sergeant Instructor Chaplin would become the Regimental Sergeant Major and was later commissioned as the Battalion Quartermaster. The Durham Company assembled on the racecourse, removed their jackets and rolled their shirtsleeves, then under the watchful eye of Instructor Chaplin began to practice squad drill. The weather was glorious and the men made rapid progress. Rumours, which proved true, circulated that Lord Southampton from the Reserve of Officers had accepted command of the battalion.

The Bede Company opened an office in a house in Mount Pleasant, Spennymoor and ex

College men came from all over the region to sign on many of them bringing friends with them to join the company, Frank Raine recalled how he came to be in the Bede company,

> *Nothing would have kept me out, I wanted to get away from life, to see something different and have an adventure. I set my inseparable friend Neesham off too. It was going to be over by Christmas that's what we were told, so we called from work, at the recruiting office every night. I weighed about 8 stone and had a 32inch chest and a 13 inch collar. They were quite rude at the finish, 'You again!' 'Out'. I was a member of a football club and the fellow that ran it was a school teacher – an Ex Bede College man and eventually he said to us one day, 'Stop trying to get into the Army, Bede College are going to form a company, I am joining and I will get you into that.' So suddenly we got word and on the Friday we went up to Spennymoor and we joined – just signed on in the Army and got the King's shilling. We hadn't a medical examination of any description. We just went up to this house 'Mount Pleasant' there was quite a crowd there and we just went into this room and a chap called Dobbie – a school teacher just filled a form in. I think there was a doctor there but he didn't really look at you. My young friend Neesham was 17 and he put 19 down and I had a 32 inch chest and they put down 36 inches.*

It was now Lord Durham offered to let the battalion use his land at Cocken Hall, north east of Durham City, as a training area and camp. Lord Durham although he owned the property did not live there. The house was last occupied by a Mr Hudson, a Sunderland ship owner, and it had stood empty for over eight years, Some time earlier in 1914, the house had been the target of an arson attack by suffragettes. The caretaker, his suspicions aroused by a number of leaflets scattered on the lawns, found a window had been forced and the staircase and corridors were full of smoke as a fire tried to take hold. An alarm clock attached to a fuse and battery was found in the stair well and some flooring had to be taken up before the fire could be brought under control.

On the following day the men again assembled on the racecourse for more drill and some physical training, during the course of the morning Colonel Bowes visited the men and drilled them himself for a short time, declaring that, 'I see no reason why the company should not become the smartest in the battalion.' The men of the Darlington Company were also drilling; the Corn Exchange was the chosen venue and upwards of 100 men were present. Now the battalion had been accepted by the War Office the men were informed that they were expected to undergo about four hours of drill daily whilst billeted at home, the instruction provided by an ex Colour Sergeant of 5/DLI and the daily routine and orders were published in the local press.

After the parade Captain F T Tristram complemented the men and informed them that he hoped to be appointed to the battalion as an officer and that although Kitchener's army were going to be wearing Blue uniforms, the raising committee had secured War Office permission for the battalion to be clothed in khaki. 'The Chester le Street Chronicle' reported that the contract for the clothing had been awarded as follows,

> *Messer's Stewart Clothe Limited, the King's tailors have been successful in securing the contract for khaki clothing for Lord Durham's Battalion. Owing to workroom pressure some difficulty was experienced in the handling of the underwear order, but this was successfully overcome by distributing the order in the Middlesborough area, among the wives and mothers of those now serving. Although normally outside their usual sphere this order has secured the continuing employment of the 600 strong workforce.*

Men who had now been waiting two weeks to join the battalion were beginning to get restless, some of them having given up good positions of employment to enlist and to them it seemed unfair to keep them hanging about uncertain as to when they would be called up. However things began to change when the local press announced that when they paraded at 6.30 p.m. on 18

The street of Old Elvet, the 'Pals' marched down the street towards the cameraman.

September attestation forms would be filled in and afterwards at eight o'clock they would march to the Town Hall where the Mayor Alderman J G Harbottle would swear them in. It was also announced that Darlington would commence raising a second company for the battalion.

On 24 September the Durham detachment held another parade on the racecourse this time with a photographer in attendance. The move to camp was immanent and an advance party of twenty men was selected to leave at once for Cocken Hall in order to begin preparing for the arrival of the main bodies from the other recruiting offices.

The departure of the Durham detachment which soon would become C Company, was recorded in the *Durham Chronicle*, under the heading:

COUNTY COMRADES' BATTALION, A HEARTY SEND OFF.

'*The streets of the old city presented an unwarranted aspect last Friday morning the occasion being the departure of a draft of the Durham City and District contingent of the County Comrades Battalion for Cocken Hall. The Comrades had been ordered to assemble on the racecourse at 8 a.m. and to bring their implements with them, and a wondrous collection of baggage it was, even cricket bags have been pressed into service. Instructor Chaplin soon had the men in formation on the University cricket ground around the main entrance to which a large crowd of Dunelmians were gathered. Col Burdon, The Mayor of Durham, Col Bowes, Councillor McLean, Mr and Mrs Tristram and Councillor Thwaites occupied positions of vantage facing the men who were inspected by Col Bowes and afterwards stood at attention whilst the Mayor delivered a short address.*'

At the end of a stirring and patriotic address by the Mayor, Sergeant Instructor Chaplin cautioned the men that whilst marching through towns and villages they must march at attention but outside they could march 'at ease' and enjoy a smoke if they wished. The men were then photographed and when this was completed they formed fours and the order 'Quick March' was given. Whilst the men leaving for Cocken Hall were the main centre of attraction, some attention and comment was passed about the newer members of the battalion drilling on the football and cricket fields.

As the 'Pals' marched off the racecourse the command 'Right Wheel' rang out and as the column turned into Old Elvet the men broke into song 'We are all Pals' to the tune of 'Auld Lang Syne'. As the column reached the Shire Hall the staff turned out and gave a rousing cheer, to which the Pals responded to enthusiastically. The song changed to 'It's a long way to Tipperary' and then many other popular airs as led by Sergeant Instructor Chaplin they marched over Elvet Bridge through the Market Place, down Silver Street and over Framwellgate Bridge. As the column reached North Road they tried to sing the 'The Marsellaise' but the paper recorded 'It was not a very successful vocal effort.' However the best was yet to come, as the comrades received the most stirring reception from the Sisters and Nurses of the County Hospital and in reply caps were doffed and one comrade proudly waved the Union Jack.

Meanwhile the Darlington Company had set up headquarters in Albion Street and the Pals were to be found drilling and doing physical training between 10 a.m. and 12 a.m and from 2p.m until 4 p.m. at the Darlington football ground and the Grammar School. Time was drawing near for them to join the Durham detachment at Cocken Hall and the day prior to their departure a Drum Head service was held at Feethams the home of Darlington AFC. The *North Star* recorded the event with these words,

> *It was an unusual type of church parade in many respects; the men were in plain civilian dress. The only pretension to uniform lay in the band (Hoggett's), which was strengthened by the addition of a few Territorial bandsmen. But it was an inspiring scene in the bright sunshine and amid the well-*

Hoggett's Military Band played the men of A Company to Darlington railway station.

preserved athletic grounds. The stands were crowded with onlookers and they followed the service with reverence.

In the centre stood the Reverend D Walker, the Vicar of Darlington, assisted by the Rev's H Clarke and Norman Vasey and supported by churchwardens. After introductory prayers and the singing of 'O God our help in ages past' he delivered a helpful address. He recalled the past history of County Durham in times of national crisis and the ready response of her sons. That day they had the evidence of the same spirit. They were engaged in a fight of moral righteousness, and he did not doubt that they would acquit themselves like men. At the close, the National Anthem was heartily sung by the crowd.

The newspaper then gave the information that the following morning the Darlington detachment would leave by an early train to join the main body at Durham.

So it was the following day that the Darlington detachment left the town, the streets were lined with enthusiastic crowds as the members of the two Darlington companies assembled at the Corn Exchange. The men each carrying blankets and other necessary baggage as uniform and military equipment would not be immediately available, paraded at eight o'clock and the baggage was then load on to a large two horsed wagon and transported to the railway station. Then led by Hoggett's Military Band the 140 members of the Darlington Pals Company marched through enthusiastic crowds to Bank Top station. At the station the band played martial and patriotic airs as the 'Pals' boarded the train and as the train moved slowly away they struck up 'Auld Lang Syne'. The crowd on the platform cheered and waved hats and handkerchiefs, as the train neared the end of the platform the engine ran over fog signals, which exploded giving the signal to the band to strike up the National Anthem. On the way to Durham the train stopped at Ferryhill Station and collected another 44 men and their baggage.

THE 'PALS' IN TRAINING AT COCKEN HALL

Now that the men were in regular training at Cocken Hall, letters began to be published about camp life; an unnamed Darlington Private sent this report to the *North Star*,

The grub is much better than we expected and we have an exceedingly lot of decent chaps in the whole battalion.

The Colonel is a sport and any of us would do anything for him. He always has a word for us when he passes and tho he gives us beans when we drill he stops us now and then and chats awfully pleasantly with us.

We do have some fun in barracks and one of the greatest jokes is to listen to the chaps talking in their sleep. By the way we are sleeping on an oak floor but there isn't a grouser amongst us. To give you an idea of what the fellows are like about dinnertime today a chap stuck up a notice that he had lost half a sovereign. A few hours later he got it back. I had a flask of whisky whilst on guard. As soon as the sergeant heard of it he fainted and of course needed a reviver. We are enjoying the training immensely and I wouldn't pitch it for worlds.

Cocken Hall uninhabited in 1914 Earl Durham offered it to the battalion as billets until the huts were erected.

In the south west of the county at Barnard Castle the scenes were not as enthusiastic but a large

Still in civilian clothing at Cocken Hall, capless is Private Jack Wilson who will be wounded 4 July 1916. All these men became 9 Section of C Company.

crowd did gather to witness the departure and wish God's speed to a number of 'Old Boy's' who had joined the North Eastern County Boy's School Company. The Headmaster the Rev F J Brereton and members of the staff were at the railway station to bid farewell to the company. Similar scenes took place at the other side of the county at Hartlepool where 110 men gathered on the platform for an enthusiastic send off, where they were addressed, by Colonel Robson and the Mayor Councillor J W Coates. Colonel Robson expressed his gratification at the magnificent response made by the men of Hartlepool to Lord Kitchener's appeal. The Mayor expressed the immense pride felt by the citizens of their town at the splendid recruiting results there and the Lady Mayoress presented each man with a packet of cigarettes. Among the Hartlepool contingent, joining D Company, were over a dozen ex regular NCOs whose previous experience was proving very useful indeed. Now they were in camp the men were settling down very quickly and letters and postcards to family and friends were telling what a grand time they were having, some even persuading friends to enlist. An unnamed Hartlepool recruit of the County Battalion quoted in *The Northern Daily Mail* wrote,

> *We are having a ripping time here; get here as sharp as possible. We have arranged to get you in our company. The uniforms have been dished out and the grub is fine.*

Whilst yet another wrote in *The Northern Echo*,

A new recruit reports to the Orderly Room at Cocken Hall.

Recruits drawing clothing.

It is proving quite a picnic, how would you like to write sitting on the polished oak floor in a mansion drawing room with a marble mantle as a backrest? That is how I am writing for we are billeted in the drawing room with about 20 others. It is as hard as nails on the floor but we don't mind as it means there is no temptation to sleep in.

There isn't a grouser in the batch and we simply laugh and joke at what we have to put up with. Really we are enjoying ourselves splendidly and with plain but good grub and plenty of it and tons of exercise, we are as fit as we can possibly be and it is proving quite a picnic.

The training at Cocken Hall in the autumn of 1914 was carried out in beautiful fine weather in the woodland and fields of the old country house, the men rose early and for an hour before breakfast physical training and running in the open air took place. Pickets were posted at the main gate and fatigue parties kept the grounds and rooms clean and tidy. Those not so employed took part in drill and other forms of field training and entrenching, although unlike other battalions of the Durham Light Infantry who were largely recruited from miners, the artisans and clerks of the County Battalion did not take easily to the last named.

With the rapid increase in numbers Cocken Hall was soon overflowing with men so to ease the congestion the Darlington men, now known as A Company, were moved

to Newton Hall another unoccupied country house closer to Durham City. Likewise the Bede men, now parading as B Company, were moved to the Dill Hall in West Rainton. Frank Raine and others who were joining the Bede Company met at Hartlepool Railway Station to begin the journey to Durham, Frank recalled,

> I joined B Company of 18/Durham LI there was a fair proportion of Bede College men but not enough to form a whole company. We came to Hartlepool station on the Monday morning and entrained for Durham City. I can remember lining up on the Durham City platform and somebody shouting 'Form fours' and there was a right old mess up as quite a few had no knowledge [of foot drill] at all. Then we marched to a village called West Rainton where we were billeted in the village hall.

This detachment under the command of Captain Neville quickly made themselve's at home and very soon was organising entertainment for themselves.

One of the company 'smoker's' was recorded in the *Durham Chronicle* this was presided over by Captain Neville with Lieutenants Burden, Tait and Harraton in attendance along with Doctor Sutherland. Private Oliver May of Durham City was the musical director and the songs both gay and grave were of the highest order and greatly appreciated by those present.

Another incident at West Rainton recorded in the press was the day the 'Rainton Hare' appeared on parade. This animal was said to be famous in the district, the largest Hare ever seen and for the last twenty years it had outrun every Greyhound and Whippet for miles around. One morning as the company fell in the Hare popped up between a startled soldiers legs. Immediately everyone present broke ranks and a wild hue and cry commenced, the animal twisted and turned, bobbed and weaved in and out between the legs before finally making an escape.

The two outlying companies had to remain away from the battalion until such time as the huts could be completed, those artisans amongst the men were put to work to assist in the rapid construction of the camp. In the meantime foot drill and Swedish drill were the order of the day and route marching commenced. In the City a ladies committee collected tin baths for the use of the men and others residents provided books, footballs and tables and chairs to help make life comfortable. Church services were held in the local Parish churches and for the Methodists and Wesleyans the Leamside Primitive Methodist church was made available. When the sleeping accommodation was completed, other huts were added to the camp one of which was a miniature rifle range. To enable the battalion to make best use of this facility Colonel Burdon had the following appeal printed in the press,

Castle Eden
County Durham

> Dear Sir,
>
> I shall be much obliged if you would let it be known through the medium of your valuable paper that the County Battalion will be very grateful for the loan of eight or ten miniature rifles for practice purposes. These would be used during the period of their training and will be returned in six months time or earlier. Any clubs that would be good enough to do this service to their country should send them to myself at the above address.
>
> Yours faithfully
> Rowland Burdon.

With these rifles, musketry was quickly brought to a high standard and the work of the Instructors, Lieutenant D E Ince and Sergeants W Greenwell, W L Allen and T W Pickles paid off in the excellent shooting at Ripon and Salisbury Plain later on.

Among those from Hartlepool who joined at this time was 18/888 Private Robert Webster who

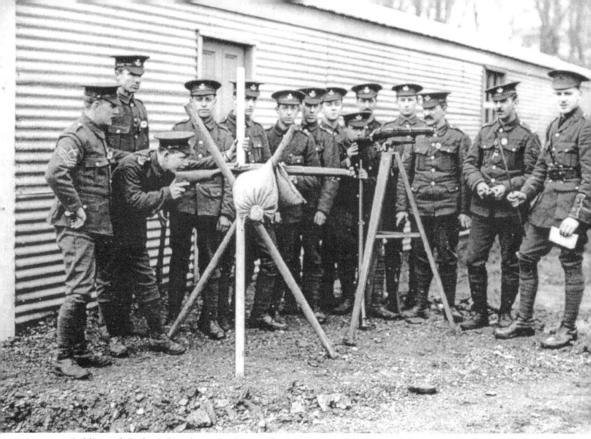

Soldiers of the battalion learn to site a rifle. Lieutenant D E Ince and Sergeants W Greenwell, W L Allen, T W Pickles were the instructors.

recorded that his billet was,

> *A mucky hayloft. We wore our own clothes and our own blankets. Parades were a scream all shapes and sizes. My pals were Bert Johnson, G Spark, Jack Lazonby, Bob Taylorson, Reg Birks and Bert Young The Wesleyans Joe Jackson, Charlie Coverdale Merryweather etc sang Sankey and Moody all night while we swore and blasphemed to annoy them. Eventually we were given huts and I was put in Number 4 Section, 13 Platoon of D Company.*

The various sections of the battalion were now being formed and training was carried on in earnest, signallers, who practiced with their flags, cooks, under Sergeant Moscrop, the transport, Regimental Police, the Quartermasters stores and the band and bugles as well as the four rifle companies were working from early morning until evening.

Friends and families, as well as members of the press, who wrote accounts of camp life that left an impression of an idyllic existence, visited the camp,

> *Away upon an eminence overlooking the Wear, which winds lazily round its base, Cocken Hall, hidden within a sweeping woodland is an ideal place for the purpose it is at present serving in the military world. The "Pals" are inhabiting its numerous rooms and outhouses and indeed, are in possession of practically the whole estate.*

> *The khaki uniform is everywhere worn by stalwart fellows with smiling, contented faces. Cocken Hall which but a short time ago was the scene of an alleged Suffragette attack, and which still bears interior traces of the fire is now re echoing words of military command and the laughter and chatter*

of gallant young men who have left their homes and warmth and luxury to face the hardships and privations of active service, preparing themselves for the time when they will be called upon to take their real practical share in the defence of our King and country.

The fine old hall with its seemingly endless variety of rooms, is erected upon the edge of a beautiful tree covered hill and down in the valley is Cocken Ford Bridge, and a picturesquely situated farmhouse near by, while in another direction is the beautiful Finchale Abbey. For Military purposes it would be difficult to improve upon Cocken and the fields adjacent are well adapted for every kind of drill and exercises.

In the distant part of the field detachments of troops were marching and nearer the hall joiners were engaged upon erecting sleeping huts, which will serve in conjunction with the building itself to accommodate the whole of the 'Comrades Battalion' sections of which are at present quartered at Newton Hall and West Rainton.

In and about the huts soldiers were busily engaged gathering the dead leaves together and clearing the surface and among them taking a keen interest in all their doings is the regimental pet or mascot as he is generally termed by the Pals at Cocken, a young retriever. The dog hailed from Rainton where he joined the soldiers on a route march and followed them into camp, declining to return home under any circumstances. It has been presented with an appropriate collar and an officer attached a badge bearing the magic letters "DURHAM".

The spectacle among the huts was one of considerable activity men busily employed clearing the decks, brightening their weapon, always preparing. They have fixed duties and fixed hours and all is happiness. Wherever one turned young men, who in normal times followed varied professional and other pursuits, appeared to have taken to their entirely fresh duties as ducks to water. 'Not a care in the world', called out one merry soldier. "I feel like I am just beginning to live," said another, his face tanned and eyes gleaming.

At the present time there are two companies quartered at Cocken of about 250 men each. C and A Companies are from Durham and Darlington districts respectively and are quartered at Rainton and Newton Hall, though it is expected that when the 28 sleeping huts are completed the whole battalion will be stationed at Cocken Hall.

Lord Southampton is in command and one cannot but be impressed by his fine physique and military bearing. It is interesting to stroll round the camp and see the provision made for the men. On the right is a marquee which serves the purpose of a canteen and which boasts a piano; on the left, in the various outhouses, are the armoury with its hundreds of death dealing instruments, and the cookhouse with its giant ovens, huge quantities of provisions and energetic staff. Turning to the rear of the hall we see the orderly room and as we stand we see a young man heavily laden report himself. He is another addition to the battalion and a fine specimen too. A little distance away are two well

A Company with Framwellgate Moor Colliery in the background.

RSM Chaplin joined 106th Light Infantry in 1881 and was Commissioned as the Battalion Quartermaster on 14/6/15.

dressed young men clearing leaves from the west lawn, they had come from Shields and already felt the experience was doing them good.

Officers were being rapidly appointed and all four companies now had a commander, A Company, Captain Roberts, B Company, Captain Tilly, C Company, Captain Neville and last but not least command of D Company was given to Captain Hutchens. The Acting Adjutant was Captain W D Lowe and several subalterns had been appointed among them Lieutenants R Burdon, J R Harraton, F S Beadon and B S Roberts.

When the huts were completed the two outlying companies returned to Cocken Hall and training progressed from platoon drill to company drill and then whole battalion sized route marches and field training. Once again a local reporter from the *Northern Daily Mail* was allowed to visit the men,

Swish-swish-swish, It might be the sighing of the night-wind through the trees; the music of some rapid running stream or other of nature's night noise, but in this case it was the rhythm of the feet of some 600 of the County Battalion out for a night route march that fell upon the wayfarers ear. Needless to say this was a new and interesting experience to the young fellows, many of whom are more accustomed to the glare of the electric arcs of the city and town, than to the absolute solitude – solitude amounting almost to uncanniness – in the heart of the country upon a dark night.

Not a star was to be observed in the heavens when the companies, each unit of which was as silent as a Sphinx paraded for the march. A quiet, almost noiseless shuffling of feet and the advance guard were off. Then came the connecting file – a yard apart – then the main body, another connecting file then the rear guard. In this manner the gloomiest of country lanes were traversed, each man keeping his eyes skinned in order to remain in touch with his neighbour. A whispered 'Halt' from the commander is passed down the line, and gradually the tramp of feet dies away until an eerie silence again reigns supreme and no one would dream that the huge body of men clad in khaki were within 20 miles of them. The command 'Forward' is whispered along the line and they are off again, after a detour they reach the parade ground once more.

But this is only a tithe of the work being done by the battalion. Squad drill, extended order and skirmishing work and rifle drill are being rapidly brought to a state of efficiency and in a manner which is a credit to both instructors and men.

As well as military training, sport also played its part in battalion life both Rugby and Association Football teams flourished, several well known players of both creeds having joined the 'Pals', from Hartlepool Rovers RUFC came Corporal Heal as well as several of the Durham City team. On the other hand, Robson of Newcastle United and Timms who was a former Barnsley player, as well a number of Northern League men like Private J E Smith who played

Lieutenant Colonel Hugh Bowes took over command from Lord Southampton.

Many well known local footballers were serving in the battalion including Robson of Newcastle United and Herbert Timms who had played for Barnsley.

for Shildon and Crook, represented association Football. From the world of local Cricket, Fred Smith of Shiny Row, who played for the Bournmoor Cricket Club was prominent; he was commissioned into the 19th Battalion and would be killed in action in 1916.

Owing to ill health Lord Southampton was forced to resign the appointment of Commanding Officer, command of the battalion passed to Lieutenant Colonel H Bowes late of the 1st Volunteer Battalion Durham Light Infantry who was at that time Second in Command.

But Colonel Bowes was not happy about the battalion's marching and wrote the following memorandum to all Officers and NCO's,

MEMORANDUM

1 The marching of the unit in column of route is far from satisfactory or creditable.

2 The chief faults are the cramped movement of the men resulting from their slovenly carriage and want of soldierly bearing and want of care in covering off.

3 All these faults lead to fatigue and affect mobility.

4 The want of freedom of movement is caused by the men bending the head forward and looking down or casting the eyes on the ground when marching. Men must be taught to look their height thus affecting the carriage of the body and giving that freedom of swing from the hips which is an essential feature of good marching (see sections 21 & 13 of Infantry Training).

5 Officer's and NCO's will at once take such steps as are necessary to see that the term of the paragraphs in Infantry Training quoted are complied with.'

The battalion on a route march near Fencehouses. The colonel's memorandum on marching had the desired effect.

From this time on the marching improved and there were no more complaints.

It was in the middle of November that units all over the north were put on the alert and moved to defend the coast. The locally raised units were still partially trained and were, in many cases, unable to deploy the whole battalion strength. In 18/DLI Colonel Bowes selected those NCO's and men who had fired the range course, these were formed into two companies under the command of Major Tristram and Captain Neville and on 16 November they marched to Leamside Station and were moved by rail to Hartlepool.

KITCHENER'S ARMY UNDER FIRE

On arrival at Hartlepool the men were quartered in Hart Road and were put to improving the trenches along the coast. Guards for strategic points were provided and some training was carried out. Shortly afterwards one company moved into billets in Old Hartlepool providing sentries and duty personnel in the docks area.

On the morning of 15 December The Admiralty passed information to the War Office, who in turn informed all Garrison Headquarters on the East Coast to expect a raid by ships of the Imperial German Navy. All along the coast trenches were manned and units stood to, but that day no enemy were sighted.

The armament of the Hartlepool forts was very weak, manned by men of the Durham Royal Garrison Artillery (TF), who were commanded by Lieutenant Colonel Robson, in the Heugh Battery were two six inch guns and about a hundred yards south of this position in the Lighthouse

Battery was mounted a single six inch gun. Three and a half miles away across the Tees estuary lay another fort, the South Gare, which mounted two 4.7 inch guns. This along with the infantry units was all that defended the marine engineering and steel works that lay along the river banks up to Middlesbrough.

On the night of 15 – 16 December four German battle-cruisers, Moltke, Seydlitz, Derfflinger, Von der Tann accompanied by the cruiser Blucher crossed the North Sea and gathered off the North East coast. The ships split up into two squadrons, Derffflinger and Von der Tann steamed south and at 8 a.m. on 16 December attacked Scarborough and take no further part in this story. The three remaining headed north and managed to get inside the British patrol line before dawn.

That morning the North East coast was covered in a dense mist, there was hardly a breath of wind, the sea was flat calm and the tide was exceptionally low. When just before 8 a.m. the German warships with Seydlitz leading followed by Moltke then Blucher crossed Tees Bay from the south east the mist considerably hampered the gunners of the two 4.7 guns at the South Gare. The British destroyers HMS Doon and HMS Hardly and the gunboat HMS Patrol attacked the German ships from seaward, although they tried to fight they were forced back by the shear weight of the German guns. Because the Germans were firing to seaward the British gunners on shore at the South Gare Battery thought that the German ships were British cruisers under attack from German destroyers. Through the mist it was difficult to tell the difference between the Imperial German Ensign and the British White Ensign. It was only when they turned their fire on the Hartlepool forts that it was realised that the ships were in fact German, but by that time they were out of range of the South Gare Battery. The gunners in the Heugh Battery took on Seydlitz and the Lighthouse fired at Blucher. With their third shot the Lighthouse gunners scored a hit and flames shot up from Blucher's after-deck where an ammunition supply had been hit. But the Germans now commenced shelling the town, the Gasometers were hit and long columns of flame shot skyward. Many shells were fired into the town hitting houses, schools, railway yards and shipyards. The enemy also claimed the destruction of the Cemetery Battery, firing a number of shells, which were wasted for this position had been dismantled in 1906. While this was going on a fishing smack was run aground on the beach, the crew abandoning the vessel. One man was left wounded on the beach and Sergeant W E Heal along with Corporal M Brewerton of the 'Pals' ran down the beach and brought him to safety. The 'Pals' manning their positions came under fire and Private Theo Jones, a teacher and member of the Bede contingent, who hailed from Hartlepool, became the first man of Kitchener's New Army to fall to enemy fire. Shortly after this a machine gun position was hit and another four men were killed, two days later another of the Bede men Private Thomas Minks died from the wounds he received.

Amongst those of the battalion deployed to the coast was 18/888 Private Robert Webster from Hartlepool, in his small diary he recorded his view of the bombardment;

> *Dawn 16 December manned trenches on sea front at Spion Kop. On sentry look out on top of sea bank, about 0820 Hrs reported three big ships off Tees mouth signalling with lights. Shortly after ships fired seaward. This was followed in a few minutes by shells fired inland. I was ordered into a trench and watched the bombardment of Hartlepool from there. Our trench was hit by a light shell and Corporal Scott was wounded and nearby the Gasometers were blazing. Fishing vessels at sea ran for the shore and men jumped into the water and ran for it. One man hurt or broke a leg and Sergeant Heal and Corporal Brewerton immediately went to his rescue.*

Derrflinger, Seydelitz & Moltke make their way towards the British coast.

Hartlepool Gasometers destroyed by enemy fire, 16 December 1914.

On top of the casualties to 18/DLI further deaths occurred to men of the Durham Royal Garrison Artillery and The Durham Fortress Company, Royal Engineers. In the town there was over 100 men, women and children killed with around 300 wounded along with much destruction to the houses and buildings of the town.

Bob Webster also wrote about going into town;

'After the bombardment we were sent to the Borough Hall and were detailed off into Rescue Parties, Stretcher Bearers, Demolition parties and Guards. At night there was another scare. The battalion lost 5 killed and 11 wounded and one died later of his wounds, Theo Jones was amongst those killed.'

All along the Durham coast folk inland watched in awe as the enemy ships pounded the town, reports came in from Horden, Hart Station and Blackhall Rocks whilst further inland as far away as Durham City the sound of the guns was plainly heard. In the offices of the Durham Chronicle news was received from Hartlepool and notices, that attracted large crowds, were put up in the window. The newspaper stated that,

'throughout the afternoon there was a continuous stream of citizens anxious to know the latest details. The anxiety was increased by the fact that the Durham Comrades Battalion are at present stationed at Hartlepool and with the Pals are a number of well known young Dunelmians.'

Within days Lord Durham visited the men at Hartlepool and complimented them on their steadiness throughout the action, however the real heroes were the Gunners of the Durham RFA (TF) who had stuck to their weapons and kept them firing.

I was in charge of one gun during the action which lasted about 50 minutes – quite the hottest 50 minutes I ever experienced and we did not half pepper them with Lyddite shells. The German ships which were all battle cruisers appeared off our battery at 8.15 a.m. and spread out like a fan one on the right, one on the left and one in the centre and opened fire on us at about 3,000 to 4,000 yards with the broadside of their guns. One shell dropped about two yards from me and ricocheted right over the heads of our chaps handing up the ammunition. They saw it pass right over my head and thought I was gone, however it did not burst. Nearly all my detachment were Territorials and I had my eye on them during the action and I must say they worked like heroes. The Germans got the range splendidly but their shells kept falling left and right. We kept at it until two of them turned and cleared off. Our casualties were very few, three 'Terriers' and six Durham Light Infantry men standing just outside the battery were blown to pieces. Our battery escaped with little damage.

Wrote Bombadier Frederick Mallin a Regular Reservist and Police Constable from Penarth, Glamorgan. For their part in the action both he and Bombadier J J Hope received the Military Medal in April 1916, whilst Sergeant T Douthwaite was awarded the Distinguished Conduct Medal for extracting a live cartridge from a gun that had miss fired. One man from 18/Durham LI, 18/559 Sergeant Albert Miles was transferred to the Royal Defence Corps and did not serve overseas, however in 1920 he put forward a case to the Army Medal Office that he had been under enemy fire at the Bombardment of Hartlepool and as such was entitled to the British War Medal. The case was investigated and on 27 February 1922 the medal duly awarded.

At 11 o'clock on 19 December 1914 the funeral took place at Saint Aidans Church, Hartlepool of Private Theo Jones. The service was conducted by the Reverend W J Knowes the vicar. Over 500 members of the 18/Durham LI were present under the command of Major Roberts and both Major Tilly and Major Neville were present, as well as numerous friends of the late Private Jones, including members of the Schools Athletic Association and the West Hartlepool Cricket Club. A large crowd lined the route from the church to the cemetery, where at the end of the internment a salute was fired by a party under the command of Sergeant Wilson, then the 'Last Post' was sounded. The coffin was covered in floral tributes including one from the Officer Commanding and Officers of the battalion, whilst another was from The NCO's and men.

Assistance was given to help clean up the damage in town, many unexploded German shells were collected and further training was carried out until Christmas when most of the men were granted leave and went home until they returned to Hartlepool after the holiday. One event that happened at this time concerned 18/1127 Private Joseph Fail, a Seaham man and devout Weslyan. One evening on guard he remembered that it was Christian Endeavour meeting at the church, so he decided to leave his rifle in the sentry box and went off to the Christian Endeavour meeting. While he was away the Orderly Sergeant came round and found the post abandoned and the rifle left behind. When Private Fail returned he was put under close arrest and the following morning, he appeared before the Colonel, who said, 'Private Fail you have broken serious laws of the Army

On the 19 December 1914 the funeral took place of Private Theo Jones, the first man of Kitchener's New Army to be killed by enemy action. He was caught by an exploding shell whilst manning the defences on the beach.

Soldiers pose behind unexploded German shells at Hartlepools.

18/1127 Private Joseph Fail who prefered the Lord's work to sentry duty.

Orders – deserting your post, breaking bounds, absent without leave etc etc'. He then said, 'What were you up to?'

Joseph Fail replied, 'Well there was nowt gannin on so I went to do the Lord's work.'

The Colonel, exasperated, exclaimed, 'I hardly know what to do with you,' then turning to Private Fail he said, 'What would you do if you were in my place?' Joseph replied, 'I'd forgive you sir' To which the Colonel replied, 'I believe I will,' – and he did!

It was around this time that 18/Durham LI joined 122 Infantry Brigade commanded by Brigadier General J G Hunter CB, as well as the Durham Pals, 122 Brigade comprised 16/NF (Northumberland Fusiliers) (Newcastle Commercials), 18/NF and 19/NF(1st and 2nd Tyneside Pioneers). The Brigade was one of the three brigades of the 41st Division of the Fifth New Army, the other two being 123 (Tyneside Scottish) Brigade and 124 (Tyneside Irish) Brigade.

On 30 December 1914 Headquarters 122 Brigade published the following congratulatory order,

The Brigadier General has been much pleased with the general turnout of the battalions of his Brigade that he has inspected. The men are clean, smart and keen and are fine soldiers. The outfit, equipment and housing arrangements reflect the very highest credit on those whom they have been entrusted. The physique and the health of the men in general are excellent.

The news was now circulated that the 'Pals' battalion was full and that no more recruits would be accepted, however the War Office decreed that each Service Battalion would now raise Depot Companies in order to supply reinforcements to the battalion once it went overseas. The recruiting offices again picked up the baton and E and later F companies were formed from the later recruits increasing the strength of the battalion to around 1500 all ranks. However this figure was being reduced as a number of the original enlistments applied for and were granted commissions. Among those to enlist around this time was Arthur Durrant of Sunderland, who eventually became a Sergeant in the battalion.

I joined the 18th Battalion of The Durham Light Infantry, 'The Pals', in 1915 by then the battalion was complete, they were a fine set of fellows and the Colonel, Colonel Bowes was very, very much liked and it was a pleasure to be in such a battalion. There was quite a number of Hartlepool lads and quite a number of Sunderland lads but there wasn't any particular one type, they were a very varied lot.

On 13 January 1915 the GOC Northern Command who expressed his regret that they were leaving Hartlepool and complimented them on the manner in which they had conducted themselves during the past two months inspected the men of the battalion stationed at Hartlepool. They were then given an enthusiastic send off by the people of Hartlepool as their train pulled out of the station. Travelling by way of Shincliffe and Sherburn the train eventually reached Leamside Station where they were met by the battalion band who played them back to the hutted camp at Cocken Hall.

After the 18th Battalion returned to Cocken Hall further field training was carried out, these field exercises generally took the form of an enemy advance with the battalion repelling the invaders. In early February one such scheme took place. The general idea was that a KHAKI FORCE based on Bishop Auckland , with a strength of about one division was operating against a WHITE FORCE of the same strength based on Sunderland. The Khaki Force had advanced troops of 122 Brigade as far as Durham Meanwhile the White Force had advanced from Sunderland in the direction Durham, but their advance was blocked by the blowing up of the railway bridge over the road due west of Belmont Hall. A further obstacle to the advance was that all the bridges over the River Wear except the bridge at Finchale Abbey had been blown up.

18/Durham Light Infantry on parade at Cramlington when part of 122 Brigade , 41st Division.

The 18th Battalion were to deploy and oppose any enemy crossing of the bridge until reinforcements could arrive. When the 'Pals' reached Crook Hall they were informed that the enemy were already over the river with a strength of two companies and supported by a section of Field Artillery and furthermore they were entrenching in the neighbourhood of East Moor Leazes, to cover the crossing of the main body. Of course 18/DLI drove the enemy back and won the day. Similar exercises were carried out throughout February and March, the enemy attacked from various directions, Chester le Street, Durham, Consett and Darlington. Advance guards and flank guards were put out, convoy's were escorted and outposts defended by rearguards. These field days were often in conjunction with units stationed nearby, the Scottish Horse (Lord Tullybardines Yeomanry Brigade) stationed at Lambton Park and 160 (Wearside) Brigade Royal Field Artillery from Houghton le Spring provided the support troops so that the infantry learned to cooperate with other arms. It was during one of these training days that Private Charles Todd, of Browney Colliery, accidentally stabbed himself in the leg. He had somehow put an open clasp knife into his pocket and when he jumped up the blade went deep into his leg. Later that night the pain was so bad he went to see the doctor, as he was being examined the main artery in his thigh burst and sent blood in a bright jet across the room. The doctor called for an orderly to squeeze the artery and immediately wired to Durham for an ambulance to take Private Todd to the VAD Hospital at Chilton Moor. He made a recovery and although the doctors wanted to discharge him, he wanted to remain with the 'Pals' and was allowed to do so.

When in barracks close order and ceremonial drill was the order of the day and gradually the battalion improved. However on an inspection of 122 Brigade by the GOC Northern Command things were not quite what the inspecting officer wanted. A long list of criticism was forwarded from HQ Northern Command to GOC 122 Brigade and from there to the various battalions of the brigade. The last paragraph of this letter pointed out faults with the men,

'2, Turn Out
   The following further points also need attention:-
Hair in many cases far too long.
Buttons and badges and other brass work not properly cleaned.
   The dirty state of the service dress.   It should be remembered that because service dress is old it is not necessary for it to be black with grease in which case evident want of attention on the part of the company commander is displayed.
   Trousers should be pulled down over the top of the puttees.
Signed J S Talbot Colonel
AAG Northern Command'

The fact that the men only had one set of service dress seems to have escaped the inspecting officer, even the Brigade of Guards couldn't have remained spotless wearing the same uniform day in day out, in camp and out on manoeuvres.

In April an open day for friends and families was arranged, the band played on the lawns of Cocken Hall and the men went through various movements to entertain their visitors, There was to have been a regimental dance that night, but a despatch rider arrived at great speed with the news that there was another coast defence scare. The Duty Bugler sounded assembly and three

'Come to the cookhouse door boys!' The duty bugler 18/1053 Arthur Dale of York, sounds the popular call to the battalion. Orderlies carry piping hot stew and bread to the huts.

*C Company at Cocken Hall. In the doorway L/Cpl Curry and Private M. Fullerton. **Middle row left to right:** L/Cpl R. Maughan; Privates J. S. Curry, A. L. Richardson, A. Clarke and S. Bates, (unknown). **Front row:** Privates Jewitt, A. Blackburn, T. Stobbs, T. Aspey, J. Wilson, T. K. Mellor, G. Butler and F. Brown.*

The Orderly Room staff 18/Durham Light Infantry. Left to right: 18/547 Private W. R. Moody, Private J. Oliver, 18/632 Sgt T. Wilson, 18/903 Cpl F. West, 18/284 Private W. Hall, (unknown)

companies, A, B & C were ordered at short notice to deploy in the Cleveland area. Entraining at Leamside in the evening of 21 April they were moved to Middlesborough and an outpost line was established to the east, south and south west of the town. Company headquarters were set up as follows, A Company in Cargo Fleet Iron Works, B Company at Marton Bungalow and C Company near Marton Hall. The men were sleeping in fields and the weather was extremely bad at this time and although the local authorities and local townsfolk did all they could, the conditions were described as 'unfavourable', so much so that after a week in the field, the detached companies were ordered to return to Cocken Hall once more, but it would be for the last time. On 3 May the battalion was ordered to join the rest of 122 Brigade in a tented camp at Cramlington in Northumberland. With the departure of the main body, which comprised A,B,C and D Companies. The reserve companies E and F were moved to Ravensworth Park alongside the Territorial reserve units to continue training.

The weather at Cramlington was cold, wet and miserable and the battalion devoted much time to ceremonial drill in preparation for an inspection by His Majesty the King and Lord Kitchener. There was a pre-inspection by the GOC Northern Command on 17 May and this time he was highly satisfied with the turnout of the Brigade, all the officers commanding battalions received a message from the GOC, relayed by Brigadier General Hunter, expressing entire satisfaction with what he had seen. Three days later on 20 May the Brigade marched into Newcastle upon Tyne to take part in a review of troops by the King. The troops on parade came from all the different arms stationed locally, and marched past in order of seniority, the cavalry were represented by 1/1 East Riding Yeomanry and the Scottish Horse Brigade. The Second Line Northumbrian Division provided four brigades of Royal Field Artillery and three field and one signal company of Royal Engineers. Following these troops the second line infantry of the Northumberland, York and Durham and Durham Light Infantry Brigades, with the Divisional Train of the Army Service Corps and Field Ambulance units of Royal Army Medical Corps following close behind. The New Army followed behind those of the Territorial Force. Led by Brigadier General Hunter's 122 Brigade, 16. 18, 19/NF and 18/DLI followed by 123(Tyneside Scottish) and 124(Tyneside Irish) Brigades.

This was the last time that 18/DLI would parade with the Northumberland battalions, the first four New Armies had been raised so quickly that nothing had been done about reserves for them. The War Office answer was to turn the battalions of the Fourth New Army, 30th – 35th Divisions into Second Reserve Battalions to provide the reinforcements for the First, Second and Third New Armies, the original divisions of The Fourth New Army being broken up. The Fifth New Army then became the Fourth New Army and the Divisions broken up or renumbered. In the 41st Division the Tyneside Scottish and Irish Brigades became 102 and 103 Brigades of the 34th Division, but 122 Brigade was broken up and the battalions posted to other formations. 16/NF went to 96 Brigade in 32nd Division, 18/NF became the Divisional Pioneers to 34th Division and 19/NF became Divisional Pioneers to 35th Division.

Ripon, 93 Brigade, 31st Division
On 22 May 18/DLI left Cramlington and moved to Ripon in Yorkshire, joining 93 Brigade in 31st Division, this division was made up of Yorkshire and Lancashire 'Pals' Battalions. 92 Brigade comprised the four 'Hull Pals' battalions the 10, 11, 12 and 13/East Yorkshire Regiment. Along with 18/DLI the other battalions of 93 Brigade were 15/West Yorkshire Regiment, the 'Leeds Pals', the 16 and 18/West Yorkshire Regiment the 1st and 2nd 'Bradford Pals'. The third brigade of the division was made up by 11/East Lancashire Regiment, the 'Accrington Pals' and three

Four soldiers demonstrate the wearing of full marching order. On the left is 18/801 Private A. Merriweather from West Hartlepool. In 1917 he was commissioned into 7/Wiltshire Regiment.

battalions of the York and Lancaster Regiment, the 12th Battalion, the Sheffield City and the 13th and 14th Battalions, the 1st and 2nd 'Barnsley Pals'.

During June 1915 the Battalion concentrated on field training at company level, the general scheme of things was that an enemy force had landed and moved inland raiding Yorkshire as far inland as Ripon, the various companies were deployed to attack the enemy known as White Force. It was while this training was taking place at Ripon that the sad news was received that Captain Edward Dickenson was missing at Gallipoli. He had originally enlisted in the 'Pals' Darlington Company but had very quickly reached the rank of Sergeant. He had applied for and been given a commission as a Lieutenant in 11/Green Howards, but on the despatch of the Expeditionary Force to Gallipoli he had been given a Captaincy in The Royal Dublin Fusiliers, it was with this last unit on 28 June that he was posted missing during the action at Gully Ravine when 1/RDF lost almost all of its officers.

On 16 July A Company moved southwards from Grewelthorpe to attack an enemy convoy, which the company advance guard had located at Aldfield. The advance guard moved into Spa Gill Wood and carried out a reconnaissance of the White Force, this was completed by 7.00 p.m. and the OC decided to attack just after dark, when the enemy were assaulted south west of Aldfield near Spa Gill Wood. The next night D Company were doing similar exercise between

Low Gate and Sawley Hall driving back the White Force, while a few nights later C Company moved via Morker Grange to Raventofts Hall and took up defensive positions allowing the rest of the battalion to deploy behind them. An inspection by General Sir Archibald Murray brought favourable comment on one hand but a sharp rebuke from Lieutenant Colonel Bowes on the other. For the inspection it was said that, 'The men looked well, stood steadily in the ranks and showed considerable soldierly bearing and on the whole were well turned out.' Despite some criticism about the fitting of uniforms and equipment the inspection had gone well but then the men had been asked to open their packs. The report on the inspection records,

> *The Commanding Officer was distressed to note that in many instances men were not carrying the prescribed clothing, equipment and necessaries in their packs. This dereliction of duty points to the fact that men are not taking their training seriously. Entrenching tool helves from this date will be scrubbed. If necessary daily, again all minor defects in equipment should be immediately reported and no stone left unturned in order to have the defect attended to. Platoon Commanders and NCO's are at all times to assist their men in having defects remedied forthwith. It should be clearly understood that a broken buckle, a torn strap or bad stitching renders a man non-efficient who has to be fed and clothed and is of no use for fighting.*

Towards the end of July 31st Division carried out a major training exercise in trench warfare. A trench system was dug in the fields south of the Bishop Monkton – Markington Road, each Brigade was given a section of the front line and every battalion was allotted a section of trench to dig. The battalions of 93 Brigade moved off with 15/West Yorks leading followed by 16/West Yorks then 18/West Yorks and bringing up the rear came 18/DLI. The digging continued day and night until the trench system was complete, then the battalions practised manning the trenches and relieving each other at night. Opposite this line the Divisional Royal Engineers had

The Commanding Officer Lieutenant Colonel H. Bowes and Adjutant Captain Lowe ride ahead of the battalion into Ripon.

The band played the battalion into Ripon. In the centre of the front row is 18/105 Private G. H. Layfield from Blackwellgate in Darlington.

The battalion tug-of-war team won 93 Brigade competition beating the Leeds Pals in the final by two straight pulls.

'Spud bashing' the time honoured task of thousands of soldiers. Here men of 18/Durham Light Infantry prepare a meal.

At recreation in the River Ure.

constructed an enemy line and each battalion in turn provided the enemy for the rest of the brigade. Sap heads were constructed and the throwing of grenades at enemy positions was practised, all movement and work was carried out as close to active service conditions as possible, second line trenches and machine gun positions were also constructed. The various battalions of the brigade manned these trenches and took their turn in the enemy trenches until such time as they were considered proficient. Musketry and courses of instruction had also been carried out during the last weeks of July and the end of August. One of the notable figures during the 'Pals' stay at Ripon was that of RSM F J Carnell 3/COLDSTREAM GDS. At that time he was the senior RSM of the British Army and his fine commanding presence and powers of drill and instruction could never be forgot by any NCO or soldier who attended one of his classes or parades. On 15 August the battalion was taken over by the War Office and ceased to be the responsibility of The County Durham Parliamentary Recruiting Committee. Of the original cost of raising, feeding and equipping the battalion the committee refused to accept a refund thus, presenting the nation the only battalion raised completely free of expense. The Fourth New Army began to move south to complete its training prior to departure overseas. On 19 September, D Company under the command of Captain W G Hutchence assumed the role of advance party and left South Camp, Ripon for Fovant Camp on the Southern edge of Salisbury Plain.

Bob Webster recorded the task of being the Battalion advance party in his diary,

Advance party to Fovant Camp Wilt., New Camp a hell hole, rain and mud no roads. All Fatigue work, cleaning up and carrying stores, blankets, tables, trestles, chairs. pots, pans, coal, buckets, mops squeegees etc etc by the thousands to all camps. Raided orchards for apples by the ton.

A few days later the rest of the battalion followed. Fovant Camp was in a deplorable state the roads were unmade and the weather was atrocious although some entrenching was possible it certainly wasn't in good conditions. However some diaries of work undertaken by the battalion at this time have survived and do give some idea of what was going on, for example on 18 October Colonel Bowes reported as follows;

8.28 am	Advance Guard left camp
8.32 am	Head of Van Guard at cross roads PICTURE PALACE
	Depth of advance guard about 1,200 yards
8.47 am	Remainder of battalion left camp throwing out a small rear guard
8.52 am	Head of Column arrived cross roads PICTURE PALACE and halted until 9.5 am.

A Machine Gun Section of 15/West Yorks joined the battalion. The Officer in Command stated he had received orders to that affect. I had not been informed of this action.

10 20 am   Battalion less Advance guard arrived COMMON BARN FARM, went into Brigade reserve and outspanned. Rearguard withdrawn.

12 noon	Advance guard withdrawn and joined reserve at 1.15 pm.
3.25 pm	Orders received to return to barracks.
3 50 pm	Battalion marched off on return, outward route being kept.
4 45pm	Arrived barracks.

Fovant Camp
18-10-15   Lieut Colonel
Comdg 18th (S) Btn

                                     Durham LI (County)

But all was not as simple as the diary recorded, in a report written later Colonel Bowes complained that, '16/West Yorks arrived at 8.27 am instead of 8.45 and blocked the road, this meant that Number 1 Column head by 15/West Yorks could not start on time and further complications were met when Number 2 Column started too early.'

About three weeks later there was another scheme this time a RED FORCE based on Warminster had defeated a BLUE FORCE based on Southampton. The BLUE FORCE had to conduct a retreat and 93 Brigade supported by 1 Squadron of cavalry, a Field Company of Royal Engineers along with a Brigade of Royal Field Artillery were to delay the RED FORCE on the line Fonthill Bishop – East Knoyle. Once the main body was clear of the cross roads near Fonthill Gifford the Brigade would withdraw. The enemy RED FORCE this time was provided by 16/West Yorks who would hamper the withdrawal. 18/DLI provided two platoons as advance guard followed by the remainder of the battalion. Behind came 18/West Yorks followed by 15/West Yorks. The officers commanding made their dispositions and took up positions as required in the instructions. By 10.24 am 18/DLI had halted North of Fonthill House with the advance guard covering the front about 1200 yards to the North. By 10.50 am the battalion scouts reported an enemy platoon about 900 yards North of Fonthill Bishop. C and D Companies moved into position to cover the rest of the battalion and Brigade was informed. By 11.20 am both companies reported that they were in position but that the enemy were developing an attack. Brigade now ordered B Company to be attached to 15/West Yorks and C and D Companies to retire to a new position covered by A Company and the Machine Gun Platoon. Around the same time Battalion Headquarters moved into Fonthill Gifford. Then all companies retired to a new position from where D Company enfiladed the enemy attack on 15/West Yorks. Then when the Divisional Staff Officers acting as umpires were satisfied the men were marched back to Fovant Camp which was reached by 4.40 pm. These exercises carried out on Salisbury Plain were recorded in the form of a War Diary and preserved by the then Adjutant Captain W D Lowe .

As late as the end of November the battalion had not received their complement of Mark III Lee Enfield rifles, in fact only D Company had been fully equipped with these. Battalion orders for 22 November stated that all Officers and specialists would return to their platoons and fire Part III of the range course. A and B Ranges at Fovant were allocated to 18/Durham LI and in order to do this 100 Mark III Lee Enfields were borrowed from another unit. The men being instructed to take great care of these weapons. The same Part One Order stated that 18/683 Private J W Backhouse and 18/842 Private W H Rushton both of D Company, were discharged from the Military Hospital in Salisbury and sent on five days sick leave. Also serving with D Company was Private Joe Ramshaw, he managed to get a card away to his wife at Single Burdon Street, Heseldon, Castle Eden Colliery, which said 'Dear Wife A few words to let you know I am alright; hoping everything is alright at home. Best love to you and all the children. God be with you till we meet again. Joe.'

The time was now near for embarkation, Staff Officers went to France on reconnaissance and twice gas helmets were issued and withdrawn. As 31st Division Artillery was not fully trained and the division was about to proceed overseas the 32nd Divisional Artillery which was ahead in its training joined the Division. In the first days of December, Lord Durham visited and inspected the battalion to bid them farewell as they were about to proceed overseas. The men were expecting to get a forty eight hour pass and many had sent word home that they were coming, when with less than three hours notice all leave was cancelled and the advance party that had left for France was recalled. Then on 5 December the day at last came. They were ordered to the Land of the Pharaoh's, Egypt.

Men of 10 Platoon C Company, 18/Durham Light Infantry at Fovant, Wiltshire, November 1915. The last group photograph before embarkation.

BOBS DURHAM BANTAMS

On 13 January the War Office authorised the Durham County Parliamentary Recruiting Committee to raise another battalion for the County Regiment. The height and chest measurements for recruits into the army had been reduced to allow the formation of 'Bantam' battalions. In these units the minimum height being 5 feet and the maximum height 5 feet 3 inches tall with a chest measurement of 34 inches. At a meeting of the Durham County Recruiting Committee a resolution was passed that the War Office should be approached with a view to forming a Bantam Battalion for the Durham Light Infantry. Generations of many Durham families had been employed underground in the collieries found throughout the county. This work led to whole families being small in height but muscular in the upper body and it cannot be denied that they like many others were keen to do their bit. So it was that on 13 January the news came that the War Office had agreed to the request. At a meeting in the Old Shire Hall in Elvet, Durham City, the following committee was constituted, Lord Durham(President), Mr C R Barrett, Chester le Street(Chairman), Mr J Wiseman, Barnard Castle(Vice Chairman), Mr A B Horsley, Hartlepool(Hon Treasurer), and Messers Corrie, Slater and Dowson(Hon Secretaries).

Mr Barrett opened the meeting and recapped on the above resolution to raise a 'Bantam' battalion in the county and confirmed that sanction had been given subject to War Office conditions being fulfilled. Accordingly the Chairman moved that the battalion be raised and that the organisation be left in the hands of a sub-committee to be appointed.

The following were then elected to the sub-committee, The High Sherriff of Durham, Captain Rogerson The Hon Secretary of the Durham Territorial Force Association, Colonel Burden, Major Tomlinson, Doctor Gibbon, Alderman Harbottle, Mr J Ness, Sir H Elverston MP, Lord Barnard, Sir Lindsay Wood Bart, Mr M Dillon, Sir W Runciman Bart MP, Alderman J Samuel MP, Mr U A Ritson, Mr W Milburn, Mr J Raine junior and MR J H Ouston.

Colonel Sir Eric Swayne KCMG CB, representing the GOC Northern Command addressed the meeting and indicated that the first task would be to secure a headquarters for the battalion, along with that the major concern was accommodation for the men. He stated that the men could be enrolled at once but should not be attested until the accommodation was secured. The committee was authorised to make financial arrangements for feeding and clothing the battalion A few days later Mr C R Barrett again presided over a meeting in Old Shire Hall when the committee met to appoint a Commanding Officer for the new battalion. On the motion of the chairman and seconded by Sir Lindsay Wood it was decided that Major W Thomlinson of Seaton Carew be appointed as commander of the battalion. Major Thomlinson accepted the position subject to War Office approval and intimated that his first priority would be the appointment of officers to the battalion. The meeting then decided that the battalion would be known locally as 'Bobs Durham Bantams' whilst the official title would be 19th (Service) Battalion Durham Light Infantry (2nd

County). The sub-committee was divided into three sections (1)Finance, (2)Billeting and Feeding and (3)Clothing and Equipment. The Hon secretaries reported that every post was bringing in names of men anxious to join the battalion and further names were being added by recruiting officers throughout the county. The 'Bantam' Committee set up Offices at 37 Sadler Street, Durham City, and the work of raising another 'Kitchener' Battalion commenced. The early recruits were initially quartered at West Hartlepool, where the Baltic Chambers in George Street were made available as billets for the battalion. Initially the 'Bantams' were attached to 122 Brigade for administrative purposes. The kitting out and early training of the 'Bantams' took place in Hartlepool, but little except foot drill and route marching could be achieved in the town. The formation of a battalion of men under the height of 5 feet 3 inches gave many such as Arthur Riddle the chance they had been waiting for, for months. Arthur recalled the times he tried to enlist,

> Every time I went to join up, 'How old are you,"19 and 5 months Sir,' 'Go on get out.' 'Three times I went round different regiments, they didn't believe I was old enough, I wasn't. Any way I had this interview for the Durham's, two doctors, first one said, 'What's your age,' '19 and 5 months Sir', 'Tell me another one.' The second doctor said, 'Let's examine him,' then he said to the other one, 'This ones pretty tough he'll be going when some of those big ones drop.' Which proved true in the long run.

The men joining the battalion were recalled by Arthur Riddle,

> We had people from all over the world, who were too short to get in other regiments, but we were mostly young miners, like myself, who came straight from the mines and were pretty hard, but we also had people who came from Australia to do their bit. I got in with one chap who was supposed to be 49 and he told me he was actually 62.

But other young men anxious to join up, like Jimmy Frater now 16 years old, were 'knocked back yet again', this was probably due to the fact that an Army Council Instruction was issued that stated,'It is notified for the information of all concerned that the practice of enlisting boys for 'Bantam' battalions is not permissible and should be discontinued.'

Whilst later on another ACI was issued giving the height standard of the 'Bantams' to be between 5 feet 1 inch and 5 feet 4 inches.

It was at Hartlepool that the first Regimental Sergeant Major joined the battalion, Harry Webb, a 43 year old Londoner had already served 22 years with the 1st and 2nd Battalions of the 'Faithful Durham's'. Enlisting in 1891 into the 1st Battalion, he transferred at Mhow in India to the

D Company, 19th Battalion Durham Light Infantry returning to billets at West Hartlepool.

2nd Battalion in 1893. In 1902 he then served with the 3rd Battalion as an instructor and transferred to the 5th Battalion in 1909 as a Colour Sergeant Instructor before retiring on pension as a Colour Sergeant in 1912. He became the Licence holder of The Dawdon Hotel in Seaham Harbour and on the outbreak of war took over the duties of recruiting officer for Seaham at the request of Major Byrne. Between that date and 31 December 1914 he obtained no less than 700 recruits from Seaham district and then decided to re-enlist himself. Harry Webb was appointed as a Company Sergeant Major to 16/Durham LI and on 10 March 1915 as Regimental Sergeant Major to 'Bob's Durham Battalion'. He remained with the battalion until he was commissioned into the 2/7/Durham LI in September 1915.

In May with the departure of 18/Durham LI to Cramlington, Cocken Hall camp became empty so the 'Bantams' were moved from Hartlepool into the hutted camp. Here they began field training, which followed closely along the lines of that of the 'Pals'. 19/1603 Private Arthur Riddle from Chester le Street recalled that,

> When the Bantams were marching at 140 paces to the minute it looked as though we were running.' He also remembered that the words sung to the regimental march, 'The Light Barque', were changed slightly to,

> Oh look at the Bantams Oh look at their feet,

> Poor little Bantams never get owt to eat.

But the 'Bantams' barely had time to settle down at Cocken Hall. They had been allotted to 106 Brigade of 35th Division. In June this formation began to gather near Masham in North Yorkshire and 19/Durham LI moved from Cocken Hall to train with the rest of the Division. 35th Division was comprised of Bantam battalions and in 106 Brigade along with 19/Durham LI were 17/R Scots, raised in Edinburgh by Lord Rosebury, 17/West Yorks (2nd Leeds) raised in the City by the Lord Mayor of Leeds and 18/Highland LI (4th Glasgow), which was raised by The Lord Provost of that City. The

WO I RSM H. Webb, 19/Durham Light Infantry.

departure of the battalion was recorded in the *Durham Chronicle* under the following heading;

Goodbye to the Bantams

The 19th Battalion of the 'Faithfull Durhams' the 'Bantam Battalion' quit their quarters at Cocken Hall on Tuesday morning for the county of broad acres where their predecessors 'The Pals' have already established themselves. They departed from Leamside in fine style being headed by the battalion band. Thanks to the military and railway authorities the entraining of a large body of troops was conducted most admirably. The spirit of these diminutive warriors appears to be in reverse ratio to the body for they are full of fight and exuberance of life, and will without doubt, when their training is complete give an excellent account of themselves. Leamside district is proud of the honour of having battalions of the 'Faithful Durham's' for neighbours and crowds flocked to the station to cheer the departing troops and to wish them good luck. The reserve companies of 'The Pals Bantams' still remain at Cocken Hall.

The Battalion Band consisted of those men who had played an instrument before enlisting. They were keen to be properly dressed as bandsmen, so much that they were buying their own badges. Corporal William Pine wrote to his wife Lydia at Shakespeare Street in South Shields.

Dear try and get me a harp badge for my arm at the Army and Navy Stores. It is a band badge for they all have got them at Durham. If you get one send it in your next letter Pet.

Given that the 'Bantam Division' had only started forming in February they were a long way behind the other locally raised battalions, who had been in being since October and November 1914, in their training, the Instructions issued by Headquarters Ripon Training Centre for the training of the Fourth New Army left out the 35th Division, the orders stated that;

Parts 1 and 2 of the General Musketry Course will be fired by the infantry of all Divisions (except 35th Division) under arrangements already notified.

Private Richard Hawksley. His daughter's birth certificate shows that he was serving with 19/Durham Light Infantry in 1915 but no other information has come to light.

Although by June the battalion had recruited over 1300 men the orders to return men to munitions and the fact that some had been medically discharged had taken a toll on the numbers in the battalion and further recruiting had to be undertaken.

After only a short period in the Masham area the division moved south to Perham Down Camp on Salisbury Plain, but 106 Brigade were sent to the northern edge of the plain and 19/Durham LI were quartered at Chiseldon Camp. Here the training was very much the same as that of the 18th Battalion further south. There were mock battles with one brigade pitted against another and a lot of time was spent on musketry. Like their predecessors 'The Pals', it was on 15 August that they were taken over by

The original postcard is simply marked 'Billy 19/DLI 1915'.

Bantams prepare their Christmas dinner. On the left is 19/66 Corporal W. Pine from South Shields.

A platoon of 19/Durham Light Infantry, identified are RSM Webb and CSM Cunningham. Somewhere in this group is Private Swinhoe who owned this photograph. Also seated third from the right is Corporal P. Goggins who is featured in chapter eleven.

the War Office and although money was recovered for food and equipment Lord Durham refused any compensation for Cocken Hall thus saving this cost to the nation.

In a letter to The Durham County Parliamentary Recruiting Committee the War Office expressed its thanks for the raising of 19/Durham LI. Lord Durham read this out to the committee at a meeting in September,

'The Army Council appreciated the spirit which had prompted their offer of assistance and felt sure that when the battalion was sent to the front it would maintain the reputation of the distinguished regiment of which it formed part.'

Afterwards the Hon Treasurer Mr A Beresford Horsley submitted a report on the finances of the battalion. The total amount passed by the Finance Committee had been £12,547, of which £11920 had been recovered from the War Office, so that taking into account the £400, which the committee had in hand there, was a debit balance of £200.

Late on in December 1915 the 'Bantams' were kitted out for the east and it was remarked that when on parade a battalion of bantams wearing sun helmets looked like a field of mushrooms. But plans were changed and it was decided to send the 35th Division to France. Before they could go however, tragedy struck. There were a number of fatal accidents involving men of the battalion, one of these occurred on Thursday 27 January just five days before the battalion embarked for France. There was an accident on the bombing range and 27 year old, Lance Sergeant Joseph Curtis, a married man with three children was severely wounded. In Murton Colliery his father, Jacob Curtis received a short letter from Lieutenant A D Trenchmann,

You will doubtless have been appraised of the sad accident which has befallen your son, Lance Sergeant J S Curtis. I have just returned from the hospital, but was not allowed to see him, his condition being much the same as last night. He has been attached to me now since last March and has always proved a keen and good soldier and very trustworthy. In my work as grenadier officer we have always worked together and I am more grieved than I can say at the ill luck he has had. We can

only hope that with his strong constitution he will pull through.

Sadly he did not pull through, Lance Sergeant Curtis is buried in Tidworth Military Cemetery, but it is highly likely that the battalion didn't have time to arrange the funeral for they left for France on the Monday morning.

ONE MORE BATTALION, THE 22nd (PIONEERS)

With recruiting for the 'Wearside' Battalion well under way the War Office again approached the Durham County Recruiting Committee and asked for the raising of a battalion of pioneers. On 17 August, The Earl of Durham KG, presided over a meeting of the Durham County Parliamentary Recruiting Committee at the Shire Hall in Durham City. Most of the committee were present to hear Lord Durham read out a letter from Major General W N Congreve VC CB MVO, on the gallant feats of the Durham's at Hooge. Afterwards Lord Durham said that he had received a letter from the Army Council to the effect that pioneer battalions were urgently needed for the new armies. In view of the success, which had attended the efforts of the committee in raising battalions, they asked them whether they could again come to the assistance of the Army Council and raise a pioneer battalion under local conditions.

Mr Malcolm Dillon asked how many men would be required for the battalion as they did not wish to clash with the battalions already forming. To which Mr J Butterfield of Sunderland said that 1350 men would be required. He regretted that this request had been brought up at the present juncture because they were just completing the arrangements for the Wearside Battalion. During the last two months recruiting had not been so robust as in the earlier stages of the war, and it seemed a pity that a request like that was made when they were endeavouring to raise another battalion. Other members of the Committee spoke and then it was agreed unanimously to take steps to form a pioneer battalion from the county and Colonel Thomlinson was appointed Commanding Officer. Lord Durham then announced that Mr Andurin Williams MP had given £100 towards the cost of the new battalion and that he, Lord Durham, would like to emulate the example and also give £100. Then a further letter was read asking Durham to furnish a platoon of 75 men for the Yeoman Rifles Battalion of The King's Royal Rifle Corps. Lord Durham said that he had been unable

to find a suitable officer for the platoon, they should have conscription it was no use going on the way they were, for if men were wanted they must bring them forward.

The problem in the County now seemed to be that other regiments, unable to raise recruits in their own counties were actively recruiting in County Durham. All the Yorkshire Regiments had strong Durham contingents, Sir Thomas Oliver had raised men for The

---

The Chief Recruiting Officer in Sunderland Wishes it to be known that Recruits are still URGENTLY WANTED, and that arrangements can now be made to deal immediately with all Recruits presenting themselves, who, when finally approved, will be sent direct to their Regiments.

Corps Open For Recruiting.

20th (Service) Battalion DURHAM LIGHT INFANTRY (Wearside).
Men are Urgently Required for this Battalion. Ordinary Infantry Standards.

22nd DURHAM LIGHT INFANTRY (Pioneers).
Recruits are required for this Battalion. Ages 19 to 40 years. Ordinary Infantry standards.

13th (Service) BATTALION YORKSHIRE REGT. (Bantams).
Height 5ft. to 5ft 3in., Minimum Chest Measurement 33 inches Expanded.

GENERAL SERVICE INFANTRY.
Height 5ft. 2in. and upwards; Minimum Chest Measurement 33½in. Age Limit 45.

ROYAL ARMY MEDICAL CORPS.
Open for the following Specialists:—Cooks, Dental Mechanics, Dispensers and Chemists' Assistants, Electrical Mechanics, Laboratory Attendants, Male Nurses, Masseurs, Mental Attendants, Operating Room Attendants, Sanitary Inspectors, Splint Makers, and Men holding Certificates in First-Aid and Nursing.

ROYAL GARRISON ARTILLERY.
Open for General Recruiting.

ROYAL FIELD ARTILLERY.
Saddlers and Shoeing Smith at 5s a day are required.

ROYAL FLYING CORPS.
Military Wing Open for Ordinary Enlistments and Duration of War for certain trades only

ARMY VETERINARY CORPS.
Men who have been accustomed to horses and are able to ride are required. Ages 40 to 47 years. Standards of height and chest measurement to be waived provided the men are organically sound.

ROYAL ENGINEERS.
Re-opened for certain trades, which can be ascertained at any Recruiting Office. Ages 19 to 40 years. Height 5ft. 6in. and upwards. Wheelwrights, Saddlers and Harness Makers at 5s a day, Office Telegraphists at Ordinary Rates up to 45 years of age. Height 5ft. 4in.

ARMY ORDNANCE CORPS.
Open for Armourers, Armament Artificers, from 21 to 60 years of age, Blacksmiths, Saddlers, Tent-Menders, Fitters, and Hammermen from 18 to 45 years of age.

1st LIFE-GUARDS.
Open for Duration of War only. Height 5ft. 9in. to 6ft. 1in.; Minimum Chest Measurement 34½in.; Age 19 to 40 years.

CAVALRY OF THE LINE.
Closed, except for ex-Regular Cavalry Soldiers.

FOOT GUARDS.
Open for Duration of War and Ordinary Service Enlistments. Standards: Coldstreams and Scots 5ft, 8in.; Irish and Welsh Guards 5ft. 7in.

ARMY SERVICE CORPS.
Open in all areas for Supply Section (except clerks). Shoeing Smiths and Saddlers up to 45 years of age at 5s a day. Drivers, who must produce references as to care and management of horses, ages 40 to 45 years, height from 5ft. upwards, are required.

DURHAM COUNTY BATTALION LIGHT INFANTRY.
Height Standard Reduced to 5ft. 3½in. Minimum.

WEARSIDE R.F.A. BRIGADE.
Closed except for Saddlers.

ROYAL ANGLESEY ROYAL ENGINEERS.
Open for All Trades except Boilermakers.

TERRITORIAL FORCES.
Recruits Required for the 5th, 6th, 7th, 8th, and 9th Durham Light Infantry. Ages 19 to 40.

Apply, John Street, Sunderland, and Bridge Street, Sunderland, Recruiting Offices.

Inniskilling Fusiliers and the 13/Gloucestershire Regiment, The Forest of Dean Pioneers had recruited a large number of men from the Thornley and Wingate area of the county. Darlington was now raising its own Heavy Battery for the Royal Garrison Artillery, with men enlisting in the Engineers, Army Service Corps, Ordnance Corps and others there could not be enough left over for the Durham Light Infantry. Then Mr A F Pease said, 'What is the use of raising new battalions when we cannot keep the others up to strength.'

By the autumn of 1915 the problem for the Government was how to maintain a constant and sufficient supply of men to the army to replace the casualties in France and other theatres of war. The response to Lord Kitchener's appeal had been truly magnificent with hundreds of thousands of men volunteering. Every avenue for obtaining recruits had been explored, recruiting marches; posters, public lectures and private appeals had all brought men to the colours. If there had been a truly great response to the call, the need at the front was still greater. The average Infantry battalion in France and Flanders was, in late 1915, losing approximately 15% of its fighting strength every month, to maintain those battalions around 30,000 men were required every week. There were around two million single men of military age who had not offered themselves for enlistment and many married men with families, who felt in unfair for them to go when so many single men were still civilians. Lord Kitchener put the facts and figures and the needs of the Army before the Government. Backed by Mr Asquith, Lord Kitchener warned the Government that if recruits could not be acquired voluntarily then conscription would have to be introduced. But it was at this time that Lord Derby, at the request of the Secretary of State for War, undertook the direction of recruiting for the army. Within a few days of this appointment there followed radical changes and details of these were issued in a speech by Lord Derby at the Mansion House, London on 19 October.

Earlier in the year a National register had been taken and this was to be used as the basis for a canvas of those willing to enlist.

Men were to be asked to volunteer under a group system. There would be 46 groups, 23 for single men and 23 for married men, arranged according to age. They would be called up in group order, men in their twenties before men in their thirties, no married men would be called up until all the single men had gone. Those who so desired could enlist immediately. The others could return to their civilian job until called up. Some men, those working in munitions, shipyards and other trades required for the war effort were classified as 'Starred' were sent back to their employment and exempt.

There was much doubt about the system particularly from married men, who thought that if not enough single men volunteered, then the married men would be taken first and single men would still be at home in safety.

Lord Derby and his followers thought that some badge was required to show everyone that a man had registered as a volunteer and was not hanging back, to this end Sir George Pragnell came up with the idea of a khaki armlet.

The scheme led to a rush of recruiting as men went to attest, but the question was who or how was it to be decided which men were indispensable to the war effort. The decision was taken that this was to be by local tribunals and that men should attest and then submit their case to the tribunal. As the last date for attestation, Saturday, 11 December drew near there was a final rush and many towns saw long lines of men, young and single through to middle aged and married waiting to attest.

But what was the effect of Lord Derby's scheme and the advent of conscription on recruiting for 22/Durham Light Infantry? Recruiting for the battalion slowed down, so much so that it was not until the spring of 1916 that the numbers were finally made up and the battalion never achieved 1350 of its own men. The numbers being made up from the 3rd, 4th , 16th and 17th (Reserve) battalions of the regiment.

It was on 11 October that the 22nd Battalion Durham Light Infantry began to assemble. Their first home, like the 19/Durham Light Infantry before them, was in the Baltic Chambers, George Street, West Hartlepool. These quarters were described as most comfortable and the food supply was said to be on similar satisfactory lines to those of the 19th Battalion. A good response was expected as being a pioneer battalion, the men would receive an extra two-pence per day pioneer pay.

Darlington was well to the fore in the recruiting campaign and advertisements for tradesmen from the town were carried in *The North Star* which also identified that 'Lord Derby's' scheme was having an effect on the numbers enlisting. Other factors also played a part. On 26 October it was reported that a party of 19 men from Tow Law had walked to Crook to enlist, but as the officer in charge of recruiting was understaffed he was unable to deal with them and the whole party had to return home without signing on. On the afternoon of Monday, 31 January a recruiting meeting was held in the open air near the Miners Hall in Durham City on behalf of 22/Durham LI. The meeting was for grouped men and unattested men and there was a fairly large gathering. Major C R Harding presided and Councillor George Watkin supported him. The speakers included Mr John Farnworth and MR James Dockett.

The battalion was taken over by the War Office on 9 March but remained in Hartlepool until 22 March 1916 when they left the town by train at 1.15 p.m. and moved to Scotton Camp at Catterick in North Yorkshire. The previous day Colonel Thomlinson had inspected them for the last time and handed over command to Lieutenant Colonel C B Morgan late West India Regiment.

On arrival in Yorkshire, 22/278 Private Matthew Robson, a native of Killingworth, Northumberland, wrote to his sister at Rose Deep Cottage.

> Dear Sister, Tuesday night, 9 p.m. We left Hartlepool and got to our new billet at 6, it is 5 miles from the station among the hills, it is an out of the way place and nothing but mud. There are thousands of troops here. I will write when I get a chance I hope this finds you all keeping well as I am. At present it is a miserable night, snow and sleet. Kind regards to you all Matt.

Lieutenant Colonel Morgan had spent some time attached to a battalion of The Worcestershire Regiment, and he wrote to Captain Gerard Davidson, asking him to transfer to 22/Durham LI and to bring some subalterns with him. Captain Davidson's memoirs describe the camp at that time.

> Catterick was a bleak and desolate place, the huge expanse of hutments extending mile upon mile over lonely and exposed upland crowned at last by Bardon Moor where were the ranges often obscured in the clouds! These Durhams were nearly ready to proceed overseas and I understand a few officers had been weeded out as in some way unfit, whilst the C.O. myself and the three officers following were to take their places. I found myself the senior Captain in command of D Company, while a major who had been out as a sergeant with the Honourable Artillery Company early in 1915 was the senior company commander and junior major. Together we were a happy family for a busy month.

Further recruiting meetings took place across the county and in Durham City at a recruiting meeting in the Market Place members of the battalion distributed handbills. These were especially aimed at the grouped and unattested men. Mr John Farnsworth remarked that for its size he had seen more armlets being worn that afternoon in Durham City than he had ever seen. He went on to say that he believed that a County of Durham Regiment should be made up of County Durham men. The recruiting party especially appealed for young men to join the 22/Durham Light Infantry. He then asked those who had not attested under the Derby scheme to consider the

A Section of 4 Platoon, A Company, 22/Durham Light Infantry at Hartlepool 1915.

Outside the accommodation of 13 and 14 Sections 22/Durham Light Infantry at Catterick.

claims of the Durham Pioneers and asked that they volunteer instead of being pressed into service. Major C R Harding then explained the numbers of men required to bring the battalion up to full strength, whilst Mr James Dockett made a speech about the Lord Kitchener and his volunteer army, saying that 'The average Briton does not like compulsion and he did not envy the position of a man who had to be compelled to do his duty.' However the meeting and others like it only brought in a few extra men. In Catterick training continued, but the battalion being pioneers they were unattached to any formation. At the beginning of June word came to be ready to entrain at short notice, that day eventually arrived and the battalion marched out of Catterick very late on the night of 25 June 1916, the event being recorded by Captain Davidson,

> *Officers were to have dinner at 6.30 p.m. and then sandwiches at 10.30 p.m. I was glad when my company marched off in the dark night to the station three miles away. We were headed by Scottish Pipers with their drums, this music was lent to us for the occasion by a Reserve battalion of the Cameron Highlanders billeted nearby. It was a wonderfully still starlit night and at the head of my men, close behind the wild music, that yet is so incomparably splendid to march to, one was romantically thrilled to be at the threshold of a great adventure. It was too, a great privilege. The train left on its long journey to Southampton at 1.30 a.m. and almost at once nearly all the rank and file were asleep. We were six officers in our compartment – the four platoon commanders, my second in command and myself. Except for the RTO, the stationmaster and a few porters the platform was deserted; a great blessing, for above all things I fear the emotional and passionate scenes of farewell. When we arrived at Southampton we embarked in two paddle steamers, which in the days of peace had no doubt been pleasure trip boats. My company and most of the rank and file were in the transport first to leave, the second boat embarked our horses, transport, details and rear guard. It was a roughish crossing made sad by a catastrophe, for the boat following ours, perhaps a mile astern, rammed its escorting torpedeo boat as the latter crossed her bows – she rolled over and went down like a stone*

Lieutenant Colonel Thomlinson commanded the battalion until forced to retire owing to ill health.

Although life belts were thrown out the transport did not stop to effect a rescue as strict orders had been given that under no circumstances would transports loaded with troops stop.

So the last of the four locally raised battalions of the The Durham Light Infantry left for the fields of France.

Lieutenant Colonel C. P. Morgan, DSO, took over and commanded until killed in action in 1918.

Chapter Three

Foreign Fields

'Its special train for Atkins '
When the troopers on the tide.'
Kipling

ON 5 DECEMBER, DURING A TERRIFIC DOWNPOUR, 18/Durham Light Infantry paraded for the last time at Fovant. The regimental transport left the battalion and under the command of the Transport Officer, Lieutenant F S Beadon, proceeded to Devonport and embarked on His Majesty's Transport *Shropshire*. Under the command of Brigadier H B Kirk,

HMT Empress of Britian.

93 Brigade along with 12/KOYLI, the Divisional Pioneer Battalion, proceeded by train to Liverpool where they embarked on the Liner *Empress of Britain*. The departure was recorded by Sergeant William H Brown one of the Bede men in the battalion.

As you know we were to have gone to France on 29 November. Well we were suddenly 'switched off' so to speak and on Monday December 6 we left Fovant amid drenching rain, and we were whirled away to Liverpool, which we reached by 4 pm. We embarked at once on The Empress of Britain. Oh how packed we were – the whole Brigade less Transport men and their animals! We moved off next morning at 10 o-clock escorted by two destroyers, which stayed with us until we were well out of danger.

The *Empress* sailed out into the Atlantic then turned and head for the Straights of Gibraltar. Following a long route and continuously zig zagging which combined with heavy weather meant that 18/888 Private Robert Webster, of West Hartlepool, was not having a good trip, in his small diary he recorded,

Suffered terrible seasickness almost at once, saw nothing, ate or drank nothing and no wees or evacuation for four days. Pals and Police searched the ship for days. Found at last in a lifeboat; don't know how I got there. All beard and dirty. Lance Corporal Benny Loudon (an Irishman from Dundalk living in Hartlepool), and another man were detailed to wash and shine me as I was all in. After some sort of clean up I was taken below to hospital and fed on beef tea. Slept and then put up on deck for fresh air and soon recovered. More beef tea and attended hospital for two days.

Another Hartlepool lad, serving in the same company was also writing in a small diary, 18/1215 Lance Corporal E C Bell noted those suffering from sea-sickness in these words,

Getting well into the swell of the Atlantic many fellows developed a marked inclination for the company of the ships tail. Many white faces being the object of despair wondering what they had done to deserve such a fate.

The fact that there was five battalions of infantry on board meant lifeboat drill and physical training could only be carried out by companies and owing to the fact that the ship was greatly

Men of the Lewis gun section B Company 18/Durham Light Infantry on board the **Empress of Britain** *ready to set sail.* **Top left:** *Private Wilkinson.* **Left:** *18/344 Corporal L Peart from Blackhill near Consett. He was commissioned in to the battalion and was killed in action 12 April 1918.* **Above:** *During the voyage on submarine watch 18/410 Lance Sergeant J Wharton, who would lose an arm in a shell explosion in 1916.*

overcrowded and the food was totally inadequate many men suffered further discomfort; Robert Webster also noted this, 'The ship's grub was terrible, Pals and I bought good grub from the fireman.'

Although Sergeant Brown put down the feeding problems to the recovery from sea sickness,

> The great drawback by now was the fact that the men had all recovered from their attacks of sea sickness and were unable to satisfy their huge appetites – as food was so scarce – owing I suppose to lack of kitchen space.

So the voyage continued, the ship steered a course that took them through the Straits of Gibraltar, they passed the Rock during the hours of darkness, which many of those on board wished they had seen in daylight. On they sailed into the Mediterranean where owing to the submarine threat everyone had to wear a lifejacket and at night the troops were brought up on deck to sleep in the open. Nothing much happened apart from passing two well-lit Hospital Ships until at around midnight on 13 December the ship's siren sounded and suddenly a loud grating sound was heard and the engines stopped. The troops stood to in their quarters although many at the first alarm had gone on deck to see what the trouble was. The Empress of Britain had collided with a French troopship the Djuradjura, which was on its return journey to France from Salonika; The Empress had almost cut the Frenchman in two. The event was recorded by a number of the 'Pals' on board.

Sergeant William Brown wrote,

> 'We got up speed again only to see the stranger was signalling SOS – SOS very slowly. We turned and then we had to wait for their coming. A flare was thrown out showing the black hulk of a sinking vessel and boats of escaping crew. The flare died out and we were obliged to show lights to guide them to the side of the Empress. All the while the vessel stood still. The stranger proved to be a French transport returning empty to Marseilles with a crew of sixty-four all told. Sixty two were saved, the chief engineer being killed by machinery and a stoker drowned.'

Private Robert Webster also remarked on the collision, 'We were all turned in on deck and the CSM was patrolling the deck saying 'Keep cool men, keep cool, we've cut the bugger in two.'

Whilst an unnamed soldier wrote to *The Durham Chronicle*,

> We had crashed into another boat amidships, many of us were on deck but there were many below. Everybody

Above: *18/1117 Corporal R Storey looking somewhat seasick in his lifejacket.*
Below: *18/1071 Private H Whitham and 18/278 Lance Corporal R Gilbert on submarine watch. Both would be killed in action in July 1916.*

A group of unidentified Durham Pals on leave in Port Said.

remained steady, though it was a nerve wracking ordeal and stood there either on deck or below in the inky darkness and in steady rain wondering what would happen to our boat in the next moment, we slipped on our lifebelts and stood ready while our ship reversed engines and pulled away from the doomed ship. A distress flare from the sinking ship lit up the sea with a lurid glare for miles and it was seen that boats were leaving her. These gradually approached us and about sixty survivors were taken on board before we steamed away into the darkness.

Sergeant Brown also made mention of the survivors as they came on board,

What a row the crew made as they embarked on our boat and how our officers swore and told them to be quiet! I needn't say that the sighs of relief were numerous when once the light was extinguished and we were moving again.'

The lookout on the bows of *The Empress* had given a warning to the bridge about four minutes before the collision but neither vessel understood what the other vessel was going to do. Whilst the large liner was stood and still lit up showing lights, about thirty mile away to the north a German U Boat was active and HMS *Dublin*, a Town Class Cruiser, was unfortunate to be torpedoed twice but although damaged she didn't sink.

As the liner went on her way to the east the sea became choppy and then rough until the next afternoon the island of Malta was sighted. As the troopship made its way into Valletta she passed HMS *Terrible*, some submarines and the French flagship. Sergeant Brown watched as the crew of the French man of war gathered on the bows of their ship.

We came into harbour and with much cheering as you may imagine and we were alongside the French flagship by the time her crew were sure who we were. Then commenced the most laughable rush on the bow and we noticed first one then another Frenchman with an instrument. Presently they formed some sort of circle and whilst the latecomers were tumbling over themselves and everyone else, the first half of the Band struck up 'It's a long way to Tipperary'. Although we were obliged to cheer in response no one could help laughing.'

An inspection of the damaged bows revealed that the damage would have to be repaired before the ship could put to sea again and that they would be there for at least two days. Brigadier General Kirk applied for permission for the men to go ashore but this was refused. The Maltese, now came out in their bumboats selling fruit and sweet things at exorbitant prices, whilst young Maltese boys flocked to dive for pennies thrown by the troops.

Some soldier's however decide to throw more than pennies and at the harbour police, not the boys. Private Webster takes up the tale,

'On December 16 I was mess orderly on the Empress of Britain, *after dinner there was spuds in jackets left over from dinner and I went to throw them overboard. Spied the Harbour Police in a motorboat and threw them at him together with others. Later he came on board with the Orderly Officer. Who threatened all then went off. Then a West York accused me of throwing and I said I'd throw him overboard. Then there was a melee bloke turned out to be a Regimental Policeman and*

with the help of other Regimental Police I was arrested. I was put in a dungeon over the propeller and next morning before the company commander 'Hutchence'. I was warned but received no punishment.

On the night of December 16 the Officers of 18/DLI hosted a dinner for all officers on board to commemorate the battalions part in the Bombardment of Hartlepool exactly one year earlier, then next morning at 0600 hours the ship up anchored and pulled out of Valletta harbour.

In the early afternoon of 18 December a lookout sighted a submarine and the 6-inch gun mounted on the stern of the *Empress* was manned and opened fire. Three times the gun fired which forced the submarine to submerge, at which the liner crammed on full speed and made good her escape. Below decks the firing caused men to rush the ladders and for a short time panic took over which was recorded by Private Robert Webster,

Below deck it was beer time when the 6 inch gun fired, panic broke out below, rushing men blocked the stairs to the deck. Another explosion, greater panic and shouting then another explosion. Panic gradually cooled and died when we were made aware of what was happening. Bert Young had just got his head through a porthole trying to see anything when the second explosion occurred and he got the full blast from the gun and a big bump on his knapper. The panic was an awful scene to witness and showed what little chance there was if we were hit when down below.

Captain A. H. Watton and Lieutenant L. C. Warmington, B Company, 18/Durham LI. Captain Watton was awarded the MC in 1918 and became the Brigade Major. Lieutenant Warmington, who came from a family of solicitors, was promoted captain and became a Courts Martial officer. His brother served with 19/Durham LI and defended Lance Sergeant Stones at his Courts Martial in 1917. (See Chapter Eleven)

On the upper decks where the Officers and Senior NCOs were there was little fuss Sergeant William Brown in his report to Bede College wrote,

I was sitting on deck reading when suddenly there was a terrific report! We got up and donned our life belts and found our way aft to see what had happened. People were anxious to see whether the gun had made a good shot or otherwise when – BANG and a second shot followed the first and fell just a few yards short of a submarine, which was soon submerged to keep from danger. Our mixed feelings for the next hour or so are better imagined than described! We are told two torpedoes were fired at us and that we passed midway between them each missing the boat by a matter of twelve to twenty yards.

The submarine had in fact fired two torpedoes at the crowded troopship one of which just missed the stern, with five battalions of infantry on board the loss of life if they had hit would have been tremendous. The ship now steered a course to the northeast and when the island of Crete was passed many onboard assumed their final destination would be Salonika. Again Sergeant Brown confirms this.

Towards 5pm we came in sight of the Cretan Mountains. What glorious heights they were quite

69

forty miles away but with the aid of glasses the crevices and precipices and the patches of snow unthawed by the midday sun were quite plain, and the brush of the crimson sunset completed a picture which won't be forgotten in a hurry.'

But the course changed and they now headed for Egypt, but before they could get there the ship was again attacked by another submarine, which fired two torpedoes before making off. At 7.30 pm on 19 December the boom across the entrance to Alexandria Harbour was opened and the great liner slowly made its way into the port. However the orders were that the troops on board were to disembark at Port Said and no one was allowed ashore. When this news reached the men on board they started to ask if the 'Forgotten Brigade' were going to spend the whole war on the boat. On Sunday prior to leaving Alexandria there was a thanksgiving service on board to celebrate the safe arrival. At sundown the great liner left for Port Said where they eventually arrived at 6 am on the Monday morning. It took quite a long time to disembark all the troops on board and when 18/DLI eventually found itself on the quayside they marched to a tented camp, which went by the name of Number 5 Camp, south of Port Said. The first training carried out was company and battalion close order drill and there were several opportunities for the men to go bathing. Christmas day was hardly celebrated none of the Christmas supplies had arrived and the men were on hard rations, a large number of supply ships and mail boats having been sent to the bottom by enemy submarines.

By the way. We have not received one iota of news from home as yet! We firmly believe that its all been sunk! The Egyptian Mail (It beats our 'Daily' out and out) informs the public that all parcels posted before 15th December and all letters posted between 15th and 22nd Dec have gone down! Its awfully hard lines and some of the men are getting very anxious about their home affairs.

Wrote Sergeant William Brown to Bede College. Indeed most of the mail addressed to men of 93 Brigade was on the 'Persia' another ship sent to the bottom by the enemy submarines.

Private John Davison, before the war, a teacher at Sacriston School and a former Bede man, wrote to the headmaster, Mr F J Bailey,

We spent Christmas such as it was at Port Said. But really the weather was so brilliant and the life in town extraordinary that one could scarcely imagine it was the festive season. I commenced things by attending Holy Communion at seven-o'clock in the morning and then attending the only parade of the day, Divine Service. It was great to hear the good old Christmas hymns, although in such surroundings.

During the afternoon I enjoyed what I scarcely ever expected to do on such a date, the pleasure of a bathe in the sea.'

However the men were allowed into Port Said but the Arab quarter was out of bounds, John Davison continued,

At night I had a walk round the town and tried to imagine Christmas dinner by visiting a hotel where an English dinner was advertised. It was certainly the best we have had since leaving England, but it was only a poor reminder of past events.

Whilst Private Robert Webster remarked on the town,

Port Said remarkable place all nationalities. Arab quarter out of bounds There are fantastic stories of Can Cans, Brothels and Drinking dens and gambling with the lowest of the low.

Men of 18/Durham LI bathing in the Mediterranean.

Above: Number 12 Section, B Company, pose for the camera.

Below: Bath time in the desert, half a pint of water per man for his ablutions.

18/341 Private H. H. Palmer at the entrance to his tent. By the end of the war he was an RSM in the Machine Gun Corps.

Whilst Sergeant William Brown wrote,

> *Its not a very prepossesing place. One isn't surprised at its questionable reputation Still there is a good deal to instruct and amuse. Our first few weeks there were spent in piquet duties, which were fairly arduous at times. We practised a fair amount of marching over the desert sands which were distinctly soft.*

One of the great hazards of active service began to make itself known to the men in this tented camp, an enemy that would prove to be unbeatable appeared and his first appearance was recorded by Private Robert Webster,

> *On the 22nd I discovered I was crawling with lice, I washed my shirt, pants and socks and disinfected with Jeys Fluid which I had bought in Port Said. 23rd Felt Cleaner but still many crawlers. I found blankets were full of them. The nights are quiet cold. 24th Lousy as ever, more washing and disinfecting.*

This battle with lice was never won and one of the lasting memories of most men was the time spent 'chatting' hunting lice in the seams of the clothes.

On 27 December the battalion moved inland, the journey was mentioned by Private John Davison in his letter to the headmaster,

> *Our stay in Port Said ended on 27 December when we entrained in open trucks for the 'somewhere' where we are at present stationed. Though naturally this mode of travelling is a good means of viewing the country I cannot say the 'beauty' of the scenery thrilled me as it was most uninteresting and devoid of any striking features. I can say that we are now encamped in the desert.*

The arrival of the 31st Division in Egypt had coincided with the withdrawal of the Imperial and

ANZAC forces from the Gallipoli Penisula. This withdrawal meant that large numbers of Turkish troops would be free to engage in offensive operations and they were expected to be used against the Suez Canal. In January 1915 the Turks had attacked the canal, which had been defended from posts mainly on the west bank. After some fighting the enemy had been driven off. By the end of the year shortly before the arrival of the 31st Division the policy of defending the canal from its own banks had been abandoned. The line had been pushed far enough to the east to protect the canal from any hostile enemy artillery fire. By the middle of December Major General H S Horne had completed a reconnaissance and the proposed lines of defences had been telegraphed to the War Office. To cut a long story short it was proposed to construct three lines of defence, the outer line 11,000 yards east of the canal. The second line at around 4,500 yards and the last a series of mutually supporting posts covering bridgeheads and vital points on the east bank of the canal. This was a tremendous task not only had defences to be constructed but also pipe lines for water supply as well as railway lines.

The canal defences were divided into three sections, each section being held by a corps. The Southern section was held by IX Corps, commanded by Lieutenant General Sir J G H Byng. Anzac Corps, commanded by Lieutenant General Sir W R Birdwood, held the Central section and finally XV Corps, commanded by Lieutenant General H S Horne, held the Northern section. Having spent a short time getting acclimatised 31st Division came under command of XV Corps and at 08.50 on 28 December 18/DLI entrained at Port Said for El Kantara. After spending their first night at El Kantara half of the battalion, C and D companies, marched out to a place known as Hill 70 where they relieved men of the 2/2 Gurkha Rifles. They only spent one day there before men of 12/KOYLI relieved them and the Durham's returned to El Kantara to rejoin the battalion. On the way back they escorted one Arab spy and two Arab families that had deserted from the Turks. The main employment at El Kantara was fatigue work digging trenches in the outpost line as well as unloading barges and constructing a light railway line towards Hill 70. A number of small diaries have survived from this period but most men only had time to write single line entries on a daily basis. Thus 18/641 Private Jack Wilson of C Company recorded,

1/1/16 On Redoubt guard
2/1/16 Church Parade
3/1/16 Dodger and I pinched oranges, D Company went to Ballah.

This last entry refers to the fact that at 11.30 on the morning of 3 January, 5 Officers and 199 men of D Company embarked for Abu Raidhar a few miles to the East of the town of Ballah where

Infantry men getting the hang of marching across the yielding desert sand.

they were to take up defensive positions to guard the light railway. The move was also recorded by 18/242 Private Arthur Corner serving with B Company in his diary, over the period from 3 to 5 January he made the following entries,

3/1/16	On Fatigues, D Company leave for higher up Suez.
4/1/16	Deserter from the Camel Corps caught.
5/1/16	Thompson and Siddle crimed, improving trenches and working on new trenches.

What great offence Privates Thompson and Siddle had committed against King's Regulations or The Army Act hasn't come to light nor has their punishment. Late in the afternoon of 6 January a small detachment of 1 Officer and forty men of C Company were ordered to march to Point 40 about four miles North East of El Kantara where they were to protect a party of engineers who were sinking a well. One of those in the party was Private Jack Wilson again the short entries in his diary tell part of the story, but tantalisingly leave the reader wanting more.

6/1/16	Route march, saw locusts, left for Point 40 a rotten march across the desert.
7/1/16	Life at Point 40 guard every other night. Played a joke on Peter Brown Lanaghan and I digging out rats.
8/1/16	Sinking well, sports at El Kantara C Company won tug-o-war for the third time.

Sergeant William Brown wrote at length to Bede College about the battalions move into the desert,

We were marched into the desert well away from our base and there we set to work on the wonderful scheme which has been laid down. There was no water within miles though from the

observation post it was visible to the west. All cooking water was brought up on camels and stored, whilst once a week a water cart came over with sufficient water to allow half the men in camp to bathe.

The bath day was a sight! You took out your ground sheet and after moulding a 'bath' in the sand the ground sheet was put down into it. Into the basin thus formed was poured a few bucketfuls of clean water, which served to wash four to six men! If you were fortunate to be one of the four parties you managed to get some clothes washed afterwards.

Whilst John Davison of the same company had this to say,

We find it pretty difficult to cross the desert, as sand is by no means the easiest matter to walk on. Practically all our transport is carried by means of a camel corps and the animals carry tremendous loads. The mules revel in the sand but will scarcely pass the camels and seem to have a decided objection to them.

Each camel was supposed to carry twenty-four gallons of water, in two fantassies. Many of these water containers carried up by the camels leaked and a great deal of water was lost in this way. This

Men of B Company, 18/Durham LI, constructing defences at Kantara.

loss caused a serious shortage among the troops and the water ration was reduced.

The bathing situation and the lack of water was also mentioned by 18/544 Lance Corporal Charles Moss from Pelaw, near Chester le Street, serving in C Company. In a letter to Mr W Lowes, published in the *Durham Chronicle* he wrote,

> *You need not send any more soap. We only get two pints of water per day now for a tent of 10 men to wash in and so you may judge what it is like when it comes to the turn of the last man. The allowance will probably be reduced later. We have transformed the place where we are camped from a lifeless waste of sand to a moving town of life and it is such a mixture of life.*

Another soldier to send word home about the march into the desert was Private William Wilkinson, who wrote a short letter to friends in Willington,

> *We have moved eight miles further into the desert. In places we were over the boot tops in sand, not to mention anything about the blazing sun. Eight miles may seem a short distance but I tell you every man of the company was done up. About three o-clock in the morning it started to rain, and a sand storm swept over the desert. I was about frozen to death. Some of our lads take an interest in catching chameleons or lizards. These animals are perfectly harmless but we don't fancy these things creeping over us at night.*

The parties that had been detached into the desert gradually rejoined the battalion as others were sent out to relieve them. The party at Point 40 was relieved on 15 January by another from the same company, and then on 20 January, D Company returned from Abu Raidhar. However they were not given long to settle down for on the morning of 21 January 1 Officer and 40 other ranks left Kantara for Hill 108 as advance party to the battalion. The next afternoon the detachment from Point 40 rejoined the battalion. Then over the next four days A & B Companies moved in two parties to Hill 108, then Battalion Headquarters with The Signal and Machine Gun Sections followed, leaving the Quartermasters stores and Transport section and the Machine Gun Officer and C and D Companies in Kantara. As before the events of the last few days were recorded in the small diaries as one-line entries. Private Arthur Corner wrote,

22/1/16   Divisional supply fatigue

23/1/16   4.30 am A & B strike camp and leave Kantara. Devilish march 8 miles into the desert.

24/1/16   Hellish night rain and sand.

18/402 Private William J Weatherley another of the Bede College contingent wrote about the move of A and B Companies in the College magazine in June 1916.

> *On January 23, A and B Companies, with more than a full pack and under a burning sun, moved a few miles into the desert. The march, which occupied the better part of four hours proved to be very heavy, there were deep sighs of relief when our lonely destination was reached. Tents were pitched, blankets and baggage sorted, and then came a welcome sleep. That we had not become expert in erecting tents was clearly proved during the following night, for a heavy storm of wind and rain broke over us, and there was much rushing to and fro to hammer in pegs and save a falling tent or re erect one already down. At 'stand to' on the following morning, the camp presented a scene of desolation and*

Mail call in the desert. Most of the mail destined for the 31st Division ended up at the bottom of the Mediterranean when the ship carrying it was sunk by a U-Boat.

some unfortunates who had been out on piquet all night returned to find their tents blown yards away and there goods and chattels wet through.

Whilst Private Jack Wilson who had been sent to hospital on 17 January wrote in his Diary,

23/1/16   Out of hospital today, A & B Coys went to Point 108. Baths every day.

25/1/16   Orderly this week

26/1/16   *Malaja* stopped off at Kantara and threw off heaps of baccy etc.

27/1/16   Short rations.

This act of kindness by the homeward bound passenger ship *Malaja* was also mentioned in the letter to Mr Lowes by Lance Corporal Charles Moss,

18/315 Private Ted Little from Ebchester, stands by his tent. He was promoted Lance Sergeant and eventually taken prisoner in 1918.

> *We had a treat the other day as the passengers of a liner homeward bound from the east sent ashore any amount of tobacco and sweets and biscuits for the troops.*

The men of A and B Companies of 18/DLI out in the desert at Hill 108 were now put to work on the defence system that was being constructed to the east of the Suez Canal. The first task carried out was the construction of three machine gun posts for the defence of the battalion as they were working. The orders for the manning of the posts were as follows:

1 Gun pits will be lettered A, B and C

2 Guns will be mounted at 6.00 am and dismounted at 6.30 pm.

3 Captain Ince will satisfy himself with respect to the supply of SAA.

4 Each gun will have a gun crew of 2 selected NCOs or men. There will be 2 men in reserve. One NCO not below the rank of sergeant will be in charge of the three pits.

5 The gun crews will mount at 6.00 am and dismount at 12.00 noon. The relief will dismount at 6.30 pm. The NCO in charge will remain on duty from 6.00 am until 6.30 pm.

6 The gun crews will not leave their posts under any pretext whatever without the direct authority of the Sergeant in charge who will temporarily replace any man absent from the two waiting men.

Having constructed the gun pits work began on the trench system, the trenches, which had to be dug in loose sand, were lined with hurdles and grass matting to prevent the sand running back into the trench. To construct a trench, which was five foot wide at the top in the loose sand, meant that the initial excavation had to be twenty-four feet wide. Sergeant William Brown sent home this description of the work at Hill 108,

> *Whilst we were here we worked from 8.30 am until 4 or 4.30 pm daily and every second day we 'stood to' from 5.30 am until 7 in the morning. There was a host of things to interest other than the work which itself was enough. The work I might here say was the most interesting and the best executed that the battalion has yet experienced – There was an abundance of small animal life, hosts of lizards, beetles and other strange insects, whilst the scrub consisted of many kinds of small plants each more interesting than the other. One in particular was a specimen of vetch, the leaves of which resemble the lupin at home, only were perhaps more juicy whilst the flower was large and a glorious golden colour.*

> *The first week was spent in ordinary routine, but the remaining three weeks of our stay there was*

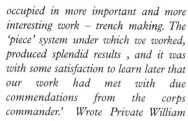

occupied in more important and more interesting work – trench making. The 'piece' system under which we worked, produced splendid results , and it was with some satisfaction to learn later that our work had met with due commendations from the corps commander.' Wrote Private William

B Company rest on the Canal bank after work on the machine gun positions.

Weatherley in the June issue of the same magazine.

It was at Hill 108 that Major C W Tilly started the regimental canteen that supported the battalion both in Egypt and throughout its time in France. The canteen ran by 18/1066 Sergeant, later CQMS William Morgan, from West Hartlepool proved to be a boon to those on their way to the front line and on the return journey. A soldier could get a hot drink or some small snack at a reasonable cost. All profit being put to the benefit of the whole battalion.

A few letters were beginning to reach *The Durham Chronicle* at this time and one was published from Private J E Smith the well-known local-footballer who played for Shildon and Crook Town, in a letter to his parents written on New Years Eve he wrote,

This spot is out of the civilised world I think and I don't know how long it will be before you get this letter. It does not seem like New Years Eve; in fact nobody seems to know what day it is. If it were possible to get away tonight I don't think I'd chance the sea again until the war is over. I'm not stuck with submarine chases.

Meanwhile C and D Companies back in El Kantara were not having a holiday they were put to work laying a light railway line but some like Jack Wilson found time to socialise with the Mysore Lancers, his dairy records not only this but the ability of the Durham Light Infantryman to obtain extra rations when the situation arose,

1/2/16	George Butler fishing some chaps took tent bag, Geordie indignant. Geordie thinks the fish will be 'ignerent' about here. (18/441 G Butler Broompark.)
2/2/16	Rail fatigues, Watty and J Harper had a row. (18/521 J Harper, Shadforth)
3/2/16	Chapatti in Bari Sahibs tent. Nobby and I had bath in about 1 pint of water by the side of lake. Bathe afterwards. Rail Fatigue.
4/2/16	ASC fatigue, 5 tins of jam, tin of butter, 2 tins of milk, dozen candles, had to make two journeys.

One of the sad events recorded by both diaries at this time was the accidental shooting of a soldier from the Leeds Pals. This tragic event occurred when a party of C Company of the Leeds Pals had returned from guard duty at Point 80. A soldier who was cleaning his rifle had failed to remove a live round from the breach. The round was accidentally fired and killed Private Edward Wintle. As in all such incidents rumours were very quick to circulate and the event is mentioned in the diaries of men from 18/DLI. On 2 February Arthur Corner wrote,

'Two Leeds Pals killed by sentries', this probably refers to the fact that another shot had been accidentally fired although there was no one injured. The funeral of the unfortunate Pal was witnessed by Private Jack Wilson who wrote on 9 February, 'Saw funeral of Leeds Pal who was accidentally shot, also RAMC man who died after falling into the canal.'

On 17 February the two companies at El Kantara, with a strength of 12 Officers and 386 other ranks, were ordered to proceed to Spit Post, on the east bank of the canal between Kantara and Tinch. The work here consisted mainly of laying a water pipe line with some work on the light railway. After a few days at Spit Post C & D company's were joined on 18 February by Battalion Headquarters, who were followed a few days later by a party of 12 Officers and 477 other ranks. Sergeant Sergeant William Brown writing in the *Bede Magazine* recorded the march of the main party through the soft desert sand,

> *'We had to march or rather trudge 2,000 yards or so to the task – only those who have marched over sand know what it means – then we were ordered to complete another task of a different nature elsewhere. Headquarters moved off to the new place and one of our number had charge of the escort to the camels which were to convey the baggage. During the day a camel escort to the water convoy was considered somewhat of a snip for the men came back in their own time. This however proved otherwise. The camels came and by 12 noon were loaded ready to start. Perhaps for the first five miles all went fairly well and then the camel drivers got annoyed about something or other until by the end of the seventh mile the poor, tired escort, were faced with the fact that the drivers thought they had gone far enough. It took some explaining that there were still some three or four miles to go, but they could rest while the escort had something to eat. – These drivers seem to be able to travel all day with nothing. – After a short rest it was deemed time to move on but one camel – loaded with kerosene tins – some of which were empty but still very useful – took it into his head that he had no right to work. Now a camel in a bad temper ought to be seen to be appreciated. He ducked, backed, raced to this side, then to the other and almost became the means of landing part of the escort down the slope into the canal, for by this time they were travelling along the canal side. The animal eventually got himself into a ditch, out of which he came in peace, for the fall had sobered him up.*

Rumours now were circulating that the 31st Division was earmarked for service in Mesopotamia, but these were dispelled when the 13th Division, which had been withdrawn from Gallipoli and refitted passed by in liners bound for Mesopotamia.. Battalions of the 52nd (Lowland) Division also withdrawn from Gallipoli, having refitted, began to relieve the 31st Division so that at 0815 hours on 29 February, D Company left for Kantara, in barges, to be followed at 1400 by the rest of the battalion.

On 9 January Lieutenant General Sir Archibald Murray arrived in Egypt and assumed command of all troops assembling or refitting in Eygpt and was to be responsible for the defence of the canal. This effectively put him in command of all formed divisions in the country. Sir J Maxwell was to take over command of the forces defending the Western Frontier, his force to comprise all unattached brigades and units. General Murray brought with him instructions from the War Office that the troops in Eygpt were now regarded as the Imperial Strategic Reserve and that the Imperial General Staff regarded France as the main theatre of war.

Headquarters MEF were warned to prepare to move troops from Eygpt to other theatres but until it became clear what direction the Turkish Army would attack from or which theatre of operations they would choose for their main effort no decision as to which troops would be sent, or where to, could be taken. As was mentioned earlier the 13th Division, which was ordered to Mesopotamia, was the first to leave in early February. Then on 28 February orders were issued for the transfer of 31st Division to France. Private Weatherley wrote this about the forthcoming move,

> *Rumours of a move either to France or Salonika were now very strong and it came as no great surprise when once again we found ourselves en-route for Kantara prior to our departure from Egypt after less than three months in the land of the Pharaohs.*

Whilst Sergeant Brown said 'We were shipped off to Port Said in the same kind of wagons that brought us some nine or ten weeks before.'

On 2 March 18/Durham LI began their move from Kantara to Port Said and as the battalion left Kantara the Mysore Lancers lined the route and cheered the battalion on its way. At port said some time was spent resting in the docks waiting to board and Jack Wilson and some pals borrowed a rowing boat and took a trip round the harbour for a look at the warships moored there. Eventually the battalion was embarked on HMT *Ivernia*, but owing to engine trouble the convoy left without them and HMT *Ivernia* sailed alone at 0500 on 6 March.

Conditions on board this transport were altogether superior to those obtaining on the 'Empress of Britain' which had taken us out. There were fewer troops on board and sleeping accommodation and food were better. Prospects of a pleasant voyage were good indeed, provided there was no molestation by submarines such as was our lot on the outward voyage. Nothing worthy of note took place until we arrived off Malta. We did not enter the harbour, but the ship's course took us very near the land, and thus we obtained a splendid view of these interesting islands. A heavy sea was running and this kept many below, the few on deck being those whose internal system was feeling the effects of the rocking. Fine weather broke on the following morning, and excitement ran high as Sardinia hove in sight. Again we kept close to land and saw the island to advantage. For some days now it had been evident that our destination was France and having passed Sardinia we were looking forward to our arrival at Marseilles. But a thick mist and a drizzling rain set in to spoil our view of the port and town which we reached on 11 March.

Wrote Private William Weatherley in the *Bede Magazine*.

As HMT Ivernia *came alongside she was in collision with a destroyer moored in the dock where she was to berth, this and the comments of the destroyer crew caused some amusement among the troops on board.*

Men of 18/Durham LI taking it easy on the deck of the **Ivernia** during the voyage to southern France, March 1916.

Time for some Swedish Drill.

A rocket signals the sighting of land as the French port of Marseilles appears on the horizon.

BANTAMS ABROAD

At 0300 hours on 31 January 1916 19/Durham LI paraded on Salisbury Plain for the last time. They entrained for Southampton where transports were waiting to take them to Havre, where they arrived the following day. After disembarkation the battalion proceeded to Number 1 Rest Camp where they spent the night. At 2.50 pm on the afternoon of 3 February they entrained in the famous, 40 Hommes - 8 Chevaux, horse boxes of the French railways and began their journey up the line. St Omer was reached at noon the next day, here they detrained and marched about four miles to the village of Campagne where they went into billets. Some training must have taken place during the stay here but nothing of interest is recorded in the War Diary. On 8 February four officers, Major Osler and Captains Kinch, Warmington and Cameron along with two sergeants from each company, Sergeants Green and White, W Company, Sergeants Rogerson and Armstrong, X Company, Sergeants Johnson and Thorley, Y Company along with Sergeants Wrightson and Thomas from Z Company, were attached to the Guards Division for instruction in trench warfare. Obviously the trench parapet could not be lowered for the 'Bantams' so the Guards Division ordered that each bantam would have two sandbags which would be placed on the fire step for him to stand on.

Other officers and men were sent on courses at Schools of Instruction, Lieutenant Carroll to the Trench Mortar School, whilst Lieutenant Ryall and 50 men of Number 7 Platoon X Company were attached to the Forestry Control Centre at Le Parc Forest de Nieppe.

Meanwhile the battalion moved billets and marched to Thiennes where they were inspected by Sir Douglas Haig and Prince Arthur of Connaught on the road east of Aire, the following day the inspection was repeated with Lord Kitchener being the inspecting officer. Nine days were spent in billets at Thiennes, before another march took them to the village of Les Lauriers where another nine days were spent training.

It was at 10.45 am on 27 February that 19/Durham LI paraded for its first experience of trench warfare, the battalion marched out from Les Lauriers to Pont de Hem where they were attached to 57 Brigade of the 19th (Western) Division. The companies of 19/Durham LI were distributed throughout the brigade as follows,

CO, Adjutant and X Company	attached to	10/R Warwickshire Regt
2i/c, MG Officer and W Company	''	8/Glosters Regt
MO, Signals Officer and Y Company	''	10/Worcester Regt
QM and Z Company	''	8/N Staffordshire Regt.

The weather whilst they were in the line was very cold and there was some snow but the time in the line passed safely and they returned to billets in Pont de Hem without casualties. By 11 March the battalion had reformed and although still under command of 19th Division they were no longer attached to 57 Brigade. The next day the whole battalion went into the front line trenches at Tilleloy, the weather warmed up a little and the next day around noon the German artillery opened up causing two men to be wounded, one of whom, 19/121 Private Matthew Kemp, from Hamsteels, died the next day.

Major E A Maxwell the Battalion second in command who was attached from the Indian Army was now ordered by GHQ to rejoin his own unit and he left the battalion. The next day the enemy explode a mine in front of the trenches to the right of 19/Durham LI and they then opened a heavy barrage on the Durham's in the front line trench, this consisted of a mixture of High Explosive, Tear and Gas shells which caused 17 casualties among the Bantams. The fumes of the gas hung about the trenches throughout the night and the next day, which passed quietly until in the evening 10/Worcestershire Regiment arrived and began the relief of the Durham battalion, who moved back to billets at La Gorgue where they spent the night.

The next few days were spent moving back to rejoin 106 Brigade, this was done in stages, first to Les Lobes and from there to Calonne. After six days at the last named village they moved via Estaires to La Croix Les Cornet. Here on 28 March the first draft of 3 NCO's and 68 men from 23/Durham LI, the reserve Bantams arrived. A couple of days later on 31 March they commenced the relief of 17/West Yorks in the front line. The first day in the trenches was described quiet and uneventful but 19/918 Private William Daglish of Gateshead was killed. On 2 April 19/54 Private Joseph Simpson became the third Bantam fatality and two other men were wounded. The next day 21/177 Private John Lowes of Catchgate was also killed. These three men the first of what was to become known as 'Daily Wastage', were buried in Rue Pettillon Military Cemetery. More Officers and men were being sent on courses, a Brigade Bombing School had been formed at Rouge de Bout and Second Lieutenant R Cross and 8 men from each company attended for ten days. Likewise Lieutenant W J Oliver and 5 men from Z Company went to the newly formed Brigade Trench Mortar School. Also Second Lieutenants W V Falkiner, J W Ryall and R C MacLachlan along with three NCOs attended the 35th Divisional Field Engineering School at Nouveau Monde.

By 8.25pm on 4 April the battalion relief had been completed by 23/Manchester Regiment and the battalion marched back to billets in Sailly. Here the next day six of those who had been wounded earlier in March rejoined from the base hospital. It was at Sailly on 10 April that Major E L Maxwell rejoined the battalion a second in command his orders to rejoin the Indian Army having been cancelled. From Sailly the battalion moved to support billets in Laventie from where two men of Y Company were sent on a sniping course at Steenbecque for a week. The stay out of the line was not long and on 16 April the relief of 7/Loyal North Lancashire in the left sub sector of the Neuve Chappelle trenches took place. During the relief or shortly after 19/1216 Private Andrew Smith of Tweedmouth was killed. Having completed the Field Engineering course Lieutenant Falkiner was now attached for duty to 255 Tunnelling Company Royal Engineers. This

An unidentified group of 19/Durham LI taken on Salisbury Plain prior to embarkation.

tour in the front line was very quiet with only one more man being wounded and on 20 April the battalion was relieved by 17/West Yorks. As the battalion marched to billets in Croix Barbee one man was wounded. Four days were spent here and on the last day, 25 April although the enemy shelled the village and one man was wounded no great damage was done. That night at 9.20 pm the Durhams relieved 17/West Yorks in the front line without incident. This spell in the line was relatively quiet and during the six-day tour of duty only five men were wounded. It was during this time that Captain E Cameron was appointed as Adjutant prior to the battalion being relieved by 17/Lancashire Fusiliers and returning to reserve billets at Vielle Chappelle. Here they remained until on 6 May the battalion moved to Richebourg St Vaast and took over billets fro 15/Cheshire Regiment. This last named battalion was the first 'Bantam' unit and contained a number of Durham miners who had walked to Birkenhead to enlist and had been the catalyst for the raising of 'Bantam' battalions.

Five days later guides met the leading company at Whiskey Corner and led the companies in at three minute intervals so that by 9.00 pm the Durham Bantams had again taken over the front line from 17/West Yorkshire Regiment, the relief being completed without incident. The next few days are described in the war diary as 'Situation Normal', however on 11 May, three men were killed in action and on 13 May another three died, two Sunderland lads, two from Hetton and one each from Leamside and Tynemouth just more examples of 'daily wastage'.

After a four-day tour of duty on the 17/West Yorkshire Regiment arrived to replace the Durhams, who were no doubt glad to return to the reserve billets in Richebbourg St Vaast. After the same interval the process was repeated with 19/Durham LI taking over from the Yorkshire men in the front trenches. This was done in stages, the first to go in were the battalion snipers, by 10.30 am the signallers were in position, who were followed at noon by the Lewis gunners and bombers. All these specialist had moved up in daylight, in parties of not more than six men at 200 yard intervals. In the late afternoon one Officer and NCO from each company went forward to take over trench stores. Then at 8.40pm the battalion began its march into the line, Z Company was to relieve the left front and moved off first. When Z Company was clear, X Company commenced the relief of the right front. Likewise when Z Company was clear, W Company began relieving the centre company. With the front line relief completed, Y Company relieved the reserve company position in the support line. Each man carried in his pack, his rations for the following day and had a full water bottle, so the routine of trench warfare went on. On 23 May 17/Lancashire Fusiliers came in once more and 'Bobs Durham Bamtams' went back into Divisional reserve at La Fosse. After some days here word came to be prepared to move at short notice, closely followed on 28 May by orders from 106 Brigade Headquarters for the battalion to move to Le Touret and take over billets from 1/1/Cambridgeshire Regiment. At 8.30pm on 30 May the battalion 'stood to' in case of hostile attack on the left front, which at that time was under heavy bombardment. Instructions were received in the case of an attack the battalion would come under command of 118 Brigade and Lieutenant Mundy would report on bicycle to the Brigade Major at 118 Brigade Headquarters. However the attack never came and on 1 June the process of relieving 17/West Yorks began again, this time in the left sub sector of the Festubert trenches. Now Officer replacements were beginning to arrive from the base, on 1 June Lieutenant C W Pollock joined and was posted to W Company. Five days later Second Lieutenant W Braidford arrived and joined Y Company. Yet again the 'Leeds Bantams' came to the relief of the Durhams who moved back to the same billets in Le Touret, where on 11 June Second Lieutenant K Smith joined for duty from 17/Durham LI.

Billy Braidford had now been with the battalion for four days, one of three brothers serving with the regiment, the other two Frank and Percy were serving with 10/Durham LI. They had all enlisted in the University and Public Schools Brigade of the Royal Fusiliers in 1914 and eventually had received commissions in the Durham Light Infantry. On 10 June Billy wrote to his sister Emily, after the family news he described the conditions in the reserve positions,

It is nearly a fortnight since I came over now but I spent a week at the base before coming up to the firing line. At present I am at a farm not far behind the firing line and have been up once at night. There was a lot of shooting going on but we had no casualties. Our artillery was peppering away at the Huns and gave them a hot time. Its very funny that I am in the same place as Frank and Percy were. It is quite a nice little place and has not suffered much from shellfire. You would be surprised at the thousands of birds here which whistle all day long in spite of the guns roaring nearly all day. You will see I came to the 19th Battalion, they have been out here for some months and we are going back for a rest in a day or two. They have had a hard time and are in need of a rest so it is lucky for me.

19/170 Lance Corporal G. Appleby from Easington Lane, killed in action 13 May 1916, age 25.

Second Lieutenant William (Billy) Braidford, a well known rugby player tipped for an England cap, he would be killed in action in July 1916.

Billy was well informed, after relief in Brigade reserve by 15/Notts & Derby Regiment on 16 June, 19/Durham LI moved right back into Corps Reserve at Gonnehem. Training was undertaken in earnest in preparation for a move south to the Somme. During this time whilst out at training some of the men committed offences contrary to the various sections of the Army Act and King's Regulations, these men were charged and brought before the Commanding Officer to be sentenced. Among them was 19/877 Private Thomas Spours of Hugh Street, Fulwell, who for his trouble received seven days Field Punishment Number 2.

Still more junior officers were arriving on the 22nd of the month Second Lieutenants G R Chester and P French arrived from 3/Durham LI and joined W and X Companies respectively. The following day Second Lieutenant L Brotherton from 3/Durham LI and Second Lieutenants S H Smith and T H Moorwood both from 16/Durham LI joined being posted to W, Y and X Companies. The next officer to arrive was Second Lieutenant L Millar from 17/Durham LI on Cannock Chase who went to Z Company on 25 June.

With the training completed 19/Durham LI spent 1 July 1916 in billets and the following night at 10.30 pm entrained for the Somme.

THE PIONEERS ARRIVE

The two paddle steamers carrying 22/Durham LI arrived at Havre on 17 June and the battalion quickly disembarked and marched through the port to the railway station, where they entrained for the front. Captain Davidson continued the story in his memoirs,

'Through the great base passed the battalion, entraining once more; this time, the rank and file, in cattle trucks on which were painted the legend 'Hommes 30 Chevaux en long 8', and in chalk, much obscured by time 'a Berlin'!

Small children ran alongside calling for 'Biscuits and Bully Beef' of which from our windows and

One of the sections of 4 Platoon A Company 22/Durham Light Infantry taken in Hartlepool 1915.

doors they received from time to time meagre showers. Word having been passed that rations were not to be given to civilians. On we went at a slow speed past Rouen and Amiens both of which I recognised by their great churches till we reached in about twenty hours some obscure place which was, if I remember rightly, Freslincourt. Here we had our first casualty, one of the Company Commanders seizing his freshly detrained charger too eagerly, the horse swerved and slipped upon an iron plate let in the ground, causing it to fall heavily, crushing the officer's foot severely. We then marched a mile or two to billets in a small village – the ranks had barns, byres and sheds lately occupied by other troops who left them littered with rifle ammunition. Of this we gathered up a quantity in sandbags and bestowed on our transport.

The officer that was injured was Captain Hurford who was taken to Number 2 General Hospital RAMC, from where, after a short stay, he was evacuated to England.

The battalion had not been allocated to any particular division at this time and so was temporarily attached to the 19th (Western) Division. The battalion spent time checking stores and getting ready for the coming offensive, picks and shovels were issued in readiness for the

Men from the Bishop Auckland area serving with 22/Durham Light Infantry at Hartlepool in 1915.

reconstruction of captured trenches. At night although they were still quite a way behind the line, flashes and reports of artillery gun fire could plainly be seen and heard. A company were the first to deploy when they were sent forward on a working party to unload shells at a railhead.

As the train carrying the men of 22/Durham LI arrived in the siding at Frenchencourt the men prepared to alight, somehow 22/403, Private J Irwin slipped and broke his leg and had to be evacuated to 59/Field Ambulance RAMC. Two casualties and the battalion wasn't even in the line. On 21 June two officers and 120 men marched to Contay and relieved men of 8/Norh Staffordshire Regiment, they took over the Staffordshire's billets and their task of unloading ammunition. The following day a working party of similar size moved off to Baizeux, where they were employed on road repair, twenty four hours later another 75 men joined this party. At the same time all available officers proceeded to the trenches at Albert under instruction, as Major Davidson recorded,

> One of these days the C.O. took the bulk of us officers for a tour of inspection of the front line where we were to go in. For this purpose an old London Omnibus was provided and a jolly ride it was, over the white roads of Picardy in La Belle France, very soon however the countryside was deserted of civilians to be replaced by huge ammunition dumps, veterinary corps and what not and then we saw a few cemeteries. At length we came in sight of the Virgin leaning at from the tower of Albert Cathedral. At the outskirts of that shattered town we debussed. The Colonel taking one party, left me to conduct the remaining officers through the town, up a communication trench called St Andrew's Avenue to the support line where there were certain redoubts. On the way up we passed batteries of artillery firing desultorily. We spent about three hours in various parts of the trenches, heard the whistle of an occasional rifle bullet, still it was quiet as a whole, though the temperature was insufferably close until a great thunder storm broke over head. We were not as used to a drenching as we were to become!

Whilst the majority of the officers were 'up the line', the rest of the battalion went on a route march and on the following a large working party of 400 men went to the sandbag hangar at Contay, where they worked filling sandbags for the front line.

All ranks knew the 'Big Push', was about to begin, it was just a question of 'at what hour', so that there can have been little surprise, when at 2000 hours on 30 June the battalion left Bavelincourt and marched up through Baizeux and Henencourt to Millencourt, a distance of sixteen miles, arriving at midnight, they bivouacked in open fields for the night, although many would have found it difficult to sleep owing to the noise of the barrage.

Seated 22/1025 Private T W Holmes from Gateshead he was transferred to the Labour Corps in 1918.

84

Chapter Four

The Somme Front

'Where the hell is everybody, I can't see anybody, I'm not going out there by myself'
Private Frank Raine B Company 18/Durham LI
1 July 1916

HMT Ivernia, *carried 18/DLI from Egypt to France.*

O N 11 MARCH 1916, His Majesty's Transport *Ivernia* carrying 18/Durham Light Infantry, having docked in Marseilles began to disembark her human cargo. First to land at 6.30 p.m. were D Company who were to form the advance party. They quickly entrained and set off for Pont Remy. The rest of the battalion landed about 10 p.m. that night and immediately entrained for the same destination. The battalion were crowded into cattle trucks of the French railways, which moved at a leisurely pace, northwards through the countryside. In fact the train moved so slow that two men who fell out were able to run alongside and arrive at the next station the same time as the train. Private W J Weatherley continued his writing for the *Bede Magazine* with this account of the journey,

We entrained the same night for a ride through France. The accommodation was perhaps not of the best, - there was 30 men with full kit and baggage in each cattle truck – but there was a great deal to interest and amuse us on the way, especially through the Rhone valley; and we forgot the small inconveniences at least during the day. At night the trouble arose when everyone was wishing to sleep for to lie at full length was out of the question altogether. Hopes of seeing Paris ran high but again we were disappointed.

Men of 18/DLI on board a French cattle truck which carried 8 Horses or 40 men.

Other reports of the journey appeared in the local press, Private Andrew Skeen sent this letter to his parents in Silver Street, Murton Colliery,

At 12 o-clock we boarded the trucks, which were to convey us across France. With 30 men in each truck we left Marseilles about 1.15 a.m. We lay down as best we could with knees up and before going very far I began to feel the bumping of the wheels, which was worse than riding in bye in the set with a bent axle. I should know a bit about that having done a good deal of it at, 'Canny Dalton'. As soon as daylight began to appear, I was on my feet and looking through the iron bars of our saloon, similar to animals at the zoo, looking for newcomers and sights. We were soon running by the foot of some hills and in the distance we could plainly see the snow capped mountains of the Alpine Range. The sight of the mountains with torrents of water roaring and flowing down and the tunnels and bridges was fine. I sat with my legs dangling over the side of the truck all the way so as to miss nothing. We had a grand reception when passing through Lyons and in one case a woman, who was standing beside her husband cheering us, completely broke down and sobbed like a child. Our train journey lasted slightly over two days through the most beautiful part of France.

Eventually the station of Pont Remy was reached and the battalion began detraining, stiff and tired limbs were stretched in preparation for the march to billets in the village of Citerne. This proved to be a trying march as the men's feet were not used to the hard French pave. The billets taken over were described as very poor and even old hen houses were pressed into service to provide shelter for the battalion.

18/615 Private Charles Todd, from Browney Colliery wrote home to his mother,

We were not sorry to get off the train and we all had a drink of tea, which made us feel sick. Then we set off to march carrying a full pack, without anything to eat. It was five o-clock on Tuesday morning when we marched into a village eight miles from the station. We were very hungry and tired out. The battalion were billeted in farm buildings, stables and cow byres, some of which were swarming with rats. My section of 10 men were luckier than most for we were given an old hen house, which was better and cleaner than what some of the men had. The people in the farm were kind and gave each of us an egg. I am not allowed to tell you the name of the village where we are.

Snow was falling and after the hot sun of Egypt the men found the weather very trying indeed.

Private Weatherley also provides observation of this period.

We were not altogether sorry to reach our destination after fifty hours under such conditions and it was some relief to get one's legs stretched again. A march of eight miles brought us to our first billets in a small village well behind the line; and here a fortnight was spent in refresher drill. Our feet were not in good condition for hard roads so that route marching formed a conspicuous part of the routine.

Two unnamed Pals had short extracts about the billets published in the *Durham Chronicle*. The first soldier reported

The people here seem to have made a practice of setting up trees in long avenues. On the journey up we were supplied with tea, with a strong taste of rum about it. I got quite a liking for the mixture. Our billet is in a barn and we have quite a tidy little room. The parcels have arrived safe and sound.'

The second man had this to say, 'We had to march seven hours to reach our billets which are infested with rats. An extra blanket was given out and we enjoyed a good rest. We are 'somewhere in France', and are happy and bright.

After almost a week in Citerne a party of 10 Officers and 39 NCOs went forward into the front line for instruction in trench warfare. The party moved forward in buses to Fonquevillers and went into the trenches with 5 and 8/R Warwickshire Regt who showed them all aspects of trench life and looked after them very well indeed.

Whilst this party was in the line the battalion packed up and began moving forward, the first march took them to Longpre where the night was spent in good billets. The following morning the march continued to the village of Flesselles, which was reached after two days, here the party from the line rejoined in the middle of a snowstorm. These marches were done in incessant rain and sleet but the spirit of the battalion asserted itself and each night they marched in without any stragglers, led by the band, which had played almost continuously throughout the day. The march continued to Beauquesne and on the following day via Louvencourt to Beaussart, this last portion of the route being done in darkness to avoid detection by enemy aircraft. As the battalion marched into the village they were met by the Regimental Band of 10/Royal Irish Rifles who played them into billets. Once again Private Weatherley recorded the events for the *Bede Magazine*

We had expected to escape all snow and slush by going to Egypt, but when we left the village for a few days march to the line snow was very much in evidence. The march was done in stages and we rested at nights in barns and lofts in the villages through which we passed. We spent the last night and the following day in a village about three miles behind the line. It was here that we had our first casualty, one of our men being killed by a bomb dropped by a German aeroplane.'

This, the first fatal casualty the battalion suffered abroad, was Private Arthur Armstrong of Crook, County Durham, who was killed by shrapnel from a German bomb and was buried in Bertrancourt Military Cemetery. That morning, 29 March, the Commanding Officer and Adjutant went forward to the White City sector, north west of Beaumont Hamel to arrange the hand over of the front line to 18/Durham LI by 9/R Irish Rifles. Then early that evening, in a foul snowstorm the 'Pals' paraded and marched up through Mailly Maillet and Auchonvillers for their first time in the line in France. The relief was completed very quickly and the battalion soon started to settle down to trench life. Not long after taking over the line, Captain W G Hutchence, commanding D Company, went out to visit a forward post, where unfortunately he was wounded by a rifle bullet. 'Daily wastage' was the term the army used as the casualties began to mount. On 31 March, 22 year old, Corporal Harold Leake of York, had the sad misfortune to become the battalion's second fatality in France. On the whole though this was a quiet time, the one piece of excitement was when the German's erected a sign, on the battalion front with the information, 'Kut Taken, Many Prisoners'.

Even Private Weatherley recorded that things weren't too bad,

We were prepared for some rough weather. Fortunately the weather was bright and warm, and continued to be so for the rest of our stay in the trenches. On the whole and compared with what we

18/1063 Corporal H. Leake the battalion's second fatality through enemy action. Below, his original grave with the early wooden cross grave marker. He is buried in the Sucrerie Military Cemetery at Collincamps.

Germans in deep dug out, the enemy made very strong and deep dug outs which were hardly touched by the British shells.

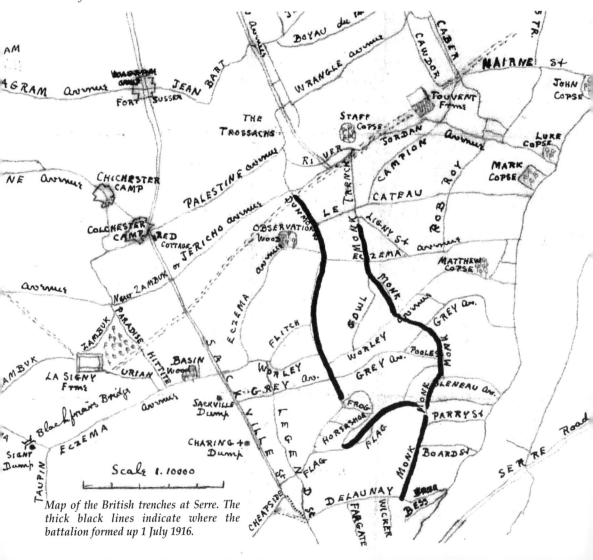

Map of the British trenches at Serre. The thick black lines indicate where the battalion formed up 1 July 1916.

experienced later, we had a very quiet time during this, our first visit.'

So the first five days of trench warfare passed and on the evening of 3 April the 12/Yorks & Lancaster Regiment arrived and took over the line, the Durham's moving back to the village of Beaussart and from there to Bus-Les-Artois, for a 'rest'. This was the first time that the battalion moved into what the Army termed 'rest' and they found it was anything but a rest. Carrying parties taking all sorts of stores to the line became the routine and some in the battalion wished they were back in the front line.

Then followed a sixteen days 'rest' – strange how the army has developed a habit of misinterpreting the meaning of certain words. Fatigues and working parties were again in vogue. During this time we lived in huts, comfortable in many ways, but not altogether waterproof, a feature, which greatly added to the discomfort of those who returned to camp, wet through, though the rule rather than the exception at that time.

Perhaps this served as a kind of preparation for our next spell in the trenches, for the elements during the first few days were very unfavourable and we gained some idea of what trench life at its worst was like. Water and mud were almost knee deep and added to the danger of being shot, was that of being drowned, especially those of us engaged on carrying rations. 'Keep to the right,' 'keep to the left,' 'mind the sump,' were oft-repeated warnings, but in spite of such, many went up to the waist in water and had to be pulled out. The humorous side of this was not entirely lacking. To see two men hugging a heavy container, and endeavouring to pass safely by stepping on floating boards was to witness a smart piece of juggling. To prepare dug-outs in the side of the trench in order to provide some protection from the elements, and to return at 2 a.m. to find the same dug-outs fallen in, all ones belongings buried and the rain still falling was almost beyond the limits of endurance and speech. Easter Sunday however introduced us to another spell of fine weather and matters gradually improved.

One could almost detect sighs of relief, when the next move to the trenches was announced. We were going into the firing line, but that implied something approaching a real rest compared with what we had had.

So wrote Private William Weatherley, recording the time spent 'resting', this was his last entry in the *Bede Magazine*, for he was wounded on 19 May and evacuated to England.

The battalion moved back into the line taking over from 11/East Yorkshire Regiment.

The enemy trench mortars were very active during this period, however they were only in for four days before relief arrived in the shape of the 18/West Yorkshire Regiment and 18/Durham LI moved back to billets in Colincamps and from there a few days later to Bertrancourt. Some time was spent here until on 6 May the huts were vacated and the battalion moved to Bus-les-Artois. Where they remained until the middle of the month when they moved back into the front line, relieving 16/West Yorkshire Regt.

It was in the middle of May that Lieutenant Colonel Bowes went to command the Brigade as Brigadier General H B Kirk went sick and sadly died of meningitis. The Colonel commanded the Brigade until to Brigadier General J D Inglis late Devonshire Regiment arrived to take command.

'The remainder of the month of May we spent in 'rest' huts in a large wood well behind the line, from which we travelled daily to the trenches on working parties. As the weeks passed it became patent to all that our efforts - for once at any rate were directed to a definite and important end.'

On 19 May the battalion was relieved and moved back to Colincamps, it was here that the enemy artillery sent over a heavy barrage that destroyed D Company's field cooker. This was reported to his family at home in Browney Colliery, by Private Charles Todd.

We had a lively time of it in the village where we are billeted, one afternoon four shells were fired in but we all rushed for the cellars. They only damaged the field kitchens and killed four horses. One poor beast was practically blown to pieces. Last time we were in the line one of the company a brave lad from Durham, F Lockey fell in action, we brought him off the battlefield and saw him laid in a soldiers grave, side by side with many a brave hero who has given his life for his country.

It was on a Tuesday when Private Frank Lockey of Durham City was killed. His party were repairing the barbed wire when he was shot through the head, presumably by a sniper. One of his comrades Private E C Bell and Lieutenant Scott, one of the old Barnard Castle boys, were close by when he was hit and stayed with him until he died about twenty minutes later. His sorrowing comrades were granted permission to remain in the line for the funeral and one of the 'Pals', writing home said, ' Every time we go to the trenches we can see the spot where poor Frank lies in his last resting place.'

Private Lockey although a resident of Durham City had been educated at The North Eastern County School, Barnard Castle and afterwards at Skerry's College in Newcastle, before entering his fathers business in Durham City. He was one of the first volunteers for the 'Pals' from the City

On 24 May the Durham's moved back from Colincamps and went into the hutments in Warimont Wood. The time here was once again spent 'resting'. Lance Corporal W E Marshall recorded these spells behind the line for the *Bede Magazine*.

The remainder of the month of May we spent in 'rest' huts in a large wood well behind the line, from which we travelled daily to the trenches on working parties. As the weeks passed it became patent to all that our efforts - for once at any rate were directed to a definite and important end. The first three weeks of June our battalion was occupied in sapping work – or rather constructing large dug ñouts on the plan so often described in the press and generally supposed to be used by the Germans. Each dug-out was to be thirty yards long, with two staircases placed well apart, so as to provide an emergency exit. The depth below the surface was about thirty feet and the staircase had bends half way down to guard against bombs being thrown into the dug out. Such a place is almost impregnable, and will sleep a platoon forty strong quite comfortably. Unfortunately it was not our lot to complete these palatial residences or to dwell in them.

When not employed on working parties the battalion practised for the coming attack, first by companies then the battalion and finally the whole Brigade. Officers and NCOs were walked over models of the enemy trenches marked out with flags. They were also shown scale models and were taken to observation posts in the line to view the ground to be taken. Everything possible was done to ensure every man knew his job and place in the attack.

Lance Corporal Charles Moss recalled this period,

A miniature copy of the German Trenches had been prepared for this purpose on open country a few kilo's behind our billets. A few brass hats explained the plan of attack, the timing of the attacking waves, the concentration of the artillery barrage and the formation of each battalion's waves.

Leeds - Bradford's – Durham's our battalion was to follow and make strong points to hold the enemy counter attacks. I was shown exactly where my Lewis Gun post was to be, but when I asked the officer what my field of fire was to be, he couldn't tell me. I pointed out that the sort of country in front was the most vital thing for me to deal with the counter attacks. He resented me calling his attention to this and all he could say was that I would find out when I got there'

The Big Push

The 31st Division had been brought from Egypt to France to take part in the forthcoming 'Big Push'; the plans for the summer offensive on the Somme had been put forward at an inter-allied

German infantry in a well constructed trench.

conference at Chantilly. The French had originally wanted the British to make a series of preparatory attacks beginning in April. However after a series of meetings it was decided that the attack would take place on a broad front. The French on the right, would attack on a twenty-five mile front with forty divisions. The British, on the left, would attack on a fourteen-mile front with twenty-five divisions. Before the Allied attack could begin the Germans attacked the French at Verdun in February of 1916, as the French Army was drawn in at Verdun they asked the British to take over that part of the line around Arras held by the French Tenth Army. The British now held a continuous line from Ypres to the Somme and as pressure on the French at Verdun increased so its share of the Somme offensive decreased to an attack by fourteen divisions on an eight-mile front.

General Haig had allotted the greater part of the coming battle to the British Fourth Army, under the command of General Sir Henry Rawlinson. The plan was for an attack on a ten-mile front, which would capture Pozieres Ridge. But this would be an uphill attack against strongly dug in and prepared German positions. General Rawlinson was in command of five Army Corps, from south to north was XII Corps commanded by Lieutenant W C Congreve VC, next in line was III Corps commanded by Lieutenant General W P Pultney, then X Corps commanded by Lieutenant General T L C Morland. Finally on the left came VIII Corps commanded by Lieutenant General Sir A G Hunter Weston, under his command was the 4th (Regular) Division, the 31st Division and the 48th(South Midland) (Territorial Force) Division. The Corps Commander placed the 4th Division on the right next came the 31st Division and on the left one brigade of the 48th Division, which at zero hour would stand fast and not attack.

31st Division were placed opposite the village of Serre and in the line Major General R Wanless O'Gowan, had on the right 93 Brigade and on the left 94 Brigade with 92 Brigade, the Hull Pals, in reserve. 93 Brigade would have the Leeds Pals and the 1st and 2nd Bradford Pals as in the first and second lines with the Durham Pals ready to follow them.

On 4 June 18/Durham LI moved to Courcelles where they were supposed to go into billets, but the village was receiving a lot of attention from the German Artillery gunners, so trenches were dug just outside the village and the battalion lived here whilst the some further training was carried out. But there was much work to do and this meant not a lot of time was spared for training.

Lance Corporal Moss again,

The billet I was in received a direct hit while I was out on a fatigue party with the result that we had to dig some trenches further in the rear in which to live. It was impossible to get any sleep during the night because of a heavy long distance battery and a great Howitzer belching all night long. We were on fatigues during the day carrying ammunition and 'Plumb Pudding' mortar shells to dumps in the line, the shells were brutes to carry; they were about the size of a football with a steel shank attached. Many of these never reached the dumps because some of the carriers, to save themselves from struggling down the trench with them, just tipped them into the deep gully's that crossed the communication trenches.

During the latter part of June the weather started to turn wet and conditions in the trenches outside Courcelles became bad and Corporal Wilf Barker and Lance Corporal Charles Moss recorded their stay here, LanceCorporal Charles Moss said,

18/544 Lance Corporal Charles Moss who wrote to the local [papers about the battalion. This photograph was taken after his promotion to segeant. Note the bombers badge above his stripes and the wound stripe on his left cuff.

Everybody remained in good spirits despite all the rain and mud and bad feeding arrangements and the filthy verminous condition we were all in. Whilst Corporal Wilf Barker remarked,

'Rain in wartime it is a punishment of which you can form no idea, when it starts you can do nothing but shiver and shrink and you must carry on. To sleep in a trench full of water has no equivalent, but that is nothing really to the moment of awakening when you have to watch to kill or be killed.'

During the last week of June the British artillery carried out a heavy and systematic bombardment of the German trenches and wire, unfortunately for the British the bad weather meant that the attack had to be delayed and this resulted in the start of the battle being put back until 0730 Hours on the morning of 1 July.

On 20 June the three Officers and 197 men of D Company left the Battalion to join 16/West Yorkshire Regt, D Company would be attached to the 1st Bradford Pals in the attack and they were to receive special training for their part of the assault.

The Germans however were not sitting waiting for the British assault and during the last weeks of June were moving numerous batteries of Heavy and Field Artillery into positions around Serre, Puisieux and Gommecourt. These batteries were camouflaged and kept silent until the British attacked.

About this time 18/1490 Private William Ewbank, in peacetime an oiler at the LNER Shildon Depot, was badly wounded by shrapnel in the abdomen. He was evacuated from the firing line and after passing through the

Regimental Aid Post and the Casualty Clearing Station he arrived at one of the three hospitals in Abbeville, from where a nurse wrote to his parents,

'Your son has been admitted to hospital here suffering from severe wounds. His condition is very dangerous. He is so anxious you should know he is here. He does not suffer much pain and on the whole is wonderfully cheery. I shall write you again in a few days as I know you must be very anxious for he is such a good fellow.'

But the promised letter from the nurse never arrived, the next letter Mr & Mrs Ewbank received was from an Army Chaplain informing them their son had passed away.

Private Jack Wilson of C Company kept a small diary of this period before the battle, no comments just one-line entries of his daily activities,

9/6/16   Leeds chap hit in front of us, two done, the other hit in the side, head, leg and arm, dressed him.

10/6/16   In dugout

14/6/16   Cleaning cellar steps, fell down cellar steps.

15/6/16   Town commandant, didn't go in, others in trenches.

16/6/16   On guard at night, great aerial activity.

24/6/16   Shelled during the night, had to get up. Two of B or D Company killed in a cellar.'

This last entry referred to the deaths of Privates George Lowton of Sunderland and Frank Plows of York.

Meanwhile in Courcelles the battalion prepared to move forward and reconnaissance parties prepared to move off, Lance Corporal Charles Moss was asked by his Platoon Commander to go out into No Man's Land but when the officer learnt that Moss had been on a working party all day he was stood down.

There was an incident on the night of 29 June that might have stopped me being in the attack. Lieutenant Simpson one of our officers who knew of my previous exploits asked me if I would go with him across No Man's Land that night to examine the German wire. He asked what duties I had been on and when I told him, 'bomb carrying working party', he said I would be too tired for such a dangerous job. It seemed to me that whoever examined the wire it would be a miracle if they got back alive. I took it as a compliment that he asked me to go.

A Company moved into a farmyard where Wilf Barker with his back against the wall of the barn enjoying the summer sunshine, watching as his comrades of A Company wrote letters home, for many it may be their last. He wrote in his diary,

They are contemplating the possible fate that awaits them. They think of it resolutely and coolly, these young men are talking very low to one another and with slow and very infrequent gestures. To those who are returning to the rear, those going into action are entrusting the letter with their final commission. One says 'You will send that letter to my Dear Mother?' Another, 'You will write and tell my dear little wife so and so'! Each thinks he is going to his death and all are writing their last will and testament.

Later that afternoon Wilf sat down in the barn and wrote his own letter,

June 30 1916 4 p.m.

My Dear Mother and Father

In the uncertainty, which hangs over our lives out here today, I want to send you a kiss and fondest love + say a few words to you. First I want to tell you I am confessed. I am going into tomorrow's attack with quiet confidence and a good strong heart. I know what I have to love in you and Father and my dear sisters and brothers. I am offering the sacrifice of my life not lightheartedly but with the conviction that it will save you all whom I love dearly.

You will tell this to all the others then perhaps they will understand. I know the sharpness of the sorrow that will pierce your hearts if I have to go down, but that is left to our God, but on the other hand if he thinks otherwise then I shall be spared. I have thought of the possible fate, which awaits from many points of view, but we can do nothing, it is not in our hands, so just hope for the best. I send you all my love and kisses

I am your ever-loving son, Wilf.

Lance Corporal Charles Moss also recalled that time before the move up to the line,

During Friday the 30th we moved to the south side of Colincamps, in the ruins of a badly straffed chateau, where during the evening our CO. Lieutenant Colonel Hugh Bowes, gave us instructions for our conduct during the attack. There was to be no turning back every man must advance at a steady pace, all officers had the authority to shoot anyone who stopped or tried to go back. The wounded had to be left, to be attended to by the stretcher-bearers and the RAMC. The grimmest order to me was that no fighting soldier was to stop to help the wounded, the CO was very emphatic about this, but I realised this would be an order to the CO as well as to us from the General. We spent the rest of the evening being issued with Field Dressings, extra ammunition, picks and shovels, camouflaging over our tin hats with sandbags and getting the bayonets sharpened. There was a good deal of light-hearted talk amongst groups of us. We did not get our rum ration that night our CO did not encourage the use of it. The rum was to be carried into action by one man in each section and dished out when urgently needed. I did not get any of it but it was the cause of B Company CSM being reduced to the ranks through getting dead drunk on his company's ration while we were in the line. The main thing we all looked forward to was to get away from the trenches to fight in open country and to get on the move.

If Charles Moss with C Company didn't get any rum then Private Frank Raine recorded that A Company did and he had this to say about it.

I didn't like rum, I couldn't take it and I also didn't want to die a drunken hero, because that rum did all sorts of extraordinary things to them y'know. It altered the complexion altogether of a man, some of them wanted to go and fight all alone. You see. I couldn't take the damn stuff, it upset me. I hated the smell and the stink of it. I only touched it once and it all came back on me and never again would I touch it. You got the ration which was about equivalent to an egg cup full and it was very potent, you were standing with an empty tummy and you swigged this stuff down and it immediately came back, it was really dangerous. I remember my great friend Broomhead, I used to give him my ration. I remember he had a high-pitched voice and he used to get these two rations and his voice used to go high and he started to shout. So I said, 'If you can't contain yourself I'm going to cut this off. If you can't carry this stuff properly your not going to get anymore and that's how I started with the flask after the Somme, after he had been wounded. I was the only one handing my ration on that I knew, most of them lived for it. There was a ration of cigarettes also but I didn't smoke either.

The first of 18/Durham LI to move forward were D Company who at 8.45 p.m. on the evening of 30 June followed 16/West Yorkshire Regiment into their positions in the second line. Those that were LOB, the Left Out of Battle and what was termed in the army as 'the details', those men that were to form the nucleus of the battalion if heavy casualties were suffered, left Courcelles at 6.30 p.m. and marched to Bus les Artois where they joined the 1st Line Transport. Then at 10.15 p.m. the Battalion, with a trench strength of 789 all ranks, left Courcelles and began moving forward.

The battalion moved forward by a route to the north of Colincamps, this had previously been marked and cleared of obstacles and debris to facilitate the forward movement of the heavily laden soldiers. Each man was carrying his haversack and pushed down between his back and the haversack was either a pick or a shovel, ready for the work of consolidating the captured enemy trenches. In his ammunition pouches were 120 rounds of .303 rifle ammunition and hanging on the belt was a bayonet and an entrenching tool. Across his chest was an extra bandolier of 100 rounds and in his pockets were two, possibly more in some cases, Mills Bombs. Specialist Bombers however carried canvas buckets of grenades and the Lewis Gun teams carried extra drums of ammunition for the guns. The Battalion Signal Section had to hump reels of signal wire into the line ready to establish communication between the Battalion Headquarters and the companies and also rearward to Brigade Headquarters, and as some one remarked, 'And they call us Light Infantry'.

The heavily laden column moved slowly past Colincamps, which was blazing after being set on fire by German shells. The march in was recorded by several of the battalion.

Lance Corporal Charles Moss, serving with C Company had this to say,

The Germans had intensified the bombardment of Colincamps and the village was soon enveloped in flames. The explosions had a shattering effect and the particular rattling effect of the small arms ammunition added to the shrieking and whining and crashing of both British and German artillery fire made the deafening pandemonium complete.

We moved off from our billets at 10 p.m. and marched in sections to the entrance of a light railway trench which led for about half a mile across open ground to the entrance of a communication trench called 'ECZEMA' all the time we had used it for front line duties but it had been renamed 'SOUTHERN AVENUE' for the attack. As we approached the railway trench we found the Germans were straffing it, especially the entrance, which meant that we had to time the bursts of the shellfire and hurry in between salvoes. It was slow work to get along that railway trench. We so often had to fling ourselves down in the trench as the shriek of the shells sounded as though they could not miss us. When we got into 'SOUTHERN AVENUE' the area was so crowded with troops it was some time before we got into it. It was marvellous how each section kept together in such a mix up. After many stops and much struggling, falling down and getting caught in signal wires we reached our assembly trench at about 4 a.m. on Saturday 1 July.

Germans unloading artillery amunition.

18/918 Corporal Wilf Barker from Darlington, a fitter in civilian life with the North Eastern Railway Company, serving with A Company recorded that the Company paraded in the village of Courcelles at 8.45 p.m. to begin their move to the front line.

> Fall in and march to the trenches, Germans shelled the battery to the left of the village. All in the pink and the best of spirits. Now we are ready, in Indian file we slowly ascend the communication trench. Arrive in our assembly trenches at 4.30 a.m. 1st of July or somewhere about that time, I cannot say exactly as I have no watch.

It was about now that signals were received from the Generals commanding the Army and the Corps that the battalion belonged to. General, Sir Henry Rawlinson, Commanding Fourth Army, wrote,

> In wishing all ranks good luck, the Army Commander desires to impress on all infantry units the supreme importance of helping one another and holding on tight to every yard of ground gained. The accurate and sustained fire of the artillery during the bombardment should greatly assist the task of the infantry.

Whilst the General Officer Commanding VIII Corps, Lieutenant General Sir A G Hunter-Weston sent the following,

> My greetings to every officer, non commissioned officer and man of Thirty-first Division. Yours is a glorious task in the battle. Stick it out, push on each to his objective, and you will win a glorious victory and a name in history. I rejoice to be associated with you as your Corps Commander.

The Battalion War Diary records that Battalion Headquarters reached their assembly trench, 'Maitland' at 4.50 a.m. the HQ being set up near the junction of 'Warley' and 'Maitland' trenches. The assembly trench was just a temporary one about four feet deep without any fire step or proper parapet. It was made just to afford a bit of protection from machine gun and rifle fire while the battalion waited to move forward to its jumping off trench in readiness to go over the top. As soon as things were sorted out, around 5 a.m. special bombing parties under the command of Lieutenant J B Bradford went forward and reported to 15/West Yorkshire Regiment at Sap A.

Lance Corporal Charles Moss again,

> They must have waited until we were all in position then they opened fire on us. Along on my left there was soon word being passed along for stretcher-bearers. We heard several of the company had been hit by the first salvo. The trench was so shallow I had to crouch low into the front of it. Regardless of danger Lieutenant Simpson kept moving up and down the trench with head and shoulders in full view of the Germans. I told him he was asking for it, but he took no notice and kept having a word here and there with the fellow's as we waited. At about 7.30 a.m. Zero Hour, the time for the first wave to go over we heard a heavy rumbling thud which was the exploding of our great mine.

Nearby A Company crouched in their portion of the shallow trench waiting for the order to advance as enemy shells started falling around them, 18/918 Corporal Wilf Barker wrote in his diary;

> My sleeve was torn by a piece of shrapnel and I was also hit in the shoulder by a piece but not wounded. The rum ration was served out and then came the order to get our packs on and move up to the ladders.'

When they were all in place Wilf noted the feelings and reactions of those about him;

> Moved up to the ladders waiting for the word 'Over' all feeling relieved... Nobody seems to care if they get hurt or not.

Then at 7.20 a.m. the great mine at Hawthorn Redoubt near Beaumont Hamel was exploded, the Tunnelling Companies of The Royal Engineers had worked for months to construct the mines that

When mines were exploded under the trenches the first side to occupy the rim of the crater had an advantage over the enemy. When Hawthorne Ridge mine was blown under the Germans, Saturday morning 1 July 1916, survivors quickly manned the rim and were able to repel the British attackers.

were exploded on 1 July 1916. All along the front a series of mines were blown that day. All were scheduled to be blown at 7.28 a.m. but on VII Corps front Lieutenant General Hunter-Weston had other ideas. He originally wanted the mine blown some hours before the advance, so that his men could capture and consolidate the crater before the main advance. But that plan was over ruled and so as a compromise the mine was fired eight minutes early. This gave the German defenders time to man their machine guns and for word to be passed to the hidden artillery pieces to prepare to fire.

At 7.30 a.m. the British Artillery redoubled its barrage on to the German line, but the enemy fired a triple barrage that simultaneously hit the British Front line, support line and reserve trench. A deadly barrage of steel hit the leading battalions as they were clambering out of the trenches. Those of the Leeds Pals and Bradford Pals that did survive the enemy barrage walked straight into the German machine guns and the battalions literally disappeared. D Company 18/Durham LI, going over with the 16/West Yorkshire regiment was also badly hit.

18/706 Lance Corporal Bob Clark was wounded and had this to say.

'When we got over the top of our trenches we could see nothing of the Leeds who were supposed to be in front of us although we could see our fellows going over in fine style on our right. We came under a terrific machine gun fire as well as the bombardment and it quickly thinned out the ranks. Sergeant Hall from Hartlepool was soon hit and Lance Sergeant Brydon from Sunderland almost immediately afterwards, so I was in charge of the platoon, but only for two minutes, when I also stopped one, I was shot in the left hand within ten minutes of going over.

97

I took cover in a shell hole and made myself as comfortable as possible, it was no good trying to get back to our trenches. Just then they were sniping at anyone who showed as much as an eyelid, but whilst there I was hit in both legs by shrapnel. It was not until dark that I got back to our trenches. I got down to the dressing station on Sunday morning and from there moved in easy stages and was evacuated on a New Zealand Hospital Ship and finished up at the Endell Street Military Hospital in London.'

This seems to be the only account from D Company to survive. Some of the company were seen moving near Pendant Copse, well inside the enemy lines, by artillery observers but they disappeared into the smoke and were never heard of again.

At 9.20 a.m. Brigade Headquarters instructed the battalion to move forward in support, but it wasn't until 9.47 a.m. that A Company left 'Maitland' and began to advance towards 'Monk', Private Frank Raine was among those to go forward,

'We walked all night up through the trenches ready to go over at daybreak. I remember we got into a side trench, which was in a bit of a dip and there was two officers there, the Adjutant and his nephew, who disdainfully helped us out of the trench, because we had this weight on. We went over from a support trench in a dip, they helped us up a home made ladder, I only remember seeing Broomhead and myself, we went over the top together, we walked along a bit and the only thing I remember after that was this terrific bang and a great black cloud of smoke above us. I felt a knock on my hip, which I didn't take much notice of and walked on. I turned round a bit after that and Broomhead had gone. I walked on a little bit and looked round, I could not see a soul of any description, either in front of me or behind me or anywhere. Oh my God, the ground in front of me was just like heavy rain, that was the machine gun bullets and up above there was these great 5.9' shrapnel's going off and I think that deadened me as I have very little recollection. However I had much sense to know and as I looked round I said, 'Where the hell is everybody, I can't see anybody, I'm not going out there by myself', and I turned round and came back to our own trenches. I didn't meet a soul. I rested in a shell hole for a bit and still nobody came and when I looked a piece of shrapnel had hit the knife on my hip and just penetrated the flesh.' Where everybody had got to I don't know. You reach a stage where you get beyond being frightened, but I felt guilty at dropping into the shell hole. The Adjutant and his nephew [Major Lowe and Captain Ince] never stepped out of the trench; those two officers should have been leading us.

I never saw the British Front Line; I don't think I reached it. I think our lot had gone a bit further than me and dropped into our front line. I think that's what happened to them.

Corporal Wilf Barker was probably in front of Frank Raine and he wrote in his diary,

Over at last, the suspense over and we begin to walk forward as if walking up the street towards the German trenches, only to drop and take cover now and again, lads lying all over, some groaning, others are quietly praying. I saw poor Billy Blewitt lying in the entrance to a dug out shot through the leg. I wished him 'the best of luck' and told him the stretcher bearers would be along shortly to get him.

Wilf didn't get much further before he was badly wounded in the stomach. Eventually the stretcher-bearers reached him and he was evacuated to a casualty clearing station, when he woke on a hospital train he found that all his money and his watch had been stolen, the thief had left only the diary behind.

18/913 Corporal A. R. Wood, a Sunderland policeman killed in action 1 July 1916.

18/730 Privaye G. W. Duthie, wounded wih D company 1 July 1916.

Three minutes after A Company advanced they were followed by B Company, who met an identical fate out in the open ground, Sergeant Arthur Durrant a Sunderland man had this to say about his part in B Company's advance,

I think my company was the third line over and we didn't have any particular training for that, all we knew was that at a certain time we had to get out of our trenches and go over the other line and consolidate what had been captured, otherwise we as a company had no particular training for the job. When we reached the trenches we felt a little tired but we weren't unduly perturbed. I had a couple of bottles of rum and we distributed those when we did get to the trench of course. We received a message early in the morning, I have forgotten the time, that D Company had succeeded in capturing their objective, whether this was true or not we did not know, but we certainly believed it at the time, and that of course increased our moral and kept our spirits going and again we thought it was money for nothing.

Somewhere between 'Maitland' and 'Monk', Sergeant Durrant was wounded however in the fog of the battle he thought he had reached No Man's Land and he continued,

No Man's Land was a wonderful sight, however that wasn't too safe so I dragged myself out of the trench and saw in the distance the entrance to a dug-out, so I thought well! Lets see if I can get myself in there. So again I dragged myself along to the steps of the dug out and I managed to get my legs so that I was in a half-lying, half sitting position on the steps leading down to the dug out. But suddenly the mouth of the dug out fell in and put me into a doubled up position. I think some kind of high explosive shell must have burst nearby and upset the mouth of the dug out. So I thought, Well, I am not any further hurt, so I better get myself out of this lot, the dug-out was not very safe because the rest of the entrance down into the dug out was blocked, so again I dragged myself out and rested a while in the open, still nothing else hit me, this kind of thing went on until the evening, I don't know the time, but I eventually dragged myself in the right direction I am glad to say and eventually crawled to safety.

The battalion war diary records that between 11 a.m. and 11.30 a.m. the German Artillery was very effective A and B Companies had been heavily shelled in the open between 'Maitland' and 'Monk' and the enemy was beginning to predominate.

C Company were still in 'Maitland' and had not been instructed to move when at 11.57 a.m. a message was received that B Company were to hold 'Sackville' in conjunction with 4th Division and 'Legend' would also would be held by 4th Division. Lance Corporal Charles Moss was still in 'Maitland' and he wrote,

I wanted to see how our attack was going so I moved some of the chalk in such a way I would be protected from the sniper fire and took a good look at the German Line in front of me. But all I could see was fountains of chalk and smoke sent up by our artillery barrage. As the barrage got clear of one the German trenches over the German third line, out on the top came scrambling a German machine gun team. They fixed their gun in front of their parapet and opened out a slow and deadly fire on our front. The gunners were without tunics and worked in their shirtsleeves, in quiet a different manner to their usual short sharp bursts. Their fire was so slow that every shot seemed to have a definite aim. Except for that gun team there wasn't another soldier in British Khaki or German Grey to be seen.

Just as I spotted the German gun team come into action we got the word to move to our jumping off trench, to be ready to go over the top. As I got into this trench I nearly bumped into a soldier who seemed to be carrying a big piece of raw meat resting on his left arm. He was doing a sort of crying whimper. Then I realized it was the remains of his right forearm he was carrying in such a way. Many more soldiers were making their way back up the trench, they were the walking wounded going back to the advanced dressing stations of which their were several dug into the side of the communication trench. When we got into our jumping off trench I found it was in one of those deep hollows that were peculiar to this part of the front and was called dead-ground because of the protection it afforded. Part of it was occupied by our Battalion Headquarters and the Commanding Officer and the Adjutant were there. A little further along the trench there was some scaling ladders up which our fellows were climbing. "Big Lizzie" a nickname we had given this officer, was brandishing a pistol and shouting and urging them up the ladders. I watched for a minute or two when down the trench came Corporal Forshaw one of the battalion runners, he was very excited and was shouting as he came, something to the effect, 'the whole shows a bloody balls up'. The CO spoke to him but I couldn't hear for the infernal row of the shellfire, but the CO came and spoke to "Big Lizzie", "Wait a minute Mr Ince a minute or two will neither win nor lose this battle." The officer at once stopped waving his revolver and stopped the fellows who were climbing the ladder. Then they all crouched down in the bottom of the trench. In a minute or two along came an Army Corps runner and handed the CO an envelope. The CO opened it and read the message it contained, then striking a dramatic attitude he turned to the Adjutant and said,

18/988 Private J. Davison, wounded 1 July 1916.

"Ah Ah Mr Lowes this is where we come in", then he read the message, "Your attack has failed 18/DLI take over the front line from point X.35 a 3.7 to point K.29.c.8.0". The CO and the Adjutant had a brief consultation and then the CO gave "Big Lizzie" an order to muster as many men as he could and occupy the part of the front allotted to us.

There was now a danger of a German counter-attack, so the battalion was moved into defensive positions. The Commanding Officers of both 'Bradford Pals' battalions had been killed and the Commanding Officer of the 'Leeds Pals' was badly wounded, so Colonel Bowes issued instructions that the survivors of these three battalions should be gathered and reorganized. A company of 11/East Yorkshire Regiment was sent forward by Brigade Headquarters to provide cover for the guns of 159 Battery, Royal Field Artillery and C Company, 18/Durham LI moved up into the old front line. By 3.43 p.m. a report from C Company reached Battalion Headquarters stating that, 'the front line trench was blown out of existence as a fighting trench and that it was full of dead West Yorks.'

Lance Corporal Charles Moss and his Lewis Gun team moved forward with C Company,

The artillery fire was much quieter by the time we reached the front line trench, but it was nearly impossible to tell it from No Man's Land, most of the revetting and fire steps had been blown in. The whole of the front was an awful chaos of duckboards, sandbags, and stakes, wire netting and dud shells strewn about. It was impossible to recognize a revetment from a fire bay. Among the wreckage were the dead bodies of a 'Leeds Pals' Lewis Gun team with their gun and drums of ammunition

18/467 Lance Corporal H. Colwell, wound 1 Just 1916. He was posted to 2/Durham LI where he won the Military Medal. His medal rolls show no evidence of service with a Highland regiment.

lying near them. One of my team picked up the gun and we took it with us making two guns in our team for the rest of the time we were in the front line.

Major Tilly reported to Battalion Headquarters bringing up with him about 66 reinforcements who joined their companies. By this time an initial count put the casualties of A, B and C Companies as 5 Officers and 126 Other Ranks wounded and 11 Other Ranks, killed. Of D Company the four officers were all wounded and only 17 Other Ranks had reported back to the battalion, but compared to the other battalions of the brigade the Durham's had got off lightly.

In the early hours of Sunday, 2 July, B Company moved forward and joined C Company in the front line. The men spread out along the front line and stated to prepare defensive positions.

I was surprised to see a black retriever dog roaming about, but it disappeared down a dug out when we got near it. Most of the West Yorks and our D Company had been killed or wounded in their assembly trenches during the intense bombardment before 7.30 a.m. I kept on struggling along the trench past several bodies of West Yorks until we reached a position well to the left, the position we reached hadn't suffered near so much as the part we had come from as the width of No Man's Land was up to 1,000 yards in places here. We set up our Lewis Gun a bit to the north of 'Rob Roy' communication trench. A good deal of webbing equipment was lying about in this sector so we stripped off our leather equipment and put on the webbing in its place. We thought the Germans might send over a bombing raid so we struggled out into No Man's Land where we got into a big shell hole and set to with picks and shovels to make it into a Lewis Gun post. One of my gun team got the wind up very badly; he would dash himself from one side of the hole to the other at each shell burst. I was urging him to keep still in the bottom of the hole when he gave a great gasp and groaned, 'Death Oh Death, they've knocked a bloody great hole through me.' He scrambled out of the shell hole before anyone could help him and I saw no more of him until I reached the 3rd Battalion at South Shields in 1917, where I found that the shrapnel had wounded him in the shoulder and given him a Blighty that got him to England. We came out of the shell hole at daybreak and joined the rest of the company who were 'Standing To'.

Wrote Lance Corporal Charles Moss.

18/1308 Private M. Colwell, brother of the above, was also wounded 1 July 1916.

18/623 Lance Corporal W. Thompson wounded in the face with C Company, 1 July 1916.

18/1392 Private J. Tombling wounded with D Company 1 July 1916.

18/686 Lance Corporal T. Baggot, killed in action 1 July 1916.

Below: standing centre is 18/907 Private R Weatherall and belonging to D Company, also wounded 1 July 1916.

Above: front centre, 18/117 Corporal R Storey, B Company, having been wounded 1 July 1916, recovers in hospital.

As daylight broke the British Artillery fired a special bombardment to cover the front but a number of shells dropped short and 1 Officer and 9 men of C Company were wounded and one man killed. The enemy began firing gas shells and 94 Brigade on the left and 12 Brigade on the right both suffered from the effects of the gas. In the sector held by 18/Durham LI the work of collecting the wounded was undertaken, many West Yorks were gathered and the dead were buried. The Divisional Pioneer Battalion 12/King's Own Yorkshire LI came up to assist with this work. During the night, Sergeant Charles Cross, a resident of Allergate in Durham City, heard a cry from No Man's Land; at great personal risk he set off over the parapet and crawled out into No Man's Land. Once out there he came across Lieutenant H W Tait of D Company, who had been badly wounded early on the morning of 1 July. Sergeant Cross managed to get the officer on to his back and proceeded back across No Man's Land to the British lines. It was later reported in the *Durham Chronicle* that the officer presented Sergeant Cross with a suitably inscribed watch and chain as a token of his thanks.

At daylight on the morning of 4 July C Company were moved back to Monk Trench, Jack Wilson noted that he was woken up in a dug out and told to move. He had nearly got to Monk when he was hit in the hand by shrapnel. He made his way out to a dressing station in Colincamps where he had the wound dressed and he was evacuated to England. As he left the trenches suddenly a terrific thunderstorm broke and a deluge of rain filled the trenches with water, which poured in from higher ground. Charles Moss was also moving back to Monk and wrote,

> *'As we struggled along the trench I noted a ground sheet covering a long body lying on the parapet. I wasn't surprised to be told that it was the body of Lieutenant Simpson and that a sniper had got him in No Man's Land.'*

Word came through that 31st Division was to be relieved and go into Corps reserve and move to the Bernaville area joining II Corps and become GHQ reserve. 93 Brigade was to be relieved by 144 Brigade of 48th Division on the night of 4 – 5 July. Initially the Brigade was to concentrate in Louvencourt and then move on 6 July to Bernaville. During the four days in the line the losses of 18/Durham LI were 12 Officers and nearly sixty percent of the 789 men, which had gone into the line on 30 June. Less than 70 were dead the majority of these being in the ill-fated D Company.

On arrival at Louvencourt the men were fed with beef rissoles and tea and then allowed to sleep in the rat infested barns.

On 6 July the battalion cleaned themselves up as best they could and an inspection took place. Lance Corporal Charles Moss received a ticking off when it was found out that he had left his Lewis Gun behind in the front line, the gun that his team had brought with them was the one they had picked up from the dead 'Leeds Pals'. The Corps Commander visited the battalion during the day and addressed the men and thanked them for the part they had played in the battle. The next day the Brigade moved further back to Fienvillers, whilst 18/Durham LI moved slightly further to the village of Berneuil where they arrived at 11.45 a.m. Thus ended the 'Durham Pals' part in 'The Great Push'

Now the letters came home, The General Officer commanding 31st Division, Major General R Wanless-O'Gowan wrote to Lord Durham as follows,

31st Division
BEF
July 7th 1916

Dear Lord Durham
I know you will be interested in the doings of the 18th D.L.I. last Saturday. One of their

companies (D) was attached to the 15th West Yorks for a particular objective and went into action on the extreme right of 93rd Brigade. Most of this company got as far as the third line. They all gave a very good account of themselves, the men going on after they had lost all their officers and most of their N.C.O's.

Nothing could equal the dash, coolness and extraordinary bravery of our men, both the 93rd and 94th attacked and suffered very heavy losses, in spite of which at the end of the day they were as cheery and as full of fight as at the beginning. The other three companies of the D.L.I. were in Brigade Reserve.'

Yours sincerely
R W O'Gowan
Major General

The raising committee also received letters from the front; Colonel Rowland Burdon received this note from Brigadier General J D Ingles, Commanding 93 Infantry Brigade.

'Dear Colonel Burdon,

Having the honour to command the Brigade in which the battalion of The Durham Light Infantry, which you took so leading a part in raising, forms a unit I feel sure you would like to hear the of the most gallant behaviour of the battalion in its first serious engagement. From the first I knew by the keenness and military bearing of all ranks, that when the time did come to which they were looking forward with so much fervour, they would render a good account of themselves. The opportunity came on July 1st and right gallantly every officer, non-commissioned officer and man behaved.

I attach a copy of the message of our Corps Commander and also one from the GOC of the ANZAC Corps. It would be presumptuous on my part to add to such messages. I would, however add how deeply I sympathise with the parents, wives and families of those gallant men who have lost their lives. I also sympathise with all those gallant men who have been wounded and I hope that the very great majority will return to us to help accomplish their and our hearts desire.'

Attached was a message from the Commander of the ANZAC CORPS,

'Just a line to say how sorry we are to hear of the losses which your magnificent Corps has recently suffered, in its gallant fighting on the German trenches. They are indeed heroes and their name will live for evermore.'

With so few killed in the battalion compared to the Leeds and Bradford Pals there a very few letters to relatives for 1 July. Lance Corporal Marshall continued his account for The *Bede Magazine*,

''Many a fine fellow died in Britain's cause that day, and many are the tales of heroism which since have come to light. Sergeant Duke of the Brigade Machine Gun Company was killed by machine gun fire whilst advancing across No Man's Land. Sergeant Richard Corker was badly wounded by shellfire and was found in our front line trench. He must have suffered terribly and it was the third day before he could be moved back to the advanced dressing post, where he died a few hours later. Fine fellows both, and good soldiers - they will be known to the younger generations of Bede as Tennis Captain and Hockey Vice-Captain respectively. They died as they had lived – 'playing the game'. It is also my sad duty to report the death of Arthur Corner who was badly wounded after leaving the trenches to meet the Bosche. He lived to see England again, and we thought all was going well with him, when the sad news came through to us that he had passed away at Colchester. Lance Corporal A D Vickers was also amongst the wounded and was last seen having his wound dressed in our trenches. Since then no one has heard of him, and we can discover no trace of him. '

Lance Corporal Marshall then listed all the 'Bede' and other University and College men who had, been wounded with the battalion, making particular mention of 18/384 Private Tom Stanfield, one of the Maryport Contingent, who had been at Hartley University in Southampton. Twice voluntarily he had re-crossed the shell swept ground, under extremely heavy fire, between Brigade and Battalion Headquarters carrying messages between the Brigadier and the Commanding Officer. 'He fully deserved the Military Medal that was awarded him.'

So the Durham Pals left the Somme. But! For the survivors the war was not over yet.

THE BANTAM'S ENTER THE COCKPIT

When the Somme battle opened on 1 July 1916 the 35th Division were still up north, but it wasn't long before they were summoned south. Bob's Durham Bantam's entrained at Chocques at 10.30 p.m. on 2 July, and after a short journey detrained, at Frevant around about 2.30 a.m. on 3 July. From there they marched to billets in the village of Le Souich. One day was spent here before they shouldered their packs and route marched to bivouacs in the Bois du Warnimont where they arrived at 2.30 a.m. on the morning of 6 July. Three days were spent here, presumably training, but the battalion War Diary gives no indication of what was done. On10 July the battalion

A well-constructed German trench before being hit by British artilley.

marched to Varennes, where they spent two days, before marching to Bresle at 6.0 p.m. on the evening of 12 July.

On 13 July the battalion moved yet again, this time via Bois du Tailles and on in the evening to Billon Copse where they billeted overnight. Moving into the forward area the battalion reached Talus Boise, where they spent the night of 14 July before moving up into the trenches just behind Montauban on the morning of 15 July.

That day Second Lieutenant A S Carroll was wounded and 23/182 Private John Gillon died from wounds he received.

Three days were spent in these reserve trenches where there was very heavy shelling and 19/Durham LI suffered half-a-dozen casualties from this enemy fire. Most of who died from shrapnel wounds. Among the dead was 19/1005 Sergeant Robert Yule, a resident of Hawthorn Terrace, Durham City, he was the battalion bandmaster and also in charge of the battalion stretcher-bearers. Some short time after the Sergeants death, Mrs Yule received a long letter from the Battalion Medical Officer, Doctor Barss, who wrote,

I have been thinking of you and the children ever since he passed away and I am taking the chance of writing you a few words of sympathy, because the sergeant was one of my best friends. He was not only my best stretcher-bearer, but he was also a personal friend of mine. I thought an awful lot of him and he was one of the favourite sergeants of the battalion. As soon as we came out to France I got him to stay along with me and my medical Corporal. We slept together in the open many a night and we have had many a meal together. He was a thoroughly brave man and I never once saw him show the least sign of fear, even under the most-heavy shelling. We used to go into the trenches together, to attend to any who were sick and I used to marvel at his fearlessness. I am so sorry that he is gone, first because of your sake and the children, and also because I have lost a true friend.

Many a night we have sat in front of a little fire and filled our pipes. Then he would tell me of his wife, his girls and his home. He used often to tell me what a fine Bible student you were and he was very much interested in the girls and their schoolwork. He tried his best to buy one of them a French Testament. The various parcels you sent him from home used to be a great comfort to him and he never failed to share them with me and the other boys. It will comfort you, I am sure, to know just how he passed away. We were getting ready to lie down. The sergeant was filling his pipe, outside my lean-to at about 9.30 p.m. When suddenly thousands upon thousands of shells began to fly overhead. They came so swiftly it was impossible to count them. Suddenly I heard an explosion,

19/1005 Sergeant Robert Yule, NCO i/c stretcher bearers.

followed by some groans. Corporal Scurr and I rushed out and found someone lying there wounded. It was to dark to recognise who it was, but we got hold of him and started to lift him along out of danger. Then I got an awful mouthful of poisonous gas and we both of us fell over. We got on our gas helmets and finally got him to a place where I could dress his wounds. It was then I recognised the sergeant and it took the good right out of me. I got him bandaged up, but his strength was failing fast because of internal haemorrhage. He said, 'Where is the Doctor?' 'I am here.' I said. 'Oh Doctor,' He added, 'I am done.' Then as he thought of you and his girls he kept repeating, 'God bless them all.' Afterwards he said, 'Oh I feel so much easier.' These were the last words I heard him speak. I placed him on a transport wagon and told the driver to get him to an ambulance at once, but he died in a few minutes. He had practically no suffering, and was not disfigured or mangled like so many poor lads out here. The wound was in the chest.

His funeral was attended by quite a number of the Red Cross men and his grave has been properly marked. Since the sergeants death I have experienced two or three days of actual hell. The sights are too bad to relate and no pen can describe it all. When I was out looking after the sergeant a shell went clean through my bed. It would have killed me for sure if I had been there. Fifteen of my stretcher-bearers have been wounded and about 200 of the battalion are killed, wounded or missing. I have had one or two of the most miraculous escapes.

Earlier before his death, Sergeant Yule, in the midst of a heavy barrage of enemy fire, had bravely went with Doctor Barss to the rescue of a wounded soldier, who was lying exposed to the enemy fire. Sadly before they reached him he was blown to pieces by the bursting of a shell, which also wounded Doctor Barss in the leg and Sergeant Yule in the hand.

North of the 'Bantams' positions at Montauban, the Germans had subjected the front line positions in Longueval and Delville Wood to an extremely intense artillery barrage which had turned the wood and the village into an inferno, 3rd Division had assaulted the village and taken most of it, but had not occupied the orchards to the north of the village. The South African Brigade serving with 9th (Scottish) Division had advanced through the wood to its northern edge where most of them were killed or wounded. In the late afternoon the Germans counter-attacked from the direction of the Ginchy Road and others from the sunken portion of the Flers Road. After a fierce struggle the South Africans were forced to fall back, although a few did hang on until morning.

Meanwhile another enemy attack was being made against Longueval and after close fighting 27 Brigade was forced back to the southern edge of the village. The situation became critical, but was saved when 5/Cameron Highlanders of 26 Brigade, advanced at 6.00 p.m. and regained the centre of the village. The General Officer Commanding 9th (Scottish) Division was determined to attack again and take the village and was given the assistance of 19/Durham LI from 106 Brigade.

On the morning of 18 July, the Commanding Officer of 19/Durham LI, Lieutenant Colonel Stoney was forced to report sick and command of the battalion passed to Major E F Osler. Then late in the afternoon a signal was received for the battalion to move forward, the actual text being,

19 DLI will move to Longueval to reinforce the remaining units of 26th IB and assist to regain our old positions gradually aaa Care being taken that the flanks are well protected aaa O/C 19DLI will report to O/C 10 A&SH aaa Touch with 18th Div must be maintained throughout at S-18-c-5-7 aaa Every effort is to be made to finally re-occupy Delville Wood which is to be held at all costs stop

6.15 p.m. signed J S Drew B/M'

19/886 Lance Corporal Scurr, a stetcher bearer who treated Sergeant Yule, later awarded the DCM.

Very quickly the men were gathered together and by 7.00 p.m. they were on the move towards the village of Longueval.

The German bombardment was so heavy and the confusion was so great that the battalion could do nothing that night, they moved into trenches in the village and the wood but casualties were mounting from the heavy artillery fire. Amongst the officers, Second Lieutenant L Millar was killed and Second Lieutenant H Heaton was wounded, also wounded, by a gun shot in the head, was Captain J W Waller, the son of the Deputy Chief Constable of the County and an assistant school master at Easington Lane School. Whilst 9 Other Ranks were killed and an unspecified number wounded.

The next day, 19 July, was spent in the same trenches, 53 Brigade of 18th Division came up and attacked from the southwestern edge of the village and after a struggle regained the southern portion of the wood. But the Durham's were still under fire and four officers were wounded, Second Lieutenant W F Reeve, Lieutenant J Mundy and Captain C Taylor with Second Lieutenant P V French dying from his wounds, as well as seventeen other ranks being killed in action. The next day one of those wounded on 18 July, 19/19 CSM Stephen Cunningham died from the wounds he had received. His obituary in the *Durham Chronicle* recorded that he was an esteemed sportsman and had played for Bearpark and Durham Rovers winning many trophies. He had trained as a teacher at St Mary's RC College Hammersmith and had been appointed to St Joseph's RC School in West Hartlepool, two years before the outbreak of war. He had tried to enlist many times but had always been rejected in consequence of his height. When the 'Bantam's' were formed he was among the first to volunteer, he was very quickly promoted and was as popular as an NCO as he was a sportsman.

19/19 Company Segeant Major Cunningham, a school teacher killed in action 20 July 1916.

CSM Cunningham's father received a short letter from the RC Padre, Father John Cotty, at the CCS where his son died,

To me belongs the sad task of conveying to you the news of your son Stephen's death. He came in early this morning with terrible wounds. In spite of all the doctors could do he passed peacefully away today. I was able to give him all the last sacraments, which he received with the greatest of piety and devotion. A strange thing was that in spite of his wounds he seemed to suffer little or no pain and was quite conscious to the end, May God in His infinite mercy grant him eternal rest and may He also help you bear your heavy loss.'

The same day 20 July, the battalion was relieved at 2.00 a.m. and moved back to Caftet Wood. A number of replacement officers arrived during the day,

Lieutenant H C V Hall from 21/Durham LI, was posted to W Company,

Lieutenant P V Day from the same battalion was posted to X Company.

Second Lieutenants, R A Wilson, R F Somerville and R M Middleton from 16/Durham LI, went to Z, Y and HQ respectively, whilst Second Lieutenant J C Corringham from 17/Durham LI was posted to Z Company. At the same time a draft of 10 Other Ranks arrived from 15/Notts & Derby's.

The next day they had to provide a working party of 300 men to work between Trones Wood and Waterlot Farm. With the continued absence of the Commanding Officer in hospital, Major S Huffam arrived from 17/West Yorkshire Regiment, to assume command. Two days were spent in Caftet Wood prior to moving on 24 July, at 1.00 a.m to Bernafray Wood, again in support of 9th (Scottish) Division. Here the battalion came under heavy shelling and Second Lieutenant W Braidford and two men were killed in action, Billy Braidford's obituary in the *Durham Chronicle* recorded that he was a well known player for Tynedale Rugby Club and had also represented the County, prior to enlisting in the Public Schools Battalion. The following day Lieutenant C W Pollock was wounded and a further thirteen men were killed, Lieutenant C W Pollock was an old boy of Bede School, Sunderland, and a B.A. of Durham University, this was the second time he had been wounded. At 6.30 p.m. 23/Royal Fusiliers took over the position and the 'Bantam's marched back to the camp in Caftet Wood. Here they spent the day cleaning up and resting before moving out that night to Silesia Trench, which was the Old German Front line on 1 July. The next few days were spent refitting and then on 30 July, 19/Durham LI were attached to 89 Brigade of

30th Division to support them in their attack on Maltzhorn Farm and Guillemont. At 7.30 a.m. the Durham's moved up to positions south of Trones Wood and stood by waiting to be called upon by 89 Brigade. Despite being heavily shelled with gas and shrapnel, in their assembly positions, the troops of 89 Brigade combined with the French on the right to take Maltzhorn Farm. They advanced in thick fog and troops from 20/King's Regiment overran the German front trench and reached the Hardecourt – Guillemont road. German counter attacks took place and some withdrawal took place but in hot sunshine and under a heavy bombardment 89 Brigade consolidated the ground it had won from Arrow Head Copse along the sunken road to Maltzhorn Farm. 19/Durham LI had not been called upon to assist the attack and remained south of Trones Wood until 8.30 p.m. when orders were received to return to Caftet Wood. The arrival of the 55th Division allowed the Corps Commander to pull both 30th and 35th Divisions out of the line and move them further back consequently on 31 July, 19/Durham LI were ordered to move to Sand Pit Valley. Casualties for the month amounted to 12 Officers and 250 Other Ranks these were light compared to many other battalions, but

Captain J. W. Waller, son of the Deputy Chief Constable of Durham wounded on the Somme. July 1916.

for the Bantams they were very hard to replace. Almost all the dead were original enlistments of 5 feet 3 inches or under, the majority being coalminers by trade and those that came to replace them were not of the same physique.

In the month of August it would seem that the Grand Old Duke of York took command. Having left Sand Pit Valley the battalion marched to Morlancourt south of Albert, three days were spent there and on 5 August they marched to Mericourt station where they entrained for Saleux. Detraining they marched to Foudrinoy where they arrived at 11.0 p.m. That day Second Lieutenant C M Drabble left the battalion to join the Royal Flying Corps as an Observer. After three days at Foudrinoy the battalion marched to the railhead at Hengest and entrained for Mericourt. Upon arrival there they got off the train and marched back to Morlancourt arriving at midnight. A further five days were spent in camp here, but there was little rest as a large number of working parties had to be found. On the last day at Morlancourt a draft of twenty-four men arrived from the Infantry Base Depot. The next move was back to Sand Pit Valley again, where Second Lieutenant F Bates and Second Lieutenant W E Harding both joined from 17/Durham LI and were posted to X and Z Company's. After a few days in Sand Pit Valley, when they again had to provide a lot of working parties the battalion again moved to bivouacs south of Caftet Wood. The 35th Division relieved the 3rd Division in the front line and made an unsuccessful attempt to capture the German strongpoint opposite Arrow Head Copse and on 21 August they discharged smoke to cover the right flank of an attack by the 24th Division.

On 22 August 19/Durham Light Infantry began moving up to the front line trenches on the eastern slope of Malzhorn Ridge and by midnight had completed the relieve of 23/Manchester Regiment. The Germans put a heavy barrage on to the 35th Divisions positions and this caused numerous casualties among the Durham Bantams. Having spent so much time on working parties all the infantry battalions of the division were very tired indeed and arrangements were made for an early relief. 17/West Yorkshire regiment arrived and relieved the Durham's who marched back to Silesia Trench where they arrived at 3.0.a.m. Casualties on Malz Horn Ridge amount to 3 Officers wounded and 110 Other Ranks, killed, wounded and missing.

Although they had not been called on to make any attacks, gallantry had been in evidence, particularly amongst the battalion stretcher-bearers, two of whom were awarded the Distinguished Conduct Medal. 19/798 Private Charles Imeson was awarded his for, conspicuous gallantry and devotion to duty during operations. As a stretcher-bearer he tended the wounded and carried them to the aid post along a road heavily shelled and swept by machine gun fire. When his battalion was relieved he stayed behind with another brigade to assist with their wounded.

19/886 Lance Corporal H F Scurr received his medal for, conspicuous gallantry and devotion to duty as medical orderly. He not only attended the wounded at the aid post, but went out and brought in wounded men under heavy fire.

A third stretcher-bearer, Lance Corporal Robert Embleton who before the war had been a rolleyman at Ludworth Colliery was also reported to have been awarded the same medal. After he had been wounded, with shrapnel in the arm and shoulder on 24 August, he attended to another wounded man and as he assisted him to the rear they were both buried and suffered further wounds through the explosion of a heavy German shell. Having managed to extricate himself and the man, Lance Corporal Embleton was eventually evacuated to England, where he ended up in The Scottish General Hospital in Aberdeen. It was reported in the *Durham Chronicle* that he was presented with the ribbon of the DCM whilst in the hospital. However no official citation of the award has been traced. The award of The Military Medal was made to 46872 Corporal W Beasley, 19/803 Private R Lambert, 19/594 Private E Wilsby and 19/1130 Lance Corporal Arthur Russell. The last named was the Labour Master at the Durham City Workhouse and writing to the Clerk of the Board, Mr H E Ferens, he said,

19/134 Lance Corporal Robert Embleton, a stretcher brearer.

> It has been hell on the part of the line we have just left. There are no trenches as they have all been flattened out and we had to dig ourselves in as quickly as possible so as to cover ourselves from the fire of the Huns. I will never forget the first time we went into that particular part of the line. The Germans bombarded with such violence that I thought it would be impossible to get out, but we managed and I cannot say how pleased I was when we reached a place of safety. At present I am in a place that was beautiful before the Huns gave it their unwelcome attention and I feel I could stay here until the war ends if the military authorities would allow. No doubt you will be pleased to hear of one of the union staff being awarded the Military Medal. I got quite a shock when I heard about it but I am also proud to think I have done something to keep up the good name of the DLI.

On 26 August a very under-strength battalion moved further back to Happy Valley where they spent three days. Here a draft of forty men arrived from the base and two more officers, Second Lieutenants W W Watson from 23/Durham LI and Second Lieutenant E Welbourne from 17/Durham LI. The battalion eventually marched to Heilly Station, where on 30 August they entrained for Candas and bid adieu to the battlefields of the Somme.

3 Section C Company 22/DLI Marked X 22/433 Private W Conroy from Darlington and standing in the centre of the rear rank is 22/463 Private "Big George" Ward.

FIRST OF JULY 1916, 22nd BATTALION, BAPTISM OF FIRE

On the morning of 1 July 1916, 22/Durham L received orders from the CRE 19th Division, to send three companies forward, to the Japanese Gardens in Albert. These companies were to be ready to go up and help consolidate positions captured by the front line infantry, accordingly B, C and D Companies moved forward, whilst A Company remained in reserve at Millencourt. They stood by all day, but were not called on, as just over the ridge the 34th Division was taking the highest casualties of the day. On 2 July, the three companies were employed carrying engineer stores up to a dump in the captured German trenches at La Boiselle. They also assisted to carry out the wounded of the Tyneside Irish and Scottish as noted by Major Davidson,

'Two days later, at dawn, it being the First of July 1916, we went up in earnest, three companies strong, my company leading. As we entered Albert, deployed with intervals between platoons, myself being at the head of the column, when a great gun, probably a twelve incher, fired from a railway cutting below us – this was the first we had heard and seen of such monsters; the result was certainly surprising. We were still wearing the ordinary cloth cap; all the other troops had iron helmets affectionately known as 'tin hats'. We got safely to the forward edge of the town to deploy in our allotted positions behind a line of field batteries in advance of some vacant warehouses and a brewery.

Here there were some shelter trenches – our field cookers and water carts I parked in a convenient ruin of a warehouse in our rear, nevertheless a cook of my company was our first casualty in action – he received a stray bullet in the thigh. Occasionally the enemy guns retaliated upon our batteries, thus our men were getting their baptism of fire, especially when shells, pitching beyond their objective, showered us with earth – it was not severe and most of us seemed to enjoy the experience, for all our men were in good spirits and fettle. La Boiselle was just to the left of our front and at first report and rumour that reached us was of great successes, though actually it proved that all the British left had been pretty well 'washed out' with high casualties from flank machine gun fire directed from Thiepval of unhappy memory. At dusk I was commanded to send up one company carrying barbed wire and pickets to consolidate and reinforce the trenches captured from the enemy by a battalion of the Tyneside Scottish NF. This I did personally, crossing what had so lately been No Man's Land, it could be seen even in the dark that here the land lay rather lower and was thus sheltered from the flank fire that had shattered so many of our service battalions that had gone over on the left. The Tyneside Scottish had penetrated deeply into the Boche position but by night fall could hold only what had been the enemy front and support trenches with one rather isolated outpost on their right. [Scots Redoubt held by survivors of B Company, 24th (1st Tyneside Irish) NF and details of 16th Royal Scots (Macrea's Battalion)]

I encountered the officer commanding NF who later received the VC for the most gallant way he led his men over and held his position. [Lieutenant Colonel M Richardson Commanding 26th (3rd Tyneside Irish) actually received the DSO.]

After an hour I made my way back to my advanced headquarters leaving my company in charge of Captain Baines my Second in Command, with orders to retire before dawn unless otherwise directed. Our stretcher bearers did not seem to be urgently required and as there was an officer of the NF gravely wounded, I employed a party with a stretcher to carry him back to a dressing station in Albert. [Probably the Second in Command of 25/Northumberland Fusiliers (2nd Tyneside Irish) Major Edmund-Jenkins died of wounds 3 July 1916 in Albert.]

It was as well that I came back for at 0200 hours the Colonel arrived with further commands which he gave me personally – they were to deploy a company in our old front line, for an enemy counter attack was believed possible – other parties drawn from the remaining company were to evacuate wounded. Digging out the blown in entrance of a trench shelter a man was blinded, I feared permanently by a bomb which his shovel struck as he worked in the trench we manned.

Towards dawn heavy masses of infantry from another division marched up into the trench – no doubt they were to go over that day. I got a message to retire all the Durhams – this was not difficult until we were half way back to Albert, heavy stuff was dropping about our forward gun position and I observed that a warehouse, adjoining the one we used as a cookhouse, had collapsed. I wrote my first report for the CO, found myself giddy for lack of sleep, refused some hot stew which my batman had brought me and lay back on the grass under my British Warm and in spite of guns to the right and guns to the left fell sound asleep.

Orders came that the battalion was to be relieved by 5/South Wales Borderers (Pioneers) and that the battalion was to march to Alonville under orders of 8th Division, however it proved impossible to get all the men out of the line, Major Davidson continued his story of the first days in action in this fashion,

Our last day, of the opening of the Somme battle, was spent more to our left. We were partly employed carrying wire and pickets to the line and in evacuating wounded. Upon what Brigade front this was is lost in oblivion, but their infantry had been terribly cut up – I think they advanced into, and even beyond La Boiselle but could not hold their places under the terrible rain of machine gun

German prisoners are escorted back across the battlefield.

fire. We got down about eighteen men and one officer, all of the same battalion if I remember rightly, wounded who had lain out amongst many more that had joined the great majority. Passing the HQ of this battalion in its old position, in our old lines, the result was reported (what was I hoped our success in the rescue work) to their commanding officer. He greeted me hopefully, but became speechless with grief, his eyes full of tears, no doubt he had continued to hope others, and many others perhaps, would be saved. That moment brought home to us the horrors of war more than the sights we had seen and moved amidst – grief is more moving than death or pain. One reflected upon all those who, at home, mourn – the wives, sweethearts, mothers and sisters.

When we were evacuating the wounded men, it was then that a Medical Officer asked us to take down the one and only officer we carried back. This Medical Officer told us he had done for him all he could in the line and feared gangrene. When we asked the Doctor the possibility of searching in front of the trenches he insisted that it would be certain death, quite impossible and I fear it was... None of us were sorry therefore when, that night we got the order to march out. Our three companies went in six hundred strong and came out about five hundred and seventy five. Personally my only loss was a wrist watch. Compared to the battalions that went over the top, our losses were trivial, *nearly half of us had captured 'tin hats' gathered off the field from those poor fellows, who having borne the brunt of the day and paid the price, would want them no more.*

Having got the battalion back together, it was at 1800 hours on the night of 3 July that they commenced to march towards Allon Ville, the route was practically the reverse of the march up, - Henencourt – Baizeux – Frenchencourt – and St Gratein and into Allon Ville at 0200 hours after a march of some sixteen miles. There was not long to rest though, the following morning orders were received to continue on to Camps-en-Amienon. At 1100 hours the leading company set off, on a Cook's tour of the villages of Picardy, Lampre – Montieres – Saveuse – Ferrieres – Briquemesnil – Floxicourt Molliens, where after twelve hours on the road, marching four abreast, they arrived and went into billets. All the next day they were allowed to rest and most of 6 July, they left the billets at 1700 hours, all through the night they marched until they arrived at Longveau station in Amiens at 0630 hours the following morning.

Major Davidson commented on the march,

So merrily along the roads, our band at the head playing "La Marseillaises" as we trudged along the dusty roads and through the small towns. The playing of their National Anthem called out the shopkeepers and their customers to see us, perhaps hoping that war was soon to be ended.

A day or two in bell tents and then, a forced march into Amiens. I call this a forced march because we carried on in full pack for very long stages. Numbers of our men showed acute distress, indeed through the Cathedral City, it was all we could do to keep the exhausted men in ranks. An early exhibition that the infantryman's load was too heavy – ninety pounds. To which has now been added tin hat and gas mask, last straws as it were. At our destination our fellows literally fell into their cattle trucks to lie higgle de pigglde like dead men. I think the forced pace was on account of some miss timing or, possibly of mistaken route.

The train carried the battalion to Dieval which was reached at 1300 hours, here they detrained and moved on foot again, marching to Divion, a village about six miles south west of Bethune. Here they were billeted for a few days, the time spent cleaning up and improving the billets.

Here they remain for the time being, as we catch up with the other battalions.

Chapter Five

After the Somme

A Flare went up; the shining whiteness spread.
<small>SASSOON</small>

THE PALS AT NEUVE CHAPPEL AND FESTUBERT. The last heard of 18/Durham Light Infantry was when they arrived in Bernuil on 7 July having left the Somme Front. The next evening they left that village and marched to Conteville where they entrained for Berguette in the First Army Area. The train pulled into the sidings at 11.30 a.m. the following morning and the stiff and weary battalion marched to La Pierreiere arriving at 1.30 p.m. As D Company had practically ceased to exist the first job was to reform the battalion. Private Charles Todd wrote home,

> *I have been taken from C Company and moved to D Company and I am in the machine gun section again. We have been highly praised for the good work we did in the battle on 1 July, and for our pluck and courage. Six of us were with a machine gun and four of them were knocked out, only leaving me and one other unhurt. But now we are back in the trenches.*

In B Company, Private Frank Raine estimated that the battalion was at about 20% of its normal fighting strength saying, 'Well I can only recollect twelve in our platoon out of the original sixty and I can remember all the names, I was also very worried about Broomhead for I had heard nothing at all about him since we went over together.'

Enemy aircraft were active, bombing ground targets, and so it became practice for the battalion to dig trenches for the men to use in the event of an air raid. The battalion moved again, on 15

The German soldiers had canteens in the front line at Neuve Chappel.

July, a long and dusty march took them to poor billets in the village of Fosse. Here training started in earnest as the new reinforcements were put through their paces and absorbed into sections and platoons.

Lance Corporal W E Marshall recorded this time for his fellow students of the Bede Contingent.

> We were indeed glad when at last we settled down in a quiet little village in a mining district to rest, train and re-equip for further service. We spent a week thus and then marched up to a village about five miles behind the line – a village which we later came to regard as a sort of second home.

The Army Commander, General Sir Charles Monro, inspected the Brigade and welcomed them to First Army and was followed on 25 July by, Lieutenant General Sir R C B Haking Commanding IX Corps, who spoke to all the officers of 93 Brigade and impressed on them the value of raiding for wearing down enemy morale. The next day word came that the Durhams were to take over the trenches at Neuve Chapelle from 14/York and Lancaster Regiment. The 'trenches' here were mere sandbag breastworks, easily knocked down by the enemy and very difficult to drain and maintain. The handover was done in daylight and by mid-day the relief was complete. The battalion had from the right A Company, B Company then C Company holding the left front. In the Support line was D Company.

A report on the handover of B Company's sector, written by Corporal James Sanderson, appeared in the *Bede Magazine*,

> What sort of time have you had here? "I said to the Corporal of the York & Lancs whose sentry group I was taking over." "Oh it's been all right until the last two days. It's been awful since then. There's nothing you need be afraid of except those Minenwerfers. You can see 'em coming, so if you keep a good look out you'll have a chance to dodge 'em." "Right Oh!", I replied.
>
> The Y & L men filed out, very relieved to get out of the trenches which they had held for the past thirteen days. "They hadn't half the wind up about these trench mortars!" said Skinnaw. "They must be awful things the way they've bashed the trenches in!" added Bill. "Well we'll have to keep a sharp look out for them."

The battalion settled down but in the late afternoon the enemy started a heavy trench mortar barrage, which continued until around 7.30 p.m. Corporal Sanderson continued his letter,

> Everything was quiet until late afternoon when they commenced to shell our communication trenches with high explosives. They had the range accurately and there was practically no trench at all in places. Soon after tea our curiosity concerning Minenwerfers was satisfied forever. From half-past five until half-past eight we were subjected to a strain almost beyond endurance. As soon as the first Minnie burst we jumped to our feet. We realised what the unfamiliar explosion was. Then we craned our necks upwards searching the sky for the new thing. Fortunately they began to fall on our right at first. From spotting the first one we could see them coming. They were of two shapes, one like a big shell, the other a cylinder nipped in the middle. The first kind rarely revolved but came from a great height point downwards. The cylindrical type slowly turned over and over. As soon as they fell we heard an ear-splitting report more terrible than anything we have known. The ordinary trench mortar was as nothing to these things. They exploded as if the earth itself had burst. Soil, sandbags and anything they fell upon splashed upwards to an enormous height, like some devilish subterranean fountain. Our trenches crumbled like an empty box. As long as these horrible things fell away from us we watched them with an absorbed impersonal interest. We watched the minenwerfers falling away from us with more interest than fear. But when one seemed to be coming straight for us our whole being concentrated on our safety. "It's going to land in the bay," shouted Frank. "Run to the right," I yelled. We ran,. The rushing, swishing sound of the mortar became

louder, until we knew without a word that the time had come to duck. There was an alarming report: the trench shook; it had fallen just behind; it had missed us. The black smoke and earth were blown thirty feet above; soil and sods fell on us but we did not care. It had missed us. Rising to our feet we watched for another.

"Listen for the report of the gun," said Arthur. Presently was heard a sound resembling a rifle shot except that it was duller and longer. "There she goes!" we exclaimed together. "I can see it!" cried Bill pointing at the sky. "Oh it's going well over," I said. "We'll stay here."

The shell reached its height and for a moment was lost in low cloud. We waited with anxiety until it was seen to emerge, making in our direction but over. We had a fine view of it. As it dropped we crouched to the side of the purados to escape flying splinters. The sound of the explosion was terrifying; it threatened to blow in our ears. Afterwards we found a base plate measuring nine inches across.

In such a manner we listened for the report of the gun; searched the sky for the shell; judged its destination and acted accordingly. It was difficult to dodge one coming very near. It's falling a few yards in front or behind meant life or death to us. On one of these occasions Lance Corporal J Hall was hurled against the door of a shelter and pinned up to the neck with the debris. He was soon dug-out and we were very relieved to see he had sustained nothing worse than a few bruises and slight shock.

At the beginning of the bombardment we had one of the finest men in the company killed, Lance Corporal Fairless, a Saint John's College man. His death was an instance of how fine may be the boundary between death and safety. Fairless was standing in the middle of a bay; on his right and only a few yards away was a comrade. The shell that knocked trench in and killed one, left the other shell shocked but with no other hurt. Sergeant R N Thompson was near Fairless too and was fortunate to escape.

Later, at 9.30 p.m. the German Artillery launched a very heavy barrage of Trench Mortar, Field Guns and 5.9cm Artillery on the battalion positions. The Trench Mortars and Field Artillery were used against the front line, mainly on B Company and the heavier 5.9cm guns concentrated on the Support Line. All communication between the front line companies and battalion headquarters was cut almost immediately and the only communication was by runner, these brave individuals had to go out in the open, over the top, avoiding the communication trenches.

At 10.25 p.m. the enemy were reported to be in the front line, but were ejected within five minutes. Twenty minutes later a message came in from 18/West Yorkshire Regiment on the right of the Durhams stating that, the enemy were in their lines between Hun Street and Oxford Street and that they would counter-attack at 11.15 p.m. The right hand company of 18/Durham LI were ordered to cooperate with the West Yorkshire battalion. Before the counter-attack could take place the battalion bomb store, located in 'Hush Hall' was hit by shells and set on fire. The fire was tackled and put out, but! Re-ignited and had to be extinguished a second time. By 1.30 a.m. a report reached Battalion Headquarters from B Company stating that, 'The Germans had entered the left of B Company but were forced out and that C Company trenches had also been entered. At this stage it was thought the enemy had taken no prisoners. A dugout had been blown in between B and C Company's; this had prevented B Company from coming to the aid of C Company. The report also said that all communication trenches had been blown in and the support line was badly damaged.

At last, at 4.00 a.m. C Company were able to report that they had had a number of bays blown in and quite a number of men buried and casualties were heavy, at that time the wounded were to many to estimate. The enemy had attacked in some strength but owing to the Company Lewis

Above: 18474 Pte M. Carney who tried to save three of his mates when they were buried alive in a collapsed dugout.

Left:
1. 18/605 Pte T. Stobbs
2. 18/471 Pte J. S. Curry
3. 18/488 Pte M. Fullerton
4. 18/579 Pte A. Richardson
5. 18/627 Pte A. Wilson
6. 18/543 L/Cpl A. Metcalfe
Casualties of the German raid 28 July 1916. All were killed.

Above: 18/468 Pte A Clarke who was wounded in the Geman attack.

Gun Section only a handful of them were able to get into the British Line. Men using the bayonet and the rifle butt had swiftly dealt with these intruders. When a party of about fifty enemy raiders were spotted by C Company, the Lewis Gunners were able to enfilade them perfectly and accounted for most of them before they could enter the British trench. In a letter to Mr W Lowes at Chester le Street, Lance Corporal Charles Moss wrote of his part in the action,

You will no doubt have heard about our scrap the other night, and what a bad knock the Chester chaps got. Poor Jimmy Curry, Matt Fullerton and Tot Stobbs. But it was a bit of satisfaction that I, a Chester lad should help to get a bit of our own back. We had a terrific two hours preliminary bombardment, a most fierce affair, in the midst of which the Chester chaps went down. Well, I seemed to have a presentiment that the square heads were coming across to us, so I chanced all, to have a look over the parapet, and sure enough, there they were, about thirty of them, crouching forward with their helmets on and in full battle gear, not fifty yards away and right across the line of fire of my machine gun. So I just lashed a full magazine of forty-five rounds into them and that started the fun. What a joust it was. Our fellows fought like fiends, as there was parties like the one I had dealt with all along our front. It was a veritable game of ball, with hand bombs. What a smashing up we gave them. There were only about four Germans got into our trenches and they met a horrible fate. We were gathering their dead in from No Man's Land for two nights. We got plenty of spike helmets, daggers, revolvers and all sorts of "Alleman" souvenirs. We have had two or three recommended for the D.C.M. as there were some noble deeds done. The Chester chaps had the breastwork knocked on top of them. One fellow managed to pull himself out and spent the night trying to get the others out and scraping sandbags and earth off their heads. While those that were buried would say, "Shoot us, Martin, and save yourself." But he would not leave them and kept saying, "No I'll not leave you, I could not leave a Rainton lad. Pray like Hell Monty; Pray like hell." All the Germans who got in, jumped on, and ran over them, but he managed to get some of them saved.

This last piece of the letter refers to an act of gallantry that took place when a German shell exploded and half buried Privates, Martin Carney of Brandon and Monty Williams of Middle Rainton, along with the Chester le Street lads named by Lance Corporal Moss. Lance Corporal Jack McKeag another Rainton man, and a member of The Durham Harriers, who although wounded, started to dig them out. Having got Martin Carney out and because of his wounds he was told to stop and go back and get his wounds bandaged, 'I couldn't leave a Rainton chap', he said, and he stuck there until he had dug both of them out, unfortunately the others had perished.

Corporal Sanderson continued the description of the action in B Company's sector of the line.

'When 'Stand to!' was passed along, everything was quiet. We sat on the fire step staring at the dusky, golden sunset, wondering how long we were to be left in tranquillity. 'Stand to!' said a member of another sentry group. We dispersed to our posts, fixed bayonets and mounted double sentries and settled down. Suddenly the full fire of the enemy's artillery was opened out on us. The dark night was lit up with flashes purple and yellow, which seemed enough to blind us. We opened the Grenade boxes and dealt out the bombs. We had two dozen. We took our bandoliers from our pouches and secured a plentiful reserve of ammunition. Then with the exception of two sentries we cowered in the side of the parapet and waited. We were all ready.

Rear left, 18/597 F Sinclair; rear right, 18/552 Cpl J McKeag, West Rainton; front left, G E Williamson, front right 18/373 Private A Rotheram, Durham City, in hospital at Hastings recovering from wounds.

"Everybody all right here Jimmy?" shouted Sergeant Ashley, as he rushed past on his way to the other groups. "All right – and the others?" "No one hurt as yet."

Presently Sergeant Ashley came to us again. He had a look over the parapet from the next bay. "Watch out lads, they're here," he yelled. "Up you get boys," I cried, "Give 'em hell." In the next bay on the left was a Vicker's Gun manned by two men of the M.G.C. At the time of warning they were smoking cigarettes. At once they leaped into position. Luckily there was no need to alter their aim. Before the gun's rattle song, rang out, we had thrown our first bombs. In the very dark night we could make out the unsubstantial shadows of a group of running men, some twenty yards away. A strong party of the enemy had crept towards us under cover of the darkness and their own fierce barrage, evidently making for the broken part of the trench on our left. Owing to our lack of a Very Pistol they had mistaken their direction and had rushed to the first manned bay on the right of the untenable stretch of trench, into the mouth of the Vicker's Gun and in front of an alert sentry group.

When we had beaten off the attack Sergeant Ashley, loath to give any of his men such a task, went down to Headquarters in the open, though the bombardment was still proceeding and the attack had not finished on the left. Having reported, he returned to us news that C Company had suffered heavily, the enemy had got in and had been subsequently bombed out and that one of our men suffering from shellshock had been captured.

This man was 18/256 Private John Dinnin of B Company, who had been partially buried by a shell, which also buried his rifle and bombs and left him badly shocked. Eventually he was able to let his comrades know he was all right and in a Prison Camp at Dulmen, in Westphalia.

Another survivor of B Company, Private Frank Raine recalled that night,

No sooner had we got in than he started to belt stuff over at us. Then he raided us, what he was after was prisoners for identification and he got through into our trenches and we give him the walloping of his life. We vented our anger at what had happened [on 1 July] on him. We didn't lose a man that night. We gathered the dead in and those bloody generals said, 'leave them there.' They were all laid out behind the trenches regimental fashion about thirty of them in very hot weather and they stank like nothing on earth. These Generals were about three days in coming to see them, there they were all decked out like Christmas trees, saying, what a lovely sight they were, That's what I remember.

According to the battalion history published after the war, sometime after the raid D Company managed to capture a German, equipped with signalling apparatus, in the ruins of Neuve Chapelle. From this man it was learned that the Germans had used one and a half battalions in the operation and that the intention had been to remain and form a salient in the British Line. However Frank Raine insisted it was he and Billy Taylor that captured him and it happened like this.

Billy Taylor and I were looking out at the back of Neuve Chapelle which was flattened level. I said to him, "Do you see what I see Will," and he looked and said, "Aye, what is it", "It's a fella poking about in these ruins". I said, "Lets go and see." We went across, it was a German Officer, and You're not going to believe this. I said, "Keep him covered Will". We came up behind him and I got within a few yards and shouted and he turned round quite unconcerned. Bill Taylor came up alongside me with his rifle cocked and I said, to this German, "Put your hands up". He had a German Luger and I said, "I'll have that for a beginning", and he had some German binoculars and I had heard about German binoculars, so I took those as well. So I said, "What do we do now Bill". He said, "We'll have to take him back to Headquarters". So we took him back to Headquarters. Now then this story was in the "History of the 18th DLI", bit it didn't mention Bill Taylor and it didn't mention me. Now Bill finished up as a Captain, but I finished up as a Lance Corporal. Now then there was never a word said, there was never an enquiry into it and we never heard another word. But he was definitely behind the British Lines and he was in the village of Neuve Chapelle, which was in ruins.

After the enemy trench raid several awards were made for gallant conduct. The D.C.M. went to Corporal Pinkney, in command of Number 8 Platoon of B Company, who had a number of his men wounded and his section of the line had been knocked in. Corporal Pinkney was standing in a bay when he saw some of the enemy jump into his trench led by an officer. Drawing his revolver he shot the Officer and the man behind him, the others made off. Meanwhile another party had entered the trench behind the Corporal and a scuffle was taking place between the enemy and some of the platoon who had lost their weapons, when they had been buried. Corporal Pinkney rushed to the rescue and shot one of the attackers and chased off the others. Awards of the Military Medal were also made, one to a stretcher-bearer for attending to the wounded and one to a runner, for delivering messages across the open in spite of the heavy barrage.

If the relatives of the 'Durham Pals' had evaded the vast amount of letters of condolence from the fighting on 1 July, now less than a month later they made up for it. Particularly in Durham City and the surrounding colliery villages that C Company drew its manpower from, the letters came bearing the sad news of the death of a loved one.

Mrs Wilson living at Newcastle Row, Framwellgate Moor, heard from the Battalion RC Padre, Father R M Gallagher, about the death of her son Albert.

'He was severely wounded on 27 July and died the following day. Albert was one of my boys and came to the sacraments regularly, so I am sure he died a good Catholic death. His poor brother is well, but naturally very upset, so I promised to write to you. I said Mass for your poor boy this morning.'

Writing from the Casualty Clearing Station at Merville, another RC Padre, Father H Tigor said,

> He was brought in early in the day badly wounded but quite conscious. I gave him the last sacraments and the last blessing and fervently did he receive the consolation of the church. He was very patient and brave.

Another letter written this time by a wounded officer, from his hospital bed, was delivered to the parents of Private Matthew Cummings in Sacriston,

> I am writing to tell you how awfully sorry to hear of your son's death. I am sure it will be a great blow to you. I heard about it by letter some days ago sent me by one of my men. I had sent your son some cigarettes and they received them the day he was killed. Your son was my servant for four months at the front and I can truthfully say he was the best one I have ever had. Further he was a brave boy and I liked him very much indeed, and was very cut up when I had the news sent me of his death. With deepest sympathy, in your sad loss. Yours truly
>
> James B Bradford, Second Lieutenant

Second Lieutenant James B Bradford, who wote to Mrs Cummings about the loss of her son.

Similar sad news reached Hartlepool Street, Thornley, where Mr and Mrs J G Cook learned of the death of their youngest son Percy. His elder brother James had fallen in May 1915 with the 1/7/Durham LI. Both were members of the teaching profession, on the elder brothers death his position at the Thornley Council School had been given to his younger brother who had just finished teacher training. However he had been anxious to enlist and with that in mind had cut short his course at Westminster Training College. His death came in his twenty-second year at the threshold of a promising career. The Battalion Church of England Chaplain, The Reverend C R Chappell wrote,

> Dear Mr & Mrs Cook,
>
> You will probably have already heard the sad news that your son was killed in action on July 27th, He fell in a big attack doing his duty bravely. I feel deeply sorry for you. It is that we have to lose so many fine young men. I buried him in the Military Cemetery just near the lines, where his grave will be looked after and a cross erected. Later on I hope to be able to tell you the exact spot where he rests. May God support you in your grief.

The father of another 'Pal', Mr John Craig, resident at Number 56 Tudhoe Colliery, had a short note about his son Corporal Alex Craig, from the Platoon Sergeant, there being no officer to write. 'All the lads in our platoon join with me in sympathy for we have lost a staunch pal.'

It was estimated that the battalion had inflicted over two hundred casualties on the enemy for the loss of nineteen men killed and about eighty wounded, the majority of these in C Company.

On 4 August relief arrived in the shape of the 'Second Barnsley Pals' the 14/York & Lancaster Regiment, by 1.30 p.m. the hand over was complete and the battalion was on its way to billets at La Fosse. On 7 August a draft of fifty Other Ranks arrived from the Infantry Base Depot.

It was on 8 August, Lieutenant Colonel H Bowes handed over command to Lieutenant Colonel R E Cheyne of 29/Lancers, Indian Army, saying farewell to the battalion he had been with since its raising. The next day the battalion marched to new billets, HQ and C Company went to the village of La Hamel and the other three rifle Companies to Essars, where the accommodation was described as very poor. During the evening of 10 August at 8.05 p.m. 2/Wiltshire Regiment arrived and took over the battalion billets. After handing over, the fighting portion of the

A severely wounded British soldier in the German Trenches, just like the British, on this front, they had to build their trenches up but seemed to do a much better job of it.

battalion, less transport and 'details', marched into the trenches east of Festubert.

The trenches in this sector were in a very bad condition and consisted of 'islands', or unattached posts held by a few men. The communication trenches were non-existent and in some places were just Hessian sacking, suspended on posts so as to obscure the enemy view. Most of the sandbags in the area had rotted away and all posts and what trenches existed were in a very poor condition.

By this time Private Frank Raine had got himself into the battalion 'Sniper Section' which manned a number of small post behind the British front line, and he had strong words to say about the reinforcements, 'We always looked on the newcomers as foreigners, they were never the same as the originals'. But he was even harsher about the new Commanding Officer and used this as a way of leaving the snipers that until then had been a somewhat cushy job.

'We got an old idiot of a Colonel from India, who came and inspected us one day and said that it was no good, snipers couldn't do any good from there, snipers had to go out in front, into No Man's Land at early dawn and stay out until night fall. Firing from shell holes where they ought to be able to see something. The only ones that I knew that did that were both killed immediately. As soon as they fired one or two shots, the Germans put rifle grenades on them. I said, 'I am getting out of this, I want to go back to the company for promotion.' I went back to the company and got a stripe straight away.'

On 10 August, B Company took over the right and D Company the left of the front line positions. Whilst C and A Companies were in the right and left support sections. The mornings were misty but later on it became clear and hot. In the German positions there was a point named Popes Nose (there was another Popes Nose near Arras), from here the enemy kept up a harassing fire with rifle grenades, so it was planned to shell the post. All unnecessary men were moved back into the disused, old front line for protection. Then at 7.30 a.m. on 13 August a number of the battalion rifle grenadiers assisted 93/Light Trench Mortar Battery attacked the German position. This brought swift retaliation from the Germans. The operation was repeated on 15 August and again the German Artillery quickly replied, only this time it was a much heavier bombardment and a number of posts and dugouts were blown in. Fortunately only three casualties were suffered. Near the front line at Island Number 12, there stood a line of six willow trees. These were considered as being useful to the enemy as ranging marks, it was therefore decided to blow them up. This was done in the early hours of 17 August, and later in the day the British Artillery and Trench Mortars shelled the enemy positions again. The front line was again thinned out and the German counter-barrage caused no casualties. The next night, 15/West Yorkshire Regiment relieved the battalion, less B Company, who remained behind as support for the Yorkshiremen. The battalion marched back to Le Touret and took over billets from 11/East Yorkshire Regiment.

18/68 Private H. P. Goodwill, killed in action 3 August 1916.

Throughout 20 August the enemy kept up a heavy barrage on the front lines and Brigade Headquarters issued instructions for those battalions behind the front to 'Stand To'. B Company sent two platoons up to the Front Line and 18/West Yorkshire Regiment, sent up 100 men to replace them in the support line. At 8.40 p.m. the enemy attempted a raid which, although thrown out by the Yorkshire's, resulted in quite a bit of damage to the some British posts. The battalions in reserve were eventually stood down just before midnight. C Company now took over the support trenches from B Company. The battalion now started to rest, carrying stores and rations up to the line and going out into No Man's Land repairing and laying new barbed wire. After some days 18/Durham LI again took over the line from 15/West Yorkshire Regiment, C Company remained in the right support line, B Company took over the right and D Company the left of the Front Line. A Company moved in to the left of the support line. Apart from desultory shelling by both sides the next several days were quite, the only thing of note that happened was when a German deserter gave himself up to B Company.

Once more on 1 September, 15/West Yorkshire Regiment arrived and took over the Front Line, this time D Company remained behind as the battalion moved back to Le Touret. Two days later 17/Manchester Regiment arrived and the battalion moved still further back to billets in La Fosse, here in the very early hours of 4 September they were joined by D Company. A pleasant week was spent here, most of the time being spent in training a raiding party. The next move came on 11 September when A, B and D Companies took over the front line, from 13/York and Lancaster Regiment, in the Neuve Chapelle sector, with C Company in reserve. Autumn was starting to draw in and the weather started to get wet and cold, but this tour of duty was marked by a very strange incident recorded in the *Bede Magazine* by Lance Corporal William Marshall,

It was a lovely morning about the middle of September, and B Company were holding the reserve line, when a French soldier in an immaculate blue uniform was seen by one of our sentries coming down the communication trench towards him. He was challenged and produced passports, which were undoubtedly bona fide, authorising him to enter the ruined village just behind our line for the purpose of removing certain valuables. It was to a corporal and a battalion scout, who accompanied him as escort, that he unfolded his story.

In the days before the warlords thought fit to plunge the world into the mighty conflict, there lived in the chateau of the village a wealthy soap manufacturer, who was also the local squire and landowner, being possessed of valuable estates. The headlong advance of the Kaiser's hordes in 1914, and the shelling of the peaceful villages and homesteads of the Pas de Calais, made the inhabitants seek safety in flight and that right soon. The soap king encumbered with various title deeds and documents relating to his world's goods, decided to bury them, so he sent for his gardener, the soldier. Together they packed up all the important papers of the estate and the valuables to the tune of about £1,000 in three deed boxes – two small and one large. They wrapped the boxes in several thicknesses of brown paper then sewed them in sacking, then deposited them beneath a certain apple tree in the garden of the chateau. The tide of battle surged forward and again receded, so that now the ruins of the place were once again behind our lines Meanwhile some eventuality had arisen which demanded the production of these title deeds and documents, hence the soap magnate had secured permission for his henchman to dig up the boxes.

21/260 Private R. Richmond, killed in action 3 Septemberr 1916.

Being assured of the veracity of his story and the validity of his passports, the soldier was allowed to proceed with the corporal and the scout above mentioned as escort. He was supplied with tools, and the novel little party went on its way. What a shock it must have been to him to see the village, he had once called home, in ruins – the houses almost without exception raised to the ground – the trees shattered – the roads scarcely recognisable for shell holes – the church a mere gable. The Crucifix at the west end of the churchyard is still standing intact, as if in silent protest against the awful carnage and destruction which had taken place in the once beautiful village.

However he must perform his task, and soon he located the orchard – or what remained of it. He commenced to dig feverishly. After a few minutes he stopped. 'I believe this is the wrong tree,' he said. Then he tried another – then returned to the first. He said his hesitation was due to the disappearance of various directing objects, which he had noted, when burying the boxes. A few more minutes digging and the spade struck something hard and metallic. The escort lent a hand and soon the three boxes – strongly padlocked, but intact save that the coverings had rotted away.

The Frenchman showed signs of alarm when the scout told him jokingly that he was going to shoot if nothing had been unearthed, in order to claim a month's leave for capturing a spy. As souvenirs of the occasion he presented them with his identity wrist plate and a 'ConfraternitÈ' medallion. Imagine the feelings of the RE's and the working parties that had dug a trench within five yards of this treasure trove when they heard about it. The boxes were removed without accident from the trenches, since when we have heard no more of the case. It was certainly an unusual and welcome diversion from the monotony of trench life.

The battalions on the right and left extended their fronts so that 18/Durham LI could be withdrawn. The night was spent in billets at Vieille Chapelle and the next morning motor buses arrived to carry the battalion to Gorre. On debussing they moved on foot to 'The Village Line', here they took over from 18/King's Liverpool Regiment. The sector taken over consisted of a series of posts that the battalion had to hold, from south to north, Pont Fixe South, Ponte Fixe North, Givenchy Keep, Hilers, Herts and Le Plantin Redoubts and finally Moat Farm. The next day Orchard keep was taken over from 16/West Yorkshire Regiment, the garrison being found by B Company.

After a few days in these posts the battalion moved forward and took over the front line from 18/West Yorkshire Regiment. This was a new experience for the battalion recalled in the *Bede Magazine* by William Marshall,

18/1054 Corporal W. Dodsworth and his father taken after he was sent home to be commissioned.

> *We had our first experience of holding the line on a mine crater front, which was comparatively quite save for the trench mortars, which were the cause of several; casualties. One morning just after "Stand Down" three of B Company were killed by a minenwerfer bomb in the support line.*

This refers to an incident on 24 September, when the British Trench Mortars had shelled the enemy between 8 and 9 a.m. When the enemy retaliated one bomb killed three Privates, 16218 Edward Evans of Ushaw Moor, 18/1740 Joseph Miles of Kibblesworth Colliery and 24779 James Scott of Gateshead. In the battalion history Colonel Lowe recorded the death of one of these men, 'In the case of one, his hair turned grey and though death was instantaneous, it went on turning colour until it became completely white.'

In this sector the German tunnellers had gone deep below the British tunnels and the Royal Engineers were still working hard to gain the upper hand. Above ground the saps and listening posts were liable to be cut off by any determined enemy raiding party. So time passed and on 26 September the battalion was relieved and moved back to billets in Gorre Chateau, recalled by William Marshall.

> *It has usually been our lot to be billeted in ramshackle barns and out houses with badly perforated roofs and open work walls not to mention damp and uneven floors. Only once or twice have we had the luxury of a battalion billet with respectable rooms and wire beds – such as we found in a certain*

chateau, which was a shooting box before the war. We are now preparing ourselves for the trials and hardships of winter in France, which will seem doubly severe to those of us who spent last winter in sunny Egypt.

On 29 September the battalion commenced what would be its last tour of duty in the trenches of this sector. Two days later sixty much needed reinforcements arrived, but at the same time Captain J B Hughes-Games, one of the original company commanders was severely wounded whilst in charge of a wiring party a sad loss for the battalion. On 4 October 1/Duke of Cornwall's LI took over and the battalion moved into the Village Line for the night prior to being relieved by 12/Gloucestershire Regiment before marching to billets in Bethune where the Transport Section and Battalion Details rejoined. Now they started to move back towards the Somme.

LATE 1916, THE BANTAMS ON THE ARRAS FRONT

On 30 August, 19/Durham LI detrained at Candas Station and marched to Vagquerie and Epecamps where they billeted for the night, then the following day they continued the march to Beaudricourt. Two nights were spent here before the march continued to Sus St Ledger, At this place lorries arrived to transport the battalion to Agnes. From the last village they moved forward into Arras where they became Brigade reserve with companies in St Nicholas and Roclincourt and one each in Thelus and Observatory Redoubts.

The sector taken over by 35th Division had to be held on a three-brigade front, with I, J and K sectors taken over by 104, 105 and 106 Brigades respectively. A pattern was now established whereby the battalions took over the same sectors, so that each time 19/Durham LI were in the line they took over K2 sector. 'Bob's Durham Bantam's' spent six days in brigade reserve before moving forward into K2 Sector for the first time, relieving 18/Highland LI during the morning of 10 September. This front had been the scene of much mining activity and the front line had been badly damaged so that it was the support line that was strongly held. Only outposts were held in the front line and in front of that, the condition of the barbed wire varied considerably. Along the front of K2 sector the mine craters were named from right to left, Katie, Kent, Kick, Kite and King, which had all been consolidated and held by the British as the front line. The original support trench 'Spook Avenue' had been badly knocked about and had been abandoned, a new support line the 'Works Line', which consisted of a series of posts E, F, G, H, I, K and L had been dug. The reserve line, was named the Redoubt Line, with company positions at Observatory and Thelus Redoubts and Roclincourt Village defences. The main communication trenches leading to the rear from K2 sector were Cecil Avenue and Bogey Avenue, these were joined by Fathers Footpath just behind the Works Line.

During this first tour in K2, the battalion lost seven men nearly all of them original Bantam's, on 10 September, 19/439 William Appleby of Fatfield, on 12 September 23/122 Albert Coulson of Dunston, 19/1186 Henry Munro of Sunderland and on 13 September 19/221 Alexander Alderson of Jarrow and 19/1221 Alfred Wenington of Darlington to name just few. The trouble was that it was the stature and physical fitness of these original Durham coalminers, which had brought about the formation of the 'Bantam' battalions, and they were extremely hard to replace.

After a week in the Front Line, 18/Highland LI replaced the Durham's, who moved back to Divisional Reserve in Duissans, where five days were spent providing working parties and training, before moving back to K2 to replace 'The Devil's Dwarf's' as the Highland LI were known. The relief was completed without incident and the battalion settled down to a tour in the trenches without any fatal casualties. On 29 September the process was repeated and 19/Durham LI moved back to the Redoubt Line, becoming Brigade reserve, where they remained until taking

An infantry transpot section delivers canvass for the battalion to build bivouacs on newly captured ground.

over K2 once more on 5 October. During 8 October, a Sunderland man, Private Robert Armstrong was killed in action, as was Second Lieutenant Fred Smith, of Shiney Row, he had originally enlisted in the 'Pals' in 1914 and had been commissioned into the 23rd (Reserve) Battalion prior to being posted to the Bantams. He was a keen cricketer and had played Bournmoor Cricket Club in the Durham League. Later that day at 9.0 p.m. Gas was successfully discharged towards the German lines.

Throughout October this was the routine for the men of the Durham Bantams. Fatal casualties among the men were light, only four more men were killed in action and two died of wounds. But replacements of the required physique were hard to find and drafts arriving from the base were few in number. Eight men arrived on 2 October, followed by twelve on 11 October and seven on 19 October, so that the battalion was still well below strength. The only officer reinforcement in October was Lieutenant James Mundy, who had been wounded on the Somme in July, on return he was posted to Z Company.

The beginning of November found the battalion holding K2 sector once more, during this tour Privates William Adey and William Harris were both killed in action. On 4 November 18/Highland LI took over again and the Durhams moved back to Divisional reserve billets in Arras. On 8 November Lieutenant J M Roberts left the battalion on transfer to the Machine Gun Corps and the next day a draft of eight men arrived from the Infantry Base Depot. A few days

Second Lieutenant F G Smith a well known Durham cricketer, enlisted in the Pals as a private and was commissioned into 23/DLI he was killed in action 8 October 1916 with 19/DLI.

later the battalion was back in the line for another week before becoming Brigade reserve again. As the battalion arrived in the rear trenches, Second Lieutenant W E Harding reported for duty and was posted to Z Company. During this spell in reserve, training commenced for a raid on the enemy trenches which would take place during the next tour in the front line. The aim of the raid was to try and take an enemy prisoner, to destroy machine guns and collect anything considered useful for information. The weather had been rather wet and the trenches were now very muddy but still passable.

The day before the battalion moved back into K2 sector, the Germans commenced a heavy trench mortar bombardment of the front line and support trenches along the whole of the divisional front, paying particular attention to the area around King Crater, where the opposing lines were only some fifty or so yards apart and the British barbed wire was only a very thin belt. The enemy were preparing to carry out their own trench raids and were softening up the intended objectives. On 22 November 19/Durham LI took over the front once again. Along the front line held by Z Company, there was a series of posts, A, B and C, these were normally held by six men, in each post, but on the night 25/26 November, the night of the battalions planned trench raid and a release of gas by the Royal Engineers, the manpower was reduced to avoid unnecessary casualties from the enemy retaliatory barrage.

19/598 Private W. H. Harris, killed in action 4 November 1916.

Post A was manned by Corporal Stevenson and one man, In Post B were Lance Corporal Hopkinson and Privates Harding and Hunt. Post C was the largest; Lance Corporal McDonald was on duty with Privates Ritchie and Spence and nearby in a dugout was Lance Corporal Goggins and Privates Davies, Dowsey and Forrest.

At 1.00 a.m. on 26 November, Lance Sergeant Willie Stones, in peacetime a miner, from Crook, relieved Acting Sergeant James Staff as NCO of the watch in the front line. The enemy reopened the trench mortar barrage at about 2.00 a.m. Then at 2.15 a.m. the officer on watch, Lieutenant James Mundy, accompanied by Lance Sergeant Stones set off to visit the front line posts. They made their way to Post A, where the officer must have spoke to Corporal Stevenson, before setting off towards Post B. As they entered King Crater, Lieutenant Mundy was shot by a member of a German raiding party, who had used the trench mortar barrage as cover to get into the British Line. As he fell, according to Sergeant Stones, Lieutenant Mundy ordered the NCO to alert Company Headquarters. In later evidence Lance Sergeant Stones stated he wedged his rifle across the trench and then turned and ran back past Post A, yelling a warning to Corporal Stevenson as he went by, and continued back to Company Headquarters. To his credit Corporal Stevenson went to Lieutenant Mundy's aid and brought the badly wounded officer in, although he subsequently died from his wounds.

The German raiders blocked the trench towards Post A and moved down towards Post B. They must have been spotted, for Lance Corporal Hopkinson and Private Harding left the post and ran down the line to Post C, shouting, 'Run for your lives, the Germans are on you'. Meanwhile the raiders had taken prisoner Private Hunt who had stood his ground. Having gone some way from his post Private Harding stopped and returned to find Private Hunt had disappeared. In Post C, the sentries on duty, Privates Ritchie and Spence, who had been taking cover from the trench mortar barrage, heard a shouted warning that the enemy were in the trench, most likely from the passing men, from Post B. An exploding bomb had blown Private Spence off the fire step, however he picked himself up and rushed along the trench to where men of 17/West Yorkshire Regiment were manning a bay south of King Crater and warned them to 'Stand To'. Private Ritchie however, went to warn the men in the dug-out and together, they all headed down Cecil Avenue until they were stopped at a post manned by Private J Kidd of 17/Royal Scots, at the junction of Cecil Avenue and G Work.

Lance Sergeant Stones had by now reached Company Headquarters, where he shouted down into the dugout. On hearing the shouting the Company Sergeant Major, WOII Holroyd, reported to Lieutenant Howes, who was in command of the support platoon. The officer then ordered the signallers to alert Battalion Headquarters. The platoon 'Stood To', and then formed up in the communication trench, where bombs were issued and the Lieutenant gave the order to follow him. Having made his way up Ghost Avenue, Lieutenant Howes turned round and found that only four men had followed him, so he returned to collect the rest.

The last man to emerge as the platoon filed out was Private John Pinkney of Easington, as he came out, Sergeant Stones asked him to show him the way to the HQ in Fathers Footpath in order to alert the cooks. Private Pinkney accompanied Lance Sergeant Stones to the HQ dugout, but when they got there the cooks could not be found. At this point in time Lance Sergeant Stones took ill and seemed to lose the use of his legs. He sat down for quite a while and eventually asked Pinkney to go with him to try and find the doctor. Private Pinkney set off down Bogey Avenue followed by Lance Sergeant Stones, who seemed to have trouble keeping up, eventually at about 2.30 a.m. the pair reached the junction of Bogey and Wednesday Avenues. Here they ran into a Regimental Police Battle Post, manned by Sergeant Robert Foster. The purpose of these posts was to stop unauthorised men leaving the front line. Sergeant Foster stopped them and noticing that Lance Sergeant Stones was without his rifle and bayonet, asked where they were there and where they were going, he then ordered both of them to return to the line. Sergeant Stones requested permission to rest awhile and Sergeant Foster allowed him a few minutes before sending him back. Some time after this another man approached the Post, this time Sergeant Foster had to stop Lance Corporal Hopkinson, who had also made his way down Bogey Avenue. Again the questions, why was he there and where was he going. Sergeant Foster also noted that the Lance Corporal was without his rifle as well. He too was ordered back up the line.

Having captured Private Hunt, some of the enemy raiders made their way into Cecil Avenue, where they came across Second Lieutenant Harding and Sergeant Napier who were doing their rounds unaware that anything untoward was happening. The British pair challenged the enemy but were both shot, the NCO managed to escape and made his way to Cecil Avenue where he found two stretcher-bearers in a dug-out. The officer however was searched by the Germans and then left for dead, but although badly wounded he was still alive and he had the presence of mind to count how many of the enemy went past him, as they made their way back to their own lines, having bombed a couple of dug-outs in the front line.

Lieutenant Howes had by now reached the Front Line, near King Crater, where he met Second Lieutenant Maclachlan, who was leading a party of bombers, the latter reported that all was quiet, but just then a noise was heard in the wire and with one of the bombers, Second Lieutenant Maclachlan went into the crater and threw bombs into No Man's Land, whilst Lieutenant Howes re-established the line and reported back to Battalion Headquarters.

Private Kidd, having stopped the men from Post C, called down into the Platoon dug-out for his Platoon Commander Second Lieutenant Bryce. When he found the six Durhams in his position Second Lieutenant Bryce put them on the fire step in a bay and issued bombs to them. About forty-five minutes later he called them into the dug-out and took their names. Then, accompanied by a corporal of the Royal Scots they were sent back to their own company headquarters and from there they returned to their post in the line.

The raid planned by the battalion was to take place about 700 yards north of King Crater and preparations were well in hand when word reached Battalion Headquarters that the German raid was taking place. Who ever was in command halted the raid. It is not clear who was actually in command on that night as Lieutenant Colonel Dent had been called away to Brigade Headquarters. However once it was confirmed that the enemy had left the British lines, the raid was resurrected and the raiders set out into No Man's Land, Lieutenants Welbourne and Forester took out a Bangalore Torpedo and positioned it in the enemy wire. At precisely 3.02 a.m. Lieutenant Dillon, Royal Engineers, fired the Bangalore Torpedo and blew an excellent gap in the enemy barbed wire. Immediately the torpedo exploded the party advanced to the German trench. Second Lieutenant Johnson and four men dropped into the trench and moved to the right, whilst Second Lieutenant K Smith, followed by three men entered the trench and moved to the left. It was now that the rest of the raiders were prevented from getting into the enemy position. A heavy barrage fired by 158 Brigade, Royal Field Artillery, began dropping all around the raiding party in No Man's Land and round the entry point into the German trench, this caused some casualties and someone shouted the order 'Get Back', which caused confusion and the remaining men ran

'Your son in the front line trench.' Hans writes home to his parents.

back to the British Lines, the confusion prevented the officers from regaining control and they were unable to lead the men forward again. In the meantime inside the enemy trench Second Lieutenant Johnson had reached the first traverse, where he bombed an occupied dug-out and on looking round found himself alone, so he returned to the entry point. When Second Lieutenant Smith went to the left, he found the entrance to a dug-out, a man appeared on the steps and Smith shot him. Moving on along the trench he threw a bomb down the next dug-out and he moved round the traverse into the next bay, where he shot a sentry. He now had only two men with him so he went back to the entry point to collect more. There he met up with Lieutenant Johnson who was on the same task. After a quick discussion it was decided to withdraw, there were no more men available and now the British barrage was falling on the German front line. As those members of the raiding party left the enemy trench they picked up the body of one of their number who had been killed on the enemy parapet and brought him back to the British line. Casualties among the raiders had been, Second Lieutenant Welbourne and eight other ranks wounded, and two men killed.

The Germans had not only raided the sector held by 19/Durham LI, but to the south, in I Sector they had got into the trenches held by 17/Lancashire Fusiliers. From the enemy point of view this was an even more successful raid, for they killed two and wounded eight men and succeeded in capturing twenty-four who were hurried over No Man's Land before their comrades could come to their aid. The third raid that night took place on J Sector and was the least successful for the enemy, for although they got into the trenches held by 15/Sherwood Foresters and forced the sentries to retire. The British Artillery was alerted by the sending up of SOS rockets by the front line company commanders and was able to disrupt the enemy progress. The Foresters then mustered all available men, cooks, signallers and storemen and forced the enemy out of their lines.

The next day was quiet for the front line infantry, they had time to check the wire and try and repair the parapets that had been blown in. During the day Lieutenant J Blenkinsop arrived from 22/Durham LI (Pioneers) and took over duties as the Battalion Transport Officer. During the morning of 28 November, 18/Highland LI arrived and took over K2 Sector the Durhams moving back to Divisional reserve billets in Arras.

The next day Second Lieutenant W G Wiseman was admitted to hospital and second Lieutenant T H Moorwood left the battalion on transfer to the Royal Flying Corps.

The battalion was now employed providing working parties, sometimes for Army Signals Companies and other times for the Royal Engineers Tunnelling companies who were constructing tunnels up to Vimy Ridge in preparation for the forthcoming offensive planned for the spring of 1917.

At some stage there must have been a court of inquiry and all those who had left their posts on the night 25/26 November were arrested and charged.

19/647 Lance Sergeant J W Stones was charged with,

When on active service shamefully casting away his arms in the presence of the enemy in that he in the front line trenches K2 sub sector on 26 November 1916 when as NCO of the watch and attacked by the enemy shamefully cast away his rifle and left the front line and ran away. Army Act Section 4(2).

19/158 Lance Corporal P Goggins
19/420 Lance Corporal J McDonald
19/1311 Lance Corporal E Hopkinson
19/625 Private A Davies

19/1429 Private H Dowsey
19/653 Private D Forrest
19/505 Private T Ritchie
were all charged as follows,

When on active service leaving his post without orders from his superior officer, In that he in the field on 26/11/16 when one of a sentry group in a front line trench left his post without orders from his superior officer Army Act, Section 6(1b).

Not content with charging these men of Z Company, the powers that be, also charged no less than sixteen of the unsuccessful raiding party with cowardice.

19/137 Sergeant R Rumley
23/36 Lance Corporal M Dempsey
19/880 Lance Corporal J W Richardson
Privates,
19/298 W Bates, 19/1409 J Dunn, 19/380 T Garrity, 19/1274 G W Giggens,
19/233 H Greaves, 19/884 B Hewitt, 19/950 J G Lumley, 19/885 J McNally
19/1605 J Oldknow, 19/190 C Spence, 23/203 T Surtees, J G Mann, W Potts,
23/44 P Wilson.

The events of that night were to have far reaching effects on the 35th Division, for a long time commanders had been complaining about the physical standard of the reinforcements arriving and now the process of weeding out the unfit began. On 8 December the GOC 35th Division and GOC VI Corps inspected battalions of the division, Major General Landon informed his Brigadiers that it was 'the GOC's wish that in re-organising the division 'Bantam' standard must be disregarded for good and all.'

Between 9 and 15 December the Assistant Director of Medical Services inspected the infantry of the division, and 2784 were recommended for transfer as unsuitable both mentally and physically for service as Infantry soldiers. Of those recommended for transfer, 334 were from 19/Durham LI. The next inspection was carried out by, General Allenby the Third Army Commander, this inspection was set up by Lieutenant General Haldane, Commanding VI Corps who wrote,

The men who had been combed out were therefore drawn up in a line by companies along some steeply sloping ground and care was taken that the army commander, who was not lacking in inches, should view them from above and not below. On the flank of certain companies were disposed a few files of tall cavalrymen. The Bantams looked at from above seemed more the dimensions of young chickens than dwarf poultry. Only one contretemps occurred which almost upset my carefully arranged plan, when one of the brigade commanders, who had been with the division from the time of its arrival in France when it was at its best, failed to support my selections, and when asked by Allenby his opinion of human bantams began to praise them. Before he committed himself too deeply he got a gentle reminder by a kick on the shins that he was spoiling sport.

There were many among the Bantams who some Regimental Officers would have been glad to keep and many of the men themselves were disappointed at being forced to leave. Those to be transferred were sent down to the Base Area and posted to new Regiments and Corps. For some months they must have been used on labouring duties in the rear area for it isn't until the formation of the Labour Corps in the spring of 1917 that any evidence is found of these men. Army Council Instruction 611 of March 1917 gave the orders for the formation of the Labour Corps and Appendix 106 gave the block numbers to be issued to men transferred from Infantry units. The 'Bantams' of the 35th Division formed several Labour Companies with the companies numbered between 184 Labour Company and 200 Labour Company. A number of those original Bantams still serving with Labour Companies in 1918 can be traced in the Absentee Voters List, when they were serving with 188 and 195 Labour Companies. Despite the Army doing away with the Bantam standard and Battalion Commanders ordered to reject previous Bantams, many of those transferred found their way back to the battalion. For example 19/146 Private Richmond Barton, from Medomsley, served with 298 and 196 Labour Companies before he was transferred back to the Durham LI and posted back to his old battalion. 19/1500 Private Alex Jennings was transferred to the Royal Engineers, then back to 2/Durham LI from that Battalion he was transferred to the Labour Corps and then managed to return to 19/Durham LI. Others, such as 19/898 Corporal William Yule, from Fulwell, went to 188 Labour Company and although he didn't get back to 19/Durham LI, he served with 22 and 18/Durham LI, before he was killed four days before the end of the war with 15/Durham LI. One to survive was 19/9 Private Thomas Pounder, of West Hartlepool, who at the time of transfer at the base was transferred to 195 Labour Company, however he was to finish the war as a front line infantry soldier with the Cameron Highlanders. Of sixteen men traced as having transferred to Royal Engineers Tunnelling Companies, one was killed with the RE, one went to the Machine Gun Corps, eleven went back to 19/Durham LI and three to other battalions of the Durham's, others had transferred to the Cameron Highlanders with Private Pounder, and yet others are found in the North Staffordshire Regiment and the Royal Fusiliers.

The policy of rejecting physical disabilities was also overlooked in some cases, In early 1916, 23/173 Private James Frater enlisted with a deformed arm, it had been smashed when a wire rope, hauling loaded tubs of coal, snapped and hit him, when he was working underground aged fourteen. On account of this he could not hold a rifle at the present arms position, so he was discharged. When conscription came in he was called up renumbered 40379 and posted to 19/Durham LI, badly gassed in 1918, he was eventually transferred to the Labour Corps, because of the gas, not his size.

But many original Bantams were still serving and would either be killed in action or see the

A 35th Division Christmas card sent home at the end of 1916.

war to its conclusion with the battalion.

As these inspections were taking place a small draft of 5 men arrived from the base and on 18 December Major W B Greenwell reported for duty from 1/Durham LI in India. Then on Christmas Eve, in the village of Foufflin Ricametz some miles from the battalions billets in Arras, the Court Martial of Lance Sergeant Stones and Lance Corporal Hopkinson took place (These are dealt with in depth in a later chapter).

On Boxing Day Second Lieutenant R Law left the battalion on transfer to the Royal Flying Corps, The remaining six men who were involved with leaving their posts were tried on 28 December. The next day the battalion took over billets in Maisnil St Pol from 18/Highland Light Infantry. Further drafts were to arrive to replace those sent away, so a period of training and reforming took place. With so many men to be trained a Divisional Depot Battalion was formed, command being given to Lieutenant Colonel Dent, his instructors and staff were drawn from all the battalions of the division, each battalion providing one platoon. The aim of the battalion was to give instruction to all reinforcements and to put them all through a musketry course. It was also to be used to train men from the battalions, whilst the division was in the line, each battalion would send back one platoon at a time. This would allow the men some respite from the trenches for a short time.

The weather turned at Christmas and thick frost set in which got worse as the month lengthened. There was periods of heavy snow which added to the trials of those on working parties, slipping and sliding under heavy loads, and for others trying to dig in ground as hard as iron. On 30 December the Courts Martial of the sixteen members of the ill-fated raiding party took place. All of them were sentenced to Death, however the sentences were commuted to ten years penal servitude, this sentence was then suspended in order that the men could be returned to the fighting line. Several of these men were among those that were sent down to the base for transfer to the Labour Corps, but the others remained with the battalion and one Lance Corporal Michael Dempsey went on to win the Military Medal in 1918.

So ended a sad year for 'Bobs Durham Bantams', the first few weeks of the New Year would prove even sadder.

RETURN TO THE SOMME, THE 'PALS' MOVE SOUTH

At 9.30 a.m. on 5 October 18/Durham LI and 15/West Yorkshire Regiment set off on their journey back to the battlefields of the Somme, a four hour march took the battalion to billets in La Pierriere, the next days march took them to Lillers where in the afternoon they entrained for Doullens, arriving just before midnight. There then followed a two-hour march to a tented camp in the village of Orville. The 31st Division had now joined XIII Corps of the Reserve Army. On 11 October the billets in Orville were required for another unit and 18/Durham LI moved to shelters in Orville Wood, they had hardly arrived when the weather broke and everyone was cold and miserable. Training began and the wood was used to good effect by the companies, but higher command did not leave them alone very long and on 17 October the Brigade began moving forward in atrocious weather along water logged roads towards St Leger. After a few days in billets at the last named village 18/Durham LI relieved 12/East Yorkshire Regiment in the Left Support of the Left Sub-Sector of Hebuterne, taking over billets and bivouacs in Sailly-Au-Bois. The weather was extremely wet and owing to the enemy artillery billets in the village were vacated in favour of bivouacs away from the shelling. On 26 October the battalion moved forward and relieved 18/West Yorkshire Regiment in the front line, facing Gommecourt, which was very wet and muddy, A and B Companies being in the line and C and D in support. The enemy commenced shelling the battalion using gas and tear shells, particularly on D Company.

With both Lance Corporal W E Marshall and Corporal J Sanderson wounded the responsibility for reporting to the 'Bede Magazine' now fell to Lance Corporal J Rotheram, who recorded the move south,

'On leaving the north with its stirring memories, this battalion with an enhanced reputation again found itself on the edge of that furnace known as the Somme. Just a short distance to the right lay the scene of our first adventures and experiences of trench warfare, where we learned all the tricks of the trade and prepared for the Big Push. It was still noisy, - at times nearly as bad as last June, but now only in spasms when the artillery were indulging in a strafe, firing away fortunes every minute.

It is a matter of opinion as to what was the more troublesome, the weather or the Germans. Owing to many days of steady rain, all the land in the danger zone was a quagmire, the roads almost impassable and the trenches themselves like so many irrigation canals. To the civilian it would seem impossible that men could live even for a few days in such ditches – they don't live; they merely exist, hang on to life in spite of everything.'

Over the next few days the weather was very wet and the trenches filled with water, fighting patrols were sent out by both B and C Companies but no trace of the enemy was found and finally on 30 October 12 York and Lancashire Regiment arrived, the relief being completed by 3.30. p.m. 18/Durham LI moving to billets in Rossignol Farm.

November began with the training of raiding parties but priority was given to working parties, the condition of the front line trenches needed so much attention. However the battalion had only one case of trench feet. Meanwhile 30 reinforcements arrived and were shared out amongst the companies and Second Lieutenant J B Bradford rejoined from hospital and was posted back to C Company. On 7 November the battalion returned once again to the front line, which was now in a terrible condition. The relief of 14/York and Lancaster Regiment took place, with A and B Companies deploying in the front line with C and D in support. The communication trenches became so bad that the carrying parties brought the rations up at night, over the top of the trenches, in the open. The enemy artillery shelled the Battalion Headquarters during the evening of 9 November but did little damage.

Lance Corporal Rotheram continued his letter,

There is always the consolation of knowing that it is as bad on the other side and certainly the Huns have more steel flying about their ears, for our artillery give them no rest even in the worst of weather. The trenches themselves were to put it mildly – in a very neglected condition, so busy had we been in preparing and continuing the advance to the detriment of everything else. In that sector the communication trenches pass through a village and are at first sight everything that could be desired, but further on they become worse until the advanced posts present the last word in wretchedness. In most parts the quality of a trench seems to vary inversely with its distance from headquarters. Day and night working parties are fighting the water and mud, a task of overwhelming difficulty, and which must be undertaken with great caution for if Fritz spots any signs of working he is bound to let us know.

By 3.55 p.m. on 11 November, 18/West Yorkshire Regiment had completed the relief of 18/Durham LI who moved back to huts and shelters in The Dell at Sailly, the wet conditions were proving troublesome and the men's feet were in poor condition with some suffering from 'Trench Foot'. The battalion was now in Brigade reserve and under 20 minutes notice to move. The Battle of the Somme was now in its dying stages with the last actions known as 'The Battle of the Ancre' taking place. To provide a defensive flank and support 3rd Division, 92 Brigade of 31st Division were ordered to attack, their objective being to take, on the right the enemy reserve line and on the left the support line. To assist the attack of the Yorkshiremen, Second Lieutenants Weddell and Bushell along with 50 men of 18/Durham LI formed a 'smoke barrage party' and proceeded to the front line at 6.15 p.m. on 12 November.

'Soon after our arrival here the increased artillery activity made it quite clear that there was going to be an attack in this part of the line, for at times all the guns would open out as though all hell had been let loose. One would think nothing could live on the other side. Most of the fire seemed to be directed on the front which we attacked on 1 July, just to our right.'

Wrote Lance Corporal Rotheram in *The Bede Magazine*.

At 5.45 a.m. on 13 November the two assaulting battalions, 13/East Yorkshire Regiment on the right and 12/East Yorkshire Regiment on the left, went steadily forward and fought their way into the support trench. Some of 13/East Yorkshire Regiment fought their way into the reserve line where they held on waiting for support but only a few managed to fight their way back. Meanwhile owing to unfavourable wind conditions the smoke barrage party from 18/Durham LI were not needed and were ordered to rejoin the battalion.

Having been spared taking part in another assault Lance Corporal Rotheram continued his letter,

Our battalion did not take part in the actual attack, but merely 'stood by' ready for any emergency and thus we had an opportunity of seeing the work behind the scenes during an attack. What traffic along these sunken roads of Picardy! One continuous stream of ammunition columns drawn by gasping horses or mules, varied now and then by motor wagons with shells for the heavies. Day and night for about a week this continued, becoming more feverish as the hour of the attack drew near. Then a few days before the attack we saw a sight, which always gives the infantryman food for thought – a big batch of RAMC marching towards the line.

When the final bombardment was at its height the thought in all minds was – 'Now they'll be going over. Wonder how they've got on?' Then followed the usual speculation and rumours; We have taken the third line and the village; Our attack has been wiped out by the German barrage- and so on. Soon the Red Cross vans are coming back with their loads of human wrecks, or in some cases smiling 'Blighties' and from these latter the true version of the fight is obtained. We have so far succeeded because one of these was wounded while crossing the third German Line. Then followed one of the most wretched and pitiful sights – a party of three prisoners. Poor devils, bareheaded, plastered with mud and slightly wounded hardly able to put one foot before the other. But what does it matter! They may have seen the same thing on the other side.

On 14 November the Durhams vacated The Dell, HQ, A and B Companies moved to billets in Bus – Courcelles and C and D Companies moved into bivouacs at Rossignol Farm. A and B were placed under command of 94 Brigade, with orders to move at 20 minutes notice, whilst the other two rifle companies were placed at the disposal of XIII Corps to provide working parties for the front. Lance Corporal Rotheram described these working parties as follows,

During the time we were not actually holding the line there was always working parties preparing for the attack by carrying in footboards, wire, and 'iron rations' for the trench mortars. To carry one of these 'football bombs' to the gun is at times quite a labour of Hercules, and an unusually deep pool is always a temptation to get rid of ones burden. The will to 'carry on' is only revived by the thought that this shell will probably clear the way for our men tomorrow and may even send some of the Boches to the happy hunting grounds.

Three days later the companies were switched round, this brief period of rest improved the moral of the battalion, but when they next went into the line on 21 November, many men went sick owing to exposure. The trenches taken over, the Northern subsector at Hebuterne were in a terrible condition and caused Lance Corporal Rotheram to write,

In the bad weather it is quite easy to find parts of the trenches where the mud is above knee deep and in such places to halt is fatal, for then one sinks deeper and deeper. It is policy to get through quickly. But in spite of all difficulties work must be carried on in communication trenches, which must be kept open at all costs, for there is one thing that the men cannot do and that is live without rations. As long as these come up regularly and in good condition i.e. 'thick and heavy' we are winning no matter what else may happen. However if there is any shortage a feeling of depression sets in and uncomplimentary remarks are passed about the transport. On this sector the transport had very often a dangerous task having to come up every night to a village on which the enemy used to send all his spare ammunition. This village for six months had been a hot spot and so had a sinister reputation, which was thoroughly impressed on us during our three months stay in the district.

The village was a most unhealthy spot where everybody used to bustle, where even the most lackadaisical have been known to do even time. Of course the most dangerous spots were the cross roads and the church, which are always well registered by the enemy's artillery. The church being in between communication trenches has been absolutely smashed up and now there are only two thick walls protruding from a heap of stone and plaster. Just behind the ruin in the cemetery is the church bell still intact, among the graves, which are here and there ruthlessly torn up by the shells. In the same street is a billet, i.e. a cellar under some ruined walls were there was evidently a school of some kind for the writer, in prowling about the ruins found several exercise books and a school register dated 1891. In most of the books the following had been written as an exercise, 'La patrie me demande de grande sacrifices.' How many who wrote that more than quarter of a century ago have made the sacrifice.

After nine days in the line the battalion was relieved and moved to billets in Rossignol Farm, here the time was spent providing working parties for the battalions holding the Front Line The amount of men reporting sick, over 100 each day, meant there was plenty of work for those fit enough to carry on. On 28 November a draft of sixty Other Ranks arrived from the base, they were described in the War Diary as a 'fairly good set of men, though mostly very new.' On 3 December the battalion was on its way back to the line and they took over the same sector again. Plans were now made for a large raid on the enemy trenches and over 100 officers and men of the raiding party were left behind to begin training for the raid. On 7 December reconnaissance patrols from the raiding party went out in No Man's Land to familiarise themselves with the layout of things. On 9 December, 18/West Yorkshire Regiment took over the line again and 18/Durham Light Infantry moved to billets, A and D Companies in Sailly and B and C Companies in Hebuterne Keep. The following day a draft of thirty-eight Other ranks joined the battalion, followed on 14 December by Second Lieutenant Busby and twenty-three men reported to battalion Headquarters, whilst 130 men considered untrained were left in billets at Couin. The preparations for the raid were well under way and the British Artillery began to bombard the enmy trenches and carry out wire cutting . The enemy did not take the shelling lying down and replied in kind, unfortunately a shell hit the dugout containing the left front Company HQ and Captain Douglas Phorson from Roker in Sunderland and Second Lieutenant Reginald Busby of Sheffield, who had only been with the battalion two days were killed. Both were buried in Sailly au Bois Military Cemetery. During the same incident Second Lieutenant G H Lean was lucky to escape with a few scratches from shrapnel and command of the company passed to Second Lieutenant Waggott.

The plan for the raid which was to take place on 19 December was as follows and this was the biggest that the battalion had taken part in so far. The objective of the raid was the German dugouts in the Gommecourt Salient in particular the two dugouts in FIT Trench between the junction of FIT and FIND and the dugouts in FIND Trench between the junction of FIT and FIND with Zero Hour set for 8.30 p.m.

Further to these objectives the raid had four main tasks,

To take as many prisoners as possible.

To kill any Germans not taken prisoner.

To bring back papers and machine guns and especially a MG belt filling machine.

To destroy dugouts and damage defences.

The raiders were in two main parties, manning the parapet and passing signals were 1 Officer, 1 Sergeant, 6 Runners, 2 Signallers and 4 Stretcher Bearers.

Whilst the main party consisted of 2 Officers, 7 NCO's, 60 Bombers and Riflemen, 2 Lewis Gun Teams (8 men), and 6 Stretcher Bearers.

The raiders were dressed as follows, Steel Helmet, Leather Jerkin outside the tunic, Cardigan, 2 pair of socks, mittens or gloves, rifle bayonet and a bandolier of 50 rounds. Certain NCO's had revolvers with 24 rounds, web belt, gas helmet and four bombs.

The artillery barrage was planned to begin at 5 36 p.m. and the first phase to last until 6.05 p.m. While this was going on the raiding party gathered in Kellerman Trench and at 6.05 p.m. moved via Howard Street, Thorpe Temple Street and New Cut to the jumping off point. Between 7.31 p.m. and 8 30 p.m. in Arrowhead Formation, led by Corporal Lawson, the main body moved silently out into No-Man's Land and lay down 100 yards in front of the British wire. Corporal Lawson with four men then went forward and laid a tape to the gap and cut and cleared the wire to let the raiders through. The main party was divided into groups each with a specific task.

Group A, 2 NCO's and 15 men

One NCO and six men move to the left and go along the outside of the parapet till the trench makes a big loop about 50 yards from the junction of FIT and FIND. Drop into the trench here and work up it till they get to the entrance of dugout at the corner of the communication trench. Bomb dugout and make prisoner any enemy.

Advanced bombing section, One NCO and four men go further along parapet past the junction until a communication trench goes off to the right, under the parapet is a dugout they drop into the trench and make a trench block.

Right Bombing Section comprising five men cross the trench move along the parados drop into the communication trench and block it.

Group B, 1 NCO and 10 men plus 2 stretcher-bearers.

This party pass through the wire and form up on the right of the leading man, the first seven men drop into the trench and make for the dugout entrances. The leading two men using only the bayonet clear the trench up to where Group A are, then return to their own Group. The remainder cross the trench and search the wood within twenty yards of the dugouts.

Group C, 1 NCO and 10men and a Lewis Gun team.

Their objective is the dugout known as FIT No 3, they cross 4 Tree Sap and move along the parapet for 70 yards, the leading six men drop into the trench and immediately bomb the dugout. The Lewis Gun team are to provide cover against attack from the wood or along the outside of the parapet and the spare riflemen provide cover by watching the wood.

Group D, 1 NCO and 8 men

Their objective is the dugout known as FIT No 4, at the mouth of Four Tree Sap the two leading men of the group drop into the trench and work down FIT using only the bayonet. The remainder cross Four Tree Sap and drop into the trench at the further side of the loop and drop into the trench and bomb the dugout.

Group E, 5 men

They enter Four Tree Sap and move down it towards the British lines, they are to look for the gap in the wire said to exist in front of the sap. Two men return to the report centre the others are to take any prisoners from the sap back to the British Lines via the gap in the wire.

Group F, Lieutenant Bradford, 1 NCO and remaining men.

They remain at the mouth of Four Tree Sap as a report centre, five men search the communication trench. The signallers open up communications with the party on the British parapet, for this purpose 400 yards of signal wire has been laid as they crossed No Man's Land. The remaining two stretcher-bearers remain near the mouth of the sap.

That was the plan, in the early evening of 19 December the rain that was falling turned to snow, but as all preparations had been made the raid went ahead.

Everything went off perfectly, except one thing, the enemy had gone, despite entering the German lines and going much farther than expected no enemy were met and further more the enemy trenches were in a state of ruin. It is probable that the handful of enemy infantry holding the position, withdrew when the British barrage began at 5. 36 p.m. The raiders withdrew, without prisoners and without casualties and doubtless great relief back to the British lines.

Two days later on 21 December, 12/East Yorkshire Regiment took over the line and 18/Durham LI were transported in buses to rest billets in Famechon. Lance Corporal Rotheram recorded the move back in this way,

> What a relief it was to find buses waiting for us on coming out, to take us far away from harm for Xmas and the New Year. There, almost out of sound of the guns, most of us spent a happy festive season. On leaving that village for another short spell in the trenches we said 'Good-bye' to Sergeant Ashley who was leaving for England to take up a commission.

On Christmas Eve the Commanding Officer handed over command to Major W D Lowe and proceeded home on leave, the following day The GOC 31st Division visited the men at Christmas Dinner, afterwards the 31st Divisional Ammunition Column Concert Party provided a show for the troops. The battalion remained out at rest for the remainder of 1916, a year which had seen them pass through the land of the Pharoahs, to the hell of the Somme and the breastworks at Neuve Chappelle and Festubert to the muddy trenches of Hebuterne.

PIONEERS UP TO THEIR KNEES IN MUD

The last heard of 22/Durham LI was when they marched to Divion after leaving the Somme. As they entrained orders were received that the battalion Second in Command, Major S L Whatford was to take command of 8/York and Lancaster Regiment, whose CO had fallen on 1 July. Major Davidson wrote a very personal passage about this regular officer in his memoirs, accusing him of being, a harsh disciplinarian coldly aloof and unhelpful, who looked upon men lately in civil professions as intruders. 'Not at all like the CO, the difference as frozen water from wine.'

One memorable event in 22/Durham LI was about this time,

> One of our companies was almost wholly composed of [Durham] miners and they were amused when some RE's were sent to instruct them in the use of the pick and the shovel! To hear them welcome their instructors with their Durham miners humour would have burst the sides of a Rhinoceros. We were now served out with gun cotton in bricks and with fuses and detonators. Under RE instruction we spent a pleasant day in a field burying this unwholesome stuff deep in the earth! In constructing shell proof cover over the pit produced the RE's were certainly good instructors and we learnt something.

A sentry uses a make-shift periscope to watch for movement in No Man's Land.

Wrote the OC D Company, Major Davidson.

Having spent a few days in Divion, resting in billets, orders came from HQ 8th Division, for two companies to move to Noyelles and two to Mazingarbe, to comply with this order, the following morning, A and C Companies marched to Noyelles and reported to the Officer Commanding 9/Gordon Highlanders, the Pioneer battalion of the 15th (Scottish) Division, whilst Band D Companies moved to Mazingarbe for duty under the CRE of 16th (Irish) Division, Battalion Headquarters, the stores and transport moved to billets in Bethune. On 14 July the headquarters moved again this time to Beuvry where they took over from 13/Gloucestershire Regiment and were joined by D Company from Mazingarbe.

Major Davidson told this story of the time,

One night at Divion, and then on to Mazingarbe. I was leading D Company as a rear guard and as we reached this half ruined town buzzing with concealed batteries, the doctor rode back to deliver a message, this was to the effect that D Company was to billet in Mazingarbe, which we proceeded to do in some fairly habitable houses and out building's in a lane off the high or principal street, the Doctor staying for dinner and bridge. There was the remainder of what had been a very fine small medieval church with a tower in the centre – always an interesting structure. After some rest and refreshment I set off with the MO to have a look at this half ruin. Medieval things are in my blood – however our venture was ill advised for we only just escaped leaving our blood in its littered interior. We were half up the tower – and perhaps observed – when heavy stuff was hurled at the church, shells we were to fear all through the war and known as 5.9's.

The next morning the Colonel arrived complete with Adjutant and very fortunately the MO also. The CO demanded of me why I had not detailed C Company to Mazingarbe and so come on with D Company to the next village, somewhat further along the road. Without looking at the Doctor, who was a particular chum of mine; I was able to say, 'I did not get that command'. Then our most excellent Colonel said, 'Well! The fault is mine, for I ought not to have dispatched an order by the Doctor.' After the CO had had a look round we were allowed to remain as we were, the CO staying to lunch for which my enterprising batman had acquired fresh vegetables and fruit. How he did it I can not think.

140

In this location the companies were at the disposal of 251/Tunneling Company RE for clearing spoil from the mines. This work continued throughout July, the casualty list lengthened daily, men were wounded or died by various ways and means, snipers claimed some, trench mortars got others and enemy artillery had their share. But on 29 July the enemy tunnelers broke into a British tunnel, there must have been hand to hand fighting underground, a working party of 22/Durham LI were down in the mine and in the ensuing fight, three Durham miners were killed, Corporal John Bolton from Hartlepool, Private Robert Laidler a Sunderland man and Private Albert Tate who although born in Skelton, North Yorkshire, was resident in the small mining village of East Howle, near Ferryhill in County Durham. Another unnamed soldier of the battalion disappeared totally and it was presumed that he had been taken prisoner of war by the enemy tunnelers. Under orders of 8th Division HQ, 2/Manchester Regiment took over the work being done by the battalion, who were redeployed, still working for the Royal Engineers but now for the divisional Field Companies. A Company, 22/Durham LI were at the disposal of 2nd Field Company, B Company, were allotted to 1/1st Home Counties (TF) Field Company and D Company of the battalion worked for 15/Field Company RE, poor old C Company were left toiling below ground with the tunnelling company. The work for the rest of the battalion now consisted of trench repair and work on defensive positions.

On 3 August word came through that 8th Division was on the move once more and they would be relieving the 32nd Division in the Guinchy sector, however before they could be relieved the Durham's lost one man when the enemy exploded a small mine in the Auchy sector prior to being relieved by 17/Northumberland Fusiliers. Moving back to Noyelles, 22/Durham LI took over a hutted camp and although the huts needed a great deal of work to make them waterproof, the camp was considered good.

Work was allotted as before, C Company joined B Company working for the 1/1st Home Counties (TF) Field Company but a number of men were detached to 180 and 179 Tunnelling Companies. The pioneers detailed 3 Officers and six NCO's as 'spoil' officers, to superintend the disposal of the spoil from the mines, and ensure it was disposed of properly, out of sight of the enemy.

> In this section mining and counter mining was highly developed and we had on out side, as I have no doubt the enemy had also, special mining companies RE these could generally be identified by the state of their uniforms. Our battalion used to send up men at night to assist in evacuating spoil – the earth, principally chalk, was brought to the shaft bottom, loaded into sandbags and hauled up to trench level where in turn our men carried the bags away to an allotted dump perhaps quarter of a mile, but often of a lesser distance in our rear. Both sides were anxious to know where the shafts were and strafed then with trench mortars.

Was how Major Davidson described this period in the battalion's sojourn in France.

As the work continued, on the night of 20/21 August, a stokes mortar, in the rear of a working party from D Company, opened fire, the front line infantry having been warned previously were all safe underground in their dug outs, but no warning was given to the pioneers, the British Mortar fire brought swift retaliation from the German Artillery, in an instant three members of the working party were buried. The Officer in charge, Lieutenant Bernard White, displayed great bravery and promptly rallied all hands and within minutes all three were dug out alive. At the end of the month three subalterns, Lieutenant's J A Findlay and J A Crutchley, along with Second Lieutenant W G Conway were taken on strength from 1/3/Monmouthshire Regiment. The weather had turned, a lot of rain was falling, the huts were dry and the tracks and pathways muddy, but the trenches were in a bad state and beginning to fall in.

September continued in the same way, owing to the condition of the trenches, men who had been employed on the improving the huts were returned to the companies and every available man was employed in the trenches. However one officer and fifty-four men were moved to Vermelles to assist with driving listening galleries under the Hulloch Road, leaving about 500 all ranks for work in the line. It was now an unusual incident took place, recorded by Major Davidson, the death of a staff officer in the line.

I remember in front of Arnequin and near the Hohenzollern Redoubt, being in the line with our CO, who was doing one of his periodical 'look rounds', turning a corner of the trench we met a very tall officer wearing a rain coat – (it was drizzeling) – which disguised his rank. Addressing our CO he asked 'Who are you?' to which, perhaps a trifle indignantly, the CO replied 'CO Durham Light Infantry – 8th Division' – and then reposted 'Who are you?' to this the staggering rejoinder was 'I am the Corps Commander!' Almost like saying I am God. However the sequel was sad for hearing that my company had been digging sap trenches into the craters left in No Man's Land after mines had been exploded, the Corps Commander demanded to be shown them. There were three of these sap trenches which converged on what was to be made that night into an advanced bombing post. Two of these saps had been glimpsed, they were all very dangerous in the daylight, and the third, I hoped, would be safely passed without any inspection, when the Corps Commander said, 'Wasn't that the third sap?' pointing to an opening we had just passed; and I had to agree that it was. Overhead the sap was camouflaged with supported sandbags. The GSO I of our division who was accompanying the Corps Commander was next behind me and the last of our party – he said 'Alright I'll have a look' and put his head up over the top for a glimpse. He was immediately shot dead a bullet entering his forehead. This was a front made very dangerous by snipers on both sides and by the irregularity of the trench lines, divided by only by huge craters.

[Major, Brevet Lieutenant Colonel, Hugh Hill, DSO MVO, Royal Welch Fusiliers, GSO I, 8th Infantry Division, was killed in action 10 September 1916 and is buried in Bethune Town Cemetery.]

Although no other ranks are recorded as joining the battalion on 19 September six officer replacements arrived, Second Lieutenants, E Parr, F R Richmond, R Watson, G R Burnett, C Jarah and G Fitzbrown, however the diarist gave no indication to which company they went. Most of this time was spent by the battalion constructing deep dugouts for the infantry, the only notable event was when the gas gongs were sounded at 2230 hours on the night of 25 September, however this proved to be a false alarm and the battalion soon 'stood down'. On 27 September the battalion received a draft of 80 other ranks from the 6, 8 and 9/Durham LI in 50th Division. As the Adjutant recorded, 'They appear to be a most useful type of man'.

The work on the dug outs continued into October, Second Lieutenant E Hartley and thirteen men were detached to Mazingarbe, where they worked on repairing huts until a new division arrived, and eventually word came through that 21st Division would be taking over that section of the line held by 8th Division. Therefore on 9 October officers of 14/Northumberland Fusiliers, 21st Division's pioneers arrived to carry out a reconnaissance of the work under way and the following day their battalion moved up and had taken over by 1400 hours. Thirty minutes later A Company moved off to Mazingarbe, followed at thirty minute intervals by the remaining companies. The 8th Division was moving south once more, back to the Somme. The first days march took the battalion to Burbure where two days were spent training, then at 2030 hours on 13 October the battalion complete with the Transport platoon, but less D Company, took to shanks pony once more and marched to the railhead at Fouguereuil where at 0310 hours they entrained for Heilly Station near Albert, arriving at the former at 1520 hours the battalion moved via

Infantry move up a congested road on the Somme.

Meaulte to Citadel Camp.

D Company followed on two days later, recalled by Major Davidson in these words, however after some years his recollection of dates and places is a few weeks out.

> *Leaving Bethune in mid September we marched by road, with rests at little towns called if I remember rightly, Barbuse and Singpre; altogether we Durhams were about a week on this pleasant tour with its halts – all ranks felt the relief – the fresh scenes, the comparatively smiling countryside and the fairly frequent buildings and villages of interest which we passed, offered so great a contrast to the shattered towns, farms, orchards and minefields which we experienced. One reflected upon the many village churches which we had seen in the battle areas shattered beyond hope of repair. This made me think of that glory of our home countryside – its many places of worship – what hopeless piles of rubble war makes of them – God grant our land and its churches from a like fate.*
>
> *We were nearly the whole time out of the hearing of gun fire, and this too, was no inconsiderable rest after the night and day racket made both by our own as well as the opposed batteries. One day while on this march a car passed us flying a Union Jack, this car was said to be General Haigs – if so, he saw us better than we could see him. Of the other trioops of the Division we saw nothing, and of course we speculated upon our destination – some said Ypres – but then we should hardly be going continually SW! Others suggested Plug Street – or Neuve Eglise -= but as I knew nothing of either of these places I mad no comment to this – then the Somme was generally agreed to be the most likely goal, and this proved to be right.*

143

But before we got there we had a day or two in billets in some pleasant small town,

where advertisements that Guinness was on sale, were frequently to be seen, but repeated drafts of that dark fluid proved this to be a cruel illusion, it had not come from Dublin. Here the Colonel left my company to enjoy ourselves for one day longer and then come on – a sort of rear guard. We played the last game of cricket that I remember to be played either in France or anywhere else.

One day while we were resting in this town the Padre temporarily attached to D Company suggested that the rations should be dished out raw; and that under their section leaders, the men should themselves cook their mid-day meal. This was a good idea and we put it into practice. It had about it something of the gypsy – the Boy Scout and the picnic. About a hundred and seventy men therefore could be seen spread over nearly a a quarter of a mile of quiet roadside cooking over small fires composed of twigs, leaves and dry grass. A very savoury odour wafted on the breeze, almost without exception the ranks enjoyed the novelty and We, that is the Padre and I, walked along to see how things were getting along. I don't think any of the dinners could be called a failure though I fancied our own, cooked by batman, was a bit smoky! It was, perhaps as well that we indulged in these lighter and amusing tasks where we could do so for a very grim time was ahead!

On 1 October [actual date 15 October] I brought our rear guard to the rendezvous with the rest of our Durhams at a place south of the front, the Division had occupied on the Somme in July, but still north of that river. It was already 1600 hours when we passed through Maricourt, an overcast evening with a very still atmosphere, a slight mist, damp and close. Vision was limited to perhaps a quarter of a mile. I dismounted, reported at HQ, fell out our water cart, field kitchen and transport wagon and then almost without pause, marched on to Montauban, the road was soft and rapidly breaking up under a constant stream of traffic – lorries – guns – wagons, troops moving in both directions; we proceeded in single file, hugging the left, often splashed with showers of mud and water. It rapidly grew dark but not before we had glimpsed the awful scene of desolation and destruction. I had to report to an advanced brigade HQ amongst other things, to be allotted and area in which we could bivouac. Finding this brigade HQ, also just arrived took a considerable time, while the mist turned into a very wetting rain. Enquiry, of the Military Police led to several mis-directions. Accompanied by one subaltern we floundered about for more than an hour, ill advisedly taking what promised to be short cuts across shell shattered ground interspaced with crumbling trenches and concealed remnants of old barbed wire. Entirely unsuccessful, we found on our return, that my excellent second in command had located the Brigade only a few hundred yards to the left of the spot where we had halted the men. Very properly he had marched the men on to the area and the men were alredy undercover in curious wig-wams which they found ready. Too exhausted to be particular we also soon found cover of sorts.

The battalion was now under orders of XIV Corps and was put to work repairing roads until on 18 October they came back under command of their own division for the attack beyond Warterlot Farm. On 20 October HQ and B Company moved to Waterlot Farm, this was the remains of a sugar refinery and old German trenches, hardly recognisable on account of the large amount of shell craters. Here three cellars and a dugout provide headquarter accommodation, whilst the men were in bivouacs in the ruined trenches. Division had now determined that the enemy trenches at Le Transloy could be taken and the attack would commence on 23 October.

The various reports of the Company Commanders tell the story of 22/Durham LI's part in the action. A Company were told off to work for the Assistant Director Medical Services 8th Division as stretcher bearers, heavy casualties were expected.

B Company moved up under the command of Captain Robson, who submitted this report after the action,

Infantry in a reserve line Stand -to.

Sir

I have to give a report on the company from the night of the 22 inst to morning of the 25th.

I reported the arrival of the company to the OC 2/Lincolnshire Regt about 2330 hours on 22 inst. He showed me the position along which the company had to dig the assembly trench. The men were at once put on this task and by dawn had dug themselves in very satisfactorily. During the morning of 23 inst, I , accompanied by the three officers of the company made a careful reconnaissance of the trenches in connection with our work was to lie. At 1425 hours I sent forward Number 5 Platoon under Second Lieutenant Watson to proceed to Gusty Trench with instructions to commence a communication trench from the right towards Zenith Trench as soon as the 1st Objective was taken. Shortly after 1430 hours the enemy commenced an intense bombardment of the support and assembly trenches and this lasted until after 1700 hours. Several times men were buried by exploding shells during this time and were dug out with difficulty. About 10 casualties occurred.

At 1700 hours I reported to Battalion Headquarters to find out whether the objective had been reached and whether I should send forward the remaining platoons. I was informed that it had not been reached and therefore withdraw the company, first toio the sunken road and later to a trench in the rear of the road. At 2200 hours OC 2/Royal Berkshire Regiment asked if I would send a platoon to the assistance of 2/Rifle Brigade, where a new communication trench had to be dug. A party was at once sent and dug until dawn next morning, the trench connecting the old front line with the new one.

The assault was renewed at 0350 hours on the morning of 24 inst. At 0230 hours a party was sent to the support line to take up a position enabling it to go over with the second wave and dig the

145

trench originally planned on the right of this sector. This poarty was commanded by Second Lieutenant Hartley, they went over in the assault with the 2/Royal Berkshire's but as the assault was repulse, they withdrew to the original position and later on information that the attack was not to be renewed returned to the trench in the rear of the sunken road.

Instructions were received about 0700 hours to with draw the company to Rose Trench and top carry on with the carrying on with the carrying of stretchers for the wounded. Several parties were sent up to the front line and many wounded brought down to the advanced dressing station.

B Company were ordered out of the line, however owing to the exhausted state of his men, and that the way back was uncertain, Captain Robson kept them in position until dawn so that they could come out in daylight, arriving back at Waterlot Farm at 0730 hours 30 October. Despite Captain Robson, recommending Second Lieutenant Hartley for a gallantry award, he received nothing. Two NCO's were also mentioned for awards, 22/237 Sergeant Clifford and 22/1133 Sergeant Rowe, were recommended because when the company had suffered several casualties from direct hits by the enemy's shell fire, they assisted very coolly in the organising the men under their command, and at great personal risk they greatly assisted the officers in moving the company to a place of safety. These two NCO's also displayed gallantry in assisting the disposal of the wounded.

The other man recommended 379, Bandsman Tarn actually received the Military Medal for his work as a stretcher bearer.

Captain Perkins led C Company up to Brigade HQ on the right sector, by 1930 hours on 22 October; they remained here until Zero Hour when they went over with the second wave. Zenith Trench was found to be clear of the enemy and at once work commenced on the new communication trench. However the location was subjected to a heavy barrage by enemy artillery and Second Lieutenant Fitzbrown and five men were killed and the Company Commander and a further fourteen men wounded.

D Company meanwhile had left their billets at 1630 hours on 22 October. They picked up a guide at 23 Brigade HQ, the guide led the company forward until he came to a point where he acknowledged he was lost! Sooner afterwards the guide disappeared. The company pressed forward and by sending out parties discovered 1/East Lancashire Regiment, who could not supply guides to Bulford Trench, which was finally discovered about 0700 hours. At 0800 hours, Number 14 Platoon went forward to Cloudy Trench where they remained until 1430 hours when they received orders to 'stand to' in Shine Trench remaining so until 0230 hours. Number 16 Platoon went forward at 0800 hours

22/779 Private P. Alderson from Eldon near Bishop Aukland, killed in action 23 October 1916.

Pioneers finish building a bridge over an old German trench.

to Mild Trench, taking cover in Polish Trench, they waited for orders and started their task at 0630 hours and cut a trench between the strong point at 24D Central and Mild Trench.

Numbers 13 and 15 Platoons were ordered to be held in reserve in Bulford Trench which they deepened. Ordered forward, direction was lost in the dark and they eventually made their way out.

Captain A. Tait-Knight killed in action 26 October 1916.

A Company, who had been detailed off to work a stretcher bearers had lost Captain Tait Knight, killed on 26 October and Lieutenant Robert Thwaites wounded the following day, but they earned a mention from the ADMS, and probably from every wounded man they carried out. As the companies returned to billets Captain Southwood was reported wounded.

Orders came through that the battalion less one company would move to Citadel Camp, the remaining company, B Company, would join XIV Corps Composite pioneer battalion. A Company were then detailed for battlefield clearance, burying the dead and salvaging equipment. Whilst burying the dead, the company lost, 28251 Private George Stephenson, from Langley Park who was killed and three men wounded by shell fire.

22/Durham LI spent the next few days resting and refitting, A Company rejoined, reporting they had buried a number of men, all unidentified, as their identity discs and other personal effects had been removed. Divisional Operations Orders now arrived stating 33rd Division would take over from 8th Division.

As soon as 18/Middlesex, the 33rd Division's, pioneers took over 22/Durham LI were on their way back, not to far however, they found billets in the Bricqueterie in Montauban. The good thing about this camp was it had a drying room and all shelters and dugouts were in good condition. Then on 8 November, three companies were put to work digging a communication trench, known as Flank Trench. C Company however, were laying a double plank road up to the beginning of Flank Trench, for which they were allowed to use four of the battalion transport wagons.

Lieutenant R. Twaites wounded 27 October 1916. When he recovered he returned to the battalion and was promoted to captain. He was killed in action 24 March 1918.

Casualties mounted daily, even walking along a duckboard track attracted the enemy artillery, A Company had six killed and nine wounded on 10 November in this way, while D Company lost nine men to one shell. On 13 November the GOC 8th Division visited the battalion and shortly afterwards the news came in that 8th Division was to be relieved, but once more the pioneers were to stay 'in', remaining in the forward area under command of HQ XIV Corps. The companies now found themselves employed on road repair under command of an unspecified Army Troops Company, Royal Engineers. They continued this work until the end of the month when eventually they rejoined their own division, who had by now moved north. As they moved out of the line 22/Durham LI were met by motor buses of the Army Service Corps who gave them a lift to Hurnoy, where the battalion transport rejoined at 1630 hours on 30 November.

The final comment on 22/Durham LI's activities near Warterlot Farm comes from Major Davidson, who pulls no punches!

It was the stupidest of battles in which I have been engaged; indeed it was hardly a battle, for although organised as such, and actually opened, it was arrested instantly. An ordinary infantry

Men of 22/Durham Light Infantry take a break from their labours on the Somme battlefield, late 1916.

officer does not hear of the ins and outs of things; still, it became significant when the Divisional General and two of the Brigadiers were changed shortly afterwards.

[This statement does not tie in with official documents or orders of battle, none of 8th Divisions Generals or Brigadiers were replaced at this time.]

About this time Major Davidson found time to write about his NCO's

I had some splendid sergeants – first class men, two of whom I later recommended for commissions, both had been at Durham College and were good sportsmen as well as sergeants. Another also a good man, at about the end of November 1916 came to me with a letter from home

in which some girl enquired if he was coming home to make her an honest woman. The sergeant was willing to do so, so I got him special leave through the CO, before whom I laid the matter- this NCO also was a good soldier of a less educated type. Then I remember a very burly young fellow who later became a corporal – he was modest and retiring in spite of the probability that he was physically the strongest man in the company and perhaps the battalion. Often he refused promotion on some plea, which as far as I could see was modesty rather than shirking of responsibility.

Throughout December the battalion moved and eventually their route march took them through the town of Meault.

'All our uniforms were ragged and we must have looked a sorry sight. In Meault the Guards were billeted, occupying the half ruined houses – they seemed to have mounted guards for each company, for us we dragged our weary way through the town, smart guards turned out , right and left very properly to salute the armed party we were – the contrast between ourselves and these splendid men in smart uniforms and equipment was extraordinary – especially as every other man of us was quite lame. The experience passed into a bye-word with us as the "Retreat to Meault". Here the RSM unintentionally amused us, for while we were still lame and exhausted and waiting to embuss he addressed my company saying, 'In a day or two he would show us some real soldiering! Every man broke out into derisive laughter.

So as 1916 came to an end 22/Durham LI sent parties forward to take up positions in Savernake Wood, as they went up the RSM became a casualty.

On the evening of Christmas day – indeed at midnight, when the battalion was marching in darkness en route for the line, the RSM missed a corner and fell into a deep ditch – he was left there – no one went to his help, no one cared for him, no one missed him, no doubt 'wounded' he was evacuated to England.' Wrote Major Davidson as the year came to an end, for it is here we leave the pioneers and return to the activities of the 'PALS'.

Chapter Six

1917 – January to June

THE PALS', AT THE GARDE STELLUNG and Gavrelle It was not until 2 January 1917 that the 18th Battalion vacated their billets and moved forward to reserve billets at Bayencourt, the roads were found to be heavy for marching as the men were fresh from the recent rest. Whilst in Bayencourt the battalion supplied working parties for the font line and it was here that the news came through that Major W D Lowe and Captain Hughes-Games had been awarded the Military Cross. The next day a small draft of 26 Other Ranks arrived before the battalion vacated billets at 8.00 a.m. on 6 January and moved forward into the left sub-sector trenches at Hebuterne. The relief of 18/West Yorks was completed by 10.45 a.m. with B and C companies in the line and A and D in support. At this time it was reported that the battalion was extremely short of officers, with only six available in the rifle companies, including the Company Commanders. After two days the companies changed round in heavy rain, a difficult relief with the trenches almost impassable. On 10 January 18/Durham LI were relieved by 10/Worcestershire Regiment of 57 Brigade and moved back to Bayencourt where they were met by motor buses. These buses eventually turned up at 1.00 a.m. on 11 January and transported the battalion to rest billets, three companies to the village of Outrebois and B Company to the village of Frohen-Le-Petit, it was here that Major Tilly rejoined the battalion from England and at the same time, officer reinforcements in the shape of Second Lieutenants, Neal and Hitchin, reported for duty. Now in

Wurtemburger's on the Arras Front in 1917, posing with a barrel of beer.

very cold and frosty weather the battalion commenced training. Over the next few days the battalion moved to Thrievres and then to Mariuex, in this latter place an 18-mile route march took place, prior to moving to Heuzecourt. Extensive training took place at this latter place and some time was given over to Divisional sporting competitions. In the Divisional football cup 18/Durham LI were defeated 1-0 by 18/West Yorks. A few days later, on 8 February, the Divisional Cross Country Run took place. Despite Sergeant Reay of the Durhams coming home in first place, the battalion team was pushed into second place by 15/West Yorks. A church parade was held on 11 February and the same day working parties that had been detached from the battalion, rejoined. With the weather beginning to thaw the sporting competitions continued, in the Brigade Cross Country Sergeant Reay was again the first man home, but the same thing happened and the team was placed second. In the Divisional boxing, Privates Middleton and Christie both won their events, whilst at shooting Number 8 Platoon won through to represent 93

18/685 Sergeant A Beaumont from Weardale after being wounded was posted to 20/DLI.

Brigade in the Corps competition and at Bombing the Durhams won the Divisional title. On 15 February the news was received that Lance Sergeant George Allison, of Ryhope, had been awarded the Croix de Guerre for his gallantry at Neuve Chappelle the previous July.

On Monday 19 February the battalion left Heuzecourt and marched to Beauval, then the following day a very wet, long and heavy march took them to the huts at Couin. Having spent over a month out of the line it was now time to go back in and B and D companies took over from 7/Loyal Regiment of 19th Division in the KEEP at Hebuterne. The next few days were quiet, but reports were coming in that the Germans were withdrawing and the battalion was warned to be ready to advance, as part of this operation 18/Durham LI, moved up to Hebuterne, but before any advance could take place the operation was cancelled and the battalion was ordered to relieve 18/West Yorks in the L.4 Sector, Mouse Trap – Wood Street. The enemy were seen to be observing the British Front Line and some time later they shelled No Man's Land and their own trenches around Nameless Farm. On 26 February observers in the British Lines reported that there were Germans standing about in the Garde Stellung, a trench which linked their first and second systems. The enemy were apparently watching the British Lines for movement; sometime later the enemy shelled No Man's Land and their own trenches

18/1422 Sergeant R. Shield having recovered from his wounds was posted to the 6th Battalion York & Lancaster Regiment and was killed in action 1 February 1917.

around Nameless Farm again. During the afternoon, six platoons of 18/Durham LI, under the command of Second Lieutenants D H Keith and G H Lean, were ordered forward to take up positions around Nameless Farm. This movement was observed and the enemy artillery and trench mortar batteries put a barrage down on the position. The men sent forward were able to link up with 15/West Yorks in the old German Front Line and that night supplies were brought up and a dump of ammunition, rations and water was established by Second Lieutenant R Armstrong. Reinforcements, in the shape of two platoons commanded by Second Lieutenant N Richardson were made available and these men crossed No Man's Land and joined up with the others. In the morning 18/356 Lance Corporal Tyson Rigg, a Wallsend man, who was an assistant school master at Stanley Council School and 18/536 Private Harry Lawler a resident of Chester Le Street volunteered to go forward and reconnoitre the Gommecourt Salient, the park and village. Having gone forward across No Man's Land, they entered the maze of German trenches and pushed forward right to the edge of the British artillery fire. They found the area totally deserted by the enemy and returned to their starting point to report the facts. As soon as this news was received two platoons under Second Lieutenant C G Findlay and Second Lieutenant J H Ruby were ordered forward to occupy Gommecourt village.

The next morning the village was handed over to 4/Leicestershire Regiment and the platoons in Nameless Farm sent out patrols and established touch with the Leicester's in Gommecourt Cemetery, and before 1930 hours the whole of the German trench known as the Motlke Graben was occupied by 18/Durham LI from Crucifix Corner to Gommecourt Cemetery. The battalion now commenced attacking the First Garde Stellung, B Company sent a platoon up the Rom Graben on the left, but a strong German bombing party, assisted by two machine guns, strenuously resisted all attempts by the Durhams to force their way into the main position. Two enemy communication trenches on the right were practically obliterated and two platoons that tried to use them got lost in the darkness. The battalion kept trying all night and most of 1 March, to enter the enemy position, but that afternoon a patrol from D Company reported that First Garde Stellung was strongly held, by many Germans armed with several machine guns. It wasn't until 0200 hours on 3 March when 18/West Yorks got into Rossignol Wood that the Durhams were able to make progress. At 0600 hours Second Lieutenant H E Hitchin MM with a party of men worked his way up Pionier Graben, but was stopped by wire and a strong bomb block west of First Garde Stellung. Then at 0725 hours, 18/1040 Sergeant Frank Reay, a Sunderland man, leading a platoon of D Company, was able to force his way in. Bombing to the left and right he was able to link up with another platoon that had forced their way in via the Becker Graben.

The Officer Commanding, D Company, Second Lieutenant E Shields, reported that the first man into the trenches on the right was 18/1567 Lance Corporal Thomas Hutchinson, a resident of Thornley Village, Wolsingham. He was in charge of a Lewis Gun Section, and when he entered the trench he saw the enemy snipers firing and the others throwing bombs at the British bombing section, who were attempting to get up to the hostile barricade, but were, in the face of the enemy's fierce opposition unable to advance along the trench. Writing a citation for gallant conduct Lieutenant Shield's report recommending Lance Corporal Hutchinson for an award for gallantry can be found in Colonel Lowes' papers,

'With level headed determination and coolness he immediately grasped the situation and he himself carrying the gun crossed the trench and took up a dangerous fire position and opening fire made the enemy keep their heads down, thereby enabling our bombers to get up to the barricade. He remained in this position throughout the day, even when they opened intense shellfire on the captured trench and in spite of shells actually bursting in the trench which had been consolidated. His ready and clearheaded grasp of the situation undoubtedly had practical effect and was a considerable factor in our successful and permanent occupation of this important trench.'

These two platoons extended their flank to the left and at a point near Gommecourt Cemetery were able to link up with 5/Sherwood Foresters, who had taken over from 4/Leicesters. All efforts by B and D Companies to work along the First Garde Stellung to link up with C Company, who were trying to get in via Pionier Graben and Schweikert Graben, were held up by enemy bomb blocks and strong barbed wire entanglements. Battalion Headquarters arranged for a bombardment, and to this end, the British had 9.5 inch mortars carried up over the water logged and shell holed expanse of No Man's Land, with a supply of ammunition. The companies were pulled back to a safer position, then in conjunction with the 4.5 inch Howitzer batteries the enemy strong points were heavily shelled. The infantry began creeping towards the enemy position and when the barrage lifted, stormed forward and entered the position. Under the fine and outstanding leadership of Second Lieutenant's H E Hitchin MM and J B Bradford the garrison was overpowered and 35 of the enemy with two machine guns were made prisoner.

18/459 Pte N. Curry from Fencehouses was killed in action 3/3/17.
The original metal cross, made out of a petrol tin was erected over Newrick Curry's grave.

At 1725 hours the Germans launched a counter attack, from the Second Garde Stellung. This was repulsed and the Durhams immediately followed and assaulted this trench, forced the enemy out and captured it. The work of consolidating the position commenced and the night was spent in this position. The next morning 12/York and Lancaster Regiment arrived to take over the new front line. With the hand over completed by 0740 hours 18/Durham LI made their way out to Rossignol Farm for a well earned rest.

Three days were spent resting, cleaning up both men and equipment and refitting at the farm and then on 7 March Second Lieutenant Dugdale led a party of one hundred men to Euston Dump for work on the tramway behind the line. The next day the battalion moved to Euston but as the accommodation was unsuitable the returned in the evening to better billets, known as 'Magnolia Camp' in The Dell in Sailly. The battalion worked on the broad gauge railway between the Sucrerie in Colincamps and Serre for three days , then on 12 March Second Lieutenant Dugdale's party rejoined. The next five days were spent providing working parties until on 17 March the battalion was

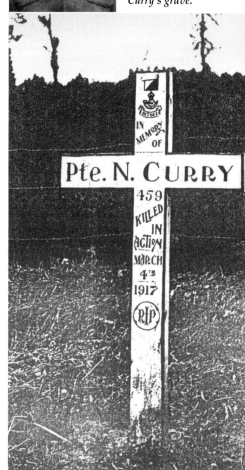

put on four hours notice to move. Orders were received that the 31st division was to join First Army and on the morning of 18 March the battalion commenced its move by route march. This was done in easy daily stages until on 22 March they rested for the day at Bours. Two days later they reached Bethune having marched eighty two miles in a week, fortunately the weather had been kind to them, bright and frosty with little wind. Here they were attached for defence purposes to the 66th Division and placed at four hours notice to move. Training commenced, although the weather had turned bad and the training ground was in poor condition.

The preparations had been taking place for some time for a battle in the area of Arras to remove the German Army from the heights of Vimy Ridge. The Third Army, under the command of General Allenby with VII, VI and XVII Corps from right to left were to be the assaulting troops on the low ground from the River Scarpe up to the higher ground near Roclincourt; whilst the hardest task, that of capturing the ridge itself would fall to The Canadian Corps of First Army. On 9 April the attack commenced and the ridge fell to the Canadians, south of them the British made inroads into the enemy lines. Three days later 31st Division left Bethune and began moving forward, by 22 April 18/Durham LI had reached St Nicholas and were set to work on the light railway between Arras and Bailleul. After a week of this work at 1200 hours on 28 April word came that work was to cease and that they were now under command of 63rd (Naval) Division. As soon as possible the battalion was to parade in fighting order and rendezvous at B.27.a. At 1515 hours the battalion marched out of camp and had arrived at the rendezvous by 1715 hours. On the way up six men had become casualties. At 2300 hours A Company, guided by Captain Vibart from the G Staff of 63rd Division, left the battalion and proceeded to take over a position on Hill 80 near Gavrelle. The next day the battalion spent most of the time improving the trenches and although the shelling was heavy no casualties occurred. At 2100 hours 93 Brigade began relieving 188 Brigade, 63rd Division, Two battalions, 15 & 16/West Yorks took over the front line and 18/West Yorks were in immediate support. 18/Durham LI remained in reserve supplying carrying parties. A Company having been relieved on Hill 80 by B Company 18/West Yorks, returned to the battalion at 0300 hours having had one man killed and two wounded. The battalion sheltered in a cutting for most of 30 April and was heavily shelled most of the night, four other ranks were killed at battalion headquarters, which led to a move to a better position 200 yards south west of the position in the cutting. On 1 May there was a further move back to Bois de la Maison Blanche, where preparations for the coming attack took place.

That night every available man was on carrying parties taking stores forward to the dumps near Gavrelle and Bailleul. Enemy artillery was very active and at 2100 hours, when a British barrage commenced, the answering enemy barrage came within a few minutes. Despite the heavy shell fire 18/Durham LI left for the front line at 2230 hours but by good navigation and even better luck they avoided any casualties on the way up. By 0145 hours they were in position as reserve to the three West Yorks battalions of the brigade, with 92 Brigade on the left and troops from 9th (Scottish) Division on the right. The British barrage opened again 0345 hours but was answered by the enemy within two minutes and came down on the Durhams as they were getting into position to advance. The main attack was overwhelmed by a furious bombardment and the enemy regained the Windmill in Gavrelle. At 0515 hours an exhausted runner arrived at 18/Durham LI HQ from 16/West Yorks, with a verbal request for help from the Commanding Officer of 16/West Yorks, Lieutenant Colonel A C Croydon. Immediately B Company, 18/Durham LI were ordered to go forward and report to Lieutenant Colonel Croyden. Fifteen minutes later a message was received from 93 Brigade HQ that 18/Durham LI were to retake the Windmill. The task was allotted to C Company under the command of Second Lieutenant H Hitchin MM. The

Having been awarded the MM and a Bar with 12/DLI and been commissioned Second Lieutenant H E Hitchin went on to win the DSO and an MC and ended the war as a Major.

reports were arriving thick and fast at Battalion HQ, at 0550 hours Brigade report that a company of 12/York and Lancs had moved off as reinforcements, and then at 0605 hours that D Company 18/Durham LI were moving up to the Battalion Headquarters. Then at 0630 hours news came in that the Left Flank of 16/West Yorks was, 'in the air' and that the enemy were counter attacking in strength from Oppy Wood. Everything was very disorganised and that Lieutenant Colonel Croyden was holding on with about a platoon strength in a position near the railway. B Company 18/Durham LI were now sent to the trenches to the west of the battalion position to prevent a turning movement round the battalion left rear. D Company having arrived were sent up to occupy Flabby and Flurry Trenches, thus providing cover from the North and North East. A Company meanwhile sent half of its strength to support B Company and the remainder were kept as a reserve at Battalion Headquarters.

At 0730 hours observers reported that C Company, 18/Durham LI could be seen approaching the Windmill in a very soldierly fashion, advancing in bounds. As Second Lieutenant Hitchin reported,

I was ordered to take my company along the trenches leading to the Windmill and retake it. I accordingly took the company along as far as C.19.c.1.0 where the trench became so shallow that it was impossible to proceed further without loss . I went forward with an observer to take reconnaissance but saw no signs of the enemy at the Windmill; time did not, however, permit a thorough reconnaissance.

I therefore decided upon a frontal attack and issued orders to the platoon commanders:-

INFORMATION	*Enemy the same as forepart of report.*
OWN TROOPS	*Garrison at Windmill may be still holding out.*
GROUND	*No cover whatever.*
OBJECTIVE	*To take Windmill at all costs.*

Company will attack in two waves with right flank resting on the right of the houses south of Windmill. Front wave to consist of Number 9 Platoon, led by Sergeant Elliot, on the right and Number 10 Platoon, led by Sergeant Cross, on the left, each in two ripples.

Second wave, Number 11 Platoon under Second Lieutenant G F Lean, who was also in charge of the attacking platoons.

Third wave, Number 12 Platoon under Sergeant Cornforth. I kept this platoon in reserve at C.19.c.1.0. which was the position of my Headquarters.

ZERO 0645 hours Front platoons extend North and South of trench C.19.c.1.0.rear waves seventy five yards behind

ZERO + two minutes Platoons move forward to assault. 1st bound, Road, 2nd bound, Railway, 3rd bound Windmill.

At the time stated the Company moved forward to the assault, and the Germans sent up SOS flares from West and South West of the Windmill and there was an immediate retaliation on No Man's Land with overhead shrapnel. The first bound was reached with no casualties, but on crossing the road a hail of machine gun fire was directed from C.19.c.5.2. approximately, C.25.a.9.1 approximately, C.25.b.1.7. We reached the railway where Second Lieutenant Lean and company retired to the road and re-organised; they again moved forward as far as the railway but had to retire from machine gun fire. Here I reached and took charge of the first wave. A third attempt was made and we succeeded in getting fifty yards from the Windmill where we had to halt.

At this point the enemy began to retire which evidently attracted the attention of our observers, for immediately 4.5 inch Howitzers were turned on the Windmill and our casualties were so heavy that I decided to retire on to the railway and eventually had to with draw to the road. I again re-organised and found that I had fifty percent casualties so decided to get the Windmill by small fighting patrols, and as the enemy were not now in front of the Windmill these moved forward as best described in the diagram.

No 1 moved first, creeping from shell hole to shell hole, and finally stopped at a point previously pointed out from the road. On reaching the destination every other man of the party sniped whilst the second man consolidated, likewise 2, 3, 4, and 5 at half hour intervals. At 1130 hours, the enemy were still holding the house south of the Windmill but were dislodged with rifle bombs. Our snipers dealt effectively with the enemy who were reinforcing the line East of Gavrelle and also men retiring from a trench North of the Windmill. During the afternoon I undertook a patrol accompanied by Sergeant Spurgeon, our objective being a reconnaissance of a line eighty yards North of the Windmill. We, however, found four Vickers Guns lying in shell holes, and after we had dismounted them they were dragged into a small trench twenty five yards North of number 3 post. They had been taken from this trench by the enemy who had failed to get them into his own line. We also found two Stokes Mortars in shell holes close by. Snipers were detailed to guard these taking up their positions in shell holes in front of their posts and when dusk fell, the guns were removed to safety. I advanced my headquarters to C.19.c.42.12 and at dusk I strengthened posts by calling on my reserve platoon. A wire was also run from C.19.c.1.0 where we tapped into Kell, this doing away with runners to a great extent.

Word was received at Battalion Headquarters that Second Lieutenant Hitchin had taken the

Artists impression of the fighting at the Windmill in Gavrelle when it was captured by C Company, 18/Durham Light Infantry, 3 May 1917.

Windmill and late in the afternoon A and D Companies 18/Durham LI were in a strong position East of Gavrelle under command of Lieutenant Colonel Taylor of the 15/West Yorks, also with them were three machine guns and one hundred men of the West Yorks and in support one company of 12/York and Lancaster Regiment. Lieutenant Colonel Croyden with about 200 men was covering the left flank to the North East and reaching a point well North of the railway. B Company in the mean time had sent out a patrol of five men, under the command of Lance Corporal Taylor, They proceeded up the trench to a point near B.18,d.4.4 where they found the trench blocked. Crossing the block they moved slowly further along the enemy trench until they met a party of enemy soldiers. They killed two of these men but were heavily bombed themselves and forced to retire. B Companies position was heavily shelled killing twelve men and the OC retired the company to a trench a little further back.

37746 Private W Burton, a Yorkshireman, from Keighley was killed in action 3 May 1917.

So far during the day 18/Durham LI had suffered the following casualties, Second Lieutenant Lean wounded in the arm, forty other ranks killed, eighty four wounded and nine wounded and missing. One of the fallen was a thirty five year old, miner, Private Robert Wilson from Old Pit Framwellgate Moor, whose brother Albert had been killed in the fighting during July 1916. His Platoon Commander, Lieutenant Iveson, writing to Mrs Wilson, said, 'Your Husband met his death with all the bravery and fortitude of a true, gallant soldier. His loss would be greatly mourned by his section and his company.' The battalion RC Padre Father R M Gallagher wrote, 'I saw a great deal of Private Wilson when he was the old Quartermaster's servant. May Almighty God console you and your little ones in your sad blow. I had a similar sad duty to perform when his brother was killed last July.'

On 4 May 12/York and Lancaster Regiment relieved Battalion Headquarters and by 0135 hours on 5 May the relief of 18/Durham LI was complete and the battalion moved to a 'very poor' camp North of the village of St Catherine, two days rest and reorganisation followed but on the evening of 7 May they were on their way back into the line, East of Gavrelle. To the right the line was held by the South African Brigade of 9th (Scottish) Division and on the left the 94 Brigade continued the 31st Divisional Front. The next three days were shattered by artillery barrages from both sides, firing would open up at one point in the line and then rapidly spread along the front, lasting two, sometimes three hours. Then there were gas alarms also, with the front eventually falling quiet for three, four, or five hours before another barrage would break out. Relieved by 16/West Yorks on the night of 10 May, they marched back to Bois de la Maison Blanche and then a further move was made to Ecurie. Here a day was spent resting, reorganising and refitting, followed by three days practicing for a night attack.

On a very dark and wet, miserable night the battalion marched out of camp and began making their way back to the front line, here they relieved the 12/East Yorks with all four companies taking up positions in the front line. The take over being completed by 0430 hours, on the way in Second Lieutenant's Welford and Apperley were wounded, whilst 18/1598 William Horn and 18/639 William Watson were killed during 17 May. .

In an attempt to cover the right flank of the Windmill, a night attack to capture Gavrelle Trench, had been planned. With A Company deployed on the right and D Company on the left, they moved into position prior to the British artillery barrage. This barrage was to open at Zero Hour and last just four minutes to Zero + 4. As the attack commenced Second Lieutenant J W Imeson was killed and a further four officers, including both Company Commanders, were wounded. The Germans facing A Company threw volleys of grenades and forced the British back. A Company quickly reorganised and attacked a second time, forcing their way into the enemy held trench. As they tried to work their way along the trench they were counter attacked on both flanks; the enemy brought up a machine gun and opened a terrific fire on the attackers, this forced them to retire and eventually forced them return to the British Front Line. Meanwhile D Company had reached Gavrelle Trench, which, especially on the right was totally destroyed and they over ran it in the dark. On the company left the attackers were held up by a machine gun post and a belt of thick barbed wire. Those on the right then fell back and began bombing along to try and link up with the left. The fight had lasted about an hour and then the Germans brought up more men and counter attacked, on both flanks and a frontal assault, which drove the Durhams out of Gavrelle Trench and back to their own lines. Apart from the officers already mentioned, the battalion had eight other ranks killed, forty one wounded and seventeen wounded and missing. The majority of the latter died from their wounds as did six of the wounded who died in the next few days. The following day was quiet until an enemy aeroplane came over and began spotting for the enemy artillery which shelled the close support trench during the afternoon. Once darkness fell the Howe Battalion of 188 Brigade, 63rd (Naval) Division commenced to relieve the battalion. This operation went well and was completed by 0400 hours.

The battalion now marched to a camp in the old No Man's Land near Roclincourt and had a spell of rest and reorganising, this was followed by working parties, every night for a week 300 men were sent to work on the green line. The weather was very good and fortunately they had no casualties. On 27 May the whole of 93 Brigade moved to Mount St Eloi, leaving early in the day to avoid marching under a hot sun. The period from 28 to 31 May was spent training and constructing a rifle range at near Bray. Having moved back to Roclincourt, the first week of June

Below: 18/554 Private C. Morris from Durham City killed in action 18 May 1917.

Below: 18/597 Private F Sinclair left the battalion to be commissioned into the Green Howards.

Above: 18/200 Private F. Walker survived and was transferred to Class Z Reserve.

Above: 18/364 Private J. A. Rickaby having recovered from his wounds was posted to 1/5/Durham LI and was killed in action 26 June 1917.

was spent working on the Red Line and then on repairing roads. The relief of 188 Brigade took place on 9 June and 18/Durham LI went into reserve and supplied working parties, this went on for four days until at 2140 on 15 June the battalion moved up into the front line, after four days the left front company extended its front, taking over 150 yards of trench near the Windmill from 12/York and Lancs. This period was uneventful, the days were hot and fine, with the odd thunderstorm and some artillery activity. Inter battalion relief's took place, 16/West Yorks came into the line and the Durhams went into reserve in the Green Line near Point du Jour. Here the news came through that Lieutenant Colonel Cheyne was to return to India and Major Headlam, East Yorkshire Regiment took over command, but a few days later Lieutenant Colonel Cheyne was in command again On 27 June the battalion again went back and took over the same sector from 16/West Yorks, which is where we will leave them for the time being.

19/DURHAM LIGHT INFANTRY, NO LONGER 'BANTAMS'

The year 1917 started with 19 Durham LI in billets at Maisnil St Pol, here working parties were provided for the tunnellers working in Arras and any other body that required large numbers of men for labour. Drafts were slow in arriving, on 9 January Second Lieutenant W McBay joined from 6/Durham LI and was posted to Y Company. Whilst Lieutenant A S Carroll, who had recovered from his wounds, returned from hospital in England and was posted to Z Company. The next day eight Other Ranks, described as 'Casuals' in the War Diary, joined from the base,

followed two days later by another fifty-five and two days after that a large draft of 144 men arrived. On 15 January two new officers were attached from 3/Highland Light Infantry, Second Lieutenant J Robertson joined X Company and Second Lieutenant W Gray went to Y Company. They were followed the next day by another large draft of 115 Other Ranks from the Infantry Base Depot. For all the instructions about not accepting men of Bantam status this draft contained a number of Bantams from 23/Durham LI based at Atwick, near Hornsea, on the Yorkshire Coast. Among them was Private John Wardell, whose documents have survived at the Public Record Office. They show that the draft was intended to join 14/Durham LI, but that when they arrived at the IBD someone realising they were Bantams, and probably not aware of the new instructions, redirected them to 19/Durham LI. These new men were sent to the Divisional Depot Battalion for further training before joining the battalion.

In a reserve trench in bitterly freezing conditions, January 1917, German soldiers are issued a warming drink.

German soldiers having their wounds dressed at an advanced dressing station a horse drawn ambulance waits to take them away.

At dawn on a bitterly freezing 18 January the executions of Lance Sergeant Willie Stones and Lance Corporals John McDonald and Peter Goggins took place and they were buried next to each other in St Pol Communal Cemetery Extension. (See Chapter Eleven)

Before the end of the month another three officers reported for duty, Second Lieutenants, W G Legat, R H Wright and E L H Jones were posted to W, Z and X Companies respectively. On 5 February the last draft of 136 Bantams who had been marked unfit left the battalion and proceeded to the base depot at Boulogne.

It wasn't until 6 February that 19/Durham LI left Maisnil St Pol, the 35th Division had received orders to move south, to the St Quentin sector. The first day's march took them to Bonnieres where they billeted for the night. The following day they moved via Hem to Vignacourt and took over billets, here they spent nine days training, before entraining for Marcelcave, on arrival here they spent two nights in billets prior to matching to the huts at Camp Decauville, some time was spent at this hutted camp before the battalion moved, via Caix and Rosieres and became Brigade reserve in the Limons Sector, the relief being carried out without incident. Battalion HQ and one Platoon of 19/Durham LI were located in Caroline Trench. 12 Platoons were in Iris Trench, with the three remaining platoons dug in, in the rear of Iris Trench. From these positions working parties were provided for the front line. The supply of reinforcements slowed down seven signallers arrived on 9 February and two NCO's joined four days later. On 14 February Second Lieutenants M H McBain and A C Paterson reported from 3/Durham LI and were posted to Z and X Companies respectively. The next officer to move was Second Lieutenant D C MacLachlan who left the battalion on 21 February to join the Heavy Branch, Machine Gun Corps.

On 1 March Captain J W Waller rejoined from hospital in England and took over command of W Company. The following day Second Lieutenant M McBain was reposted to 2/Durham LI and left the battalion just as it was preparing to move. During the day the battalion moved up and took over the left sub sector of the brigade front, relieving 17/West Yorkshire Regiment. This was a difficult relief carried out under enemy shellfire. Only one casualty is recorded when during the day 37426 Private Thomas Snaith of Chester le Street died of wounds. No sooner had the battalion settled in than the enemy carried out a raid. Later at 5.30 a.m. on the following morning a tremendous bombardment took place and the raiders, estimated at between forty and fifty men, came again.

The main point of attack was the left of 16/Cheshire Regiment, but also took in the right hand platoon of 19/Durham Light Infantry. The Durhams lost a machine gun and two men killed, Corporal Charles Nobbs a Londoner and Arthur Williams from Tetbury in Gloucestershire, both recently joined reinforcements since the purge of the Bantams. However the battalion captured a badly wounded enemy soldier, the prisoner turned out to be a Pole who for some reason was wearing a Russian cap badge, but unfortunately for him, his wounds proved fatal and he subsequently died. The next couple of days were quiet and on the evening of 6 March the battalion moved back into Brigade reserve at Rosieres, being relieved by 17/West Yorkshire Regiment.

Two small drafts arrived during this period, on 5 March twelve other ranks joined and on 7 March a larger group of 42 men arrived from the Base Depot. The next three days were spent providing working parties it was now that Lieutenant Colonel B Dent left the battalion and assumed command of 16/Cheshire Regiment, command of 19/Durham Light Infantry passed to Major W B Greenwell who had joined the battalion as 2i/c in December. Once again on 10 March they moved forward, back into the left sub sector of the Limons Sector, after a few days in the line the whole brigade was relieved by 105 Brigade. On completion of the relief 19/Durham Light Infantry marched back to the Camp Des Ballons near Caix, where they were accommodated in huts. Towards the end of the month the march back to the front line commenced, this time to the sector north east of Chilly, where one night was spent before moving to Hallu where the battalion was employed repairing roads. For over a week this work was carried on until on 29 March they moved to billets in Morchain, where the working parties continued. Captain A F Davey left the battalion on posting to 3rd Army Infantry School and the following subalterns joined from 3/Durham Light Infantry, Second Lieutenants G F Golightly and M Wharton on 21 March and Second Lieutenant J R Ozzard on 30 March, all three being posted to Z Company. Another small draft of 50 Other Ranks arrived at the same time from the base.

The Battalion Band of 19/Durham Light Infantry march through a French village.

April 1917 began with the battalion still employed on working parties, Battalion Headquarters and two companies moved to Quivieres and the other two companies and the battalion transport section went into billets at Douvieux. The battalion specialists, the signallers, machine gunners, stretcher-bearers, the battalion specialists, began training for a planned attack. By 8 April the battalion had regrouped at Flez and a practice attack on Ugny Wood and Ugny Village was carried out. Two days later the battalion was back in the front line at Mareval Copse, with Battalion Headquarters at Bihecourt and one company in reserve at Vadencourt Chateau and one in support east of Vadencourt. The other two companies held the front line, which had been the Old German Line, at Mareval Copse. On the night 14/15 April 17/West Yorks relieved all but one company, which remained in reserve to the Yorkshiremen, the remainder of the Durhams moved to billets in Soyecourt, where they yet again commenced working parties. After a few days in reserve they returned to the same sector with one company of the West Yorks in reserve. The War Diary records that there were few casualties but, 54098 Lance Sergeant Thomas Sawyer, 19/201 Private William Berry and 38959 Private Alfred Chapman all died of wounds and then on 22 April Second Lieutenant R Ozzard was wounded.

On the 23rd of the month the Durham's were relieved by 23/Manchester Regt and moved to billets in the village of Trefcon where they were in Divisional Reserve. The first two days were spent training in attack formations but on the third day they were put to work repairing roads. By the end of April the War Diary was reporting that the battalion specialists were under training and on 30 April the Battalion moved forward by night and relieved 15/Sherwood Foresters becoming reserve to the right battalion in the right brigade, with 3 companies deployed in the sunken road South West of Fresnoy-Le-Petit. The Battalion Headquarters and HQ Company were in reserve at Maison-DuñGarde. On the night of 4 May the battalion took over from 17/West Yorks, deploying two companies in the front line, one in support in the Brown Line and one in reserve in the sunken road. A raid had been planned and the following night two companies, Y and Z moved out to attack a new enemy trench. Zero hour was at 0030 hours and the raid went in with artillery support. However the enemy trench was very strongly held and the raiders suffered over sixty casualties, three of them officers, Second Lieutenant's F Blenkinsop, killed, G F Golightly, died of wounds and W F Gray was wounded. However W Company was able to establish a line of posts north west of Les-Trois-Sauvages. The next two days were quiet, but just prior to the battalion being relieved on 8 May, the enemy drove in the posts established by W Company. The arrival of 15/Sherwood Foresters sent 19/Durham LI back into divisional reserve at Trefcon, where the next ten days were spent on repairing roads and training. The 35th Division was now ordered to move to another sector of the front line accordingly on 19 May 19/Durham LI marched with 106 Brigade to Peronne. The next day W Company proceeded to Templeux-la-Fosse to erect tents for the rest of the battalion. The remainder of the battalion caught up the next day and then spent a day in camp at Templeux-la-Fosse. The following

19/742 Private J. Naylor from West Cornforth, badly gassed he died from the effects of gas poisoning 1 April 1919.

evening the battalion moved forward and relieved 11/Yorkshire Regiment, The Green Howards, in billets at Villers Guislain and became the Brigade support. At night working parties were provided for 175 Tunnelling Company, and 205 Field Company Royal Engineers, these working parties carried on for four days until the battalion moved into the front line east of Villers Guislain, taking over from 17/West Yorks.

A four day spell in the front line was uneventful and on 31 May the Brigade boundaries were altered, halving the frontage of 19/Durham LI prior to handing over to 18/Lancashire Fusiliers. In the evening of 2 June 14/Gloucestershire Regt took over the line and 19/Durham L I moved into reserve at Aizecourt-le-Bas. After cleaning up and refitting the next week was spent training, with sport each evening. It was here that a draft of sixty-four other ranks arrived from the Infantry Base Depot on 3 June. Captain C E Noakes and Second Lieutenant Robertson had a narrow escape on 6 June, both were lucky not to be killed when a Mills bomb prematurely exploded wounding both men. The next move on 10 June took the battalion forward into Brigade Reserve in the Gauche Sector, where they relieved 17/Lancashire Fusiliers. In Brigade Reserve the battalion provided working parties digging in the 'Green Line' each night. After four days of this work the battalion went into the front line in the Left Brigade sector of the Gauche Sector, Battalion Headquarters being deployed in a sunken road near the Cemetery. Eight very quiet days were spent in the front line before a move was made back into Brigade reserve, where another four days were spent digging before moving back to Divisional Reserve where we will leave them for the time being.

1917 THE PIONEERS SLOG ON

We left the Pioneers at the end of 1916 in an area known to the troops as 'Savernake Wood', as the New Year broke the work continued on the communication trenches, however it was realised that effort was being wasted owing to the condition of the ground. After the CO 22/Durham LI, Lieutenant Colonel C B Morgan DSO conferred with the CRE 8th Division, Lieutenant Colonel C M Browne, a halt was called and the decision was taken that no new work would be started, and that as it was difficult to keep the present trenches clear, in lieu of regular lines of trenches a series of 'islands' would be constructed, so sited as to enable flanking fire to be brought to bear on any part of the post in case of attack. If and when the weather improved these islands could be joined together to give a continuous trench once more. Accordingly A and B Companies commenced work, this continued quite satisfactorily until around 4 January, when it was reported that the working parties were having trouble finding suitable material for revetting the islands. Another shortage that was keenly felt was that of 'A' frames to line bottom of the trenches and support the duckboards. As many as twenty islands were under construction when orders were received that 8th Division would be replaced but that the two Royal Engineers Field Companies and the

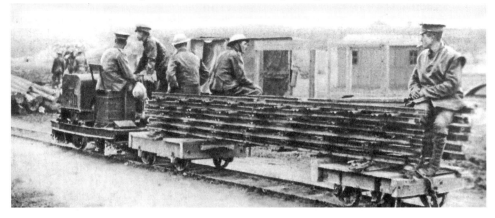

Pioneers laying more track for the light railway.

Pioneers would remain behind for another four days. On 7 January a reconnaissance party of officers from 4/Coldstream Guards (Pioneers) from the Guards Division, arrived to arrange taking over billets and work from the Durhams.

As work continued on the islands the first fatalities for 1917 occurred on 9 January, when a shell landed among a working party, killing three and wounding another. The three dead, 22/974 Private, Joseph Paylor, from Willington, 22/188 Private, John Goldsbrough, from Shildon and 22/127 Private, Charles Moore, from Darlington, were taken away for burial. As the burial party were about there task another shell landed and killed 43458 Private, Peter O'Neill, from Lintz Colliery. After the war no trace of the grave was found and they are commemorated on the Thiepval Memorial to the Missing.

By 1830 hours on 10 January the Coldstreams had taken over the work and 22/Durham LI moved off by companies to an area known as Camp 12 near Chipilly.

Here the huts were of a large French construction designed to hold 150 men – but there was no accommodation for the officers. The following morning the CRE came round and inspected the camps, owing to the amount of mud and the accessibility problems it created, it was decided that 2nd Field Company assisted by 22/Durham LI would move the lines of huts nearer the road and that one company of the pioneer battalion would make a new road into Camp 14. The work proceeded slowly as the new ground had to be drained before moving the huts. Whilst employed on this work a warning order was received that the 8th Division would be relieving the 40th Division in the Bouchavesnes and Rancourt sectors on 26 – 27 January. On 22 January Captain J F Grindell and Second Lieutenant Jameison reported for duty from the base and Captain J J Everatt also rejoined about this time.

Work on the huts ceased on 26 January and the battalion moved forward via Bray and Maricourt to Maurepas Ravine. In the last place they found shelters and splinter proof dug outs manned by 12/Yorkshire Regiment (Pioneers). All but two platoons were billeted here, the two remaining platoons were sent forward almost three miles to an area known as Andover Place. The work here consisted of repairing two communication trenches, Agile and Abode and work on dug outs at Andover, Craniere and Hospital Wood. Owing to the weather work was

22/127 Private C. V. Moore from Darlington, taken at Hartlepool in 1915 he was killed in action 9 January 1917 aged 19.

reported to be slow and extremely difficult, the trenches had insufficient revetting and no berm had been made. The work continued without anything special occurring until 1 February when a change was made to the working arrangements. A Company took over the work at Andover Place, B Company continued the mining at Hospital Wood , C Company worked on Abode Lane and D Company started on Agile Avenue, burt all reported slow progress due to the condition of the ground. At this time the Pioneers were 'No Body's Child', A Company were moved out of the dugouts they had dug at Andover Place and they were handed over to 4th Division, the pioneers

52999 Private W. Parker from Barnoldswick, a reinforcement from the 32/Northumberland Fusiliers the North East Railway Reserve Battalion originally 32/949 killed in action 27 January 1917.

being crowded in to accommodation at Craniere. The working parties on this quiet front were not without danger and there was a steady trickle of wounded, among them on 6 February was Second Lieutenant G R Burnett, who was wounded whilst in charge of a working party from A Company. Four officer replacements arrived when Second Lieutenant's H S Bruce, P Minor, F D Summerscales and A H Talbot reported for duty. Over the next few days work continued as usual until 12/Yorkshire Regiment, the 40th Divisional Pioneers arrived to take over the work. Work continued as usual for the next few days, an additional task fell to C Company, who were required to dug a battery position for the Royal Field Artillery complete with dug outs. On 14 February Second Lieutenant's J Williams and W Sheriff reported from the base and on the following day 42899 Private Thomas Fairbank from Bishop Auckland, was Killed in Action. During the middle of February great difficulty was experienced, by working parties, especially those trying to get engineering stores up into the line. Many of the Infantry working parties simply failed to reach their destination owing to the mud, which choked the communication trenches, making them impossible to move through. Towards the end of the month the battalion received a warning order from Headquarters 8th Division, this advised of an attack on the enemy trenches East and North East of Bouchavenes with a view to gaining ground from which the enemy can observe the Bouchavesnes Valley. The part to be played by 22/Durham LI was very straight forward, A and C Companies would support 24 Brigade on the left front and B and D Companies would support 25 Brigade on the right front. The work assigned was for all companies to work on communication trenches from the British Front Line to the newly captured line. Preparations for the attack continued, stretcher bays were constructed in the communication trenches and those trenches partially blocked by falls were cleared and where possible kept clear.

Zero Hour for the attack was set for 0515 hours on 4 March. At that time the leading waves of both brigades went forward and stormed into the enemy trenches. A Company, 22/Durham LI went forward at 0810 hours and commenced digging. The

At 0810 hours A Company 22/Durham LI went forward and commenced digging a new communication trench.

position of the communication trench had been reconnoitred by Captain G P Baines, which enabled the company to go straight into No Man's Land and commence digging, initially under a desultory barrage, which grew, until by early afternoon it was a heavy barrage. By then though the new communication trench was 240 yards long and had a depth of five feet. The old German Front Line was renamed 'Pallas Trench' and the communication trench became 'Pallas Alley', the German second line was renamed 'Fritz Trench' A Company were with drawn overnight, but next morning came up to assist 25 Brigade consolidate the captured positions. C Company, commanded by Captain B B White, made their way forward but met with heavy shell fire. Captain White sent Second Lieutenant A J Allcock, accompanied by his batman, forward, to locate the site of the company's task. The pair pushed forward and found the location but in doing so attracted the interest of a German sniper, who shot the unlucky batman in the leg. The men of C Company were forced to crawl out into No Man's Land, and under a German bombardment dug a new communication trench 150 yards in length. An attempt to wire the work had to be abandoned, owing to the night not being dark enough.

22/407 Private W. Glendinning from Coxhoe, County Durham, killed in action 4 April 1917 aged 21.

The B Company task was reconnoitred by Captain A H Robson accompanied by 22/377 Lance Sergeant Arthur Stephenson from Howden le Wear and a company runner. Their task, to lay mine tape marking the communication trench to be dug by B Company. The task was done in the middle of a heavy enemy barrage and could only be done by moving from shell hole to shell hole. On this right flank there was considerable enemy machine gun fire, this forced the company to move up in small parties and to commence digging lying down. By late afternoon the trench was down to a depth of five feet six inches and some 240 yards in length. At 1830 hours D Company led by Captain J J Everatt, came up and took over, working through the night, by next morning the trench was down to a depth of six feet along its length.

Casualties had been fairly light considering the work was done under fire, Second Lieutenant's C A B White and A G Mullen were wounded along with twenty eight other ranks, and fourteen men were killed or died of wounds.

The work carried out earned praise from the Army Commander, General Rawlinson and further praise from the GOC 8th Division was passed along by the CO, Lieutenant Colonel Morgan.

Captain Everatt and Second Lieutenant R Hodgson were both evacuated to hospital sick on 6 March, working parties continued to go forward and wire positions and dig new ones. On the night of 9 March Second Lieutenant A F Summerscales took a wiring party out into No Man's Land. There must have been an enemy patrol in No Man's Land that night for the officer simply disappeared. An enquiry into the events of the night found that, 'all are of the opinion that he was taken prisoner.'

Major Davidson had by now returned from a detachment away from the battalion and recorded the story with these words,

In effect we had advanced our line about 150 yards and we now had to consolidate the position. To do this D Company drew iron cork screw pickets and reels of barbed wire. The procedure was for an officer to lead a party carrying pickets and at certain number of paces, along the intended line to stick up a picket and proceed. Those who followed threaded the eye of the picket with the helve of an entrenching tool and turned it round and round until, like a cork screw it was well driven into the ground. Them others brought forward the wire which with the addition of small pickets made a belt about ten feet wide and five feet high in its centre – a very formidable barrier to pass.

The first night all proceeded very well, though when Verry lights were very active we had to drop flat for a few minutes to escape stray shots. The second night the young subaltern ahead, leading the picket carrying party, must have taken a wrong turn in the confusion of broken trenches, out in what now was a new area of No Man's Land, and advanced right up to the Boche occupied hollows; for heavy machine gun and bursts of rifle fire opened up. All the wiring party had to seek shelter in shell holes and old trenches, as best they could. It was not for an hour or more that wiring could be continued and in the meantime we had men knocked out and others wounded, whom we managed to drag back to our line. An examination made it evident that an error of direction had occurred. With the help of a few NCO's and my orderly we rectified the line of pickets observing the line of those previously set up by the original party, had wandered straight towards the Boche line, these we left. By dint of setting out the wirers from the other end we fixed all up, pretty well, by 0500 hours. I was, however, rather concerned about the fate of the young fellow who had led the original picket party for he had not returned, so when his absence was reported to me, taking one man along, we set very cautiously out again to examine and search. Reaching the point where the earlier error had been made – I sent my companion along our line, wired that night, to make sure that it joined up correctly, myself going on down an old trench alongside the general line indicated by the abandoned pickets. It was very quiet, no Verry lights were being sent up by either side, one could see a certain distance and objects against the sky more clearly. A low sound, as of several men moving in muddy ground, reached me and peering over the top, I could just observe four or five men in single file advancing towards me. It was soon evident that this was a German patrol, out to see what we had been up to, they came steadily towards me. To my consternation I remembered that I had no arms or anything more formidable than a walking stick! If an isolated man or even a small party is trapped in such a position as I was then a sharp command to 'Come Out', has to be obeyed! Otherwise a couple of hand grenades settle all argument. Indeed the days of throwing first and enquiring afterwards had arrived! My raincoat and tin hat were practically the colour of the soil – so I crouched down in the bottom and hid my face. The patrol passed along the side within a yard or two of me, but I escaped discovery. It was a critically alarming few minutes during which I ran the very lively chance of ignominious capture. I determined never again to go out into No Man's Land again unarmed. Had I my revolver it would have been effective to fire all six shots, possibly winging one and certainly scaring all so that they scattered, believing they were surprised by a superior and un-located number of Britishers. There was no sign of the young fellow so far, but I dared not go any further, moreover dawn, or the grey light that proceeds dawn, was nearly due. My orderly had also seen the patrol, but they were separated from him by some distance and by the wire we had put up.

Over the next few days the weather turned to rain and the companies were exhausted trying to keep them passable. On 12 March, Lance Sergeant James Lawson from Hetton le Hole was killed, before enlisting he had been a trainee teacher at Sunderland Day College, further casualties occurred the next day, when Second Lieutenant R Richmond and 22/705 Private James Spencer from Hebburn were killed and seven other ranks wounded. By 18 March the enemy were reported to be withdrawing and several trenches in front of 8th Division were known to have been evacuated.

> *Strange accounts reached us and I was requested by the Infantry Commander in our front to come forward and occupy the fire trench, for the message read that the line was out of touch with the enemy, so, forward we went, all agog to find the strangest of sights – our infantrymen were openly strolling about in No Man's Land and had penetrated some depth into the so lately hostile lines!*

Recorded Major Davidson.

This withdrawal was followed up and 22/Durham Light Infantry were set to work repairing the main Bethune – Peronne road from Rancourt to Bouchavesnes. This work was important and the personnel of two infantry battalions and two trench mortar batteries were also allocated to the task. When the village of Moislains was reached, the grave of an English officer, buried by the Germans on 9 March, was discovered.

> *In a garden we found a newly made grave marked with a simple cross of sticks, bearing our Durham regimental badge, this proved to be the remains of our subaltern missing during our wiring operations of less than a fortnight ago. He had been shot, probably confused by the intricacies of the torn up and entrenched ground, the poor lad had walked straight upon Jerry's trench and as I hinted earlier, we had reached the period of shoot first and ask afterwards,*

Orders were received for the scattered battalion to move into the forward area on 26 March, at the same time Second Lieutenant L W Andrews reported from 20/Durham Light Infantry. Consequently A and C Companies moved to Haut-Allaines and B and D went to Vaux Wood. The roads in the area had suffered, during the enemy withdrawal they had blown many craters in them. These roads had to be repaired and 24 Brigade supplied 400 men to assist the pioneers. Four officers, Captain G Hurford, Lieutenant Thwaites, Second Lieutenant J C Whillance and Second Lieutenant H F du Mosch along with a draft of 100 men arrived on 27 March. The draft was an exceptionally good one, as the Battalion War Diary records 'The draft includes a good number of miners and most of the men have already seen service out here.

Work on the roads was hampered by the lack of transport and progress was slow on 30 March an enemy aeroplane flew very low over Moislains and dropped bombs and although the Durham's replied with rifle and Lewis Gun fire the enemy pilot escaped.

April opened with 22/Durham Light Infantry employed filling in craters, these were mainly located at cross roads and road junctions. The craters were filled in using rubble and material from nearby destroyed villages this enabled the British Artillery to move forward, closer to the infantry. The companies were living in tents and shelters and when a move was made the men carried these forward with them, in order not to delay the work. The enemy shelled the bivouacs in Ville Wood wounding four men, one of whom, 22/401 Acting Corporal Walter Green from West Hartlepool died the following day. A number of officers joined the battalion in April, on 3 April Second Lieutenant G Adamson reported from GHQ Cadet School, and Second Lieutenant Fosbrooke from the Base Depot, a week later Second Lieutenant J Scott, and then on 16 April, Lieutenant Birchall and Second Lieutenant Roscoe both reported from the Base. Drafts of other ranks were in short supply and only twenty six men arrived with the two officers.

Major Davidson wrote about the move forward and the craters in his memoirs,

> *The German command had taken adequate precaution, however that we British should not unduly pursue them. The entire cross roads had enormous craters blown by explosives so as to block all roads – these craters were sixty to seventy feet across and thirty to forty feet deep and were very cleverly sited. Many dug outs and cellars, in the villages and hamlets, if not already destroyed, were mined and liable to 'go up' at any moment, while wells were poisoned with the carcasses of dead horses, all piped water supplies being destroyed. Across the roads whole lines of trees were felled and a*

number of 'booby traps were left about for us to fall into, such as a helmet with a bomb beneath it, so that if one incautiously lifted the trophy the bomb exploded. I suppose there is military justification in the complete destruction of numbers of farmsteads, hamlets, railways and even towns, so that these are no longer of any use to the enemy, it certainly applies to bridges – but it seemed wantonly unnecessary to cut down orchards. Of course all telegraph standards and poles were smashed.

This work continued through until the end of the month, as work was completed the companies moved forward to tackle next series of obstacles. On 23 April work was redistributed, A Company were on the Lieramont – Meddicourt road, B Company in Heddicourt, C Company Sorel – Heudicourt road whilst D Company was on the Heudicourt – Revelon – Gouzeaocourt road. Whilst working on the roads the news came in that Captain Robson, Sergeant R Garbutt, Lance Sergeant Stephenson and Private R Hopps all of B Company had been awarded gallantry medals for their bravery the previous month. At the same time a congratulations letter from GHQ BEF, came in via Headquarters Fourth Army, Headquarters XV Corps and Headquarters 8th Division,. The Commander in Chief wrote,

I congratulate you and all concerned on the successful operations carried out by XV Corps on the 12th instant. Ends. Please convey this message to 8th Division.

At each level Army, Corps and Division the commanding General had attached his comments on the fine fighting qualities, gallant spirit and cheerful way in which the men overcame all difficulties and obstacles.

At the beginning of May some men who had been evacuated wounded, returned to the battalion, but those at work were still at great risk, D Company were employed on road repair as usual, when they came under heavy artillery fire, a shell burst among a platoon the men, both the wounded and unscathed displayed great coolness, the wounded had their wounds dressed and were prepared quickly for evacuation, the general good conduct of the men reflected greatly on the platoon commander Second Lieutenant Fosbrooke and his NCO's. However singled out for particular mention by the Commanding Officer were 30150 Private W Moore and 30134 Private C Nelson.

22/327 Corporal C. E. Peace. Note the Battalion battle patch on his upper arm.

At another place rather earlier a platoon of mine occupied an old German deep dug out but they mighty soon evacuated it when Jerry opened upon it with his big stuff. I think both sides had delayed action shells of about 9' calibre, these shells penetrated deeply into the ground – perhaps twenty feet before detonating – they were intended to burst in the sides of a dug out below ground level. Very nasty stuff indeed. With some exceptions, I generally preferred to take my chance 'on top'. If you lie down or squat in a hole, a shell, even a 'big-un' can pitch very close to you to do no more than shower you with the earth it upheaves, you may have your lungs burst if you keep your mouth open.

We made Haverincourt our Company HQ for a spell of ten to twelve days, partly revetting a causeway over its newly blown crater and its two roads and another across a railway track which otherwise could have been used as an alternative road by us. We suffered rather badly here, for aeroplanes with the greatest cheek and daring used to fly overhead quite low and apparently indifferent to our rifle fire, drop a light to indicate where we were to the artillery who would reply at once with a 'packet' of four or five 5.9 shells by battery fire – that is to say; all at once. After one experience of this sort, when I lost one of my best Sergeants with a number of men, we used to evacuate these confined depths when we saw an inquisitive plane overhead. As yet the destruction of communications had made it difficult to get up more than a very few of our anti-aircraft guns; while our own aerodromes were still many miles back.'

So wrote Major Davidson of this period in May 1917.

On 10 May Second Lieutenant J A Findlay 1/3/Monmouthshire Regiment left the battalion on posting to the staff of Director General of Transportation, at the same time orders were received to prepare for a move., for which the warning order was duly received on 11 May. In accordance with these orders the battalion marched to Vaux Wood where they bivouacked in tents and home made shelters, the Adjutant, the officer responsible for the battalion war diary recording bitterly, 'The position is not too good for a camp on account of it having been previously used for a horse lines and left fouled.' A training programme was worked out and the usual training of specialists began. On 18 May the General Officer Commanding, XV Corps, Lieutenant General H S Horne, inspected the training and at a battalion parade presented the ribbons of the gallantry awards to Sergeant Stephenson, Lance Corporal Tarn and Private Hopps. As well as training the battalion held a church parade on 19 May and the next day a sports day, at which the GOC 8th Division, Major General W C G Heneker, [replaced Major General H Hudson on 10 December 1916] presented the ribbon of the Military Medal to Sergeant R Garbutt.

Events were now moving fast and 8th Division was transferred to XIV Corps, which held a sector of the Ypres Salient in Belgium. Before they left the Fourth Army, the Army Commander, General Rawlinson, sent a long letter, expressing his appreciation, of all the work done and enemy positions taken by the Division. He ended by saying 'I regret that the Division is leaving the Fourth Army, but I hope that on some future occasion I may again have the good fortune to find them under my command.

After a few more days training, the battalion received orders to move on 26 May to Peronne, where they would board a train for the north at about 1800 hours. The battalion paraded at 0945 hours and marched into Peronne, arriving at 1315 hours, they bivouacked in a field by the railhead until 1930 hours, when the train arrived and the battalion began to entrain. The train slowly pulled out of Peronne at 2145 hours but there wasn't enough room for the whole battalion and Major Davidson, four officers and 109 other ranks of D Company were left behind to follow up on an empty supply train. The Major recalled in his memoirs, some time later,

'The second day in Peronne saw our CO lead out three companies and most of the transport, together with our chargers, to entrain for an unknown destination. As trains were now running almost into Peronne they had not far to march. Early next morning except for a few details, D Company comprised almost all the troops that remained in the ruins. Two Frenchmen ostensibly civilians were arrested 'prowling about', in a ruin and brought before me, one was a quite elderly man and the other his son aged about fifty. They produced a permission signed by General Haig, Supreme Commander of the British Army and altogether their credentials seemed quite in order. I invited them to breakfast with me. They had left Paris the day before and journeyed the portion of the way up the war side of 'Romes Camp' in a troop train of cattle trucks. The old man was the Mayor of Peronne and the younger his son. They had permission to search for some archives buried in the floor of a cellar of the Hotel de Ville, now completely in ruins. D Company supplied them with a dozen men with picks and shovels and, after a time a box was abstracted from beneath a brick floor. The old mayor had fought in the French artillery during the Franco – Prussian war of 1870 and remembered that previous

occupation of his native town by foreign soldiers, but then the town had not been utterly destroyed, Church, Town Hall and many fine houses, as it was now; even including drainage system, water supply, indeed everything, even the roads.

Major Davidson offered the two Frenchmen a ride in the train taking his company north and the two men rode with the officers to Amiens, where they left the train, D Company however continued to the very north and eventually pitched up at Calais. Here they found tea and refreshment before the train headed south east along the Belgian border and eventually into that country, where they eventually arrived at the XIV Corps railhead, somewhere near the small town of Poperinghe in the back area of the Ypres Salient.

The day generated into nightfall, all lights were extinguished, there were repeated long halts, gunfire became audible – doubtless we were somewhere behind 'Wipers'. At length about 2300 hours a Railway Transport Officer came along in some siding to tell us we had reached our destination. Poperinghe was under shell fire – Vlamertinge a little further on was said to be impossible for the same reason – all roads and tracks were reported to be gassed; the RTO did not know where even our Division was; it was nearly midnight – all ranks had only emergency rations, these I dared not allow to be broken into despite my field rank. The RTO telephoned Army or Corps - and we were directed to doss down in a large brewery warehouse only one hundred yards away – it was a warm still night – and except that a soldier resents being hungry we had no real grievance.

Soon after dawn we were on the move again, this time on 'Shanks' Pony' through Poperinghe – over the pave between the bordering trees to Vlamertinge – a beautiful summer morning of late May or early June. As we approached the cross roads in Vlamertinge we were halted by the Military Police; we were marching with a gap of 150 yards between platoons, they ordered that we now proceed two by two like animals entering the ark, however it appeared to be an army order. At intervals of thirty paces we advanced two at a time, but no ark was in sight.

Officers had left their kits at the railhead but our rankers were marching in full kit, our pace was necessarily slow. Captain Hurford, [who had recently returned to the battalion after his injuries had

Captain G. C. Reay mounted right and another Captain of 22/DLI, possibly Captain Robson, ready for the battalion to move out of a French town.

healed] sent on ahead located our turning and later on battalion headquarters. We were all glad to get in, for marching as we had been for about three hours on empty stomachs we were feeling the need of nourishment.'

The main party had arrived at Hopoutre station at 1900 hours the previous day, met by the Forward Area Commandant they were directed to a field near Pioneer Camp where they bivouacked for the night. During the night 30147 Private G Harrison, was run over by a light railway engine and killed. The area was surrounded by guns and came under enemy shell fire among which was a number of gas shells and one or two men became casualties The CO's batman, a good soldier, who looked after the CO, became upset when he realised he had left the CO's gasmask packed in his kit which was on the transport miles behind the battalion. When the CO made light of the matter and refused to take his batman's gasmask in its stead, the devoted soldier servant burst into tears. But all was well for the CO was not affected and seemed no worse for his exposure to what turned out to be tear gas.

The battalion was allowed no rest and immediately were allotted tasks, A Company were to construct water troughs and lay a water pipe line. B Company moved to Brisbane Dump and took over from a company of 11/South Lancashire Regiment, the task of laying a light railway to 'Woodcote', a distance of 2300 yards. C Company relieved a company of the same battalion, but their task was laying a corduroy road from Kruisstraat to the Zillebeke road. D Company was placed under orders of the 67th Heavy Artillery Group making gun emplacements for the coming battle. The camp came under fire from enemy artillery and the MO and his stretcher bearers found work bandaging casualties from a passing Divisional Artillery Ammunition Column, only two men of the battalion were injured, one of whom, Corporal Wilby, died of his wounds the next day.

The work continued into the first week of June, each day a steady trickle of wounded was evacuated, until on 5 June the 8th Divisional Operations order Number 197 was received at battalion headquarters. This was the instructions for the coming assault on the Messines – Wytschaete Ridge. The battalion was to cease work and return to 8th Division. The battalion, less 5 Officers and 200 men of A and C Companies, marched via Reninghelst, - Boesschepe, - Berthen and Meteren to Strazeele where the majority of the men were billeted in tents but there was insufficient for the whole battalion. The party left behind were brought on to Strazeele by motor lorry and X Corps also provided lorries for the mens packs. Whilst resting here a draft of eighty-five men, the majority of whom had been out to the BEF previously, arrived and were allotted to the various companies and leading the draft was one of the original battalion officers, Second Lieutenant J Stirland, rejoining the battalion after being evacuated sick.

They remained here two days and then on 11 June the battalion marched, under orders of 24 Brigade to Caestre, where they arrived at 1300 hours. Further orders were received to move again the next day via Ecke – Godeswaersvelde – Reninghelst to Ouderdom, where they were billeted in Winnipeg Camp. On 14 June they moved about one mile down the road to Pioneer Camp, 'this is one of the best camps to which the battalion has been consisting of huts and farm buildings,' wrote the Adjutant in the war diary. Having been left out of the attack at Messines the Division was transferred to II Corps in Fifth Army. Whilst most of the battalion rested reconnaissance parties went out to look at the position of two new communication trenches to be dug on the far side of Ypres, to do this A and C Companies moved to billets at the Esplanade in Ypres, here a shell fell and killed two and wounded seven and in addition five were wounded at work on the new communication trenches. The work could only be done at night, for during the day the whole area was under the observation of the enemy from balloons behind his front line.

Command of this work was given to Major Davidson who wrote at length about the work undertaken at Ypres,

'The brigades of our division went back to practice for the attack, but the RE, Pioneers and artillery remained 'up'. The DLI moved forward to a ruined court-yarded farmstead close behind Ypres It was a better billet than our last for though nearer the line the greater attraction of the majestic pile of ruins which within its ramparts and canal was Ypres, drew most of the enemies spite. True we had, like so many others, to pass through its reverberating streets, twice nightly to get to our task, threading our way out through the Menin Gate or else running the gauntlet of Hell-fire Corner. Nor did we envy the Military Police who controlled and directed Dead Man Corner in the city's midst. Half a mile on and at the summit of a rise was an old sandbagged breastwork know as The Wall of China, more or less parallel with the road in its front. From this point forward the land fell for half a mile to our line – all absolutely open to the view of the enemy who seemed to crouch upon a further rise almost holding our positions in his clasp. In day light movement had to be by ones and two and no guns could have lived a moment in front of The Wall of China. So while the Boche artillery fired at visible targets ours had to reply by map reference.

From this road by The Wall of China, down the falling ground to our line, a half ñmile measured straight, we were to construct two well zig - zagged communication trenches and under the Menin Road we were to excavate a tunnel. As the senior company commander the CO made me personally responsible for these works. They were for the purpose of developing a grand attack in which our Division would be included. Down these trenches Brigades and Battalions would 'march in', followed by stretcher bearer companies, ammunition supplies, ration parties and what not. 'Out' by these means would come wounded and troops when relieved for division was to go through division as the attack developed.

We were working each night for a fortnight upon these trenches and the tunnel – in some hollows, because of the water logged nature of the ground – the trench was more than half a double breastwork of sandbags. Just as we completed laying down the trench boards and all was finished, perfect and complete, as the company filed out at the rear end, the platoon in our rear was caught in the last bay and its officer and seven men blown to pieces – the whole bay was knocked out. [This was Second Lieutenant R V Hodgson as well as those killed there was twenty-three wounded, from a sudden enemy barrage]

The tunnel I entrusted to a subaltern who was a mining engineer, who inspite of his exposed position made a good job of it. It had to be cut with 18' of the road surface supported upon by massive timbers lining the tunnel on both sides as well as on top and the passage had to be wide enough for two men to pass. I was very proud when the CRE inspected and praised the result.'

Also killed the same day as Second Lieutenant Hodgson was Captain J F L Grindell and Second Lieutenant C Jarah who were leading A Company up to work when they too were caught by enemy artillery. A Company were taken off the communication trench and set to making accommodation at Swan Chateau where they had a further two men wounded. As June drew to a close each day saw one – two sometimes more men wounded and evacuated but perhaps the unluckiest was 27963 Private Henry Carney, a Sunderland man who was employed as a clerk at XV Corps Headquarters some way back from the front line, he was reported killed, by a stray shell on 27 June.

So ends the first part of 1917 it is now time to return and catch up with the other battalions.

Chapter Seven

1917 – July to December

A S THE SUMMER WORN ON, July found 18/Durham Light Infantry still holding the trenches in the Gavrelle sector close to the Windmill. Throughout 1 July the enemy artillery shelled the Windmill area and the trenches were badly blown about. It was expected that the enemy would launch a night raid to retake the position, but it never materialised. The next day was much the same, then at 1730 hours on 3 July, Howe Battalion, Royal Naval Division took over the front line, the Durham positions in the support line were relieved by men of 2/Royal Marine Light Infantry. The relief was complete by 0215 hours and18/Durham LI began moving back, unfortunately they lost three killed and six wounded during the tour, among them 18/464 Lance Sergeant Walter Carrick MM, whose family ran a well known bakers shop in Durham City. The move took the battalion back to Roclincourt, where they arrived early in the morning, after sleeping most of the day a general clean up commenced. Work resumed on the Roclincourt- Bailleul light railway, daily a working party 300 strong went out to work in the wet and cold weather. On 14 July, 31st Division relieved 1st Canadian Division, in the Vimy sector, but 93 Brigade were left in support and did not go straight into the line. To comply with these movements 18/Durham LI moved to Mont St Eloi, where they moved into indifferent

On 21 July 18/Durham LI moved back up the line and resumed work on the Roclincourt-Bailleul light reilway. Here 11/Durham LI are transported on a Light Railway.

old French camp, situated in a clay swamp below the ruined abbey of Mont St Eloi. The next week was spent training, with plenty of sport going on in the various Brigade competitions the battalion fared well, the most impressive performance was by the Tug-o-War team who defeated 16/West Yorkshire Regiment after three magnificent pulls.

On 21 July they moved back up the line, 93 Brigade relieved 94 Brigade with 18/Durham LI moving into brigade reserve positions at Thelus, from where they nightly sent out working parties, carrying the stores and rations up to the line. After a week of this work they moved up to the L4 sector, where they relieved a battalion of the Hull Pals. This tour in the line was exceptionally quiet, the only fatality was when, 8014 Private George Burnham, a Jarrow resident, was accidentally killed. The line was held until the night 6/7 August when 13/East Yorkshire Regiment came up to relieve the Durhams. Those in the line moved back down the communication trenches to the transport lines, located in the village of Aux Rietz, here they were met by motor buses of the Army Service Corps, who transported them to Winnipeg Camp, Mont St Eloi. The next week was spent in company training then on 16 August they marched to Laurel Siding, where they entrained at 1600 hours. The train carried them to Neuville St Vaast, by 0030 hours 18/Durham LI had completed relieved 13/York and Lancaster Regiment in brigade support in the Acheville sector. The position of Battalion Headquarters was near an old concrete, dome shaped, pillbox that had received a direct hit from a large shell and been stove in. Being in support meant the battalion once again had to find working parties to carry stores up the line, consequently the next few nights were taken up carrying up gas bombs for the Special Company Royal Engineers. Two nights later over 1000 of these bombs were fired at the German line between Fresnoy and Acheville, each bomb contained 30 lbs of gas, which appears to have kept the enemies heads down, for there was hardly any retaliation. On 21 August, 11/East Lancashire Regiment took over in support and 18/Durham LI moved, sideways and forwards to the north, into the line in the Mericourt sector. At 0230 hours during the night 30/31 August the enemy attempted a raid on 18/West Yorkshire Regiment, who were holding the sector on the right. The raid was expected and was easily repulsed. In front of 18/Durham LI, an enemy party was fired upon and several men, including one officer were killed, a patrol went out and found a wounded German, who they took prisoner, along with some equipment, a machine gun and a Bangalore Torpedo. The Durham's had three men wounded and sadly one officer, Second Lieutenant Douglas Keith, was killed. The 27 year old, Highland Light Infantry officer, hailed from Edinburgh and was buried in the British Cemetery in Neuville St Vaast.

Private Rotheram having left the battalion the narrative for the *Bede Magazine* was continued by Private Lattimer who mentioned the raid and the casualties to those at home,

Mention was made last time of Vimy Ridge, and I should just like to record certain things in connection therewith. In rambling round, some of the chaps came across a small plantation on the steep or far side of the ridge. On wandering through this it was surprising to find some of the finest blackberries one could imagine. I have never before seen them growing to such a size, and they were also very plentiful. In fact one never thought of touching any of the size of those generally found in our own country. There were shell holes all round, and only three months previously this had been one of the hottest places on the Western Front, yet this wild garden was bearing fruit as though it lay in one of the most desirable spots on the globe.

Our stay in this particular sector was very quiet – the opposing Front Lines being about 1000 yards apart. Fritz did try one raid towards the end of our stay but it was beaten off by the battalion on our right, and the only casualties sustained by our side were inflicted on one of our companies which had sent out a protective patrol that got into the fringe of the barrage.

Of course one had the opportunity of visiting many old German gun positions here, and they were noticeable for their strength and the amount of labour which must have been put into them. Clearly they were not the work of a week for every one was made of concrete and was well made. As a matter of fact they provided splendid and tolerable safe mess rooms for the HQ officers. Whilst here also we saw some of the finest Very Light displays one could wish for. Lens not being far away on the left it was quite a common occurrence for our people to indulge in 'Joy Strafes' etc putting the wind rigt up the enemy. We came to the conclusion on such occasions that Fritz must keep a battalion behind each sector to keep up the supplies of lights for these firework displays. Many a pound has been spent in England and a worse show provided.

The battalion cooks now unintentionally caused a slight epidemic of diarrhoea; they had devised a way of making meat pies, in artillery fuse tins. These were ideal sizes for carrying up to the line and several various types of pie and pasty were concocted. However a contaminated batch of Maconochie went through, undetected until numbers of men were incapacitated by the latest batch. The battalion cooks worked hard at devising new meals to send up the line instead of the same old stew. Cheese rissoles, savoury pasties, scones, jam tarts and roly poly pudding, helped give those in the line a bit of variety. Apart from the usual shelling the next few days were quite quiet, only the back areas received any shells. Then late on the afternoon of 4 September, there was a dog fight, between a British scout and a German two-seater, in the air above the battalion. The

Battalion cooks worked hard at devising new meals to send up the line. This cook samples his wares for the benefit of the camera man.

German Field Kitchen, the enemy troops were fed from mobile field kitchen's nicknamed by the troops, 'Goulash Kanon'.

scout was victorious and the enemy plane was brought crashing to earth, right behind a trench held by members of the battalion, known as Teddie Gerard. The plane burst into flame when it crashed and both crewmen died instantly, but the heat was so intense that the immediate area of the trench had to be evacuated.

Later, that same evening a burial party was detailed to collect the remains of the pilot and observer, from the burnt out wreck and give them a decent burial. The Germans must have heard or suspected what was going on, as the burial was taking place, the party came under fire and 18/32 Company Sergeant Major, Fred Curry, received a blighty wound that would take him back to England. When he recovered he was posted to 51/Durham LI. As the night drew on 2/Canadian Mounted Rifles and 4/Canadian Mounted Rifles, relieved the West Yorkshires in support and reserve respectively, both Yorkshire battalions were able to get out of the line before a heavy gas bombardment began. Two bursts of heavy shelling hit the line, the first from midnight to 0040 hours and the second from 0130 to 0150 hours, indeed the whole of the Vimy area came under attack, the barrage being mustard gas mixed with high explosive. The very front line seemed to have missed the heaviest fire, 18/Durham LI lost a Lewis gun post, one NCO and seven men being evacuated, but in 4/Canadian Mounted Rifles in reserve at La Chaudiere brick stacks, lost a whole company, owing to the fact that their dug outs were not protected sufficiently. The shelling went on intermittently throughout the day, as there was little wind the gas hung about in the trenches. That night 4/CMR moved forward to relieve 18/Durham LI, even though the Canadians had lost a whole company, their trench strength was still greater than that of the Durhams, by 2330 hours the relief was complete and moving off by companies 18/Durham LI made their way out of the line to Vancouver Camp, where the battalion cooks were waiting with a hot meal ready for each man as they arrived. Unfortunately, the enemy must have got wind of the relief and as they made their way towards the rear area the battalion came under enemy shell fire and was fortunate to get out with only three men wounded. Most of the day was spent sleeping, the battalion did not parade until 1700 hours, they then marched off, in a terrific thunderstorm, to Territorial sidings, here they entrained on the light railway and were transported to Bray, where they found accommodation some in huts and others in billets. The next two weeks were spent training, mainly tactical exercises for officers and NCO's and for the men musketry, bayonet fighting and gas defence. The highlight of the period for a select few officers and NCO's was after a lecture by a colonel of the Royal Flying Corps, they were taken for a visit to a nearby aerodrome and taken up in an aeroplane, and no doubt afterwards into their respective mess's. On the final day before going back into the line inter company boxing and tug-of-war competitions were held.

The advance party, consisting of one officer and the Company Sergeant Major from each company, the Signals Officer and two signallers, along with the Regimental Sergeant Major, gathered at the battalion horse lines on the night of 18 September. Under special instructions from the Adjutant they left there at 0830 hours the following day. The companies began entraining at 1015 hours and after detraining moved via Zehner Weg, Ouse Alley and Tired Alley, the order of march being B, D, C, A companies, the rear being brought up by Battalion Headquarters. By 1400 hours the whole battalion was east of the Lens – Arras railway line and by 1500 hours, in very fine weather, the battalion had taken over completely from 13/East Yorkshire Regiment in a position known as Sandbag City, on the Bailleul – Arleux Road. Here they were in support to 16/West Yorkshire Regiment in the Arleux Sector. The companies were deployed as follows, B Company in the Arleux Loop, D Company as the Right Company in the Red Line, C Company in the centre in the Red Line and A Company as the Left Company in the Red Line. B Company were placed under the tactical; command of 16/West Yorkshire Regiment with the Company Commander receiving instructions that if the enemy attacked and got into the front line, B Company would counter attack and he was to report the action to both Battalion and Brigade Headquarters.

Private Lattimer recorded the time spent in this sector also,

'The time out of the line hereabouts was passed in the organisation of Cricket matches. With the return of A P Ashley, as an officer, the team received a great addition to its somewhat meagre strength. At any rate strong or weak, we had many enjoyable games.

About September we moved to the sector on the right. Here we were once more lucky, as Fritz behaved himself quite decently as a rule, varying the monotony now and again with heavy gas shelling of the batteries. Thus 'Reserve' was often more lively than the Front Line. Indeed here it was more exciting behind the Lines, for in Brigade Reserve we were close to an Observation Balloon, and it was a daily practice of the enemy to shell this with his long range guns. When this was put up our feelings and remarks may be imagined. It was almost a relief to have a dull or even a wet day. Despite this, however, we managed to have a comparatively good time, concert parties and picture shows being quite numerous. By now the Battalion had been reduced to fairly low strength and on the occasion of our second visit to the sector, the Companies in support had a very rough time, about half-a-dozen carrying and working parties, each day being the lot of practically every man. To make matters worse the enemy had made a mess of the trenches in his effort to silence our Trench Mortars. In this he was entirely unsuccessful as there was not a hit to be recorded.

The sector they were now holding was regarded as vital ground, if lost to the Germans; they would have had a clear view of the British Gun positions at the foot of Vimy Ridge. A series of strong positions had been built here, deep trenches, well wired, with machine gun positions. Owing to the lack of observation, the enemy had numerous aircraft patrols over this area, which caused a lot nuisance to those men working in the rear areas, little happened until 23 September, The Battalion Headquarters Signals Sergeant, 18/1200 Thomas Knaggs, a Sacriston man, and one of his signallers 21/270 Private Robert Lamb, who came from Gateshead, were walking on a track that led from the Red Line to the Arleux Road. Some way along the track the Royal Engineers had a cookhouse, which had a fire going, this fire was producing a lot of smoke, the enemy observing the smoke, sent over a number of shells, Sergeant Knaggs was killed instantly, Robert Lamb, who was only twenty one years of age, was badly wounded and taken to the Casualty Clearing Station in Duissans, but sadly succumbed to his wounds two days later. In the support position there was a constant requirement for working parties and a regular routine was established

1 Officer and thirty two men	wiring nightly
1 Officer and fifty men	carrying for the above
2 Officers and fifty men	day work on Arleux Loop improvements
2 Officers and fifty men	night work on Arleux Loop improvements
1 Officer and twenty five men	day work Tired Alley – Red Line
In addition fifty – sixty men	any odd carrying required
B Company twenty five men	stood to in posts night and day

B Company only to work in the trench they occupy.

It can be seen from the above that there was more than enough work for everyone.

The day Private Lamb died; the battalion moved forward, relieving 16/West Yorkshire Regiment in the front line. Patrolling became the main activity, whilst in turn the Germans brought their trench mortars into play, particularly against A Company, but caused no casualties, that is until 28 September, that morning they fired at one of the Durham's patrols, from B Company, out in No Man's Land, A South Shields man, twenty three year old, 18/981 Lance Corporal Thomas Vockuich, who had been awarded The Military Medal for his work at The Guarde Stellung, was immediately killed, whilst twenty eight year old, 18/408 Private Thomas Wrench, from Bishop Auckland, was brought in badly wounded, but died shortly afterwards. Over the next two nights there was some sporadic shelling with the enemy sending over gas shells which caused the battalion to wear respirators for a short while. So as September drew to a close and October arrived, 11/East Yorkshire Regiment came up and relieved the battalion, who marched back down Tired Alley, as they were on their way out, they came under some enemy shelling, but this time thankfully, there were no casualties. The main part of the battalion went into Ecurie Camp, a lot of work had been done on this camp and it now contained baths, cinemas and at least four huts acting as theatres for concert parties. B Company however, had been left behind, two platoons in Long Wood and two platoons in Sunken Road, providing working parties for the line. They had only been in Ecurie for a day or so when the battalion had to provide large working parties, the Royal Engineers, Royal Field Artillery both claimed men from the Infantry as labourers. Between 1 and 13 October each company in turn rotated on the task given initially to B Company. Other tasks given to the battalion included the wiring of Total Post; this was undertaken by Second Lieutenant Agar and 32 men, whilst one officer and fifty men were sent back up to the Red Line, where they remained for three nights, employed in wiring jobs each night.

Under the command of Major Ince, the battalion moved up into the Arleux L2 Support Sector, where on 13 October they relieved 11/East Yorkshire Regiment. The next two days were uneventful The Adjutant; Lieutenant J T Thorman left the battalion on posting to the Deputy Adjutant General's department at Army Headquarters, the duties of Adjutant being taken over by Second Lieutenant Freer. On 16 October, at midnight, the enemy launched a hurricane

Lieutenant J. E. Waggott joined the battalion in 1917 but was posted to the staff of DAQMG at XIII Corps HQ, he eventually became Staff Captain 'Salvage' at XIII Corps HQ.

bombardment of gas and high explosive shells all along the battalion front and the artillery batteries in the rear, around the Red Line. The shelling lasted until 0150 hours, casualties were very light, two sergeants slightly wounded by shrapnel and one Lance Corporal and two men affected by gas. Two days later, the battalion moved into the L2 Sector Front Line, where they relieved 16/West Yorkshire Regiment, this was a trying tour in the line, the enemy trench mortar batteries kept up a heavy barrage, particularly a night, concentrating on the southern end of the battalion front, their bombs being a mixture of gas and high explosive and at night their machine gunners fired occasional bursts. But they didn't have it all their own way; British Heavy Artillery shelled the enemy wire and the 18 Pounder batteries of the Divisional Field Artillery hit enemy positions in Fresnoy Park, as well as at night opening up on tracks and roads used by enemy carrying parties. The strength of the battalion had now fallen really low, during this tour the actual trench strength was only 350 men in the line. On 25 October, in wet, stormy weather, 11/East Yorkshire Regiment came up and 18/Durham LI moved back out of the line, by 1900 hours they had reached the railhead, where they boarded the light railway and were transported to Ecoivres, a very poor camp in the middle of a swamp. After cleaning up and bathing, working parties were supplied to the Town Major. Various inspections took place, kit, stores and company equipment, all came under the eagle eye of the Officer Commanding Lieutenant Colonel Cheyne. In heavy rain the battalion paraded and carried out company drill and later bayonet fighting. Owing to the shortage of manpower the companies were reorganised, Company Headquarters now had two Lewis Gun Sections but there was only one platoon in each Company, each consisted of two Lewis Gun Sections, one rifle section and 1 bombing section. The training continued well into November, a practice attack by the battalion, in fine weather, was watched by the GOC 31st Division and the Brigade Commander. Just before the battalion went back into the trenches, they held an inter-platoon competition, consisting of tactics and skill at arms, in heavy rainfall the platoon representing A Company, commanded by Second Lieutenant J Pattison took the honours.

The move back into the Support Line, scheduled for 8 November was put back twenty four hours, owing to a raid taking place by the 11/East Yorkshire Regiment. Accordingly on 9 November the relief of 16/West Yorkshire Regiment took place in the Red Line, however the sector taken over was slightly to the north of that previously held and included positions up to Willerval North, in wet weather, the relief was completed by 1430 hours. The European winter was beginning to make itself felt, the recent wet weather was leading to trenches beginning to fall in, consequently large working parties were required to work on trenches new to the battalion, Brittania Trench and Sapper Dump where over 200 men were employed. The Germans however were using a hurricane bombardment for several minutes on a location and then moving on to another sector. L2 and L3 were shelled in this way on a number of occasions. On the slightly misty morning of 14 November, C Company suffered the battalion's first fatal casualty for seven weeks, when 23863 Sergeant Ralph Brewis was killed. The following day ten men, who were collecting water from the water tanks in Tired Alley, had to be evacuated slightly gassed, later that evening the enemy again put shells over on Willerval and Arleux between 2000 and 2200 hours. On 16 November 18/Durham LI took over the L1 Sector, Front Line from 16/West Yorkshire Regiment. The battalion was deployed with A Company on the left front and B Company on the right front. C Company was in left support and D Company in right support. During the afternoon the enemy launched a very heavy artillery attack, which broke the railway line in three places near the Arleux – Sugar Factory Road and then at night there was heavy machine gun fire on the flanks, throughout the night. The enemy division in front was suspected of being relieved so British Artillery shelled the enemy back areas during the night. The Germans however replied by shelling the area where battalion headquarters was located, fortunately there were no casualties. The work allotted to the battalion during this tour had been the construction of defended localities, trenches were wired over and only certain trenches held, it had been realised that weak battalions could no longer hold long lines of continuous trenches. Carefully wired and patrolled, posts were constructed between 400 and 1000 yards apart with banks of barbed wire to prevent

outflanking. By the time 18/West Yorkshire Regiment came in, on 23 November, to relieve 18/Durham LI, the work on OAK Post was almost complete. The Durham's moved back into support positions, where they came under heavy enemy artillery fire, On the afternoon of 24 November the final fatal casualty for 1917 occurred, the unfortunate man, 20/964 Private Thomas Clear, from Sunderland, was killed by shell fire. Having gone out with 20/Durham LI in May 1916, during the fighting at Flers in September 1916, he was evacuated to 139 Field Ambulance with appendicitis and from there via 1st New Zealand Stationary Hospital; he had made his way back to England. Having recovered from the operation he was sent out once more and wound up as reinforcement to 18/Durham LI.

Over the next few days the enemy artillery was extremely active, even as the battalion moved back into the Font Line to relieve 18/West Yorkshire Regiment, the shelling barely ceased. On the evening of 29 November over 200 gas shells fell on the battalion, but only one Corporal was reported wounded. On the last day of the month the artillery was quiet during the day but as night fell high explosive and gas shells fell all about the battalion area.

18/1393 Private S. Ryder was awarded the Military Medal for his good work in the autumn of 1917.

At the beginning of November the Divisional Front was greatly extended with the result that our spells in the back areas became few and far between. The chaps in consequence got into as bad a condition as ever before, bathes and clean changes becoming absolute luxuries. Then towards the end of the month Fritz livened things up considerably with his Artillery, although on the other hand he almost ceased using Trench Mortars, so that to use a somewhat vulgar expression, what we lost on the swings we won on the roundabouts.

So wrote the correspondent to the *Bede Magazine* recording this time in the trenches.

The first four days of December continued in the same way, almost ever trench and position in the battalion area was targeted by the Boche Artillery, using both gas and high explosive. On 3 December an enemy working party had been observed working on No Man's Land, so the following night a patrol went out from 18/Durham LI's, right company, having previously arranged a system of signals with the Brigade Machine Gun Company, stealthily they made their way out into No Man's Land , where they observed about twenty German soldiers working on some defensive task. Quickly and quietly they returned to the British line and fired two flares one red, one white, whereupon the machine gunners let loose a terrific barrage and it was thought it caused a large number of casualties among the enemy working party. This operation was repeated two nights later, the first patrol didn't locate any enemy soldiers, but a later patrol came across a large working party. Retreating a short way they fired two flares, this time green and white. However that night there was a haze and the signal wasn't seen, the patrol waiting for the machine guns to open fire, returned to the British Line and telephoned the Machine Gun Company with the location of the enemy working party, although they opened fire the results were unconfirmed. While this was going on at the southern end of the battalion position at the northern end a soldier was wounded by machine gun fire, but this came from behind and it was supposed from the left rear, or the Canadian part of the line.

56th (1st London) Division was now coming into the line and 8/Middlesex Regiment of 167 Brigade arrived to relieve the battalion, however C Company, who were holding Oak Post and Manitoba Road were relieved by a company of 1/London Regiment. 18/Durham LI moved back to York Camp at Ecoivres, D and B Companies travelled by light railway, whilst A, C and HQ were met by motor buses of the Army Service Corps who dropped them off at Mont St Eloi and they completed the journey on foot. After a day off and then a Church Parade on 9 December, the next day company inspections were the order of the day, then off for a route march under company arrangements. Over the next nine days all sorts of training took place, on 19 December the Medical Officer inspected the battalion for Scabies, a skin disease which could quickly reduce the trench strength of a battalion. On 22 December moved to Ecurie Wood Camp and became Brigade Reserve taking over from the London Rifle Brigade, here training continued and working parties were supplied to several dumps and tasks.

It was at this time that 18/976 Private Fred Poole, of West Hartlepool, started a small record of the last year of the war.

Jerry shelled camp with long range gun from Doura when getting ready for the do Christmas Day, but kept quiet after airman reported gun position had been bombed and destroyed. Ecurie was once a village but there was nothing left to show what it had once been, being close to the main road from Arras to Lens and Bethune, there was also a railhead there. There were several picture shows and Concert Parties, also baths for the troops. It was a nice target for Jerry with his high velocity shells just to put the wind up the troops, on several occasions we had to take cover but I found it was one of the most comfortable places I had been in both for billets and amusements. I found the Arras front the best of any front I had been on, with the light railway running close up to the front line. After the taking of Vimy Ridge, it took away all ground observation from Jerry, which enabled the troops to get a good system of light railways and broad gauge line, close up to Tired Alley, the first communication Trench.

The work continued on the morning of Christmas Day, but that afternoon a special Christmas Dinner was held, followed by a performance by 'The Owls', the Leeds Pals Concert Party. Time off didn't last, having been in reserve over Christmas it was back into the line over New Year. On 28 December, two companies took over Brierly Hill, one company was in Willerval North and one in Sugar Post, Battalion Headquarters went into dug outs in Tunnel Dump. The relief was spotted by the enemy and heavy shelling took place. The next three days were very quiet but very cold, two platoons carried stokes mortars shells up for 93 Light Trench Mortar Battery, but apart from Major Gibson/ from 15/West Yorkshire Regiment assuming command of the battalion the year ended very quietly.

Private Lattimer wrote his last entry for the *Bede Magazine* at this time, for he was posted to XIII Corps Headquarters,

> On 7 December, the Division was relieved for a move to another part of the line, rumour said Cambrai. We were to depart from our rest billets in two days, but at the last moment we received orders to take over the old sector again. Before doing this we were given about ten days training some eight miles behind the Lines, this was well spent in football, interest in which had grown greatly. On the occasion of our previous Divisional Reserve, boxing and football had been properly organised so that now all that was necessary was to 'carry on.' Through the medium of the canteen gear had become quite plentiful. I ought to mention that the Football Team seldom won a match, but that mattered little, so long as we had the games and derived the consequent enjoyment.

> The Battalion moved up again into Reserve about 20 December. Here they remained long enough to enjoy a good Xmas spread. One man said he thought it was the best that had ever been laid out in France. As far as my information and memory carry me, the Bedeites are gradually growing less in number and the following are all that remain with the Battalion: A P Ashley, Second Lieutenant, W H Brown, Second Lieutenant, L Oliphant, RQMS, W Forrest, CSM, T Cook, MM, Stretcher bearer.

> Further than this I am unable to go, for I left the Battalion on 15 December.

The 'Pals' had been very lucky throughout the summer and autumn of 1917, battles had raged around Ypres in Belguim, Messines, Menin Road, Polygon Wood and Passchendaele , all consumed thousands of British Infantrymen, but 31st Division had not been called upon, even when the Battle of Cambrai took place in November, they remained on the Arras Front, however the dark days of March 1918 were still to come.

19/DURHAM LI, THE HINDENBURG LINE AND PASSCHENDAELE

We left 19/Durham LI in Divisional Reserve, however they were not settled, each day they moved to a different camp, until they settled in a camp at Longavesnes, a couple of days training and brigade tactical schemes took place before they were back in the support line as the right support in the C1 sub sector North East of Hagricourt. They took over from the 12/Lancers and Queen's Own Oxfordshire Hussars of 5 Cavalry Brigade, of 2nd Cavalry Division. The Cavalry with less men in a units ranks, had also to leave about half their strength behind to look after the horses, hence two cavalry units were relieved by one from the infantry. For seven days 19/Durham LI were in support each night they sent up working parties, who were employed on digging and wiring in the front line. Then on 15 July the battalion relieved 17/West Yorkshire Regiment in the right front line, occupying, A B and C posts with one company in reserve in Orchard Post and Toine Post. The front was very quite for two or three days and then on the night 19/20 July a heavy artillery bombardment was unleashed on Rifleman Post, which was about 1500 yards north east of Hagricourt. Under cover of the barrage a large enemy raiding party launched an attack. Immediately the post fired a warning SOS rocket, but no counter fire came down so a second rocket was fired. As the attack came in, the post commander Second Lieutenant Harry Heaton, who was awarded the Military Cross for his defence of the post, moved about among his men, encouraging them and giving fire orders, until the portion of the trench he was in was blown in, which restricted his movements. But another man assisted controlling the defence, 26714 Private G B Bell, a Newcastle man, gained the Military Medal for his conduct during the defence of Rifleman Post.

Casualties among the defenders were quite heavy, ten men killed and sixteen wounded, the enemy left two dead and a lot of equipment in the vicinity of the post. The front went quiet over the next few days and on 23 July 14/Gloucestershire Regiment took over the front line. 19/Durham LI went back into Divisional Reserve near Aizencourt-le-Bas, where the first day out of the line was completely free, the following week being taken up cleaning up and training. The next move on 1 August was into the Birdcage Sector, south east of Epehy, where they relieved elements of 15/Cheshire Regiment and 19/Northumberland Fusiliers in Brigade reserve. It wasn't until 5 August that 19/Durham LI went into the front line of the Birdcage left sub sector, here over the next six day the situation was described as normal, however, two Yorkshire reinforcements, 40745 Private Joseph Ellis of Barnsley, 43818 Private John Appleyard from Batley, both lost their lives on 7 August. On

Original card marked 'Private J. Wastel 19/DLI, but no trace on Medal Rolls.

the same day a thirty four year old, Gateshead man, 36403 Private James Errington was also killed. On 11 August, III Corps Cyclist Battalion moved into the line to relieve 19/Durham LI, the Cyclists were under strength and W Company was left behind in support of the Cyclists when the battalion moved back to Villers Faucon. The normal round of cleaning up, bathing, inspections and training took place as well as supplying working parties at night. It was soon time to go back up the line and on 19 August 19/Durham LI relieved 18/Highland LI in Gillemont Farm, this position had been taken by 18/Highland LI the previous day. The relief was carried out without incident, except that 19/441 Private Wilkinson Bestford, from West Auckland was killed in action.

Over the next few days there was little activity, two men died of wounds and one was killed in action, on 24 August, 18/Highland LI came back and took over from 19/Durham LI, who marched back to billets in cellars at Lempire. Once again W Company were left behind, this time holding a position known as Cat Post a little to the south of the main position. That night the Germans attacked Gillemont Farm in strength and drove 18/Highland LI out of the position that they had fought hard to take; as the men of the Scottish battalion withdrew the Germans followed them and were able to gain a foothold in what had originally been the British Front Line. Word was sent back to 19/Durham LI that they must come up and endeavour to retake what they could of the lost positions. During the day, British Artillery bombarded the enemy positions and as the evening drew on, three companies of 19/Durham LI formed up for the assault. At 1930 hours, the whistles blew and the Durhams went over the top, immediately fire from the west side of the ruins caused casualties in the leading platoon of Y Company. Among the first to fall was Second Lieutenant G W Berry, attached from 5/Durham LI, the Company Commander, Captain G R Forster, who had been with the battalion since it formed was next to go. Also seen to fall was the Platoon Sergeant, Albert Hogg. At this point anything could have gone wrong, but Corporal Fred Ramsden, a Lancashire Lad from Bolton, grasped the situation, took command of the platoon and led them onto the objective, the Germans fought hard for the position but were eventually driven out.

Shortly afterwards the opened a barrage of artillery fire and immediately they launched a counter-attack, trying to bomb their way down the trenches on either flank. This attack was repulsed and later at 2030 hours they attacked once again, this time from the South East, the defenders opened fire and the attack dispersed, leaving 19/Durham LI holding the old British Front Line. Here they remained throughout the night until 17/Royal Scots came up and relieved them, 19/Durham LI then moved back to Lempire once more and became the Brigade reserve battalion, providing working and wiring parties at night, it was on one such party that Second Lieutenant G E Brown was wounded on the night of 27 August. During the attack at Gillemont Form the battalion were able to capture one heavy machine gun, and recover two Lewis guns and three Stokes Mortars, taken by the enemy from 18/Highland LI.

The beginning of September found them once again holding the front line at Gillemont Farm, on the night of 1 September, 14/Gloucesters moved in and 19/Durham LI went back to Villers Faucon, here they remained training, bathing and resting where possible, until 6 September, when they took over in the Birdcage sector, relieving 18/Lancashire Fusiliers in the Front Line. This tour was remarkably quiet; a few casual drafts of ten or less men joined the battalion before it moved back into Brigade reserve again. On 18 September they were relieved by 15/Cheshire Regiment and moved back to Divisional Reserve at Templeux La Fosse, where they carried out training, musketry, bombing and wiring, along with the training of specialists, Signallers, Lewis gunners and stretcher bearers. On 22 September a Brigade parade was held at which medal ribbons were presented to those who had won gallantry awards. Then on 26 September they moved back to the front line, relieving 20/Lancashire Fusiliers who were holding Fleecall and Grafton Posts south east of Epehy. It was three days later when they moved back to Brigade reserve once more the same cellars in Lempire as they had used previously. Here a large draft of 120 men arrived from 22/Durham LI, all trained infantrymen, who had been replaced in the pioneers by class B2 men of the Royal Engineers.

A dead German, taken with a 'Box Brownie' camera. The body is hard to make out against the mud.

It was now that 35th Division was ordered north, to Ypres, all through the late summer and early autumn battles had raged in the Ypres Salient and 19/Durham LI and their comrades of the 35th Division were headed for Passchendaele. On the night 3 October the battalion was relieved by 7/King's Liverpool Regiment of 55th Division and moved back to Aizecourt-le-Bas. The next morning a convoy of motor lorries collected them and the battalion was carried to Peronne, where they found billets for the night. The next day they entrained for an unknown destination, which turned out to be Arras, where they arrived in the early hours of 6 October, after detraining and forming up in column of route they set off for the village of Montenescourt, south west of Arras, near the town of Avesnes. The battalion now embarked on a period of intensive training, preparing for the coming battle.

The next move came on 14 October, when they foot-slogged their way north west, to Aubigny, at the railhead here they were met by a train which took them to Ziggers Cappelle, where on 15 October another large draft of pioneers joined the battalion, this time the powers that be had combed out 210 trained infantrymen of 11/Durham LI.

Moving from the billets in Ziggers Cappelle, the battalion marched on to Areke and entrained for Proven, where on arrival they were billeted in P4 area for the night. The next day they crossed the rear of the salient and up the western edge to Woesten, where they prepared to move into the front line. As they moved into the line, to relieve 17/Lancashire Fusiliers north east of Koekhuit, they were met with heavy shelling. Battalion Headquarters was established at a point known as Veebend, but beyond that point it was difficult to know where anyone was. In the forward area there was little resembling trenches, the battlefield was simply a crater field, with the majority of the craters full of water, the majority with dead bodies or pieces of body in them. In these conditions the battalion had to live and when called upon to do so, fight. Throughout 19 and 20 October the battalion positions were continuously shelled with a mixture of high explosive and gas shells. Among those gassed was the Commanding Officer, Lieutenant Colonel W B Greenwell, who although quite badly affected, remained at duty. On 21 October 23/Manchester Regiment, 17/Lancashire Fusiliers and 16/Cheshire Regiment, all came up and took over portions of the front held by 19/Durham LI, who quickly moved out of the line and made their way to Emile Camp near Elverdinghe. Here they rested for a day and were then ordered to move back into the front line, taking over a sector south east of the Houthulst Forest, held by 15/Cheshire Regiment and 15/Sherwood Foresters. This relief was heavily shelled, the Durham's lost a large number of killed and wounded, many of those wounded died over the next two or three days before they could reach the base hospitals on the coast. At length the battalion got themselves settled in position, but all the time there was an incessant barrage of high explosive. At 1800 hours on 24 October the Germans launched a large counter attack under the cover of a heavy barrage; the leading enemy wave sent up red flares and came over the top. However 19/Durham LI were ready and waiting, with Lewis gun and rifle fire they drove the attackers back to where they had started, leaving between sixty and seventy men dead on the field. No more attempted counter attacks occurred over the next two days, but the artillery hardly ceased fire and it was a sadly depleted battalion that welcomed 7/Lincolnshire Regiment when they came in to relieve the battalion on 27 October. Making their

A Gas Cloud drifts towards the British Lines, taken with a 'Box Brownie'.

way as best they could over the craters full of water and through the deep glutinous mud the battalion, or the remnants of the battalion eventually arrived at Boesinghe, here they boarded a light railway train and were carried back Proven, arriving at 0515 hours on 28 October. Marching to Palma Camp they began cleaning up and refitting, the estimated losses over the last four days were 120 killed, wounded or missing and 110 sick with gas poisoning.

Two days later they moved to a hutted camp known as Dykes Camp and began preparing to go back into the line, however the Commanding Officer's health deteriorated and owing to the gas he had inhaled nearly two weeks earlier, he was forced to report sick. Command now passed to Major S Huffam, who led the battalion back up to Koekhuit on 1 November. Relieving 15/Cheshire Regiment, W and X Companies manned support posts at Koekhuit and Y and Z Companies, along with battalion Headquarters held support positions at Wijendrift, North West of Langemarck, here Second Lieutenant G M Allan was wounded during 2 November. The same night the enemy unleashed a heavy barrage of gas shells, the battalion must have been caught unprepared, for there was a long list of officer casualties, Major Huffam and all the company commanders, the Adjutant and the Medical Officer as well as nine subalterns had to be evacuated, along with approximately 125 other ranks mainly in Y and Z Companies. Relieved by 7/Essex Regiment from 53 Brigade, the survivors trudged back once more to Boesinghe and the train back to Proven, where they entered Number 4 Camp and after three days they moved into Number 3 Camp, Here Major V E Gooderson 18/Highland LI joined the battalion and took over command. The main activity at this time was providing protection against air raids and the building of

Lieutenant Colonel W. B. Greenwell, although badly gassed, continued in command.

sandbag walls around tents too up most of the time. The front held by 35th Division had moved slightly to the right and when the battalion went back up the line on 16 November, they relieved 17/Royal Scots in Brigade support in the Poelcappelle Sector. W X and Z Companies took over a position known as Kempton Park and Y Company went into Pheasant Trench, these positions were held, without loss, for two days and then they went forward and took over the front line from 17/Royal Scots along the line of te Poelcappelle – Westroosebeke Road. The battalion was deployed as follows, on the right, X Company with their Company Headquarters in Gloster House. In the centre, Z Company, their Headquarters were in a position known as Poelcappelle East. On the left, were W Company, who's Company Headquarters was located in The Brewery, or what remained of it. Each platoon was holding a line of posts located in pill boxes or ruined farm buildings.Y Company was deployed in support, Numbers 9 and 10 Platoons, behind W Company and Numbers 11 and 12 Platoons behind X Company. The relief was completed by 2330 hours with out incident. The battalion hadn't been in position very long when the shelling commenced.

During this shelling on the morning of 19 November, the Germans sent a patrol towards the left half of X Company. This position was commanded Second Lieutenant R Smith, who reported,

A strong officer patrol approached the pill box on the right flank front line, where Private Pinkney [Probably 19/362 John Pinkney from Easington Colliery] was on duty as sentry to Number 5 Platoon, holding the centre post of our line. At 0515 hours he challenged the enemy who opened fire. He immediately fired and killed one of the enemy and on a brisk fire being opened the enemy withdrew. They were again led by their officer round the rear of the pill box right up to the centre post. Private Pinkney again challenged and the enemy officer replied in English, 'Oh it's alright!' Private Pinkney however noticing his soft cap immediately called to the platoon and fired, killing the officer and the enemy were again driven off. Later in the day the enemy patrol was completely wiped out, leaving twelve dead and six prisoners.

The next part of the battalion to come under attack was the centre, held by Z Company, the post at Meunier House, was on the alert and observed a large enemy force, estimated at about thirty men. Later that afternoon another four prisoners were captured, this time by W Company, the Company Commander, Captain F Moore, wrote,

> At 1535 hours a party of Germans estimated as four, possibly six, was seen approaching our left platoon post at Helles House. They had come from a pill box at Grid V.14.b.9.0. On approaching, they noticed the machine gun on the right of our post and halted behind two tree stumps, pointing to it. Corporal Coyle covered one of the men with his rifle, when they saw him they turned to run away. He fired, dropped one, another put his hands up and advanced to our left post, where he was taken prisoner. The other two ran southwards and in passing our right post at Nobles Farm, were again covered and challenged, upon which they put up their hands and came in and were made prisoners. Meanwhile, Corporal Coyle and some men had gone out after these Germans. They brought in the wounded German, who was attended to by our stretcher bearers at the centre post, but died on his way to the Field Dressing Station.

Throughout 20 November there was heavy shellfire, later in the evening,18/Lancashire Fusiliers arrived and took over the line, the relief being complete by 2130 hours 19/Durham LI set off for the rear area, as they made their way out they came under shell fire. This caused some casualties in Y Company and one of their original 'Bantams' 19/724 Lance Corporal John Humphries was killed. Moving back to Siege Camp the battalion started a week of musketry training and range practice before relieving 14/Gloucestershire Regiment in reserve at Canal Bank. Here Lieutenant Heaton with one officer per company took a very large working party of 225 men to work for the Royal Engineers and the Royal Artillery.

At the beginning of December, they still occupied the position at Canal Bank, another large working party, of 220 men, under Captain Smith, marched to Kempton Park to work for the CRE. On 5 December the battalion came under the tactical command of 104 Brigade but were not called upon. The next day Lieutenant Colonel Greenwell returned from hospital and resumed command, Major Gooderson having handed over rejoined his own battalion of the Highland LI. For the next several days the working parties continued but on 9 December 19/Durham LI were relieved and all the working parties rejoined at Caribou Camp. They now began bathing and cleaning up and commenced training and recreation, only one move was made on 11 December to Road Camp, where they settled down for a good break. On 13 December the GOC 35th Division Major General G M Franks inspected the battalion, and after that they were left alone. They were brought up to strength with drafts from the base among them was 19 year old Fred Plows from Ilkley who wrote this letter to his sister Lily,

A Working Party carry dugboards across a shell cratered landscape. taken with a 'Box Brownie'.

> 27 Dec 1917. Pte F Plows 75058, 8 Platoon X Coy, 19th DLI, BEF
> Dear Lily
> I received your letter and paper dated 23 Dec today. You don't seem to be having a very fine time this Christmas but you are lucky to have three days holiday.
> George will be alright if he gets home. It will be nice for him to be at home the same time as Norman. As you say, George is very lucky. He sent me a letter, and said that he was fed up, but he does not know what it is like in the army. We had a decent time on Christmas Day. The food we got

X Company, 19/Durham LI.

was fine. You must be getting very short of food at home if you could not get mince pies and plum pudding. I saw a piece in the paper about Thwaites being killed. I wonder who will be next. There seems to be some one every week killed from Ilkley. We are alright just yet, as we are some way behind the firing line. I don't know when we are going into the trenches; we may stay here for some time yet. We have an NCO from Ilkley I think his name is Stapleton or something like that. I went to see him one day this week and he said he was some relative of Batty's in Middleton Road. I think there are four Batty's of the Dukes stationed near here, and there is sure to be someone from our place with them.

I must close now

From your Brother Fred

As Fred said in his letter, the Quartermasters staff ensured there was beer and food for Christmas and the majority would have seen at least one show by a Divisional or Brigade Concert Party. So 1917 came to an end for 19 Durham LI, in November they had been particularly unlucky, especially from the gas, but many lived to fight on into 1918.

THE 22nd BATTALION, PIONEERING AT PASSCHENDAELE

We left 22/Durham LI, located at Pioneer Camp, on 1 July A and C companies were at Swan Chateau, B and D Companies were still working on the right flank communication trench and C Company on the left flank communication trench. Owing to the nature of the ground a lot of sandbag breastwork had to be built up. A Company was employed building more accommodation at Swan Chateau. The next day A and C Companies changed over and during the day they came under enemy shell fire which killed Company Sergeant Major, James Woods and two other ranks as well as wounding six men. Over the next couple of days additional work was allotted to the battalion and each company had to provide a platoon to work on road repair. By July 8 the battalion was sending out small parties to work in the early morning, because of their small size they were left alone by the enemy artillery. Also this day a draft of thirty men arrived from the base, all of whom had previously served with 7/Durham LI (Pioneers), to receive so many trained men was a welcome addition to the battalion. A deviation in Hellfire Trench the communication trench previously constructed between the Menin and Zillebeke Roads had to be undertaken as the original trench was filling with water, it was to be 350 yards in length and to assist with the task the pioneers were allotted 100 men of 1/Wiltshire Regiment. On 13 July C

190

Company were sent back to a training area north of Poperinghe, where they underwent a course in light railway construction. The task on Hellfire Trench continued and three platoons of 11/South Lancashire Regiment arrived to assist in deepening the trench. During the day Captain W H Perkins rejoined the battalion fro England and took over command of A Company. Work practically ceased over the next three days, this was owing to the large amount of shell fire sent over by the enemy gunners, among which was a new type of gas shell, this attacked the eyes and nostrils and also caused vomiting in many cases, which rendered work impossible. Work was eventually recommenced on 19 July when it was found that the trenches that were to be worked on had been very badly knocked about and that progress would be impossible, however work commenced and Second Lieutenants W Sherriff and C Fosbrooke were both killed by shrapnel. This shelling, particularly the gas shells, slowed down the work on Hellfire Trench, meanwhile at Battalion Headquarters a small draft of sixteen men arrived, all of whom were returning to the battalion after being evacuated wounded. But these men didn't bring the strength up for as they arrived nineteen gas cases, including Second Lieutenant Roscoe, were evacuated. Orders came through from HQ 8th Division the battalion were to prepare to move and on 25 July they moved to Winnipeg Camp and by 1515 hours they were accommodated in wooden and 'Nissen' huts, A B and D Companies were in the camp, whilst C Company was located at Belgian Battery Corner and had progressed the light railway to the north of Zillebeke Lake, sharing the work with 7th Canadian Railway Construction Company. Further orders came in that on Y/Z night the battalion would move back up to Swan Chateau. It was at this time all the preparations were coming together and the British Army was going to recommence the

attack against the German Army in Flanders.

All was now ready for the British Army to deliver its great shock – unfortunately Mr Jerry was also ready to counter with another, The scheme seemed to be based upon a very rapid assault with one division passing through another and then the first through the second again in what was referred to as 'Leap frog.' At the same time field guns and field mortars were to advance to ever more forward positions and so maintain the creeping barrage ahead. All this was to take place on a wide front, many divisions being employed – this was a FIFTH ARMY show – we had the reputation of delivering "Hammer Blows." My company were detailed to clear felled trees known to lie across a road between the 2nd and 3rd objectives and to clear the way generally for the advancing artillery. As we should be just behind our most forward infantry and might fight with them, we took up one of our four Lewis guns, which we drew from Battalion HQ for the purpose.

Major Davidson wrote, recording his activities at this time.

Each Company of 22/Durham LI was ordered to work with one of the Divisional Field Companies, Royal Engineers. A Company, under Captain Perkins was to work with 490 Field Company, B Company, led by Captain Robson MC were to work with 15 Field Company and D Company commanded by Major T Davidson cooperated with 2 Field Company. At 0350 hours the Divisional Infantry went over the top, but they ran into a large number of concealed concrete pill boxes, although the leading troops got to the far side of Bellewaarde Lake and the second wave passed through, they came under observation of the Germans on the high ground at Westhoek, who called down artillery and machine gun fire on the attacking British troops.

At Battalion Headquarters reports came in that the work was proceeding quite well, although they were under considerable shell fire.

'The night before zero hour we moved up by a well defined track to 'Swan Chateau' and got into shelter there safely – another DLI company arrived almost simultaneously. Very big and numerous guns of ours were all around, these soon opened fire and continued firing hour by hour. Very soon

corresponding big stuff was retaliated and as Swan Chateau and its miniature 'lake' was exactly in the centre of their target we had a very thin time indeed. The other company lost its sergeant major, while both companies had six to ten men knocked out. A man who was badly hit was dragged inside the Chateau and a subaltern very pluckily volunteered to fetch assistance for him from a dressing station on the road 200 yards away. To do so he had to scramble over trenches and walls, through illuminating flashes and smoke, under fire all the way and back again. Shells of the calibre that were raining down on our area are very intimidating. I mentioned this youth in a report to the CO for I knew this was by no means a solitary brave act of his. He did not get any award – had he doe so and had an award been made once or twice before, it would have encouraged us all. After this restful night we marched forward one hour after dawn, I think zero hour for the attack was dawn plus thirty minutes.

We went forward in single file by the trench D Company had dug – the over land pipe laid for water supply was shattered from end to end. I doubt if one single pipe had escaped – here and there a bay or so had got it in the neck and thereby lay some infantry dead – hit on the way up. These we lifted out to lie on the top – others of us were to repair and maintain this main artery of communication. Until we reached our old front line we came under no fire except the big stuff still

An unidentified Sergeant stands on a diuckboard track across the Flanders swamp.

going over towards "Swan Chateau," and areas of that kind in the rear – these shells are readily identified by old troops and disregarded unless there is a certain increasing note – then' look out' you have only a second to get down... .

I halted the company while they were still in the trenches to have a look round. I could see that heavily laden men like ourselves carrying two handled saws, axes, picks and shovels as well as arms , would be terribly slow in crossing that embogged 150 yards – more over some might stick fast in it. Two hundred yards to the left a causeway crossed the bog and along it stood half a dozen chargers held by their grooms – I decided to cross there. We did so to march into a gassed area in which already crouched the Infantry of a division which was to 'leap frog' through the advanced infantry of the division immediately on the left of ours. So I was off our area – all these troops were wearing their gas masks and we had to assume ours too – however, it was important for me to pass the craters at Hooge on time. I endeavoured to get on; leading in my mask, after pitching head first into one or two shell holes I removed the mask to below the eyes and proceeded, as I though, on our course. After a while machine gun fire whistled about, but it seemed overhead and we paid no heed to it – I mean no obvious heed.

I began to lose my bearings, to miss expected landmarks. We emerged out on to higher ground beyond the gassed area. Momentarily we were protected by a heaped up breastwork like a redoubt – now quiescent and abandoned. We had been marching for well over an hour with only one very short halt. Under this breastwork I fell the company out for a moment so that I could go forward myself to explore. To tell the truth I feared to lead my company in single file under direct observation, round the corner perhaps at any moment to have machine guns opened up on us. Looking back I could see I was more than quarter of a mile too far to the left and judging by what I could remember of distances, in length I had about arrived. We were also due in ten minutes time at the summit of the Bellewaarde Ridge – when some few hundred yards along to our right I thought I identified first a cluster of shattered trees which had once surrounded Bellewaarde Chateau and then, O blessed sight! The little ornamental lake that had been in its park. As we crossed this little lake and the foundations of the otherwise vanished chateau we came once more under the unpleasant fire of black smoke shrapnel and half a dozen men were hit, none killed as I remember. Just here I encountered a lance corporal of the RE Field Company with whom we were to work and under whose command I was to take and receive orders that day. This very junior NCO had brought me a verbal order that we were late – twenty minutes in fact and must move up at once.'

This was how Major Davidson recorded the march up of D Company, to the position where it started work.

D Company soon got to work to clear the road; parties had already been told off to the various tasks, some two man teams to saw trees in half to make them easier to move. Other groups spread out along the road filling in craters, and all the while just over the crest was the roar of battle, machine gun fire and shells exploding, and most of the time a steady trickle of walking wounded making their painful way to the rear and the advanced dressing station. However having cleared the road to the top of the ridge they could go no further as to do so would bring them under German observation

A Company began their march up at 0715 hours on 31 July and were soon at work, just behind the Royal Engineers who were marking the track. The work proceeded satisfactorily but slowly. Captain W H Perkins reported the following,

'For the first two hours HE shell was falling heavily in the neighbourhood, but fortunately appeared to be aimed mainly into the valley on our right and into the neighbourhood of the craters on our left. Casualties were quite light and the Company worked very well. During the early afternoon enemy shell fire caused much less disturbance, although there was some interruption owing to machine gun fire, probably aimed at the ridge on our right front. The ground near Idiot Reserve Trench was badly cut up and progress there was very slow, but by 1800 hours the track was made good and was passable for light guns up to but not over Jacob Trench at about J.7a.2.6. An hour was then spent on improvements and settled down to draw rations and to rest in the neighbourhood of Idiot Support Trench. The men were fairly comfortable until rain commenced and before midnight they were all wet through. Just after midnight the line in this neighbourhood was occupied by a battalion of The Border Regiment, which resulted in a considerable scattering of the company and in still greater discomfort, as the rain still continued to be very heavy. At 0600 hours on 1

22/681 Private H Alnwick from Seaham killed in action 30 August 1917.

August an attempt was made to assemble the company and it was found that ten men, including one Corporal, were missing. The runners were set to find them, whilst the remainder set to work to extend the track to Ziel House and to affect such improvement as was possible along the whole line. The track which had been perfectly passable for light guns at 1800 hours on the evening of 31 July was now a perfect quagmire, owing to heavy mule and pedestrian traffic all through the night and morning.'

Having done as much as they could A Company received orders to move back to Pioneer Camp and set of at 1030 hours. The report supplied by Captain Robson, the Officer Commanding B Company was very similar,

'The Company proceeded from Winnipeg Camp to Swan Chateau, on the night 30/31 July arriving at the latter place at 0200 hours on 31 July. At 0700 hours a message arrived from OC 15 Filed Company RE giving instructions to proceed to Track 4 at a point just north of Zouave Wood.

An officer briefs his platoon for the task ahead.

> On arriving there at about 0830 hours, the company were at once allotted tasks, from the old British Front Line forward across the Old German Line. This continued throughout the morning and afternoon until 1830 hours. The enemy had been shelling all day, and progress was very difficult. Rain commenced about 1630 hours. At 0830 hours I was wounded through the left wrist by a piece of shell. About 1000 hours I left to proceed to the Dressing Station, leaving the Company in charge of Second Lieutenant L S Wood. Later Second Lieutenant L W Andrews was sent up arriving about 1600 hours and took over command of the company until the return to camp next day, Second Lieutenant L S Wood having been wounded in the course of the afternoon. The Company took shelter for the night in the Old German Line. Work recommenced the following morning at 0415 hours. The rain had continued without interruption from the previous afternoon; and the condition of the ground made the work of levelling very hard. The men were allotted tasks round the southern end of Chateau Wood and round the Eastern edge to the Westhoek Road. The work was completed by 0715 hours progress having been greater owing to the fact that the enemy was not shelling very much.

Major Davidson's company started on the tasks allotted and by 1400 hours the hostile small arms and machine gun fire was so great, that a number of men were wounded. When Major Davidson and the OC Field Company, Major Brown, observed an enemy advance, they decided to withdraw. Eventually as far back as China Wall owing to the fact that the tasks set could not be carried out owing to the enemy fire.

Orders came through on 1 August that 8th Division was to be relieved and arrangements were made with the Officers commanding the RE Field Companies for the pioneer companies to withdraw during the night. C Company were at this time still working on the light railway with the Canadians, but the other companies had already rejoined in time to leave Pioneer Camp and march to Halifax Camp where refitting and cleaning up commenced. On 4 August the Corps Commander, Lieutenant General, Sir Claude Jacob Commanding II Corps visited the Division and came round all the battalions including 22/Durham LI. The next day they moved again to Dominion Camp where they found accommodation in huts and tents. A party of one officer and fifty men were now moved to Lock Number 9 on the canal bank for the task of clearing the battlefield of unburied dead, the party was changed twice and the task lasted until 12 August when they rejoined the battalion.

At 0830 hours on 13 August the battalion moved up to Belgian Chateau to carry out tasks detailed by CRE 8th Division, Task A1, was allotted to D Company, constructing a double duckboard track to Inguana Lane and from there to Sexton House. Task A2 was allotted to A Company, constructing a double duckboard track South of Etang de Bellewaard to Sieben House and then forward. A Company were allotted to task A3, which was to work on improving the camp throughout the day and then to construct a duckboard truck from South of Etang de Bellewaard to Sexton House. The main part of the work was carrying up the duckboards and trestles, these were constructed by the Royal engineers at Acton Dump and carried up to Birr Cross Roads before the working parties arrived, which saved much time on the work.

On 16 August, 8 Division was ordered to attack again; the problem was that the leading battalions would have to get across the Hannebeek before they could get to grasps with the enemy. To achieve this 22/Durham LI were tasked with bridging the stream prior to the attack. Major Davidson's memoirs recall the events of the day quite vividly,

> No doubt it all looked moderately simple to Division, quite simple to Corps and no hindrance at all at ARMY HQ where maps wee studied. But we DLI thought otherwise. The CO was on leave and Major Mitchell commanded us. Together we studied the subject on the spot. I was asked to make a model of the area to scale, this I did on a sand basis confined in a frame of boards about 8'x 6' – it was rather fun making it and it showed as much detail as seemed useful or guiding. We came to the conclusion that two of our proposed bridges should as often as possible be set in line together making a twelve foot space – the centre or junction resting upon a cross piece calculated to spread the pressure widely. To do this we drew one hundred 'one man bridges' and two hundred trestles – to carry these two hundred men would be needed, with other details to act as guides, leaders etc. Corporals and Sergeants carried hammers and six inch spikes, we also had a few axes dished out. Then with ammunition reduced to 100 rounds per man, we were properly equipped for the job.

Three minutes before the Zero Hour fixed for the infantry, the DLI went very silently over the top in the first faint light of dawn and without confusion or shouting of commands, got to the swampy ground and laid these bridges upon their trestles – most of these bridges were fairly effective, but because of the depth of the slime, even more than because of its width, a certain proportion were less so. The work was extraordinarily well done in practically complete silence – our men were a picked lot, drawn from all companies, most of them the rather older men.

There was no advanced barrage and at Zero Hour two battalions of 23 Brigade went over the bridges with bayonets fixed, they advanced towards the enemy line and shook out into formation ready to attack, then the German Artillery opened fire most of it coming down on the area of the bridges. In anticipation of this barrage the pioneers had withdrawn slightly but were still stood by to maintain the bridges. In the swampy conditions not a lot of damage was done to the bridges unless they received a direct hit. However the attack ran into well sited German pill boxes, echeloned and able to support each other both in line and in depth. The Pioneers of 22/Durham LI remained in position repairing the bridges and assisting the wounded infantrymen who came trickling back from the fighting in front.

> 'Our stretchers, of which we had drawn the whole quota from battalion strength, were admirably employed by their bearers. These operations of Pioneers do not have the glamour of those charging with bayonets fixed, nor do they engender that hot blooded mixture of funk and fierceness which an assault upon the actual enemy position calls out. All the same the endurance and cold determination to remain for long periods under fire, without retaliation, takes a deal of supporting. But again no one received any award though the battalion was 'thanked' by the General of the Division.'

This was how Major Davidson ended his account of the Hannebeeke crossing.

It was now time for the battalion to be on the move again, consequently the pioneers of 47th Division, 4/Royal Welsh Fusiliers came up and took over the work being done by 22/Durham LI. On 22 August, C Company rejoined the battalion and a convoy of motor buses conveyed the whole battalion from Halifax Camp to the Caestre area, where they were accommodated in tents in an old internment camp. Here they were joined by a draft of five officers and 131 other ranks, a number of whom had served with the battalion previously. Time was spent overhauling equipment, cleaning up and bathing. Further orders came in to the effect that the battalion would move to Nieppe and take over from the New Zealand Pioneer Battalion. 22/Durham LI marched down the Bailleul – Armentieres Road and eventually reached Nieppe at 1115 hours on 26 August, the personnel of the battalion being accommodated in the empty houses of the small town, where a few die hard civilians still clung on to their homes. A and D Companies were soon at work repairing and maintaining two communication trenches, Ultimo Trench and Vancouver Avenue, that ran up to the line. A Company were on the left of the Divisional Front and their communication trench had been badly knocked about and required more work than that of D Company, where the trench only required general maintenance. Meanwhile B Company were employed on road repair and C Company on the tramway forward of Ploegsteert Wood. A further task was loaded onto the battalion by the CRE on 3 September, when they were told to provide a 'Divisional Drainage Officer and 1 Company of men to work draining the land, the task was given to B Company, but they had to wait for, 'Gum Boots Thigh,' to be issued in order to start work. Every morning the men marched out to a light railway siding and were taken up the line by train to their work. Each section of the line was repaired by an NCO and several men of the battalion. One night heavy shell fire fell on one section,

> 'One of our tasks was keeping the narrow gauge railway which was still employed at night to take up all manner of stores to quite close to the line, but this use of a steam engine became more and more precarious until at last, it was caught by a shell, tippled over pinning its driver below, in a shell hole, where the poor fellow was scalded to death. We made great efforts to extract him, but the engine was heavy, emitting scalding steam and shells continued to fall all around, adding greatly to the confusion and alarm. The section employed by us on this job of track maintenance only consisted of eight men under a corporal.'

So wrote Major Davidson, describing part of this task given to the battalion.

The work continued in the same way well into September, C Company worked with 8th Canadian Railway Troops, cutting, grading and laying a track through Ploegsteert Wood. Work was delayed on 15 September, when all carrying parties were diverted to carry gas for the Special Brigade Royal Engineers. On 19 September, one other rank, 22/159 Private William Scott, from South Shields was killed and Second Lieutenant H S Bruce was wounded. As the work continued on 20 September an enemy aircraft appeared over the battalion, it was engaged by British Anti Aircraft Batteries who opened a rapid fire on it. Two officers Second Lieutenants, J Williams and P T Marston, were wounded, whether by a bomb dropped by the aircraft or by and anti aircraft shell that came down and exploded when it hit the ground was uncertain. The unfortunate Second Lieutenant Marston died from his wounds later in the evening, at Number 2 Australian Casualty Clearing Station, to where he had been evacuated. On 22 September a large draft of 210 ex Royal Engineers reported to the battalion, none of whom had previous service in France, originally they were destined for 11/Durham LI and 20/Durham LI. This brought the strength of 22/Durham LI up to 1218 other ranks, but not for long, an order was received that an equivalent draft of 'Trained infantrymen', to be posted as follows, 120 other ranks to 19/Durham LI and 90 other ranks to 14/Durham LI. These drafts left on at 0600 hours on 25 September, when the entrained at Steenwerck for their new units.

As October started enemy aircraft were regularly strafing the communication trenches at night, the battalion machine gun section with their Lewis guns, set up six anti aircraft posts. Another task loaded on to the pioneers was responsibility for the drainage of the trenches where they were working. The month continued in the same fashion and they were still employed in the same way in November, when work started on duckboard tracks, one of which was to run rearwards to the Messines – Ploegseert Road. Also in November work started on the Support line, which High Command wanted finished before winter set in. All through these two months there was a steady trickle of killed and wounded men, which reduced the amount of effective men available for work. On 12 November the advance party of 3rd Australian Pioneer Battalion, arrived to take over from 22/Durham LI, who proceeded to La Blanche Maison near Bailleul. Major Davidson recalled the way they left the town where they had been billeted for two long months,

> We left Pont Nieppe with regrets – a war under those conditions might continue sometime without inconvenience. We set out at night, quite late at night, marching along the Route National, our boots on the pave echoing amidst the darkened houses. Our transport jolted and lumbered behind, our band was with us, but not playing out of respect to the sleeping friendly people we were leaving. Yet as we left behind the last of the buildings a dark figure stood silently with hand raised, offering us a blessing – it was the good village padre. So too he had watched all the young men of the town go.

The march continued northwards back towards the salient, the Second in Command, Major Mitchell and the Officers Commanding B and D Companies, Captain Robson and Major Davidson along with their grooms, were ordered by HQ CRE 8th Division, to ride on ahead to Ypres, to the Headquarters of the 3rd Canadian Pioneer Battalion, to take over the work being done by the Canadians. On 18 November the battalion entrained at Caestre Station along with units of 23rd Brigade and were carried to Brandhoek, on arrival they marched to billets in Vlamertinghe, where they spent the night, being joined by the Battalion Transport Section, who had moved independently by road, later in the evening. The next day they set off for Ypres, where Headquarters, A and B Companies found shelter in cellars near the station. C and D Companies kept going and marched on up to the St Jean area, where sandbag shelters became their new home. The transport Section was near Goldfish Chateau, between Vlamertinghe and Ypres. There was no rest however, immediately they were put to work on the duckboard tracks that led up to the forward area. Since they had last been here, the whole area had become one vast sea of liquid slime and filth, pock marked with thousands of shell holes and littered with the wreckage of two armies, broken wagons, dead horses and mules, field guns, rifles, tin hats and webbing and of course not far below the surface, bodies, English, Australian, Canadian, French, Belgian and German, in every stage of decomposition imaginable.

Through all this then the companies started work, C and D Companies on Number 5 Track, 600 yards of which had to be laid to link up with the forward portion now being constructed by 2nd Field Company, Royal Engineers. B Company worked on the repair of the plank road. Having had previous experience of the enemy aircraft employed in this area, the Lewis guns were deployed in an anti aircraft role in the neighbourhood of Gravenstafel. After three days Number 5 Track had less than 100 yards to go, in spite of very difficult conditions and the nature of the ground, the men had worked extremely hard. The main delay was caused by enemy artillery, which not only destroyed sections of the track that had been completed, but caused numerous casualties among the infantry, employed as human mules, to get the planks up to where they were needed. On 23 November, a carrying party from 23 Brigade lost almost fifty men killed and wounded in this way and no stores reached the point where they were required. A Company in the meanwhile were providing working parties in the back area in addition to carrying up trench boards and trestles to Number 5 Track. The work continued until the end of the month, each day bringing a mounting toll of dead and wounded, on 28 November, 22/411, Sergeant John Matthews, a resident of West Hartlepool, died of wounds and then two days later 22/367, Lance Corporal Joseph Brown, from Willington and 42877, Private Edward Henderson, a Haswell man, were both killed by shell fire, when a party from B Company were working on the duckboard track north of the Gravenstafel Road.

On the night of 1/2 December 32nd Division on the left of 8th Division were to attack the enemy held line, 25 Brigade were ordered to cooperate with this forward movement.. Accordingly work on the track ceased and B Company provided two platoons to act as escorts for any prisoners taken. C and D Companies were detailed to keep the routes clear. They were able to establish small dumps along the track; this greatly aided the swift repair of damaged sections. On 3 December 8th Division was relieved and went back for rest, 22/Durham LI, less D Company were retained in the Ypres area. D Company were sent back to rest in the Watou area. C Company started work on a new hutted and transport lines at the Dixmude Gate in Ypres. The work continued over the next few days, during which a letter of congratulations was received from the GOC 8th Division. C Company commenced work on the Frezenberg – Zonnebeke Road, draining it and laying metalling, they were assisted by men from 187 Labour Company, among whom were a number of Bantams, combed out of 19/Durham LI earlier in the year. From 10 December the shelling grew heavier and a lot of time was spent on repairing the tracks. On 14 December, D Company returned from Watou and C Company went out to rest. A shift system was put in place with six platoons working during the mornings, two platoons in the afternoon and only one platoon at night. Over Christmas, the Commander of VIII Corps, Sir Aylmer Hunter Weston, DSO, MP agreed that the battalion could reduce its work to two companies, this allowed as many of the men as possible to sit down to Christmas dinner.

> We were able to make great preparations for Christmas day. All the companies were to have roast pork, served with fresh leeks, subscribed for out of battalion funds. By placing a sheet of iron on brick supports and lighting a fire below we made a capital hotplate upon which carving took place – all getting a bumping hot plate full – even those served last. Those up the line got theirs later in the day. We officers were to assemble in a fine cellar at 1930 hours for a similar repast with one or two embellishments. Major Mitchell asked me to turn up at 1900 hours as he had a communication; this was news of my leave and a Senior Officers course at Aldershot – I was to leave next morning, and upon the Colonels order the news had been with held till then. A nice Christmas present... . My Pioneer days were over.'

Major Davidson, wrote as he prepared to leave the battalion.

The last few days of December 1917 were spent working in the mud of the Ypres Salient, B Company were tasked with cleaning out old German pill boxes in order to provide forward billets for the British infantry, Others were hard at work between Gravenstafel and Mosselmarkt. On the last day of the year the German Artillery put down a heavy barrage in the region of the Abraham Heights which delayed the working parties getting to their tasks. The last word for the year was a long message wishing all ranks good luck, for the New Year and exhorting them to better things in the future, from VIII Corps Commander, Sir Aylmer Hunter Weston, DSO, MP.

Now it is time to leave the Pioneers to see what 1918 brings.

Chapter Eight

1918 – The German Onslaught

'Backbone of the Empire, the old PBI'
WIPERS TIMES

F OR THE GERMAN ARMY THE COLLAPSE of the Russian Army in 1917 released large numbers of men who could be transferred to the Western Front. The danger for the Allies was that the Germans would breakthrough before the American Expeditionary Force arrived in numbers, as late as December 1917 there was only four American Divisions in France, a total of around 130,000 men. In late1917 with the Bolsheviks asking for an armistice it was practically a certainty that a large scale transfer of enemy troops to France would take place. By the end of December at least ten if not as many as fifteen German Divisions had been moved from east to west.

THE SITUATION IN FRANCE, JANUARY 1918

With the arrival of these divisions General Ludendorf was able to begin planning a spring offensive and eventually decided that it would be against the British.

Behind the British front politics was playing a leading role, the War Cabinet was arguing with the Army Council about reinforcements, Sir Douglas Haig was worried about the number of men arriving in France and also that the Germans might regain the initiative and attack in 1918. Whilst General Petain was proposing plans and insisting that the British Army should take over more of the line and at a conference in Boulogne on 25 September 1917 Lloyd George met M Painleve the French Prime Minister and it was agreed in principal that the British would extend their front. The French held roughly 350 miles against the British 100 miles; however the French Front was largely a quiet one. However on 10 January Lieutenant General Sir I Maxse's XVIII Corps, with 36th (Ulster) and 61st (2nd South Midland) under command, began taking over the sector opposite St Quentin from the French III Corps, then later in the month British III Corps, under command of Lieutenant General Sir R H K Butler, with 58th (2/1st London) and 14th (Light) Divisions, took over from the Groupement d'Ugny le Gay and French I Corps, the sector astride the Oise. The British were busy reorganising the defences and their army at the beginning of 1918, the front line defences were organised in three zones of defence, the Forward Zone, the Battle Zone and the Rear Zone, each was to be prepared and organised in depth, with lines of trenches – strong-points and machine gun emplacements. In view of the shortage of manpower the Rear Zone was only marked out and in a few places wired. After the battles of 1917 the British Expeditionary Force was woefully short of men, those reinforcements that were arriving at the front lacked training and their skill in musketry, in particular, was considered to be below a reasonable standard. The BEF had mainly trained for offensive action and therefore training for defence was urgently required. Furthermore the actual numbers that were arriving hardly replaced the losses of the previous year and almost all of the British Divisions were below strength. To get round the manpower shortage the Cabinet Committee recommended a reduction in the number of infantry battalions in each division from twelve to nine. This new organisation was objected to by the Army Council, who protested that the Army was accustomed to the twelve battalion division for

German troops with a light machine gun advance through a French village. Note the wrecked light railway engine in the background.

both tactical and administrative reasons and that the surplus of men made available would barely bring the other battalions up to strength. It was not as simple as it sounds because the orders did not disband one battalion in each brigade and send the men to the other three battalions. The new establishment decreed that no regular or first line territorial battalion would be disbanded the axe would fall on the battalions of the New Army and some second line territorial units. This created a logistical nightmare for the staff as many battalions were camped a long way from their new divisions. In some divisions as many as six battalions were to move, amalgamate or disband. The reorganisation began on 29 January and was final completed on 4 March just seventeen days before the Germans attacked. In all 115 Battalions were disbanded, 38 were amalgamated and seven were converted to Pioneers. The Pioneer battalions in each division had not escaped the reductions either for they were reduced from a four company establishment to a three company one. The Empire divisions however retained their twelve battalion organisation. The Canadians broke up their 5th Canadian Division in England to supply the men required, the New Zealanders with one division in France broke up 4 New Zealand Brigade also in England, whilst the Australians were able to maintain drafts for all five of their divisions. These changes would affect all of the Durham battalions as will become clear as the story unfolds.

18/DURHAM LI, THE KAISER'S BATTLE

New Year's Day 1918 brought no rest to 18/Durham LI, with the ground to hard for digging and wiring, the working parties set to converting sump holes into fire bays, thus turning Tired and Tommy communication trenches into defensive fire trenches. A few heavy shells fell near Tunnel Dump at about 2200 hours and the left sector battalion 'stood to' for about an hour. The next day the same working parties were ordered, but there was little success, then on 3 January, 12/East Yorkshire Regiment came up and relieved the battalion. The enemy Forward Observation Officers were on the alert and as 18/Durham LI made their way out down Tommy and Ouse the communication trenches leading to the rear, they came under a heavy artillery barrage. Fortunately there were no casualties and by 1800 hours they had taken over York Camp at Ecoivres. Here the usual cleaning up and re-equipping began, then over the next week training at all levels took place, even though there was a considerable amount of snow falling, the men went out on the ranges and practiced musketry. The final tactical exercise was an imaginary counter attack on Arleux Post, which had supposedly fallen to the enemy.

> We were in the Brown Line, in German dug outs on New Year's Eve, it was snowing and pretty cold. We were having a game of cards till 12 o-clock when our guns were going to let the New Year in. About 10 minutes to go when the old lad on the other side put a big one over, too near to be comfortable and made us all get off the floor, not waiting for another, we went into a deep dug out and had a sleep. Got relieved two days after, having been in the line six days. Jerry did not strafe much except for blowing in one or two dug out entrances. We went back to rest billets at Ecoivres where we stayed till the 14th. Had a very decent twelve days out of the line, had several football matches, the principal one being with the 5th Squadron Royal Flying Corps after a very close game we were beaten by 1 goal. We had several concerts and picture shows. The weather was very cold and frosty.

So wrote Fred Poole, in his small diary recording his time with the battalion.

By 1200 hours on 15 January the battalion were moving back into the Red Line, two companies between Willerval South and Willerval North and the other two companies holding the Arleux Loop, where they relieved 13/East Yorkshire Regiment. That night heavy rain fell and a thaw set in, this had a dire affect on the state of the trenches, working parties were put to work shoring up the sandbags and sides of the trenches. These working parties continued for two days and then the battalion took over the front line from 18/West Yorkshire Regiment. The trenches forward of the Henin – Levin line were impassable and to carry out the relief 18/Durham LI had to get out of the trenches and go over the top, the relief started at 1700 hours and was completed by 2000 hours with out any casualties. A and D Companies were holding Arleux Post, C Company, under the command of Second Lieutenant Oldfield, were in Oak Post, whilst Lieutenant Armstrong with D Company were holding Tommy Post. The next night a patrol of one officer and twenty five men went out into No Man's Land in the direction of Lone Tree; their mission was to discover if the series of consolidated shell holes and a post in the German Front Line were occupied. The patrol returned to report them unoccupied. While the patrol was out, one NCO and six men went out and repaired and extended the wire between Oak and Arleux Posts. Over the next two nights patrols went out to try and ascertain if Chump Trench was manned by the enemy. On the night 21 January, the patrol was in No Man's Land, when the moon broke through the cloud, in the bright moonlight they were unable to get close enough to the enemy wire and so, were forced to return. The next night the patrol went out through Arleux Post, again in bright moonlight they proceeded into No Man's Land, but this time they came under heavy fire from Chump Trench. The last day of the tour was wet but very quiet and then at night 15/West Yorkshire Regiment came up and relieved the battalion.

Went in the line again on the 14th. Very wet day. Got up early about 3 o-clock, relieved in daylight, went up on the light railway through Arras and Roclincourt to daylight railhead, the communication trench there is called 'Tired Alley', which was rightly named. Pretty quiet during relief, observation being very poor. Had a very good time in the line, just a few strafes to keep things going. After the first few days it got muddy and wet, in places it was knee deep in water and slush. Just before being relieved it cleared up and got pretty lively. Had to look after No 1. Relieved after twelve days and got leave to England.

This was how Fred Poole remembered the first tour in the line for 1918.

At Ecurie, Major Ince MC assumed command of the battalion, which for the next four days provided working parties for the Area commandant and another large party, worked on 'Tired Alley' forward of 'Long Wood'. On 27 January they moved from Ecurie to Ecoivres, into York Camp once again. Here equipment inspection was the first thing on the agenda, which was followed by reorganisation of the companies into three, platoons each. The first day ended with Box Respirator drill. The next two days were given over to tactical training and following the pattern set the last time it ended with the battalion counter attacking an imaginary enemy at Arleux Post.

It was now that the disbandment and moves mentioned earlier mentioned took effect in 31 Division. In 92 Brigade the four 'Hull Pals' Battalions were reduced to two, the two junior battalions disbanded and 11/East Lancashire Regiment, the 'Accrington Pals' transferred in from 94 Brigade. In 93 Brigade, 15/West Yorkshire Regiment amalgamated with 17/West Yorkshire Regiment to become 15/17/West Yorkshire Regiment, 14/York and Lancaster Regiment, the 'Second Barnsley Pals', transferred in from 94 Brigade, whilst the two 'Bradford Pals' battalions both disbanded, for 18/Durham LI, there was no change. In 94 Brigade the remaining battalion, 'Sheffield City' and 'First Barnsley Pals', both disbanded. Thus 94 Brigade ceased to exist. To bring 31 Division back up to three brigades, three battalions of the Guards Division, 4/Grenadier, 3/Coldstream and 2/Irish Guards were transferred in and became 4 Guards Brigade.

Having reorganised the battalion prepared to go back into the line, this time into Close Support in the Arleux L1 Sector. This was another daylight relief, entraining at 0800hours in Ecoivres they were carried up on the light railway to the 'Daylight Railhead', from where they proceeded on foot to the Red Line and Arleux Loop by 1230 hours the relief was complete, no sooner were the East Yorks out of the line, than the enemy artillery opened fire, both 5.9 and 4.2 cm guns being used. They managed to score twelve direct hits on the sector held by 18/Durham LI, then later between 2100 and 0200 hours they dropped gas shells along the Red Line. The next day the shelling continued, Sapper Dump, received one shell every three minutes between 1300 and 1600 hours, but the remainder of the front was quiet. Next day a draft of seven officers and 143 other ranks arrived from 14/Durham LI, which was one of the battalions that had been disbanded. On 8 February the enemy shelled Arleux Loop South with high explosive and gas shells, whilst another draft of forty four men reported to Battalion Headquarters. Three days later the battalion moved up and took over from the West Yorkshire Regiment in the front line, this relief took an exceptionally long time, commencing at 0300 hours it was not completed until 1200 hours. In the early hours of the following morning at about 0315 hours, a large enemy patrol came through the British wire and set up an ambush on the parapet just north of the junction of Beer communication trench and Brandy Trench. Here they lay in wait for any unsuspecting Durham to come along. The next fellow to pass that way was the leading man of a three man ration party. However even though it was early morning and he was on a routine boring task, he was wide

German sign warning of gas in Armentieres.

awake! He spotted the Germans and rushed down Beer CT and reported to the Officer Commanding Arleux Post. Meanwhile the other two men, with a container of food slung between them, had fallen a little way back, they too spotted the enemy and dashed past them to the next post, here they delivered the rations and raised the alarm. OC Arleux Post sent out a patrol of one NCO and six men and a sharp fight ensued in a position just south of Beer CT. The enemy were forced to retire, leaving the NCO wounded and one man 18/1398, Private, Alex Crawford, dead. The enemy must have removed his tunic for identification for the following day it was found in No Man's Land by a patrol from the battalion. Another patrol found an enemy rifle and some bombs and a hat. At this time the battalion snipers were active along the battalion front, claiming hits on enemy soldiers at Fresnoy Park and in front of the wire in front of Fresnoy. The snipers and observers, watching the enemy line reported seeing movement and timber being carried up to the front line, and a listening post reported the sound of a very large amount of timber being dumped. On 16 February, the enemy artillery shelled Tunnel Dump and Sucerie Road between 100 and 1600 hours then later that evening the same places were treated to a dose of gas shells, which were also fired on Arleux Loop. The next day 4/Grenadier Guards relieved three company's of 18/Durham LI who were back at the railhead by 1530 hours, the remainder of the battalion being relieved in the evening, reached the railhead at 2130 hours. The battalion was then transported to Bray, where they arrived in camp at 2300 hours.

Fred Poole having arrived back in France from his leave wrote,

'Went back to Bray for rest, stayed there a short time and marched to Manicourt [Magnicourt] well behind the line for month's rest, where we had to do some training etc. Had a very decent time

well out of the way of the war, had some very good football matches. After staying in Manicourt a fortnight moved on to Bajus about three kilometres away. A very small village, stayed in the Mayors house in a very decent little billet. Got on very well with the people, pruned the vines and fruit trees for Madame. Got plenty to eat and drink from the old lady.'

As Private Poole had recorded the Battalion spent ten days at Bray training and then on 28 February, they became GHQ reserve battalion at Magnicourt. On 1 March Lieutenant Colonel Cheyne relinquished command of the battalion he had command for over eighteen months and command passed to Lieutenant Colonel Carter MC, KOYLI, who had lately commanded the disbanded 18/West Yorkshire Regiment. The billets in Magnicourt were reached after a long and tiring muddy march, and the condition of them was very poor indeed. After more cleaning up and training, large working parties were sent away to assist the RE Tunnelling Companies, these were being employed on trench repair. On 11 March the battalion proceeded to Bajus and Frevillers, where they took over billets from 13/York and Lancaster Regiment, A, B and HQ Companies were allocated billets in Bajus, whilst C and D companies found accommodation at Frevillers. A couple of days were spent doing more training and then they started practicing ceremonial drill. On 20 March a large Brigade Ceremonial Parade was held. Major General R Wanless O'Gowan, who had commanded 31st Division since 24 August 1915, had come to say farewell, on handing over command of the division to Major General R J Bridgford CMG DSO. That night the word was received to 'stand by to move.'

In the very early hours of 21 March along the front of the THIRD and FIFTH Armies, German patrols were active in No Man's Land, there was a ground mist, in some places a thick fog, which covered them and made observation for the British quite difficult. However most were driven off by British patrols, but then at around 0430 hours, the storm broke. A massive artillery barrage, high explosive and sickly gas landed all along the Front Line. It hit the full front of FIFTH ARMY and V, IV and VI Corps of THIRD ARMY. Slightly to the north, the FIRST ARMY around the La Bassee Canal and Armentieres were also shelled. The enemy had made his preparations very well

and the barrage hit many important points, the British battery positions and telephone exchanges, headquarters both divisional and brigade, railway stations and many cross roads all were under fire and communication with the front line all but broke down. At 0940 hours the enemy assault came and many forward positions were quickly over run. The code word 'Bustle' was sent to those troops held in readiness in the rear, this meant, 'man battle stations.'

Having had a warning order the night before, when 'Bustle' arrived at the HQ of 18/Durham LI, they were ready. The battalion was issued with extra ammunition and paraded at 0715 hours on 22 March and marched to an embussing point between Berlea and Tinques.

18/436 Pte Fred Brown from Chester le Street was killed in action 25 March 1918.

'After being at Bajus about a fortnight ready to move at 12 hours notice, got orders around midnight to get ready for the line. Got all ready, drew extra ammunition and moved off early in the morning while all the people were in bed. About 23 March marched into Tanks [Tinques] where the buses were waiting to take Div where they were wanted.' Recalled Fred Poole.

A long column of London Omnibus' met the various battalions of 31st Division and transported them through St Pol, Frevent and Doullens to Pommier, at the last named orders were received to continue on to Blairville, where they arrived at 2100 hours. After debussing, packs were dumped and the battalion, less first reinforcements and the nucleus, re-boarded the busses and were carried up to Boisleux St Marc, here they again debussed and this time marched into the

ARMY Line near Boyelles. The 31st Division had moved up behind the 34th and part of 59th Divisions who had been making a fighting retreat since the morning of 21 March. The 31st Division was deployed with 4 Guards Brigade on the right and 93 Brigade on the left. 93 Brigade had 15/West Yorkshire Regiment on the right and 13/York and Lancaster Regiment on the left with 18/Durham LI in support. 92 Brigade were in reserve. 18/Durham LI established Battalion Headquarters in a sunken road.

As far as I remember from debussing that night we immediately moved forward leaving packs etc at this point. A Coy had Captain Dick, Myself, Second Lieutenant Fletcher and Second Lieutenant Brown, leaving Lieutenant Welford with the details. After a decent march up the Brigade assembled at a certain cross roads and where emergency rations were issued and Colonel Carter took to sleep, wrapped in a blanket on the roadside. I can remember distinctly kicking this parcel and much to my surprise and his annoyance discovered it was the CO. after a short rest the Brigade moved off in the following order WYR – Y&L and ourselves. In the early hours of the morning we took up a position in some very broad trenches, towards midday we moved a little further back and took up position in a sunken road which I can remember was just west of the main road.

Is how Captain Alfred Everatt told the story to Colonel Lowe in April 1920.

The next day 23 March was quiet for the battalion, no rations had come up the previous night and the men were ordered to break open their 'iron rations' which were replaced later in the day. A reconnaissance of a position known as 'Maison Rouge' was carried out by B Company officers and orders were issued for a move there but this was later countermanded. During the day two men were wounded by shell fire, and later they were ordered to side step south and occupy another section of the ARMY LINE, once 1/Welsh Guards had taken over 18/Durham LI moved along the Arras – Bapaume Road to the new position. The new position ran East – West across the Arras – Bapaume Road with Hamelincourt directly west of the position. A and D Companies were west of the road and B and C Companies on the east side together with Battalion HQ, who were in a cabin in a sunken road. But another move was ordered and they eventually had all companies on the east side of the road. D Company left this position and in the afternoon to dig a position for the West Yorkshire Regiment, running south from Judas Farm, to where 13/York and Lancaster Regiment held the line. They returned that evening. During the night of 24 March, 18/Durham LI, which had been subjected to some shelling, relieved 2/Irish Guards

Standing is 18/1215 Lance Corporal E C Bell from West Hartlepool who was awarded the Military Medal for his work manning a Battle Block for the Assistant Provost Marshall 31st Division. The identity of the seated soldier is unknown.

placing two companies on each side of the Arras – Bapaume Road, but an unfortunate incident occurred when Brigade Major Ramsden ran along the trench and ordered men to vacate it, taking their rifles and leaving their equipment. Some of the men formed up to move – much to the disgust of a nearby Scots Guards Officer – fortunately the Durham's, B Company Commander, Lieutenant McConnell was able to follow up the Brigade Major and put things right, whilst Second Lieutenant Everatt got A Company 'stood to'. Apparently the Brigade Major was badly shell shocked having just survived being blown up by a heavy artillery shell.

That night information came through that the enemy had broken through. Consequently slightly different positions had to be taken up to meet this new situation. The next order received was for the battalion to relieve 13/York and Lancaster Regiment in the front line, but this was soon cancelled and the next morning they were ordered to take up a position East of Courcelles, along the railway to prevent an enemy advance from Gomiecourt, where they had broken through.

Recalling D Companies position, Second Lieutenant Quentin Cooper wrote to Colonel Lowe in March 1920,

> We had moved from the Green Line to the right, something over a mile I should say though of the distance I am uncertain; until we came to a railway embankment running I think I am right in saying down to Achiet-le-Grand. We marched down the railway embankment on both sides of it, half the battalion on the side next to the Boche, half on our side with scouts out. One of our planes appeared at intervals in the light of the moon between fleeting clouds and dropped two bombs on us. The first burst in the front of the column next to the Boche, killing I believe some ten men, all stragglers who had joined us at various times. The second burst some distance in front of our column on the inside of the embankment, hurting no one. We passed a team of horses lying close under the embankment, lying dead and in pieces, the work of some very powerful shell or an aeroplane bomb, a question which excited some debate. Passing these we came to a level crossing over which we went diagonally turning left. We then strolled about, Colonel Carter and the other officers on the Boche side of the cutting, endeavouring to get the hang of affairs. All were in low spirits, bad news of the retirement further south having made us feel rather fed up. However the Colonel remarked cheerily that the war was not lost yet and we set to work acting on his orders to fashion a few out post pits, about one hundred yards in front of the embankment, in which we put a few men, not more than ten or fifteen, with one Lewis gun. Wilson was in command of them. The remainder of the company dug ourselves in along the lip of the cutting immediately behind a spare hedge which ran along it clearing spaces in the lower part of the hedge to see and shoot through. During the night one of Wilson's men shoot a Boche officer through the head and captured his servant who was out with him. They were evidently out patrolling and had crawled quite close to our outposts. The man was hit in the ammunition pouch and was much alarmed, Kamerading speedily. The officer was shot in the head poor chap and as good as dead. The next morning we retired from the cutting soon after dawn and made our way back to our own artillery past some old gun pits a mile to the rear or more.

On the morning 26 March at 0830 hours, orders were received to move back in support of 13/York and Lancaster Regiment, who were to dig a line from A.3.d.9.8. to S28 central and that the battalion should retire to the high ground about Moyenneville. These orders should have been received at midnight, allowing the battalion to move in the dark. The late receipt meant that the battalion had to move in daylight. So off they went B Company leading, A Company next and then D Company, coming under heavy shellfire as they went. The shelling wounded Lieutenant Colonel Carter and he had to be evacuated. Command now fell to Captain Dick, OC A Company and he received orders for a general retirement, to be made to a line roughly between Adinfer and

Ficheux. The battalion were to fight a rearguard action and conform to the units on either flank. Although they were in touch with 13/York and Lancaster Regiment, but no contact was made with 15/17/West Yorkshire Regiment. They commenced to retire leaving half off C Company behind to cover the withdrawal. Indeed C Company led by Captain Stafford and Lieutenant Allbeury put up a stiff fight and gave a good account of themselves, the Lewis guns of two platoons taking heavy toll of the advancing Germans as they came out of Gomiecourt, until they ran out of ammunition and were forced to withdraw. Early in the action Captain Stafford was wounded and he too was evacuated, with a bullet in the knee. As they retired they came to trenches held by The Guards Division roughly 500 yards behind where they had started, and retired through them. Captain Dick and the Adjutant went to Brigade Headquarters and spoke with the Brigade Commander, who thought that the orders to retire should not have been given. He therefore ordered the two battalions to return to their original lines in Moyenville. A reconnaissance party consisting of Captain Dick and the Adjutant 18/Durham LI, the Officer Commanding 13/York and Lancaster Regiment and 93 Brigade Intelligence Officer, went forward of the line held by the Guards and as they moved towards Moyenville they came under heavy rifle and machine gun fire. The enemy having realised that the British had pulled out of Moyenville had quickly filled the void and rushed a large number of men into the village and reached the top of the ridge to the south west, from this position they were able to enfilade the West Yorkshire Battalion. It was obvious that 18/Durham LI and 13/York and Lancaster Regiment could not cross the crest of the ridge in daylight and the Brigade Intelligence Officer went back to seek instructions from the Brigade Commander.

> On arrival in Moyenville we manned the best set of trenches I had seen in the district and thought at last we should make a show. At this point Colonel Carter was wounded, Captain Dick taking over the battalion and myself A Company. Shortly after the Y+L's came upon the scene and we again moved further back this time in artillery formation to a place called Valley Wood. We got in touch with the Brigade here after having lost them temporarily who at once ordered us forward in the direction of Moyenville and we dug in behind the Y+L's. Towards the afternoon we came under 'heavy' light gun fire and two of my No 1 Lewis gun team were killed, Davies and another man. That night I was ordered with my Company to report to the CO Y+L's and had orders to dig a trench round Moyenville, the instructions I got left me half an hour in bright moonlight with ninety men and two officers a task impossible in the face of it. The CO Y+L decided with me and I reported back to the battalion. The following day I took A Company up too reinforce the Y+L's taking over their right front with two platoons, here we had a few casualties including CSM Warwick. Captain Dick came up from Battalion HQ to become Liaison Officer. After two long days here we were eventually relieved by 15/West Yorkshire Regiment who could only muster one company with no Lewis guns, they taking one of my company's. However, eventually later in the evening the WY's and the Y+L's were relieved by 2/KO Yorkshire LI. I reported the relief complete that same evening and the following day at dusk the battalion moved off in pouring rain for Bienvillers, before eventually going to Frevillers. This is just about as much as I can remember.

This was how Captain Alfred Everatt recalled the events of those two hectic days in March 1918. [He has 2/KOYLI arriving earlier than they did.]

In the early hours of 27 March, Captain Dick was taken from the battalion and the Brigade Commander sent a message that the next senior officer was to assume command. Thus, to the Adjutant, Captain F G Stone fell the responsibility of commanding the remnants of the battalion. As Captain Everatt explained they were ordered to dig a trench round Moyenville, but this was cancelled by the OC 13/York and Lancaster Regiment, Captain Braithwaite and those members

Hier links
ein ge-
schützfüh-
rer von
unsere
Batterie

'On the left
is the fire
position of
my battery.'

Gef. Engl. gehen zum Sammelplatz

A German gunner watches as English prisoners of war march back to the collecting point. He wrote on this card to his parents "English Gefangen gehen zum sammelplatz."

of 18/Durham LI returned to the start point. It was now that Major W D Lowe MC came up and assumed command of the battalion. B Company had become somewhat detached from the battalion during the preceding days and Lieutenant McConnell and Second Lieutenant Turnbull brought the company out of action without passing through the battalion lines, but had rejoined by the morning of 28 March.

That morning found what was left of the battalion dug in on either side of the Boiry St Rictrude – Ayette Road. 13/York and Lancaster Regiment had moved up into the line with the Guards Division and A Company 18/Durham LI sent up two and one half platoons in line with them. Twice that morning, the Guards and 13/York and Lancaster Regiment were attacked, on the second occasion the enemy got in, but were ejected at bayonet point, during a counter attack, when D Company 18/Durham LI went up in support of 13/York and Lancaster Regiment. Later 2/Irish Guards reported that 13/York and Lancaster Regiment were falling back, but they were advised that this was D Company 18/Durham LI taking up new positions. Major Lowe went up to look at the position and found the line thinly held by the Irish Guards so he ordered C Company to fill in between 13/York and Lancaster Regiment and 2/Irish Guards, the Irishmen moving up to make room for them. With both A and C in the line a company from the East Yorkshire Regiment was sent up to Major Lowe as a counter attack force. The East Yorkshiremen dug in about 200 yards behind the Durham's in a dried up river bed and so spent a reasonably quiet night.

Fred Poole recalled this time with a long detailed passage in his diary,

The boys were ready to move up the line, the guns were lighting the skies up and everything looked as if somebody was in for a rough time. Felt a bit tired after the long march at both ends of the long bus journey, had been on the go for twenty two hours. It was very dark and being in a strange place it was rather a job finding our way. We marched back a bit, those of us who were left behind, got down in a field and went to sleep. Next morning we were stiff with cold, had a good breakfast and got ready for lines at night. Had a long march up, got shelled in different places on our way up.

Found ourselves somewhere near Monchy, plenty of shelling. Did not really know what was in front or what strength Jerry had, but soon got to know when Jerry came over. We were in a hole with Jerries all round and a very heavy shelling. Had pretty rough time of it – shelled by our own and Jerries artillery. Our gunners were not to blame as we were in such a mix up with Jerries behind us.

The Guards division and a Brigade of Guards with our Division would not retire, although losing very heavy. Our machine guns doing good work among the Jerries, firing over our heads. It would be about the 26th when it got that hot that we had orders to retire during the night. Just before retiring our guns opened up on us and rained shrapnel on us. Helped us out rather quicker than we intended to go. Retired through a village where a black kitten followed us for a long way. Our aeroplanes were flying about during the night to bomb any enemy movement as we were as we were halting for a rest near a station. Some of the lads resting on the railway, others laying down on the road side. Our airman kept flying round us, we could not see him but he loosed his bombs, several all together, killing and wounding several of our lads. I sat on the road and did not get hit. We got the wounded away and went along the railway to a position about a mile away on the railway. A good position, everybody needing a sleep. We were allowed to have an hour or two but were wakened up by shrapnel and high explosives. Got orders to retire again as we were surrounded, if we did not look sharp Jerry having captured some troops on our flank. Retired best way we could not to let Jerry see us. His balloons spotted us and we got strafed all the way. The Colonel getting wounded and several more men also. Retired in artillery formation, got shelled all the way with heavies and dug in on some high ground near an aerodrome. Things were quiet that day but next morning Jerry attacked several time, being beaten back every time and losing very heavy. We lost rather heavy, mostly wounded. A continual stream of wounded leaving the line getting shelled on the way. I had some very close shaves but never got hit, only by pieces of earth. Kept Jerry back till relieved by another division near Ette, raining rather heavy when relieved. Marched back to Bienvillers very tired after eight days. Got shelled in billets at Bienvillers but nobody got hit. Rest for onne night and marched back behind the line where we rested another night and marched all the next day. Then we got another bus ride to Freivilliers [Frevillers] a place not far from where we started for the trenches.

It is interesting to compare the word of the officers and that of the private soldier, the officer's state 'two bombs' were dropped, whilst Fred Poole quotes 'several'. Whilst in Captain Everratt's account, the relieving troops seem to arrive two days earlier than they did.

The relief of 18/Durham LI was complete at 0340 hours on 30 March, having handed over to 2/KO Yorkshire LI and 11/Border Regiment from 97 Brigade, the battalion moved off in pouring rain, with instructions to be through Monchy au Bois by 0530 hours. That morning they arrived in Bienvillers where the rest of the day was spent resting. Instructions were received thet the battalion was to parade at 1500 hours to march to Souastre, but these instructions were cancelled and replaced with orders to clear the village by 0400 hours and march to Ivergny. As Fred Poole has already stated, on 2 April at Ivergny the battalion was met by a convoy of motor buses and transported to Frevillers. The next ten days were spent refitting, cleaning up and training replacements for the specialists that had been lost during the previous weeks.

Whilst 18/Durham LI were out of the line the German Army launched the next phase of their offensive operations. On 9 April a massive barrage fell on the British lines in the north between Armentieres and Lens. The heaviest barrage fell on the Portuguese, who were attacked under cover of fog. At least one Portuguese battalion fought on when all ammunition was spent and fought with the bayonet until totally overrun. Despite gallant stands by various units the German Army pushed forward and once again the British Expeditionary Force was in retreat. The 31st Division was now ordered back into the line and orders were issued to the various battalions of the Division.

At 1230 hours on 10 April 18/Durham LI was ordered to move to the embussing point at Tinques once more, the buses were supposed to take the battalion to Lillers, but on reaching that place they continued on and eventually stopped at Vieux Berquin.

When the battalion arrived at Vieux Berquin the CO reported to 31st Divisional Headquarters, which had been established in the Brewery, here he was ordered to move to the village of Outtersteene, where the battalion arrived at about 1700 hours.

The move north and up to the line was recorded by Fred Poole,

About 8 April, after having a few days rest we got orders to move back to the buses at Tanks [Tinques], landed there about 1400 hours where we had to stay till the Div got in the buses, about 300 buses in the convoy. A lot of old London buses and motor lorries. Travelled all night. Did not know where we were going but noticed the country was very flat when it began to break daylight. Several of the buses broke down. The one I was in ran into a ditch at the side of the road and threw us all out, most of us were asleep and we gathered ourselves in a field next to the road, waited a short time to see if there was any chance of pulling it out, but it could not be done, so we continued to march after the convoy, after walking a few kilometres another bus picked us up. Marched on to another village passing lots of refugees wwho had to leave their homes and everything behind on account of Jerry breaking thrugh. Some people were leading cows, others had wheel barrows with a few things they had packed in a hurry, others with children hanging on their aprons, several were sat at the roadside, some crying, while others gave us a cheer as we marched past.'

18/159 Private Joseph Southern from Bishop Auckland was killed in action 12 April 1918.

On arrival at Outtersteene, A Company moved slightly forward and established an outpost line beyond the eastern edge of the village. The next morning the Commanding Officer, Major Lowe was summoned to a conference at Brigade Headquarters in the Convent in the village of Merris. Around 1600 hours the CO returned to Battalion Headquarters with the news that the battalion had been ordered to attack on two enemy positions in conjunction with 13/York and Lancaster Regiment, and when these positions had been taken to continue on to a position in line with the Farm Du Bois. The attack was to be supported by a machine gun barrage, but by the time the Company Commanders had been briefed there was little time to spare as the attack was to commence at 1930. Messages came in giving the times and extent of the Artillery barrage, but at 1910 hours the 13/York and Lancaster Regiment began to advance. C Company 18/Durham LI conformed to the attack of the Yorkshiremen, whilst the remaining companies of the DLI conformed to C Company. D Company on the left of the attack, advanced somewhat slower than the others, but C Company advanced over easy open ground. At La Rose Farm, 18/506, Sergeant George Gillespie from the little village of Quebec in County Durham, mopped up and took a number of German soldier's prisoner. At the other end of C Company attack Second Lieutenant Arthur Freer won the Military Cross for his part in the attack at La Becque,

'His initiative and resolution in mopping up a farm and some houses, which were garrisoned by the enemy, gave a magnificent example to his men. Later, in spite of a harassing machine gun fire, he materially improved the situation by a thorough reorganization of the company'.

Meanwhile Second Lieutenant Seymour found an enemy heavy machine gun which he managed to bring back into action against its previous owners, but when they came out of action it had to be left behind owing to a lack of manpower. C Company advanced so fast they passed straight through the first objective and went on to the second objective. D Company reported that they were in touch with troops from 74 Brigade on the left, but then some time afterwards reported that the men of 74 Brigade were pulling out, saying that they had been relieved. This left a large gap on the left of 18/Durham LI and to cover it all the companies were ordered to reform and extend their fronts. C Company was unable to carry out the order as they were in an open position and to do so would incur heavy casualties. They therefore proposed to carry out the order when darkness fell.

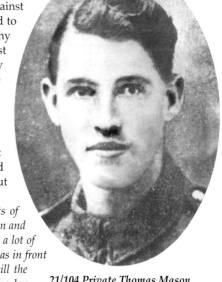

Towards night we got ready for the line, still meeting lots of refugees on the road. It was getting dusk when we got in position and counter attacked straight away, taking a village and capturing a lot of prisoners, which was useful giving us information as to who was in front of us and what numbers we were up against. All went well till the next morning about 1100 hours. Got up, after an hour or two lay down; found a cow in a field not far away. I went and milked her, getting a jug full of milk, a few bullets came pretty near but seemed

21/104 Private Thomas Mason from Darlington was killed in action 12 April 1918.

only stray shots so continued the good work. No rations came up so ate our iron rations. Found a hen house, full of hens which had been fastened in, waited a short time to see if they would lay, but there was nothing doing, so killed a nice plump one, got the feathers off and boiled it. Found some seed potatoes and boiled a pan full, when things were about ready for the troops, got word that Jerry was massing for an attack. Had to leave everything and stand to.

This was how Fred Poole recalled the attack on the village and the start of the German attack.

At around 0730 hours on 12 April, runners from A, B and D Companies arrived at the battalion headquarters to say that the enemy were massing in front of them, at the same time the same message was received from C Company, by telephone. Another message, this time from Second Lieutenant Freer with C Company, stated that 13/York and Lancaster regiment on his right flank were falling back, and that a large enemy patrol was advancing through Grand Beaumart. He was holding on, but fifteen minutes after 13/York and Lancaster Regiment retired, he was forced to do likewise.

D Company held on the longest, but, having inflicted heavy casualties on the enemy, they too were forced back once 15/West Yorkshire Regiment on their left flank fell back.

B Company too inflicted casualties on the enemy, but had to conform to the retirement of the other companies. As they withdrew the battalion was forced to leave three badly wounded officers behind, Second Lieutenant's Leonard Peart, William Wilson and John Long, all of whom died from their wounds. The companies fell back to the line of the previous night's first objective, which they held for a while, but once again with the flanks exposed they had to fall back. As they did so, they were heavily shelled by the British artillery. Behind this position ran a river, the Rau du Leet and here the CO and Adjutant attempted to form a line, the companies being told to hold the line of the road running along the Rau du Leet. The attempt to form a line here failed as most of the men were already behind the line so another attempt was made to form a strong point near a cemetery. However this message did not get through to all companies. D Company Commander held the line of Rau du Leet with fifteen men north west of Maison Blanche and B Company with remnants of 15/West Yorkshire regiment held on near the cemetery, holding up the enemy main body long after the bulk of the battalion had retired. A new line was established along a railway line and a quick reorganisation took place, 15/West Yorkshire Regiment were placed on the right, in the centre 13/York and Lancaster Regiment and 18/Durham LI on the left. At this stage there was only about 400 all ranks in this position, which was held for over an hour, until 15/West Yorkshire Regiment reported that their right flank had gone and the enemy were across the railway. 18/Durham LI split into two, the right half battalion commanded by Major Lowe held their position, whilst the left half, led by the Adjutant, withdrew fifty yards and turned facing east and then covered the with drawl of the right half. They were now under fire from farm buildings 300 yards to the south, where the enemy had set up a machine gun position. The right half battalion covered the withdrawal of the others, who set up along the north side of the Bailleul – Outersteene road facing south east.

The whole of this period was written up in his diary by Private Fred Poole who wrote,

It looked pretty rough for some of us as Jerry had broken through on both flanks and practically surrounded us. Looked to me as if the whole fatherland had broken in on us, machine guns firing on us from all sides and the ground we were on being very flat could get very little cover. Got orders to retire which we did as best we could, sections giving covering fire while the others retired to continue firing while the others fell back. Considering the heavy machine gun fire we had to go through very few got hit, while we had targets which were very hard to miss.

It was very exciting and plenty of sport. We tried to hold on after retiring a short distance in a corn field, making little holes with our entrenching tools to get a little cover, making the holes as we lay down under very heavy machine gun fire and some shelling. Finding ourselves nearly surrounded again on our flanks. Had order to retire again, Jerry closing in on us and leaving us very little space to get out Jerry being not 200 yards away and some behind us had to retire a good distance. I ran up against a rather deep stream and could not get over and on looking round saw the Jerries close on me. A thick hedge held me up, a thing which I have very seldom seen out there but I had struggled through somehow and landed in the water, bullets pouring through the hedge. I think it partly saved me as I got across the next field without any direct fire, but on climbing up a railway embankment at the other end it looked as if I would stop a bullet as the bullets were sending up soil and hitting everything but me. Still, I could not help but smile the way they seemed to miss. On getting to the other side of the railway I found several there who were keeping up a good fire on the Jerries. I was dead beat when I got laid down. On looking up the Jerries were still coming on, fired all my ammunition away, my rifle getting very hot, got up to find some more and got two bandoliers nearly full from chaps who had been killed or wounded. On getting down to it again one of my mates fell back, shot through the chest, killing him right out. We succeeded in holding Jerry up for a time causing him very heavy losses. We lost very few, a few odd ones being killed and several wounded. There was not many of us left, the machine guns having fired all their ammunition and the rest of us had not much left. Jerry seemed to have taken cover as we could only see odd ones which sniped at us. It seemed to quieten down for a time till a couple of machine guns opened up behind us. They must have got right through on our flank. We had nothing else to do but retire. The fire came from a farm so we all opened out on it, sending the tiles on the roof flying. It seemed to do some good as the firing stopped for a time and let us retire. We lost a few in retiring but had to be careful to get away, it looked as if we could be surrounded, but our Colonel said 'stick it to the last', which we did and succeeded in getting out of the ring all right. The darkness helped us as it was just beginning to get dusk and observation was not very good.

It was now that Major Lowe and the Officer Commanding 13/York and Lancaster Regiment, Major Nutt, held a conference and decided to try and work North and North West, and try and find 93 Brigade Headquarters in Merris. With an advance guard, flank guard and rear guard out they made their way behind hedges and after moving around 400 yards, they came upon 15/West Yorkshire Regiment and their Commanding Officer, Lieutenant Colonel Tilly late of 18/Durham LI. Another conference took place and it was decided that the remnants of the three battalions should report to 33rd Division defending Meteren. Consequently they joined with 18/Middlesex Regiment and took over a number of rifle posts facing South East and began improving them. The night was quiet and they held the position taken up but throughout 13 April these positions came under heavy artillery fire. That night patrols were sent out to search a wood to the front, which was found to be clear of the enemy and another patrol of eight men led by Sergeant Dickenson established contact with the Queens Regiment of 19 Brigade, thus restoring touch all along the line. On 14 April, Lieutenant Colonel Tilly was killed by a shell splinter and Major Lowe took over command of what was left of 93 Brigade. At 0630 hours on 15 April, C Company 5/Tank Corps came up in an infantry role and took over from the battalion, who having been relieved, marched to the village of Borre, where they reported back to Headquarters 93 Brigade. Here they were warned for further operations and the battalions of the brigade were reorganised as companies, becoming known as 93 Composite Battalion, which was commanded by Lieutenant Colonel W D Lowe, who had just been promoted.

Over the next two days they worked on the Hazebrouk defences and at one stage were detailed to relieve an Australian battalion, although the Commanding Officer went forward and reconnoitred the position to be taken over, these orders were cancelled .

On 19 April they moved again to the North West of Hazebrouk, to the village of Le Grand Hasard, where they were joined by the battalion details and two drafts who had come up from the base area. On 20 April there was time for reorganisation back into the original brigade and to allocate the new men to the companies, but no time was allowed for rest, the next day they were ordered forward to fill a gap in the line. They went forward and joined with B Company

18/260 Private W A Dodd from Ryhope he had been transferred to the Machine Gun Corps and he died of wounds on 28 April 1918.

Number 4 Battalion Tank Corps. D Company went into the front line and A an B held a strong point at Petit Sec Bois with orders that it must be held at all costs. C Company was in reserve, carrying wire for the front line. Throughout this time the enemy were shelling very indiscriminately with gas shells, and their aircraft were actively bombing targets in the back areas. During the night of the 23 April a patrol, consisting of one NCO and five men went out to look at some houses in No Man's Land, but were unable to find any evidence of enemy activity. This patrol was repeated the following night when some enemy soldiers were seen coming out of a haystack, but they were to far away to do anything about. C Company went up to relieve D Company and both companies laid about 150 yards of a barbed wire belt in front of the battalion position. Then at 0445 hours on 26 April an officer and twenty men went out to try and rush the house where the enemy had been spotted, the accompanying barrage fell to far behind the house and alerted the enemy, who were in strength with three heavy machine guns, which drove the attacking party back and the attempt failed. Later that day the Officer Commanding and the Company Commanders of 1/Border Regiment came up to organise the relief of 18/Durham LI the following day. During the day there was heavy shelling around the Regimental Aid Post and Battalion Headquarters, then at 2130 hours men of 1/Border Regiment arrived and began taking over the positions. This relief took a long time and it wasn't until 0330 hours that 18/Durham LI were clear and able to march back to a tented camp near Sercus. Placed on one hours notice to move the battalion began cleaning up and resting. The next week was spent training and digging defences, each day two companies carried out training and two went out to work, this went on until Sunday 5 May, when Church Parades were held and then on 7 May work was cancelled owing to heavy rain. On 9 April orders were received to relieve 2/Australian Infantry that night, so at 1545 hours the battalion moved to the embussing point on the Wallon Cappell – St Omer road. The convoy moved of at 2030 hours and eventually arrived at a point 600 yards North West of Caestre, where the battalion debussed. They eventually moved off at 2330 and marched to Fletre, where they were met by guides and led into the support system North West of Meteren, where they completed the relieve of the Australian battalion. Joining the battalion at this time was Second Lieutenant Arthur Borrell who kept a small diary of events at that time,

> Ordered for the line and posted to 18/Durham LI, left Etaples for the line at 0645 hours on 6 May. Travelled to Burgette via St Pol and the enemy shelled the station just after we arrived. On 7 May went through Gas tent and then visited a magnificent church in Aire. Sent up to the Corps Reinforcement Camp near Cirus and in the evening visited an estaminet, then later the battalion where I met several officers and the Commanding Officer, later dined with Kitchen of C Company. On 9 May joined battalion and was posted to D Company and travelled up to the support line near Meteren, the relief was complete by 0300 hours and we were shelled on the way up.

In this position 93 Brigade was disposed with two battalions in the line, 15/West Yorkshire Regiment on the right, 13/York and Lancaster Regiment on the left and 18/Durham LI in support. On the Brigade left were the Australians and on the right the French 160th Infantry Regiment, with its 1st Battalion in the line and 2nd Battalion in support. Captain Dick of 18/Durham LI went to the French Regimental HQ as a liaison officer and at the point where the two nationalities joined liaison posts were established. The next week was fairly quiet as both sides were drawing breath for the next round at night digging was done and wire was laid out in front of the trenches. On 21 May they went into the front line, where the battalion was active in patrolling and then on 24 April the battalion was relieved by 7/Seaforth Highlanders, the battalion marched to Caestre where they were met by motor buses and they were transported to Heuringhem where they debussed and marched to billets in the village of Campagne. For the next three weeks the battalion carried out training, particular attention being paid to musketry and a number of inter platoon and company competitions. This led up to a full scale battalion attacks through woods.

By 18 June they were once more employed on working parties in the line near Morbecque. The orders were received to relieve 1/Lancashire Fusiliers in the reserve line behind Grand Sec Bois, with A Company detached under command of 13/York and Lancaster Regiment to hold the Swartenbrouch Defences. B Company were then allocated to 15/West Yorkshire Regiment and moved up to Petit Sec Bois, C Company moved into the positions vacated by B Company. Meanwhile D Company took up positions around the Farm La Promenade. On 22 April orders were received to relieve 13/York and Lancaster Regiment in the front line left sub sector. This was owing to two companies of 13/York and Lancaster Regiment being withdrawn to practice an attack on the enemy held Ankle Farm. Between 24 and 26 April there was some shelling by the enemy, both gas and high explosive, more posts were taken over on the left when 15/West Yorkshire Regiment were relieved to go out to practice for an attack on La Becque, which would follow up the attack of 13/York and Lancaster Regiment. During the night of 26 June the front line companies left the trenches and lay down behind the parados, in order to make room for the two companies of 13/York and

Lieutenant A C Borrell joined the battalion on 6 May 1918.

Lancaster Regiment who were about to launch their attack. Two platoons of C Company, Numbers 9 and 11 Platoons were ordered to form a defensive flank linking up with the York and Lancaster companies. Zero hour was planned for 0030 hours and the party advanced in small columns slightly in the rear of the York and Lancaster second wave.

The British barrage opened up and the party occupied some pre dug posts and began digging in. The barrage passed over some German positions which opened up at close range. Captain H Hitchin DSO, MC, MM, and Second Lieutenant W Alleubury, organised parties to tackle these positions. In one a light machine gun and three men were captured and although they had thrown hand grenades at the advancing Durhams, they did not put up a hand to hand fight. Immediately another German post opened fire and Captain Hitchin was wounded. By 0045 hours the left post was in touch with the right of 13/York and Lancaster Regiment. Two success lights were fired in the air and the same signal was sent by buzzer to Battalion Headquarters. Captain Hitchin made his way to the Headquarters of 13/York and

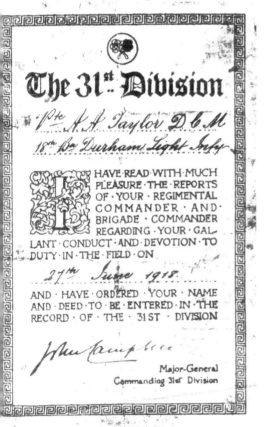

31st Division Card of Honour for 9938 Private A A Taylor 18th Battalion.

Lancaster Regiment and reported that the flanks were in touch with each other and he then made his way back to 18/Durham LI headquarters and reported the same. The next day to conform to the attack of 15/West Yorkshire Regiment, five small columns were formed to advance in alignment with the West Yorkshiremen. The advance achieved complete success and met little opposition. Those of the enemy that stayed in their positions were shot or bayoneted in their shell holes. During the attack Sergeant H Goldsborough showed great gallantry, having led his Lewis gun team to capture his objective he then carried on over the Becque and into a field of standing corn, where he located an enemy machine gun post. He rushed the post, captured the guns in it and accounted for the teams. His actions undoubtedly saved many casualties and allowed the consolidation of the position to carry on unhindered. Another leader showing great leadership skills was Second Lieutenant Arthur Everatt, who skilfully organised the consolidation and sent back valuable reports to Battalion Headquarters. During the next night, 30 June the battalion was heavily shelled with gas and high explosive as they moved sideways to relieve 15/West Yorkshire Regiment.

It is now time to leave 18/Durham LI and return to 19/Durham LI.

19/DURHAM LIGHT INFANTRY, FIGHTING ON IN FLANDERS, BACK TO THE SOMME

On New Year's Day 1918, 19/Durham LI were still in the Ypres Salient, behind the lines training, resting and preparing to go back into the line.

Fred Plows was able to write to his brother serving with the Royal Flying Corps at Farnaborough,

Dear George...

We are still getting along alright; we have a very easy time just now. In the morning we go for a run. After that I go to a Lewis Gun class which lasts until dinner time and then we have finished for the day. The food we get is rather scarce but is very good. I don't know how long we shall be before we go into the firing line. The worst of this place is that we can't go out and buy a decent feed. All we can get is eggs and coffee. There are lots of coffee houses, but one gets fed up with coffee without anything to eat. The YMCA hut is the same, only the coffee tastes like soap. I was sorry to hear you were not so well, but the leave was worth the sore feet; and a rest will be alright. I must close now

From your brother, Fred

Then two days later he was writing to his sister Lily at home in Ilkley,

Dear Lily

Thank you all at home for the parcel which I received last night. It came in fairly good condition and it could not have come at a better time, as bread was scarce and I was without anything for tea when the parcel came. I don't think that you could keep me warm. We have plenty of clothes and each of us has a leather coat. When we first arrived here we were given a pair of mittens and a scarf. They were a present from the people of Durham. The scarf was fine but the mittens were too large, but as I already had a pair that did not matter. I think our rest is nearly over. We expect to go into the firing line next week. It will not be very nice but we will have to make the best of a bad job. We were very lucky to get with the battalion when they were having a rest, so we can't grumble now we have to start work. We are still having very cold weather out here. You seem

78358 Private F Plows from Ilkley was killed in action 21 March 1918 according to the Army, however, the battalion did not move south until 22 March.

to be having it like winter at home.

I must now conclude with kind regards to Mother and Father

Yours Truly

Fred

Fred didn't have to wait too long to move up the line, for on 8 January that move was made, when they relieved 6/London Regiment in the Canal Bank area, leaving Proven they were transported by light railway up to Boesinghe and from there marched forward, HQ, Y and Z Companies going to a camp at Turco Huts and W and X Companies to Wilson's Farm. The Companies at Turco Huts provided working parties for the Royal Engineers and Divisional Pioneers, whilst the two companies at Wilson's Farm worked for 255/Tunnelling Company RE. The Quartermasters stores and the battalion details remained at Red Chateau and the Transport lines were at Bridge Camp from where they took rations up the line nightly. The working parties lasted until 18 January when the battalion assembled at Bridge Camp, prior to moving into the front line. On 21 January they took over as the right front battalion in the Westroosebecke Sector from 12/Royal Sussex Regiment who were part of 39th Division. At this time the front line in the Ypres Salient was just a series of defended posts, mainly in shell holes that weren't too water logged. There was no actual line of trenches, the company and platoon headquarters being established in captured enemy pillboxes, each of which was given an identifying name. The position taken over was held with two companies in the front system, with one in support and one in reserve. W Company, commanded by Lieutenant Waugh held eight posts on the left front; the right front consisted of ten posts under the command of Captain Smith with X Company. In support near Varlet Farm was Z Company led by Captain Heaton MC and back in reserve was Y Company under the leadership of Lieutenant Jopling MC, who were established in and around Albatross Farm, with one platoon holding Inch Houses. These positions were held for two days and then an inter company relief took place with Z Company taking over from W Company and Y Company exchanging with X Company. Whilst the battalion was in the line, Second Lieutenant C Fox and twenty seven men of the battalion details were ordered up to join the 106 Brigade wiring party at Hilltop Camp. After two more days sitting in the middle of the crater fields of the salient, 4/North Staffordshire Regiment arrived to relieve the battalion, who made their way back to Hilltop Camp, where they became the Brigade reserve battalion, which meant they were to provide working and carrying parties. On 29 January they moved forward into the Poelcappelle Sector and completed the relief of 17/Royal Scots by 2145 hours. Battalion Headquarters was established at Hubner Farm, but the line was held with three companies again in series of posts. On the right, W Company held Bray Farm, Bamff House and Vacher Farm along with six associated posts. In the centre X Company were responsible for Berks House and Burns House and another six posts. Whilst on the left front X Company held Shaft House, Oxford House and Unnamed Pillbox and a further six posts. In reserve was Z Company at Winchester House with one platoon at Inch Houses. This platoon at Inch Houses was relieved by a platoon from 4/Worcestershire Regiment on the night of 30 January, and rejoined Company Headquarters at Winchester House.

On 1 February 18/Highland LI took over the Poelcappelle sector and moved

Back to brigade reserve where by 2130 hours they had relieved 4/North Staffordshire Regiment in the Corps Line. This position was held for three days and then they went further back top a position known as California Dugouts and X Company to Hilltop Camp. It was now that the reorganisation of brigades from four battalions to three battalions took place in 35th Division. In 104 Brigade, 20/Lancashire Fusiliers (4th Salford) and 23/Manchester Regiment (8th City) were both disbanded and 19/Durham LI were moved to the brigade from 106 Brigade. In

105 Brigade, 16/Cheshire Regiment (2nd Birkenhead) and 14/Gloucestershire Regiment (West of England) both disbanded and were replaced by 4/North Staffordshire Regiment from 106 Brigade. This latter battalion had replaced 17/West Yorkshire Regiment (2nd Leeds) who had left the division to amalgamate with 15/West Yorkshire Regiment in 31st Division. This left 17/Royal Scots (Lord Rosebury's) and 18/Highland LI (4th Glasgow) in 106 Brigade, to bring this brigade back up to three battalions 12/Highland LI joined from 15th (Scottish) Division. The disbandment of other battalions also affected the battalions of 35th Division and 19/Durham LI were brought back up to strength by a draft of ten officers and 200 other ranks from the newly disbanded 14/Durham LI.

By 10 February they were moving back into the line this time in the Langemarck Sector where they relieved 17/Royal Scots in the left front sub sector with Battalion Headquarters located at Egypt House. They were only in the line two days before being relieved by 18/Lancashiire Fusiliers and moved back into support. At the start of this tour each company had left one officer, two NCOs' and twenty men behind, these formed a large raiding party which commenced training for a raid planned for late in February or early in March. The objective of the raid was to kill or capture the garrison of some of the enemy's posts at a position known as 'The Huts', in the Langemarck Sector, at the same time secure identification and information and when that was done destroy the posts. There was to be a heavy artillery barrage as well as one by the 35/Machine Gun Corps firing on fixed lines. The raiding party was to move up as close to the barrage as possible and when it lifted at Zero + 10 the posts were to be rushed. Between Zero +25 and Zero + 45 the raiding party was to withdraw. The party was to be lightly armed, with rifle and bayonet. Only ten rounds of ammunition in the rifle and twenty in the pockets was to be carried and no equipment except a box respirator. The steel helmet was to have a white line painted on the front and back for recognition purposes. Each man was to have piece of paper in his pocket, with Number, Rank and Name and Durham Light Infantry but no battalion number on it. There was also a detailed instruction for the disposal of prisoners and the handing in of documents and information. Captain Smith, Officer commanding X Company was tasked with laying out a white tape line as a jumping off point and providing guides from a position known as Vee Bend to the jumping off point. He was also to provide a covering party which he was to put in place himself.

While the raiders were training 19/Durham LI went back to the front line this time to the right front sub sector where they relieved 17/Lancashire Fusiliers the relief being completed by 1935 hours on 14 February. Battalion Headquarters were at Souvenir House, Z Company at Millers House, Y Company at Taube House, with W Company at Olga Houses and X Company at Double Cotts. On 16 February 12/Highland LI relieved the battalion and they moved back to Huddleston Camp where they started work in the Battle Zone under the CRE after a week of this they again moved back to Bridge Camp where they carried out training and recreation until the end of the month. Although there had been a steady trickle of wounded over the last two months there had only been three fatalities, 375825, Private Wilfred Hobson, from Leeds, who died at the end of January and on 15 February, 17778, Corporal Jacob Robson, from Gateshead, along with, 19/404, Private Thomas Mould, of Washington, who died from his wounds on 13 February.

At the beginning of March the battalion was once more ordered to take over the left sub sector at Langemarck and by 2200 hours they had successfully relieved 4/North Staffordshire Regiment, Battalion Headquarters being at Pascal Farm. Z Company had taken over at Colombo House and here on 2 March they managed to capture a German soldier. At 0315 hours on 5 March the long planned raid took place. At 1600 hours the previous evening the raiding party assembled at Ney Cross Roads and the Commanding Officer, Lieutenant Colonel W B Greenwell spoke to the officers, who handed in duplicate nominal rolls of those men taking part in the raid. Two parties of stretcher bearers were put in place, the first at the unnamed pillbox near Angle Point and the second at the pill box known as 5 Cross Roads. There were several amendments to the original instructions, the main part being that the raiders would report back to their own companies at the end of the raid, rather than to battalion headquarters. One additional item was that hot tea laced with rum was to be available after the raid.

At the beginning of the raid, when the barrage opened up, the Germans manning 'The Hutts' withdrew back to their own main line, so that by the time the barrage lifted and the raiding party rushed the position there was no one there. A counter barrage came down and must have caused mayhem and confusion among the raiders, Second Lieutenant G L Hounam, a Platoon Commander in X Company and three men were wounded and one man, Sidney Plumpton, a nineteen year old, Private, from the Albert Hill area of Darlington, was killed. It was now that two of the party showed a great deal of bravery and devotion to duty, 15751, Sergeant W Dixon, a resident of Old Penshaw, and a young Newcastle man, 70587, Private J Pearson, carried the wounded out under fire. Sadly the young officer, who hailed from Sunderland and was only 21 years of age, died from his wounds later. Both he and Private Plumpton now lie side by side in Cement House Cemetery, Langemarck, not that far from where the raid took place.

The following night 17/Lancashire Fusiliers came up and took over the front line and 19/Durham LI went back to support positions, Headquarters was established at the 'Pig and Whistle' Langemarck, whilst the companies were established as follows, W Company at Gruyterzale Farm, X Company at Langemarck, Y Company at York House and Z Company at Eagle Trenches. By 2030 hours the relief was completed without incident. Two days later 18/Highland LI came up and 19/Durham LI moved back to Bridge Camp at Elverdinghe becoming Brigade Reserve, they then became Army reserve and were placed at twenty four hours to move. Working parties were sent up to the Battle Zone to work for the Royal Engineers. On 11 March they were placed at twelve hours notice to move. The German attack was expected any day – but where they would strike was uncertain. In the north, at Ypres, 19/Durham LI practised manning the Army Line in the Battle Zone. Company training was taking place and over the next

week or so the battalion carried out training daily. The men seem to have been unable to get many letters away at this time and Fred Plows had to tell his relatives that, 'This week our officer told us that we were not to say when we were in the lines, or when we were having a rest. We will be able to get all the news on a Field Post Card soon. Hoping for the end of this job soon'.

As has been seen in the previous section in the early hours of 21 March the Germans attacked the FIFTH and THIRD ARMIES, with the main thrust on the Somme. In Flanders the 35th

A German Storm Division moves up to the front.

Division received orders to move south on 22 March. In 104 Brigade, 19/Durham LI received orders that W Company were to move to Peselhoek Station and act as the brigade loading party. Then at 0915 hours on 23 March 19/Durham LI marched to the station and entrained at 1300 hours. The train slowly steamed south and at 0300 hours on 24 March the battalion detrained at Corbie, from where they marched to Sailly le Sec, where they were met by a convoy of buses, which carried them to a point 1000 yards west of Bray, where they arrived at 1145. At this point orders were received to march up to Maricourt and report to 104 Brigade Headquarters. On arrival the battalion was ordered up to the Maricourt support line 600 yards East of Maricourt, with Battalion Headquarters in the Maricourt Defence Line. During this time the battalion only had one fatal casualty; nineteen year old Fred Plows was hit in the head by a bullet and killed outright. It wasn't until 26 April that any positive news was received, a short article in the local newspaper told the story, under the heading 'PRIVATE PLOW'S DEATH PRESUMED',

> *From information received during the past week there is every reason for believing that Private Fred Plows, Machine Gun Section, Durham Light Infantry, has been killed in action. He was the youngest son of Mr and Mrs Arthur Plows, 2 Grosvenor Terrace, Bridge Lane, Ilkley, and up to joining the Army on reaching military age was in the employ of Mr William Lawson, Plumber of Brook Street, Ilkley. Private Plows was in his 19th year, and had been in France since December last. About a fortnight or so a comrade from the Keighley district wrote home stating that his 'pal' had been shot through the head and killed, and the news was sent on to Mr and Mrs Plows. Nothing more was heard until last week, when his company officer wrote, stating that Private Plows had taken part in the heavy fighting during the German offensive and was missing. Last Saturday morning, Air Mechanic George A Plows, the brother of Private Plows, who is stationed at Farnborough, received more definite information from a very unexpected source. This was in the nature of a letter from an Australian Non Commissioned Officer, who stated that he had buried a British soldier shot through the head by an enemy bullet, on whose body he had found the address portion of a letter sent by 1st Air Mechanic G A Plows Farnborough, England, which he now forwarded to the person named, in the hope he would be able to identify the dead soldier and inform his parents. The address was the top part of a letter Air Mechanic Plows had sent to his brother, which he at once forwarded to his parents. No official information of any kind has yet been received.*

Fred Plows is recorded as dying on 21 March but this has to be a mistake as the battalion was still in the Ypres Salient, but he must have been the first casualty after moving south.

Having spent a quiet night in the support line, the next morning orders were received to move up to Talus Wood, where they would come under the command of 106 Brigade. Battalion Headquarters went on ahead and reported to Brigadier General Pollard, Commanding 106 Brigade and were told they were under his immediate command. The companies moved independently to Talus Wood, by the time they arrived, at 1530 hours, the enemy had launched an attack and had driven in part of the line. 19/Durham LI were ordered to make an immediate counter attack and restore the position. The attack was quickly planned with a two company front, one in support and the fourth in reserve. The two front companies moved off in two waves and advanced over 1000 yards under a storm of shell fire. The leading company halted and waited for the second company to arrive, at this point they established a strong firing line and then fixing bayonets advanced with great dash and drove the Germans back. One Lewis gun in particular, killed a lot of the enemy as they retreated. By the time the officers established control and the men were taking cover they were over 200 yards further than the line that had been lost.

In the early hours of the morning word was received from the GOC 106 Brigade that it was his intention to withdraw towards Bray. The reserve company formed a screen to cover the withdrawal and formed the Brigade rearguard. In order to get the rearguard away safely it was divided into two parties, A and B. Party A set off across country towards the main road. When it reached the road it moved down the road to the Carnoy cross roads. Party B set off down the valley to Carnoy and when it reached the village, moved to the cross roads and linked up with Party A once again. Having reformed as a company they marched down to Bray and rejoined the battalion, which by now had come under command of 104 Brigade once more. A number of officers and men had particularly distinguished themselves during the counter attack and the withdrawal, Captain K Smith, Captain H Heaton MC, Second Lieutenant's W G Dyer and H R Cunliffe, Corporal A Burt, Lance Corporal W Marsden and Privates J Scott, J Bowditch and A Ridddle. Indeed Arthur Riddle a Lewis gunner was responsible for many of the enemy soldiers who were now lying dead, and when the company withdrew he volunteered to cover them and was the last man out.

When we first went up two or three waves of Germans were coming up and they were piling up in front of our position and we never shifted. We stopped there and fired all the time, the lads were going there with their rifles and I had my machine gun. The Lewis Guns did terrific work. I was too young to realize the horror of that kind of work, but it was a job we had to do. I felt early on that I hated Germans but it wasn't until we were retreating on the Somme and I was asked with another chap to stay and keep them back. The other chap was killed and I was left there holding them back, giving the others time to get away. I had to wait until night time to ease my way back. On the way back I came across a German Officer in the trench, I was there with my Lewis gun and he was sitting there. He looked terrible, he had a wound in the groin, I suppose I had done it earlier on because they had been creeping round trying to stop my post from firing. I looked at him and I got no hate. He looked at me and pointed at my water bottle and said, 'Wasser, Wasser'. I took my water bottle off and gave it to him, he had a good drink and nodded, but I had to go, to get back and I left him. When we were retreating on the Somme we were leaving behind all sorts of equipment and I remember the French coming out of their cottages and cursing us.

Having reached Bray, the battalion received orders to continue withdrawing and were ordered to take up a line along the road running due west from Buire-sur-L'Ancre. It took until 2000 hours for the battalion to reach this position and then W and X Companies were pushed forward to hold the line of the railway running South West from the village. Here they settled down for the night, which passed quietly without any major incidents. The next morning X Company were ordered to move forward across the river and to take up positions in the village of Treux with one platoon deployed to a wood on the high ground South West of the village. One platoon was pushed up to the Eastern edge of the village and the other two were held back in reserve. In these positions they were heavily shelled throughout the day bu there was no infantry attack. The following morning at dawn the expected infantry attack commenced, the enemy obviously hoping to surprise the defenders. In this they failed completely and Z Company was sent up to relieve X Company in the village. X Company then moved up in support of the platoon on the high ground. Later Y Company came up in close support. All day long the enemy artillery was very busy and the village was under a constant bombardment, but in spite of this the position was held until 15/Sherwood Foresters came up at dark to relieve the battalion. This was completed by 2230 hours and 19/Durham LI went back to rest in a quarry behind the main positions. They spent a quiet day here and on the night of 29 March they relieved 17/Royal Scots along the railway line, from a point 1000 yards East of Buire-sur-L'Ancre to a point 1000 yards South West of Dernancourt. All four companies were along this line, with one post from each company pushed forward, down to the line of the River Ancre. In spite of being heavily shelled during the day the

20/376 Sergeant E W Brown from Tindale Crescent near Bishop Auckland, having been wounded with 20/Durham LI he was killed in action 29 March 1918 with 19/Durham LI.

battalion had no casualties and by 0130 hours on 31 March they had been relieved by 51/Australian Infantry Battalion. Having been relieved 19/Durham LI moved to La Houssoye, where 104 Brigade were in reserve. On arrival the battalion rested and then began cleaning up after a hectic week, during which they had the following casualties,

Second Lieutenant E Walton – killed. Lieutenant W Legat and Second Lieutenant R Coke-Harvey and H Womack, wounded. With Lieutenant and Adjutant, E Parke and Second Lieutenant H Cunliffe, both wounded but remaining at duty. Among the men there had been thirty five, killed or died of wounds. 100 wounded and twenty missing.

Resting in this position Second Lieutenant Cecil Pugh managed to find time to write to his father:

B.E.F 1/4/18
Dear Dad,

At last there's a chance to write a few hurried lines...Well I am alright, very fit hardly lost any kit, and enjoyed this little bit of the war more than any other. Physically it's been a pretty tough strain, mentally also, as the adjutant was hit and I had to do his work, though he's taken over again.

We marched along the dusty chalk road, whilst on the other side came a constant stream of refugees, old farm carts, babies, bundles, blankets, beds all the pitiful little goods and chattels which war exposes to our neighbours. They utter no complaint, but wearily trudged along, with their lifeless faces full of dull despair. Still we marched on and the dust clouds settled like snow on our clothing and equipment. Now came long streams of funny looking old men without rifles, officially known as The Labour Corps, and on the sides of the road some of these poor devils lay full length in the sun, trying to recover their lost strength. The streams grew thicker, a band of prisoners marched past singing 'Der Wacht am Rhein', but our men uttered never a word. Then came great lumbering ASC carts and lorries and evil looking guns, men on horses, men on cycles. Still we marched ever going forward, along into the unknown, as the opposite stream flowed back, came little groups of unkempt, wild eyed men, some wounded, with bloody bandages, some not. Still the streams grew, past burning stores and burning houses, until the shells beagn to drop. Then we halted, staff rode up and slowly we moved into position on the crest of the forward slope, lying in the grass. But you have no idea, though one reads of it in books, of the impression that ever backward stream has upon the fighting man. I can understand now just a little of what Mons meant in 1914. So we waited and little figures came running hither and thither on the crest of the opposite slope, a few thousand yards away. Soon little groups appeared wandering here and there, always coming closer. When behind them a thin line of men and another thin line, line after line, until suddenly the Lewis guns opened; crack rapped out the rifles. Death's scythe mowed down the lines, as the old reaper whistled the old, old tune. Soon the sunlight flickered on steel, the noise grew greater, men detached went wandering back, a red trail marking their way. After that is a confused memory, more ammunition came up, now all were fighting, fighting and then lo and behold! We were fighting thin air. All those little figures lay on the ground stark still as Old Man Death read their silent burial.

Well then, after night drew in we went back, along the soiled roads, figures silhouetted against a blaze of burning huts, alone utterly alone, the rearguard of a retiring army. We took the wrong road and had to retrace our steps, peering furtively, straining our eyes to see what lay in the pitch black beyond the blaze. Slowly we wandered back and as dawn broke over the hills we passed the outposts

– beyond which we found a little breathing space. We lay down on the grass and slept, horrible sleep, runners always coming and going. Then in the afternoon the whole thing started again, in the evening we went back, and so the following day.

At last a General rode past and said 'Now we stop boys'. So we stopped and the Boche stopped, to his credit let it be said he tried hard not to do so. Since then we've been fighting hard but holding our ground in spite of some of the heaviest artillery barrages I've known. We lived in a house and had our first hot meal for five days, slept for the first time for five days, even had time to think. Now its over for the while, and I'm afraid the regiment has taken few prisoners. You see we had a lot of old debts to pay off. Well cheerio, everybody and forgive me if my letters are a bit irregular.

Yours affectionately

Cecil

Three days were spent training and cleaning and then on 4 April they were moved to Bonnay and from there moved up to Vaux where the brigade was in support of the ANZAC Corps. This position was held until the evening of 8 April, when they were relieved by 51/Australian Infantry again. After being relieved they marched via Lahoussoye to Querrieu where they embossed and were transported to Axheux, having debussed they set off for Hedauville where they found billets for the night. Two days later the battalion was back in the front line having relieved 18/Highland LI south of Martinsart. Three days were spent in the line, the sector was very quiet and no casualties occurred. In the rear, at the battalion details a draft of sixty six men arrived from the base and after some training was allotted to the various companies. On 17 April 4/North Staffordshire Regiment moved in and 19/Durham LI moved to a tented camp in the valley near Hedauville. After cleaning equipment and kit inspections the battalion began practicing for an attack. If the Germans had gone quiet, the British were not going to for long. Plans were already being made to retake the ground lost the previous month.

On the night 21/22 April the battalion moved up to the front line and support trenches in Martinsart Wood and remained there throughout the day, waiting for the time to go over the top. At around 1915 hours the enemy must have seen movement in the wood and opened fire with high explosive on the rear support trenches, this barrage did not last long and things died down. At 1927 hours, three minutes before Zero Hour the British Trench Mortars launched a rain of steel on Aveluy Wood. Then the Artillery barrage came down right on time. From the enemy front line green rockets went up and at 1935 hours the counter barrage started. Thee minutes later the two leading companies went over the top. The right company 'W,' came under very heavy machine gun fire from both flanks and suffered many casualties, including the Company Commander, Captain C W Howes, who was killed. The Company being held up some 250 yards from the jumping off point. On the left Y Company advance much further, almost 400 yards and had to halt as the

23/138 Private W Edgar from Gateshead was killed in action 23 April 1918.

British barrage had failed to lift onto its next target. The Officer Commanding then realised that he had lost touch on both flanks, he therefore pulled both his flanks back to form a defensive line, while he tried to find out what was happening. News was then received from Lieutenant Bell, who was acting as liaison officer with 14/R Welsh Fusiliers that they were held up too. At this stage a gap appeared to be opening between Y and W Companies and X Company were ordered to send up a platoon to fill it, this was duly done and at the same time a platoon from Z Company went up to reinforce W Company, who had many casualties. Later it was found that 15/Cheshire had been unable to move forward. Orders then came through from HQ 104 Brigade to dig in and make a line of posts on the position reached. This was done, but in daylight the posts on the left had to be vacated as they were under enemy observation and came under enfilade fire from rifles and machine guns. When 19/Durham LI had moved forward 18/Lancashire Fusiliers moved into the support line and then at 0400 hours Y Company withdrew to the original front line, X Company moved back to the support trench, leaving W and Z Companies holding the line of posts. After being relieved they moved back to reserve positions in a sunken road and then after two days back to the tented camp at Hedauville, where three days were spent resting. Casualties during the period in the line had been four officers and over 117 men, killed, wounded and missing.

11007 Warrant Officer II Acting Regimental Sergeant Major W C Mason served from 1914 in France and Flanders. He was awarded the Military Medal in 1916 with 2/Durham LI and the Distinguished Conduct Medal with 19/Durham LI.

On 29 April 19/Durham LI moved back to the front line where they relieved 18/Highland LI in the Aveluy Sector, which they held for two days until relieved by 16/R Welsh Fusiliers. After spending one night back at Hedauville the battalion marched to Toutencourt and made a camp in a wood. For the next twenty days they remained here. The normal training was carried out, with a lot of time given over to sport and on 16 May the Divisional shooting competition was held, but four days later they were back in reserve in the Aveluy Sector, having relieved 13/Welch Regiment. Having spent four days in the reserve line, after being relieved they were once more moved to the valley at Hedauville, unfortunately this time the enemy shelled the camp with heavy artillery, killing Privates Watkiss, Taylor and Hebb and wounding two officers and four men. On 27 May Lieutenant Colonel W B Greenwell who had commanded the battalion for almost eighteen months was sent back to England to a Senior

18/1610 Company Sergeant Major G Walker from West Hartlepool posted to 19/Durham LI he was awarded the Distinguished Conduct Medal.

Officers course at Aldershot and command of 19/Durham LI passed to Major H R McCullagh. The next day enemy aircraft flew low over the battalion and an alert Lewis gun crew from Y Company had the pleasure of bringing one of them down, the plane hitting the ground near Bouzincourt. It was then into the front line where they relieved 18/Highland LI in the Aveluy left sector. On 1 June 17 and 18/Lancashire Fusiliers made an attack on Aveluy Wood and although

19/Durham LI were in support they were not called upon, they did however lose a number of men to enemy shelling later in the day when they had been withdrawn to the reserve lines in the rear. The following morning the enemy artillery again hit the battalion position and a large number of men were wounded. Over the next two weeks, the battalion twice went into the front line, each time relieving 15/Sherwood Foresters. Then on 17 June one officer and twenty one men carried out a raid on the enemy trenches in the hope of gaining identification of the enemy units opposite them. The raiders entered the enemy trenches and found them empty, those holding the position having withdrawn. The journey back to the British lines was quite hazardous and a number of men were wounded by the enemy machine guns and trench mortar fire. The battalion moved to Beauquesne and spent some time training and refitting and then on 30 June they began preparing to move, for the 35th Division had been ordered to move north.

18/584 Lance Corporal T Reavely from Langley Moor posted to 19/Durham LI he was awarded the Military Medal and Bar after the war.

22/DURHAM LIGHT INFANTRY – FIGHTING TO THE FINISH

The New Year of 1918 saw the Pioneers of 22/Durham LI still at work in the Ypres Salient. On New Year's Day, A Company was working on Number 5 track from Godley Road to St Jean and Number 6 track, which led from Spree Farm to Canal Bank. B Company was still cleaning out the old German pillboxes. C Company employed one platoon on Number 5 Track from Berlin to Mosselmarkt and two other platoons on draining the mule track from Panet Road to Bellevue, this was a very difficult task owing to the frozen nature of the ground. The work allotted continued through until the middle of January, when A Company sent two platoons to work on the Gravenstafel Mule Track, as a thaw had set in the drainage work on the mule tracks became a lot easier and a lot of progress was made. A number of instructions were received from the Deputy Adjutant General's Branch regarding manpower and the battalion was forced to make the following transfers, nineteen NCOs and men, the last of the Royal Engineers posted in the previous September, were sent to the Base Depot Rouen on 12 January. The same day one

Pioneers taking duckboards up to the front line in the Ypres Salient.

sergeant, one corporal and forty eight men were posted to 18/Durham LI and two corporals, one lance corporal and forty seven men were sent away to 19/Durham LI. To bring the battalion back up to strength 100 Class B1 men were sent up from the base depot. Unfortunately from the battalion's point of view, they were not fully fit, nor were they trained as pioneers. The weather turned really bad and heavy rain fell in the salient which flooded the already water logged ground; the Gravenstafel mule track was completely underwater. Matters were not helped by the continual shelling of the German artillery. The CRE 8th Division then ordered 22/Durham LI to take over the whole of the work on the tracks in the divisional area and they companies had to carry many duckboards up to enable the front line infantry battalions to be relieved.

On 19 January, 8th Division went out for a rest but the pioneers were left behind to keep working, they were however allowed to send one company back at a time to rest and clean up, the first to go out being B Company. The rest of the battalion commenced work on a new plank road from Devils Crossing to Seine, all the material being brought up as close as possible on the light railway to reduce carrying time. The enemy was actively shelling all the roads in the area and a system of patrols went up and down the roads looking for and repairing damage. If a repair could not be affected by the patrol then an emergency party was available from 20/Labour Company. Manpower was also allocated from A Works Company, 110/Labour Company and 4/Labour Company. The work on the new plank road proceeded very slowly mainly owing to the muddy condition of the ground. On 26 January, D Company, along with 20/Labour Company commenced work on the Army Defence :Line in the region of Wieltje, and further work taken on was the repair of the Frezenberg – Zonnebeke Road, whilst further assistance came in the shape of 187/Labour Company, which had a number of ex 19/Durham LI men in its ranks. As the month came to an end good progress was reported on the Devil's Crossing – Seine plank road, but on the Frezenberg – Zonnebeke road the working parties were forced to withdraw owing to the enemy artillery fire.

On 1 February, A Company marched back to Trappistes Farm and relieved B Company, who in turn went up the line and commenced work on the Army Defence Line under the command of the Chief Engineer VIII Corps. The following day some of the labour companies were taken away for other tasks and a redistribution of the work took place 110/Labour Company taking over from 189/Labour Company on the Zonnebeke Road. About a week later seven officers and 150 other ranks arrived as reinforcements from the newly disbanded 14/Durham LI, this brought the number of officers serving with the battalion up to forty nine. During the first two weeks of February very good work was done on all the tasks being carried out by the battalion. So much so that the Chief Engineer VIII Corps, Brigadier General; R A Gillam, late Royal Engineers, wrote to the Corps Commander, singing the praises of the Durham pioneer battalion.

I wish to bring to the notice of the Corps Commander the very excellent work carried out by the under mentioned unit during the past 24 days on the Army Battle Zone and the Forward Roads, and the exceptionally good services rendered by the officers of this unit specified here under,

22nd Durham Light Infantry (Pioneers), 8th Division

Commander Lieut Colonel C B Morgan DSO

During the greater part of the above period three companies of this battalion have been employed on A, Construction of a new double plank road forward from Devil's Crossing.

B, Construction of bridge east of Frezenberg.

C, Generally supervising the labour allotted to various sections of forward roads for maintenance work and the construction of a diversion near Kansas Cross.

For the last few days one or two companies have been employed on the Army Battle Zone, chiefly on wiring. The results produced by this battalion have exceeded all expectations and have been due not only to the sound, steady, solid work which has been carried out by all ranks with such consistent energy and unfailing good spirit. But also the careful and conscientious supervision, which has invariably been exercised by the officers and Non Commissioned Officers of the battalion.

I would particularly bring to notice the energetic manner in which Major J D Mitchell (2nd in Command) has personally superintended the work throughout and the keen interest he has shown in getting the new double plank road at Devil's Crossing pushed forward. I would also like to specially mention the good services rendered by Captain A W H Cooke and Second Lieutenant W H Gibson in the work of general supervision and the construction of the new bridge on the Frezenberg Road respectively. On the occasions I have visited the forward roads I have been much impressed by this battalion's capacity for work and the cheerfulness, good spirit with which it has met all demands made upon it.

R A Gillam Brig Gen

Chief Engineer VIII Corps.

No sooner had the battalion been praised so highly, than they were given even more work to do. A Company took over work draining the Gravenstafel - Bellevue – Mallard Cross Roads from 1/2/Monmouthshire Regiment and B Company started constructing Divisional Defences on the Abraham Heights. C Company were given the task of extending the light railway towards Passchendaele, whilst one officer and fourteen men were attached to 24 Brigade to supervise the construction of a new Divisional Reserve Line. On 16 February, the early shift men of C Company were making their way back through Ypres to their billets when the enemy put down a heavy artillery barrage, four men were wounded and one of them, 22/950, Private, George Dorr later died from his wounds. A twenty two year old Darlington man, from Brighton Road in the town, he was taken back and buried in Ypres Reservoir Cemetery.

It was now the reorganisation of the Army took its effect on the 22/Durham LI, under the Authority of War Office letter 121/France/1388 S.D.2 dated 6/2/18 all the pioneer battalions serving in France were to be reduced from four companies to three companies. Rather than send surplus men away it was decided that the reduction would be best achieved by 'natural attrition', so as casualties left the battalion, they would not be replaced until the battalion was three companies strong. Another new task was given to the battalion when they were ordered to construct dams on the Ravebeek as part of the defence works, however a major problem was the reliability of the light railway, and working parties were left without material for long periods and in some cases eventually had to march back without doing any work, the trudge back being under shellfire as the enemy artillery sent it hail of daily high explosive and shrapnel towards Ypres.

On 1 March a number of men were attached to 245/Tunnelling Company to assist with the construction of deep dug outs, whilst C Company was constructing four strong points, the next morning as the men were preparing to march up to work the enemy shelled the area of Ypres Station near D Company billets, one man was killed, 22/697, Private, Raymond Norton of Grangetown, Sunderland and the Company Sergeant Major was wounded. At the end of the week in accordance with the previously received instruction, D Company was disbanded and the officers and men distributed between the other companies. The battalion now changed places with 1/2/Monmouthshire Regiment, the pioneer battalion of 29th Division and took over the work of constructing various 'keeps' and machine gun posts in the Army Battle Zone as part of the defence plan. This work continued until 21 March when word came through of the massive enemy assault on THIRD and FIFTH ARMIES to the south. Headquarters 8th Division put the battalion on five hours standby to move. That afternoon they took the light railway to Poperinghe where they spent the night. At 1300 hours the following day they marched to Hopoutre sidings and entrained in two trains for an unknown destination. The first train carried, A and C Companies to Marcelcave and the second train took B Company and the Battalion Transport to

British infantry were rushed south to the Somme from the Ypres Salient by train.

Guillaucourt, about ten miles due south of Albert. Quickly the battalion sorted itself out and set off for Rosieres where they found billets for the night. At 0400 hours under the orders of Headquarters 8th Division the battalion marched to Fresbnes and then on to Omiecourt where a halt was called for a short while and then the proceeded on towards Pertain. A reconnaissance party went forward and then at 1500 hours the battalion moved forward and A Company took up a defensive position West of Morchain. Here they came under attack from the enemy, the rifles rattled and the Lewis guns opened up but eventually under strong enemy pressure they were forced to withdraw. The last man to leave was 22/184, Private Walter Ransome who firing his Lewis gun with great coolness and deliberation inflicted heavy losses on the advancing enemy. He then brought the gun out of action under heavy enemy machine gun and rifle fire. In a similar position was 22/1016, Sergeant James Mackie who having commanded his two Lewis guns with great tenacity was unable to get them away when ordered to fall back, so he damaged them and put them out of commission so that they were of no use to the enemy. In one position two Lewis guns under the command of Corporal Thomas Stonehouse were holding up the enemy, when the crew of one gun were completely wiped out by an enemy shell. The gallant Corporal rushed forward alone and continued to fire his gun until all his ammunition was gone, he then brought his gun out o action and arranged for the other gun to be collected and brought out too.

Lieutenant H G Legg killed in action 24 March 1918.

At 1845 hours they moved back on B Company and dug a trench 500 yards west of Potte Wood. When the trench was completed A Company took up positions on the right with B Company on the left, with their left flank across the Pertain – Morchain Road. C Company meanwhile was in reserve at Pertain. The night passed quietly, but an expected counter attack by the French failed to take place, That night Second Lieutenant William O'Dell MM led a successful patrol and located the enemy in the village of Mesnil-St Nicaise and brought back valuable information, later the same night he took another patrol out in to Potte Wood where he was heavily fired at by the enemy but the patrol was able to return with accurate positions for the enemy. The enemy had occupied Potte and in the thick mist next morning, the Germans started attacking once more, bombing their way up old communication trenches abandoned in 1917. At 0900 hours they reached the positions held by 22/Durham LI and attacked in strength. As the enemy came down the communication trench 22/240 Corporal Joseph Green, a Pelton man, along with Lieutenant T W Howey went forward and constructed a block in the trench and they were able to protect the flank of the company with a Lewis gun. Another man showing great coolness was 22/325, Corporal

Edward Dodds, from Hebburn, who although wounded remained with his men and by his doggedness stiffened the resistance to the enemy at a critical stage of the withdrawal. As in so many other positions the battalion very soon found that its flanks were in the air and was compelled to withdraw. This time they moved back to a line North East of Pertain, all the while suffering casualties, the killed, lying still and remaining behind as the battalion went back and those wounded to badly injured to move, being left to the mercy of the attacking enemy. The walking wounded were able to get away and make their way out to the Battalion Aid Post and from there to the Casualty Clearing Station. The line at Pertain was only held for about one hour, when again with flanks in the air and under strong enemy pressure they were forced back once more. It was decided that the battalion should take up a position near Omiecourt and by noon they were established on this line. Here they held on until 1600 hours when orders came in that they must retire once more and they moved back and took up a position on Chaulnes Ridge, north east of the village of Chaulnes. In the three days since leaving Belgium it was estimated that the battalion had suffered over 400 casualties among the other ranks and that four officers had been killed and at least ten wounded. Having spent a restless night at dawn word came to retire on Lihons and by 0700 hours they were in position, the infantry brigades of the division started to fall back and as they did so the enemy attacked, but was repulsed with heavy losses, covered by 25 Brigade both 23 and 24

22/197 Private H Scollen born in Seaham and living in Easington Colliery was taken prisoner during the enemy attacks.

Brigades had passed through Lihons by 1400 hours and at 1530 hours, 22/Durham LI also left that village and withdrew in a south westerly direction to a new position west of the Brick Factory in Rosieres. At noon on 27 March, one officer and three NCOs from each company went up to the line north east of Rosieres to carry out a reconnaissance. Then at 1330 hours the Commanding Officer received orders direct from Division to move the battalion to a point north east of Harbonnieres and link up with 2/Devonshire Regiment, with a view to launching a counter attack. The move was made and the counter attack launched. With B Company on the Devons right and the others on the left, advancing with fixed bayonets they drove the enemy infantry back for over 1000 yards, as far back as the main Amiens – Estrees Road. Here the advancing British managed to seize and hold a trench. As they went forward, taking casualties many acts of courage and leadership occurred, some that will never be known, but 22/799, Lance Corporal Ernest Lambert when both his Platoon Commander and Platoon Sergeant became casualties, took over and led the platoon onto its objective where he reorganised them and secured the objective. The second wave was led by Second Lieutenant George Eastwood, who in spite of the heavy enemy machine gun fire walked about encouraging the men regardless of danger and setting a fine example to all ranks. Throughout this swift advance a large number of prisoners were taken and the battalion's casualties were relatively light. Sadly though the Commanding Officer and Second Lieutenant Scott were both wounded and unfortunately they both later died from these wounds. The battalion stretcher bearers were working exceptionally hard and displaying great gallantry as they went about their work. 22/928, Private John Gibbons tended the wounded faithfully under heavy fire and saved many of them from falling into enemy hands. Another stretcher bearer 27007, Private Barnard Sharp, was also showing great bravery tending the wounded and although both men were recommended for the award of The Military Medal, they received no recognition for their efforts. One who received a Parchment Certificate for his work as a stretcher bearer was 22/423, Private Arthur Chapman, who was always well to the front assisting the wounded as soon as possible after they were hit.

Orders came through that both A and C Companies were to withdraw in a south easterly direction to a point north of Harbonniers and from there due south to Caix. This was done in an orderly manner and when they arrived at Caix they marched back to Morisel. In the early hours of the morning and having lost around fifteen men B Company found their left flank was in the

22/532 Private T Robson from Thornley Colliery transferred to the Labour Corps and Royal Engineers.

air. They managed to get in touch with Brigade Headquarters and received orders to fall back on Caix and from there they moved to Jumel where they found billets for the night. The next day B Company was joined by A and C Companies from Morisel and a further night was spent at Jumel. On the morning of 30 March, at 0945 hours orders came in from HQ 8th Division, that 22/Durham LI was to move to Cottenchy, which was done by march route, the journey being completed by mid-day. Then at 1600 hours further orders were received from Division, the battalion was to move to Castel and report to Headquarters 25 Brigade, under whose orders they would operate for the time being, the battalion set off for the new location at 1700 hours. When the battalion reached 25 Brigade, the Commanding Officer, Major Mitchell went in and reported, where upon he was ordered to take up a position North West of the Moreuil – Demum Road, with the battalion's right flank resting on the edge of the wood North – North East of Moreuil. The battalion moved up into this position with B and C Companies in the line, A Company being placed in support. The night passed quietly enough, as did the morning of 31 March, but around mid-day the German Artillery opened up on the battalion positions. Prominent among the battalion at this time was 22/267, Private Harry Peart, from the small Weardale town of Stanhope, employed as a company runner, on numerous occasions he bravely went back and forth across the battlefield, braving shot and shell to relay messages to the platoons and back to battalion Headquarters. A strong barrage came down on the Durham's position, for almost forty five minutes and then the enemy infantry came. Masses of them stormed forward and the under strength battalion found it difficult to hold them. Rifles, Lewis Guns and grenades, every weapon they possessed was brought into action in an attempt to stem the flow, but eventually the hard pressed Pioneers were forced to give ground and fell back for almost 1000 yards, to a position where they could reorganise. This was quickly done and then in conjunction with a cavalry unit on their right, they turned on the foe. Forward they went straight into the advancing enemy, who must have had a shock to see, what they considered to be an enemy in full retreat, turn and come back at them with bayonets flashing. The tables were turned and the Germans, in their turn, were sent backwards, as the Pioneers of 22/Durham LI regained much of the ground they had just lost. They consolidated the position under very heavy fire but managed to hold on despite a number of casualties.

22/147 Private W Brabiner of West Hartlepool came through unscathed.

Prominent among those showing great bravery at this time was the Battalion Medical Officer, Captain R W Pearson RAMC and his orderly 22/669, Lance Corporal Fred Armstrong. As they were dressing the wounds of one man two shells hit the Regimental Aid Post and killed the wounded soldier and later as the pair followed up behind the attack they tended men wounded and inspired the stretcher bearers so that many wounded men's lives were saved, the MO was awarded The Military Cross and Lance Corporal Armstrong who was also one of those listed among the wounded, received a Divisional Parchment Certificate.

Among the wounded officers were, Major Mitchell and Captain Robson MC, who had spent the day encouraging his men to hold on and had inflicted a large number of casualties on the enemy, was wounded during a heavy bombardment, along with Lieutenant Crutchley and Second Lieutenant Adamson. There was also seventy five other ranks wounded or killed. Throughout the following day, although the British artillery was busy shelling the enemy and British aircraft were flying low and strafing the German infantry, there were no attacks on the battalion forward positions.

On 2 April, the 8th Division was relieved by a French Division and 22/Durham LI left the line and marched to Sains-en Amienois where they were met by a convoy of motor buses; that took them to Ailly-sur-Somme, here they debussed and marched to billets in Fourdrinoy. The next day was spent refitting and cleaning up and then on the afternoon of 4 April a move was made to Conde where they arrived at 1645 hours. Here they were joined by a large draft of 450 other ranks, all well below the physical requirements for front line infantrymen. It was here that the battalion received the news that the Commanding Officer, Lieutenant Colonel C B Buckley, had died, at Rouen, of the wounds, he had suffered on 27 March.

With the death of the CO and the Second in Command, Major Mitchell in hospital wounded, Lieutenant Colonel Boucher Charlewood James, 2/Devonshire Regiment was appointed to command the battalion. The first act was to allocate the new drafts to the companies, and then having spoken to all the officers, he inspected the new men. A training programme was put together and the companies set to training the new draft, musketry and gas drill receiving special attention. The battalion also provided, at the express request of the GOC, a guard of one sergeant, one lance corporal and six men for Divisional Headquarters. Three officers, Lieutenant W K Taylor, Lieutenant P Minor and Second Lieutenant V Vincent along with nineteen other ranks joined the battalion from VIII Corps Reinforcement Camp. Ceremonial drill was practised on 9 April and again on the morning of 10 April, after the parade the battalion spent time on spit and polish so that in the afternoon they were spick and span when the GOC 8th Division arrived to inspect the battalion. At 1445 hours the battalion paraded en-masse and at 1500 hours the GOC arrived. He inspected the battalion and then gave a short address in which he thanked those who had taken part in the operations of the previous weeks, for the splendid way the battalion had fought and hoped the new men would endeavour to emulate their comrades. Then afterwards the battalion gave three hearty cheers for the GOC. The battalion then marched past in column of fours, with the Battalion Band playing, 'The Light Barque', The Regimental March of The Durham Light Infantry. The battalion was placed on short notice to be ready to move although no move was made and training continued over the next two days. At 0300 hours on 12 April, 8th Division came under command of The Australian Corps and the Battalion Transport of 22/Durham LI was placed under command of 24 Brigade to march via Crouy and Montieres to Bussy-les-Daours where they arrived about 1830 hours. The rest of the battalion moved under command of 25 Brigade and marched to Hangest Station where they entrained and were moved by rail to St Roch Amiens, which was reached at 1130 hours on 13 April, after detraining they moved on foot to Bussy-les-Daours. After marching for roughly six kilometres they were met by the company cookers and a meal halt for dinner was made. The march continued and when they arrived at

Bussy-les-Daours, at 1900 hours they were met by guides who showed the companies to their billets. The next day after a late breakfast and a foot inspection the battalion rested, although there was a voluntary church service for those of the Church of England faith. On 15 April training started once more and new Lewis Gun sections were formed, as the number of guns in the battalion had been increased. Musketry and Box Respirator Drill again were given special attention with every man firing the rifle whilst wearing the respirator. Five days were spent here as each company went through the various courses and exercises set out for the battalion and it wasn't until 20 April that under orders of 23 Brigade, B Company relieved one company of 15 Australian Brigade in the reserve line at Aubigny, the remainder of the battalion moved to billets in Blangy-Tronville taking ammunition and tool wagons needed for fighting, the remainder of the battalion transport moving back to Camon.

28256 Private W Tinkler from Consett killed in action 26 April 1918.

The companies were reduced to 200 men per company and the remainder were allotted work, under Numbers 1 and 3 Sections of 256 Tunnelling Company, Royal Engineers, at regular periods these parties were relieved by the main part of the battalion who were still in billets. Here four new officers joined the battalion, Lieutenant S G Highmoor and Second Lieutenant's T Riley, A G Rowley and S R Wyld. B Company held the position in the Aubigny Reserve Line until St George's Day, 23 April when A Company took over the position and the work in progress. B Company returned to the billets in Blagny-Tronville. Another six new officers, Lieutenant C V Grimshaw, and Second Lieutenant's H Stuart, J P Cotton, P Blades, J R Armstrong and G Foster joined the battalion on the same day. The next morning at 0400 hours the order to 'stand to' was received and then at 0430 hours the companies moved off to join A Company in the reserve line. On the way up they came under a very heavy bombardment of gas shells, but they pushed on and C Company moved in to the line on the left of A Company, B Company being placed behind in support positions. At 1155 hours 22/Durham LI were placed at the disposal of 25 Brigade who at 2000 hours ordered the battalion to take up a line along a sunken road running South South East where they spread out to avoid the shell fire. The CO ordered patrols to be sent out towards Villers Brettoneux and they returned with the news that the town was held in strength by the enemy and that they had a number of machine guns in strong positions. The battalion was being heavily shelled and they were ordered to cooperate with 15/Australian Brigade in attacking Villers Brettonuex. 22/Durham LI being allocated the task of mopping up with A Company tasked to maintain touch with 2/Northamptonshire Regiment on the southern flank. At 2200 hours the attack commenced and several attempts were made to gain a footing in the village but none was successful until the next day. At 0200 hours on 25 April a strong fighting patrol went out and succeeded in knocking out two heavy machine guns. This greatly assisted the attack and by 1000 hours the battalion had fought its way into Villers Brettonuex, inflicting heavy casualties on the enemy and taking six officers and eighty men prisoner. Throughout the day, yard by yard and house by house the battalion fought its way into the village and by 2300 hours most of the village, except for the south east corner, was back in Australian and British hands. 22/Durham LI had done well but had suffered a number of casualties, Second Lieutenant A G Rowley, who had only joined a few days earlier was killed, The Battalion Medical Officer, Captain R W Pearson RAMC, and Lieutenant S G Highmoor were wounded but remained at duty and forty other ranks were killed or died of wounds, eight men were missing and 138 men were evacuated wounded. They were now ordered to return to the start position and began moving back, shortly after they arrived back in this position word came that they were to move, and hold a line along a railway embankment south east of Villers Brettoneux. A reconnaissance party went forward and then the battalion followed as they went forward they came under shell fire and a number of casualties

Group photograph of officers, non commissioned officers, and soldiers of 'B' Company, 22nd Battalion, The Durham Light Infantry, 'who were in the original Battalion', c.1918.

occurred. When the new line was reached A Company took up position on the right and B Company on the left, with C Company in support on the western edge of Villers Brettoneux. A post on the flank held by another battalion requested assistance and under extremely heavy machine gun fire Major C C Hall and Second Lieutenant S G Highmoor got together some 20 men with a Lewis gun and a machine gun and led them forward over an embankment and across a road which was being badly sniped and machine gunned. As men fell wounded and killed Major Hall went back and brought forward more men, and conveyed an important message from Brigade headquarters. A Company were shelled out of their position and were forced to take up a position in a trench a few yards back from the railway embankment. As the enemy made for a gap in the embankment 22/715, Sergeant, Acting Company Sergeant Major Robert Whereley was ordered to fill the gap, this he did, disposing his men with great coolness and disposing his men with a skill that stopped the enemy and restored the position. By the end of the day fourteen other ranks were dead and thirty wounded and among the officers Second Lieutenant A J Hossack MM had died of wounds, he had been recommended for the award of a Military Cross for his work on 25 March when he had gone forward under very heavy rifle and machine gun fire to establish communication with the battalion on his company's flank, and then on 27 March he had fought his platoon on to his objective and reorganised them when the objective was gained. Other officer casualties were Second Lieutnant's V Vincent and L Hickman who were both evacuated gassed. During the night patrols went out, one of these spotted an enemy patrol moving about and opened fire on them. The 27 April passed quietly, although the front line was under heavy shell fire and then in the afternoon orders were received that 45/Australian Battalion would relieve 22/Durham LI that night. The relief duly took place and by 0100 hours the battalion was on its way back to billets in Blagny Tronville unfortunately on the way out Lieutenant E Minto was wounded and two men were killed and eight wounded. After the action they won the praise of many Australian soldiers, some, who had a very low opinion of the British Tommy, were made to change their attitude, one 'Digger' is reported as saying, 'I never had any time for the Tommies, reckoned they were hardly worth their tucker, but I'll take my hat off to those chaps.'

Captain Andrews, 22/Durham LI, standing in a trench near the River Aisne, France, 'the day before the big German attack'.

The billets were reached at 0300 hours where the battalion rested until ordered to move to Daours. The battalion marched to the new location but on arrival they found that the billets to be taken over, had not been vacated, and it wasn't until 1800 hours that they were able to bed down in their new accommodation. Training commenced once more and on 30 April a letter was received from the GOC 8th Division which expressed total satisfaction with the battalion's fighting at Villers Brettoneux.

On 1 May the battalion paraded in full marching order and began a march to new billets in Boutillerie where they arrived at 1300 hours, later that afternoon a foot inspection took place and again the following day, when every man washed his feet. Another draft arrived, this time 160 men who were inspected by the Commanding Officer at 1100 hours on 3 May and then allocated to the various companies. A number of Divisions of XIX Corps that had been heavily involved in the fighting of March and April, 8th, 19th, 25th and 50th were considered to be in urgent need of a rest and refit and they were to be moved south and take over a quiet sector of the Chemin-des-Dames from the French. At 1600 hours on 4 May, A

Company marched to Saleux Station and entrained at 1940 hours for an unknown destination. The remainder of the battalion marched to the station at 1900 hours and left there at 0030 hours on 5 May arriving at Fismes at 1340 hours where they left the train and marched to billets in a hutted camp at Villesavoye arriving at 1510 hours. The next four days were given over to the usual training programme and at 1730 hours on 9 May a concert was held in the recreation hut.

The next day Major Davidson returned from the Senior Officer Course in England,

C Company, 22/Battalion, The Durham L I, June 1918. Named Officers: Brown; Leach; Reay (seated centre); Rothing; Palmer; Owen.

A special telegram came from the old Division demanding my return to France. Perhaps to be specially asked for is complimentary; about a week before this telegram arrived I had seen in the casualty lists, the death of my CO and the wounding of the Senior Major. I had to catch the boat train from Victoria that same night. It was dusk when we entered the harbour at Boulogne, immediately all ranks were marched off to the Gas School then the train left for a destination unknown. I do not remember the names of the wayside stations through most of which our train slowly steamed that early morning of 10 May 1918; but a length we arrived at the railhead – Fimes – here the comparative few left of us finally alighted and our personal luggage was also put out. Divisional HQ was said to be a few miles further on – we were on the fringe of the country still occupied by the native inhabitants, it was pastoral country mixed with vineyards.

As a somewhat senior officer it was supposed that a groom from my battalion

236

would appear with my charger, but during half an hour no such appeared, so after partaking of a cup of tea and a biscuit with the RTO I set off on 'shanks' pony' to report to Divisional Headquarters, leaving my baggage to be picked up later – amongst this was a very new suitcase of scarcely military appearance in spite of its inscription of name, rank and battalion! I soon made Divisional Headquarters where the CRE whom I knew quite well, entertained me for an hour over a few cigarettes and a drink, while he telephoned our show to let them know of my arrival. My charger arrive and I rode about four miles to Bouffilliers, a tiny hamlet in a shallow ravine, through which a brook flowed. Our horse lines and transport were a little further up the ravine along a very minor and rough road, quite off the beaten track. I discovered certain ruins had been made into strong points for machine guns, One company, that is to say the company in reserve, was billeted in barns, byres and stables and this lot had its company mess in a ruined farmhouse where also a guard was posted. At the HQ I found only the Adjutant 'at home' – he was a stranger to me and had only been posted to our Durhams a fortnight earlier, he still wore the badges of another regiment which somehow one resented, perhaps foolishly! Here I met our late CO's batman, Crisp of whom I have spoken earlier, he told me of the death of the CO and also many others – there seemed only four of the old officers left , Captain Adams, Lieutenant Rae, and a Lieutenant who had been Transport Officer and Captain Hall lately adjutant and now junior Major. Of the NCO's and men perhaps sixty remained not counting Transport Platoon, Quartermasters details and the clerks of the Battalion Orderly Room.

Returning to our HQ I met our new CO who was a Regular aged about thirty four or five, a pleasant cheerful man, he almost apologised for assuming command, which was quite unnecessary for I had been junior Major, not Second in Command. The CO told me we had reverted to Infantry of the Line pure and simple and were likely to remain so, nevertheless we were still not brigaded and received our orders direct from Division.

Despite the fact that they were operating as infantry and not pioneers the battalion took over the work of a French battalion in the village of Gernicourt. A Company took over the digging of a trench from the outskirts of the village towards the Aisne Canal. B Company took over the maintenance of the Decquaville track and roads leading up to the front line. The remainder of the battalion moved to Bouffignereux . On 14 May one platoon of C Company went up and relieved one platoon of B Company. Over the next four days tasks such as wiring the trenches of the Gernicourt defences and draining the trenches in the Bois des Pies as well as working on the RE Grand Bellay Dump. Work on the light tramways was also undertaken and a dump of rails was made ready for repair work. On 19 May a draft of 109 other ranks joined the battalion. The work on the tramway was given priority and any damaged rails were quickly replaced. Whilst others were employed on the trenches around Gernicourt, the party employed here paid special attention to the barbed wire defences. On 24 May the 25th Company of the 25th French Machine Gun Battalion was allocated to the Gernicourt defences and came under the command of the Commanding Officer 22/Durham LI. The work continued until 2000 hours on 26 May when a signal was received from Headquarters 8th Division that the enemy were seen to be massing and that an attack should be expected imminently.

Major Davidson described the position of his command post in this way,

A few yards in front of where I stood, an old cart track led for quarter of a mile down into an old gravel pit, along the track which was deeply hollowed out ran a number of wires for batteries and to connect infantry in the line with their HQ in the rear etc. Here a number of signallers had splinter proof shelters and there was an advanced aid post, but a more complete and far more secure aid post had been hollowed out of the advanced side of the gravel pit in the form of deep caverns divided from

Germans advancing on the Chemin des Dames.

one another by adequate spaces unexcavated. All these opened into at the level of the bottom of the gravel pit, but secured against splinters with a massive sandbagged wall, encased in wire-netting. These shelters were used by various details of our own forces, Machine Gun Companies, advanced ration stores, artillerymen, together with more than one cookhouse. The ground was the lower slope of the rise under which an immense dugout had been made by the indefatigable French – running for a hundred and fifty yards parallel with our moated front and was not more than a hundred yards in the rear of the canal. There were lower entrances at both ends of its length, reached by a few steps only, for most of the length there was an upper floor, still quite twenty feet below the crest of the rise; and from the top three separate stairways led down to this upper floor while a few carefully contrived observation galleries were tunnelled to the canal side of the mound or hill. Just below the summit were a set of well constructed trenches, the lower depth of which penetrated in to the chalk. Everything about these huge underground barracks was very stoutly constructed and strengthened with timber. There were quantities of beds in two tiers, mattressed with chicken wire and there were tables and forms. The whole was electrically lit from a special plant controlled by French Engineers.

At 0100 hours on 27 May the enemy opened a very heavy bombardment on Gernicourt with high explosive and gas, the bombardment continued until 0500 hours when it eased off. The two platoons of A Company holding the Bois des Pies, Numbers 1 and 2 platoons had practically all become casualties and it was impossible to get any messages through as every runner that was sent became a casualty. The two platoon commanders, Lieutenants Hickman MC and Willmer MC were both wounded and evacuated. Numbers 3 and 4 platoons were in Boyon St Rigobert and a trench running parallel with the Aisne Canal respectively. No information could be got from these platoons but at 0900 hours information was received that the enemy were through on the right. At 0910 hours the enemy were seen crossing the Aisne Canal and were heavily engaged by Number 4 Platoon, a machine gun was placed on top of the P C Corneille but all the crew became casualties and the gun put out of action. By 0930 Lieutenant Highmoor MC reported the enemy entering Gernicourt and that most of the platoon along the canal bank had been wounded or killed. Then at 0945 hours word came in that the enemy was round on both flanks and the company was down to forty effective men. Major C C Hall DSO gave orders to withdraw and took a small party of men towards the Bois de Geais, this was the last seen of either Major Hall or the Adjutant Captain Atkinson. The remainder of the company eventually withdrew under the command of Captain Elliff and Lieutenant Highmoor MC.

It was while I was awaiting developments that Major Hall in the rear of his company, turned about with some twenty men to lead a bayonet charge upon a party of Boche who suddenly appeared on his left rear, coming as it were from the area we had but recently vacated. Unfortunately he received a direct hit from a shell which carried away his head, so that the charge faltered and those who survived fled into the cover of the trees. I heard this much later, when I was up at South Shields in October from a private who took part in this. Major Hall had been our Adjutant for a full two years and was a most painstaking officer.' Major Davidson wrote in his memoirs about this incident.

C Company under the command of Captain Heighway and Lieutnant Grimshaw held on until they found the enemy attacking them from the rear, so they made their way along St Dennis trench to a position south of Bouffignereux at which point they numbered around fifty six men. They managed to hold the enemy until 1630 hours and as the left flank had gone a retirement was ordered to the high ground above Guyencourt. Here they found the remnant of a brigade of 25th Division. Then a further retirement was ordered as the enemy were occupying some high ground.

At the start of the barrage B Company was occupying a position at La Violette in L Butte Aux Vents, the Company Commander got in touch with 24 Brigade Headquarters and by 0330 hours the three platoons of the company were manning their battle positions, all three being in the line Number 8 platoon on the right, Number 7 Platoon in the centre and Number 6 Platoon on the left. By 0530 hours the front line troops were falling back through B Company positions and the enemy started shelling the company with high explosive and gas. By 0630 hours German Infantry were seen crossing the La Miette River and were engaged by Number 7 and 8 Platoons, this held the enemy up but not for long and soon a number of German soldiers forced their way into the trenches at La Miette. At 0800 hours the OC Company ordered the company to fall back towards Canal Bank as they went back the Company Commander was wounded and Lieutenant Minor took over and managed to establish a position on the edge of the Bois de Gernicourt. By now the company was down to fifty men and at 1000 hours they were ordered to take up another new position astride the Roucy – Ventelay Road, here they managed to get in touch with the Border regiment and at 1400 hours they were able to get a re-supply of ammunition from the farm at La Faite. The line taken up was manned by a hotch-potch of units 5/Northumberland Fusiliers and 5/Durham LI from 149 and 150 Brigades of 50th Division and 22/Durham LI from 8th Division. At 2230 hours the two 50th Division battalions withdrew covered by 22/Durham LI who followed them at 2300 hours and no sooner were they out of the position than the enemy, with a number of heavy machine guns were in. The next day the remnants of B Company were ordered to report back to 8th Division and they marched to Montigny, but Divisional Headquarters had moved. They moved on to Jonchery where they managed to get information that the survivors of A and C Companies were at Lehry. They marched to that place and rejoined what was left of the battalion.

Also moving back was Major Davidson, who wrote at length about this period of the battle.

I was soon joined by a few men, who had drifted across and then some of my own headquarter group, including my own batman, Robson. Later a further fifty or so had turned up by twos and threes so that we became perhaps seventy men with three officers – I heard that two young officers who I liked very well had been lost off in our rear with their platoons, all believed to have been killed or captured, I was glad later to meet them both at Catterick after the Armistice, both had been taken prisoner – I remember both their names, O'Dell and John Cotton. The Sergeant Major also turned up bringing with him a Lewis gun and two of its crew, carrying with them one box of ammunition.

We remained under intermittent shell fire, but there was a sufficient spell to rest for a time. I had learned that most of the rest of our strength had melted away partly by shell and machine gun fire

Officers of C Company prior to disbanding.

and by men seeking shelter within the wood, all these latter would be captured, for the whole of that ridge or tree covered hill was by now encircled by the enemy and none within its boundaries could escape capture. Only those who had run the gauntlet across the valley had a chance. So the day drifted on, we could hear the roar of the battle away on our left rear, enemy aeroplanes flew low backwards and forwards quite low down and towards sunset we could identify Boche transport actually a mile away on the road we used to employ between our positions and HQ in Bouffillierees. To remain where we were was to be left high and dry, out of the show, yet cut off and eventually to be located and wiped out. We therefore continued to slowly and cautiously retire half right, which was south west. Just as darkness descended we struck a rough track-way which crossed our direction obliquely. On this we halted to take stock of our position. It seemed we had retired perhaps a mile and a quarter with an inclination of about three-quarters of a mile to the right – so if this was so, Joncery-sur-Vessle lay ahead of us distant two or three miles – one arm of the track-way led more or less in that direction. Even in the darkness of the night, so long as the track continued and did not diverge too greatly, we could continue more towards possible British Forces. We might also meet others of our own unit, for remnant of the support company might be ahead and after all there was the reserve company, the transport etc which hours ago must have departed in some direction from Bouffillieres.

By now most of us were very exhausted men and the line straggled away badly in the rear; so, when after a short distance we came upon a cluster of hovels and huts we decided to halt for a long rest. Some time after midnight, Mr Jerry began once more to fill the wood with gas by shelling. Exhausted men lying prone and asleep had to be roused up and warned to assume their respirators. Bye and Bye high explosive shells were mixed in with the bombardment and one of our occupied hovels was directly hit, this contained my batman Robson, he with his two companions was instantly killed.

[18203, Private, William Robson, who came from Dunston on Tyne.]

A moment later another man came running up screaming with a severe gash on the forehead and the confusion became confounded – to add to the trouble machine gun bullets began to strike the trees all about us and for a time it was difficult to locate the direction from which they came. I sent two signallers off to try and identify this but neither rejoined us again.

About this time faintness came over me and as I was wearing my respirator I could not account for it. However a man gave me some support and I sat down for a time. I was certainly suffering from ga. I found that the tube connecting the cylinder with the mask had been pierced by a bullet or splinter so I asked my companion to fetch me another for me, taking it off one of the dead in the hut. This he did but not before I had been violently sick. We remained where we were for perhaps an hour, then a lighting through the trees showed us that dawn was not far off and that we were much nearer the fringe of the forest than we had known during the night. Also the shelling had died down and the gas had almost cleared away.

Taking the Sergeant Major with me I went to the edge of the tress to look around – two hundred yards off stood a barn or byre with haystack and wood. Towards these rode four mounted Britishers – we advanced to meet them. They were the CO, the Adjutant, OC reserve Company and an orderly. We were astonished and so were they. I gave a brief report to the CO, seeing my condition he sent me off on his own horse accompanied by his orderly to Joncery. When I arrived at the dressing station, I was just in time to have a label tied on me and be pushed into the last ambulance to leave.

Also recording the German attack was Second Lieutenant Sam Wyld, who kept a small diary of events, mainly one line entries,

27 May German Attack – Withdrew to Rouncy – Only seven left out of platoon of fifty. Andrews, [OC B Company] *broken jaw, Smart and Armstrong wound, Minor, killed. Met John Robinson of*

Welsh Regiment he was afterwards killed. Colonel James the only officer left from HQ. Major Hall, one of the best, killed. Blades and self with twenty three men hunt for Divisional Headquarters ran into Germans in Ventilay, hundreds of dead about. – Lost all kit stuck at Thery and also Romigny. Burned hospital on road out – Transport blown to pieces. Germans favoured by the weather conditions. Rushed into sunken road, - death trap machine gun fire.

When A, and C Companies were falling back, Lieutenant Grimshaw was wounded quite badly and had to be left behind. Second Lieutenant Sproat, who was also wounded, was lucky to get evacuated. The battalion was scattered among a number of units one party of around 100 men was found in Savigny. Having been sent back to Divisional Headquarters the previous night, they had avoided the worst of the enemy barrage. They moved back to the battalion transport lines at Tramery where Major Mitchell DSO was collecting stragglers and details under orders from Headquarters XIX Corps. The next day at 0500 hours the remnants of the battalion, around 220 all ranks reported to the Advanced Headquarters of 8th Division at Tramery, here they were organised into two Companies under the command of Captain Elliff and Lieutenant Reay, The

Original NCOs 22/Durham LI before disbandment.

Commanding Officer took charge of these men and they came under the orders of Headquarters 74 Brigade who ordered them to take up positions near Coemy commanding the woods to the south of the Chateau Prin. Here they were in close touch with French troops on the left. The enemy attacked the French and drove them back which in turn meant 22/Durham LI had to fall back too. Ordered back to a position North of Romigny they again dug in and tried to hold on. At 0400 hours the next day the enemy shelled the battalion position and soon after that attacked again. The unit on the west side of the road fell back and 22/Durham LI adjusted its front accordingly and found troops of 19th Division on its right. They managed to hold on until afternoon, when the enemy worked a machine gun into a position from which they could enfilade the Durham's position. This forced the battalion to withdraw to high ground south of Ville en Tardenois. This position was held until the next day. On 31 May they were instructed to hand over to French troops and report back to 74 Brigade, it was found impossible to hand over to the French until the situation was explained to a French Commandant at Boujacourt. The battalion was then relieved and reported at Nappes at 0900 hours, during the day they dug positions North West of Chanterine where they remained for the night.

While all this had been going on Number 5 Platoon had become completely detached from the battalion, the platoon commander, Lieutenant Howey, had been asked by a Major of 25th Divisional Engineers to help him fill a gap in the line, which he did, taking up a position on the ridge in front of Ventelay, two hours later under orders from the RE Major he moved to a position in front of Montigny where he came across some men of 8th Division. On 28 May, the enemy attacked at 0500 and after holding them for an hour or more they were forced back north of Jonchery. The enemy outflanked the platoon once again and picking up all the stragglers he could find, Lieutenant Howey reported to Headquarters 23 Brigade. They ordered him to take up a position defending the road into the village. In this position he held on taking a good number of casualties but by 1600 hours they were once again outflanked and had to withdraw again, this time to the ridge about one mile north of Savigny. This position was held until 1000 hours on 29 May, when an orderly retirement was made to the ridge in front of Treslon. The enemy made several attempts to take this position but they managed to hold on for four hours until yet again the Germans forced their way in on the flanks and another retirement was found necessary. By now Lieutenant Howey's command had ceased to be a platoon of 22/Durham LI as he had men of nearly every unit of the division with him. He moved these back to another ridge just north of Bouleuse, where they were reinforced by a company of 8th Divisional Details. After holding on all night the next day Lieutenant Howey reported to Major Edwards the officer in command of 8th Division Details and became his Liaison Officer for a short while.

The end was almost in sight for 22/Durham LI, on 1 June the survivors became the Durham Company of the 1/8th Divisional Composite Battalion. Throughout the first weeks of June they fought on in some holding actions but eventually on 13 June the survivors were brought back together to refit and take a long awaited bath. At 0600 hours on 14 July the Transport moved by road to Sezanne to entrain, they were followed by the remnants of the battalion at 0900 hours, who entrained at 1130 hours. They were moved back north behind the British held portion of the line where it was easier to re-equip and bring them back up to strength. Having detrained they moved to Marchville and Doudlainville but there were no training facilities in these places, so limited training was carried out On 22 June they moved to Helicourt Camp and were joined by the survivors of 1/7/Durham LI the 50th Divisional Pioneer Battalion. The two Commanding Officers agreed to operate as separate units until a decision was made as to what was going to happen to them. A move was made to Friacourt on 23 June and over the next week training continued. On 28 June the Battalion Transport paraded for the last time to be inspected by the Commanding Officer. He thanked the NCOs and men for all they had done and then they proceeded to Etaples for disbandment.

On 1 July 1918, 22/Durham Light Infantry held a battalion sports day, which all ranks thoroughly enjoyed and the next day the Officers Mess held a final dinner. On 3 July the youngest Service Battalion of The Durham Light Infantry ceased to exist, that day the battalion was absorbed by 1/7/Durham Light Infantry, who transferred from 50th Division and became 8th Divisional Pioneer Battalion. 22/Durham Light Infantry had only spent two years at the front, but, in that time they had suffered, sixteen Officers and 526 other ranks, killed, missing or died of wounds. With over twenty four officers known to have been wounded along with well over 1500 men wounded and that number does not include those evacuated gassed or medically sick. These are the highest figures for any of the Infantry Pioneer Battalions raised or converted during the First World War.

Chapter Nine

July – November 1918 – It's all over now

HAVING RELIEVED THE WEST YORKSHIRE BATTALION 18/Durham Light Infantry settled down in their positions, but during the morning of 1 July they were heavily shelled by both the German and the British heavy artillery, then at 1100 hours some 18 pounders fell short on them near La Becque. However the next three days were fairly quiet apart from the usual inter-company relief. It was then at 0315 hours on 4 July 10/East Yorks took over and 18/Durham LI were able to move back to Morbecque. Here they were able to have a bath and generally clean up, the following day being a Sunday, Divine Service was held for all ranks and denominations and the GOC 31st Division paid a visit to the battalion. Two days were spent training and refitting and then on Wednesday 10 July they moved back towards the line once more, by 0230 hours on 11 July the Durhams had relieved 12/Norfolk Regt in the right sub sector. This battalion along with 12/Scots Fusiliers and 24/R Welsh Fusiliers were formed in Palestine from dismounted Yeomanry Regiments and had formed a new 94 Brigade which had replaced 4 Guards Brigade in the Divisional Order of Battle.

Captain A C Borrell.
After only a short time with the battalion Arthur Borrell was promoted to the rank of Captain.

18/DURHAM LIGHT INFANTRY 'PALS' TO THE END

In very wet weather the men moved up into the trenches and no sooner had the battalion taken position, when an enemy light machine gun team walked down the road from Vierhouk towards A Company's right hand post. The men in the post waited and held their fire until the enemy were almost on top of them and then let them have both Lewis gun and rifle fire. They captured one unwounded and three wounded Germans and their gun. In the early hours an officer patrol went out and inspected the shell holes for enemy occupation, but there was nothing to report when the patrol returned. Patrols were active over the next two days and on 13 July a Corporal and two men went out and silenced an enemy machine gun which was causing trouble. They killed one of the crew but the others fled, leaving them to carry the gun back to the British lines. The next day 15/West Yorks came up and relieved 18/Durham LI. It was now that A and D Companies began training for an attack and went back to the Transport lines at Wallon Cappel to practice. Along with two companies of 15/West Yorkshire Regiment they were to advance behind a barrage and clear the ground of the enemy from La Plate Becque Farm southwards to the Vierhouk road. In preparation for this the battalion moved back into the line on 18 July. The original plan called for an artillery and trench mortar barrage but at the last moment the barrage was cancelled, which, as was later learnt, was very unfortunate as a new enemy division, and of much better fighting quality had taken over their side of the front. On the front 18/Durham LI, A Company attacked on the right half of the battalion sector and B Company on the left half.

245

By 0650 hours, A Company was in position and at Zero Hour commenced to advance, at which time they were in touch with the left company. The left Platoon commanded by Second Lieutenant Henderson reached a point about eighty yards from a stream which crossed their front, here they were held up and suffered very heavy casualties from a machine gun and were much harassed by an enemy sniper in the trees. Second Lieutenant Henderson and his Platoon Sergeant Wilf Barker managed to pull a number of the wounded into a shell hole and took up position with them there. Suddenly, at 0745 hours two Germans appeared and called on them to surrender. Second Lieutenant Henderson shot one and Wilf Barker got the other, but now a party of approximately sixteen German soldiers attacked throwing grenades. One grenade landed in the shell hole beside a wounded Durham, without a second hesitation, Wilf Barker picked the grenade up and with a great throw returned it directly to its former owner, where it exploded killing the German soldier and the man alongside him. This scattered the enemy attack and the officer and sergeant were able to hang on, although out of touch on both flanks, they held the position until ordered to withdraw at 1000 hours. For his gallantry Wilf Barker received The Distinguished Conduct Medal.

Sergeant Wilf Barker managed to pull a number of the wounded into a shell hole and took up position with them there.

The right platoon of A Company advanced very successfully and actually overrun their objective with few casualties. Second Lieutenant Brown the platoon commander took part of his platoon, and worked round to the left to try and assist Second Lieutenant Henderson but was seen to fall apparently severely wounded. The rest of the platoon came under very heavy fire from the flank. Behind Second Lieutenant Henderson the right mopping up platoon had come under a very galling flanking fire and had been unable to get very far forward. On the platoon's right, one section managed to get into position between the right and left platoons although they were a little behind them, but here they were held up by a number of enemy MG posts and therefore dug in. The right mopping up platoon was most ably led by Sergeant Whitfield and they thickened up the line held by the front platoon. It was now that a Durham Bantam proved that 19/DLI was formed from good stock – 19/698 Lance Corporal William Harper, a Spennymoor man who had been wounded on the Somme with 19/DLI came into his own, unable to get back to his own battalion he had served with 22/DLI and then joined 18/DLI. He had managed to get to within 50 yards of Plate Becque and had observed a series of six

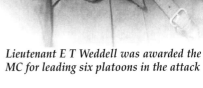

Lieutenant E T Weddell was awarded the MC for leading six platoons in the attack

machine gun posts. He ordered his team to enfilade them while he worked round to the left, from where he could bring fire to bear. Then he and another man stalked a machine gun through the corn, shot two of the crew and dismantled the gun. Their section being held up again, they went forward and successfully dealt with this second machine gun, killing three of the crew. The splendid courage and resource of these two men saved many casualties. He too was awarded The Distinguished Conduct Medal.

The platoon suffered heavily but dug in despite the right flank being threatened when the West Yorks withdrew, but Lance Corporal Ditchfield, with his Lewis gun team held the west end of the ditch, refused the right flank and accounted for a number of the enemy and forced them back. Company Headquarters which was located on the right to maintain contact between the battalions was held up in No Man's Land, but any movement attracted heavy hostile machine gun fire and nothing could be done. Meanwhile on the left, B Company left their trenches at Z-1 and got into position ready to advance. Precisely at Z Hour the advance started and within three minutes the hostile enemy machine guns had opened fire on the company left. B Company then established contact with A Company near some houses on the edge of the road. At this point B Companies left flank was very well forward and advancing towards the enclosure which was one of the objectives. They were within fifty yards of the enclosure when the enemy machine guns in side opened fire and wiped out a complete Lewis Gun Section. The Platoon commander Second Lieutenant Turnbull led a rifle section along the hedge line and charge the machine gun post but every man, except the officer, fell dead or wounded, the officer was pinned down ten yards from the post and unable to get any closer. He managed to get into cover and then fell back to another section. At 0815 hours he led this section in an attempt to work round to the flank to put the gun out of action. However the attempt was doomed to failure, owing to the highly sustained and accurate enemy fire.

In the centre of the company, Lance Corporal Adams and his Lewis gun team got inside the enclosure and seeing the enemy machine gun firing on Second Lieutenant Turnbull, they engaged

A supply tank takes stores forward saving the infantry much work in providing carrying parties.

it immediately. They had hardly opened fire, when an enemy platoon came out of one of the houses, charged Lance Corporal Adams section and bombed them out of the enclosure. The other enemy machine gun in the enclosure also switched targets and switched onto the left flank with deadly accurate enfilade fire.

On the right, Second Lieutenant Langley reached the south west corner of the enclosure without casualties, at this corner he observed two German soldiers mounting a machine gun, he shot one, but simultaneously another enemy machine gun opened fire on his left flank. This gun appeared to be positioned in the hedge running out westward from the centre of the enclosure; the fire from this gun killed all but two of the men with Second Lieutenant Langley. The next order given by the officer was for his left rifle section to push along the hedge and deal with the machine gun post; the section moved off as ordered and moved along the hedge line, but the gun turned on them and at least two men were killed, which brought the movement to a halt. Meanwhile Lieutenant Armstrong brought up a number of rifle grenadiers and Lewis gunners in an effort to drive the enemy out of the enclosure; however the Germans had sighted their positions with great tactical skill and had provided excellent cover behind the hedge, so the Durham's efforts were completely wasted. Meanwhile the extreme right of B Company had finished beyond the southern edge of the enclosure; here it was hit in the left rear by a hostile enemy machine gun. Seeing that they had got too far forward of the rest of the company and were out of touch, they took cover and worked their way back to where they could align with the rest of the company. Lieutenant Armstrong now ordered his men to dig in, with the intention of working forward at dark or if the situation altered. However word came through from Brigade Headquarters that the West Yorks attack had failed and they were now back at the start line. Plans were made to reinforce A Company, but before anything was done word came in that their position was critical and a gradual withdrawal was ordered. A Company received these orders around 1300 hours, but only a partial withdrawal took place as posts remained out to cover wounded men in shell holes. Many of these came in or were brought in by the stretcher bearers once darkness fell. On the left B Company fell back to the original front line, this was done by the men working in pairs and moving slowly back through the corn. However Second Lieutenant Crierie was unable to bring his platoon out as they were right up against the enclosure and any movement would have attracted enemy

The four Company Sergeant Majors and a Company Quarter Master Sergeant of 18/Durham LI near the end of the war.

fire and possible casualties. By 2200 hours with the exception of a few men the companies were back where they started, and had paid a high butcher's bill.

	Second Lieutenant W Brown		*wounded andmissing*	
	Lieutenant C L Welford		*badly wounded*	
	Second Lieutenant R W Langley		*slightly wounded*	

	A Company	B Company	Total
Killed	20	12	32
Wounded	25	26	51
Wounded and missing	4	1	5
Missing	10	1	11

Other Ranks 99

The report issued after the action highlighted a number of points, Wardogs had been used and one dog and its handler had been killed, a second handler was killed but the dog broke free and returned to his kennel at Brigade Headquarters, the third dog successfully brought in his message. Signals on the whole worked well, as did the medical arrangements, with particular praise for the stretcher bearers. In a number of cases the enemy held up their hands and offered to surrender and then fired pistols or threw grenades, in one case shouting 'Not this week Tommy!' A large number of wounds were caused by bullets being turned by the standing corn; these were much more serious than if they had been a straight forward bullet wound. Further information came in from Brigade that on the night prior to the attack the German 187 Regt had taken over and completely changed the system of defense, which accounted for the unexpected resistance that was encountered.

Having returned to the front line A & B Companies were relieved by C & D Companies, 21 July was a very quiet day but that night there was very heavy machine gun fire, and then the following day 11/East Lancashire Regt relieved 18/Durham LI., The Durham Pals now went back to Morbecque and were able to clean up and have a bath and the training started again. After a church parade on 28 July the battalion received orders to move back into the reserve line where A and B Companies replaced 24/R Welsh Fusiliers at Grande Marquette Farm, D Company took over La Promenade Farm and C Company were in trenches at Grande-Sec-Bois, the relief was complete by 2256 hours in front of the Durhams on the right was 13/York and Lancaster and on the left 15/West Yorks. To the right the 92 Brigade held the line and on the left 119 Brigade of 40th Division continued it northwards. On 1 August they moved forward and took over the right sub sector from the 13/York and Lancaster Regiment, the relief being completed 0230 hours, A held the right front and B the left front, with C in support and D in Reserve. They had only been in position for a few hours when orders were received that they were to take over the R2 sub-sector from 11/East Yorks. In preparation for this move 12/Norflok Regt relieved the front two companies and 23/Lancashire Fusiliers took over in support, 18/Durham LI then moved sideways to complete the move. At the end of the move C and D companies were in the front line, with A and B Companies positioned in right and left support respectively. In order to familiarize the men with the ground to their front patrols were quickly sent forward to establish where the enemy was located. On 6 August D Company was withdrawn and over 600 gas bombs were fired at the enemy held line, from their location. They remained clear of the danger zone for over two hours, owing to the gas lingering about and when they returned they found a badly gassed German soldier had wandered into the British position. Unfortunately he was not carrying any means of identification and he died before he reached the Casualty Clearing Station. The following day, acting on information received from Brigade, a patrol of two snipers was sent out to watch the enemy, who were rumored to be likely to be withdrawing. The patrol came back some time later and reported that the enclosure did not appear to be held. The OC D Company, Captain Neal, DCM, ordered Second Lieutenant Perry and six other ranks to go forward and check this out. When they arrived at the enclosure they came upon a party of Germans, who indicated that the British should surrender. However four of the Durhams had worked round to the flank and the tables were turned on the Germans, in all fourteen of them surrendered to Second Lieutenant Perry and his men. For his ability and securing a vital recognition of the enemy unit opposite he was awarded The Military Cross.

The battalion was now able to move its posts forward some 200 to 300 yards, where they dug in. Over the next two days patrols were actively looking for a way forward, but! The enemy machine gun fire was very heavy and the patrols established that the enemy had an observation post high in a tree on the La Couronne road, from which any movement could be observed. On the night of 9 August 11/East Yorks came up and completed the relief of 18/Durham LI by 0200 hours on 10 August. 18/Durham LI then moved back to Morbecquem where after baths and a general clean up musketry and training took place. Whilst the battalion was out of the line 40th Division took over the Vieux Berquin sector from the 31st Division, who in their turn took over from 9th (Scottish) Division in the Meteren sector. So it was on the late afternoon of 22 August that 18/Durham LI began moving forward, marching via Hazebrouck and by 2330 on 23 August they had taken over the front left sub-sector from 12/Royal Scots Fusiliers. The next day the front was extended northwards by taking over a portion of the line held by 5/Cameron Highlanders. On 25 August the day was fairly quiet but towards evening the rain started and it fell all night, There was some shelling near battalion headquarters but no casualties occurred, whilst a patrol out in No Man's Land spotted a larger group of the enemy, however as they were outnumbered the Durhams held their fire and returned to their own lines. The bad weather continued as did the shelling and on 27 August two men were killed at Battalion Headquarters, when it was shelled heavily all day, that night A and B Companies were relieved by 1/King's Own Scottish Borderers and D Company by 12/Royal Scots Fusiliers, this allowed another sideways move and on 28 August at 2300 hours A Company took over a new portion of the front line with D Company on their left and the other two companies in support positions, with Battalion Headquarters in a location known as Kelso Cottage. Later that night a patrol went out from D Company and identified an enemy post some 300 yards in front of the company position. It was arranged for an artillery barrage to fall on the enemy post; however there was no follow up action and the results of the barrage remain unknown. During 29 August a large number of fires were observed in the German lines and it was thought that the enemy was burning stores and equipment prior to withdrawing. The next morning both front line companies reported that the enemy was withdrawing rapidly and they were ordered too follow up and try and keep touch. Patrols were pushed out as far as the town of Bailleul but no enemy was encountered. C Company pushed on to the Mont De Lille and by 2015 hours two platoons were trying to get to the top of the hill. In Bailleul a German spy was found dressed in British uniform at the entrance to a cellar, which was full of rations and telephone equipment, with wires running back into the German lines. After a quick court martial, the man was executed. The month ended with the advance continuing right across the front, on the left the 36th (Ulster) Division took Ravelsberg and 18/Durham LI met heavy machine gun fire as they pressed forward 31st Divisions advance at Mont De Lille, likewise to the south the 'Incomparable' 29th Division kept up their sectors advance.

Sergeant Parker and Orderly Room Quartermaster Sergeant Allison both served with the battalion throughout the war

At 0425 hours on 1 September, 1/Border Regiment completed the relief of 18/Durham LI, after which the Durhams moved back to a rest area east of Meteren, where they arrived at 1800 hours. They were now employed as navvies clearing the roads of rubble between Meteren and Bailleul, which came under long range shell fire from the enemy. These working parties continued until the battalion began erecting a new camp at Neuve Glease on 13 September, however the enemy forced them out by shelling the place heavily and by mixing in a large number of gas shells, they caused no less than forty casualties in D Company alone. On the night of 15 September, D Company went forward and moved into support positions behind 15/West Yorkshire Regiment, whilst in a similar move C Company took up positions behind 13/York and Lancaster Regiment. The next two days were fairly normal but on 18 September, 15/West Yorkshire Regiment made an attack in which they took a number of prisoners, which caused the enemy to shell the British lines and thinking there may be a counter attack, all four companies of 18/Durham LI were 'stood to'. Later that night 12/Norfolk Regiment took over and 18/Durham LI moved back to a bivouac camp, as C Company moved back they came under fire from a long range gun and suffered some eighteen casualties of whom, four died from their wounds, After one night in this camp they were moved to another camp, from where they started work clearing debris and salvaging equipment. The signs that the war was close to its end showed clearly when all companies were treated to a lecture, 'Education after the war.' By 25 September the men were at work clearing the Grande Place in Bailleul, even though it had been a large town with thousands of inhabitants, there was not one building left that could provide cover for the men. During this period when two companies were working the other two were training and generally at lunch time they would change over, so that some form of tactical training would take place each day. After a visit by the GOC 31st Division on the afternoon of 26 September, the battalion began preparing to move back into the line under command of 92 Brigade.. Taking over from 11/East Yorkshire Regiment the battalion placed C Company and two platoons of A Company in the right front line and D Company, along with one platoon of B Company held the left front. The remaining two platoons of A Company were in support and the rest of B Company in reserve. At noon next day command passed to 93 Brigade Headquarters, who ordered an attack to be made on Ploegsteeert Wood, Touquet Berthe and Maison 1875. The attack started well, D Company reached all its objectives and the left of C Company advanced buut were later forced to withdraw, the enemy launching a hurricane bombardment and two very threatening flank attacks. On the right however this company met serious opposition and was unable to make any headway. During the night command passed back to 92 Brigade, who ordered that the attack should be resumed at dawn. This time the companies pushed deeper into the wood and reached the objective and pushed out advanced posts.

The tactical situation now required a re-alignment of line of the battalion advance, leaving only two platoons to cover the line they had just taken, they made a night tactical march, in atrocious weather conditions, torrential rain and a sea of muddy tracks, all ploughed up by marching feet. Led by Captain Killick and D Company, they moved up the western edge of the wood and then along the northern edge, then turned south and moved to the south eastern corner they eventually lined up for an attack south eastwards towards the Lys. They linked up with 12/Royal Scots Fusiliers on the left, but the unit on the right suffered a number of mishaps and failed to cross the start line. On 1 October B and D Companies advanced towards the River Lys. They had a brilliant advance, but enemy artillery observers were able to bring down a heavy barrage particularly on the right company. There was four men wounded and it was now that the last three men of the battalion were killed in action, 18/679 Sergeant Ernest Bushby, who was aged thirty and came from Thornley, near Wheatley Hill in County Durham and two nineteen year old Yorkshire men, Privates, 91221, John Horsfield from Mirfield near Halifax and 91229, Harry Iredale who's parents lived in the High Street in Golcar. Although a number of others would die from wounds received these were the last three men of 18/Durham LI killed by the enemy.

After the attack the position was held until the night of 1 – 2 October when they were relieved by 11//East Yorkshire Regiment and the net two days were spent in cleaning up and reorganising. On 4 October the battalion relieved three companies of 13/York and Lancaster Regiment and one company of 29/Durham LI in the front line. The battalion placed A Company on the left, C Company in the centre and B Company on the right with D Company in support. That night patrols went out and every bridge over the River Lys was reconnoitred and reported on. After another quiet day on 6 October the battalion moved back into Divisional support and began cleaning up and re-organising, on 7 October the Brigade commander visited the battalion and then the inspections started as well as training and tactical schemes. The training continued right through until 16 October when they moved back in the morning to Ploegsteert, that afternoon they moved again to Deulemont. Each day they followed the advance and marched to a different location by 28 October they had reached Steenbrugge at 1330 hours and had great difficulty securing billets. On these marches they were greeted with great enthusiasm by the local people and wine, beer, coffee, cakes were all pressed onto the liberating troops. They remained here for five days and then advanced again moving on 3 November to the Roncq area where they arrived at 1300 hours. Training took place over the next four days and then on 8 November word of an Armistice started to spread. The battalion left Roncq and moved to Sweveghem and took over the front line on 9 November. However the enemy retired and the battalion followed up and crossed the River Scheldt and it was here that the news came in that the Armistice had been signed and for 18/Durham LI 'the war was over.'

19/DURHAM LIGHT INFANTRY – 'THE END IN BELGIUM'

At 0400 hours on 1 July 1918, 19/Durham LI entrained at Doullens and after a four hour train journey, in the luxurious cattle trucks of the French Railways detrained at 0800 hours at St Omer and marched to billets in Tilques. The following day they were picked up by motor buses of The Army Service Corps and were carried to Watou where they moved into camp prior to moving into reserve in the Locre Sector. The battalion war diary for this period is very sparse indeed over the next twenty six days the battalion went from support to the front line and back to reserve without any additional information.

It wasn't until the night of 27 July when the battalion carried out a trench raid on the enemy trenches on the left of Locre Hospice that any new information comes to light. The preparation for the raid took place under the watchful eye of Captain H Heaton MC and consisted of two parties. The first consisting of twenty eight other ranks led by Captain Smith MC and Captain J W Ryall was found by X Company and the second party was thirty two other ranks of Z Company commanded by Second Lieutenant W G Dyer MC and Second Lieutenant Jordan. Zero hour was set for 2330 hours at which time a heavy and accurate stokes mortar barrage fell on the objective, at the same time an artillery barrage was brought to bear on the Brigade SOS lines of fire. Two gaps were blown in the enemy wire by Bangalore torpedo and the raiders entered the enemy line at two different points with the X Company men on the left and those from Z Company on the right. There were an unusually large number of enemy soldiers in the trench and it was thought that they had also been planning a raid or an attack, or it was possible that a relief was taking place. With such a large garrison in the trench a fierce hand to hand struggle commenced and at least twenty German soldiers were killed. On the left Captain Ryall with a small party of men rushed an enemy machine gun post and killed the crew. The Captain himself was badly wounded but with the assistance of his batman he carried the captured gun back to the British lines. Four prisoners were sent back across No Man's Land but, on the way two of them started to struggle and unfortunately their guards were forced to shoot them. As well as Captain Ryall, both subalterns and twenty one men of the raiding party were wounded, mainly by shrapnel from the bombs they themselves had thrown. Identification of the prisoners and other captured

273060 Private Delar Simmons, a Londoner, was killed in action 2 July 1918.

How Captain Ryall won the Military Cross. Captain Ryall and his batman carried in an enemy machine gun

material showed that the line opposite the battalion was held by 103 Reserve Infantry Regiment which was part of the 58th Division, which recruited its men in Saxony.

Immediately after the raid the Brigade Commander sent the signal 'Well done Durhams', to the battalion The following day they were relieved by 18/Lancashire Fusiliers and moved back into Brigade Reserve and then two days later another relief took place, this time by 27/Canadian Infantry Battalion and 19/Durham LI went further back into Corps Reserve at Terdeghem where they began refitting and cleaning up. On 3 august a convoy of motor lorries carried the battalion forward to Boeschepe and the next day they relieved 17/Lancashire Fusiliers in the Front Line of the Locre Sector. The line was quiet but the enemy were suspected to be withdrawing. Divisional Headquarters sent orders that the battalion should send out patrols, to try and find out what was happening. Two patrols were sent out one from each front line company. On the left Second Lieutenant R Shield and twenty other ranks tried to get to the German Front Line but were held up by an enemy machine gun. On the right however Second Lieutenant W Reid with fourteen other

19/1512 Sergeant Charles Ward from Langley Park Co Durham, discharged in July 1918 having been wounded twice.

ranks, manage to enter the enemy trench and worked along a communication trench for over eighty yards behind the line. They established that the enemy had retired to a ridge behind the line and then returned to the British trenches. After a further two days in the line they were relieved and set off for the camp at Terdeghem. Here two weeks were spent training and then they moved to the ranges at Colembert, the whole battalion being billeted at Henneveux. Four days were spent on range work and musketry before they moved back to Terdeghem for further training.

On 2 September the battalion left Terdeghem and marched to Herzeele where they were billeted for two days. They then marched to the area east of Poperinghe where they boarded a light railway train and were carried to Red Farm, here they detrained and marched to St Lawrence and Erie Camps and became the divisional reserve. On 8 September the battalion had one man wounded as they relieved 15/Sherwood Foresters in the support trenches in the canal sector; here they were billeted in what was left of some old farm buildings south east of Vlamertinghe. They remained in this location for four days and then on 12 September the battalion went forward and relieved 17/Lancashire Fusiliers in the Front Line of the Canal Sector. The relief was completed without incident and the battalion

53691 Sergeant W Rigg 19/Durham LI was the last of the raiding party to leave the enemy trenches, he was awarded the Distinguished Conduct Medal.

settled down to hold the line. Early next morning an alert sentry in one of the forward posts spotted an enemy patrol approaching. He alerted the post commander, a Marley Hill man, 18803, Lance Corporal William Cranney, who gave orders that his men should hold their fire. When the enemy patrol was less than thirty yards from the British post, Lance Corporal Cranney and two of his men rushed out and forced the whole of the enemy patrol, a corporal and four men, to surrender. For this action Lance Corporal Cranney was awarded The Military Medal.

Division now ordered that the front should be pushed forward and an operation was planned whereby 19/Durham LI and 18/Lancashire Fusiliers would advance under cover of an artillery barrage and seize a line of posts about one thousand yards in advance of the position held. The section allocated to 19/Durham LI was from Blauwe Poort Farm and Manor Halt to the embankment at I.22.a.7.0. Y Company was detailed to provide the attacking force and all four platoons were to go over the top, whilst one platoon of X Company was on standby as a support if required. Second Lieutenant Leach was to advance with his platoon along the edge of Zillebeke Lake. Second Lieutenant Shepley had Manor Halt as the objective for his platoon and he was to use the Ypres - Menin railway line as a direction guide. The Platoon commanded by Second Lieutenant Reid had as its objective the cross roads at I.28.a.15.90. They were to use the Ypres – Hollebeke road as an aid to direction. The last platoon, commanded by Lieutenant Dales was ordered to take Blauwe Poort Farm. The company formed up in a line running roughly north easterly, each platoon was in a diamond formation and each section in file. Precisely at 2228 hours on 15 September the barrage landed on the enemy front line and Y Company advanced. On the left Second Lieutenant Leach met with no opposition at all, the enemy ran away as his platoon approached. They were able to dig in and consolidate their position. The next morning a patrol from this platoon found a German soldier hiding in the bank of a stream and took him prisoner. Second Lieutenant Leach had previously reconnoitered the ground most thoroughly and during the operation led his men over most difficult ground to the final objective. After consolidating his line he personally attacked the enemy's posts and brought in eight prisoners and two machine guns. Throughout the engagement he led his men with great daring and dash and his conduct was a stirring example to all ranks. The left centre attack on Manor Farm, led by Lieutenant Dales also met with practically no opposition and was able to dig in and consolidate the position. On their right however the Platoon led by Second Lieutenant Shepley met with considerable opposition. Although they fought their way into the enemy position they were initially forced back. They immediately returned to the attack and regained the position. The fighting was very fierce and several of the enemy were killed as well as a number taken prisoner. Second Lieutenant Herbert Shepley had also previously reconnoitered the

After the attack a Sergeant and two men of 19/Durham LI consolidate their position.

Sergeant Proud, on the left, was awarded the MSM and promoted to CQMS and then to RQMS.

position and he led his platoon in the attack with great courage and was ever in the forefront of the fight. He took the enemy's posts and consolidated them, and the line was completely established owing chiefly to his initiative, dash and cheerful influences. Throughout the whole engagement he set a fine example to his men. This platoon was reinforced by a Lewis gun section from X Company.

On the right flank in front of Blauwee Poort Farm the enemy had manned a series of small posts well forward. When Second Lieutenant Reid had reconnoitered the ground the previous night the posts had not been there, and as the platoon advanced they were surprised when these posts opened fire on them. While he was in the act of throwing a bomb Second Lieutenant Reid was seen to be hit and believed to have been killed. The advance was continued but owing to the loss of the platoon commander the direction was lost. The party eventually took up a position near a building which they believed was their objective. Later that night they were reinforced by Second Lieutenant Dyer and ten men from X Company. The attackers captured over twenty five prisoners and had one officer and four men killed, with a further seven men wounded.

The next day 17/Royal Scots arrived and took over the front line, 19/Durham LI meanwhile moved back to St Lawrence Camp where they began refitting. The battalion was out of the line for eight days and it wasn't until 24 September that they took over from the Lancashire Fusiliers in the left sub sector along the Comines Canal sector. As the relief took place the enemy put down a heavy barrage and twelve other ranks were wounded before the relief was completed at 2355 hours. After two quiet days holding the line the battalion took part in the advance of the British forces in Flanders. At 0525 hours ton 28 September the British barrage crashed down onto Hill 60 and 19/Durham LI stormed forward and captured the Hill and moved on towards Klien Zillebeke. Here they were held up by enemy snipers and 18/1610 Company Sergeant Major W G Walker made up his mind to do something about them. He crawled forward and killed one and captured another, then led his platoon to its objective and consolidated. Second Lieutenant F W Blake, although gassed prior to the commencement of operations, led his men with great spirit and endurance. Having reached the final objective he immediately reorganized his platoon and rushed forward with patrols to Jehovah Trench, where he took a machine gun and an enemy sergeant major. He was also largely instrumental in capturing six officers and forty other ranks on reaching the same line. Yet more acts of gallantry were taking place all along the battalion front, 24559 Sergeant R Stoddart, from Medomsley, near Consett, commanded a platoon throughout the whole operation in a most able manner. Also, he alone rushed a machine gun post, killing three of the crew and capturing the remainder and the gun. Subsequently, he helped to get in wounded under exceptionally heavy artillery, and the battalion Adjutant, Captain E A Parke went forward and get information and so clear up the situation. In addition to this his great assistance and forethought in the arrangements in forming and forwarding of dumps of munitions and material were perfect. At 0945 hours 17/Lancashire Fusiliers passed through 19/Durham LI, to carry the attack on to Zandvoorde, however the Fusiliers were held up at the Basseville Beek by machine guns firing from the remains of Zandvoorde village. A further Military Cross was won by Lieutenant J Sharp who when the Fusiliers passed through his company took his men and acted as a flank guard to the Lancashire battalion and protected their flank for two days. The attack was continued on 30 September and 19/Durham LI were ordered to advance on the Gheluwe Switch a well defended line that ran north east to the Menin Road. The battalion marched up through Tenbrielen to America Cabaret where they deployed into line and at 1900 hours with 18/Lancashire Fusiliers on the right, the attack commenced. Both battalions were held up by the uncut wire and several machine gun positions and were forced to dig in for the night. At dawn the attack started again, but! The enemy in pill boxes and behind strong barbed wire were too strong, further more the enemy artillery now put down a very heavy barrage on the attacking British troops and all that was gained was 200 yards, where some advanced posts were established.

On 2 October 5/KOSB relieved 19/Durham LI and they started to move back, first to Kruiseke in reserve and the following day to Zillebeke where they went under canvas and began refitting. On 5 October 104 Brigade went up the line again and relieved a Brigade of Irishmen from the 36th (Ulster) Division in front of Terhand. 19/Durham LI were in Brigade reserve and were only called upon to send forward two companies W and Y, who went forward to an area near Becelaere, whilst X and Z Companies remained at Zillebeke. On 6 October however W Company went back to Clapham Junction, they were soon followed by X and Z Companies and then on 7 October HQ and Y companies also arrived there. For the next four days the whole of 104 Brigade was in Divisional Reserve at Clapham Junction.

On the night 11/12 October 104 Brigade went up the line again and relieved 106 Brigade, 19/Durham LI went back under canvas at Becelaere and began preparing for another attack. On the night of 12 October officers went forward to reconnoitre the approaches and it was while doing this that Captain K Smith MC was wounded by enemy shell fire.

At 0530 hours on 14 October behind a very powerful artillery barrage 104 Brigade began to advance. 17/Lancashire Fusiliers led the way and captured the first objective a line South of Moorseele to Tamil Farm. When this line was reached 18/Lancashire Fusiliers on the right and 19/Durham LI on the left continued the attack. Their objective was a line from Poeselhoek – Schoon Water – Kappelhoek. 19/Durham LI was advancing with X and Y

Sergeant W Wilson DCM gained a bar to his medal during the raid, he personally bayoneted a least three enemy soldiers and was the last man to leave his section of the enemy trench.

Companies in the front line Z Company in support and W Company provided 'mopping up' parties and carrying parties. The advance took place in a thick fog and it was difficult for the attacking waves to keep direction. It was then that a Trimdon Colliery man, 13672, Sergeant, J R Robertson MM, came into his own, when his company had been held up some 200 yards from its final objective by machine gun fire and snipers. He took a party of ten men and attacked the post from a flank, capturing the machine gun and three prisoners, and putting the remainder of the enemy to flight. The position was consolidated and at a critical moment under a heavy enemy barrage Second Lieutenant H Chadwick brought his platoon up to reinforce the line. Sergeant R Stoddart was in great evidence throughout the attack, alone he charged two machine guns, which were firing at him point blank, bayoneting two of their crew and taking the remainder prisoner. Later, he again rushed a machine gun post, which was menacing our left flank.

A number of abandoned field guns were found and a large number of enemy soldiers taken prisoner. The battalion had two officers wounded and around ninety other ranks with about twenty men killed in action. That night patrols were sent out in the direction of Bissinghem. The next morning at 0900 hours a further advance took place against the Shoon Water Spur and the spur South East of Poeselhoek. Sergeant Stoddart was now ordered to take a party of sixteen men to raid two farms, which were giving a considerable amount of trouble. He accomplished his task and, although severely wounded, established posts in the positions taken. The line gained was consolidated and held for the night, and then the following morning at 0530 hours, 106 Brigade passed through 104 Brigade and continued the advance until they reached the banks of the River Lys.

The next day 106 Brigade continued its advance and crossed the River Lys and established posts about 1000 yards over the river. Pontoon bridges were put into position by the Royal Engineers and at around 1100 hours 19/Durham LI and the rest of 104 Brigade crossed the river and formed up in assembly positions behind 106 Brigade outpost line.

The Brigade had three battalions in the line 17/Lancashire Fusiliers on the right, 18/Lancashire fusiliers in the centre and 19/Durham LI on the left. At 0530 hours the British Artillery fired a creeping barrage and under the cover of this and hidden in a thick mist the three battalions advanced. The first objective, the Aelbeke – Courtrai road was taken with little opposition. A large number of civilians were encountered here, the enemy having had no chance to evacuate them. The advance was quickly pushed on and the second objective the Walle – Knock road was taken. Patrols were pushed forward to the main Hooge – Courtrai road, which soon became the new front line. In taking this position a lot more machine gun fire was met and this

Lieutenant W E Lennard the Battalion Signalling Officer was awarded The Military Cross for his work in maintaining communications with the forward troops.

caused some casualties among the advancing Durhams. On reaching the road W Company sent patrols forward into Courtrai at 1100 hours, the battalion having the honour of being the first British troops to enter and liberate the town. No opposition was met and eight or nine stray enemy soldiers were rounded up. Later that day a piquet from Z Company took up position in The Grande Place. The battalion held this line overnight until next morning, when at 0700 hours the advance was resumed. 104 Brigade attacked in a South Easterly direction without an artillery barrage. The first objective was the crest running south west from Sweveghem and the second objective the Kreupel Crest. Each battalion had two field guns attached and some Vickers guns of 31/Machine Gun Battalion. On the front of 19/Durham LI enemy resistance, at the first objective, was strong and the field guns had to be called up to clear the enemy machine gun positions. As the battalion cleared the ridge and moved onto the second objective they were held up by machine gun fire from the Kreupel Ridge. Again the field guns were called up and shelled the ridge, the attackers then secured the ridge and pushed patrols forward to secure the line of the final objective, which was secured at 1830 hours. On the left of the battalion advance Lieutenant W Iley was leading his platoon forward when he came across a row of houses that should have been cleared by the battalion on the left. However they were held up, so Lieutenant Iley took some of his men and started to clear the houses, he shot one German himself and with his men routed the remainder, which enabled the battalion on his left to advance to the objective. This line was held throughout 21 October and during the day troops of 41st Division passed through the line and continued the attack. The whole of 35th Division was now withdrawn to billets in Courtrai. They began refitting and two large drafts joined the battalion, 123 other ranks on 23 October and 60 other ranks the next day, however the Commanding Officer, Lieutenant Colonel H R McCullagh was ordered to England for a six month tour of duty, Major B C H Keenlyside 18/Lancashire Fusiliers took over command.

Lieutenant James Murray was awarded The Military Cross for leading his men to the attack under heavy shell and machine gun fire.

104 Brigade moved back into the line on 27 October, but 19/Durham LI remained in reserve in the village of Krote, it wasn't until the evening of 29 October that they relieved 17/Lancashire Fusiliers in the Front Line North of Avelghem. At 0525 hours on 31 October, 104 Brigade again advanced against the enemy, under cover of a barrage from 6 inch Howitzers and an effective smoke screen. Some enemy positions fought very hard and Second Lieutenant R Wood led his platoon in a rush, under heavy machine gun and artillery fire, against some form buildings, where he captured over thirty enemy soldiers and took three heavy machine guns, to win The Military Cross. Major Keenlyside who had been wounded, led the battalion throughout the operation and continued to advance with the battalion until the final objective was reached. By 1030 hours all objectives were taken and the villages of Rugge, Trappelstraat, Waermaerde, Tenhove and Kerkhove had all been liberated from the enemy. Later that day the battalion pushed on as far as Eeuwhoek and by the end of the day the battalion had taken over 300 enemy prisoners. The casualties in the battalion were four officers and ninety eight other ranks, of which Second Lieutenant F W Blake and twenty two men were killed in action. Captain Heaton, commanding Z Company, wrote to Second Lieutenant Blake's father,

19 Durham LI
10/11/18

Dear Mr Blake

I expect you will have had the sad news of the death of your son, who was killed in action about 6 a.m. on Thursday, October 31st. May I on behalf of all Officers and men of my battalion express the very deep sympathy we feel for you in your sad bereavement. I expect you would like to know the exact details as to how and where he met his death. We had commenced the attack on the enemy at 5.30 a.m. and were a right flank guard to the Belgian Army which was attacking North of us – our right rested on the river and this was our guide.

Your son was leading the platoon forward and had advanced some 1500 yards when an obstacle in the nature of a stream was encountered – it was while leading his men through this that he fell

mortally wounded with a machine gun bullet in his head. He was taken to the Advanced Dressing Station and died there. He was unconscious throughout. His grave lies near Avelghem on the Scheldt about eleven miles east of Courtrai.

He was one of the most splendid officers I had in the Company, and his men simply adored him. He was always a thorough gentleman and I think the thing I most admired him for was his total abstinence from alcohol. Even when going over to the attack he would not join the others in having his issue of rum. His favourite words were 'you can always fight better without that stuff on your stomach. He had just been awarded The Military Cross for gallantry and devotion to duty on September 28th 1918 though he did not live to learn of this honour. He was due for leave and expected to be getting home after this attack. 'It was the only thing, he said, that made life bearable out here, was leave.

May I once more express my heartfelt sympathy for you all in your sad loss.

204000 Private John Peacock from Old Shildon was one of the twenty two men killed in action on 31 October 1918.

On 1 November 19/Durham LI were relieved in the Front Line by 20/Durham LI and some of The Queens West Surrey Regiment of 41st Division and moved back to Sweveghem and from there to billets in Courtrai. While the battalion was in Courtrai refitting Lieutenant Colonel W Rigby DSO, Royal Irish Rifles arrived and assumed command of the battalion. After several days resting and refitting the battalion moved back towards the front arriving at Berchem where they billeted for the night on 9 November. The next day the followed up the enemy and arrived at the village of Louise-Marie where the people were more than overjoyed to see them. The next day they were ordered to move forward again and secure a bridgehead over the River Dendre at Grammont. Cyclists had gone forward and secured the bridge and 19/Durham LI were moving forward, to get in touch with the enemy, when the word came through that an armistice had been signed between the Allied Armies and the German Army and that hostility would cease at 1100 hours. For 19/Durham LI the war was over and they marched back to billets at Everbecq.

Chapter Ten

Epilogue – The return to civilian life.

'When I get my civvies clothes on no more soldiering for me.'
SOLDIER'S SONG 1914-18.

No SOONER HAD THE ARMISTICE BEEN SIGNED than 18/Durham Light Infantry began a long march back across Flanders and into Northern France, by 16 November they had reached Wevelghem where they practiced a ceremonial parade and on 20 November, with all of 93 Brigade on Parade the GOC 31st Division, presented the ribbons of gallantry awards to those who had won them in the last days of the war. Menin, Vlamertinghe, St Eloi, Arques was the route taken all on foot in the last days of November 1918. With the battalion billeting party setting off early each day and the battalion marching behind, usually with the band in the centre so that the marches could be heard by all ranks and the step kept together.

THE 18/DURHAM LIGHT INFANTRY 'A LONG MARCH HOME'

In Arques good billets were found and training was carried out to keep the men busy, but as early as 11 December coal miners were being sent home, every day a batch of miners left the battalion, but time was also found for sport, Rugby., Football and Boxing, there was Brigade and Divisional tournaments and soon Christmas was upon the battalion, four separate dinners were held on Christmas Day, the men at 1230 hours, the Transport Section, nearly all the 'old hands' original enlistments at 1700 hours and the Sergeants and Corporals at 1900 hours. Whilst of the officers who would also have had a dinner the war diary makes no mention. New Years Day 1919 was given as a holiday and those Roman Catholics of the battalion celebrated Holy Mass in the Parish Church in Arques, but even that and the holiday didn't stop the miners being sent home for discharge. Soon men were on working parties salvaging material from the battlefields but the army discipline continued and kit inspections and parades were a regular feature of battalion life. However on 29 January, 31st Division was ordered to Calais, where there was unrest and strikes among the Army Ordnance Corps and Railway Operating Division men in the Base Area. 18/Durham LI paraded in fighting order at 0530 hours and marched to St Omer where they entrained at 0800 hours and arrived at Calais about 1300 hours. Every man carried a blanket and one day's rations, but trouble was expected and although the Lewis guns were carried by limber to St Omer, they were taken from the limbers and issued to companies and actually carried into Calais by the battalion. On arrival in Calais, 93 Brigade with 18/Durham LI under command moved to Beau Marais camp and on a very cold January night went under canvas. Two days later, on 31 January after much negotiation the strikers returned to work and 18/Durham LI

Bill Pearson started the war a Private and by the end was a Company Sergeant Major, still serving with 18/Durham LI.

261

Mrs C D Shafto places a Laurel wreath on the pole.

went back to Arques.

All through February men were sent home and those that remained, waiting their turn were employed on various working parties. On 19 February at Blendecques, all the battalions of 93 Brigade and the Divisional Pioneer Battalion 12/King's Own Yorkshire Light Infantry paraded for the presentation of The King's Colour. Brigadier-General G B Smyth DSO presented the Colour of 18/Durham LI to Lieutenant Allbeury MC and at the end of the parade the battalion buglers sounded the Royal Salute. By early march there was only a few men left, a draft of 300 young soldiers, under command of Captain A C Borrell joined 2/6/Durham LI on 17 March, Lieutenant Colonel Lowe had left to command 93 Brigade and what was left of the battalion was commanded by Major D E Ince MC. Eventually all the stores and animals, both horses and Mules were handed over to the Army Ordnance Corps. Time began to drag and all ranks wanted to be away, cricket against other units filled the time but it wasn't until 16 May that the stores and transport moved to Wizernes Station to begin the journey home. Two days later on 18 May the Battalion Cadre followed, they spent a night at Dunkirk and then moved to Number Three Embarkation Camp and sailed on the SS Mogileff at 1700 hours on 21 May, arriving at Southampton at 0955 hours the following morning after a very comfortable voyage. From Southampton they moved to Catterick, where all mobilisation stores were handed in and the Cadre briefed on the forthcoming Parade to lay up the Colour in Durham Cathedral.

On 27 May the Cadre entrained at Catterick and arrived at Durham at 1145 hours. They stored their kit at the station and marched, with the colours cased, through the City to the Market Place where a large crowd had gathered to greet them. Lunch was provided in the Town Hall, after which the cadre formed up inside the Town Hall and marched out into the Market Place, with the Colour uncased. The Cadre formed up facing the Town Hall, with around 120 discharged members of the battalion behind them. Mrs C D Shafto then fastened a Laurel wreath to the pole. All the Gentlemen connected with the raising of the battalion were gathered on the Town Hall balcony from where they delivered long speeches. The Mayor spoke first, welcoming the cadre home and praising their fighting prowess. Next to speak was Lord Durham, who said how proud he and the County were of the 'Pals', in a long speech. Next the Deputy Mayor added his praise, particularly remembering the fallen of the battalion. Last but by no means the shortest speech was made by Colonel Rowland Burdon VD, MP. Who had been one of the main raisers of the battalion, the last part of his speech, praised the battalion, saying 'The records of the 18th Battalion would add honour to those of their great County Regiment.'

Major Ince MC replied on behalf of the battalion, thanking the people for the hearty welcome and to all those who had sent comforts to the battalion whilst on active service. The cadre then formed up behind the Colour and followed by the discharged men, The Lord Mayor, Lord Durham and the mayor's bodyguard, and all the other nobility and gentry, marched to the Cathedral. A service was held and at the end the Dean accepted the Colours into the safe keeping of the Cathedral. At the end of the service the National Anthem was sung and then the Cadre marched back to the Market Place and from there to Old Elvet, to within half-a-mile of the racecourse from where the original C Company had marched away in 1914. The Cadre fell out,

The Colour Party formed up facing the Town Hall

Some of the officials who attended the reunion dinner of the 18th Durham Light Infantry (Pals) Old Comrades Association, held in the King's Head Hotel, Darlington, on Saturday.—[N.D.]

Every year the Old Comrades Association met for a reunion dinner, this photo was taken in 1951.

but remained in Durham overnight enjoying the hospitality of the City. The next day the Cadre entrained for the dispersal depot at Ripon and the officers went to Larkhill on Salisbury Plain. So the battalion faded away, but not for long very soon an Old Comrades Association had sprung up and many of the old battalion joined. Each year a dinner was held in a different part of the county. From 1921, the second year of existence, the annual dinner was reported in 'The Silver Bugle', the Regimental Journal of The Durham Light Infantry. That year the dinner was held at the Palatine Hotel in Sunderland, in 1922 at West Hartlepool. By 1923, the membership was reported as 337, when Lieutenant Colonel W D Lowe DSO MC gave the address at the annual reunion dinner in Darlington on 17 November. In 1924 the dinner was again held in Darlington, at The King's Head Hotel on 13 December, this time with Lord Durham in the chair, this year the membership had dropped by two, Lieutenant C Adams and Private M Strirling had both passed away, although no cause was given it is highly likely that their war service had something to do with their deaths. However the funds were healthy and a balance of £7 7s 8d in hand was reported. It was the same venue in 1925, the only change being a reported rise in the membership. In 1926, the Rose and Crown Hotel in Durham City on 13 November hosted the annual gathering and again on 19 November the following year. The election of officers always followed and the general meeting of the association. This went right through until the 1950's, with the annual meeting usually reported on in 'The Durham Advertiser'. In 1951 ex Lance Corporal, now Councillor Bob Merriweather of Scarborough, reported to the meeting that the Durham Light Infantry badge, cut into the chalk downs above Fovant Camp, by members of the battalion in late 1915, was badly overgrown. The battalion should follow the example of the London Rifle Brigade and the Australians and have it re-cut at a cost of £33. It was felt that this was a large sum to spend on something so far away that none of them could go to see it. Mr Stan Watson from Willington said that the general feeling was the money would be better spent on looking after those old comrades now in old age that needed financial help. The 18th Battalion, The Durham Light Infantry Old Comrades Association kept meticulous records and ledgers recording membership, many of these ledgers are now in the Durham County Archives, but sadly they also recall the passing away of the battalion as each old soldier has a line drawn through his name and his date or year of death is recorded. So then the meetings ceased as there was too few men to carry them on and the 18th (Service) Battalion, The Durham Light Infantry (1st County)(Pals) passed out of living memory.

THE 19th BATTALION 'SIMPLY FADES AWAY'

At the cessation of hostilities the battalion had marched to billets in Everbecq where they remained until 15 November when the moved to billets at Kerkhem. This was followed on 18 November by a move to Berchem and then the next day to Harlebeke. Nine days were spent here cleaning up refitting and training and then on 28 November orders came through that the 35th Division was to concentrate around St Omer. The battalion started by marching to Menin where they billeted for the night. The next days march took themn to St Lawrence Camp near Elverdinghe and then on 30 November to Terdeghem. From 1 December the battalion took over a succession of old XIX Corps school camps, on 2 December the XIX Corps Reinforcement Camp at Millian, on 6 December, the XIX Corps Infantry School at Merckeghem. Then on 9 December the XIX Corps Gas School, and X and Y Companies went into the XIX Corps Signal School at Volerinckhove. Then on 16 December they started to build a new camp for themselves in the last named place. The battalion war diary is very bare for this period and although the majority of the battalion were miners, no mention is made of men being sent home or of any sporting activity, or education classes. Christmas came and went without even a mention of any festivities, likewise

The Colour being presented to 19/Durham Light Infantry in 1919.

As the battalion came to its end, 20 year old, 45389, Corporal, Ralph Pearson died in England.

the New Year. Like 18/Durham LI, 19/Durham LI were called upon to move to Calais to suppress the unrest among the Army Ordnance Corps and Railway Operating Division men. They travelled to Number 5 Leave Camp where they arrived at 1400 hours 29 January 1919; they were called upon to put down a disturbance in Number 6 Leave Camp and deployed at 1030 hours 30 January but by 1200 hours they were back in Number 5 Leave Camp. They remained in Calais throughout February but of their activities nothing is known, but in March they returned to Volerinckhove. That is the last entry for the war diary, we must presume that like 18/Durham LI, drafts of younger men were sent to other battalions, those with long service, miners and others with jobs to go to were sent home for discharge, and then the Cadre returned home to hand in the stores and be dispersed. Nothing has been traced about the Colour being laid up, the Colour is in the Cathedral but unlike 18/Durham LI there does not appear to have been any formal service, or at least none that the author or the regimental museum know of. There does not appear to have been any attempt to form an Old Comrades Association and there is little information surviving about the battalion apart from a very sparse War Diary.

So ended the life of the 19th (Service) Battalion, The Durham Light Infantry (2nd County) (Bantams) they had like most old soldiers simply, 'faded away'.

21/69 Private Hanson Whittaker. Undersized Hanson Whittaker was enlisted in the 21st Battalion but soon transferred to the Bantams and then posted to the Labour Corps. Note the un-pressed uniform; likely just removed from his kit bag.

THE 21st AND 23rd (RESERVE) BATTALIONS

On 2 December 1914 the Army Council published an Instruction ACI 13 of 2 December 1914, this authorised the raising of Depot Companies for the Service Battalions of the New Armies, and the number of men enlisting into 18/Durham LI eventually totalled over 1600. In July 1915 the Depot Company of 18/Durham LI, was formed into the 21st (Reserve) Battalion and moved to a tented camp in Wensleydale, North Yorkshire. Here they were joined by men from the 20/Durham LI.

Equipment and clothing was hard to find from the normal military sources and on 28 September the Commanding Officer wrote to Messer's Bainbridge in Newcastle.

> Suits for cooks
> Officer Commanding
> 21st (S) Battalion
> Durham LI
> Messer's Bainbridge & Company Ltd

Newcastle upon Tyne
28 September 1915
Dear Sirs,
With reference to your letter of 22nd September forwarding samples of canvas, will you please
supply 16 suits of canvas as per No 1 pattern @ 6/6d each.
Chest 44'
Height as follows

Four	*@ 5'10'*
Eight	*@ 5'8'*
Four	*@ 5'6'*

Trousers and Jackets separate
D Cheverton Lt Colonel Comdg 21st Battn Durham LI. Local Reserve.

Advertisements appeared in the local press stating that men were urgently needed for 21/Durham LI but in the rush to fill the gaps in the ranks many men who were medically unfit or of the wrong height were enlisted, one such recruit was 21/69, Private Hanson Whittaker, who lived with his parents at 17 Waterville Road, North Shields. He was twenty two years of age and had a thirty four inch chest, but was only five feet one inch in height and should have been enlisted in 19/Durham LI. However, on 23 September 1915 the recruiting sergeant enlisted him in 21 Durham LI and he reported to the camp at Wensleydale the following day. He served with 21/Durham LI until 30 October, when the authorities realised the mistake and he was transferred to 23/Durham LI which had now formed as a reserve for 19/Durham LI. He was only with the second unit just over a month before he was transferred to 19/Durham LI, just in time to join them on Salisbury Plain and complete training before they went overseas. Like many of his comrades he fell foul of, the purge of the bantams in early 1917 and was transferred to 188 Labour Company. However this probably saved his life, as the Labour Corps was a lot safer place to be than the Infantry.

Some of 21/Durham LI must have remained at Cocken Hall for on 19 October there was a strange case reported in *The North Star* under the headline:

The first men to arrive pose for the photographer - note the Seregeant on the left with the Medal Ribbons.

ALLEGED THEFT OF ARMY STORES, DURHAM PORK BUTCHER ACQUITTED

There was a report of an alleged theft of army rations.

Before Mr J S G Pemberton and other magistrates at Durham Quarter sessions yesterday James Edward Edmondson, aged 49 described as a store manager was indicted for having stolen two side of bacon the property of the officer commanding 21st Battalion D.L.I. from the canteen at Cocken Hall on 8 September. Harold Ingham aged 32, pork butcher, of Durham was also charged with having received the goods well knowing them to have been stolen.

Mr R J Simey prosecuted and Ingham was defended by Mr Meynell. Mr Simey in outlining the case said, 'The supplies for the camp at Cocken Hall were contracted for by Messer's R Dickeson and Co Ltd of London, who sent Edmondson to the camp to receive the goods and hand them over to the Army stores.

The Alleged Theft

On 8 September two sides of bacon were sent by Quarter Master Sergeant Knight to Mr Edmondson's stores for the purpose of weighing them.

It was alleged that later in the day Edmondson engaged a boy named Cleckner to 'take some things for

H F Duthie joined to be with his brother in 18/Durham LI, but was posted to 14/Durham LI.

him to Durham', and between them the bacon covered with a sack was placed in Cleckner's cart and taken to Ingham's shop in Claypath, Durham. When charged with the offence Edmondson declared that the bacon had been brought to the store to be exchanged for a milder kind. With regards to Ingham counsel warned the jury, 'not to jump to conclusions that even if Edmondson was guilty Ingham really knew the stuff had been stolen.' Ingham had declared that he had no reason to believe the stuff had been stolen.

The Evidence

Evidence was given by Quartermaster Sergeant Knight that the bacon had been sent to the stores to be weighed not exchanged. According to Arthur Osborn, an inspector to the contractors, Edmondson had the power to buy from local tradesmen if the stores ran short, but had no authority to change the surplus. P S Foster of the County Constabulary spoke to witnessing the arrival of the bacon at Ingham's shop. Deputy Chief Constable Waller (his son was a Captain in 19/Durham LI) said when Edmondson was under arrest he stated that the bacon had been taken to the store to be exchanged. He, Edmondson had sent the bacon to Ingham, but the latter was not aware it was coming.

Mr Meynell on behalf of Ingham submitted there was not a particle of evidence that the prisoner had any guilty knowledge and also that there was no case to go to jury.

The case was dismissed for lack of evidence.

In November 1915, 21/Durham LI moved to Catterick and became part of 20 (Reserve) Brigade. But recruiting was not going well and the Commanding Officer took the unusual step of writing to the newspapers.

ROOM FOR 400 RECRUITS IN 21st D.L.I.

We are asked to publish the following letter which has been sent to employers of labour in which the Durham County Battalion was recruited by Colonel Cheverton of the 21st D.L.I. which is the reserve to the 'Counties' and which is at present stationed at Scotton Camp Catterick.

Dear Sir – I hear that a number of men are being enlisted in the County of Durham and are being told that the County Battalion, namely the 18th Service Battalion Durham Light Infantry which was raised for the commercial and artisan classes of the County of Durham, by Lord Durham, Colonel Rowland Burdon, Mr William Cresswell, cannot take any more recruits.

I shall feel personally obliged if you will kindly cause it to be known among the any of your clerks and employees who are thinking of enlisting that this 21st Battalion D.L.I. is the first and only reserve battalion for the 18th Battalion and we still require 400 men to complete our numbers.

The 18th (Service) Battalion will probably soon proceed abroad and this 21st Battalion will then almost immediately be required to supply all drafts to it, so that men wishing to go to the front will have an early opportunity of doing so by joining us. If desired I shall be pleased to send a representative to supply information to intending recruits. Many men are now enlisting in response to Lord Derby's appeal and Durham men who join the 21st Battalion which is run on similar lines to the 18th Battalion will be associating themselves with the popular County Battalion.

Lieutenant W G L Sear posted to 11/Durham LI won the Military Cross in 1917.

Sergeant C Smith, from Sheffield, posted to France he lost a leg.

The last statement proved somewhat untrue, for the drafting system soon broke down and men from the 21st Battalion were sent not only to the 18th and 20th Battalion's but to all the other 'New Army' battalions of the regiment and later on in 1917 and 1918 the were being sent to the Regulars and the Territorial battalions, as they were needed.

One example is a West Hartlepool man, 21/463, Private, Harry Duthie, who enlisted to be with his brother George who was serving with 18/Durham LI, when he had completed training he was posted to 20/Durham LI in France, where he arrived on 12 June 1916. He was only with the battalion three months before he was wounded, most likely at Flers, and he was on his way back to England. When he was fit again in 1917 he was put on a draft to 14/Durham LI and arrived at the Base Depot in France, but here the posting was changed and he joined 2/Durham LI on 21 September 1917 less than a month later he was back in England wounded again. His parents received a Field Postcard but no other news of him and on 29 October his anxious father wrote to the War Office.

Gentlemen,

We received a Field Card from Somewhere in France, saying my son, Private H F Duthie, 21/463 attached 2nd Durham Light Infantry had been wounded on or about the 22nd of October and admitted to hospital. We have had no word since and feeling very anxious about him we should be glad if you could give us any information as to the nature of his wounds and name of hospital and oblige.

Yours truly

Wm Duthie.

Harry survived and was eventually transferred to the Royal Defence Corps and discharged in early 1919.

21/Durham LI moved from Catterick to a tented camp at Hornsea in April 1916 and later that year on 1 September became the 87th Training Reserve Battalion. Soon huts were built and the battalion remained there training recruits and draft finding until the end of the war.

Also at Catterick were the Depot Companies of 19/Durham LI, who became the 23rd (Reserve) Battalion. In April 1916 they moved to Atwick near Hornsea and on 1 September the battalion was absorbed into the Training Reserve Battalions of 20th (Reserve) Brigade. In contemporary photographs of the period these men can be identified by a cloth '20' patch worn on the upper arms. The 20th (Reserve) Brigade consisted of 29th (Tyneside Scottish) Battalion who wore a white 20, 30th (Tyneside Irish) battalion who wore a Green 20, 31st (Newcastle Commercial) Battalion who wore a Blue 20 and 21 and 23 Durham LI who wore a red 20. In the case of the Durham Light Infantry the 20 is so dark it is hard to make out.

As with the men of 21/Durham LI drafts sent out to France from 23/Durham LI were often directed to other battalions than 19/Durham LI, however some such as John Henry Wardle, (his name appears as Wardell and Wardle in his records) as was related in chapter six were sent to 19/Durham LI, even after the purge of the bantams from 35th Division. He served with the battalion until October 1917 when he was posted to 106 Light Trench Mortar Battery. He was posted missing presumed killed in action on 28 November. His mother received no word from him after

Sgt Jock Meanor served as an instructor at the NCO School in Catterick.

that date and eventually wrote to his company commander, only to be told he had left the battalion. In January 1918 still having had no official word she wrote to the War Office.

> *Mrs C Wardle*
> *No 1 Arthur Terrace*
> *Barnsley Street*
> *Holderness Road*
> *Hull*
> *Please kind sir could you tell me any news of my son Pte J H Wardle 23/307 19th DLI Z Coy France. As I have had no news for ten weeks only last week we heard that he had joined a trench mortar battery from his CO. If only we could get a line we will be very thankful to you. His officer said he left them two months ago any news we will be thankful to you as long as he is in the land of the living.*
> *Thanking you very much for your service*
> *From his anxious Mother.*

No quick reply was forthcoming and in desperation his mother again wrote on 31 January 1918:

Would you please be so kind as to try to get to know if anything has happened to my son, Pte J H Wardle 23/307 19th Batt DLI 11 Platoon BEF France. As I have had no word from him for twelve weeks I have sent a letter to his officer but he says he left the Batt about 2 months ago so as you see we do not know his address at present so if you would get to know for me I would be grateful to you sir.

I remain yours in expectation

Mrs C Wardle.

Mrs Wardle's expectations were dashed for written across the front of the letter were the fateful words 'REPLIED ON AFB104-82.'

The Army Form 104-82 began with the words,

It is my painful duty to inform you that a report has this day been received from the War Office notifying the death of...

Her son's remains were never recovered and his name is recorded on The Tyne Cot Memorial to the Missing at Passchendaele in Belgium.

By the end of September the 23rd Battalion had been absorbed into the rest of the Brigade, mostly into the 87th Training Reserve Battalion, that was the end of the Bantam Reserve Battalion. Nothing has come to light on any old comrades associations or further history.

Private J H Wardle posted to the Trench Mortar Battery he was posted "missing" and his poor mother had to search for him.

Chapter Eleven

Court Martial – Sentence – Execution

'I'm dreadin' what I've got to watch the Colour Sergeant said.'
DANNY DEEVER – KIPLING

IN CHAPTER FIVE THE READER LEARNED of the 'Incident at King Crater' on the night of 25/26 November 1916, which resulted in the charging and court's martial of a number of NCOs and men of 19/Durham LI. Imagine the scene, it is Christmas Eve 1916 in the little French Village of Fouflin Ricametz, for a few days a number British soldiers have been held as prisoners in French barn. In the village, a room has been set up as a court room, tables and chairs have been laid out, awaiting the arrival of the officers of the court. Even though it is Christmas Eve, two of the Non Commissioned Officers, Lance Sergeant Willie Stones and Lance Corporal E Hopkinson, will face the court that day.

At some stage during the morning all the parties are assembled, The President of the Court Martial, Lieutenant Colonel Cecil Bampfylde James Riccard, who had been commissioned into the Royal Dublin Fusiliers in 1893, he had served in the South African War and had been present at the Relief of Ladysmith, as well as serving in The Transvaal, Natal and the Orange Free State, for which he had been awarded The Queen's South Africa Medal with five Clasps and The King's South Africa Medal with two

Lance Sergeant Willie Stones

clasps. He had retired in February 1911 with the rank of Captain, but on the outbreak of war he had immediately volunteered and by 1916 the Army List shows that he was commanding 2/6Essex Regiment. However on 12 December 1916 he arrived in France and took over command of 17/Royal Scots. The other two members of the court were both captains from 17/West Yorkshire Regiment; Captain George Henry Mason, the senior Captain in the battalion, had been promoted to that rank on 1 October 1915 and was another veteran of the war in South Africa with a Queens South Africa Medal and three clasps for service in the Orange Free State, The Transvaal and Cape Colony. By the end of the First World War he was a Major, Temporary Lieutenant Colonel, commanding a service battalion of The Middlesex Regiment, The third member of the court, Sydney Lara Bell had been promoted captain on 4 October 1915; by the end of the war he had won The Military Cross. Other officer's involved at the trial included. Second Lieutenant, Robert Mitchell Hill Middleton, the Adjutant and Prosecuting Officer of 19/Durham LI. He had originally been commissioned into The Nottinghamshire and Derbyshire Regiment, before being posted to the Durham Light Infantry. He was eventually evacuated gassed in late 1917. Also present was Waldo Raven Briggs, a Captain on the General List, who was employed as the THIRD ARMY, Courts Martial Officer. By the end of the War he was awarded the OBE and twice Mentioned in Dispatches. The third and arguable the most important officer from the defendant's point of view was the 'Prisoners Friend', Captain George Warmington, who was serving in Y Company of 19/Durham LI. He was by calling a solicitor but it was strange that he was there, for he out ranked the prosecuting officer.

As no records survive of the trial of Lance Corporal Hopkinson, let us assume that the senior of the two men. Lance Sergeant Stones was tried first. When all was ready a signal was passed up the street and the prisoner was brought out and placed between a two man escort. A more senior NCO or possibly a Warrant Officer took charge, giving the order 'Prisoner and Escort, ATTEN _ SHUN.' There was a crash as three studded army boots hit the pave, as the three men came to the position of attention. 'Prisoner and Escort – move to the left in file, LEFT TURN,' another crash after the men swivel on heel and toe through ninety degrees. 'By the front, QUICK MARCH, EFT IGHT, EFT IGHT EFT IGHT', the pace is called out in double time, the man in charge dropping the first letter of each word in true army style, as the prisoner and escort march towards the court room. As they near the room the door is thrown open and they march straight in. 'RIGHT WHEEL, MARK TIME,' crash, crash, crash, as the three men march on the spot. 'Prisoner and Escort, HALT, WILL ADVANCE LEFT TURN'. Another crash from three right boots as the men turn through ninety degrees to face the court. 'Escort – DIS – MISS.' The two escorting NCOs turn to the right – salute and move off to the chairs that are allocated to them. Lance Sergeant Willie Stones stands alone in front of the three officers sitting at the table. [Of course the directions are hypothetical – rights and lefts may have been different – but this is generally the sort of scene at a military trial.]

The charge against him is read out, 'Are you 19/647, Lance Sergeant William Stones, Z Company, 19th Service Battalion, The Durham Light Infantry,' 'Yes Sir.' 'You are charged that contrary to The Army Act (1914) section 4 (2), you did, when in the front line trenches, in K2 sub sector on the 26th of November 1916, shamefully cast away your arms in the presence of the enemy, in that when as NCO of the watch and attacked by the enemy you shamefully cast away your rifle and left the front line and ran away. How do you plead Guilty or Not Guilty?'

'Not Guilty Sir.'

Although the records of the trial have survived, the questions put to both the witness' and the accused were not recorded, only their replies. So this makes the narrative somewhat disjointed.

Sergeant Stones was probably allowed to sit down as the witness' were called to give the evidence against him. The first to be called was Lieutenant Charles W Howes, who would be killed leading W Company in April 1918. He made the following statement.

'On the night of 25/26 November 1916 at about 0225 hours, I was in charge of the counter-attack platoon of the right company and was standing to with the platoon in the Coy. HQ dug out. I heard a voice calling down the far entrance to the dugout. The CSM (Company Sergeant Major) came and reported to me. I went to the Signals and told them to warn Battalion HQ I called my men together in the CT (Communication Trench) known as Bogey Avenue, armed them with bombs, and passed back word to them to follow me. I went to Ghost Avenue and started to make my way across the open to the front line, but finding I only had about three or four men with me I went back to collect the rest. When I was collecting my men in Bogey Avenue I saw the accused. He was standing there and seemed very much upset. I can't say whether he had a rifle. The place where I saw the accused was about 150 yards, by the trench, from the front line. The accused was NCO of the watch that night. As such it was his duty to be in the front line with the officer of the watch. When I started to go across the open and found I had only three or four men with me, the accused was not among them.'

Lieutenant Howes was asked to study a sketch map and confirmed that it was a map of the K2 sub sector. It was now Captain Warmington's turn to question the subaltern and Lieutenant Howes remembered that he had eventually collected about ten men from the company headquarters and that Lieutenant Mundy had been the officer of the watch. He ended his testimony by repeating that it had been at the company headquarters that he had seen Stones, adding that he could not be certain that it had been Stones who had called down the entrance to the dugout.

The next witness to be called was 9129, Company Sergeant Major Holroyd, who stated that, 'the accused was NCO of the watch from 0100 to 0300 on the morning of 26 November. During the period the enemy came over into our front line. I was in the Company Headquarters dugout when the alarm was passed down. Shortly after this I went up into the front line. On looking round I missed the accused. As NCO of the watch it was his duty to be in the front line.'

He must have been asked another question for the records show he replied,

'I did not see the accused at all until next day, i.e. later on the 26th.'

The next witness, 19/1430, Acting Sergeant, James Staff, had been on duty prior to being relieved by Lance Sergeant Stones and was only able to confirm that the relief had taken place and that Stones was the duty NCO, saying,

'On the morning of 26 November at 0100 hours I was relieved by the accused as NCO of the watch. He was on for two hours from 0100 until 0300 hours.'

The fourth witness to be called for the prosecution was 19/362, Private John Pinkney, from Easington, County Durham, who made the following statement,

'On the morning of 26 November, I had just come off duty as gas guard at 0200 hours when accused came out to give me the warning that the Huns were in the Crater. I was at the Company Office. Lieutenant Howse gave the order for all of us to file out. The accused was present. We were ordered to take all the bombs we could and file into Ghost Lane. We all did so. The accused wanted to warn the HQ cook. He asked me if I would show him the way to the HQ in Father's Footpath, where the cooks were. I went with him. When we got to HQ we looked into two dugouts but could not find the cook. As we were coming out accused took ill. He seemed to have lost the use of his legs. He sat down for a good while and tried several times to get up. He thought if he could see the doctor he would give him something to ease him and asked me to go to the doctor with him. I went with him and we were stopped at the outward end of Bogey Avenue by the guard. Sergeant Foster was on duty at the time and he said the accused could not go any further. We turned round and after staying there a good while accused came back with me. He tried two or three times to get back to the Company Office but could not manage. After we got a little way past Father's Footpath he seemed to go off all again, he could not find the use of his legs. I told him I would take him to the dugout in father's Footpath. I did so and covered him up and sent word to the Company Office. I couldn't say if he had a rifle with him. I was with him a good while.'

Private Pinkney was then asked another, again unrecorded question by the court and replied,

'When I first saw accused he came running. He seemed properly put about. He seemed excited. There didn't seem anything the matter with his legs then. When we were going to where the cooks were I was four or five yards in front, accused did not seem able to keep up with me.'

The next prosecution witness, the fifth, was 19/136, Sergeant, Robert Foster, who had been manning the Regimental; Police battle post at the junction of Bogey Avenue and Wednesday Avenue.

On the evening of 25 November, I mounted a police battle post at the junction of Bogey and

Wednesday Avenues. My duty was to stop any unauthorised persons coming down the trench. At about 0230 hours on the 26 November I saw someone coming down Bogey Avenue. I halted them and found it was Private Pinkney with the accused behind. I questioned Pinkney and asked him what he was doing there and where he was going to. He said he was bringing accused down. I called accused and asked him where he was going and what was the matter. He was in a very exhausted condition and trembling. He said he had been out on patrol with Mister Mundy and that they had met 4 or 5 Germans. The enemy shot Mister Mundy who ordered accused to run and save his life. I noticed accused had no rifle or bayonet. I questioned him as to where they were. He said the Germans were chasing him down the trench and he dropped his rifle and bayonet crossways across the trench. I ordered him to get back up the line at once. He asked for permission to smoke and have a rest. I ordered him to go up the line, he hesitated, but then he went. Private Pinkney went back with accused. I let accused have a few minutes rest before sending him back.'

Captain Warmington then cross-examined, Sergeant Foster who stated,

'I am certain accused said he was 'out on patrol' with Mister Mundy. Accused seemed as if he had been running. He was afraid. He could hardly walk, he seemed thoroughly done up.'

That was the end of the case for the prosecution and it was now the turn of the defence Captain Warmington opened the case by handing the court a note from Captain G A Barss, which stated,

'This is to certify that L/Sgt Stones 19 DLI reported sick with rheumatic pains in his legs on two occasions within the last 11 months - once on Oct. 27th and once on Nov. 29th.'

Captain Warmington went on to make a submission, but! Unlike the prosecution evidence which was recorded verbatim, Captain Warmington's submissions were written down in note form, under the heading,

'Accused's friend submits no case;'

'No evidence that accused shamefully cast away his arms in presence of enemy.

One witness saw him without a rifle - not corroborated.'

Leaving the front line and ran away -

'Evidence is that he was out with the officer of the watch.

He left front line to extent of going to Coy. HQ and no further and went there to give warning.'

'That was within his duties and does not constitute leaving front line.'

Running away -

'Pinkney says he came running to him. That means to the Company Headquarters No evidence of him running any further.'

The prosecution had nothing to say in reply and there was a recess to consider the submission, which, after the re-start was declined by the court.

Lance Sergeant Stones was now called to give evidence in his own defense, after recording that he swore an oath; his evidence was recorded in a long written statement.

'On 25/26 November I had to go on patrol from 0100 until 0300 in the morning with Lieutenant Mundy. While going along the trench he told me to stay in the trench till he went to a dugout to warn the Battalion bombers to put their gas helmets on their chests. When we set off to go along the trench again there was a shot went off and Mister Mundy fell to the bottom of the trench. He said, 'My God, I'm shot. For God's sake Sergeant go for help and tell Mister Howes,' I did so.'

'I told the men in the front line that the Huns were in the trench. I came to a dugout before I came to the Company HQ and I gave the alarm there also. When I got to Company HQ I gave the alarm there also. When I got to the Company HQ the men were sitting on the steps of the dugout.

I told them to pass the word down to the CSM that the Huns were in the trench. When I got to the entrance of the dugout to warn Mister House [sic.] he was coming up the dugout telling the men to go into Ghost Lane with bombs. As the men were passing me I did not see the officer's cook. I enquired where they were and someone said they were in Father's Footpath. When the men were filing into the trench, Private Pinkney was the last man I could see. I asked him if he knew where the dugout was, and asked him to show it me. I looked in the dugout, there was no one there. He said there was another dugout further on, so I said I would look into that as well. We could not find him in that dugout. There was a stretcher bearer came from the right of the crater, wounded. I asked him what was the matter. He said ,'I have been wounded by the Huns.' I asked if the enemy were in the trench where he had come from. He said, 'Yes, they have bombed the dugout.' He left me and went to seek the other stretcher bearers in Bogey Avenue. I said to Pinkney that I wondered where the cooks had gone. He said he could not say. We turned to go to Company HQ in Father's Footpath. When I got to the end of Father's Footpath I lost the use of my legs and had to stay there about 15 minutes. I said to Private Pinkney, 'I wonder if the doctor has got anything to nourish us up and take the pains away from my leg.' Pinkney said he didn't know but he was willing to come with me to help me out. When we got to the junction of Bogey and Wednesday Avenues I heard someone shout, 'Halt!'

'Pinkney stopped. He was about ten yards in front of me. When I got up to him I asked what was the matter. He said we could not get out. Then Sergeant Foster asked me what was the matter with us. I told him I was ill and wanted to see a doctor. He told me I couldn't get past. I asked him to let me sit down for a minute or two. He said I could. After I had had a rest I turned round and came back with Private Pinkney. I could not walk by myself and had to hold on to the side of the trench as I walked. When we got past Father's Footpath my legs gave way again and I tried two or three times to get up but could not. Pinkney helped me on to my feet and took me to a dugout. He covered me up and said he would send word to Mister Howse where I was. He went out of the dugout and was away about 15 minutes. He came back with a cup of tea and said he had sent word to Mister Howse where I was . When I had had the tea it pulled me together a bit and I tried to get up but couldn't. After about ten minutes I tried again and got onto my feet and got to the dugout where I was staying before the Huns came over the Crater. I stayed there till 3 p.m. Then I tried to go on duty again with Sergeant Austin. At about 4.15 at stand to, my legs gave way again and the Sergeant said I had better go into the dugout and he would tell the officer. I went to the dugout and lay there and was never on duty any more. They did not put me on the duty roster, they gave me a rest. When we were relieved by the HLI it took me all my time to get to the billet. When I got there I lay down and reported sick next day. The MO got one of his orderlies to rub my leg with embrocation.'

After this the court adjourned for lunch and resumed at 1415 hours, when Lance Sergeant Stones was called, yet again no questions were written in the transcript only the answers given by the accused.

'No orders were issued to me when I took over as NCO of the watch. Mister Mundy told us we had to have our gas helmets on our chests in case of a gas attack.

We were patrolling the trench. The shot that hit Mister Mundy was from the enemy. I saw the enemy. When I saw them I had a rifle and bayonet. I had the bayonet but no rifle when I got to the junction of Bogey and Wednesday Avenues.

I went from the front line to Coy HQ by way of Bogey Avenue. I tried to run but was unable to do so because my leg was stiff. I wanted to warn the cook because the enemy could get round from the right of the crater and I thought they might get to Company HQ. There was a sentry-group posted on the right of the crater. So far as I knew then it was still there. It did not occur to me to tell Pinkney to warn the cook. It did not strike me that my services as a sergeant were more valuable in the front line than in personally warning the cook.

The occasion in Father's Footpath was the first time that night that I lost the use of my legs. I rested till stand to on account of my legs. I did not report sick later on the 26th because I could not get out of the dug-out.

I was going my rounds as NCO of the watch. I am quite sure Mister Mundy said what I have already stated. As I turned to go the Huns were stepping over Mister Mundy. I put my rifle across the trench so as to stop them from getting across at me so that I could get ahead of them and warn the men. When I was in the dugout on the 26th I was so bad I couldn't lift my head up. I remained like that till 3 p.m. It was no good going sick then, so as an NCO was wanted I volunteered to go on duty from 3 to 5. I said that to Sergeant Staff. I had left word with the CSM that I was going to my dug-out.'

Further questions were asked, yet again not written down but the answers were,

'The reason why I didn't go back with help to Mister Mundy was that I thought it was sufficient when I had got the men into the front line and I told them what had happened.

I saw four or five Germans. It was a narrow trench. They were one behind the other. My rifle was loaded. I didn't fire because the safety catch was on and the [protective canvas] cover over the breech. My bayonet was not fixed.

I had been NCO of the watch before.'

The reason I wanted to get the cook was that the company was weak and I wanted to get all the men I could. it didn't occur to me to send Pinkney by himself because I was properly upset.

I didn't go to the doctor on the 27th because I was too ill. It was only with a hard struggle that I got out on the 28th when the Battalion left the trenches.

I loaded my rifle with 4 cartridges in magazine and one in chamber. I had the breech cover on when on patrol because I never had orders to take it off. I can't say how long it would have taken me to take it off.'

That was the end of Will Stones cross examination and testimony now other witness' were called in his defence.

The first was CSM Holroyd who had already given evidence for the prosecution. From the nature of the reply the question must have been about Stones' disability.

From the time of the raid until we came out Sergeant Stones had to be excused duty because he was too ill to do it. He was the last man in the company; I ever expected to shirk his duty.'

This led to another question from Lieutenant Middleton to which CSM Holroyd answered,

'I excused accused from duty. The other sergeants agreed to do duty for him. When a man goes sick a sick report is sent down with him. This was not done in this case because he did not go sick.'

There was then a question asked by the court to which the CSM answered the following,

'In the ordinary case if a man was too ill to move he would be sent down on a stretcher like wounded man. We always had stretchers. Accused was not sent to the doctor on a stretcher. I didn't think he was bad enough to be out of the line.'

The court now called the battalion Medical Officer Captain G A Barss RAMC, who testified and was cross examined by the court. Once again no questions were recorded but the replies are written in full.

'I attended accused on 29 November. He complained of muscular rheumatism in the muscles of his legs. I examined him and gave him some embrocation and put him on no marching for one day. So far as I know he didn't come back.'

He had been once before for the same complaint, on 27 October.

When I examined him on 29 November, I formed the opinion that his condition was not serious. Accused had no temperature. There were no visible symptoms. I did not think that muscular rheumatism unless very pronounced, would prevent a man from walking. If it did I should expect to find some visible symptoms.'

Captain Warmington didn't cross-examine the MO, but went on to sum up; Yet again the defence's statements were written down as notes.

Accused's friend addresses the Court

'Rifle not thrown, but put across trench.

Ran - under orders to get help - did not run any further.

No hiding away. His whereabouts known to everybody. He reported sick to his CSM.

Evidence not strong enough to convict. Accused acting under orders of his superior officer.'

The court now retired to consider the verdict, when they returned to the court room they did not disclose their verdict. But the Adjutant, Lieutenant Middleton read out a statement,

'I produce a certified true copy of AF B-122 relating to the accused'

The Army Form B-122 was the Soldiers Field Conduct Sheet, the Army Form B-120, was his Regimental Conduct sheet and the Army Form B-121, was his Company, Conduct sheet, these latter two documents were forwarded to the Regimental Record Office when the soldier went overseas and the AFB-122 was maintained whilst the unit was in the field. [King's Regulations 1914 amended by Army Order 102 of 1913 and Army Order 109 of 1914.]

In the case of Lance Sergeant Stones, his AFB-122 disclosed that Stones had never committed any disciplinary offence and stated his character was 'Exemplary'.'

The next witness re-called by the court was Lieutenant Howes, who was asked about the character and service of Lance Sergeant Stones.

'I have known accused for over a year. I have found his character as a soldier at all time excellent. His work in the trenches has always been good not only in getting men to do the work but in setting them an example.

On the Somme he behaved well. He got his first stripe before leaving England. Accused has been nearly eleven months in France.'

Having heard all the evidence and the reports on Lance Sergeant Stones' character the court closed and in keeping with the usual practice did not disclose their verdict. At the end of the day the opening proceedings were repeated, the two NCOs of the escort fell in either side of the accused, the Warrant Officer or Senior NCO i/c the escort barked out his commands, and with the crash of studded boots, the three came to attention turned in the direction commanded and marched off in double time, back to the barn where the escort fell out and Lance Sergeant Stones was again imprisoned. Here he had to wait for the decision of Battalion, Brigade, Division, Corps, Army Commanders and then the final say was with Sir Douglas Haig.

At the end of the trial the paper work for both Courts martial, those of Stones and Hopkinson was completed and sent off up the chain of command for senior officers to comment on the trials and the sentence. The Commanding Officer of 19/Durham LI wrote to Headquarters106 Brigade,

'Ref your 106/c/159 dated 29/12/16. I have no personal knowledge of these two NCO's as I have only been with the battalion a short time. But I attach reports of the Company Commander on whose statements I can thoroughly rely.

W B Greenwell

Major, Commdg 19 D.L.I.'

The report attached written by the Officer Commanding Z Company, Lieutenant William

Oliver, spoke highly of Lance sergeant Stones' ability to command men and his boldness when out working in No Man's Land.

'He came out with the battalion in February as a Lance Corporal. Showing ability to handle men he was promoted over the heads of senior NCOs in the company. He has done good work on patrols & when in charge of wiring parties. I have personally been out with him in no-man's land & always found him keen and bold. In the trenches he never showed the least sign of funk. He has always been in my company. I therefore had countless opportunities of seeing him under all circumstances & can safely say that he was the last man I would have thought capable of any cowardly action. He has been in a very poor state of health lately.'

The reports and the attached paper work was forwarded to 106 Brigade Headquarters for the comments of the Brigade Commander, Lieutenant Colonel B C Dent, who was temporarily in command having recently been the Commanding Officer of 19/Durham LI. He sent the following letter to Headquarters 35th Division.

'Confidential

106/c/153

Headquarters 35th Division

Recommendations of the Reviewing Officer in the case of Sergt J W Stones 19th D.L.I.

I recommend that the sentence be commuted in consideration of the manner in which this NCO has performed his duties previously – I myself have been in command of

Major W B Greenwell, Commanding 19 D.L.I.

19th D.L.I. for the last 9 months (and am only temporarily in command of 106th Inf Bde) but have only very slight personal knowledge of this NCO. His Company Commander gives him a good character.

B C Dent Lt Col

Commdg 19th D.L.I.'

On the last day of 1916 the letter and the rest of a mounting pile of papers were sent to Headquarters 35th Division, for the attention of the GOC Major General, Herman James Shelley Landon CB.

Born in 1859, he had been commissioned into the 6th Foot, The Royal Warwickshire Regiment, on 22 January 1979, in what appears to be an average military career, he did not see action until 1898, when he was with the Nile Expedition, and by which time he had attained the rank of Major. He ended the campaign with two campaign medals and a Mentioned in Dispatches. When the Boer War broke out he was commanding 2/Royal Warwickshire Regiment, on 10 September 1901 he was again Mentioned in Dispatches, at the end of this his second period of active service he was awarded the Queen's South Africa Medal

GOC 35th Division, Major General, Herman James Shelley Landon CB.

with five clasps. In February 1906 he was placed on half pay until October that year when he became a Temporary Brigadier General. When war broke out in August 1914 he took over command of 3 Infantry Brigade in 1st Division. He commanded the brigade all through the retreat from Mons and the Race to the sea and the early fighting around Ypres, He was promoted Major General whilst still commanding a brigade and it wasn't until November 1914 that he took over, temporarily, command of 1st Infantry Division. He then became Inspector of Infantry until assuming command of 35th Division in September 1916.

This was the Victorian soldier in whose hands the life of the Durham Bantams now lay. The same day he received the papers, he wrote to Headquarters, VI Corps:

C.M. 2/10/3

VIth Corps

Ls Sergt J W Stones 19/D.L.I.

'In my opinion there is no reason on which to base a recommendation that the sentence be commuted. I consider that the sentence should be put into execution.

H J S Landon MG

31/12/16   Comdg 35th Div'

The next day the papers arrived at Headquarters VI Corps, and were received and stamped by the D.A.A.Q.M.G. department and given the serial number CM920. VI Corps was now commanded by Lieutenant General, James Aylmer Lowthrop Haldane. He was born in 1862, and

commissioned into The Gordon Highlanders on 9 September 1882, in 1894-5, as a Lieutenant he took part in the Waziristan Expediton and the Operations in Chitral in 1895, collecting both campaign medals along the way. During the Tirah operations in 1897-8 he took part in a number of actions, became the battalion Adjutant and was Mentioned in Dispatches and awarded The Distinguished Service Order. During the operations in Natal in 1899 he was severely wounded at Elandslaagte, he went on to see action at Laings Nek, Belfast and Lydenberg and was again Mentioned in Dispatches and the Queen's South Africa Medal with four clasps. When the BEF went to France in 1914, Haldane was a Brigadier General commanding 10 Brigade in 4th Division, until 22 November when he was given command of 3rd Division, known throughout the army as 'The Iron Division', which he commanded until 6 August 1916, when he took over command of VI Corps.

*Lieutenant General
J A L Haldane,
Commanding VI Corps.*

He now had to carry out one of the duties of a Corps Commander and make a decision on the case of the two NCO's of 19/Durham LI.

On a type written sheet which was given the serial number VI Corps:CM/920

and sent to Headquarters Third Army'A' Branch on New Year's Day 1917, Haldane wrote,

'Forwarded and recommended that the sentence be carried out. I am expecting no delay in forwarding proceedings.

J A L Haldane

Lieut General

1/1/17

Commanding VI Corps'

The file was now getting bigger daily on 2 January 1917 it was received and stamped at Headquarters THIRD ARMY. Here it came to another man who had served in Queen Victoria's little wars, but unlike the infantryman, Haldane, the commander of the THIRD ARMY, General, Sir Edmund Henry Hynman Allenby , was a cavalryman, born in 1861, he had been commissioned into the 6th Inniskilling Dragoons on 10 May 1882 and had seen service in Bechuanaland in 1884 and Zululand in 1888, when the Boer War broke out he was commanding the Regiment and by 1901 commanded a mobile column. He was at the Relief of Kimberley and took part in many actions and ended the war with the Queen's South Africa Medal with six clasps and the King's South Africa Medal with two clasps and a CB. When war broke out in 1914 he was commanding 1st Cavalry Division and went on to command The Cavalry Corps, before taking command of V Corps and then THIRD ARMY.

The file took a while to reach Army Headquarters but on 7 January 1917, Allenby signed a type written sheet and added his recommendation in his own hand,

'ThirdArmy C.M.5472
The Adjutant General,
General Headquarters
Forwarded.
I recommend the sentence of death in the case of No. 647 L/Sgt J.W.Stones 19th Batt. Durham Light Infantry Be carried out
E H H Allenby
Headquarters General
Third ArmyCommanding Third Army
7/1/17'

General, Sir Edmund Henry Hynman Allenby, Commanding Third Army.

From THIRD ARMY the file of papers went to General Headquarters British Expeditionary Force for the approval of the Army Commander, Sir Douglas Haig KT, GCB, GCVO KCIE, who had just been promoted Field Marshall on 1 January. Another cavalryman, who had served in the 7th Hussars. On 11 January 1917 he simply wrote one word on the front of the documents relating to Lance Sergeant Stones.

'Confirmed
D Haig F M
11/1/17'

Four days after the trial of the two NCO's, on 28 December the scene was repeated, the same officers arrived in the same village and went to the same room, to hear the case against a further six accused. This time the sound of army boots on the French pave would have been much louder, as the six accused, cap less and belt less, marched along the street in double time. A senior NCO calling out as they

Army Commander, Sir Douglas Haig KT, GCB, GCVO KCIE

went, EFT IGHT EFT IGHT EFT IGHT, Imagine the sound as all six mark time in the court room, crash, crash , crash , crash and the command 'HALT, WILL ADVANCE LEFT TURN.', another crash as they swivel through ninety degrees and resume the position of attention. All six men face the three officers of the court and the charges are read out.

Again the same pattern followed the witness' answers were recoded but not the questions, the first witness called was Company Sergeant Major Daniel Austin who stated,

'On the morning of 22 November, I was detailed to take a sentry group up Cecil Avenue to relieve the Highland LI. The sentry group consisted of 6 men and 2 NCO's. On the 23 November one of the NCO's reported sick, he was replaced by the accused, Lance Corporal, MacDonald. This was a permanent sentry group for the six days that we were in those trenches. The other members of the group were Corporal Wilson, who went sick, Lance Corporal Goggins, Privates Dowsey, Forrest, Davies, Ritchie, Spence and Todd. With the exception of Corporal Wilson and Privates Spence and Todd the persons I have mentioned are the accused now before the court. Private Todd was wounded and Private Spence is on leave. There was to be a raid by one centre company. Orders were issued on 26 November for the men to stand-to in the dugout. There was one sergeant and two lance corporals, and one officer. The NCOs changed the sentries who were left on the fire-steps. This was on account of the coming raid and of the heavy bombardment by trench mortars which had been going on for three days. This bombardment was by the enemy. The men who were withdrawn were ordered to stand-to on the steps of the dugout. I should have expected if any bombardment was going on to find a sergeant and a lance-corporal on the fire-step and the remainder on the stairs of the dugout. I can't say if this actually took place, I was on the left. I could not state the names of the men who would be entitled to be in the dugout. Second Lieutenant, Harding was the officer detailed. He was wounded. There were supposed to be two men on the fire-step and everybody else was entitled to be in the dugout. Those orders came from an officer, I think Mr Howes. I passed it on to the men. About 0235 hours on 26 November there was a very heavy bombardment. I found that our artillery seemed to be dropping short. I looked along the left of the crater and found that TMs [trench mortar bombs] and aerial torpedoes were coming over together. I returned to Company Headquarters and waited for orders. I did not turn the sentry-group out of the dugout because I did not go on to the right. I was not on duty at the time. The

19/158 Lance Corporal P Goggins had already been reduced from the rank of Lance Sergeant for going AWOL.

bombardment affected both entrances to the crater. The sentry-group was about 25 yards to the right of the crater.'

The Sergeant Major appears to have been asked a question, presumably by Captain Warmington, he replied,

'I was not on the right of the crater when this bombardment was going on. These men had no authority to leave the front line.'

Another question was put to Company Sergeant Major Austin, this time by Lieutenant Colonel Riccard, which prompted a long reply,

'Private. Spence was present on the night in question. The nearest I went to the sentry group when I was looking round at 0235 hours, was about 150 yards away. The TMs and aerial torpedoes were being sent over by both sides. The members of the sentry-group except those who were actually on sentry-go at the time were ordered to stand to on the steps of the dug-out. The dugout was about twenty yards from the place where I posted the sentry group. There were about 12 to 14 steps. There was accommodation for about 20 men in the dugout but the only persons occupying it at the time were the members of this sentry-group. The order was that the men were to go to the dugout on this night; it was not that they were to go there if there was a bombardment. No orders were given to the accused to go to any other part of the line that night.'

After the Sergeant Major the next two witnesses' were from 17/Royal Scots, the battalion commanded by the President of the Court. The next called was Second Lieutenant H Bryce, and he stated,

'On the morning of 26 November, I was in command of G Work with my platoon as a garrison and had posted a sentry at the junction of Cecil Avenue and the front face of G Work.

At about 0215 hours my sentry shouted down the dugout stairs. I went upstairs and found two NCOs and four men from the Durhams in the work. The accused now before the court are the men I saw.

I questioned them all as to why they had come into the works line, and some of them answered that they thought an NCO was leading them out of the front line. The two NCOs were without rifles. I took their names and sent them back to their company. The names were Lance Corporal MacDonald, Lance Corporal Goggins, Privates Dowsey, Forrest and Davies. I cannot remember the name of the sixth man.

I am quite sure these six men now before the Court are the six men I found in the work.

Lance Corporal Goggins had no steel helmet, the others had. All the accused were in a state of excitement.'

Captain Warmington took the opportunity to ask the young officer one or two questions to which he replied,

'I should expect men to be in a state of excitement after being bombarded for three days by trench mortars.

I kept the accused in the work for about 15 minutes, and put them on the fire-step. I gave them no special instructions. I did not give them any bombs. They all went on the fire step. I found Lance Corporal Goggins in a little bomb shelter twice. All the others were under control. I have no complaint to make as to the way in which they obeyed my orders.'

The president of the court having just arrived from England in last two weeks asked Second Lieutenant Bryce about the position of G Work, he replied,

'G Work was about 200 yards from the front line, i.e. the part of it where I found the accused. The head of Cecil Avenue is in the front line.'

The next witness also was a member of 17/Royal Scots, 24931, Private James Kidd, who had been the sentry at G Work, when the party of Durhams ran into his post. His evidence stated,

'One night about a month ago - I can't remember the exact date - I was on sentry at the junction of G Work and Cecil Avenue. I was on sentry from 0100 hours to0300 hours. At about 0230 hours some men came down the trench and I halted them. I can't say how many were there. It was dark and I could hardly recognise the men. I fetched Mister Bryce, my officer, and he took the men's names. There were not very many of them, about six or seven. The men came down the trench at a good pace, they were not running.'

He was then cross examined, and from the answer, Captain Warmington obviously asked a question about stopping the men, to which the Private replied,

'I had no difficulty in halting them.'

Captain Warmington had no further questions but the court asked Private Kidd a question to which he answered,

'I was not present when the names were given to Mister Bryce. I can't remember whether the man who was leading the party was a private or an NCO, or whether he was carrying a rifle,'

Another witness who had not been added to the summary of evidence was called, Captain Warmington making no objection. However in the trial documents the witness is described as 23180, Private, C Spence 19/Durham Light Infantry, when researching this man, the author found that the number 23180 in the Durham Light Infantry belonged to a soldier named Archibald Bamford. The witness called, was highly likely to have been 23/190, Private, Cuthbert Spence, who was on of the Bantam's from the Reserve Battalion, purged by General Landon, he was renumbered, 111631 and was transferred to 187 Labour Company. In giving evidence he made the following statement,

'About a month ago - I can't remember the exact date - I was in sentry with the accused Private. Ritchie, in the front line; from 2359 hours to 0200 hours I think. The enemy was shelling us with Trench Mortars. Ritchie got off the fire step to be out of the way of the shrapnel. Someone came along the trench and I saw none of the sentry-group after that. About half an hour after all of the group, including Ritchie, came back together. Ritchie had no orders to leave the fire-step. I saw him get off the fire-step and go along the trench.'

Captain Warmington now cross examined Private Spence and his answers were note as follows,

Lance Corporal Goggins posted me. I had no orders from Sergeant Austin.

The trenches were badly damaged at the time by enemy fire.

We had orders to get out of the way of the shrapnel and later on we had orders that we were not to leave the place. The order to get out of the way of the shrapnel was given by an NCO, I think by Lance Corporal. Goggins. The same NCO gave the second order. The two orders were given while I was on sentry. There was an interval of about an hour between the orders. The orders were given to me while I was on the fire-step. Ritchie was there when both orders were given. I am quite certain of that. I understood the orders came from Mister Harding.

I was knocked off the fire-step by a TM. When I got up the Germans were in the trench and I went into the next bay to tell the W.Yorkshires, who were on the right.

I am certain the second order was given.'

Lieutenant Colonel Riccard on behalf of the court then asked two questions to which Private Spence replied.

'I was about 10 yards into the bay where the West Yorks were. I have been with the Battalion 5 months.'

That was the end of the case for the prosecution, it was now up to the defence, and each soldier was allowed to make a statement in his own defence. The first to give his evidence under oath was 19/420, Lance Corporal, John MacDonald, whose statement considering he was on trial for his life was quite short.

'On 26 November all the men who were off duty were standing to in the dugout. I was with them. Somebody came running down the trench and shouted 'Run for your lives, the Huns are on top of you.' When I got out of the dugout I couldn't see anybody. I walked about 5 yards towards the front trench and as nobody was there I went down Cecil Avenue. When I got to the Avenue I was halted by the Royal Scots sentry. We went in to G Works and got bombs and stood on the fire-step. We were escorted to a dugout where one of the Royal Scots officers took our names. We were sent back to our company on the right of King Crater.'

He was then cross examined and gave a further reply,

'I saw no one when I came out of the dugout in the front line when I got there. The front line was very thinly held on this night, it was possible to go for 20 yards along the line and see nobody. I expected to see all the sentry group when I got to the front line because they all went out of the dugout before me. I was not on duty at the time. I heard some men running down the CT as I came up the dugout steps. I followed the men down to see where they were going. The Company Headquarters was not in G Works. I can give no reason why I went to G Works. I did not see the enemy but I heard them. That was before I went down the CT. I couldn't tell what direction they were in.'

Another question was put to the Lance Corporal, to which he replied,

'When I was on duty it was my business to change the sentries. On that night we were ordered by Mister Harding to get under cover if we could.'

It was now the turn of 19/1584, Lance Corporal, Peter Goggins to defend himself, his statement under oath reads,

'On the night in question I happened to be on top of the dugout stairs when I heard a panic in the trench. I stepped up to see what it was and I heard some men rushing out of the trench. I informed the men in the dugout and ordered them to stand-to. All I could hear was 'Run for your lives, the Huns are on top of you.' I was under the impression that the front line was held by the enemy and that we were cut off from the front line. I went down Cecil Avenue thinking that it was the sentries who had rushed out. We were detained and ordered by an officer to man a bay.'

He too was cross examined and he answered as follows,

'I was in charge of the group. I turned to go up the front line and went about ten yards towards it. I was knocked down by people rushing out [of the line]. Then I went and warned the men in the dugout. After I had shouted down the mouth of the dugout I saw three sentries running down the C.T. and was under the impression they were my sentries. I did not go to the front line to see if my sentries were there because so many men had gone past. I did not order my men to go down to G Works. I did not see them going, it was too dark.

The members of the group should have stayed in the dugout.

As I did not find them there I just followed them down. I went down to G Works because we had been there before when there had been a gas attack, I was going there on this occasion to get bombs with which to turn the enemy out of the front line.

I thought we were cut off on account of the panic and excitement. We could not fire at the enemy because there was a bend in the trench. The rifle I had was no use, it wasn't my rifle.'

Captain Warmington then asked questions about the orders for the sentry group. To which Lance Corporal Goggins gave the following replies,

'If the sentry groups had left the post the dug-out would have been cut off.

The orders we received on that night were that all men, except two on the fire step, were to be in the dugout. That order came at 2359 hours. That was the last time I saw an officer till Mister Harding came at 0155 hours. Those were all the orders I received. The sentries in the open got no further orders so far as I know.

My sole object in going towards G Works was to get some bombs and form a counter-attack with the men of my group.

I succeeded in getting all the men together. An officer told us to get on to the fire-step which we did.

The next questions to Lance Corporal Goggins were put by the court, and the answers were recorded as follows,

'I lost my steel helmet when I was knocked down, I did not pick it up because I did not think of it. I was thinking of the position I was in. The two occasions when I was in the little bomb shelter was when I was getting bombs to issue to the men. My counter-attack didn't come off because Mister Bryce wouldn't allow it. I was a guide not an escort that Mister Bryce sent back with us.'

The court then adjourned until 1415 hours and at the re-start of the trial the next man called was Private David Forrest, in the trial documents he is described as 19/653 but when trying to trace this man it was found that he was numbered 19/633 and transferred to the Labour Corps as 111971 and went to 187 Labour Company. Whether the mistake is with the Medal Rolls or the court documents remains to be seen. However his sworn testimony states as follows,

On the 26 November I was in the dugout in Cecil Avenue. At about 0230 hours some men came along the trench and shouted down the dug-out, 'Run for your lives. The Huns are on top of you.' When I got out of the dugout there was no one there. I heard some men running down Cecil Avenue and I thought that the front line was occupied by the enemy and that the dugout was cut off from the front line. So I followed a man down Cecil Avenue and when I got down to the junction of the works I found that the man had been halted and an officer put me on a fire-step. We were taken off the fire-step down to a dugout where there was an officer who took our names. We were then sent up to Company HQ and we returned to the post.'

Private Forrest was then cross examined by Lieutenant Middleton for the prosecution, he replied,

'I received no order to leave the dug-out. I simply followed the other men. We couldn't get to the bombs in the front line because the dugout was cut off. I went about 5 yards up the trench and then returned. I never went to the front line to get the bombs. The front line was 20 yards from the dugout. I thought the front line was occupied by the enemy. I took no steps to find out whether that was so or not. I did not see the enemy but I heard them. I heard them as I was going up towards the front line. There was no firing at that time. I went of my own accord down to G Works.'

The Prisoners Friend, Captain Warmington then made a further enquiry to which Forrest replied,

'I followed the other men down to G Works. I was at about the centre of the dugout when I heard a shout to run. The orders we had that night were that we were to stand to in the dugout, two of us being on the fire-step, and one NCO on duty, and one man on the dugout stairs.

One of the sentries on the fire-step told me that he had received an order to take cover from TMs if he could possibly get it. That was Private Ritchie, he told me when he was relieving me.

I had my rifle when I arrived at G Works. We had no bombs given us at G Works.'

The Private was then asked a question by Lieutenant Colonel Riccard, and responded with these words,

'When we were sent back one of the Royal Scots was sent with us. I couldn't say what he was sent for. I knew the way from G Works to Company Headquarters.'

That was the end of Private Forrest's testimony and the next man to be called was 19/505, Private Ritchie, who was sworn in and stated the following,

'At about 0130 hours on 26 November, I was down in the dugout. At about 0155 hours Mister Harding came. He told me about the raid going over and that we should be bombarded by the enemy. Private Spence and I went on from 0200 to 0300 hours, we relieved Privates. Forrest and Dowsey. We were told to take as much cover from the TMs as possible. At about 0215 hours the enemy started shelling with TMs. Spence lay flat on the trench boards and I ran round by the sap. All of a sudden as I was coming back to the step someone rushed past and said, 'The Huns are in the front line, run for your lives.

I warned the men in the dugout and went back to see if the other sentry was there. There was no one there. I heard some firing about 100 yards away. I saw nobody else there so thought it was my opportunity to go where the others had gone. I went down Cecil Avenue and we went to man a bay for about three quarters of an hour. We were fetched out of one bay by an officer and put in another bay where there were some bombs. I went into a small dugout where the bombs were and got a box of bombs. We were standing on the step about three quarters of an hour. Then the officer sent for us and we went down into the dugout and he took all our names. Then he sent a corporal back with us with our names on a paper to our Company Headquarters then we were returned to our post.'

Private Ritchie was then cross examined and he then explained,

'I don't remember any other order than I have stated being given on the night. I was about 5 yards from Private. Spence, he received no other order while he was with me. The sap to which I went was less than 10 yards from my post. I think I saw three men running past me on my way back. They seemed as if the had lost their heads. Spence was lying flat on the trench boards when I got back. The time he went on the trench boards was when the TMs came over. When I got back from warning the dugout Spence was not there. When I turned back to go the dugout I was about three yards from the post. Spence was not there then. I had no direct order to go to G Works. I didn't see the enemy, I heard them.'

The defence now asked at least three questions to which the response was as follows,

'When I got to G Works I had a rifle and bayonet with me. Mister Harding gave me the order to take cover when on sentry go. That was about a quarter to two.'

Cross-examined by the court, Ritchie then stated:

'It was the firing in the trench of rifles and revolvers and what I was told that made me think the enemy were there. I am quite sure it was for three-quarters of an hour that I was in the fire-bay at G Works.'

The next man called was 1429 Private M Dowsey again in the court documents there is a discrepancy for in the Medal Rolls it is confirmed that his name was Henry Dowsey. Also although sent to 185 Tunneling Company, Royal Engineers, and although he was a Bantam, he made his way back to 19/Durham LI, No matter what orders were issued many of the purged Bantams found their way back to the battalion.

In his defence Private Dowsey stated,

'I was in the dug-out on the morning of 26 November when I heard the cry, 'Run for your lives.' I came out of the dugout and could see no one, it being too dark. There is a trap door at the entrance to the dugout used for blocking the trench. I tried to block the trench with it. Owing to it being clogged with dirt I could not do so. I went a few yards back in the trench to the rear entrance of the dugout. Presently I heard someone coming down the trench towards me. I halted him. It was Lance Corporal MacDonald. The news he gave me of the front line gave me the impression that it was occupied by the enemy, so we went back into the reserve trench, which I thought was the best possible idea under the circumstances. Our men were standing-to and I stood to along with them until we were sent back to Company Headquarters and from there to the front line. When I got to G Works I had my rifle, bayonet, and equipment. We had an order that night to stand to in the dugout. I know nothing of orders to sentries on the fire-step.'

Dowsey went on further to explain,

'When the voice came down the dug-out, there were four other men there. I did not ask the other men to help me with the trap door. I did not think of it. I was in a queer state owing to being overworked. I did not see the other men leave the dugout. I received no order from Lance Corporal MacDonald. I did not see or hear the enemy or hear any firing.'

The last to be called to defend himself was 19/625, Private, Arthur Davies, who lived at 75 Davidson Street, Gateshead. Once he was sworn in he made the following statement,

'On the 26 November at 0230 hours, I was on the dug-out stairs when I heard three or four men run along the trench past the top of the dug-out. They shouted, 'Run for your lives. The Huns are on top of you.' I fell down the stairs with the shock. Then I came up the stairs and went down towards Cecil Avenue. When I got to the junction of G Works I met Lance Corporal Goggins & Private Ritchie who were in front of me. We were halted by the sentry. Then we went and manned a bay and stayed there for about three-quarters of an hour. Then we were taken to a dugout about two or three hundred yards away, where an officer took our names. He asked us if we had our rifles with us and sent us back to our Company Headquarters. He sent a Corporal back with us with a note of our names. Then we returned to our post. I had rifle, bayonet, equipment, and ammunition when I got to G Work.'

When he was cross examined by the prosecution Private Davies admitted he had been confused on the night of 26 November 1916 and in a further statement he said.

'It was the way they shouted that made me fall down the stairs. I did not see the other men leave the dugout. There was a candle in the dug-out. There were three men and a sergeant and an officer in the dugout. The sergeant and the officer were both wounded. I made no effort to go to the front line. I did not know what I was doing. I did not know which way I was going, for all I knew I might have been going towards the front line. I lost my head altogether. I had no orders to go. I did not see or hear the enemy nor did I hear their firing'

Davies was asked one further question by the court to which he made the reply,

'There were two entrances to the dug-out.'

Captain Warmington had no further questions and now addressed the court, as in the previous Court Martial his statements are recorded as notes.

'A raid was about to take place therefore front line was practically evacuated except for a few posts.

Enemy raided our line about half an hour before we were to start.

Found only a patrol in Crater & sentry group on each side.

Original orders varied.

Orders to take cover if fired on by TMs.

Remainder in dugout.

Novel situation.

If enemy raid in great numbers these few sentry groups were groups such as might be employed in outpost scheme.

If they had orders to take cover and knew, as they did, that front line [had been] evacuated, they were quite right to take up position & line of resistance reserve line.

Considering circumstances, bombardment for 3 hours, novel orders, and the disorder accused acted in good part and did what they thought was their duty.

All their statements agree, all have given evidence on oath.

Confinement they have already had and this charge is sufficient penalty for any unintentional mistakes they may have made

The accused have nothing further to say.

The court adjourned to consider their verdict. When they resumed the disciplinary record of each man was read out, Only Lance Corporal Goggins had any adverse entry, for he had been convicted by General Court Martial in England for Absence without Leave on 13 February 1916. The battalion had proceeded overseas on 1 February; he was reduced from the rank of Lance Sergeant to Lance Corporal.

Captain Warmington then submitted a further statement which was recorded by the court.

'1. LCpl. Goggins - aged 21, married - enlisted 1.3.15 - miner.

2. LCpl. McDonald - aged 28, married - enlisted 2.3.15 - labourer.

3. Pte. Forrest - aged 20, single - enlisted 10.3.15 - chimney sweep.

4. Pte. Davies - aged 20, single - enlisted 5.3.15 - miner, wounded 1.4.16 at Fleurbaix.

5. Pte. Dowsey - aged 35, married - enlisted 6.7.15 - miner.

6. Pte. Ritchie - aged 20, single -enlisted 3.3.15 - miner.'

The court was told that Private Ritchie had been classified as unfit for service in the front line by the Assistant Director of Medical Services, 35th Division; Lance Corporal Goggins, Privates Davies, Forrest and Dowsey had been similarly classified by the Corps Commander, and Lance Corporal MacDonald was reported by his company commander as being physically incapable of carrying out the normal work of an infantry soldier. All except Forrest and MacDonald were recommended for employment in tunnelling work with the Royal Engineers and all had been on active service with 19/Durham LI since the battalion landed in France.

Also noted was that Private Ritchie had been rejected by the ADMS 35th Division, and that Lance Corporal Goggins, and Privates Davies Forrest and Dowsey had been similarly rejected by the Corps Commander. All except Lance Corporal MacDonald and Private Forrest were recommended for employment with the Tunnelling Companies, Royal Engineers. The other two had been recommended for a Labour Battalion.

The Company Commander was allowed to give the men a character and he stated,

'Their general conduct has been good. I have never had any trouble with any of them. None of them has done anything special as soldiers but each of them is quite up to the average and has down all I have asked them to do. Goggins and Ritchie I have noticed appear to suffer from nerves, this has not been sufficient to give me any trouble in the trenches but it is quite noticeable. In Ritchie's case he was rejected by the ADMS on account of his nerves.'

The court martial was now over and it remained for the paper work to follow that of Stones and Hopkinson through the chain of command. The only difference this time was that Brigadier H O'Donnell had resumed command of 106 Brigade, and he attached the following statement,

"In each case the men have been found guilty of the charge and have been sentenced to 'Death'. I am doubtful, however, if the evidence is sufficient for a conviction. From enquiries made the men in character and behaviour appear to be of the average in their battalion. The battalion, however, has not done well in the fighting line. They suffered somewhat severely from heavy shelling while in the SOMME fighting in July and were very shaky in the advanced trenches before GUILLEMONT in August. I am reluctantly compelled to recommend that should the finding be confirmed the sentence be carried out for the purpose of example and to show that cowardice in the presence of the enemy will not be tolerated in the British Army.'

When the file went to Divisional Headquarters the GOC added his views before passing it on to Corps,

'These 2 NCO's and 4 privates have been found guilty of a most serious crime. They appear all equally culpable as soldiers, but the NCOs must be held as having especially failed in their duties, and responsibilities. There are, however, some 4000 men in the Division of whom 314 are in the Durham L.I. who are recommended for transfer as being unsuitable mentally and physically as Infantry Soldiers and it is probable that any of them would have behaved similarly under the circumstances described in the proceedings of this Court Martial. In view of the mental and physical degeneracy of these men I consider that though the sentence passed on all six is a proper one, the extreme penalty might be carried out in the case of the two NCOs only and that the sentence on the four privates be commuted to a long term of penal servitude, and this I recommend.'

Like the files of Stones and Hopkinson, the remaining files were in front of Sir Douglas Haig on 11 January 1917. In the case of Goggins and MacDonald he again wrote one word 'Confirmed' and signed and dated the forms. On the others he wrote 'Confirmed - recommend the sentence be reduced to 15 Yrs P.S [Penal Servitude] to be suspended.'

A further court martial took place when the trial of the members of the raiding party was held on 30 December.

23/36, Lance Corporal, M Dempsey, 19/880, Lance Corporal, J W Richardson

Privates,

23/36, Lance Corporal, M Dempsey. Sentenced to death for suposed cowardice he went on to win the MM in 1918.

19/298 W Bates, 19/1409 J Dunn, 19/380 T Garrity, 19/1274 G W Giggens,
19/233 H Greaves, 19/884 B Hewitt, 19/950 J G Lumley, 19/885 J McNally
19/1605, J Oldknow, 19/190 C Spence, 23/203 T Surtees, 19/1183, J G Mann, W Potts,
23/44 P Wilson.

19/13, Sergeant, R Rumley was tried separately on New Years Day 1917. As no records of the trial have survived, it is unknown if the same officers sat on his court martial.

All were found guilty and the sentence commuted to ten years penal servitude. It is interesting to note that 23/36, Lance Corporal, Michael Dempsey, a Gateshead man, remained with the battalion and in 1918 having been promoted to Corporal went on to win the Military Medal for gallantry under fire.

On 13 November The Adjutant General at GHQ sent a telegram Number A(b) 2122 to the GOC THIRD ARMY and followed up in writing stating,

'Please note that the C in C has confirmed the sentence in the case of No 647 L/Sergt J W Stones 19th Battalion Durham Light Infantry.

Please return the proceedings direct to this office after promulgation.

GHQ   J B Wroughton Colonel
13/11/17   Adjutant General'

In turn Headquarters passed the information down to VI Corps Headquarters,
Third Army C.M. 5472-5500-5501

Headquarters
VI Corps. (A)

1. The proceedings of Field General Courts-Martial in the cases of
No 647 L/Sergt J.W. Stones, 19th Durham Light Infantry
No 420 L/Cpl J MacDonald,   - do-
No 158 L/Cpl P Goggins,   -do-
are forwarded herewith for necessary action, the sentence of Death in each case having been confirmed by the Commander-in-Chief on 11/1/17.

2. Please have the instructions contained in circular Memorandum on Courts-Martial S.S.412. Part III, 2(c), page 26 complied with, and return the proceedings to this office after promulgation.

3. The 35th Division have been notified direct by wire.

Headquarters,   Waldo R Briggs
Third Army   Captain
15/1/17   for D.A.A.G Third
Army

When the file reached Headquarters, VI Corps, they in turn passed it on to Headquarters 35th Division, with a simple note 'For information and necessary action,'

Signed by the Staff Captain of the D.A.A. & Q.M.G.

Headquarters 35th Division in their turn passed the file back to Headquarters, 106 Brigade with a hand written note,

'106 Bde
 Herewith proceedings of FGCM in the case of,
No 647 L/Sergt J.W. Stones,}
No 420 L/Cpl J MacDonald,} 19th DLI
No 158 L/Cpl P Goggins,   }
To be promulgated this afternoon as arranged with APM.

After the entry has been made on proceedings they should be handed to APM
17/1/17   S   Preston
Capt'

Brigade in turn passed the file on to the Commanding Officer of 19/Durham LI. It was now time to inform the convicted and condemned men of their fate.

This was witnessed by another man held prisoner in the same barn, Private Albert Rochester, who wrote after the war.

'In the morning, after a wash and a scanty meal of biscuits and 'pozzy' [jam], three of the men - all NCO's - were ordered out through the hole [in the wall of the outhouse], and escorted by a squad of military police armed with revolvers, transferred to a more isolated cell'

Later he was ordered out of the prison and made to erect the posts against which the three men were to be shot.

'Come out, you!' ordered the corporal of the guard to me. I crawled forth. It was snowing heavily. 'Stand there!' he said, pushing me between two sentries. 'Quick march!' and away we went, not, as I dreaded, to my first taste of 'pack-drill' but out and up the long street to an R.E. dump .There the police corporal handed in a 'chit' whereupon three posts, three ropes, and a spade were given to me to carry back. Our return journey took us past the guardroom, up a short hill, until we reached a secluded spot surrounded by trees.

'Drop 'em there!' ordered the corporal. After waiting about an hour, and officer and two police sergeants rode up. Certain measurements were made in the snow after which I was ordered to dig three holes at stipulated distances apart.'

The three executed men lie together in St Pol Communal Cemetery Extension, France.

'On 17 January the intensely cold night. A heavy mantle of snow covers the earth; overhead, a steely moon. The hour is near midnight, and in the distance is heard the incessant thunder of the guns.

Down the street there comes a file of soldiers, with rifles at the slope and bayonets gleaming in the moonlight.

They wheel into the yard of the farm allocated to the military police, and are promptly ordered into military formation. Ten minutes later a luxurious car arrives with four British officers.

More orders; then from a barn close at hand emerge three handcuffed men who are led before the company. the senior officer pompously unrolls a document, and by the aid of a flash lamp read the confirmation of the death sentence, and the decrees they be shot at dawn.

A gasp from one poor trembling victim - the other two remain stiff and impassive. The officer quickly rolls up his papers and makes for the car, and the soldiers march away.'

At dawn on 18 January 1917 a number of officers whose duty it was to witness the execution gathered in woodland near the village of Rouellecourt. Albert Rochester described the scene and the execution in *The Railway Review* published in February 1922, his account is graphic.

'The motor ambulance arrives conveying the doomed men. Manacled and blindfolded they are helped out and tied up to the stakes. Over each man's heart is placed an envelope.

At the sign of command the firing parties, twelve to each, align their rifles on the envelopes. The officer in charge holds his stick aloft, and as it falls 36 bullets usher the souls of three Kitchener's men to the great unknown. The aim of the firing party is not quite steady. The medical officer quickly examines each victim, gives a sign to the officer, who with his revolver completes the ghastly work.

The last statement may not be quite true for the Battalion Medical Officer; Captain Barss when he signed the Death Certificates said that death was instantaneous.

The three bodies were transported back to the barn to be taken for burial; today they lie side by side in Row D, graves 1, 2 and 3 of St Pol, Communal Cemetery, Extension, in France.

The firing party marched back to Maisnil to their billets and so ended this chapter in the history of 19/Durham LI

Gallantry Awards

COMPANION OF SAINT MICHAEL AND SAINT GEORGE
Lieutenant Colonel Cecil Buckley Morgan DSO Commanding 22nd Bn   LG 3/6/18

THE DISTINGUISHED SERVICE ORDER
Major G Barry-Drew 18th Bn   LG 1/1/18
King's New Years Honours no citation
Temp Captain, Acting Major Cecil Charles Hatfield Hall 22nd Bn   LG 16/9/18
For conspicuous gallantry and devotion to duty. When a call was made by a neighbouring unit for reinforcement he got together some 20 men with a Lewis gun and a machine gun and led them forward over an embankment and across a road which was being badly sniped and machine gunned. He subsequently brought forward more men, and conveyed an important message from Brigade headquarters. His cool and brilliant example at a very critical time inspired all with confidence.
Major J C Hartley 18th Bn   LG 4/6/17
Temp Captain Harry Heaton MC 19th Bn attached 45th Royal Fusiliers (Russia)
On 10 August 1919 during attacks on Kochamika, Sludka and Lipovets he was commanding the battalion. He personally led his troops in all these attacks and showed conspicuous gallantry and efficiency throughout under heavy fire, taking all objectives.
Second Lieutenant Harold Everitt Hitchin, MM & Bar 18th Bn   LG 24/9/17
For conspicuous gallantry and devotion to duty when in command of a bombing party. He made three most gallant attempts to force his way into the enemy's position and himself shot four of the enemy with his revolver. Later he voluntarily joined in another company's attack and rendered invaluable assistance. He was largely responsible for the final success of the operations.
Major William Douglas Lowe MC 18th Bn att West Yorkshire Regt   LG 26/7/18
For conspicuous gallantry and devotion to duty. He was indefatigable under all conditions throughout heavy fighting. After the Brigadier and Brigade Major were casualties and the Brigade was without communication to the rear. He shouldered the whole responsibility until touch was regained.
Major John Douglas Mitchell 22nd Bn   LG 26/7/18
For conspicuous gallantry and devotion to duty during long operations when by his great personal courage and powers of leadership he assisted to hold the battalion together under most trying conditions. After the Commanding Officer had been wounded early in the operations he assumed command of the battalion and the success and praise it earned were to a great extent due to the splendid example of energy and devotion set by him.
Major E W Ormston 18th Bn transferred Royal Engineers   LG 4/6/17
Captain Geoffrey Peirson MC 18th Bn   LG 3/6/19

THE MILITARY CROSS
Second Lieutenant William Allbuery 18th Bn   LG 15/10/18
This officer showed great skill and determination in leading his men during an attack over unknown ground, under heavy fire, to an objective, which was very oblique to the front of the assembly position and was not defined by any particular feature. He accomplished his task with great success, capturing a machine gun and its whole detachment. While selecting the line for consolidation he moved about under heavy fire encouraging and steadying the men by his resolute behavior.
Second Lieutenant Leonard Wilkinson Andrews 22nd Bn   LG 26/917
For conspicuous gallantry and devotion to duty when in charge of a working party. Coming under an intense and accurate hostile bombardment, his party suffered heavily, but in spite of the shelling he remained at great personal risk helping to collect those of the party who had become scattered in the darkness. On another occasion when constructing a light railway he succeeded in spite of an intense gas shell bombardment, in maintaining the control of his party in the dark and continued to work. Although buried by a shell, he carried on with splendid pluck and devotion and rendered great assistance in dressing the wounded. He set a splendid example of courage at all times.

Captain George Philip Baines 22nd Bn   LG 1/1/18
King's New Years Honours no citation
Captain Frederick Scarth Beadon 18th Bn   LG 1/1/19
King's New Years Honours no citation
Second Lieutenant Francis William Blake 19th Bn   LG 15/2/19
For consistent gallantry and devotion to duty from September 28th to October 2nd, 1918, during the attack from Zillebeke lake. Although gassed prior to the commencement of operations, he led his men with great spirit and endurance. Having reached the final objective he immediately reorganized his platoon and rushed forward with patrols to Jehovah Trench, where he took a machine gun and an enemy sergeant major. He was also largely instrumental in capturing six officers and forty other ranks on reaching the same line. Throughout he set a splendid example to all ranks.
Second Lieutenant F Blenkinsop 18th Bn
Second Lieutenant James Barker Bradford 18th Bn   LG 17/4/17
For conspicuous gallantry and devotion to duty. He gallantly led his men into the enemy trench, capturing many prisoners and two machine guns. He himself killed thrte of the enemy. Later, he succeeded in repelling a determined enemy counter-attack.
Lieutenant J W Carroll 18th Bn
Lieutenant Colonel Herbert Francis George Carter 18th Bn
MC with King's Own Yorkshire Light Infantry   LG 18/2/15
Second Lieutenant Henry Rose Cunliffe 19th Bn   LG26/7/18
For conspicuous gallantry and devotion to duty. During a counter attack he led his platoon forward three times to the attack, successfully driving the enemy back and inflicting heavy casualties upon them. He was wounded by shrapnel in the face but remained on duty until his battalion withdrew. He set a splendid example of courage to all ranks.
22/56 CSM Percy Shalto Douglas 22nd Bn   LG 4/6/17
King's Birthday Honours no citation
Second Lieutenant William Gilbert Dyer 19th Bn   LG 26/7/18
For conspicuous gallantry and devotion to duty in action. He led his platoon forward three times to the attack, and with the help of the platoons on his flanks finally managed to dislodge the enemy. Later, when in command of two platoons he rendered valuable service in the defense of a village and with the help of a corporal handled a Lewis gun with great effect causing heavy casualties on the enemy.
Second Lieutenant Robert Anderson Edgar 19th Bn   LG 7/3/18
For conspicuous gallantry and devotion to duty in an attack. He took command when his company commander was a casualty and led his men successfully in the attack and organized the defense. He personally killed an enemy sniper who had caused many casualties.
Second Lieutenant Alfred Everatt Spec Res DLI att 18th Bn   LG 15/10/18
To this officer was largely due the success of the party from the battalion, which took part in the attack. The ground was new to the men and the alignment of the objective very oblique to the front. However he led the attackers with great dash and energy, overwhelming the positions of the enemy with such rapidity that a group of machine gunners who had not time to open fire were captured as well as many prisoners. His powers of leadership, gallantry in action and characteristic cheerfulness rendered him a platoon commander of great value to his company.
Lieutenant Walter Vernon Falkiner 19th Bn   LG 9/1/18
For conspicuous gallantry and devotion to duty when in charge of Stokes mortars during an assault on the enemy's trenches. When one of his gun positions was blown in under heavy shellfire, he took the gun out and brought it into action in the open trench thus maintaining the maximum effect of fire. During the whole of the operations this officer has consistently shown the greatest gallantry and personal disregard of danger.
Second Lieutenant Herbert Fawcett 18th Bn   LG 24/9/18
For conspicuous gallantry and devotion to duty. At a critical time he collected together a number of men of various units, and under fire led them to high ground where he held up the enemy's advance. His initiative and prompt action undoubtedly helped save an amount of transport and material which would otherwise have been lost.
Second Lieutenant Arthur Martin Freer 18th Bn   LG 16/9/18
For conspicuous gallantry and devotion to duty when in command of a platoon. His initiative and resolution

in mopping up a farm and some houses, which were garrisoned by the enemy gave a magnificent example to his men. Later, in spite of a harassing machine gun fire, he materially improved the situation by a thorough reorganization of the company.

Second Lieutenant William Forster 18th Bn
LG 24/9/18

For conspicuous gallantry and devotion to duty in command of two sections of a raiding party. He led his party forward to their objective, captured a machine gun and killed three of the team himself. After returning to his lines he found several men were missing. He thereupon led a search prty back under heavy machine gun fire and brought in his wounded. He showed fine courage and determination.

Second Lieutenant Reginald Claude Moline Gee 21st att 15th Bn
LG 25/11/16

For conspicuous gallantry in action, he showed marked courage and determination during the consolidation of the position, and set a fine example to his men. Later, he led his platoon in the attack, directing fire on a suspected position and locating snipers and machine guns.

Lieutenant Cecil Gillott 22nd Bn
LG 26/7/18

For conspicuous gallantry and devotion to duty when defending part of the line with his platoon. Although wounded early in the attack he remained with his men until hit for the third time. By his fine example of coolness and absolute disregard for personal safety, his platoon was enabled to inflict heavy losses on the enemy and tohold them up until they had worked round the flanks.

Captain T M Harbottle 18th Bn with 4th Field Survey Bn RE.
LG 3/6/19

King's Birthday Honours no citation

Second Lieutenant Harry Heaton 19th Bn
LG 17/9/17

For conspicuous gallantry and devotion to duty during a hostile raid upon his post. He moved about encouraging the men under heavy fire, until he was hemmed in by the sap being blown in. The successful defense of his post was greatly due to his fine personal efforts.

Second Lieutenant Leslie Hickman 22nd Bn
LG 16/9/18

For conspicuous gallantry and devotion to duty during a counter attack he out flanked an enemy machine gun, killing the crew and capturing the gun, thereby saving his company from heavy casualties.

Lieutenant Samuel George Highmoor 22nd Bn
LG 16/9/18

For conspicuous gallantry and devotion to duty. He brought up reinforcements through artillery barrage, machine gun fire and sniping, to seven men of another unit who were holding some houses. He also returned by daylight to get belt boxes for a machine gun which had none, crossing 100 yards of ground under close rifle fire.

Second Lieutenant Harold Everitt Hitchin DSO MM & Bar 18th Bn
LG 13/7/17

For conspicuous gallantry and devotion to duty. When in command of a company he led four successive attacks upon a position of great tactical importance. His personal daring and skilful use of ground enabled him to capture it at the last attempt after losing 50 per cent of his men. His gallantry and good leadership were most marked.

Lieutenant James Falshaw Hobson 18th Bn
LG 16/9/18

For conspicuous gallantry and devotion to duty as Transport Officer he did excellent work in bringing up Lewis guns and small arms ammunition under very heavy and concentrated shell fire.

Captain (Temp Major) Joshua Bower Hughes-Games 18th Bn
LG 1/1/17

King's New Year's Honours no citation.

Major D E Ince 18th Bn
LG 1/1/18

King's New Year's Honours no citation.

Lieutenant M B Jobbing 19th Bn

Second Lieutenant Harold Ward Jordan 19th Bn
LG 15/10/18

During a raid this officer was in command of the party on the right, which met with considerable opposition from the enemy. He attacked them with great boldness and determination, entering their trenches and killing many of the garrison. He himself was wounded in the head, but continued to command his men until they were withdrawn. His coolness and courage were conspicuous throughout the operation.

Major Clarence Gorringe Killick 18th Bn
LG 3/6/19

King's Birthday Honours no citation

Second Lieutenant George Stanley Leach 19th Bn
LG 1/2/19

This officer was in command of the platoon on the left of the attack south of Zillebeke Lake on 15 September 1918. He had previously reconnoitered the ground most thoroughly and during the operation led his men over most difficult ground to the final objective. After consolidating his line he personally attacked the enemy's posts and brought in eight prisoners and two machine guns. Throughout the engagement he led his men with great daring and dash and his conduct was a stirring example to all ranks.

Second Lieutenant William Edward Lennard 19th Bn   LG 18/3/19

His services as signalling and intelligence officer during the operations west of Courtrai, from 14th to 21st October, 1918, were admirable. In his efforts to maintain communication with all points of the attack he was indefatigable, and he was ever to the fore, showing great disregard of danger under heavy fire. His intelligence duties were performed with great efficiency.

Major William Douglas Lowe 18th Bn   LG 1/1/17

King's New Years Honours no citation

Lieutenant James Wallace Macfarlane RAMC attached 18th Bn   LG 26/7/17

For conspicuous gallantry and devotion to duty. He went through a heavy gas shellfire to dress a wounded man. Finding it impossible to perform this work with the gas mask on he removed it at great risk and completed the task before putting it on again.

Lieutenant Alexander Anderson McConnell 18th Bn   LG 26/7/18

For conspicuous gallantry and devotion to duty when his company commander was wounded he took charge and fought on until hemmed in on three sides and almost out of ammunition, when he withdrew in good order under heavy fire, successfully extricating his men from a difficult situation.

Lieutenant R R McHenry RAMC MORC attached 18th Bn

Lieutenant P Minor 22nd Bn

Second Lieutenant Acting Captain James Murray 19th Bn   LG 8/3/19

For the crossing of the River Lys in October 1918. For conspicuous gallantry as a company commander in the operations west of Courtrai between 14th and 21st October, 1918. He displayed marked courage and devotion to duty leading his men to the attack under heavy shell and machine gun fire, and his reorganization and initiative contributed in no small measure to the splendid success of the operations.

Captain Geoffrey Peirson General List late18th Bn   LG 4/6/17

Second Lieutenant James Gordon Perry Spec Res DLI att 18th Bn   LG 15/10/18

This officer was in command of a daylight patrol operating against an enemy post in an enclosure. Whilst advancing against the enclosure he sighted some of the enemy. He placed four of his men opposite the enclosure and himself with two others worked round to the left. He covered two of the enemy with his revolver and forced them to surrender, subsequently capturing another ten prisoners. He with his two men then entered the enclosure and captured two more prisoners. He led his patrol back with fourteen prisoners and a machine gun. In this operation he showed great daring and ability and secured an important identification.

Captain Frederick Cecil Prickett 18th Bn   LG 3/6/18

King's Birthday Honours no citation.

Lieutenant Harry Ewbank Raine 18th Bn,   LG 3/6/18

King's Birthday Honours no citation

Captain Adam Henry Robson 22nd Bn   LG 26/5/17

For conspicuous gallantry and devotion to duty. He personally taped out the line for a new trench under very fire and eventually succeeded in completing the trench. He set a splendid example of courage and determination

Second Lieutenant Evan William Rowlands 18th Bn   LG 1/1/18

King's New Year's Honours Award no citation.

Lieutenant Scott RAMC attached 20th Bn

Second Lieutenant Herbert Shepley 19th Bn   LG 1/2/19

This officer took part in the attack south of Zillebeke Lake on 15 September 1918. In a previous reconnoiter he led his platoon in the attack with great courage and was ever in the forefront of the fight. He took the enemy's posts and consolidated them. The enemy, afterwards counter-attacked but were driven off with loss and the line was completely established owing chiefly to his initiative, dash and cheerful influences. Throughout the whole engagement he set a fine example to his men.

Captain Kingsley Smith 19th Bn   LG 26/7/18

For conspicuous gallantry and devotion to duty during a counter-attack. When in command of two companies he advanced and attacked with great determination, driving the enemy back and occupying a line 200 yards in advance of the lost line. During the whole engagement and organization of the line he showed great coolness and skill, and by his devotion to duty saved a very critical situation.

6876 Acting RSM M A Smith 18th Bn attached 8th Duke of Cornwalls LI LG 3/6/18
King's Birthday Honours no citation

Captain Alexander William Summerbell York and Lancs Regt late att 18th Bn   LG 1/2/19
At Havrincourt on 12th September, 1918, this officer displayed great courage in working his way up a trench with only a few men and holding the enemy in check. He succeeded eventually in putting them to flight, causing considerable casualties and capturing twenty prisoners.

Second Lieutenant Roland Rockliffe Turnbull 18th Bn   LG 15/10/18
For conspicuous gallantry and devotion to duty during an advance. He twice led a charge against a machine gun, showing utter contempt of danger. Throughout a most trying day he showed marked courage, ability and determination.

Captain Albert Howard Waton General List att 18th Bn.   LG 26/7/18
For conspicuous gallantry and devotion to duty in repeatedly going forward during obscure situations and bringing back valuable information. Again; as liaison officer, he remained forward in an exposed position, continuously shelled, observing and reporting the enemy's movements, thus enabling a timely counter-attack to be launched,which restored the line.

Captain Eric Thomas Weddell 18th Bn   LG 15/2/19
During the attack on the western edge of Ploegsteert Wood on September 28/29 1918 he commanded six platoons on an exceptionally wide and difficult front. By his driving power and leadership he successfully made a series of bounds. When a strong enemy party held up the advance he organized and carried through a flank attack, resulting in the capture of two machine guns and six prisoners. Seventy of the enemy, at least were accounted for by machine gun fire as they retreated. His gallantry, able leadership and prompt action contributed greatly to the successful penetration of the wood.

Captain Bernard Burke White 22nd Bn   LG 1/1/18
King's New Years Honours Award no citation.

Major George White 13th later 18th Bn   LG 3/6/16

Second Lieutenant Clive Stanley Willmer 22nd Bn   LG 16/9/18
For conspicuous gallantry and devotion to duty during several days of fighting this officer showed considerable skill in the handling of his platoon, particularly in the mopping up of a village. He was also instrumental in putting out of action an enemy machine gun, which was holding up the attack, and in capturing the crew.

BAR TO THE MILITARY CROSS

Lieutenant, Acting Captain Harry Heaton 19th Bn   LG 19/6/19
Maricourt 25 March 1918
For conspicuous gallantry and devotion to duty. The battalion was ordered to counter attack on a portion of the line which had been lost. He led the first wave forward for a distance of 1,000 yards, drove the enemy right back and established the new line in an advanced position. During the whole of the engagement he was ever to the front and showed the greatest courage in leading his men to the attack.

Lieutenant James Wallace Macfarlane MC RAMC att 18th Bn   LG 4/2/18
Captain Adam Harry Robson MC 22nd Bn   LG 26/7/18
For conspicuous gallantry and devotion to duty during a heavy enemy attack in command of his company. Although half of the company had become casualties, and only two officers were left, he inflicted great losses on the enemy and only by his skill and courage succeeded in safely withdrawing the remnants of his men. Later, while moving about encouraging all with him to hold out during a heavy bombardment he was badly wounded.

SECOND BAR TO THE MILITARY CROSS

Lieutenant James Wallace Macfarlane MC & Bar RAMC att 18th Bn

THE DISTINGUISHED FLYING CROSS

Lieutenant J Parke RAF late 18th Bn   LG 21/9/18
This officer has taken part in 40 long distance day bomb raids and photographic reconnaissances. His work as an observer has been consistently good, and he displayed great gallantry and determination, notably in a bombing raid when he was observer to the leader of our second formation.

MENTIONED IN DESPATCHES

Captain F S Beadon 18th Bn

Lieutenant Colonel H Bowes 18th Bn   4/1/17

Second Lieutenant H C Bruce 22nd Bn   21/12/17

Lieutenant & Quartermaster J H Chaplin 18th Bn   25/5/17

Lieutenant Colonel R E Cheyne   25/5/17, 24/5/18

Captain A W H Cooke 22nd Bn   24/5/18

Second Lieutenant A Crierie   9/7/19

Lieutenant J A Crutchley 22nd Bn   24/5/18

Captain L A Dick 18th Bn   24/5/18

Second Lieutenant W G Dyer MC 19th Bn   9/7/19

Captain W Fenwick 18th Bn   9/7/19

T/Lieutenant Colonel A V A Gayer   21/12/17, 30/5/18, 28/12/18

T/Captain, A/Major C C H Hall 22nd Bn   25/5/17, 28/12/18

Lieutenant E Hartley 22nd Bn   25/5/17

Captain H E Hitchin 18th Bn   25/5/17

Lieutenant Colonel W D Lowe 18th Bn   28/12/18

Captain, A/Lieutenant Colonel H R McCullagh 2nd att 19th Bn   24/5/18, 28/12/18

QM & Lieutenant J C Mills 19th Bn   9/7/19

Lieutenant P Minor 5th att 22nd Bn   28/12/18

Major, A/Lieutenant Colonel J D Mitchell DSO 22nd Bn   28/12/18, 9/7/19

Lieutenant Colonel C B Morgan 22nd Bn   21/12/17, 24/5/18

Captain, T/Lieutenant Colonel W Rigby R Irish Regt att 19th Bn   8/7/19

Captain A H Robson MC 22nd Bn   21/12/17

Captain R Thwaites 22nd Bn   21/12/17

Captain L C Warmington 18th Bn   21/12/17

Major A H Waton 18th Bn

THE DISTINGUISHED CONDUCT MEDAL

38896 Private J Atkinson 18th Bn   LG 3/9/18

For conspicuous gallantry and devotion to duty. He volunteered to take an important message to the front line over open country, and over a light railway embankment in full view of the enemy. He was wounded, but reached the front line. He was again wounded, this time seriously, but managed to deliver his message. His loyal devotion to duty and resolute determination could not be surpassed.

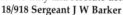

18/918 Sergeant J W Barker   LG 30/10/18

During the operation against Becque Plate, west of Vieux Berquin, on 19 July 1918 Sergeant Barker not only assisted his platoon commander in every possible way but showed coolness and personal courage of the highest order. Under galling machine gun fire at point blank range he with Second Lieutenant Henderson drew wounded men lying in an open clover field into a shell-hole and took up position with them there. Two Germans appeared on the edge of the shell hole and called on them to surrender. The officer shot one and Sergeant Barker shot the other. Almost at once sixteen of the enemy rushed up and threw hand grenades and fired, one of the hand grenades fell by the side of one of the wounded men: without a moment's hesitation and without thought of his own danger Sergeant Barker gallantly picked it up and threw it at the enemy, it burst immediately and killed two Germans. He then, with his officer, killed seven more of the enemy with their rifles and drove back the remainder. In every way both by his resolution and courage this non-commissioned officer set an inspiring and encouraging example to all who saw him.

18/918 Sergeant J W Barker served with the RE in WW2.

18/1291 Sergeant W Bell with Tank Corps   LG

18/1162 Company Sergeant Major W T Benneworth   LG 3/9/18

For conspicuous gallantry and devotion to duty. He made a personal reconnaissance under heavy machine gun fire over eight hundred yards of ground, thus saving a very dangerous position. Later, when in command of a post, he showed great courage and skill in covering the retirement of other troops, killing six of the enemy himself. He set a fine example to all.

45332 Private R W Cowling 18th Bn   LG 30/10/18

For conspicuous gallantry and devotion to duty during an attack. He and another man stalked a machine gun through the corn, shot two of the crew, and dismantled the gun. Their section being held up again, they went forward again, and successfully dealt with this second machine gun, killing three of the crew. The splendid courage of these two men saved many casualties and greatly helped the advance.

18/32 Company Sergeant Major F Curry   LG 17/4/18

For conspicuous gallantry and devotion to duty. His total disregard of danger in action and his fine soldierly qualities have always been a splendid example to his men.

7375 Company Sergeant Major B Dolan 18th Bn LG 30/10/18

For conspicuous gallantry and devotion to duty. Before our advance he personally supervised, under very server machine gun fire, the distribution of rations to the posts, ensuring by his devotion to duty that all men were properly fed before moving to the attack. When the objective was finally reached he volunteered to guide the ammunition parties, under a severe enemy barrage, to the front lines, as the men were new to the country and might have missed the way. He was entirely successful in his arrangements, and the supply of ammunition was amply provided, he himself making two journeys in full daylight under heavy fire. His courage, determination and high soldierly qualities have always distinguished him in the most marked manner.

1304 Sergeant H
oldsborough, from
shop Auckland.

18/1304 Sergeant H Goldsborough   LG 30/10/18

For conspicuous gallantry and devotion to duty. Immediately after he had captured the objective during a successful advance he took his Lewis gun team across a stream and moved up under cover of standing corn to within a short distance of a group of enemy light machine guns. He rushed the post in a most determined fashion, and captured the guns and accounted for the teams. His prompt and gallant action and skilful leadership undoubtedly saved casualties during the consolidation which was then carried on without hindrance.

18/509 Sergeant I Habron   LG 18/7/17

For conspicuous gallantry and devotion to duty. He led his platoon three times to the assault, and on each occasion reorganised them under cover whilst remaining himself exposed to close enemy fire. His platoon achieved its objective largely owing to the moral effect of his intrepid leading and extraordinary coolness under every form of fire.

22/327 Private E Handyside with 1/7th Bn   LG 3/9/19

He has repeatedly displayed great coolness and gallantry in action particularly on the morning of 25 March 1918 near Morchain. When the enemy was attacking he rallied men in his vicinity, and in spite of numerically superior forces he held on to his post, and inflicted heavy casualties on the enemy. On previous occasions he has displayed great gallantry and coolness and throughout these operations his conduct had a very inspiring effect on his comrades.

19/685 Private W Harper, with 18th Bn   LG 30/10/18

For conspicuous gallantry and devotion to duty during an attack. He and another man stalked a machine gun through the corn, shot two of the crew and dismantled the gun. Their section being held up again, they went forward and successfully dealt with this second machine gun, killing three of the crew. The splendid courage and resource of these two men saved many casualties.

19/798 Private C Imeson   LG 20/10/16

For conspicuous gallantry and devotion to duty during operations. As a stretcher bearer he tended the wounded and carried them to the aid post along a road heavily shelled and swept by machine gun fire. When his battalion was relieved he stayed behind with another brigade to assist with their wounded.

18/1276 Corporal C Lloyd   LG 30/10/18

For conspicuous gallantry and devotion to duty during an attack. An enemy machine gun was holding up his section, so halting his men in a ditch, he went forward alone and stalked the gun. He succeeded in shooting two of the team and in silencing the gun. On returning to bring on his section he found all but one were casualties, he himself having been wounded while stalking the gun. He showed great grit and determination.

11007 Regimental Sergeant Major W C Mason MM 19th Bn   LG 3/9/19

This W.O. has, from August 1917, served continuously with this battalion and has rendered yeoman service, especially in the line. On many occasions he has displayed great gallantry under fire, and his skill, initiative, and gallant bearing have been a splendid example to all ranks. He has served continuously with the BEF in France since August 1914. (MM with 2nd Bn 1916)

45306 Private H Mitchell 18th Bn   LG 3/9/18

For conspicuous gallantry and devotion to duty. His company was seriously harassed by a machine gun firing from a hedge near by. He volunteered to silence it, and went forward by himself, and by crawling along in the dusk rushed the gun team, bayoneted three men and put the gun out of action. His bold action saved the company many casualties.

18/126 Regimental Sergeant Major E Oldridge.

18/126 Regimental Sergeant Major E Oldridge   LG 3/9/18

For conspicuous gallantry and devotion to duty. Throughout a critical day's fighting this warrant officer was ubiquitous in helping to rally men and organise defensive posts. He was twice in the very last group of men to withdraw. During the next two days he was always at work in helping with the linking up of trenches and general arrangements for defence, and proved his solid value to the battalion as RSM.

BAR

For conspicuous gallantry and devotion to duty. During two year's continuous service in the field this WO's leading and conduct have done much to uphold the efficiency of the battalion. As RSM he has been of great assistance to his CO; especially in active operations against the enemy. While in the lower ranks his readiness to share in all dangerous undertakings were an incentive to others of his company to follow his example.

18/351 Corporal M R Pinkney   LG 22/9/16

For conspicuous gallantry at Neuve Chappelle in July 1916. When in a bay, on each side of which the enemy had penetrated, he cleared one side by shooting round the traverse with his revolver, and then, turning to the other side, shot two of the enemy who were taking a man prisoner.

18/826 Sergeant E C Powell   LG 10/1/20

For conspicuous gallantry and devotion to duty on 28 September 1918, during the advance upon Ploegsteert Wood. While his platoon was preparing for the final thrust in the wood it was strongly counter-attacked. He gathered a handful of men and led a charge, which drove the enemy back. Later, when his platoon was suffering from the fire of a machine gun, he worked round alone to the rear and silenced it.

53691 Sergeant W Rigg 19th Bn   LG 30/10/18

For conspicuous gallantry and devotion to duty. During a raid on the enemy line this NCO showed great gallantry and devotion to duty, being responsible for keeping the party together in spite of difficulties. He with his officer, bombed the enemy with great effect, and although wounded, he was the last man of the party to leave the enemy position. He set a fine example to all ranks by his courage and determination.

13672 Sergeant J R Robertson 19th Bn   LG 14/5/19

On 14th October 1918, for most conspicuous gallantry and devotion to duty in action west of Courtrai. The company had been held up some 200 yards from its final objective by machine gun fire and snipers. He took a party of ten men and attacked the post from a flank, capturing the machine gun and three prisoners, though he only had two men with him at the time and putting the remainder to flight. He has shown marked courage on many occasions and set a fine example to all ranks.

19/886 Lance Corporal H F Scurr   LG 20/10/16

For conspicuous gallantry and devotion to duty as medical orderly. He not only attended the wounded at the aid post, but went out and brought in wounded men under heavy fire.

18/175 Sergeant W Siddle   LG 3/9/19

From 25 February 1918 to 16 September 1918. He has throughout his service in France showed marked courage and initiative while in charge of transport proceeding to the line, and especially during the hostile operations at Ayette in March 1918, where rations and stores were brought up under heavy shell fire. At Meteren, in May 1918 when the transport was disorganised by heavy gas shelling and was compelled to scatter, he collected his wagons, reorganised the convoy, and completed the delivery of rations. He has done consistent good work.

24559 Sergeant R Stoddart.

24559 Sergeant R Stoddart 19th Bn   LG 2/12/19

For consistent gallantry and devotion to duty from 28 September to 2 October 1918 during the attack from Zillebeke Lake. He commanded a platoon throughout the whole operation in a most able manner. Also, he alone rushed a machine gun post, killing three of the crew and capturing the remainder and the gun. Subsequently, he helped to get in wounded under exceptionally heavy artillery.

BAR   LG 10/1/20

18/175 Sergeant W Siddle

For most conspicuous gallantry and devotion to duty during operations east of Moorseele on 14 October 1918. He alone charged two machine guns, which were firing at him point blank, bayoneting two of their crew and taking the remainder prisoner. Later, he again rushed a machine gun post, which was menacing our left flank. In the attack on 15 October 1918, he took a party of sixteen men to raid two farms, which were giving a considerable amount of trouble. He accomplished his task and, although severely wounded, established posts in the positions taken.

9938 Private A A Taylor 18th Bn   LG 30/10/18

For conspicuous gallantry and devotion to duty. When we had reached our objective after a successful advance, this man went forward to reconnoitre in front with his platoon sergeant. They took three prisoners in the standing corn and three more in shelter, and, working through the corn were able to attack from the rear an enemy machine gun and team, whom they also captured. Returning through the stacks of reaped corn they secured another light machine gun and two prisoners. Private Taylor worked most energetically and courageously in co-operation with his platoon sergeant and by their enterprising and determined action they crushed what might have become a serious local counter-attack.

18/182 Sergeant W Teasdale   LG 20/10/16

For conspicuous gallantry in action. Though blown back into the trench by the bursting of a shell, he got out again, rallied all the men he could find, under heavy shellfire, and led them forward with great determination. He has since been severely wounded.

18/264 Company Sergeant Major G W Tucker   LG 25/11/16

For conspicuous gallantry in action. He showed great courage and determination in assisting to lead his company in a bombing attack under intensive fire. He repeatedly went back for fresh supplies of bombs.

18/1610 Company Sergeant Major W G Walker with 19th Bn   LG 10/1/20

For conspicuous gallantry and fine work in the attack from Zillebeke Lake on 28 September 1918. When a platoon was held up by snipers at Klien Zillebeke, he crawled forward and killed one and captured another. He then led his platoon to its objective and consolidated. His conduct throughout was a splendid example to all ranks.

19/833 Sergeant W Wilson   LG 9/7/17

For conspicuous gallantry and devotion to duty in the Lihons sector in February 1917. He commanded a platoon for a lengthy period, often under the most trying circumstances, and led his men with the utmost courage and ability, setting them a splendid example throughout.

BAR   LG 30/10/18

For conspicuous gallantry and devotion to duty. During a raid on the enemy's line he distinguished himself by his gallantry and devotion to duty, which were an outstanding example to all ranks. He kept his party together with great skill throughout the operation, and inflicted severe casualties on the enemy, of whom he killed three himself with the bayonet. Although wounded he was the last to leave the enemy trenches.

245912 Corporal F Wright 18th Bn   LG 30/10/18

For conspicuous gallantry and devotion to duty. During a daylight patrol against an enemy post he boldly advanced up to an entrance and captured two of the enemy. Then he succeeded with an officer in capturing ten more prisoners and a machine gun. The total was fourteen prisoners and a machine gun, and the success of the enterprise was very greatly due to the great courage and enterprise of Corporal Wright.

THE MILITARY MEDAL

21/375 Private W Ainsley with 18th Bn	LG 21/10/18
18/422 Lance Corporal C Anderson	LG1/9/16
42434 Corporal J Aspin 18th Bn	LG 14/5/19
18/1515 Private T Batey with 14th Bn	LG 19/2/17
14447 Private R Bawn 19th Bn	LG 17/6/19
46872 Corporal W Beasley 19th Bn	LG 27/10/16
19410 Sergeant T Bedingfield 19th Bn	LG 11/2/19
325086 Lance Corporal J Bee 19th Bn	LG 19/2/17
18/1215 Lance Corporal E C Bell att APM 31 Division	LG 27/8/18
26714 Corporal G B Bell 19th Bn	LG 17/9/17
22/466 Sergeant F Benson	LG 16/7/18
22/366 Private G Bolam with 9th Bn	LG 20/8/19
54060 Sergeant C B Booth 19th Bn	LG 11/2/19

19/104 Private J H Bowditch	LG 12/9/18
3755979 Private F Bowe 19th Bn	LG15/5/19
23/399 Private H Brailey with 18th Bn	LG 14/5/19
21610 Private H Brankston 19th Bn	LG 17/6/19
22/368 Lance Corporal J A Brown	LG 17/9/17
75698 Private E Buckham 19th Bn	LG 17/6/19
21/314 Sergeant O Burdon with 18th Bn	LG 20/8/19
54063 Acting Corporal A Burt 19th Bn	LG 12/6/18
19/1525 Corporal J Carney	LG 17/6/19
18/464 Corporal W Carrick	LG 9/7/17
18/1186 Private O Carroll	LG 18/7/17
91189 Sergeant W T Carroll 22nd Bn	LG 29/8/18
19/393 Sergeant A Charlton	LG 23/7/19
18/1673 Private W C Chator	
18/1706 Private W Coates with 14th Bn	LG 6/1/17
22/363 Private R Coltman	LG 16/7/18
18/467 Lance Corporal H Colwell with 14th Bn	LG 18/6/17
18/238 Corporal T Cook	LG 28/1/18
22/949 Private J R Cooper	LG 21/10/18
18803 Private W Cranney 19th Bn	LG 11/2/19
21/318 Private G W Croft with 15th Bn	LG 18/6/17
18/1217 Private W Curry	LG 6/8/18
45347 Lance Corporal T Davison 18th Bn	LG 13/11/18
23/36 Corporal M Dempsey 19th Bn	LG 23/7/19
18/729 Lance Corporal W Dickinson	LG 1/9/16
43467 Private F Dinning 22nd Bn	LG 29/8/18
18/43 Sergeant W Dixon	LG 9/7/19
15751 Corporal W Dixon 19th Bn	LG 25/4/18
22/325 Corporal E Dodds	LG 16/7/18
23748 Lance Corporal J Dunning 18th Bn	LG 6/8/18
91197 Private F Edwards 22nd Bn	LG 29/8/18
43648 Private V Feeney 19th Bn	LG 13/11/18
19/140 Sergeant A Fenny	LG 24/1/19
53602 Corporal C Fethney 19th Bn	LG 2/11/17
18/956 Corporal C G Foster	LG 9/7/17
350633 Private T Foster 19th Bn	LG 24/1/19
18/489 Lance Corporal A Frazer	LG 26/4/17
30131 Sergeant R Garbutt 22nd Bn	LG 11/5/17
18/276 Private S Gibson with 13th Bn	LG 6/8/18
18/1145 Private W Grant	LG 21/10/18
22/248 Corporal J Green	LG 16/7/18
43637 Private W Greener 19th Bn	LG 17/6/19
45901 Corporal W H Hare	LG 29/8/17
45949 Sergeant F Harper 22nd Bn	LG 29/8/18
52611 Private F G Harrison 22nd Bn	LG 29/8/18
18/767 Corporal G E Hawkins	LG 6/8/18
80867 Sergeant S Hemmingfield 19th Bn	LG 17/6/19
18/1516 Sergeant B Hobson with 19th Bn	LG 17/6/19
20/582 Private E Hodges with 13th Bn	LG 12/12/17
30125 Lance Corporal A P Hodgson 22nd Bn	LG 17/9/17
22/370 Private R Hopps	LG 11/5/17
43462 Corporal N Houston 19th Bn	LG 14/5/19
22/354 Sergeant J H Howells	LG 17/9/17
19/1081 Corporal W Hughes with 2nd Bn	LG 7/10/18
18/1567 Private T S Hutchinson	LG 26/4/17

19/1081 Corporal W Hughes.

19/798 Private C Imeson	LG 13/11/18
45525 Private A W Iliffe	LG 16/7/18
19/200 CSM E Jackson	LG 14/5/19
203077 Private J Jackson 19th Bn	LG 11/2/19
18/782 Sergeant G H Jacob	LG 16/11/16
19/636 Sergeant J W Jobling with 18th Bn	LG 16/7/18
53648 Corporal J H Johnson 19th Bn	LG 6/8/18
9175 Private G Jones 19th Bn	LG 14/5/19
18/100 Lance Corporal J Kennick att 93 Bde HQ	LG 16/7/18
18/1601 Private F King	LG 19/7/18
18/531 Private F Kirk with 19th Bn	LG 11/2/19
18/533 Lance Corporal J Lackey	LG 26/4/17
19/803 Private R Lambert	LG 21/10/16
18/536 Corporal H W Lawler	LG 17/3/17
24075 Private D S Lawson 19th Bn	LG 14/5/19
18/308 Corporal G C Lawson	LG 19/2/17
18/315 Private E R Little	LG 30/1/20
12249 Private J Lowe 19th Bn	LG 11/2/19
301574 Private R R Lowery 19th Bn	LG 2/11/17
19/20 Private H Lyth att 106 LTMB	LG 2/11/17
31058 Lance Corporal W Marsden 19th Bn	LG 12/6/18
39442 Private T B McCallum 19th Bn	LG 11/2/19
19/1174 Private H McDonald with 12th Bn	LG 21/10/18
13435 Private W Meadows 19th Bn	LG 17/6/19
18/809 Private J Mellor	LG 11/11/16
18/120 Lance Sergeant J Milburn	LG 19/2/17
19/626 Private C W Mitchell	LG 23/7/19
203460 Private W Nash 18th Bn	LG 13/11/18
76531 Private W Naylor 19th Bn	LG 17/6/19
21941 Private F Nelson 18th Bn	LG 16/7/18
19/622 Private R Nelson	LG 14/5/19
23/488 Corporal W Nelson 19th Bn	LG 17/6/19
3/10056 Private S Nesbit 18th Bn	LG 19/2/17
18/232 Private F Newcombe	LG 6/8/18
20/110 Private G Newton with 19th Bn	LG 14/5/19
14083 Private N Ogle 18th Bn	LG 13/11/18
70587 Private J Pearson 19th Bn	LG 25/4/18
52811 Private J H Pinkett 19th Bn	LG 6/8/18
9957 Corporal W M Plant 19th Bn	LG 23/7/19
78211 Private A Porter 18th Bn	LG 24/1/19
18/1342 Sergeant Jack Potts (Ryton)	LG 28/1/18
19/348 Sergeant W Powell with 13th Bn	LG 12/12/17
22/375 Private J E Pringle 22nd Bn	LG 21/10/18
53671 Lance Corporal F Ramsden 19th Bn	LG 2/11/17
18/583 Corporal J Rand	LG 11/12/18
22/184 Private W Ransome	LG 18/9/23
18/584 Private T Reavley with 19th Bn	LG 14/5/19
18/144 Private T Reed	LG 14/5/19
19/1603 Private A Riddle	LG 12/6/18
24589 Private W J Rigby 18th Bn	LG 21/10/18
18/356 Lance Corporal T Rigg	LG 17/4/17
13672 Sergeant J R Robertson 19th Bn	LG 14/5/19
22/734 Sergeant A Robinson	LG 17/9/17
19/1130 Lance Corporal A Russell	LG 21/10/16
18/1393 Private S Ryder	LG 23/2/18
18/933 Private C H Sainte	LG 20/8/19

54096 Sergeant W E Sanderson	LG 6/8/18
18579 Sergeant G Sayers 19th Bn	LG 23/7/19
19/866 Sergeant B Scott with 20th Bn	LG 28/9/17
22/903 Lance Corporal J Scully with 1/7th Bn	LG 17/6/19
93167 Private F Sharpe 19th Bn	LG 17/6/19
204517 Private R Simpson 19th Bn	LG 14/5/19
201082 Private C Slater 18th Bn	LG 21/10/18
18/851 Sergeant J D Smith	LG 11/11/16
19/817 Private J H Smith	LG 11/2/19
245439 Corporal C Southwell 19th Bn	LG 14/5/19
18/384 Private T W Stanfield	LG 16/11/116
22/377 Lance Sergeant A L Stephenson	LG 11/5/17
22/1003 Private A W Stobbs attached 8th Div RE	LG 29/8/18
18/167 Lance Corporal A E Stokes	LG 1/9/16
22/683 Corporal T Stonehouse	LG 16/7/18
28092 Private J Sullivan 22nd Bn	LG 29/8/18
320043 Private J W Swainston 19th Bn	LG 6/8/18
22/505 Private F Sykes	LG 29/8/18
22/379 Private G B Tarn	LG 6/1/17
19/85 Sergeant C L Taylor	LG 17/6/19
36492 Private H Taylor 18th Bn	LG 13/11/18
18/1152 Private W Taylor	LG 9/7/17
18/1064 Lance Corporal W A Taylor	LG 9/7/17
85248 Private A Thompson 22nd Bn	LG 21/10/18
18/619 Lance Corporal H W Thompson	LG 16/11/16
19/405 Corporal M Thompson	LG 11/2/19
4/10075 Private M Thompson 19th Bn	LG 2/11/17
18/1655 Private F B Thorpe	LG 21/10/18
43629 Private A Tilley 19th Bn	LG 23/7/19
18/614 Lance Corporal R Topping	LG 9/7/17
43238 Corporal W Tordoff 19th Bn	LG 17/6/19
245914 Private H F Towle 18th Bn	LG 13/11/18
18/1225 Private J H Turnbull with 19th Bn	LG 14/5/19
91306 Private G Turner 18th Bn	LG 13/11/18
85259 Private G R Ure 22nd Bn	LG 21/10/18
11900 Corporal B Veasey 22nd Bn	LG 17/9/17
18/981 Private T R Vocknick	LG 27/4/17
19/178 Sergeant R Wallis	LG 6/8/18
42915 Private L Walker 19th Bn	LG 17/6/19
270090 Private S J Walker 18th Bn	LG 21/10/18
18/1488 Private I B Walton with 13th Bn	LG 23/7/19
53676 Sergeant F Warburton 19th Bn	LG 17/6/19
22/1115 Private W Watson	LG 16/7/18
22/715 Sergeant R C Wherley	LG 16/7/18
53205 CSM R C Whetter 19th Bn	LG 11/2/19
45304 Corporal F G White 18th Bn	LG 21/10/18
22/760 Lance Sergeant J Wigham	LG 16/7/18
19/594 Private E Wilby	LG 21/10/16
27078 Private F Willis 18th Bn	LG 24/1/19
10617 Private J Woodhouse 19th Bn	LG 24/1/19
106735 Private J H Workman 19th Bn	LG 23/7/19
91191 Lance Sergeant J Wright 22nd Bn	LG 29/8/18
18/1517 Sergeant R T Young with 14th Bn	LG 19/2/17
245910 Private J Yoxall 18th Bn	LG 21/10/18

18/1225 Private J H Turnbull.

19/178 Sergeant R Walli

Bar to The Military Medal

42434 Corporal J Aspin MM 18th Bn	LG 19/6/19
19410 Sergeant T Bedingfield MM 19th Bn	LG 14/5/19
325086 Lance Corporal J Bee MM 19th Bn	LG 9/7/17
23/399 Private H Brailey MM 18th Bn	LG 4/9/19
18/238 Corporal T Cook MM	LG 6/8/18
18/729 Sergeant W Dickinson MM	LG 6/8/18
22/325 Corporal E Dodds MM	LG 29/8/18
43462 Corporal N Houston MM 19th Bn	LG 14/5/19
18/308 Corporal G C Lawson MM 18th Bn	LG 18/7/17
31058 Lance Corporal W Marsden MM 19th Bn	LG 6/8/18
52811 Private J H Pinkett MM 19th Bn	LG 17/6/19
18/584 Private T Reavley MM 19th Bn	LG 23/7/19
18/144 Private T Reed MM	LG 14/5/19
22/734 Sergeant A Robinson MM	LG 29/8/18
53676 Sergeant F Warburton MM 19th Bn	LG 20/8/19

2nd Bar to the Military Medal

325086 Corporal J Bee MM & Bar 19th Bn	LG 12/12/17
18/238 Corporal T Cook MM & Bar	LG 14/5/19

Meritorious Service Medal

18/425 CQMS A W Austin	LG 3/6/19
18/432 Private E T Bell	LG 3/6/19
22/669 Sergeant R Blackett	LG 17/6/18
320034 Corporal G F Brighton 19th Bn	LG 3/6/19
18/468 Lance Corporal A Clarke	LG 18/1/19
18/1729 Private S Clarke	LG 14/5/19
18/734 RQMS A G Drummond	LG 18/1/19
18/284 RQMS W Hall	LG 3/6/19
22/357 Corporal R Imeson 22nd Bn	LG 10/10/18
53013 Sergeant A Oakes 19th Bn	LG 3/6/19
18/655 CQMS L Oliphant	LG 18/1/19
12775 Lance Corporal J Ord 18th Bn	LG 19/2/17
19/369 RQMS J C Proud	LG 3/6/19
22/412 CQMS F G Reeves with 7th Bn	LG 3/6/19
18/377 Private L H Robinson	LG 3/6/19
19/1205 Private J Russell	LG 17/6/18
22/377 Sergeant A L Stephenson	LG 3/6/19
22/463 Sergeant G H Ward	LG 17/6/18
22/1125 Sergeant H C Welsh 22nd Bn	LG 1/1/18
18/416 CQMS G Whitehead	LG 3/6/19
22/13 CQMS J Wilson with 7th Bn	LG 18/1/19

Croix de Guerre Belgium

Lieutenant William Allbuery 18th Bn	LG 4/9/19
23/399 Private H Brailey MM 18th Bn	LG 4/9/19
22/2 CQMS T Danby	LG 12/7/18
43633 Corporal J Dent 19th Bn	LG 4/9/19
14083 Private N Ogle MM 18th Bn	LG 4/9/19
19/1296 Sergeant F W Peacock	LG 4/9/19
14083 Private N Ogle MM 18th Bn	LG 4/9/19
19/1296 Sergeant F W Peacock	LG 4/9/19

18/1517 Sergeant R T Young.

ORDER OF LEOPOLD (BELGIUM)
18/1162 CSM W Benneworth DCM

CROIX DE GUERRE FRANCE
18/426 Sergeant G F Allison	LG 1/5/17
42434 Private J Aspin 18th Bn	LG 19/6/19
18/238 Corporal T Cook MM & 2 Bars	LG 19/6/19
21/318 Private G W Croft with 15th Bn	LG 14/7/17
53017 CQMS P Darling 19th Bn	LG 19/6/19
Lt A/Captain H Heaton 19th Bn	LG 19/6/19
22/357 Lance Corporal R Imeson	LG 10/10/18
18/131 CSM W A Pearson	LG 17/8/18

LEGION D'HONNEUR
Lt Colonel Hugh Bowes	LG19/3/20

MEDAL MILITAIRE
93252 Lance Sergeant W H Lawler	LG 21/8/19

BRONZE MEDAL FOR VALOUR (ITALY)
19/789 Private C Imeson DCM, MM	LG 13/11/18

ORDER OF ST GEORGE 4TH CLASS (RUSSIA)
18/782 Sergeant G H Jacob MM	LG 15/2/17

ORDER OF KARRA -GEORGE (SERBIA)
18/308 Lance Corporal G C Lawson MM	LG 19/2/17
3/10056 Private S Nesbitt MM 18th Bn	LG 19/2/17
12775 Lance Corporal J Ord MM 18th Bn	LG 19/2/17
18/1517 Sergeant R T Young with 15th Bn	LG 19/2/17

MENTIONED IN DESPATCHES
18/1185 Sergeant A E Atkin	LG 9/7/19
18/224 Private A/CQMS C B Boyce	LG 25/5/17
53683 Sergeant W Brooking 19th Bn	LG 9/7/19
21/314 Sergeant O Burdon 18th Bn	LG 28/12/18
18/43 Sergeant C G Dixon	LG9/7/19
53632 Sergeant J C Garton 19th Bn	LG 9/7/19
22/435 Lance Corporal G Green with 1/7th Bn	LG 9/7/19
18/1273 Sergeant W Harrison	LG 9/7/19
18/289 Corporal G Horner with 1/7th Bn	LG 9/7/19
26966 Corporal E Jackson 22nd Bn	LG 21/12/17
18/1775 Private J Jackson	LG 9/7/19
323055 Corporal S A Jeavons 19th Bn	LG 28/12/18
22/113 Sergeant C R Leeming	LG 25/5/18
18/812 Sergeant W Mowbray	LG 4/1/17
18/131 CSM W A Pearson	LG 21/12/17
18/389 Sergeant J A Simpson	LG 4/1/17
22/921 Sergeant G Stephenson	LG 21/12/17
18/178 CQMS H L Taylor	LG 9/7/19
18/886 Sergeant R Walton	LG 25/5/17

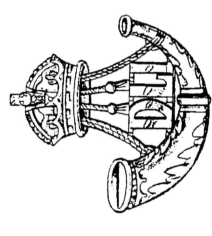

ALPHABETICAL NOMINAL ROLL OF ORIGINAL
OTHER RANKS
18th (SERVICE) BATTALION
DURHAM LIGHT INFANTRY
(1st COUNTY)(PALS)
1914 – 1919

NAME	INITIALS	RANK	NUMBER	TOWN_VILL	PLACE_&_DATE_ENL	CAUSE_&_DATE_DIS,_DIED_&_BURIED	TRANSFER_-_HOSP_-_NEW_REGT_No_-_PLACE_OF_BIRTH_ETC
ADAMSON	JohnR	PTE	/661	SUNDERLAND	SUNDERLAND 21/12/14	1/7/16 THIEPVAL MEM	AGE 35 DID NOT SERVE OVERSEAS.
AFFLECK	RobtW	PTE	/1118			ASTEOMA 28/1/19	COMMISSIONED 3rd BN 25/9/18.
AGAR	JWL	SGT	/1				
AINSLEY	JohnA	LCPL	/969	DARLINGTON	29/10/14	KR para 392 31/1/18	TO 3rd BN. AGE 25. 2nd SOUTHERN GEN HOSP BRISTOL 8/7/16
AINSLEY	Walt	PTE	/1160	WEST HARTLEPOOL		2/3/19	TO CLASS Z RESERVE. ON STAR ROLL AS AINSLIE
AINSWORTH	Wm	PTE	/4	WEST HARTLEPOOL	24/9/14	KR para 392 3/4/18	TO DEPOT. AGE 23
AISTON	Thos	PTE	/8	DARLINGTON	DARLINGTON	23/4/18 MORBECQUE BRIT CEM	TO 18th BN. AGE 24
AITKEN	Arth	SGT	/1185			5/4/19	TO CLASS Z RESERVE.
ALDERSON	Bens	PTE	/1257	SADBERGE			2nd SOUTHERN GEN HOSP BRISTOL 8/7/16
ALDERSON	Fred	PTE	/1262	COUNDON	13/1/15		TO CLASS Z RESERVE. OFFICERS SERVANT, MINER
ALDERSON	John	PTE	/1212			15/1/19	TO CLASS Z RESERVE.
ALLAN	Alf	PTE	/5	STOCKTON	STOCKTON	20/3/19	LCPL.
ALLAN	Ron	PTE	/1281	WEST HARTLEPOOL	WEST HARTLEPOOL	29/3/18 ARRAS MEM	AGE 22 BORN MIDDLESBROUGH
ALLEN	WattL	CSM	/657			3/10/16 BETHUNE TOWN CEM	BANDMSTR, MUSKETRY INSTR CONVICTED BY THE CIVIL POWER 3 MONTHS PRISON **NO MEDALS**
ALLEN	Wm	PTE	/658	WEST HARTLEPOOL		KR para 392 21/1/19	TO ARMY RESERVE CLASS P. SGT. AGE 27
ALLISON	Geo F	CPL	/426	RYHOPE		KR para 392 26/2/19	NOT IN EGYPT.
ALLISON	Robt	PTE	/6	DARLINGTON			STILL SERVING 19/2/20. RESIDENT BROWNEY COLLIERY 1914
ANDERSON	Chris	LCPL	/422	LANGLEY MOOR	DURHAM CITY		TO 4th, 52nd BNS, CLASS Z RESERVE. WOII
ANDERSON	Jos	PTE	/1094	WEST HARTLEPOOL			TO 15th, 19th, 18th BNS, CLASS Z RESERVE.
APPLEBY	JohnR	PTE	/1500	WEST HARTLEPOOL		10/9/19	TO WEST YORKSHIRE REGIMENT(1/8th BN). AGE 29. BORN BANKHEAD, W YORKS No 242819
APPLEBY	JohnT	PTE	/1211	FENCEHOUSES	HOUGHTON LE SPRING	4/11/18 ETAPLES MIL CEM	
APPLETON	Fred	PTE	/656			KR para 392 5/10/16	TO 18th BN.
APPLEYARD	Geo S	CPL	/1123	EAST SHEEN	SUNDERLAND	25/6/16 TANCREZ FARM CEM	TO 20th BN PRIOR TO EMBARKATION. AGE 23
ARKLEY	Thos	PTE	/421			20/1/19	TO CLASS Z RESERVE.
ARMSTRONG	Abt	PTE	/1159		4/1/15	KR para 392 23/8/16	
ARMSTRONG	Arth	PTE	/212	CROOK	SPENNYMOOR	29/3/16 BERTRANCOURT MIL CEM	AGE 26
ARMSTRONG	Gilbt	PTE	/1210	EASINGTON			COMMISSIONED 26/1/15.
ARMSTRONG	Jos S	SGT	/1196	SACRISTON		5/4/15	TO 20th, 18th BNS, CLASS Z RESERVE.
ARMSTRONG	Wm	PTE	/424	HETTON LE HOLE		KR para 392 1/4/19	AGE 33
ASHLEY	ArthP	CPL	/214	TRIMDON			COMMISSIONED 29/5/17. SGT. STUDENT BEDE COLLEGE 1905, IN 5 PLATOON
ASKEY	JohnH	PTE	/1158	TUDHOE COLLIERY			TO CLASS Z RESERVE.
ASPEY	Thos	PTE	/423				TO 18th BN, CLASS Z RESERVE. BN TRANSPORT SECTION
ATKINSON	Fred	SGT	/9				TO CLASS Z RESERVE.
AUBIN	MewH	SGT	/9				COMMISSIONED 30/4/15.
AUSTIN	Arth	LCPL	/425	DURHAM CITY	DURHAM CITY	12/4/19	TO CLASS Z RESERVE. CQMS
AYRE	Rich	CPL	/1307	DARLINGTON	23/1/15	KR para 392 5/2/19	SGT AGE 38.
AYTON	Wm A	PTE	/1312		21/1/15	KR para 392 17/10/18	TO 20th, 1/6th BNS, COMMAND DEPOT SHOREHAM, 4th BN. LCPL AGE 26
BACKHOUSE	James	PTE	/683			22/3/19	TO LABOUR CORPS, CLASS Z RES DIS HOSP FOVANT 23/11/15, LAB CORPS No 662090
BAGGOTT	Thos	LCPL	/686	SUNDERLAND	SUNDERLAND	1/7/16 THIEPVAL MEM	BORN NEWCASTLE AGE 38.
BAILES	Jas R	PTE	/1213				COMMISSIONED 25/9/17.
BAINBRIDGE	Fred	LCPL	/1264		2/11/14	SICK 26/5/17	TO DEPOT.
BAINBRIDGE	James	SGT	/17			11/3/19	TO MACHINE GUN CORPS, CLASS Z RESERVE. MGC No 22770
BAINBRIDGE	JohnG	CQMS	/10	COUNDON	24/9/14	KR para 392 3/12/17	TO 18th BN. DEPOT. AGE 41
BAINBRIDGE	JohnG	PTE	/1249	SEAHAM		21/1/19	TO CLASS Z RESERVE. LCPL
BAKER	HerbE	PTE	/21	DARLINGTON			TO 18th BN, CLASS Z RESERVE.
BALMER	Pring	CSM	/216	HOUGHTON LE SPRING		27/5/18 SOISSONS MEM	COMMISSIONED(1/5th BN). 27/11/17. REC FOR MM BY Lt C G FINDLAY
BANKS	Chas	PTE	/28			KR para 392 14/12/18	TO MACHINE GUN CORPS. MGC No 22768
BARKAS	Walt	LCPL	/221			KR para 392 4/2/19	TO LABOUR CORPS. LAB CORPS No 251564
BARKER	Herbt	PTE	/1621	DARLINGTON			ATT 93rd LIGHT TRENCH MORTAR BATTERY, CLASS Z RESERVE.

Surname	Forename	Rank	No.	Residence	Enlisted	Discharge / Casualty	Notes
BARKER	Jos W	CPL	/918	DARLINGTON	DARLINGTON 5/9/14	20/2/19	TO 20th, 18th BNS, No1 BN RAF(FOR COMMISSION 13/11/18),Z RES TO SPRINGBURN WOODSIDE HOSP GLASGOW 11/7/16
BARKER	Thos	PTE	/1653	WHITBY	WEST HARTLEPOOL	1/7/16 THIEPVAL MEM	TO 15th BN.
BARNARD	JohnB	PTE	/11	STOCKTON	DARLINGTON	10/8/16 STOCKTON OXBRIDGE LANE	AGE 23
BARNES	Jas W	LSGT	/1448	WHEATLEY HILL	WEST HARTLEPOOL	26/6/16 ENGELBELMER COM CEM	TO 14th BN.
BARR	Harry	PTE	/1602				TO 15th BN. CLASS Z RESERVE.
BARRAS	JohnH	PTE	/1087			KR para 392 4/3/19	TO LABOUR CORPS. LAB CORPS No 317071
BARRASFORD	Robt	PTE	/443	SACRISTON	DURHAM CITY	30/11/17 GOUZEAUCOURT NEW BRIT	ATT WEST YORKSHIRE REGT(1/6th BN), 10th, 11th BNS.
BARRASS	Albt	PTE	/437	HETTON LE HOLE		KR para 392 1/12/16	TO CLASS Z RESERVE.
BASSETT	Chas	PTE	/448	NEW HERRINGTON	DURHAM CITY	18/1/19	TO 14th BN.
BATEY	T	PTE	/1515				AGE 30.
BAUM	Alf	PTE	/22	LOUGHBOROUGH	DARLINGTON	3/8/16 ST VAAST POST MIL CEM	TO 20th BN PRIOR TO EMBARKATION. 51st BN(E COY).
BAXTER	Ewart	LSGT	/1454	WEST HARTLEPOOL		27/1/19	TO CLASS Z RESERVE.
BEADHAM	James	SGT	/444	WEST RAINTON	5/9/14	17/2/19	TO 18th, 20th, 9th BNS, CLASS Z RESERVE.
BEAUMONT	Alex	PTE	/685			SICK 6/5/16	DID NOT SERVE OVERSEAS.CHILTON MOOR HOSP 3/3/15.
BECKWITH	Harry	LCPL	/12	DARLINGTON		KR para 392 5/3/19	TO LABOUR CORPS. LAB CORPS No 599446
BEECROFT	Wm	PTE	/1142	SUNDERLAND	DARLINGTON	1/7/16 THIEPVAL MEM	
BELL	ArthO	PTE	/688	RAINTON	SUNDERLAND	16/10/17 DOZINGHEM MIL CEM	SON OF MR G BELL SUNDERLAND RATE COLLECTOR.
BELL	Chas	PTE	/445	WEST HARTLEPOOL	DURHAM CITY	24/3/19	TO NORTHUMBERLAND FUSILIERS(25th(2nd T) BN). NF No 35566
BELL	Edw C	LCPL	/1215	DAWDON		20/1/19	ATT ASSISTANT PROVOST MARSHALL 31 DIV, TO CLASS Z RESERVE. SGT
BELL	James	PTE	/674	DURHAM CITY	DURHAM CITY	17/2/19	TO 18th BN. CLASS Z RESERVE.
BELL	Thos	PTE	/432	DARLINGTON	DARLINGTON	27/9/18 UNICORN CEM VENDHUILE	TO CLASS Z RESERVE. CPL. RESIDENT 28 WESTERN HILL 1914
BELL	Wm	SGT	/1292	DURHAM CITY	DURHAM CITY	13/3/19	TO TANK CORPS(A SECT No 4 SUPPLY COY). TANK CORPS No 308323. AGE 24
BELL	Wm W	CPL	/429			14/3/19	TO CLASS Z RESERVE.
BENNETT	R	PTE	/696	BRANDON	2/10/14		TO LABOUR CORPS, CLASS Z RESERVE. LAB CORPS No 260586
BENNETT	James	PTE	/220	LIVERPOOL	SUNDERLAND	1/7/16 EUSTON ROAD CEM	COMMISSIONED 29/1/18
BENNETT	James	PTE	/230	WEST HARTLEPOOL	WEST HARTLEPOOL	3/5/17 ARRAS MEM	BORN SOUTH SHIELDS AGE 25.
BENNEWORTH	John	PTE	/226	SUNDERLAND	SUNDERLAND	5/4/19	PLAYED FOR HARTLEPOOL UNITED AFC
BENSON	Wm	CSM	/1162		17/8/15	KR para 392 17/10/18	TO CLASS Z RESERVE.
BENTLEY	John	PTE	/1171	WEST HARTLEPOOL	WEST HARTLEPOOL	19/2/19	AGE 22
BERRY	Oscar	PTE	/695	DARLINGTON	DARLINGTON	1/7/16 THIEPVAL MEM	ATT R ENGINEERS(3rd FLD&5th SURVEY COYS).18th BN.CLASS Z RES
BEST	Thos	PTE	/1230	TUDHOE COLLIERY		11/4/18 LE GRAND BEAUMART BRIT	TO 2nd, 18th BNS, CLASS Z RESERVE.
BEVAN	Chris	PTE	/1184		7/5/15	18/1/19	TO 4th BN.
BEWICK	Isaac	PTE	/440	DURHAM CITY	DURHAM CITY	KR para 392 7/9/17	AGE 28, MINER FRAMMOOR COLL. BUGLER & STRETCHER BEARER
BILTON	Harry	PTE	/446	DURHAM CITY	DURHAM CITY	23/8/16 LE TOURET MIL CEM	TO CLASS Z RESERVE.
BILTON	Geo	PTE	/1385	DARLINGTON	DARLINGTON	24/3/19	AGE 22
BINKS	Ralph	PTE	/24	PHILADELPHIA	DURHAM CITY	1/3/17 THIEPVAL MEM+GOMMECOURT CE	TO 3rd BN. AGE 23
BINNING	Harry	PTE	/1013		28/10/14	KR para 392 3/10/17	TO CLASS Z RESERVE.
BIRBECK	Edwd	PTE	/451	STRANTON	WEST HARTLEPOOL	17/4/19	COMMISSIONED BORDER REGT(3rd BN) 26/7/17.
BIRD	Geo W	SGT	/983	STRANTON	WEST HARTLEPOOL	1/7/16 THIEPVAL MEM	13 PLATOON
BIRKS	RobtG	LCPL	/663			1/7/16 THIEPVAL MEM	AGE 19
BIRKS	Arth	PTE	/687	HETTON LE HOLE		KR para 392 20/6/19	TO CLASS Z RESERVE.
BIRNIE	Har V	PTE	/15	SOUTH SHIELDS			AGE 32.
BLACKBURN	Geo A	PTE	/431	DARLINGTON		24/2/19	TO 14th, 19th, 12th, 12th, BNS, CLASS Z RESERVE.
BLAGDEN	Alf	PTE	/1627	WEST CORNFORTH	DURHAM 12/12/14	KR para 392 18/7/19	TO CLASS Z RESERVE.
BLAND	Arch	PTE	/20		27/9/14	KR para 392 28/12/17	TO 3rd BN, ATT KINGS AFRICAN RIFLES(21/5/18), DEPOT DLI. DRAPERS ASSISTANT, LCPL 6/12/16 ATT MG SCHOOL GRANTHAM 3/18
BLENKINSOP	Edwd	PTE	/1098	WEST HARTLEPOOL	WEST HARTLEPOOL	16/5/16 HORNSEA CEM	TO DEPOT. WND IN LEG LEFT LYING IN GERMAN DUG OUT
BLEWITT	Jos	PTE	/18	HOUGHTON LE SPRING	HOUGHTON LE SPRING 12/10/14	KR para 392 11/2/18	TO 21st BN. AGE 18
BOAGEY	Wm	PTE	/1590	SEATON CAREW	WEST HARTLEPOOL	1/7/16 THIEPVAL MEM	TO 3rd BN.
BOOTH	Wilf	PTE	/964				TO 15th BN. AGE 19
BORRETT	Syd C	PTE	/1611				

Surname	Forename	Rank	No.	Place	Enlisted	Fate / Memorial	Notes
BOUMPHERY	JohnG	LCPL	/671	WEST HARTLEPOOL		28/3/18 BELLACOURT MIL CEM	AGE 24 BORN BENSHAM
BOWES	JohnP	PTE	/1373	ST JOHNS CHAPEL			TO 20th BN.
BOWES	Robt	PTE	/666		18/9/14		TO 18th BN.
BOWMAN	Wm	CSM	/1555	TUNSTALL		KR para 392 27/4/18	TO 14th, 1/5th BNS, CLASS Z RESERVE.
BOWMAN	Thos	PTE	/16	DARLINGTON			BORN SUNDERLAND, BROTHER IN ASC.
BOYCE	Chas	PTE	/224			12/4/18 LE GRAND BEAUMART BRIT	TO CLASS Z RESERVE. WOII CSM
BRACEGIRDLE	James	PTE	/889	WEST HARTLEPOOL	15/2/19	1/7/16 THIEPVAL MEM	TO CLASS Z RESERVE. LCPL
BRAMLEY	John	PTE	/434	BRANCEPETH CASTLE	2/11/14	20/2/19	DID NOT SERVE OVERSEAS.CHILTON MOOR HOSP 11/4/15.
BRAMWELL	Thos	SGT	/1023		2/2/15	VDH 24/3/16	AGE 33.
BRANNEN	Harry	PTE	/1368		26/9/14	KR para 392 18/8/17	TO DEPOT. AGE 28
BREWERTON	Fred	PTE	/667			KR para 392 21/9/17	TO LABOUR CORPS, CLASS Z RESERVE. LAB CORPS No 428267
BRIGHAM	Mark	PTE	/672			12/3/19	TO NORTHUMBERLAND FUSILIERS. ACTING CSM NORTHBLD FUS No 94502
BROADLEY	Syd	CPL	/669	SPENNYMOOR		1/7/16 THIEPVAL MEM	TO CLASS Z RESERVE. CPL
BRODRICK	JohnW	PTE	/1293	NEWFIELD		24/2/19	
BROOKBANK	Frank	PTE	/435	DURHAM CITY	28/9/14		TO 4th BN. AGE 23.
BROTCHIE	Sam	SGT	/449			KR para 392 5/12/17	TO 18th BN, CLASS Z RESERVE.
BROUGH	John	PTE	/223			14/2/19	TO 20th BN PRIOR TO EMBARKATION. 20th, 20th BN, CLASS Z RES.
BROUGH	Chas	PTE	/678	WEST HARTLEPOOL		8/3/19	TO 20th BN, CLASS Z RESERVE.
BROWN	Jas R	PTE	/1773			1/7/16 THIEPVAL MEM	
BROWN	JohnT	PTE	/1358			KR para 392 21/9/17	TO 19th, 3rd BNS. AGE 39
BROWN	EdwdA	PTE	/673	SUNDERLAND	19/6/15		COMMISSIONED 19/12/14.
BROWN	Ernst	PTE	/1616			25/3/18 ARRAS MEM	
BROWN	Frank	PTE	/225	DURHAM CITY		3/2/19	TO 13th, 2nd BNS, OFF CADET, CLASS Z RESERVE.
BROWN	Fred	PTE	/436	CHESTER LE STREET		5/4/19	TO CLASS Z RESERVE.
BROWN	Geo	PTE	/1121	BLACKHILL		1/7/16 THIEPVAL MEM	
BROWN	Harid	PTE	/219			15/1/19	TO CLASS Z RESERVE.
BROWN	Harry	PTE	/1347	STAINDROP		KR para 392 14/12/18	TO MACHINE GUN CORPS. MGC No 22774
BROWN	LloW	LCPL	/1216	GREAT LUMLEY		14/5/16 BOULOGNE EASTERN CEM	TO 14th BN. AGE 31 BORN SPENNYMOOR
BROWN	Ralph	PTE	/1052			19/2/19	TO CLASS Z RESERVE.
BROWN	Ralph	PTE	/1558	BISHOP AUCKLAND			TO CLASS Z RESERVE.
BROWN	Robt	PTE	/218	CROOK		3/3/19	TO 20th BN, CLASS Z RESERVE.
BROWN	Thos	PTE	/1161				COMMISSIONED(18th BN) 30/10/17.
BROWN	Wm F	PTE	/227	DURHAM CITY	21/8/14	KR para 392 7/2/19	
BROWN	Wm H	SGT	/215	WEST HARTLEPOOL		6/2/19	
BROWN	Wm S	SGT	/662	DARLINGTON		KR para 392 25/2/17	
BROWNLESS	Edwd	SGT	/23	DURHAM CITY			TO COMMAND DEPOT RIPON. REDUCED TO THE RANKS BY FGCM 9/9/16. AGE 33
BRUCE	FredW	SGT	/449				TO CLASS Z RESERVE. RES 30 ATHERTON ST 1914
BRYANT	Sid M	PTE	/229	SUNDERLAND	22/9/14		TO ARMY RESERVE CLASS W. AGE 28
BRYDON	JohnC	LSGT	/693	BISHOP AUCKLAND		1/7/16 THIEPVAL MEM AND SERRE ROAD	AGE 24.
BUCKLE	ThosA	SGT	/19			1/7/16 EUSTON ROAD COLINCAMPS	AGE 23.
BULLAMORE	JohnA	PTE	/1733				TO CLASS Z RESERVE.
BULMAN	Jos	PTE	/1014			KR para 392 16/12/14	
BUNKALL	James	LCPL	/1334	WEST HARTLEPOOL	28/10/14	18/5/17 ARRAS MEM	
BUNT	Ezek	PTE	/1137	HETTON LE HOLE		KR para 392 16/1/19	TO 18th BN, ATT WEST YORKSHIRE REGT(1/8th BN), 18th BN.
BURDIS	Wm	PTE	/680	WILLINGTON		16/3/19	TO 20th BN PRIOR TO EMBARKATION.
BURDON	W	PTE	/1531	NETTLESWORTH			TO CLASS Z RESERVE.
BURLINSON	Ebnzr	PTE	/1265	ROKER		11/8/16 LE TOURET MIL CEM	AGE 20.
BURLINSON	Ernst	PTE	/1578	ROKER		1/7/16 THIEPVAL MEM	TO MACHINE GUN CORPS(93rd MG COY), AGE 24, MGC No 22776
BURLINSON	Geo	PTE	/694			KR para 932 16/5/17	TO ARMY RESERVE CLASS P.
BURN	Jos	PTE	/938				TO 20th BN.
BURNS	G	LCPL	/430				ATT 35th IBD,TO 2nd BN,ATT 6 DIV EMP COY,18 IBD,CLASS Z RES STUDENT BEDE COLLEGE 1910
BURNS	John	PTE	/1199	FERRYHILL STATION	20/10/14		

Surname	Forename	Rank	No.	Birthplace	Other location	Service record / remarks
BURTON	ArthR	PTE	/1608	WEST HARTLEPOOL		ATT 257 TUN COY ROYAL ENGINEERS, TO 1/7th BN, CLASS Z RES.
BURTON	Edmd	PTE	/1585	BENSHAM	COCKEN HALL	13/8/16 ENGLEBELMER COM CEM. TO 14th BN. AGE 23
BUSBY	Albt	PTE	/1410			TO 14th, 18th, 11th, 18th, DIV C GUARDS, CLASS Z RESERVE.
BUSHBY	Ernst	SGT	/679	THORNABY	WEST HARTLEPOOL	1/10/18 STRAND MIL CEM. AGE 30
BUSSEY	Rob W	PTE	/ 25			13/1/19. TO CLASS Z RESERVE.
BUTLER	Geo	PTE	/441	DURHAM CITY		16/1/19. TO CLASS Z RESERVE.
BUTTERY	James	PTE	/1583	DARLINGTON		TO 15th BN.
CAIRNS	Alex	PTE	/701		DURHAM CITY 25/9/14	23/9/16 THIEPVAL MEM. AGE 34.
CAIRNS	Geo	PTE	/480			KR para 392 2/6/17. TO CLASS Z RESERVE.
CALDER	John	PTE	/239			15/2/19. TO LABOUR CORPS, CLASS Z RESERVE. LAB CORPS NO 442754
CAMERON	Harry	PTE	/692	WEST HARTLEPOOL		27/3/19. TO ARMY RESERVE CLASS W. AGE 21
CAMPBELL	ChasE	PTE	/1034	HETTON LE HOLE	21/1/15	KR para 392 16/11/17. AGE 22
CAMPBELL	Fred	PTE	/1294		14/1/15	KR para 392 10/6/18. TO 20th, 20th, 1/5th BNS.
CAMPBELL	James	PTE	/1250	SUNDERLAND		TO CLASS Z RESERVE.
CAMPBELL	Jos	PTE	/1633	LOW SPENNYMOOR		TO CLASS Z RESERVE.
CARD	Ben O	PTE	/ 920	MIDDLESBROUGH		COMMISSIONED 28/8/17.
CARLING	Stan	PTE	/244	BRANDON		30/6/17 ROOKERY COM CEM. AGE 26.
CARLING	Wm C	PTE	/248		DURHAM CITY 25/9/14	27/6/19. TO LABOUR CORPS, CLASS Z RESERVE. LAB CORPS No 260699
CARNEY	Mart	PTE	/474		SPENNYMOOR	15/2/19. TO CLASS Z RESERVE.
CARPENTER	Wm N	PTE	/712	WEARHEAD		1/7/16 THIEPVAL MEM. AGE 23. WOLSINGHAM GRAMMER SCHOOL
CARR	Henry	LSGT	/700	TUDHOE	DURHAM CITY 25/9/14	KR para 392 1/4/19. SGT COMMISSIONED 25/6/18.
CARR	John	PTE	/246	DURHAM CITY	DURHAM CITY 25/9/14	3/4/19. RESIDENT 'THE PETH' 1914.
CARR	Wilf	LSGT	/472			23/2/19. TO DEPOT.
CARROLL	Watt	PTE	/464			1/7/16 THIEPVAL MEM. BORN PALLION AGE 21.
CARROLL	O	PTE	/1186	SOUTH BANK YORKS	18/9/14	21/1/19. TO CLASS Z RESERVE.
CARTER	ArthW	LCPL	/ 40	WHITEHAVEN	SUNDERLAND	28/6/17 BAILLEUL RD EAST CEM. TO CLASS Z RESERVE.
CARTER	Edwd	PTE	/704	CHESTER LE STREET	STOCKTON	WOUNDS 5/2/17. TO LINCOLNSHIRE REGT(7th BN). LINCOLNS No 15436
CARTER	Geo	PTE	/ 985	FULWELL	SUNDERLAND	25/8/18 VIS EN ARTOIS MEM. TO 14th BN. AGE 28
CARTMELL	Frank	CPL	/1111	WEST HARTLEPOOL		9/3/19. TO CLASS Z RESERVE.
CASE	JohnR	SGT	/ 37	EASINGTON COLLIERY	SEAHAM HARBOUR	23/10/18 COLOGNE SOUTHERN CEM. TO 14th BN. DIED WHILST A POW. AGE 26
CATCHPOLE	Fred	PTE	/1560	LEEDS	SUNDERLAND 18/9/14	PAINTER AGE 23, 5'7", DESERTED 3/4/15 FENCEHOUSES.
CATTERICK	Rich	PTE	/713	DURHAM CITY	DURHAM CITY 25/9/14	COMMISSIONED Lt & QM 18th BN 14/6/15. ENLISTED 106th BOMBAY LI 1881
CAVE	Jas B	PTE	/702			COMMISSIONED 6/7/16.
CAYGILL	Alf	PTE	/1644	WEST HARTLEPOOL	DURHAM CITY 25/9/14	KR para 392 27/1/19. TO 4th BN(A COY), 18th BN, CLASS Z RESERVE.
CAYGILL	Hny	PTE	/711	WEST HARTLEPOOL	DURHAM CITY 25/9/14	2/3/19. TO 2nd BN, CLASS Z RESERVE.
CHAPLIN	Jos H	RSM	/481			TO HOME DEFENCE LABOUR, CLASS Z RESERVE.
CHAPMAN	Cyril	PTE	/1349	DARLINGTON		TO 12th, 19th, 10th, 2nd BNS, CLASS Z RESERVE.
CHAPMAN	Geo	LCPL	/698	WEST HARTLEPOOL		28/1/19. ATT LABOUR CORPS(228 DIV EMPL COY), CLASS Z RES LAB CORP No 346027
CHAPMAN	Henry	CPL	/705	DURHAM CITY	DURHAM CITY	6/4/19. TO LABOUR CORPS, CLASS Z RESERVE. LAB CORPS No 343797
CHARLTON	John	LCPL	/1439			TO 18th BN. CLASS Z RESERVE.
CHATER	Geo	LCPL	/ 240	DURHAM CITY	MIDDLESBROUGH	KR para 392 2/5/16. TO MACHINE GUN CORPS(31st BN). MGC No 22774
CHATOR	Thos	PTE	/234	MURTON		ASSISTANT MASTER MURTON COUNCIL SCHOOL
CHATTERTON	Wm C	PTE	/1673	WEST HARTLEPOOL		20/3/19. ATT 1st ARMY SCHOOL OF MORTARS, CLASS Z RESERVE.
CHECKLEY	Alf E	PTE	/465	LANGLEY MOOR		24/3/19. TO CLASS Z RESERVE.
CHEESEBOROUGH	Wm T	PTE	/1295	TOW LAW		3/4/19. COMMISSIONED 6/5/18.
CHERRY	Jos W	PTE	/697	HAVERTON HILL		19/2/19. AGE 29
CHESTER	Wm R	PTE	/455	DURHAM CITY	DURHAM CITY 25/9/14	29/10/18 DIV COLLECTING POST BOEZING. TO CLASS Z RESERVE. CPL
CHILTON	Arth	CPL	/1386			27/8/16 NETLEY MIL CEM.
CHITTOCK	John	CPL	/1076			15/2/19.
CHRISTISON	HerbA	PTE	/453			14/3/19.
CHRISTISON	JohnJ	SGT	/720			12/11/16 HEBUTERNE MIL CEM.
CHRISTOPHER	John	PTE	/1154			21/3/19.
CHRISTOPHER	Rich	PTE	/461			

CLARK	ArthW	PTE	/ 35	DURHAM CITY		20/4/19	TO LABOUR CORPS, CLASS Z RES LAB CORPS No 599757. EMPLOYED MR STOKOE SADLER ST DURHAM
CLARK	Edwd	PTE	/1542		20/5/15	WOUNDS 28/12/16	TO DEPOT.
CLARK	Percy	LCPL	/ 473	NORTHALLERTON	DURHAM CITY 25/9/14	1/10/16 GORRE BRIT & INDIAN CEM	AGE 28.RES CONSETT 1914.
CLARK	Samp	PTE	/1729	STAINDROP			
CLARKE	Albt	LCPL	/ 468	CHESTER LE STREET	DURHAM CITY 25/9/14	9/3/19 LONGUENESSE SOUVENIR CEM	AGE 29
CLARKE	Chas	PTE	/ 707	WEST HARTLEPOOL	WEST HARTLEPOOL	16/12/14 NORTH CEM WEST HARTLEPOOL	
CLARKE	RobtD	PTE	/ 706		WEST HARTLEPOOL18/9	GSW 11/8/17	TO 3rd BN. ENDELL ST MILITARY HOSP LONDON
CLARKE	Sam	LCPL	/ 721	MARKS TEY	WEST HARTLEPOOL	1/7/16 THIEPVAL MEM	
CLARKE	Sams	PTE	/1727				TO CLASS Z RESERVE.
CLAUGHAN	Jos E	LCPL	/ 231		18/9/14	KR para 392. 11/1/18	TO DEPOT. AGE 31
CLEMENT	JohnT	PTE	/1619	WEST HARTLEPOOL			TO 15th, 3rd BNS, CLASS Z RESERVE.
CLEMINSON	Chas	PTE	/ 232	DARLINGTON	DARLINGTON	1/7/16 THIEPVAL MEM	BORN STOCKTON AGE 28, IN 5 PLATOON.
CLEMITSON	Rob H	SGT	/ 458	HEXHAM	DURHAM CITY 25/9/14	26/3/19 HEXHAM CEM	AGE 33 BORN SUNDERLAND.
CLOSE	Shep	PTE	/1164	WEST HARTLEPOOL			ATT 4th ORDNANCE MOBILE WORKSHOP, TO 12th BN, CLASS Z RES. LCPL
COATES	John	PTE	/1041	FERRYHILL		16/1/19	TO CLASS Z RESERVE.
COATES	JohnW	PTE	/1163			27/3/19	TO 18th, 22nd, 1/7th BNS, CLASS Z RESERVE.
COATES	Wm	PTE	/1706	FERRYHILL			TO 14th, 18th BNS, CLASS Z RESERVE.
COATHAM	James	PTE	/1119	DURHAM CITY	DURHAM CITY	1/7/16 GORDON DUMP CEM	TO 15th BN. AGE 34 EMPLOYED AS A JOINER BY MR INNES BEARPARK
COCKAYNE	Rich	PTE	/ 243	SPENNYMOOR			TO 2nd, 18th, 3rd BNS, CLASS Z RESERVE.
COCKERSOLE	Harry	PTE	/ 245	DAWDON			TO 4th BN(H COY).
CODDINGTON	J W	PTE	/ 38	OLDHAM	DARLINGTON. 21/9/14		MINER AGE 32, 5'6",DESERTED 27/3/15 FENCEHOUSES.
COLLING	Normn	PTE	/1337		25/1/15	KR para 392 18/4/17	TO 3rd BN. AGE 21
COLLINGWOOD	Fred	PTE	/ 722		18/9/14	KR para 392 6/5/18	TO 18th, 20th, 3rd BNS. AGE 30
COLMAN	Wm	PTE	/ 482	DURHAM CITY	DURHAM CITY 25/9/14	18/3/19	TO CLASS Z RESERVE. PRISONER OF WAR
COLWELL	Henry	PTE	/ 467	BRANDON VILLAGE	DURHAM CITY 25/9/14	KR para 392 20/1/19	TO 2nd, 14th BNS, 35IBD, LABOUR CORPS(415 AGR COY).
COLWELL	Mark	PTE	/1308	BRANDON VILLAGE		30/3/19	TO CLASS Z RESERVE.
CONNELL	Pat	LSGT	/ 984	CULLYHANNA ARMARG	MARYPORT	27/8/18 CAESTRE MIL CEM	
COOK	Adam	PTE	/ 723		29/9/14	SICK 1/9/17	TO 3rd BN.
COOK	Hor W	SGT	/ 476	LANGLEY MOOR	DURHAM CITY 25/9/14	KR para 392 1/4/19	TO 3rd BN. AGE 48
COOK	James	PTE	/1600		7/6/15	KR para 392 7/6/16	DID NOT SERVE OVERSEAS.
COOK	Percy	PTE	/1432	THORNLEY	DURHAM CITY	28/7/16 ST VAAST POST MIL CEM	ATT 3rd ENTRENCHING BN, 18th BN. TEACHER AT THORNLEY SCHOOL, BROTHER KILLED IN 1915
COOK	Thos	CPL	/ 238	WINGATE		15/2/19	TO CLASS Z RESERVE. STRETCHER BEARER.STUDENT BEDE COLLEGE
COOPER	Frank	PTE	/1495				TO CLASS Z RESERVE.
COOPER	Henry	LCPL	/1617	SUNDERLAND	SUNDERLAND	28/3/18 MOYENNEVILLE TWO TREE CEM	AGE 28
COOPER	John	PTE	/ 466	DURHAM CITY	DURHAM CITY 25/9/14	KR para 392 17/10/19	TO 19th, 19th BN.
COOPER	Wm	PTE	/ 699			2/3/19	TO 18th, 20th, 18th BNS, CLASS Z RESERVE.
COPELAND	JohnE	PTE	/ 454	FENCEHOUSES	DURHAM CITY	10/4/19	TO CLASS Z RESERVE.
CORDES	FranJ	LCPL	/ 714				TO 18th BN, CLASS Z RESERVE.
CORKER	Rich	SGT	/ 249	QUEBEC CO DURHAM	DURHAM CITY	1/7/16 EUSTON ROAD CEM COLINCAMPS	STUDENT BEDE COLLEGE 1910, TEACHER WATERHOUSES C S
CORNER	Arth	PTE	/ 242	FERRYHILL	SPENNYMOOR	10/7/16 COUNDON ST JAMES CH YD	TO DEPOT. AGE 23 DIED OF GAS,STUDENT BEDE COLLEGE,TEACHER TUDHOE COLL
CORNFORTH	Baily	CPL	/ 29	DARLINGTON		15/3/19	TO CLASS Z RESERVE. LSGT
CORNFORTH	JohnR	SGT	/ 463	NEW BRANCEPETH	DURHAM CITY 25/9/14	KR para 392 3/6/19	
CORNFORTH	Walt	PTE	/ 690	NORTON ON TEES		24/3/19	TO 18th BN, CLASS Z RESERVE.
CORNFORTH	Wm	PTE	/ 261	DARLINGTON			
CORPS	Ernst	CPL	/ 715			13/2/19	TO CLASS Z RESERVE.
COTTAM	Thos	PTE	/1431				TO 14th BN, 18th BN MGC, 251 TC RE, 18th ATT LTMB, ATT 1st SCHOOL OF MORTARS, 2nd BN, ATT LTMB, CLASS Z RESERVE
COUNTER	Jas H	PTE	/1232		9/1/15	KR para 392 28/2/17	AGE 39.
COVERDALE	Chas	CPL	/ 708	WEST HARTLEPOOL		20/2/19	TO 18th BN, CLASS Z RESERVE.
COVERDALE	Miles	SGT	/ 236		22/9/14	KR para 392 27/2/19	TO ARMY RESERVE CLASS P. AGE 32
COWAN	Arth	PTE	/ 717	SUNDERLAND	SUNDERLAND	1/7/16 THIEPVAL MEM	

Roll of men (surname, forename, rank, regimental number, residence, enlistment, casualty/discharge, and notes):

Surname	Forename	Rank	No.	Residence	Enlisted	Died / Discharged / Memorial	Notes
COWAN	Jas M	PTE	/691		24/10/14		TO DEPOT.
COWELL	Robt	PTE	/460	HOUGHTON LE SPRING	DURHAM CITY 25/9/14	WOUNDS 13/4/17	TO CLASS Z RESERVE.
COX	Alf J	DVR	/716	WEST HARTLEPOOL	WEST HARTLEPOOL	8/3/19	TO 18th BN, CLASS Z RESERVE. BN TRANSPORT SECTION
COX	Wm D	PTE	/30			5/4/19	COMMISSIONED 26/9/15.
CRAGGS	John	PTE	/233				COMMISSIONED 2/1/15.
CRAIG	Geo W	PTE	/1559	TUDHOE	DURHAM CITY 25/9/14		TO 14th, 11th BNS, CLASS Z RESERVE.
CRAIG	Wm A	CPL	/456	WEST HARTLEPOOL	WEST HARTLEPOOL	28/7/16 ST VAAST POST MIL CEM	AGE 28.
CRAWFORD	AlexB	PTE	/1398		FENCEHOUSES	12/2/18 ROCLINCOURT MIL CEM	TO CLASS Z RESERVE.
CRAWFORD	Ernst	PTE	/36	DARLINGTON	DARLINGTON	17/4/19	TO 27th BN.
CRAWFORD	John	PTE	/260	STOCKTON ON TEES	STOCKTON 24/9/14		TO 13 OFFICER CADET BN 5/3/17, COMMISSIONED 27/12/17. NAVAL ARCHITECT
CRIERIE	Adria	SGT	/31	DURHAM CITY	DURHAM CITY 25/9/14	26/1/19	TO LABOUR CORPS(124 LAB COY). LAB CORPS No 581516
CRINSON	Jos W	PTE	/479	FERRYHILL	DARLINGTON	KR para 392 10/3/19	AGE 30. RESCUED Lt TAIT FROM NO-MANS-LAND
CROSER	Arth	PTE	/41	DURHAM CITY	DURHAM CITY 25/9/14	1/7/16 THIEPVAL MEM	
CROSS	ChasT	SGT	/483		DURHAM CITY 25/9/14	3/5/17 ARRAS MEM	
CROSSLEY	Stan	PTE	/1381	NORTH SHIELDS	NORTH SHIELDS	27/3/19	TO CLASS Z RESERVE. CHILTON MOOR HOSP 2/15, LCPL
CROWE	Tom	CPL	/1728	NEW HERRINGTON	DURHAM CITY 25/9/14		TO 14th BN, CLASS Z RESERVE.
CROZIER	Jas W	PTE	/1724	DURHAM CITY	DURHAM CITY	4/8/18 LE GRAND HASARD MIL CEM	AGE 32.
CRUDDAS	Matth	PTE	/478				RESIDENT NEWTON HALL 1914.
CULBERT	Wm	LCPL	/1357			29/6/18 PLOEGSTEERT MEM	ATT 3rd ENT BN, 18th, 14th, 18th BNS, DIV C GUARDS, 18th. BORN SPENNYMOOR. AGE 28
CUMMING	Wm G	PTE	/1120	DURHAM CITY	DURHAM CITY 25/9/14	5/2/19	TO 11th, 18th, 2nd BNS, CLASS Z RESERVE. CPL
CUMMINGS	Geo	PTE	/1320	WITTON GILBERT		10/7/19	TO 18th, 11th, 18th BNS, CLASS Z RESERVE. SGT
CUMMINGS	Matt	PTE	/462	DEPTFORD	SUNDERLAND	28/7/16 LOOS MEM	AGE 26. SERVANT TO Lt J BRADFORD.
CURRAN	Fred	PTE	/718	DARLINGTON		21/3/18 POZIERES MEM	TO MACHINE GUN CORPS. MGC No 25320
CURRY	Fred	SGT	/32	CHESTER LE STREET	DURHAM CITY 25/9/14	28/7/16 ST VAAST POST MIL CEM	TO 51st BN(B COY), STILL SERVING 1920. WOII CSM
CURRY	James	PTE	/471	FENCEHOUSES	SUNDERLAND	3/3/17 SAILLY AU BOIS MIL CEM	AGE 32.
CURRY	Newr	PTE	/459	GREAT LUMLEY		27/6/19	BORN LUMLEY AGE 25.
CURRY	Wm	PTE	/1217		2/10/14		TO ROYAL ENGINEERS.
DALE	Jos A	SGT	/1053	WEST HARTLEPOOL	WEST HARTLEPOOL 10/12/14	25/9/16 THIEPVAL MEM	TO CLASS Z RESERVE.
DALKIN	Geo	LCPL	/1508			KR para 392 10/11/17	TO 14th BN.
DAND	Arth	PTE	/1102			19/3/19	TO ARMY RESERVE CLASS W. AGE 21
DANIELS	Lewis	PTE	/1166				ATT DIV CARPENTERS SHOP. TO CLASS Z RESERVE.
DARLING	Thos	LCPL	/987	SACRISTON			COMMISSIONED 22/12/15.
DAVIDSON	ArthA	LCPL	/727	SOUTH SHIELDS	WEST HARTLEPOOL	18/5/17 ARRAS MEM	BORN DALKEITH
DAVIDSON	JohnT	PTE	/485	CONSETT	DURHAM CITY 25/9/14	KR para 392 31/3/20	TO LABOUR CORPS. LAB CORPS No 599781
DAVIDSON	Jos	LCPL	/988	SACRISTON		15/2/19	TO 2nd BN,ATT 2nd CORPS HQ, 46th DIV BATHS, 2nd REINFOR CAMP 1/6 W YORKS, 18th BN. CLASS Z RES
DAVIES	Chas	PTE	/1085	SEATON CAREW	WEST HARTLEPOOL	1/7/16 THIEPVAL MEM	AGE 22 AN ARTICLED CHARTERED ACCOUNTANT.
DAVIES	Edwd	PTE	/1323	FERRYHILL	DARLINGTON	3/7/16 ETRETAT CHURCHYARD	ATT 93rd LIGHT TRENCH MORTAR BATTERY. AGE 26
DAVISON	John	PTE	/484	DURHAM CITY	DURHAM CITY 25/9/14	11/5/18	TO CLASS Z RESERVE. AGE 22 STUDENT BEDE COLLEGE 1908
DAVISON	Robt	PTE	/1036			2/3/19	TO CLASS Z RESERVE.
DAVISON	Thos	PTE	/49	OLD SHILDON			TO CLASS Z RESERVE.
DAWSON	Arth	PTE	/1540	RICHMOND YORKS	DARLINGTON	1/7/16 GORDON DUMP CEM	TO 15th BN.
DAWSON	Edgar	PTE	/1575			15/1/19	TO 15th BN, COMMISSIONED 17/12/17.
DAWSON	John	PTE	/1138	MORTON GRANGE			TO CLASS Z RESERVE.
DEACON	Rich	PTE	/42	DARLINGTON		3/4/19	TO 19th, 2nd, 15th BNS, CLASS Z RESERVE. CPL
DEE	Wm	PTE	/1532	USWORTH		9/3/19	TO 3rd BN.
DEES	Thos	PTE	/255	SPENNYMOOR		WOUNDS 7/6/17	
DEMPSTER	John	PTE	/1297				TO 14th, 18th BNS, CLASS Z RESERVE.
DENNISON	Henry	PTE	/486	DURHAM CITY	DURHAM CITY 25/9/14		TO CLASS Z RESERVE. SGT
DICKEN	Thos	PTE	/1124				TO 14th BN, DEPOT.
DICKENS	Fred	PTE	/1554	SUNDERLAND	SUNDERLAND 30/12/14	1/7/16 THIEPVAL MEM	ATT 3rd ENTRENCHING BN, 18th BN. AGE 20
DICKENSON	Edwd	SGT	/1050	DARLINGTON		28/6/15 HELLES MEM	COMMISSIONED YORKS REGT(11th BN) 24/10/14. KIA ATT ROYAL DUBLIN FUSILIERS

Surname	Forename	Rank	No.	Place 1	Place 2	Date / Memorial	Notes
DICKENSON	Wm	PTE	/729	WEST HARTLEPOOL		25/2/19	ATT WYORKS(1/6th BN), 18th BN, SGT TO UK FOR COMMISSION, CLASS Z RES
DICKINSON	Wm	CSM	/258	WEST HARTLEPOOL			TO 19th, 18th BNS, CLASS Z RESERVE.
DINNIN	John	PTE	/256			20/2/19	TO CLASS Z RESERVE. STUDENT ARMSTRONG COLLEGE 1910-12
DIXON	ChasG	SGT	/43			22/10/16 DUNKIRK TOWN CEM	TO 1/8th BN. WOII, TEACHER REED C S
DIXON	FredW	LCPL	/1551	HARROGATE HILL	DARLINGTON	12/10/16 THIEPVAL MEM	TO 14th BN(A COY). AGE 21
DIXON	Harld	PTE	/970	WINGATE	WEST HARTLEPOOL	14/5/17 WANCOURT BRIT CEM	TO 18th, 10th BNS. CHILTON MOOR HOSP 2/15. AGE 20
DIXON	James	PTE	/247	TUNSTALL			
DIXON	John	LCPL	/1552	DARLINGTON	21/5/15	KR para 392 3/10/17	TO 14th BN. DEPOT.
DIXON	Syd	SGT	/44	DARLINGTON			TO 18th BN, CLASS Z RESERVE.
DIXON	Walc	PTE	/252				COMMISSIONED 28/6/17.
DIXON	WilfA	SGT	/731				TO 18th, 13th BNS. LABOUR CORPS(89 LAB COY), BASE DETAILS BN. SPRINGBURN WOODSIDE HOSP GLASGOW 11/7/16, CLASS Z RESERVE
DIXON	Willi	PTE	/1584	WEST HARTLEPOOL		18/9/16 THIEPVAL MEM	TO 14th BN. AGE 27
DOBBIE	Robt	CQMS	/251			KR para 392 9/2/18	TO LABOUR CORPS, LAB CORPS No 343793, AGE 40
DOBBS	Sam	PTE	/949			31/1/19	TO CLASS Z RESERVE.
DOBBS	ThosH	PTE	/1126			KR para 392 24/1/19	
DOBINSON	Sid	PTE	/1770		16/8/15	WOUNDS 13/6/17	TO 14th, 3rd BNS.
DOBSON	Ed H	PTE	/1324	BISHOP AUCKLAND		18/2/19	TO 10th, 2nd BNS, CLASS Z RESERVE.
DOBSON	Norm	PTE	/254	BISHOP AUCKLAND	SUNDERLAND	23/3/18 POZIERES MEM	TO 14th, 11th BNS.
DOBSON	Thos	PTE	/1518	SUNDERLAND		27/6/19	TO CLASS Z RESERVE.
DODDS	John	LCPL	/1313	DARLINGTON		22/2/19	TO LABOUR CORPS, CLASS Z RESERVE. LAB CORPS No 599786
DODSWORTH	Benj	PTE	/728			12/2/19	TO CLASS Z RES, SGT TO UK TO BE COMMISSIONED.
DODSWORTH	Walt	CPL	/1054	YORK		26/6/17 MENIN GATE MEM.	TO 20th BN PRIOR TO EMBARKATION. AGE 20 COMMISSIONED 1/8/16
DONLEY	W	PTE	/1784	WEST HARTLEPOOL			TO 20th BN PRIOR TO EMBARKATION, 2nd, 29th, 3rd BNS, Z RES. LCPL, AGE 21.
DONOVAN	Wilf	PTE	/259		WEST HARTLEPOOL		TO CLASS Z RESERVE.
DOWNS	John	LCPL	/1378	DARLINGTON		3/7/16 COUIN BRIT CEM	TO 18th BN, CLASS Z RESERVE.
DOWSE	JohnN	PTE	/47	NORTON ON TEES	STOCKTON	23/3/19	TO 20th, 18th BNS, CLASS Z RESERVE.
DOWSON	Morri	CQMS	/1343	CROOK		24/2/19	TO CLASS Z RESERVE.
DOYLE	Thos	PTE	/726	WEST HARTLEPOOL		20/3/19	TO CLASS Z RESERVE.
DRAYCOTT	Ernst	LCPL	/939	NEWBOTTLE		KR para 392 24/1/19	COMMISSIONED 30/10/17 14th BN, ATT 11th BN. AGE 22
DRING	Robt	PTE	/1462	WEST HARTLEPOOL		22/2/19	TO CLASS Z RESERVE. CPL
DRUMMOND	Ab G	RQMS	/734	WEST HARTLEPOOL		11/3/19	TO MACHINE GUN CORPS(93rd MG COY), MGC No 22764, AGE 24. BORN WEST HERRINGTON BEDE COLLEGE 1911
DRYDEN	Geo	PTE	/1139	DARLINGTON		23/3/18 POZIERES MEM	RENUMBERED 114536 DLI ENTERED FRANCE 22/12/15.
DUCKETT	Geo V	LCPL	/989	PRESTON	DURHAM CITY 25/9/14	17/3/19	COMMISSIONED NOTTS & DERBY REGT 26/3/18. 2nd SOUTHERN GEN HOSP BRISTOL 8/7/16
DUFFY	Geo	PTE	/986	DURHAM CITY		6/5/19	TO CLASS Z RESERVE.
DUFFY	RichH	PTE	/1791				COMMISSIONED.
DUKE	John	SGT	/250	WEARHEAD	DURHAM	1/7/16 THIEPVAL MEM	AGE 26.
DUKES	Frank	PTE	/1055	STOCKTON			
DURRANT	Arth	LSGT	/1652	SUNDERLAND			
DUTHIE	Geo	PTE	/730	HARTLEPOOL		4/4/19	
DYER	Gilbt	SGT	/733	WEST HARTLEPOOL		7/2/19	
DYKE	Horac	CPL	/1442	DURHAM CITY	WEST HARTLEPOOL	11/5/18 CAESTRE MIL CEM	
EARL	Oliv	PTE	/1679	PENZANCE	SOUTH SHIELDS	29/7/16 MERVILLE COM CEM	
EDWARDS	Wm E	PTE	/1628	COCKFIELD	DARLINGTON	27/9/16 THIEPVAL MEM	TO 14th BN. AGE 28
ELLIOTT	Walt	CPL	/1048	DARLINGTON		31/1/19	TO CLASS Z RESERVE.
ELLIOTT	JohnH	PTE	/55	TRIMDON COLLIERY			TO LABOUR CORPS, 18th BN. COMD DEPOT RIPON. CLASS Z RESERVE.
ELLIS	Albt	CPL	/1269	TUDHOE COLLIERY			TO CLASS Z RESERVE.
ELLISON	Wm A	CPL	/1464			24/4/19	TO 14th, 20th, 19th BNS, CLASS Z RESERVE. SGT
ELLIS	Harld	CPL	/263			11/11/18	TO CLASS Z RESERVE. CPL
ELLISON	Arth	LCPL	/51				
ELLWOOD	Dan E	SGT	/736	BISHOP AUCKLAND			COMMISSIONED 29/5/19.

Surname	Forename	Rank	No.	Place 1	Place 2	Date	Fate	Notes
ELLWOOD	Linn	PTE	/1449					COMMISSIONED DEVONSHIRE REGT(3rd BN) 28/5/18.
ELSTOB	Jas E	PTE	/1167	WEST HARTLEPOOL		5/1/15	KR para 392 29/10/17	TO ARMY RESERVE CLASS W. AGE 22. OCA 117 RABY ROAD WEST HARTLEPOOL 1972. CPL
EMMERSON	John	LCPL	/265	WITTON GILBERT			10/3/19	ATT 257 TUN COY RE, TO CLASS Z RESERVE. CPL
ENGLAND	Edmd	PTE	/56					COMMISSIONED 23/8/15.
ENGLISH	John	LCPL	/737	MONKWEARMOUTH DAWDON	SUNDERLAND		25/4/16 BEAUVAL COM CEM	AGE 23.
ENGLISH	Robt	PTE	/1187	WEST HARTLEPOOL			10/1/19	TO CLASS Z RESERVE. CPL.VAD HOSP TENDERDEN(?) KENT 1918
ENGLISH	Wm B	PTE	/738	WEST HARTLEPOOL			8/3/19	TO 18th, 10th, 15th, 3rd BNS, CLASS Z RESERVE.
ERRINGTON	John	PTE	/487	FENCEHOUSES	DURHAM CITY	25/9/14	1/7/16 EUSTON ROAD CEM COLINCAMPS	BORN LITTLE LUMLEY.
ETHERINGTON	Thos	PTE	/54	DARLINGTON	DARLINGTON		10/4/17 COJEUL BRIT CEM	TO 15th BN, LCPL AGE 22
EVANS	John	PTE	/1011		DARLINGTON		29/3/19	TO CLASS Z RESERVE.
EVANS	Robt	PTE	/266				9/2/19	TO CLASS Z RESERVE.
EWBANK	Wm	PTE	/1490	NEW SHILDON	DARLINGTON		22/6/16 ABBEVILLE COM CEM	ATT 3rd ENTRENCHING BN, 18th BN. AGE 20. OILER LNER OPERATIONS DEPT SHILDON
FAIL	Jos	PTE	/1127			23/12/14	KR para 392 9/2/18	TO COMMAND DEPOT RIPON. AGE 24
FAIREY	Arth	PTE	/740	BARTON YORKS	WEST HARTLEPOOL		12/4/18 LE GRAND BEAUMART BRIT	AGE 24. STUDENT YORK ST JOHNS 1911-13
FAIRLESS	Edwd	PTE	/267	WESTGATE	SPENNYMOOR		28/7/16 ST VAAST POST MIL CEM	
FALSHAW	F M	PTE	/63	WHITBURN				ATT 3rd ENTRENCHING BN, 13th CORPS HQ, CLASS Z RESERVE.
FARRER	Emst	SGT	/1435	FERRYHILL	WEST HARTLEPOOL		3/5/17 ARRAS MEM	SGT AGE 25
FAWCETT	Normn	LCPL	/741	WEST HARTLEPOOL			KR para 392 29/1/19	TO 18th BN, CLASS Z RESERVE.
FEATHERSTONE	Geo M	PTE	/1006		DARLINGTON		1/3/17 GOMMECOURT BRIT CEM No 2	
FEATHERSTONE	Wall	PTE	/65	BISHOP AUCKLAND			25/2/19	TO 4th BN. AGE 24. STUDENT BEDE COLLEGE 1911
FENWICK	Peter	PTE	/739	WEST HARTLEPOOL			3/5/17 ARRAS MEM	CPL AGE 28.
FENWICK	Wm	PTE	/1745	WEST HARTLEPOOL	WEST HARTLEPOOL	8/2/15	KR para 392 11/9/17	SGT COMMISSIONED 27/7/17.
FERGUSON	Geo	PTE	/1387	MURTON		10/9/14	KR para 392 21/12/18	TO LABOUR CORPS, CLASS Z RESERVE. LAB CORPS No 12179, LCPL
FERGUSON	Jos	PTE	/990					TO 14th BN.
FERRIER	H V	LSGT	/268				9/4/19	TO CLASS Z RESERVE.
FIELD	ThosW	PTE	/59				KR para 392	ATT 257 TUN COY RE, 18th BN, CLASS Z RESERVE.
FIELDHOUSE	Tom	PTE	/742	LEAMSIDE				
FISHBURN	Chris	PTE	/1473	WEST HARTLEPOOL				
FISHBURN	ThosW	PTE	/1749	HUTTON RUDBY				
FITTON	ChasV	PTE	/62					COMMISSIONED 19/2/15. OCA SIR CHARLES FITTON OBE, MC. HUTTON RUDBY
FLETCHER	Fincs	PTE	/491	HOUGHTON LE SPRING	DURHAM CITY	25/9/14	KR para 392 22/3/17	
FORREST	Wilsn	CSM	/492	DURHAM CITY		14/12/14	29/3/18 BIENVILLERS MIL CEM	
FORSHAW	EdwdS	PTE	/1099	WEST HARTLEPOOL			KR para 392 8/11/18	TO ARMY RESERVE CLASS P. LCPL, AGE 23
FORSTER	Chas	CPL	/956	WINGATE			18/5/17 ARRAS MEM	AGE 34 BORN MIDDLESBROUGH, TEACHER NEW BRANCEPETH C S.
FORSTER	JohnJ	PTE	/1058	NEWCASTLE	BENWELL		3/5/17 ARRAS MEM	SGT AGE 34.
FORSTER	Rob M	CPL	/490	DURHAM CITY		25/9/14	14/3/19	AGE 24.
FORSTER	Thos	PTE	/1638			28/6/15	SICK 6/4/17	TO 4th BN(SIGNAL SECTION), CLASS Z RESERVE. 25 NEVILLEDALE 1914
FORSYTH	Wm	CPL	/1091				9/2/19	TO 20th BN. DEPOT.
FOSTER	John	PTE	/1234	WEST RAINTON		11/1/15	KR para 392 27/8/18	TO CLASS Z RESERVE. STUDENT BEDE COLLEGE 1908. HOSP MANCHESTER
FOSTER	Wilf	PTE	/64			12/10/14	18/1/19	AGE 35.
FOTHERGILL	S C	CPL	/812				KR para 392 20/12/17	TO 18th BN, CLASS Z RESERVE. CPL.STUDENT BEDE COLLEGE 1906
FOWLER	Robt	PTE	/1447	COCKEN HALL			KR para 392	TO DEPOT. AGE 29
FOX	Hen G	PTE	/1739	SHERBURN HILL			26/3/18 POZIERES MEM	TO 20th BN PRIOR TO EMBARKATION, 11th, 18th BNS.
FRASER	Chas	CPL	/1251	DURHAM CITY		25/9/14	KR para 392 29/1/19	TO 20th BN.
FRAZER	Alf	CSM	/489	DARLINGTON		5/9/14	12/4/18 LE GRAND BEAUMART	COMMISSIONED 30/10/17.
FREER	ArthM	PTE	/58				KR para 392 22/6/18	COMMISSIONED 3rd BN 29/5/17, TO 18th BN. 95 FLD AMB 17/7/16 - 39 G HOSP.
FUGGLE	Wm a	PTE	/743				11/2/19	TO LABOUR CORPS. LAB CORPS No 343769
FULLER	Herbt	SGT	/1081	WEST HARTLEPOOL			28/7/16 ST VAAST POST MIL CEM	TO CLASS Z RESERVE.
FULLERTON	Matt	PTE	/488	PELTON FELL			1/7/16 EUSTON ROAD CEM COLINCAMPS	AGE 21.TEACHER PELTON FELL C S,
GALLAND	ArthC	PTE	/1183	ACOMB YORKS	YORK		21/3/19	
GALLOP	Wm F	PTE	/503	DURHAM CITY		25/9/14		TO CLASS Z RESERVE.

Surname	Forename	Rank	No	Residence	Enlisted	Fate / Cemetery	Notes
GANNON	Jos E	SGT	/751			KR para 392 12/1/17	TO 22nd, 13th BNS, CLASS Z RESERVE.
GARBUTT	Chas	PTE	/1092	WEST RAINTON	DURHAM CITY 25/9/14	15/5/19	TO LABOUR CORPS(727 LAB COY), LAB CORPS No 387578. AGE 23
GARBUTT	Harry	PTE	/493	WEST RAINTON	DURHAM CITY 25/9/14	21/3/18 POZIERES MEM	TO CLASS Z RESERVE.
GARBUTT	Percy	PTE	/494	WEST RAINTON		24/3/19	TO CLASS Z RESERVE. LCPL
GARDINER	ChasF	PTE	/1341		SUNDERLAND	24/3/19	TO 10th BN, ATT 43 LTMB, CLASS Z RESERVE.
GARGETT	Tom	PTE	/752	STATION TOWN		1/7/16 SERRE ROAD No 1 CEM	
GARGETT	Thos	PTE	/1218			18/2/19	
GARRY	Robt	PTE	/273			18/9/16 LOOS MEM	
GATE	FredL	PTE	/1761	DARLINGTON	DARLINGTON 21/8/14	KR para 392 19/5/17	TO ARMY RESERVE CLASS P. CHILTON MOOR HOSP 1/2/15, AGE 27
GEE	Edwin	PTE	/274			14/3/19	TO 12th BN, CLASS Z RESERVE.
GIBBON	Thos	PTE	/271			24/6/19	TO 2/6th BNS, CLASS Z RESERVE. CPL
GIBSON	Evan	PTE	/270	SPENNYMOOR	SPENNYMOOR 19/9/14	16/3/19	TO 19th BN, CLASS Z RESERVE.
GIBSON	E	PTE	/1113			18/2/19	TO 13th BN, CLASS Z RESERVE. PL BEDE COLLEGE STUDENT 1908. TEACHER SOUTH CHURCH SCH
GIBSON	Edwd	CPL	/1143				TO 14th, 22nd, 1/7th BNS, CLASS Z RESERVE.
GIBSON	Steph	PTE	/276	BISHOP AUCKLAND			TO CLASS Z RESERVE.
GIBSON	Thos	PTE	/1574	BISHOP AUCKLAND		8/3/19	TO CLASS Z RESERVE. LCPL
GIBSON	ThosH	PTE	/279			30/3/19	AGE 18.
GIBSON	Wm O	LCPL	/272			1/7/16 EUSTON ROAD CEM COLINCAMPS	
GILBERT	RobtW	LCPL	/278	LINTHORPE		KR para 392 25/6/17	TO DEPOT. AGE 28
GILL	Fred	PTE	/1059			20/2/19	COMMISSIONED?, 11 OFFICER CADET BN(D COY), CLASS Z RESERVE. AGE 26
GILL	Jas C	BGLR	/ 67	DARLINGTON		1/24/18 PLOEGSTEERT MEM	
GILL	Wm F	CPL	/1144	NEW HERRINGTON	HOUGHTON LE SPRING	22/2/19	TO 18th BN, CLASS Z RESERVE.
GILLANDER	John	SGT	/ 73			8/3/19	TO CLASS Z RESERVE. SGT
GILLESPIE	Geo A	CPL	/506	QUEBEC	DURHAM CITY 25/9/14	1/24/18 LE GRAND BEAUMART	BORN CROOK
GIRLING	Gilbt	LCPL	/1595	HIGH FELLING	COCKEN HALL	8/5/16 BARD COTTAGE CEM YPRES	TO 14th BN. AGE 29 BORN DURHAM
GLADWELL	Wm A	PTE	/1557	BISHOP AUCKLAND	BISHOP AUCKLAND	KR para 392 17/1/18	TO CLASS Z RESERVE.
GOLDSBROUGH	Harld	SGT	/1304	BISHOP AUCKLAND		3/5/17 ARRAS MEM	TO ROYAL DEFENCE CORPS. RDC No 66900. WITH BN UNTIL 26/6/17
GOLDSMITH	Cyril	PTE	/ 70				ATT 257 TUN COY ROYAL ENGINEERS, 35IBD, 18th BN. AGE 24 BORN WEST AUCKLAND
GOODMAN	Har V	CPL	/1681	DARLINGTON	DARLINGTON	3/8/16 MERVILLE COM CEM	AGE 22
GOODWILL	Herbt	PTE	/ 68	DARLINGTON	DARLINGTON	28/7/16 ST VAAST POST MIL CEM	BORN CORSTORPHINE AGE 24, EDUCATED SKERRYS COLLEGE.
GORRIE	JohnA	SGT	/496	CASTLE EDEN	DURHAM CITY 25/9/14	26/10/16 SAILLY AU BOIS MIL CEM	BORN MIDDLETON IN TEESDALE AGE 21
GOWLING	Arth	PTE	/ 66	DARLINGTON	DARLINGTON	19/7/18 MERVILLE COM CEM	ATT WEST YORKS REGT(1/8th BN), 18th BN. BORN MIDDLETON IN TEESDALE
GOWLING	Edwd	SGT	/ 74	DARLINGTON	DARLINGTON	15/3/19	TO CLASS Z RESERVE.
GRAHAM	ChasS	PTE	/277	EDMONDSLEY		28/7/16 ST VAAST POST MIL CEM	BORN TOW LAW AGE 23.
GRAHAM	Harry	PTE	/280	WREKENTON	SPENNYMOOR	27/4/19	TO 18th BN, CLASS Z RESERVE.
GRAHAM	JohnF	PTE	/ 72			KR para 392 9/1/17	TO DEPOT. AGE 34
GRAHAM	Jos	PTE	/495		DURHAM CITY 25/9/14		ATT WEST YORKS REGT(1/8th BN), 18th, 21st, 87th TRG RES BN. LCPL
GRAHAM	Jos	PTE	/746	HOUGHTON LE SPRING	18/9/14	MYOPIA. 7/9/16	TO 18th BN. SGT
GRAHAM	Robt	PTE	/ 75	DARLINGTON	DARLINGTON	1/3/17 GOMMECOURT BRIT CEM No 2	TO 15th, 18th BNS. AGE 40. ALSO 4 QUARRY HEAD SHINEY ROW 1918 AVL
GRAHAM	Wm	CPL	/ 71	DARLINGTON	COCKEN HALL	10/7/18 PLOEGSTEERT MEM	TO CLASS Z RESERVE.
GRANT	Wm	PTE	/1145	SHINEY ROW		30/1/19	TO 14th, 11th, 1/6th BNS, CLASS Z RESERVE.
GRAY	ThosW	PTE	/1407	DURHAM CITY		29/3/19	TO 14th, 3rd BNS. AGE 22
GREAVES	Jos T	PTE	/757	HEBBURN		KR para 392 15/3/19	TO 20th, 3rd BNS. AGE 25
GREENWELL	Geo H	PTE	/497	LANGLEY PARK	DURHAM CITY 25/9/14	KR para 392 17/7/18	TO LABOUR CORPS, CLASS Z RESERVE. LAB CORPS No 476303
GREENWOOD	Thos	LCPL	/1788	DARLINGTON	DARLINGTON 30/8/15	KR para 392 12/10/18	
GREENWOOD	Wm	LCPL	/1471	DARLINGTON	DARLINGTON 23/4/19	24/2/19	
GRETTON	JohnT	PTE	/1311			16/9/16 AIF BURIAL GROUND FLERS	TO 15th BN. AGE 24 BORN HULL
GREY	Jas E	PTE	/1664	WEST HARTLEPOOL	WEST HARTLEPOOL	1/7/16 SERRE ROAD No 1 CEM	
GRIEVES	Edwd	PTE	/755	YORK	SUNDERLAND	28/6/17 LOOS MEM	TO 2nd BN. AGE 30. 2nd SOUTHERN GHOSP BRISTOL 7/16
GRIMES	Vict	PTE	/754	WORSTEAD NORFOLK	WEST HARTLEPOOL	KR para 392	TO 14th BN.
GRONBERG	Eric	PTE	/1768				

Surname	Forename	Rank	No.	Place	Date	Fate / Cemetery-Memorial	Remarks
GROODY	Wm	PTE	/502	ESH WINNING	23/12/14	DIS 5/1/17 DIED 29/3/18. QUEEN OF MARTYRS	
GUY	Thos	CPL	/1128	WHEATLEY HILL	4/11/14	KR para 392 22/4/19	TO ARMY RESERVE CLASS P. AGE 23
HABRON	Isaac	SGT	/509	LANCHESTER	10/9/14	KR para 392 25/6/17	TO ARMY RESERVE CLASS P. AGE 27
HALL	Andrw	SGT	/1042	HARTLEPOOL	5/9/14	KR para 392 26/4/18	TO ARMY RESERVE CLASS P. AGE 28
HALL	James	CPL	/1060	BISHOP AUCKLAND		18/5/17 ARRAS MEM	AGE 26
HALL	JohnH	SGT	/1783	BISHOP AUCKLAND		1/7/16 SERRE ROAD No 1 CEM	AGE 29
HALL	Reg V	PTE	/82	DURHAM CITY	25/9/14	KR para 392 10/3/18	AGE 24.
HALL	Walt	PTE	/283	DURHAM CITY	25/9/14		COMMISSIONED 10/9/18.
HALL	Wilf	SGT	/284			24/4/19	TO CLASS Z RESERVE. RQMS
HALL	Wm J	PTE	/519			21/3/19	TO CLASS Z RESERVE. CPL
HALLAM	Wm	LCPL	/1100	SPENNYMOOR		KR para 392 7/2/19	REC FOR MM BY Lt C G FINDLAY
HAMILTON	Fmcs	PTE	/523	DARLINGTON			TO LABOUR CORPS. LAB CORPS No 638830
HAMPTON	Wm	PTE	/1477	SHINEY ROW			ATT 1st ARMY SCHOOL OF MORTARS, 93rd LTMB. CLASS Z RESERVE.
HANDISIDES	Alf	PTE	/1146			18/1/19	TO CLASS Z RESERVE.
HANDS	Cecil	PTE	/1537	SUNDERLAND		12/10/17 TYNE COT MEM	TO 14th BN. DEAD ON MR
HANSON	Geo	PTE	/1356	WEST HARTLEPOOL		7/3/19	COMMISSIONED 27/3/17. TO 13th BN. AGE 21
HARDING	Wm	PTE	/777				TO CLASS Z RESERVE. SGT TO UK FOR COMMISSION.
HARDY	JohnG	PTE	/1274			18/1/19	TO CLASS Z RESERVE.
HARLAND	Herbt	PTE	/762	WINGATE			TO CLASS Z RESERVE.
HARLAND	ThosW	PTE	/78	TOW LAW			COMMISSIONED 20/9/15.
HARLE	Jos	PTE	/1147	SHADFORTH		20/3/18	TO CLASS Z RESERVE.
HARPER	John	PTE	/985	MARYPORT		28/7/16 ST VAAST POST MIL CEM	ATT 31st DIV HQ. CLASS Z RESERVE.
HARPER	Syd	LCPL	/521	WORKINGTON		17/10/18 COLOGNE SOUTHERN CEM	TO 18th, 2nd, 18th BNS. AGE 25, DIED WHILST A POW
HARRISON	H	PTE	/994	DARLINGTON			AGE 36.
HARRISON	Herbt	PTE	/94	STRANTON		16/9/16 THIEPVAL MEM	
HARRISON	Thos	PTE	/1624	SUNDERLAND		1/7/16 EUSTON ROAD CEM COLINCAMPS	TO 15th BN.
HARRISON	ThosH	PTE	/1591	WINGATE			BORN RYHOPE.
HART	Wm C	PTE	/922	WINGATE			TO CLASS Z RESERVE.
HART	Em M	SGT	/1273	SPENNYMOOR		22/3/18 POZIERES MEMORIAL	TO CLASS Z RESERVE.
HARTLEY	Harry	PTE	/1108	FERRYHILL		9/4/18 PLOEGSTEERT MEM	COMMISSIONED 3/2/19.
HARWOOD	Wm	PTE	/950			21/4/17 LOOS MEM	TO 18th, 22nd, 10th, 15th BNS. BORN BISHOP AUCKLAND
HARWOOD	Fred	PTE	/1707	ST PETERS			TO 12th, 1/5th BNS. AGE 26
HATTON	Jas	SGT	/921	STOCKTON			TO 14th BN.
HAWKINS	Wm	LCPL	/76	WEST HARTLEPOOL		1/7/16 EUSTON ROAD CEM COLINCAMPS	AGE 23
HAWKSWELL	Geo E	PTE	/767	WEST HARTLEPOOL			TO CLASS Z RESERVE.
HAY	Stan	PTE	/972				TO CLASS Z RESERVE.
HAYMAN	John	PTE	/520	WEST HARTLEPOOL	2/10/14	WOUNDS 28/2/17	TO DEPOT.
HAZELWOOD	Edwd	PTE	/785			3/3/19	AGE 27
HEATON	ThosW	PTE	/1029	WEST HARTLEPOOL	28/10/14	KR para 392 25/7/19	TO CLASS Z RESERVE. TWO BROTHERS IN EAST AFRICA
HEDLEY	Harld	PTE	/1028		28/10/14	14/2/19	TO ARMY RESERVE CLASS P. AGE 37
HEDLEY	Jas H	PTE	/518	DURHAM CITY	25/9/14	KR para 392 13/2/19	TO DEPOT. AGE 23
HENDERSON	Reg	PTE	/770			KR para 392 5/9/16	
HENDERSON	Alex	PTE	/993			5/9/16	
HENDREN	Robt	PTE	/90		13/12/14	KR para 392 13/2/19	
HENRY	Demi	PTE	/1105			24/1/19	
HEPPLE	Geo	PTE	/281		22/9/14	KR para 392 19/2/19	AGE 22.
HEPPLESTON	Geo	PTE	/1220	MOORSLEY		KR para 392 1/4/18	TO 4th BN. AGE 23
HERBERT	Herbt	PTE	/81	THORNABY	28/9/14	KR para 392 29/1/19	ATT 93rd LIGHT TRENCH MORTAR BATTERY.
HERBERT	Fostr	PTE	/776	WEST HARTLEPOOL		15/8/16 LE TOURET MIL CEM	
HERON	Mars	PTE	/779	DURHAM CITY	25/9/14	KR para 392 15/4/18	
HESLOP	ArthH	PTE	/516	DARLINGTON		13/12/16 GEZAINCOURT COM CEM EXT	TO CLASS Z RESERVE. LSGT
HESLOP	Thos	PTE	/290			18/2/19	

Surname	Forename	Rank	No	Place	Enlisted	Date	Remarks
HESLOP	Thos	PTE	/764		26/12/14	15/2/19	TO CLASS Z RESERVE.
HIBBERT	Stan	PTE	/1122		DURHAM CITY 25/9/14	SICK 26/6/17	TO 4th BN.
HILL	Edwd	SGT	/511	WATERHOUSES		20/1/19	TO CLASS Z RESERVE. LCPL
HOBSON	Bert	SGT	/1516	TOW LAW			TO 14th, 11th, 2nd(D COY), 19th BNS, CLASS Z RESERVE.
HOGG	Mart	PTE	/973	WEST HARTLEPOOL	DURHAM CITY 25/9/14	19/3/19	TO CLASS Z RESERVE. BN TRANSPORT SECTION.
HOLMES	David	PTE	/514	WITTON GILBERT		29/1/19	TO CLASS Z RESERVE. LCPL
HOPKINSON	Jos A	PTE	/1326	NEWBOTTLE	DURHAM CITY 25/9/14	24/3/19	TO CLASS Z RESERVE.
HOPPS	John	PTE	/510	DURHAM CITY	DURHAM CITY 25/9/14		TO 27th BN.
HOPPS	Wilf	LCPL	/89	ETHERLEY GRANGE	BISHOP AUCKLAND 21/9/14		COMMISSIONED RIFLE BRIGADE(5th BN) 5/6/17 TO ROYAL AIR FORCE AGE 20
HORN	Wm J	PTE	/1598	AMBLE	WEST HARTLEPOOL	17/5/17 ARRAS MEM	
HORNER	Geo	CPL	/289	TUDHOE COLLIERY		30/3/19	TO 1/7th BN, CLASS Z RESERVE. SGT
HORNSLEY	WilfH	PTE	/85	DARLINGTON	DARLINGTON	1/7/16 THIEPVAL MEM	
HORSLEY	Maur	PTE	/1272			24/4/19	TO MACHINE GUN CORPS. MGC No 22789
HOURIE	Wm	LCPL	/1061				TO LABOUR CORPS, CLASS Z RESERVE. LAB CORPS No 22769
HOURIGAN	Corni	PTE	/522	SHILDON	DURHAM CITY 25/9/14	KR para 392 14/12/17	TO MACHINE GUN CORPS, MGC No 117222, CSM COMMISSIONED TANK CORPS 3/2/18.
HOWE	Robt	LCPL	/1691		SPENNYMOOR	16/9/16	DID NOT SERVE OVERSEAS.
HOWELL	Alf	SGT	/1548	HURWORTH ON TEES	DARLINGTON	19/7/16 LIJSSENTHOEK MIL CEM	
HOWL	ThosE	PTE	/515	LITTLEBURN COLLIERY	DURHAM CITY 25/9/14	1/7/16 THIEPVAL MEM	
HOY	Arth	PTE	/77	EAST HARTLEPOOL	STOCKTON	6/3/19	TO 14th BN. BORN PENMORFA WALES. TEACHER ST JOHNS SCHOOL
HUDSPETH	Jas W	PTE	/92	NEWCASTLE		KR para 392. 17/5/18	TO TRG RES BN, COMMISSIONED ROYAL ENGINEERS. TRG RES No TR/5/3417
HUDSPITH	Ralph	PTE	/517	DURHAM CITY	DURHAM CITY 25/9/14		TO ROYAL ENGINERS, CLASS Z RESERVE. RE No 246393
HULL	Jos	PTE	/1721	WEST HARTLEPOOL		KR para 392 10/10/17	TO LABOUR CORPS. LAB CORPS No 195079
HULLOCK	Edwn	CPL	/1631		23/6/15	SICK.3/8/17	TO 13th, 3rd BNS AGE 21
HUMBLE	JohnW	CPL	/84		18/9/14	KR para 392 6/3/18	TO DEPOT. SGT
HUME	Robt	PTE	/288		22/9/14	14/2/19	TO DEPOT. AGE 22
HUNNAM	Wm	LCPL	/780			5/4/19	TO CLASS Z RESERVE.
HUNTER	Frans	PTE	/1271			27/2/19	TO CLASS Z RESERVE. SGT
HUNTER	Geo	PTE	/292	SUNDERLAND	SUNDERLAND	19/12/16 SAILLY AU BOIS MIL CEM	
HUNTER	Harld	CPL	/293	BISHOP AUCKLAND			TO CLASS Z RESERVE.
HUNTER	J	PTE	/91				AGE 24.
HUNTLEY	Eust	PTE	/991				COMMISSIONED ROYAL NAVY 10/4/15.
HURWORTH	ThosW	PTE	/1533		TOW LAW		BORN PARTICK.
HUTCHINSON	David	PTE	/87	DARLINGTON	DARLINGTON	1/3/17 GOMMECOURT BRIT CEM No 2	
HUTCHINSON	Edwd	PTE	/513	WASHINGTON	DURHAM CITY 25/9/14	24/3/19	TO CLASS Z RESERVE.
HUTCHINSON	Fred	LCPL	/773	WEST HARTLEPOOL		7/3/19	TO CLASS Z RESERVE. CHILTON MOOR HOSP 20/2/15
HUTCHINSON	Herbt	PTE	/1526	DARLINGTON			TO CLASS Z RESERVE.
HUTCHINSON	JohnA	PTE	/1084	TOW LAW	DURHAM CITY	1/7/16 THIEPVAL MEM	
HUTCHINSON	Mat H	PTE	/86	BISHOP AUCKLAND	DARLINGTON	19/7/18 PLOEGSTEERT MEM	AGE 26.
HUTCHINSON	Matt	PTE	/1237	CASTLE EDEN		25/2/19	TO 18th BN. AGE 28
HUTCHINSON	Robt	PTE	/1236	CASTLE EDEN	24/9/14		TO 20th, 18th BNS, CLASS Z RESERVE.
HUTCHINSON	Sid	PTE	/79	DARLINGTON		KR para 392 3/1/17	ATT 31st DIV HQ, CLASS Z RESERVE.
HUTCHINSON	Thos	PTE	/1567	WOLSINGHAM		11/3/19	TO DEPOT. AGE 22, LEFT ARM AMPUTATED
IBBOTSON	ThosE	PTE	/781	WEST HARTLEPOOL	SUNDERLAND	29/3/20	TO CLASS Z RESERVE.SGT. SGT
ILLINGWORTH	Arth	PTE	/1437	WEST HARTLEPOOL		1/9/18 BERLIN SOUTH WEST CEM	
INGHAM	ThosW	PTE	/1402	SUNDERLAND		13/2/19	TO LABOUR CORPS. LAB CORPS No 343769
IRVING	Jos S	PTE	/1112			5/4/19	TO 2nd BN, COMMISSIONED 9/9/18
JACKSON	Edwd	PTE	/525	BROWNEY COLLIERY	DURHAM CITY 25/9/14		TO NORTHUMBERLAND FUSILIERS(9th,26th(3rd Tl),1/5th BNS). LCPL NORTHBLD FUS No 38977.AGE 24
JACKSON	Ernst	PTE	/1702			KR para 392 19/12/17	TO CLASS Z RESERVE.
JACKSON	John	PTE	/1775	BILLY ROW CROOK			TO CLASS Z RESERVE.
JACKSON	Norm	PTE	/300		21/9/14	KR para 392 24/7/17	TO 20th, 19th BNS, CLASS Z RESERVE.
JACKSON	Wm C	PTE	/296				TO CLASS Z RESERVE.
JACKSON	Wm G	PTE	/299		22/9/14		TO 3rd BN. AGE 26 COMMISSIONED 26/2/18.

Surname	Forename	Rank	No.	Place of Birth	Enlisted	Date / Cemetery or Memorial	Notes
JACOB	Geo	SGT	/782	STILLINGTON		15/2/19	TO CLASS Z RESERVE. SHOWN AS COMMISSIONED IN 18BH
JARMAN	Chas	LSGT	/788	WEST HARTLEPOOL		21/9/17 TYNE COT MEM	TO 11th, 13th BNS. AGE 24, SPRINGBURN HOSP GLASGOW 11/7/16
JARY	Robt	PTE	/1708	SOUTH SHIELDS		7/6/16 DARTMOOR CEM BECOURT/BEC	TO 15th BN. AGE 26
JEFFERSON	Geo T	PTE	/787	WEST HARTLEPOOL		12/10/18 TYNE COT MEM	TO 1/9th, 29th BNS. AGE 23
JEWITT	Mat B	PTE	/527	LUMLEY CASTLE	DURHAM CITY 25/9/14	18/9/16 THIEPVAL MEM	TO 2nd BN. AGE 27
JOHNSON	Alf	PTE	/1468	WYNDENHAM			TO 14th BN.
JOHNSON	Edwd	PTE	/1300	DARLINGTON			TO 2nd BN. CLASS Z RESERVE.
JOHNSON	Herbt	PTE	/297	WEST HARTLEPOOL		15/2/19	ATT HQ 31 DIV TRAIN, TO CLASS Z RESERVE.
JOHNSON	John	PTE	/1397	BISHOP AUCKLAND	15/2/15	KR para 392 21/9/17	TO NORTHERN COMD DEPOT RIPON. AGE 24.STUDENT BEDE COLLEGE 1911
JOHNSON	Thos	PTE	/298			15/2/19	TO CLASS Z RESERVE.
JOHNSON	Thos	PTE	/302		21/9/14	KR para 392 1/5/17	TO ARMY RESERVE CLASS W. AGE 26
JOHNSON	Wm	PTE	/301			27/6/19	TO CLASS Z RESERVE.
JOHNSON	Wm	PTE	/1149	HETTON LE HOLE		9/9/17 FAVREUIL BRIT CEM	TO WEST YORKSHIRE REGIMENT(2/6th BN). W YORKS No 242835.AGE 28
JOHNSON	Wm H	SGT	/1717				TO 20th, 18th BNS, CLASS Z RESERVE.
JOICEY	Fred	PTE	/789	DARLINGTON	24/9/14	KR para 392 24/6/17	TO 20th, 18th BNS, CLASS Z RESERVE. NORTH EVINGTON HOSP LEICESTER 8/7/16
JOLLY	Herbt	SGT	/1520	WEST HARTLEPOOL			ATT 3rd ENTRENCHING BN, 18th BN. AGE 27 BORN NORTHALLERTON
JONES	Alf	PTE	/1419	GATESHEAD		3/5/17 ARRAS MEM	TO 3rd, 15th BNS. BORN ASHTON UNDER LYNE.STUDENT BEDE COLLEGE 1906
JONES	Alf	CPL	/1670	DURHAM CITY	DURHAM CITY 25/9/14	19/9/18 VILLERS HILL BRIT CEM	TO DEPOT. AGE 32
JONES	Andw	PTE	/526		19/9/14	KR para 392 14/2/18	TO DEPOT. AGE 21
JONES	Ernst	PTE	/303	WEST HARTLEPOOL		KR para 392 26/1/15.	TO 22nd, 19th BNS, CLASS Z RESERVE.
JONES	Hurt	PTE	/1170	STRANTON		18/3/19	TO KINGS OWN YORKSHIRE LI(2nd BN). KOYLI No 22941
JONES	James	LCPL	/1523			18/11/16 MUNICH TRENCH CEM	TO CLASS Z RESERVE.
JONES	Norm'n	PTE	/1556	WEST HARTLEPOOL			NOT IN SDGW
JONES	Reub'n	PTE	/1772	BARNARD CASTLE		16/9/16 THIEPVAL MEM	BORN DALTON AGE 30.STUDENT BEDE COLL.TEACHER STATION TOWN. AWOll
JONES	Robt	SGT	/940			28/7/16 ST VAAST POST MIL CEM	TO 14th, 19th, 12th, 12th BNS, CLASS Z RESERVE.
JONES	Sam	PTE	/923	WEST HARTLEPOOL		23/1/19	ATT 3rd ENTRENCHING BN, 18th BN, CLASS Z RESERVE. SERVED XV PLATOON
JONES	Theo	PTE	/295			16/12/14 HART ROAD NEW CEM	BORN DARLINGTON, AGE 27.
JOPLING	Edwd	PTE	/1687	TUDHOE COLLIERY			TO ARMY RESERVE CLASS P. AGE 23
KAY	Wm	LCPL	/1201	MIDDLESBROUGH	7/1/15	KR para 392 22/4/19	AGE 26, RESIDENT HOUGHTON LE SPRING 1914.
KEENE	Garth	SGT	/529		DURHAM CITY 25/9/14	12/4/18 OUTTERSTEENE COM CEM EXT	ATT 93rd BDE HQ, TO CLASS Z RESERVE.
KELLETT	Robt	PTE	/1594	WINGATE			TO 22nd BN. AGE 30
KELLY	John'H	PTE	/1452	BRANDON		18/1/19	TO 16th BN. AGE 25
KENNICK	John	LCPL	/100	SUNDERLAND		28/5/18 LA VILLE AUX BOIS BRIT CEM	TO DEPOT.
KENT	Fred'W	PTE	/790	SHEFFIELD	DARLINGTON	17/8/16 CHOCQUES MIL CEM	
KENWORTHY	Jesse	CPL	/98	HOUGHTON LE SPRING	DURHAM CITY 25/9/14	GSW 3/6/17	TO CLASS Z RESERVE.
KERR	Arthe	LCPL	/528	FERRYHILL		KR para 392 11/11/18	TO LABOUR CORPS. LAB CORPS No 351122
KIDD	Rob H	LCPL	/101			10/3/19	TO 15th, 14th, 18th BNS. AGE 21
KIDD	Wm	PTE	/1791	DURHAM CITY		KR para 392 7/12/17	TO MACHINE GUN CORPS. MGC No 22771
KILLEN	Sam	PTE	/307		DURHAM CITY 25/9/14	19/7/16 PLOEGSTEERT MEM	TO 18th, 20th, 19th BNS, CLASS Z RESERVE. BORN RIPON
KING	Fred	PTE	/1601	CROOK		KR para 392 5/12/17	TO CLASS Z RESERVE. CPL
KIRBY	Bernd	PTE	/96	DURHAM CITY	DURHAM CITY 25/9/14	10/3/19	COMMISSIONED.
KIRK	Edmd	PTE	/531	YORK		24/3/19	BORN SHADFORTH.
KIRK	Henry	PTE	/532	SACRISTON		23/9/17 ROCLINCOURT MIL CEM	
KITCHING	Gord'n	LCPL	/99				STUDENT BEDE COLLEGE 1909. TEACHER CASSOP COUNCIL SCHOOL
KNAGGS	Thos'A	SGT	/1200	DURHAM CITY		KR para 392 29/3/18	TO 3rd BN. AGE 29
LAIDLER	Wm Ed	PTE	/1275		DURHAM CITY 25/9/14	KR para 392 27/6/18	TO 18th, 19th, 18th BNS.
LAMB	David	PTE	/313	BIRTLEY	2/10/14	11/2/19	ATT 13 CORPS HQ, TO 17th BN, CLASS Z RESERVE.
LANAGHAN	Frank	PTE	/534				COMMISSIONED 13/8/18. STUDENT BEDE COLLEGE 1911.STRETCHER BEARER
LANCASTER	Ernst	PTE	/997		DURHAM CITY 25/9/14	15/1/19	TO CLASS Z RESERVE.
LATIMER	Chas	PTE	/1301	CHILTON			COMMISSIONED.
LATTIMER	Fred	PTE	/314	CHESTER LE STREET			
LAVELLE	Thos	PTE	/924				
LAWLER	Harry	CPL	/536		DURHAM CITY 25/9/14		

Surname	Forename	Rank	No	Town	Enlisted	Date / Cemetery	Notes
LAWRENSON	Chas	PTE	/108			13/4/19	TO LABOUR CORPS, CLASS Z RESERVE. LAB CORPS No 520114, ENTERED FRANCE IN 1915
LAWS	Arth	PTE	/311	DARLINGTON		19/3/19	TO CLASS Z RESERVE.
LAWSON	Cyril	PTE	/1130	LEAMSIDE		25/2/19	TO CLASS Z RESERVE.
LAWSON	Geo C	LSGT	/308				COMMISSIONED 29/11/17.
LAWSON	Wm	LCPL	/102			24/3/19	TO 18th BN, CLASS Z RESERVE.
LAX	John	PTE	/1415				ATT 3rd ENTRENCHING BN, 13th BN, CLASS Z RESERVE.
LAYFIELD	Geo F	PTE	/105	DARLINGTON		2/3/19	TO 18th BN, CLASS Z RESERVE. MEMBER OF BATTALION BAND
LAZENBY	JohnH	PTE	/793			17/4/19	TO CLASS Z RESERVE.
LEAKE	Harld	CPL	/1063	YORK		31/3/16 SUCRERIE MIL CEM	AGE 22
LEAVITT	JohnR	PTE	/1064			30/3/19	TO CLASS Z RESERVE.
LEE	Arth	PTE	/537	DURHAM CITY	DURHAM CITY 25/9/14	15/10/16 BANCOURT BRIT CEM	TO 2nd BN. AGE 22
LEE	Edwd	LSGT	/1367	THROSTON HARTLEPC	WEST HARTLEPOOL	3/5/17 ARRAS MEM	
LEE	Robt	CPL	/1541				TO 15th, 20th, 10th, 1/7th BNS, CLASS Z RESERVE.
LEIGHTON	Geo W	PTE	/1649	HETTON LE HOLE		13/10/16 BANCOURT BRIT CEM	TO 14th BN.
LENDER	Reg	PTE	/312				COMMISSIONED 7/1/15.
LEWIS	Jas H	PTE	/1140		31/12/14	9/3/19	TO 20th BN, DEPOT. AGE 31
LEWTHWAITE	Arth	PTE	/1400			KR para 392 19/12/17	TO CLASS Z RESERVE.
LIBBEY	FredJ	PTE	/974		HOUGHTON LE SPRING 2/10/14	16/12/14 DARLINGTON WEST CEM	
LIDDLE	Alex	PTE	/107			KR para 392 28/1/19	CPL AGE 25.
LIDDLE	Clar	PTE	/1467		DARLINGTON	KR para 392	ATT 3rd ENTRENCHING BN. LCPL
LINDRIDGE	Neisn	LCPL	/1677	WEST HARTLEPOOL			TO 15th BN.
LINDRIDGE	Wm H	PTE	/1039	WEST HARTLEPOOL			TO 20th BN PRIOR TO EMBARKATION.
LINDSAY	Ernst	PTE	/1586				TO 20th, 20th BN, CLASS Z RESERVE.
LINDSAY	James	PTE	/309				COMMISSIONED 13/8/18.
LINTON	Wm B	SGT	/792			30/6/19	TO CLASS Z RESERVE.
LISLE	Thos	PTE	/1546			KR para 392	
LISTER	John	PTE	/998	EBCHESTER	10/9/14	KR para 392 27/6/18	AGE 29.
LITTLE	Edwin	PTE	/315		DURHAM CITY	2/3/19	TO CLASS Z RESERVE. LSGT. PRISONER OF WAR
LIVELY	JohnF	PTE	/996			26/7/19	TO 10th, 10th, 2/7th BNS, CLASS Z RESERVE.
LLOYD	Chatt	CPL	/1276	HOUGHTON LE SPRING		25/2/19	TO CLASS Z RESERVE.
LOADER	James	PTE	/318		22/9/14	KR para 392 9/8/18	LCPL AGE 23
LOCK	James	SGT	/1790	BISHOP AUCKLAND	7/8/14		TO DEPOT. RSM AGE 45
LOCKEY	Ambr	PTE	/319	DURHAM CITY	SPENNYMOOR	KR para 392 21/12/18	AGE 34.
LOCKEY	Frank	PTE	/535	COCKTON HILL	DURHAM CITY 25/9/14	5/8/15 AUCKLAND ST ANDREWS NEW CH YD	
LOCKEY	James	PTE	/310	WEST RAINTON	DURHAM CITY 25/9/14	23/5/16 SUCRERIE MIL CEM	
LOCKEY	James	LCPL	/533				
LOCKWOOD	Henry	PTE	/1155	DARLINGTON		3/5/17 ARRAS MEM	BORN SAINTFIELD IRELAND AGE 24
LONGLEY	Walt	PTE	/1576				COMMISIONED 21/1/16. STUDENT BEDE COLLEGE 1908
LONGSTAFF	Walt	SGT	/798	WEST HARTLEPOOL		23/1/19	TO 14th, 1/5th, 2nd BNS, CLASS Z RESERVE.
LONSDALE	Harry	PTE	/1640	BILLINGHAM	MIDDLESBROUGH	18/9/16 THIEPVAL MEM	ATT NORTHUMBERLAND FUS(9th BN), 18th BN, CLASS Z RESERVE.
LONSDALE	Wm	PTE	/538	NEWFIELD	DURHAM CITY 25/9/14	21/3/19	TO 14th BN. AGE 20
LONSDALE	Wm	SGT	/1630	HOUGHTON LE SPRING			TO CLASS Z RESERVE.
LOUDON	Ben H	CPL	/796	DUNDALK Co LOUTH	WEST HARTLEPOOL	12/7/16 ETAPLES MIL CEM	TO 20th BN 139 F AMB 3/12/16 PUO TO 41 DRS SAME DAY, AGE 21
LOUNTON	Geo	PTE	/317	BISHOPWEARMOUTH	SOUTH SHIELDS	25/6/16 BERTRANCOURT MIL CEM	AGE 23. LONDON IN MR
LOVETT	Fred	PTE	/1355	HENDON	SUNDERLAND	22/2/19 RYHOPE ROAD CEM S/LAND	TO 11th, 1/5th BNS. AGE 22
LOWERY	Fred	PTE	/316	SUNDERLAND	23/9/14	KR para 392 24/6/18	TO DEPOT. LCPL AGE 27
LUCAS	ThosH	PTE	/794	HILLFIELD	SUNDERLAND	1/7/16 THIEPVAL MEM	
LUND	Alf J	PTE	/103	DEAF HILL		28/3/19	TO 18th BN, CLASS Z RESERVE.
LUXMORE	Jos	PTE	/1252	WINGATE			AGE 24.
MAITLAND	Andw	PTE	/542		DURHAM CITY 25/9/14	23/5/18 EBBLINGHEM MIL CEM	COMMISSIONED 4/3/15.
MANN	Robt	PTE	/551				TO 1st GARRISON BN. DID NOT SERVE OVERSEAS
MANSON	Hor	LCPL	/322	WEST HARTLEPOOL	DURHAM CITY 25/9/14	INJURY 2/7/16	TO 2nd BN, 21 OFF CADET BN, SERVED WITH 35th SIKHS

Surname	Forename	Rank	No.	Residence	Enlisted	Died / Memorial	Notes
MAQUIRE	Thos	PTE	/545	SUNDERLAND	DURHAM CITY 25/9/14	8/6/17 ETAPLES MIL CEM	AGE 37.
MARSDEN	Jas H	CPL	/553	DURHAM CITY	DURHAM CITY 25/9/14	18/2/19	TO 18th BN, CLASS Z RES HOSP CAMBRIDGE 28/7/16, BROS IN RAMC & GREEN HOWARDS
MARSH	Jos	PTE	/557	MONKWEARMOUTH	DURHAM CITY 25/9/14	1/8/16 ST VAAST POST MIL CEM	AGE 40.
MARSHALL	Geo R	LCPL	/803				COMMISSIONED WEST YORKSHIRE REGT 30/10/17.
MARSHALL	John	PTE	/556	DURHAM CITY	DURHAM CITY 25/9/14	17/1/19	TO CLASS Z RESERVE.
MARSHALL	Thos	SGT	/104	DURHAM CITY	DURHAM CITY 25/9/14		
MARSHALL	Thos	PTE	/320			KR para 392 24/3/19	TO 1/6th, 18th, 1/9th, 18th BNS.
MARSHALL	ThosW	LSGT	/1709				ATT 31st DIV HQ, 18th BN, CLASS Z RESERVE.
MARSHALL	Wm E	LCPL	/324	COANWOOD	ASHINGTON	3/5/17 ARRAS MEM	TO 15th, 18th BNS. AGE 23 BORN HALTWHISTLE, STUDENT BEDE COLLEGE 1911
MARTIN	Fred	PTE	/110	DARLINGTON		5/4/19	ATT 31st DIV HQ, 228 EMP COY, 18th BN, CLASS Z RESERVE.
MARTIN	Rich	PTE	/1277		13/1/15		AGE 26.
MARTIN	Thos	PTE	/1614			KR para 392 30/5/18	TO 20th, 20th, 20th BNS, CLASS Z RESERVE.
MASON	Harry	PTE	/1569	WEST HARTLEPOOL	LIVERPOOL	12/4/18 LE GRAND BEAUMART	AGE 23 SPECIAL MEM
MATHIE	Archl	PTE	/800			KR para 392 4/2/19	AGE 21.
MATSON	Chas	PTE	/113	DARLINGTON	DARLINGTON	2/3/17 SAILLY AU BOIS MIL CEM	AGE 37.
MATTHEWS	Thos	PTE	/804	WEST AUCKLAND	6/10/14	KR para 392 19/12/17	TO CLASS Z RESERVE. HEAVY WEIGHT BOXER
MAUGHAN	Chas	PTE	/1101			13/1/19	COMMISSIONED NORTHUMBERLAND FUSILIERS(3rd BN) 25/4/17.
MAUGHAN	Hit	PTE	/381				TO CLASS Z RESERVE.
MAWSON	Robt	SGT	/549	CHESTER LE STREET	DURHAM CITY 25/9/14	27/2/19	TO 15th BN.
MAY	John	PTE	/1629	PITTINGTON	COCKEN HALL	20/9/16 HEILLY STATION CEM	TO CLASS Z RESERVE. COMS SEC OCA
McCANN	Geo	SGT	/550	LITTLE STAINTON	DURHAM CITY 25/9/14	5/4/19	BORN DURHAM, AGE 30. TWO LETTERS IN DA
McCLAIN	Jo O	PTE	/558	BURNOPFIELD			TO ARMY RESERVE CLASS P. AGE 24
McCRICKARD	James	LCPL	/1572	DURHAM CITY	12/1/15	28/7/16 ST VAAST POST MIL CEM	AGE 24
McDONALD	Harld	SGT	/1239	CHESTER LE STREET	SOUTH SHIELDS	KR para 392 22/4/19	TO CLASS Z RESERVE.
McDONALD	Jos	SGT	/323	FERRYHILL	DURHAM CITY 25/9/14	28/3/18 ARRAS MEM	BORN DONCASTER.
McGEORGE	JohnS	LCPL	/548	SOUTH SHIELDS	DARLINGTON	28/7/16 ST VAAST POST MIL CEM	TO CLASS Z RESERVE.
McGREGOR	Wall	CPL	/1757	SHINEY ROW	DURHAM CITY 25/9/14	3/3/17 GOMMECOURT BRIT CEM No 2	TO CLASS Z RESERVE.
McINTOSH	Wm A	PTE	/117	WEST HARTLEPOOL		KR para 392 11/12/19	TO CLASS Z RESERVE.
McKEAG	John	PTE	/806	DARLINGTON	DURHAM CITY 25/9/14	16/1/19	
McMILLAN	Chas	PTE	/941	WEST RAINTON		19/3/19	
McNAUGHTON	Jas C	PTE	/325	THORNLEY		2/4/19	
McNEILL	Thos	PTE	/802	WEST HARTLEPOOL		KR para 392 3/3/19	OCA 32 RICHMOND STREET WEST HARTLEPOOL 1972.
McPHAIL	Don	PTE	/1106			WOUNDS 9/6/17	TO LABOUR CORPS, CLASS Z RESERVE. LAB CORPS No 31217. CPL
MELLOR	Frank	SGT	/540	CHESTER LE STREET	DURHAM CITY 25/9/14		TO DEPOT. TEACHER CHESTER LE STREET, DURHAM CRICKET CLUB
MELLOR	J	PTE	/809				OFF CADET BN(8/9/17) COMM WILTSHIRE REGT 7th BN 2Lt ROYAL ARTILLERY 1941/44
MERRIWEATHER	Anthy	LCPL	/801	WEST HARTLEPOOL	WEST HARTLEPOOL	23/5 COMMISSIONED 29/1/18	
METCALFE	Alex	LCPL	/543	NORTH BIDDICK	DURHAM CITY 25/9/14	28/7/16 ST VAAST POST MIL CEM	TEACHER FATFIELD C S. BORN SKIPTON.
MILBURN	John	PTE	/120	WHORLTON	DARLINGTON	1/7/16 THIEPVAL MEM	LSGT, AGE 35.
MILBURN	Lance	PTE	/541	NEW BRANCEPETH	DURHAM CITY 25/9/14		TO 3rd BN(No 5 COY).
MILES	AbtE	SGT	/559		DURHAM CITY 25/9/14		TO ROYAL DEFENCE CORPS RDC No 73227,NOT O/SEAS,WAR MEDAL 27/2/22 FOR W HARTLEPOOL
MILES	Jos	LCPL	/1740	KIMBLESWORTH	COCKEN HALL 13/1/15	24/9/16 GORRE BRIT & INDIAN CEM	AGE 23
MILFORD	Geo	PTE	/1253		DARLINGTON	KR para 392 28/4/19	TO ARMY RESERVE CLASS P. AGE 23
MILLER	Jos	LCPL	/698	GATESHEAD	13/1/15		TO 10th, 22nd, 1/7th BNS, CLASS Z RESERVE.
MILLER	Robt	PTE	/171	WEST HARTLEPOOL	WEST HARTLEPOOL		
MILROY	James	LCPL	/999	MARYPORT	WEST HARTLEPOOL	1/7/16 THIEPVAL MEM	TO ROYAL ENGINEERS. PUPIL CARLISLE GRAMMAR SCHOOL
MINKS	Thos	PTE	/328		NEWCASTLE		COMMISSIONED 7/1/16.
MINTO	Ernst	PTE	/1278	ROWLANDS GILL	2/1/14	17/12/14 ST PATRICKS CH YD WINLATON	AGE 25 BORN MEDOMSLEY.TEACHER HIGHFIELD C S.

Surname	Forename	Rank	No.	Residence	Enlisted	Died/Discharged & Cemetery/Memorial	Notes
MITCHELL	Ab E	PTE	/1651	SUNDERLAND	COCKEN HALL	19/5/18 COLOGNE SOUTHERN CEM	To 15th, 11th, 1/7th BNS. DIED WHILST A POW
MITCHELL	Herb	PTE	/114			WOUNDS 20/4/17	To DEPOT. CHILTON MOOR HOSP 1/3/15. 2nd STHN GEN HOSP BRISTOL 8/7/16
MITCHELL	JohnC	PTE	/604	SUNDERLAND	SUNDERLAND	9/5/17 ETAPLES MIL CEM	To 3rd, 15th BNS.
MOFFITT	Jas P	PTE	/326	ROKER		3/12/17 CAMBRAI MEM	COMMISSIONED 6/3/15 1st BN. ATT 14th BN. AGE 25
MONKS	Henry	PTE	/1222	FERRYHILL	COCKEN HALL 22/1/15	1/7/16 THIEPVAL MEM	BORN HETTON LE HOLE AGE 34 A HAIRDRESSER BY TRADE.
MOODY	Wm R	LCPL	/547	SHINCLIFFE	DURHAM CITY 25/9/14	30/4/17 BAILLEUL RD EAST CEM	BORN PENSHAW AGE 25
MOON	Ernst	PTE	/1732	COLD HARBOUR YORK WEST HARTLEPOOL		3/5/17 ARRAS MEM	To 15th, 18th BNS.
MOON	JohnW	CPL	/952	SPENNYMOOR	2/10/14		ATT 93rd LIGHT TRENCH MORTAR BATTERY. CLASS Z RESERVE.
MOORE	Em S	PTE	/1657	WEST HARTLEPOOL			To 15th, 18th, 2nd BNS, CLASS Z RESERVE. HOSPITAL STOCKPORT 7/16
MOORE	Ernst	SGT	/1131	TUDHOE COLLIERY	COCKEN HALL	19/5/18 CAESTRE MIL CEM	AGE 24
MOORE	Harld	PTE	/1136	TUDHOE COLLIERY	DURHAM CITY 25/9/14	25/2/19	To CLASS Z RESERVE. SGT
MORGAN	Ab E	PTE	/560	DURHAM CITY	DURHAM CITY 25/9/14	KR para 392 17/1/17	CHILTON MOOR HOSP 3/15
MORGAN	John	PTE	/546	HETTON LE HOLE	DURHAM CITY 25/9/14	15/2/19	
MORGAN	Wm	CQMS	/1538	WEST HARTLEPOOL	DURHAM CITY 25/9/14		To CLASS Z RESERVE. RAN REGIMENTAL CANTEEN IN EGYPT & FRANCE
MORLAND	Robt	CPL	/554	WITTON LE WEAR	DURHAM CITY 25/9/14		ATT 3rd ENTRENCHING BN. 18th BN, CLASS Z RESERVE.
MORRIS	Chas	CPL	/1132	DURHAM CITY	DURHAM CITY 25/9/14	18/5/17 ARRAS MEM	AGE 27
MORRIS	Wm P	SGT	/1012		DURHAM CITY 25/9/14	27/6/19	To CLASS Z RESERVE.
MOSCROP	Alf	CPL	/109	MORTON GRANGE		22/1/19	To CLASS Z RESERVE.
MOSES	Robt	SGT	/544	CHESTER LE STREET	DURHAM CITY 25/9/14		COMMISSIONED KINGS SHROPSHIRE LI 26/2/18.
MOSS	ChasH	PTE	/1639	STOCKTON ON TEES	MIDDLESBROUGH	17/2/18	To 3rd BN, CLASS Z RESERVE.
MOUNTAIN	Chas	PTE	/562	DURHAM CITY	DURHAM CITY 25/9/14	20/4/17 CALAIS SOUTHERN CEM	To 14th BN. AGE 19
MOWBRAY	Geo E	CQMS	/1066	STAINTON			To 21st, 3rd BNS. LCPL 9/4/15. 5'6" BLUE EYES, BROWN HAIR, GROCER. NOT O/SEAS
MOWBRAY	W	CPL	/133			VDH 24/3/16	To EAST YORKSHIRE REGT. CLASS Z RES TO UK TO BE COMMISSIONED
MURRAY	Harry	LCPL	/1502	STAINTON	SUNDERLAND	24/6/18 BERLIN SOUTH WESTERN CEM	ATT 3rd ENTRENCHING BN. 18th BN. DIED WHILST A POW
MURRAY	Thos	SGT	/561	STRANTON	DURHAM CITY 25/9/14	KR para 392 28/11/17	To DEPOT. AGE 33
MYERS	Edwd	PTE	/942		21/9/14	KR para 392 16/5/17	To ARMY RESERVE CLASS P. LCPL AGE 26
MYERS	Glbt	SGT	/1150	HETTON LE HOLE	DURHAM CITY 25/9/14	24/3/19	To CLASS Z RESERVE.
MYERS	JohnR	PTE	/1489	STRANTON	WEST HARTLEPOOL		AGE 17.
NEEDHAM	Herbt	PTE	/564		DURHAM CITY 25/9/14	1/7/16 SERRE ROAD No 1 CEM	COMMISSIONED 27/8/15.
NEIL	Geo	PTE	/189	HETTON LE HOLE			To LABOUR CORPS, CLASS Z RESERVE. LAB CORPS No 205041
NELSON	A	PTE	/1699	WATERHOUSES	DURHAM CITY 25/9/14	21/1/19	To 21st, 15th BNS, CLASS Z RESERVE.
NELSON	Fred	PTE	/1354	SUNDERLAND	SUNDERLAND		To DEPOT.
NELSON	Jonet	PTE	/814	HARTLEPOOL	WEST HARTLEPOOL	GSW 24/8/17	AGE 21.
NESBIT	Henry	PTE	/173	WEST HARTLEPOOL		15/6/16 GORRE BRIT & INDIAN CEM	AGE 21.
NEWBY	Harry	PTE	/333	HEMLINGTON ROW	11/9/14	1/7/16 SERRE ROAD No 1 CEM	To CLASS Z RESERVE. LCPL SIGNALLER
NEWCOMB	Fred	PTE	/813	WEST HARTLEPOOL	18/9/14		
NEWCOMBE	Fred	PTE	/816		21/9/14	15/2/19	3rd NORTHERN GEN HOSP SHEFFIELD 8/7/16.
NEWTON	Issac	PTE	/332	GATESHEAD	DURHAM CITY 25/9/14	WOUNDS 20/11/18	DID NOT SERVE OVERSEAS.
NEWTON	StanO	LCPL	/567	HARTLEPOOL	DARLINGTON	KR para 392 15/12/14	DID NOT SERVE OVERSEAS.
NICHOL	Chas	PTE	/818	WEST HARTLEPOOL		SICK 10/6/15	To CLASS Z RESERVE.
NICHOLSON	Edmn	PTE	/1503	DARLINGTON	11/9/14	24/2/19	To MACHINE GUN CORPS, CLASS Z RESERVE. MGC No 22767
NICHOLSON	JohnH	PTE	/331	WEST HARTLEPOOL	5/9/14	4/3/19	To 14th BN. ATT 18th BDE TRANSPORT, 11th, 18th BNS. AGE 23
NICHOLSON	Thos	PTE	/1588	DURHAM CITY	DURHAM CITY 25/9/14	2/9/16 LES BARAQUES MIL CEM	COMMISSIONED 28/8/17 YORKSHIRE REGT. ATT EAST YORKS (7th BN). AGE 24
NILSSON	Geoff	PTE	/565	WEST HARTLEPOOL		18/6/18 GOUZEAUCOURT NEW BRIT CEM	AGE 23.
NIXON	Rohd	PTE	/815	WEST HARTLEPOOL	7/1/15	KR para 392 19/8/18	To 20th, 19th BNS, CLASS Z RESERVE. CPL
NOBLE	John	CPL	/1198	DURHAM CITY	DURHAM CITY 25/9/14	18/3/19	To 2nd BN, CLASS Z RESERVE.
NORMAN	RobtC	SGT	/820	WEST HARTLEPOOL		20/3/19	
NORTHROP	FredV	PTE	/1758	HETTON LE HOLE		KR para 392 2/12/18	
OGLESBY	Chas	CPL	/126	WEST HARTLEPOOL	WEST HARTLEPOOL	11/4/18 LE GRAND BEAUMART	To 19th BN. AGE 23
OLDFIELD	JohnH	SGT	/820	HETTON LE HOLE	HETTON LE HOLE	1/7/16 LONDON CEM EXT	AGE 29
OLDHAM	Nich	PTE	/1758	DARLINGTON	DARLINGTON	30/1/19	To 15th BN.
OLDRIDGE	Ernst	SGT	/126	WEST HARTLEPOOL	WEST HARTLEPOOL	2/3/19	To 18th BN, CLASS Z RESERVE. RSM
OLEY	Robt	PTE	/334	WEST HARTLEPOOL	HOUGHTON LE SPRING		To CLASS Z RESERVE.

Surname	Forename	Rank	Number	Birthplace	Enlisted	Discharge/Death	Notes
OLIPHANT	Harry	LCPL	/ 127	MARYPORT	DURHAM CITY 25/9/14	15/2/19	TO 18th BN, CLASS Z RESERVE. RQMS.STUDENT BEDE COLLEGE 1907, SCHOOL TEACHER
OLIVER	James	CPL	/ 568		5/9/14	WOUNDS 16/5/17	TO DEPOT. CPL.
OLIVER	AlexJ	PTE	/ 819	DURHAM CITY	DURHAM CITY 25/9/14	KR para 392 24/12/18	AGE 24, RESIDENT 4 LAMPTON STREET 1914. COMMISSIONED ROYAL NAVAL RESERVE 26/7/15.
OLSSON	Ralph	PTE	/ 569	DURHAM CITY	DURHAM CITY 25/9/14	KR para 392 2/4/19	TO 18th BN. AGE 28
ORD	RichF	PTE	/ 337	DARLINGTON	DARLINGTON	KR para 392 19/2/19	TO LABOUR CORPS. LAB CORPS No 599783
ORTON	Reg G	LCPL	/ 1314			20/3/19	ATT 257 TUN COY RE. 18th BN, CLASS Z RESERVE. COMMISSIONED 25/5/18.
OSBORNE	W	LCPL	/ 1723				TO ARMY RESERVE CLASS P. AGE 23
OUTHWAITE	Lawr	PTE	/ 336	DARLINGTON	19/9/14	KR para 392 12/5/17	TO 18th BN, LABOUR CORPS(837 LAB COY), 20th BN. LAB CORPS No 446445.BROTHER IN 20th BN
OWSNETT	Jos	PTE	/ 128	DARLINGTON	DARLINGTON	29/9/18 TYNE COT MEM	
PACE	Jas H	PTE	/ 1280	HUTTON HENRY			ATT MILITARY FOOT POLICE, LABOUR CORPS, 2nd BN, CLASS Z RES.
PALEY	Roger	CPL	/ 1693				TO 18th. 18th BN.
PALLISTER	Rohd	PTE	/ 133	DARLINGTON	DARLINGTON	21/3/18 ARRAS MEM	AGE 26.
PALLISTER	Thos	LCPL	/ 1176	BISHOP AUCKLAND	DURHAM CITY	30/4/17 BAILLEUL RD EAST CEM	TO DEPOT.
PALMER	Henry	PTE	/ 824		18/9/14	WOUNDS 18/9/16	TO MACHINE GUN CORPS, CLASS Z RESERVE. MGC No 22785. AWOl
PALMER	Horat	PTE	/ 341			22/2/19	TO DEPOT. CPL AGE 30
PARK	ThosA	PTE	/ 135	DARLINGTON	20/9/14	KR para 392 21/8/17	TO 20th BN PRIOR TO EMBARKATION.
PARK	Wm	PTE	/ 1480	DARLINGTON			COMMISSIONED 4/10/15.
PARKE	Edwd	PTE	/ 347				AGE 37, BORN DURHAM CITY.
PARKER	Matt	PTE	/ 735	BLACKHILL	DURHAM CITY	4/3/16 BENFIELDSIDE CEM	TO 52nd BN. COMS
PARKER	Syndh	LCPL	/ 346	BISHOP AUCKLAND	28/9/14	KR para 392 8/3/17	DID NOT SERVE OVERSEAS.
PARKIN	E	PTE	/ 574		DURHAM CITY 25/9/14	KR para 392 16/11/17	TO CLASS Z RESERVE.
PARKIN	James	PTE	/ 1202	BISHOP AUCKLAND		24/3/19	TO 21st BN, YORK & LANCASTER REGT(9th BN). Y&L No 39865.AGE 22
PARKINSON	JohnW	PTE	/ 1785	WEST HARTLEPOOL	DURHAM CITY 25/9/14	21/10/17 TYNE COT MEM	TO 20th BN, CLASS Z RESERVE.
PARLETT	Geo	PTE	/ 577		WEST HARTLEPOOL	6/6/19	TO MACHINE GUN CORPS(32nd BN). MGC No 122908
PARR	Norm	PTE	/ 1428	WEST HARTLEPOOL		7/6/18 CABERET ROUGE MIL CEM	TO 3rd BN.
PARRY	JohnT	PTE	/ 1174				TO 18th BN, CLASS Z RESERVE. CHILTON MOOR HOSP 2/15.
PARTINGTON	Wm	PTE	/ 575	DURHAM CITY	DURHAM CITY 25/9/14	15/1/19	TO CLASS Z RESERVE.
PATTERSON	Cecil	PTE	/ 348			8/2/19	TO 3rd BN. AGE 27
PATTERSON	James	PTE	/ 340	FERRYHILL	21/9/14	KR para 392 31/3/19	
PATTERSON	M S	PTE	/ 132	STOCKTON			
PAWSEY	Herbt	LCPL	/ 1565				TO 15th, 2nd BNS. COMMISSIONED 28/5/18.
PEACOCK	Berti	PTE	/ 338	MIDDLESBROUGH			TO CLASS Z RESERVE.
PEARS	Geo R	CPL	/ 1388	DARLINGTON	DARLINGTON	KR para 392 22/1/19	ATT 275 FLD COY RE. 31st DIVISIONAL GAS SCHOOL.
PEARSON	Don L	SGT	/ 136				COMMISSIONED(3rd BN) 25/9/17. RENUMBERED 22233
PEARSON	EmW	PTE	/ 825		WEST HARTLEPOOL	6/8/15 REDOUBT CEM HELLES TURKEY	COMMISSIONED 17th BN. ATT MANCHESTER REGT(6th BN). AGE 36
PEARSON	JohnT	PTE	/ 1001		WEST HARTLEPOOL	11/4/19	TO 13th, 13th BN, CLASS Z RESERVE.
PEARSON	Rich	PTE	/ 1258		WEST HARTLEPOOL	KR para 392 26/7/17	
PEARSON	Wm A	CPL	/ 131	CORNSAY COLLIERY		5/4/19	TO CLASS Z RESERVE. CSM
PEART	Fred	PTE	/ 1336	BLACKHILL		14/2/19 HEATHERY CLEUGH CEM	ATT 3rd ENTRENCHING BN, 19th, 18th BNS. RESIDENT WEARHEAD 1918
PEART	Leond	CPL	/ 344	STANHOPE			COMMISSIONED 25/9/17.
PEART	T C	PTE	/ 953	ST JOHNS CHAPEL		3/2/15	TO 20th BN PRIOR TO EMBARKATION. LABOUR CORPS.
PEART	ThosE	PTE	/ 1372	SEATON CAREW		3/9/16 ST SEVER CEM ROUEN	TO 10th BN.AGE 38. SERVED 3rd BN COLDSTREAM GUARDS SOUTH AFRICA
PEET	Jas F	PTE	/ 1780		WEST HARTLEPOOL	4/7/16 COUIN BRIT CEM	AGE 20.
PENBERTHY	Jas	PTE	/ 977		WEST HARTLEPOOL	12/10/16 THIEPVAL MEM	TO 14th BN.
PENDLINGTON	RobtA	PTE	/ 1134		WEST HARTLEPOOL	WOUNDS 16/5/17	TO DEPOT.
PETTY	Robt	PTE	/ 1436			5/4/15	COMMISSIONED 9/12/14.
PEVERELL	Bernd	PTE	/ 345				TO CLASS Z RESERVE.
PHILLIPSON	Thos	PTE	/ 339	WILLINGTON		23/2/19	TO 11th, 1/5th, 18th BNS, CLASS Z RESERVE.
PHILLIPS	Harry	PTE	/ 1141			27/6/19	COMMISSIONED R BERKSHIRE REGT 20/9/15.
PICKARD	Thos	PTE	/ 572		DURHAM CITY 25/9/14		COMMISSIONED GREEN HOWARDS(3rd BN). 28/6/17.
PICKEN	RichH	SGT	/ 828				TO 15th BN.
PICKERING	Rich	PTE	/ 1587	WEST HARTLEPOOL	WEST HARTLEPOOL	1/7/16 THIEPVAL MEM	

Surname	Forename	Rank	No.	Place	Enlisted	Died / Discharged	Notes
PICKFORD	Geo	PTE	/1482				TO 20th BN PRIOR TO EMBARKATION. 2nd, 15th BNS.
PICKFORD	Hugh	PTE	/134				COMMISSIONED 26/3/18.
PICKLES	ThosW	SGT	/576	DURHAM CITY	25/9/14	6/6/19	TO 52nd, 53rd BNS, CLASS Z RESERVE. CSM, MUSKETRY INSTUCTOR
PIKE	Wm V	PTE	/975	WEST HARTLEPOOL		21/2/19	TO 22nd BN, CLASS Z RESERVE. TO 3rd NTHN GEN HOSP SHEFFIELD 8/7/16
PINKNEY	Arth	PTE	/1433	WEST HARTLEPOOL	6/4/15	1/7/16 THIEPVAL MEM	ATT 3rd ENTRENCHING BN, 18th BN. IN VII PLTN
PINKNEY	MarkR	CPL	/351			KR para 392 23/4/19	TO ARMY RESERVE CLASS P. AGE 29
PINNINGTON	James	PTE	/1774				COMMISSIONED 30/10/17. WOUNDED AND POW
PITT	Wm	PTE	/1096	WEST HARTLEPOOL	7/10/14	3/5/17 PONT DU JOUR MIL CEM	TO CLASS Z RESERVE.
PLAICE	JohnW	PTE	/827			SICK 1/3/17	AGE 21
PLEWS	Robt	PTE	/130	DARLINGTON			TO DEPOT.
PLOWS	Frank	PTE	/343	YORK		25/6/16 BERTRANCOURT MIL CEM	TO ROYAL AIR FORCE. RAF No 139332
POOLE	FredB	PTE	/976	HARTLEPOOL		21/1/19	AGE 18
PORTER	Arth	PTE	/978	WEST HARTLEPOOL	29/10/14	KR para 392 12/4/19	TO CLASS Z RESERVE.
PORTER	JohnG	PTE	/349			24/2/19	TO 18th BN. AGE 23
POTTS	Jack	PTE	/1342	RYTON			TO CLASS Z RESERVE, SGT TO UK TO BE COMMISSIONED?
POTTS	Wm	PTE	/1613				STUDENT BEDE COLLEGE 1911. STRETCHER BEARER
POUNDER	RobtW	PTE	/1746	WEST HARTLEPOOL	15/6/15	KR para 392 10/5/19	TO 15th, 20th, 2nd BNS.
POWELL	Ernst	SGT	/826	ST NEOTS			TO 22nd, 19th, 17th BNS, CLASS Z RESERVE.
POWELL	G H	PTE	/943	BISHOP AUCKLAND		15/2/19	TO 11th, 18th BNS, CLASS Z RESERVE.
POWELL	Harry	PTE	/822	KNARESBOROUGH			COMMERCIAL TRAVELLER
POWELL	Thos	PTE	/350	MIDDLESBROUGH			
PRIESTLEY	Ron H	PTE	/830	SUNDERLAND		1/7/16 THIEPVAL MEM	LCPL
PROUD	JohnH	CPL	/1197	SEATON CAREW		KR para 392 7/7/16	TO CLASS Z RESERVE.
PROUDFOOT	Frank	CPL	/1309	SCARBOROUGH		27/3/19	ATT 39th DIV 'G' BRANCH, 50th DIV HQRA, CLASS Z RESERVE.
PUGSLEY	Gordn	PTE	/1003				COMMISSIONED YORK & LANCASTER REGT 29/1/18.
PURDY	Robt	PTE	/1622	SUNDERLAND	10/9/14	KR para 392 2/4/17	TO ARMY RESERVE CLASS P.
QUIGLEY	O	SGT	/1855			4/7/16 SERRE ROAD No 1 CEM	AGE 26
QUINNAN	Edwd	PTE	/1563	SUNDERLAND			TO 20th BN PRIOR TO EMBARKATION.
RACE	JohnW	PTE	/1423	GATESHEAD		2/9/16 FONCQUEVILLERS MIL CEM	TO 13th, 1/9th, CLASS Z RESERVE.
RAILTON	Geo	PTE	/145	FENCEHOUSES		3/3/19	ATT NORTHUMBERLAND FUSILIERS(9th BN), 3rd ENTRENCHING BN.
RAILTON	Ralph	SGT	/149				TO LABOUR CORPS, CLASS Z RESERVE. LAB CORPS No 184909
RAINE	Frank	PTE	/355	WEST HARTLEPOOL			COMMISSIONED 29/11/17.
RAINE	Geo C	PTE	/1116	WITTON GILBERT	27/10/14	8/5/19	TO CLASS Z RESERVE. LCPL
RAINE	JohnT	PTE	/365		19/9/14	KR para 392 30/7/18	TO ARMY RESERVE CLASS W. AGE 25
RAINES	Harry	SGT	/1417	DARLINGTON	22/9/14	KR para 392 10/10/18	AGE 28
RAMSDALE	James	PTE	/359	EAST HERRINGTON		KR para 392 18/2/19	TRANSFERRED.
RAMSHAW	Geo E	PTE	/839	HESELDEN	WEST HARTLEPOOL	25/2/19	AGE 22.
RAMSHAW	Jos	CPL	/583	ESH WINNING	DURHAM CITY 25/9/14	22/6/17 MENIN GATE MEM	TO 20th BN.
RAND	John	SGT	/1331	FERRYHILL		KR para 392	TO 11th, 13th BNS, CLASS Z RESERVE.
RANSOM	Arth	CPL	/137	WEST HARTLEPOOL		19/3/19	TO CLASS Z RESERVE.
REAH	JohnT	CPL	/584	DURHAM CITY		18/1/19	TO 20th BN PRIOR TO EMBARKATION.
REAVLEY	Thos	SGT	/1040	LANGLEY MOOR	DURHAM CITY 25/9/14	18/5/17 ARRAS MEM	TO CLASS Z RESERVE.
REAY	Frank	SGT	/1365	SUNDERLAND	3/2/15	KR para 392 18/12/17	TO 18th, 19th BNS, CLASS Z RESERVE.
REAY	Harry	PTE	/376	DURHAM CITY		28/3/19	AGE 32
REDDEN	David	PTE	/587	OLD SHILDON	DURHAM CITY 25/9/14	KR para 392 4/6/18	DID NOT SERVE OVERSEAS.
REDHEAD	Arth	LCPL	/139			27/6/19	AGE 37
REED	Alf	PTE	/140	CONSETT			TO CLASS Z RESERVE.
REED	Edwd	PTE	/555	BRANDON COLL	2/10/14	KR para 392 3/1/17	TO CLASS Z RESERVE.
REED	EdwdJ	PTE	/841			5/4/19	TO ARMY RESERVE CLASS P. AGE 29
REED	Fred	PTE	/1030			15/1/19	TO CLASS Z RESERVE.
REED	Thos	PTE	/144	DARLINGTON		27/2/19	TO CLASS Z RESERVE.

Surname	Forename	Rank	No.	Birthplace	Enlisted	Died / Discharged	Notes
REED	ThosA	PTE	/317	WEST HARTLEPOOL	WEST HARTLEPOOL	AMP L THIGH 22/12/17	TO DEPOT. HUDDERSFIELD WAR HOSP 14/8/16, SCOTTISH R X 14/5/17. AGE 25
REINECKER	JohnA	PTE	/831	WEST HARTLEPOOL	WEST HARTLEPOOL	1/7/16 THIEPVAL MEM	ATT 3rd ENTRENCHING BN, 18th BN.
RENWICK	Geo	PTE	/1429				TO 12th. ATT 3rd ENTRENCHING BN, 20th, 20th, 20th, BNS, Z RES
RENWICK	Marsh	PTE	/1719				TO 20th BN. CLASS Z RESERVE.
RICHARDSON	Alex	PTE	/579	CHESTER LE STREET	DURHAM CITY 25/9/14	28/7/16 CABERET ROUGE MIL CEM	TEACHER FENCEHOUSES C S, DIED IN GERMAN FLD HOSP. AGE 25
RICHARDSON	Geo	PTE	/1204	CROOK	WEST HARTLEPOOL	18/5/17 ARRAS MEM	TO CLASS Z RESERVE. STUDENT BEDE COLLEGE 1911
RICHARDSON	John	PTE	/586	DURHAM CITY	DURHAM CITY 25/9/14	2/3/19	TO CLASS Z RESERVE. CHILTON MOOR HOSP 16/2/15. LCPL
RICHMOND	James	PTE	/363			2/4/19	TO 1/5th BN.
RICKABY	Jas A	LCPL	/364	DARLINGTON	DARLINGTON	26/6/17 ARRAS MEM	AGE 26 AS/SCH MASTER STANLEY C S. TRAINED SUNDERLAND TRG CO
RIGG	Tyson	SGT	/356	WALLSEND	SPENNYMOOR	28/3/18 ARRAS MEM	AGE 20. 5'6". DESERTED 23/7/15 FENCEHOUSES.
RILEY	EdwdA	PTE	/1427	HARPERLEY	SPENNYMOOR 30/3/15		ATT No 2 SEC ARMY SERVICE CORPS, TO 20th BN(D COY).
RILEY	Fred	PTE	/1315	GRINGLEY ON THE HILL	DARLINGTON	13/3/17 LIJSSENTHEOK MIL CEM	TO 3rd 18th BNS, CLASS Z RESERVE.
RITSON	Rich	CPL	/585	DURHAM CITY	DURHAM CITY 25/9/14	17/2/19	TO 12th, 20th BNS, CLASS Z RESERVE.
RIVERS	John	PTE	/929	THORNLEY	NEWCASTLE	14/3/19	TO 14th BN. BORN TUDHOE AGE 26 TEACHER BIRTLEY C.S. F/BALL N/CASTLE UTD
ROBERTS	Geo S	PTE	/1394	EASINGTON COLLIERY	SUNDERLAND	13/8/16 ENGLEBELMER COM CEM	TO 14th BN. ATT 5th ENTRENCHING BN, LOYAL REGIMENT(9th BN). AGE 26
ROBERTS	JohnG	CPL	/1026	CAMBRIDGE	DURHAM CITY 25/9/14	26/4/18 TYNE COT MEM	AGE 23 BORN BOSTON LINCS. LIVING FENCEHOUSES 1914.
ROBERTSON	Wm	SGT	/944	RENFREW GLASGOW	NEWCASTLE	15/6/17 DUISANS BRIT CEM	CHILTON MOOR HOSP 2/15, TEACHER HIGH SPEN WESTMINSTER COLLEGE
ROBERTSON	Archi	PTE	/371		DARLINGTON	22/7/16 CARDIFF CATHAYS CEM	TO CLASS Z RESERVE.
ROBERTSON	Robt	PTE	/1109	TUDHOE		4/3/19	TO 19th, 3rd BNS, CLASS Z RESERVE.
ROBINSON	Thos	PTE	/362				COMMISSIONED 25/12/14.
ROBINSON	Arth	SGT	/361				TO CLASS Z RESERVE.
ROBINSON	Fred	PTE	/353				COMMISSIONED 29/12/14.
ROBINSON	FredH	PTE	/1738				TO 3rd BN. AGE 22
ROBINSON	Geo C	CPL	/374	SPENNYMOOR	19/9/14	KR para 392 28/12/17	TO CLASS Z RESERVE.
ROBINSON	Geo H	PTE	/581	DURHAM CITY	DURHAM CITY 25/9/14	2/3/19	DID NOT SERVE OVERSEAS. AGE 22.
ROBINSON	Harry	PTE	/146		21/9/14	KR para 392 22/3/15.	TO 18th BN. DEPOT. BROTHER IN 20th BN
ROBINSON	JohnJ	CPL	/832	WEST HARTLEPOOL	5/9/14	1/7/16 THIEPVAL MEM	TO CLASS Z RESERVE.
ROBINSON	JohnW	PTE	/142	SACRISTON		KR para 392 11/7/18	AGE 30. LNER FREIGHT SHUNTER DARLINGTON
ROBINSON	Law H	PTE	/372	MIDDLESBROUGH		15/3/19	TO LABOUR CORPS. LAB CORPS No 439389
ROBINSON	Wilsn	SGT	/141	EPSOM		18/5/17 ARRAS MEM	TO 15th BN, CLASS Z RESERVE.
ROBINSON	Wm	PTE	/375	WEARHEAD		KR para 392 17/2/19	ATT 3rd ENTRENCHING BN, 18th BN.
ROBINSON	Wm	PTE	/1338	NEW HERRINGTON			TO CLASS Z RESERVE.
ROBSON	Chas	CPL	/1647	MONKTON	SUNDERLAND	1/7/16 SERRE ROAD No 1 CEM	TO 2nd, 19th BNS. AGE 24
ROBSON	Herbt	PTE	/138	SUNDERLAND	DURHAM CITY 25/9/14	15/1/19	13 PLATOON AGE 25. BORN SUNDERLAND.
ROBSON	JohnE	PTE	/836	CHESTER LE STREET	SUNDERLAND	31/10/18 VICHTE MIL CEM	TO 19th BN.
ROBSON	JohnW	LCPL	/582	SUNDERLAND	WEST HARTLEPOOL	1/7/16 EUSTON ROAD CEM COLINCAMPS	AGE 25. CHIEF CLERK LINGFORD & Co B AUCKLAND
ROBSON	Percy	SGT	/930	WEST HARTLEPOOL		KR para 392 6/6/18	COMMISSIONED 30/1/15. DID NOT SERVE OVERSEAS
ROBSON	RobtH	PTE	/833		21/9/14	16/12/14 BISHOP AUCKLAND	TO CLASS Z RESERVE.
ROBSON	Thos	PTE	/367	BISHOP AUCKLAND	BISHOP AUCKLAND		TO 20th, 12th BNS, CLASS Z RESERVE.
ROGERS	Walt	PTE	/369				TO 20th, 18th, 51st BNS, CLASS Z RES SGT AGE 28. BEDE COLL 1908, HOSP ARMSTRONG COLLEGE NEWCASTLE
ROLLIN	Henry	PTE	/1004	BISHOP AUCKLAND	NORMANTON	4/5/17 ST LEDGER BRIT CEM	COMMISSIONED.
ROPER	Wm	PTE	/358	NORMANTON			
ROSE	Jos	PTE	/147	BISHOP AUCKLAND	DURHAM CITY 2/10/14		TO CLASS Z RESERVE.
ROTHERHAM	Alf	PTE	/373	DURHAM CITY		18/3/19	TO 20th, 12th BNS, CLASS Z RESERVE.
ROTHERHAM	Jos	PTE	/366	NEVILLES CROSS		15/1/19	
ROUTLEDGE	H	LCPL	/148			24/7/18 LONGUENESSE SOUVENIR CEM	
ROWE	Geo	LCPL	/208	SUNDERLAND	SUNDERLAND	21/3/18 ARRAS MEM	TO 2nd BN.
ROWELL	Arth	PTE	/1549	DARLINGTON	DARLINGTON	1/7/16 THIEPVAL MEM	
ROWLANDS	JohnT	PTE	/834	SOUTH BANK	WEST HARTLEPOOL	12/4/18 PLOEGSTEERT MEM	BORN MIDDLESBROUGH IN XIII PLTN
ROWLANDS	Wm	PTE	/835	WEST HARTLEPOOL		KR para 392 26/6/18	
RUNDLE	Thos	SGT	/1434		6/4/15		TO 14th BN. DEPOT. AGE 25
RUSHTON	Wm H	PTE	/842	OLDHAM LANCS	SUNDERLAND	1/7/16 THIEPVAL MEM	DIS HOSP FOVANT 23/11/15, SICK LEAVE - 29/11/15.

Surname	Forename	Rank	No.	Location(s)	Date	Cemetery / Memorial	Notes
RUSSELL	Alex	LCPL	/150	PAISLEY GLASGOW	15/5/16	SUCRERIE MIL CEM	AGE 29 BATTALION BOXER,
RUSSELL	John	PTE	/928	DARLINGTON / DARLINGTON	24/7/17	LA TARGETTE BRIT CEM	AGE 29.
RUSSELL	Wat	PTE	/615	DURHAM CITY			TO 2nd BN, CLASS Z RESERVE.
RUTHERFORD	Thos	PTE	/1075	SPENNYMOOR			DISCHARGED AFTER HARTLEPOOL.
RYDER	Syd	PTE	/1393	BISHOP AUCKLAND	20/3/19		TO 1st ARMY SCHOOL OF MORTARS, 18th, 93rd LTMB, CLASS Z RES. CPL. BORN 1891, 11 GEN HOSP CAMIERS 20/7/16
SAINT	Clem	SGT	/933		2/3/19		ATT 13 CORPS SCHOOL, 18th BN, CLASS Z RESERVE.
SALKELD	Ernst	PTE	/1093	HORDEN 10/12/14	KR para 392 31/10/17		TO 3rd BN. AGE 33
SALKELD	Ger H	PTE	/602	DURHAM CITY 25/9/14	25/3/19		TO 18th BN, CLASS Z RESERVE.
SALTMARSH	Thos	SGT	/1748	SHILDON / DARLINGTON	10/4/17	COJUEL MIL CEM	TO 15th BN.
SANDERSON	Jas J	SGT	/378	LIVERTON MINE LOFTL / DURHAM CITY	3/5/17	ARRAS MEM	AGE 26 STUDENT BEDE COLLEGE 1909.
SANTON	Ab G	PTE	/1530	DARLINGTON	2/3/19		TO 15th, 15th, 20th, 22nd BNS, CLASS Z RESERVE. LCPL TAKEN POW WITH 22nd BN
SARGEANT	Abt	CPL	/165				TO CLASS Z RESERVE.
SAYNOR	James	CPL	/590	DURHAM CITY 25/9/14	16/3/19		TO MACHINE GUN CORPS, CLASS Z RESERVE. MGC No 22775
SCAIFE	Robt	SGT	/1543	19/9/14	KR para 392 31/3/15		TO 15th, 20th, 20th, 11th BNS, CLASS Z RESERVE.
SCHOLLICK	ThosW	PTE	/386	21/9/14	KR para 392 1/4/19		DID NOT SERVE OVERSEAS.
SCORER	Geo	CPL	/387	CROOK / DURHAM CITY 25/9/14			TO 2nd BN. AGE 25
SCOTT	Har J	SGT	/591				COMMISSIONED.
SCOTT	Henry	LSGT	/844	HARTLEPOOL / WEST HARTLEPOOL	1/7/16	SERRE ROAD No 1 CEM	AGE 31 BORN BOW LONDON.
SCOTT	John	PTE	/767	THROSTON	1/7/16	THIEPVAL MEM	TO CLASS Z RESERVE.
SCOTT	Johns	PTE	/1192	EDMONDSLEY / COCKEN HALL			TO CLASS Z RESERVE.
SCOUGAL	Fred	PTE	/1351	WEST HARTLEPOOL 18/9/14	KR para 392 17/10/17		TO DEPOT. AGE 29
SCOUGAL	Herbt	SGT	/860		13/4/19		TO CLASS Z RESERVE.
SCOUGAL	James	CPL	/1135				TO 10th BN, CLASS Z RESERVE.
SCRUTTON	Chas	SGT	/1333	WEST HARTLEPOOL	8/2/19		TO 15th BN. AGE 19
SEPHTON	Robt	CPL	/1650	SUNDERLAND	17/11/16	CAMRIN CH YD EXT	
SERGEANT	Chas	PTE	/853	WEST HARTLEPOOL	KR para 392 5/2/19		TO 14th, 2nd BNS, CLASS Z RESERVE.
SEVERS	Jos	PTE	/168		2/3/19		TO CLASS Z RESERVE.
SHARPE	Wm H	SGT	/859	WEST HARTLEPOOL / DURHAM CITY 25/9/14	27/6/19		TO 18th, 12th BNS.
SHAW	Alf	LCPL	/569	DURHAM CITY	29/10/18	TEZZE BRIT CEM ITALY	TO 19th, 18th, 3rd BNS. AGE 28
SHAW	ArthE	CPL	/1363	WEST HARTLEPOOL 2/2/15	KR para 392 22/11/18		TO 12th BN, CLASS Z RESERVE.
SHAW	Fred	LCPL	/385	DURHAM CITY	4/5/19		BORN SOUTH HYLTON AGE 22. BROTHER ALSO KIA.
SHAW	Harry	LCPL	/847	PALLION / SUNDERLAND	1/7/16	THIEPVAL MEM	TO CLASS Z RESERVE.
SHAW	John	PTE	/1461	FENCEHOUSES	KR para 392 4/2/19		TO 4th BN. AGE 25
SHEPHERD	Edgar	PTE	/1491	3/5/15	KR para 392 12/7/17		TO DEPOT. AGE 33
SHERRITT	Abt	PTE	/1241	11/1/15			TO YORK & LANCASTER REGT(6th BN). Y&L No 39881.AGE 23
SHIELD	Robt	SGT	/1422	WEST HARTLEPOOL / MANCHESTER	1/2/17	VARENNES MIL CEM	TO 19th BN.
SHIELDS	Alex	PTE	/382	WEST HARTLEPOOL	KR para 392 27/1/19		TO CLASS Z RESERVE.
SHIELDS	Robt	CPL	/1282	WEST HARTLEPOOL	4/4/19		TO 20th, 1/5th BNS.
SHIPLEY	Bertr	PTE	/1582	GATESHEAD / DARLINGTON	12/12/17	TYNE COT MEM	TO DEPOT.
SHIPLEY	John	PTE	/177	4/1/15	WOUNDS 28/3/17		TO LABOUR CORPS, LAB CORPS No 237265.PUPIL ARMSTRONG COLLEGE
SIDDLE	MichE	PTE	/1067				COMMISSIONED KOYLI, 29/1/18.
SIDDLE	Norm	SGT	/1225				TO CLASS Z RESERVE. BROTHER IN RFA
SIDDLE	Wm	CPL	/175	WITTON GILBERT			
SIMMONDS	Geo	PTE	/598	EAST MURTON / DURHAM CITY 25/9/14	25/2/19		COMMISSIONED NORTHUMBERLAND FUS, 28/5/18.
SIMMONDS	Jas H	CPL	/861				TO ARMY RESERVE CLASS W. AGE 24
SIMMONS	Owen	LCPL	/867				TO 10th, 2nd BNS, CLASS Z RESERVE.
SIMPSON	Robt	PTE	/1399	FENCEHOUSES 24/9/14	KR para 392 14/11/17		TO CLASS Z RESERVE.
SIMPSON	Chas	PTE	/854	WEST HARTLEPOOL	27/4/19		TO CLASS Z RESERVE.
SIMPSON	Fred	PTE	/388	TUDHOE GRANGE	21/2/19		
SIMPSON	John	PTE	/1017	WEST HARTLEPOOL	24/2/19		TO MACHINE GUN CORPS. MGC No 22786 3rd NORTHN GEN HOSP SHEFFIELD 7/16
SIMPSON	JohnG	PTE	/1103		13/2/19		TO CLASS Z RESERVE.
SIMPSON	Jos A	SGT	/389				TO CLASS Z RESERVE.

Surname	Forename	Rank	No.	Place / Enlistment	Date	Notes
SINCLAIR	Frank	CPL	/597	DURHAM CITY 25/9/14	17/12/14	COMMISSIONED GREEN HOWARDS.
SINDEN	Wm T	PTE	/1114		KR para 392 4/2/18	TO DEPOT. AGE 22. DECEASED WHEN MR WRITTEN 1920
SKEA	James	SGT	/1570	SUNDERLAND	9/4/19	TO 14th BN. AGE 34
SKILBECK	Andrw	PTE	/612	MURTON	23/5/19	TO 18th BN. CLASS Z RESERVE.
SLACK	WattC	PTE	/864	DURHAM CITY 25/9/14		TO LABOUR CORPS, CLASS Z RESERVE. LAB CORPS No 404597
SLATER	WattR	PTE	/593	DURHAM CITY 25/9/14	16/3/19	COMMISSIONED NORTHUMBERLAND FUS(25th BN) 5/1/15. WOUNDED IN KNEE WITH TI
SLATER	Thos	PTE	/596	DURHAM CITY 25/9/14		TO CLASS Z RESERVE.
SMELT	Geo	PTE	/1179			COMMISSIONED 25/6/18. LSGT
SMITH	Chris	PTE	/162	DARLINGTON	KR para 392 14/5/19	TO COMMAND DEPOT RIPON, 3rd BN.
SMITH	Arth	PTE	/1764	DARLINGTON	25/9/47 BRONFAY FARM MIL CEM	TO 14th BN. AGE 18
SMITH	Chas	PTE	/176	DARLINGTON	19/4/19	ATT 93rd LIGHT TRENCH MORTAR BTY,15th,19th BNS, CLASS Z RES. CPL BUGLER
SMITH	Edwin	PTE	/1486	SUNDERLAND		TO 16th, 14th, 2nd BNS, CLASS Z RESERVE AGE 22
SMITH	Ernst	PTE	/1283	BRANCEPETH CASTLE DURHAM CITY 25/9/14	DIS 11/4/19 DIED 4/11/20 MEREKNOLLS CE	TO 18th BN. CLASS Z RESERVE.
SMITH	Fred	PTE	/603	SHINEY ROW	8/10/16 FABOURG D'AMIENS	COMMISSIONED 23rd BN(7/11/15), TO 19th BN. CQMS,BEDE STUDENT,TEACHER GATESHEAD, CRICKETER BURNMOORE CC
SMITH	Fred	SGT	/946	SUNDERLAND	27/4/18 BELGIAN BATTERY CORNER CEM	
SMITH	Fred	CPL	/1579	SUNDERLAND	27/4/18 BELGIAN BATTERY CORNER CEM	TO 15th, 2nd BNS, ATT 1st ARMY MORTAR SCHOOL, 18th LTMB.
SMITH	Geo	PTE	/1226	GRANGE IRON WORKS SUNDERLAND	19/9/18 LA KREULE MIL CEM HAZEBROUCI	AGE 25.ALSO AT 65 RYHOPE STREET NORTH RYHOPE COLLIERY. COMMISSIONED 27/8/17.
SMITH	Geo C	LCPL	/945	NEW WASHINGTON	2/10/14	TO UK FOR COMMISSION. CONVICTED BY THE CIVIL POWER, 3 MNTHS IN PRISON
SMITH	Geo V	PTE	/801	DURHAM CITY 25/9/14		TO CLASS Z RESERVE. REGIMENTAL POLICE. CHILTON MOOR HOSP 5/2/15
SMITH	Harri	LCPL	/164	DARLINGTON		COMMISSIONED YORK & LANCASTER REGT, 17/9/17.
SMITH	Jas D	SGT	/851	STANLEY	5/3/19	TO CLASS Z RESERVE.
SMITH	John	PTE	/161	DARLINGTON	16/12/19	TO CLASS Z RESERVE.
SMITH	John	PTE	/932		1/5/19	TO CLASS Z RESERVE.
SMITH	Sam	PTE	/979			TO 16th, 11th, 18th BNS, ATT 13 CORPS HQ, WORK CAMP, Z RES.
SMITH	Thos	PTE	/608	DURHAM CITY 25/9/14	KR para 392 26/1/15	DID NOT SERVE OVERSEAS.
SMITH	Wm	PTE	/1528	DARLINGTON	1/10/16 GROVETOWN CEM	TO 14th BN. AGE 25
SMITH	Wm A	PTE	/856	RICHMOND YORKS		COMMISSIONED 30/10/17.
SMITH	Wm T	PTE	/606	DURHAM CITY 25/9/14	29/3/19	TO 18th, 20th BNS, CLASS Z RESERVE. RESIDENT 13 SIDEGATE 1918, SERVING 22nd BN
SMITHARD	Jas B	PTE	/160	DURHAM CITY 25/9/14	19/5/19	TO 20th, 20th BN, CLASS Z RESERVE.
SMURTHWAITE	Wm	PTE	/594	BEARPARK	1/7/16 EUSTON ROAD CEM COLINCAMPS WOUNDS 14/12/16	BORN WEST STANLEY.
SNAITH	Frank	PTE	/1374	DURHAM CITY 25/9/14	31/5/15	TO DEPOT.
SNOW	Thos	PTE	/604	DURHAM CITY 25/9/14	11/4/18 LE GRAND BEAUMART	TO 18th BN. AGE 223
SNOWBALL	Phil	CPL	/379	SPENNYMOOR	4/7/16 THIEPVAL MEM	BORN BISHOP AUCKLAND, AGE 22.
SOULSBY	Alf	PTE	/1648	SUNDERLAND	4/2/17 CAMBRIN MIL CEM	TO 2nd BN. AGE 36
SOUTHERN	Thos	PTE	/1420		24/3/19	TO CLASS Z RESERVE.
SOWERBY	Jos	PTE	/159	BISHOP AUCKLAND	12/4/18 LE GRAND BEAUMART	AGE 38
SPALDING	Ralph	PTE	/1522	DURHAM CITY		TO 20th, 2nd, 19th, CLASS Z RESERVE. 139 FLD AMB 20/11/16 EVAC 41 DRS 21/11 AGE 25.
SPARK	Henry	PTE	/1104	WEST HARTLEPOOL	13/1/17 VARENNES MIL CEM	TO ARMY RESERVE CLASS W. AGE 22
SPALDING	Geo	PTE	/845	WEST HARTLEPOOL	KR para 392 28/7/17	COMMISSIONED 27/11/17.
SPARK	Wm C	SGT	/154	DARLINGTON	11/3/19	TO 19th, 20th, 19th BNS, CLASS Z RESERVE.
SPEEDY	John	PTE	/174		29/1/19	
SPENCE	Jos	PTE	/1006	WEST HARTLEPOOL	16/9/16 THIEPVAL MEM	TO 15th BN. AGE 31
SPENCE	Wm H	LCPL	/1675	DARLINGTON	10/5/15	TO CLASS Z RESERVE.
SPINK	Sam	CPL	/155	WEST HARTLEPOOL	KR para 392 6/3/19	TO 13th BN, ARMY RESERVE CLASS P.
SPOONER	James	PTE	/1510	WEST HARTLEPOOL	16/9/16 THIEPVAL MEM	TO 15th BN. AGE 31
SPOORS	Frank	PTE	/1676	EAST HOWLE	KR para 392 13/5/17	TO DEPOT.
SQUIRES	Reg	PTE	/173	CARLISLE	23/11/17 ANNEUX BRIT CEM	COMM 30/8/17, TO YORKSHIRE REGT(13th BN).AGE 26 BORN MARYPORT. PUPI; HARTLEY UNIV SOUTHAMPTON
STAFFORD	ThosW	PTE	/384			COMMISSIONED 5/2/19.
STANFIELD	Harld	SGT	/609	DURHAM CITY 25/9/14	KR para 392 18/6/18	
STANLEY	Harld	SGT	/609	HETTON DOWNS	KR para 392 18/6/18	
STELLING	John	LCPL	/1441		7/4/15	TO 20th BN. DEPOT. AGE 30

Surname	First	Rank	Number	Place	Enlisted	Date / Memorial	Notes
STEPHENSON	Watt	PTE	/1151				TO 1/6th, 11th BNS. CLASS Z RESERVE.
STEVENSON	Geo	PTE	/1019				COMMISSIONED EAST YORKSHIRE REGT. AGE 28
STEWART	ThosA	PTE	/852			21/3/19	TO 15th BN.
STEWART	Allan	PTE	/735	WEST HARTLEPOOL	19/10/14	OTITUS MEDIA 28/1/19	TO DEPOT.
STEWART	Wm T	PTE	/846		WEST HARTLEPOOL	1/7/16 THIEPVAL MEM	DID NOT SERVE OVERSEAS.
STIRLING	Malc	PTE	/868		18/9/14	KR para 392 8/3/17	TO CLASS Z RESERVE.
STOBBS	Jos	PTE	/1007	WITTON LE WEAR	26/9/14	CHRONIC ASTHMA. 9/3/15	TO 18th BN. BORN NEWFIELD AGE 21
STOBBS	Thos	PTE	/605	CHESTER LE STREET	DURHAM CITY 25/9/14	28/7/16 ST VAAST POST MIL CEM	DID NOT SERVE OVERSEAS.
STODDART	Swint	PTE	/862		26/9/14	IRREGULAR HEART 26/1/15	
STOKES	A E	LCPL	/167	DARLINGTON			TO ARMY RESERVE CLASS P. AGE 35
STOKES	Sam	PTE	/1319		26/1/15	KR para 392 30/1/17	COMMISSIONED.
STOKOE	Wm	SGT	/592		DURHAM CITY 25/9/14		TO CLASS Z RESERVE.
STOREY	Ralph	CPL	/1117			16/3/19	COMMISSIONED 31/7/17
STOTT	Bert	SGT	/866				TO CLASS Z RESERVE.
STOTT	Geo	SGT	/611	FERRYHILL VILLAGE	DURHAM CITY 25/9/14	13/1/19	BORN EASINGTON.
STRATFORD	Thos	LSGT	/810	EAST HOWLE	DURHAM CITY 25/9/14	3/5/17 ARRAS MEM	DID NOT SERVE OVERSEAS.
STRINGER	Jos	PTE	/843	SUNDERLAND	25/9/14	KR para 392 9/3/15	IN XIII PLTN. AGE 24.
STRONG	JohnW	PTE	/1254	WINGATE	DEAF HILL	12/4/18 PLOEGSTEERT MEM	ATT 3rd ENTRENCHING BN. 18th BN.
STUART	Henry	LCPL	/1496	LOW SPENNYMOOR	SPENNYMOOR	3/5/17 ARRAS MEM	TO 4th BN.
STUBBINS	Jos	PTE	/968		26/10/14	KR para 392 8/4/18	COMMISSIONED 29/1/18.
STUBBS	John	CPL	/1470				DID NOT SERVE OVERSEAS.
SUGGETT	Thos	PTE	/1754		11/8/15		COMMISSIONED 28/5/18.
SUMMERBELL	AlexW	PTE	/607	SUNDERLAND	DURHAM CITY 25/9/14	KR para 392 18/4/16	TO 21st BN. DID NOT SERVE OVERSEAS
SURTEES	Ruben	CPL	/865		22/9/14		COMMISSIONED 22/2/15.
SUTCLIFFE	Fred	PTE	/595		DURHAM CITY 25/9/14	HERNIA 2/7/16	TO CLASS Z RESERVE.
SUTTIE	EdmdD	LCPL	/166			9/2/19	TO CLASS Z RESERVE.
SUTTON	Levi	PTE	/163	DARLINGTON		20/4/16.SUCRERIE MIL CEM	AGE 36.
SWAILES	Wm J	PTE	/172	CATCHGATE		13/1/19	TO CLASS Z RESERVE.
SWAINSTON	Percy	PTE	/169	DARLINGTON			TO 20th, 19th, 11th, 1/6th BNS. CLASS Z RESERVE.
SWAN	Robt	PTE	/153	DARLINGTON		3/9/16 THIEPVAL MEM	TO WEST YORKSHIRE REGIMENT(1/6th BN). W YORKS No 7184.BORN HOUGHTON LE SKERNE
SWANN	Roland	PTE	/1724	DARLINGTON	DURHAM CITY	22/5/16 ETAPLES MIL CEM	TO 15th BN. AGE 25 DIED OF CEREBRO SPINAL FEVER AGE 21.
SWEETING	Chas	PTE	/1193	HEBBURN COLLIERY	DURHAM CITY	13/5/17 DUISANS BRIT CEM	TO 20th, 18th, 15th, CLASS Z RESERVE.
SWINDLEY	Jos	PTE	/1037			1/3/19	TO 13th, 22nd BNS, CLASS Z RESERVE.
SYNNOTT	Pierc	PTE	/858			16/3/19	COMMISSIONED 31/12/14.
TAIT	Alex	PTE	/391	COXHOE	2/10/14		TO 14th BN, CLASS Z RESERVE.
TAIT	Robt	SGT	/955	SOUTH SHIELDS		8/3/19	TO UK FOR COMMISSION, STILL SERVING 15/3/20.
TARREN	Wm	SGT	/1227	WINGATE			AGE 35.
TATE	Chas	CPL	/875		18/9/14	MYALGIA 28/6/19	13 PLATOON AGE 22.
TAYLERSON	Robt	LCPL	/961	WEST HARTLEPOOL	WEST HARTLEPOOL	1/7/16 SERRE ROAD No 1 CEM	TO CLASS Z RESERVE.
TAYLOR	Herbt	PTE	/178			27/2/19	
TAYLOR	John	PTE	/1450			KR para 392	TO 20th, 18th BNS. BORN SPENNYMOOR
TAYLOR	JohnE	LCPL	/1659	SUNDERLAND	SUNDERLAND	26/5/17 BISHOPWEARMOUTH CEM	ATT 3rd ENTRENCHING BN. 18th BN. AGE 33
TAYLOR	Wm	PTE	/625	BRANDON COLLIERY	DURHAM CITY 25/9/14	3/5/17 ARRAS MEM	TO LABOUR CORPS. LAB CORPS No 400086
TAYLOR	Wm	PTE	/878			KR para 392 4/6/18	TO 18th BN, CLASS Z RESERVE. SGT
TAYLOR	Wm	CPL	/1152	CROOK		1/3/19	TO CLASS Z RESERVE.
TAYLOR	Wm	SGT	/1243				TO CLASS Z RESERVE.
TAYLOR	Wm A	LCPL	/1068			15/3/19	TO 15th BN. SGT
TEASDALE	Chas	PTE	/1370			KR para 392 3/12/19	COMMISSIONED 27/11/17.
TEASDALE	Wm	CPL	/182		24/7/15	KR para 392 4/1/18	TO 20th BN. DEPOT. AGE 21
TEASDALE	Wm	PTE	/1697	DAWDON	13/1/15	KR para 392 23/4/19	TO ARMY RESERVE CLASS P. AGE 23
TEMPLE	Fred	CPL	/1255		17/12/14	KR para 392 14/8/17	TO 3rd BN. AGE 22
THAYNE	James	PTE	/1115				

Surname	Forename	Rank	No.	Residence	Enlisted	Died / Memorial	Remarks
THOMAS	FredR	PTE	/1481	SHINEY ROW		28/7/16 ST VAAST POST MIL CEM	ATT 3rd ENTRENCHING BN. 18th BN. BORN PENSHAW AGE 20
THOMAS	Herbt	PTE	/621	BRANCEPETH CASTLE	DURHAM CITY 25/9/14	KR para 392 8/5/18	TO 18th BN. AGE 28 COMMISSIONED 25/6/18
THOMAS	Ivor	LCPL	/177				DID NOT SERVE OVERSEAS.
THOMPSON	Bertr	PTE	/395		23/9/14	SICK 15/12/14	
THOMPSON	Harry	LCPL	/1049	MIDDLESBROUGH	DARLINGTON	1/7/18 THIEPVAL MEM	TO 15th BN. AGE 22
THOMPSON	Harry	PTE	/1749	STAINDROP	DARLINGTON	2/10/17 TYNE COT MEM	TO ARMY RESERVE CLASS P. AGE 35
THOMPSON	Herbt	LCPL	/619	DURHAM CITY	DURHAM CITY 25/9/14	KR para 392 25/6/17	TO 20th, 18th BNS, CLASS Z RESERVE.
THOMPSON	John	PTE	/879			5/4/19	TO LABOUR CORPS. TO UNIV HOSP SOUTHAMPTON 7/7/16 LAB CORPS No 272002 RESIDENT CROOK 1914
THOMPSON	JohnG	PTE	/617	DURHAM CITY	DURHAM CITY 25/9/14	KR para 392 12/6/19	COMMISSIONED 8/9/18 STUDENT BEDE COLLEGE 1910
THOMPSON	Jos F	CPL	/622	HIGH HESKETT CARLIS	DURHAM CITY 25/9/14	3/5/17 ARRAS MEM	
THOMPSON	RichN	SGT	/397	SILKSWORTH		11/10/18 ST SEVER CEM EXT ROUEN	TO 13th BN. AGE 26
THOMPSON	RobA	PTE	/874	DURHAM CITY	DURHAM CITY 25/9/14		TO NORTH STAFFORDSHIRE REGT(8th BN).
THOMPSON	Rupt	PTE	/624	NEW SEAHAM	COCKEN HALL	3/8/15 ST MARY'S SEAHAM	
THOMPSON	Stan	PTE	/1682	DURHAM CITY	DURHAM CITY 25/9/14	18/2/19	TO 6th BN. TO CLASS Z RES SHIRE HALL 1914. WOUNDE IN FACE, HOCKEY PLAYER
THOMPSON	Wilf	LCPL	/623	LANCHESTER		KR para 392 21/12/18	TO 18th, 11th BNS. AGE 30
THOMPSON	Wm H	PTE	/616	WEST HARTLEPOOL		1/7/16 SERRE ROAD No 1 CEM	ATT 3rd ENTRENCHING BN, TO 18th BN. AGE 21
THORNTON	Abt	PTE	/882	SKELTON IN CLEVELAN	WEST HARTLEPOOL	1/7/16 SERRE ROAD No 1 CEM	AGE 24.
THORNTON	Chas	PTE	/1306	WEST HARTLEPOOL		5/3/19	TO CLASS Z RESERVE.
THORPE	Fred	PTE	/1655	DARLINGTON			TO CLASS Z RESERVE.
THUBRON	Cecil	PTE	/180			30/1/19	COMMISSIONED 17/3/15. PLAYED FOR BARNSLEY AFC
TIMMS	Herbt	PTE	/390	DURHAM CITY		11/4/19	ATT 93 LIGHT TRENCH MORTAR BTY. ATT LTMB 25th DIV. CLASS Z RES
TINDALE	ThosW	PTE	/627	FISHBURN	DURHAM CITY 25/9/14	KR para 392 10/11/17	TO CLASS Z RESERVE.
TINKLER	Chas	PTE	/980		18/1/15	26/4/18 POZIERES MEM	TO 20th BN PRIOR TO EMBARKATION. 3rd BN. AGE 39
TIPLING	JohnW	PTE	/1332	DURHAM CITY	DURHAM CITY 25/9/14	29/3/19	TO 18th, 18th, 14th, 22nd BNS. CHILTON MOOR HOSP 28/2/15
TODD	Chas	LCPL	/615	BROWNEY COLLIERY	11/2/15		TO 21st(29/7/15), 18th. DEPOT, 3rd, 2nd, DEPOT, 3rd BNS EGYPT 6/12/15-4/3/16, FRANCE 5/3/16-7/7/16-10/12/16-28/11/18
TOMBLING	Jos	PTE	/1392	WEST HARTLEPOOL		21/2/19	COMMISSIONED 23/5/15.
TOMS	James	PTE	/877				TO 20th, 20th, 20th BN, CLASS Z RESERVE.
TOPPIN	Shir	CPL	/1008	CHESTER LE STREET	DURHAM CITY 25/9/14	KR para 392 19/2/19	TO 18th BN, CLASS Z RESERVE.
TOPPING	Robt	LCPL	/614	WEST HARTLEPOOL			TO LABOUR CORPS(298 LAB COY).
TOSE	John	PTE	/947	WEST HARTLEPOOL		KR para 392 8/10/18	TO 2nd BN. CLASS Z RESERVE.
TOSE	Vic C	PTE	/873	HETTON LE HOLE	1/5/15		AGE 27.
TOSE	Wm	RSM	/181	WEST HARTLEPOOL		28/7/16 ST VAAST POST MIL CEM	COMMISSIONED 21/1/15. CAPTAIN DLI 1918
TREMBLE	ThosW	PTE	/1485	WEST HARTLEPOOL		KR para 392 8/12/17	COMMISSIONED 17/5/15. LIEUTENANT 267 PUNJABIS NWFRONTIER 1918 LETTER IN DA.
TRENCHMANN	Adolp	PTE	/396	DURHAM CITY		27/5/18 SOISSONS MEM	
TRENCHMANN	Albt	PTE	/392	STILLINGTON	19/9/14		TO ARMY RESERVE CLASS W. AGE 22
TREVITT	Sem	PTE	/620	WEST HARTLEPOOL		1/7/16 THIEPVAL MEM	
TROTTER	Chris	PTE	/869	WEST HARTLEPOOL	DURHAM CITY 25/9/14	16/12/14 ST PATRICKS CH YD WINLATON	
TURNBULL	Fm E	LSGT	/1284	GATESHEAD	SEAHAM HARBOUR	3/5/17 ARRAS MEM	
TURNBULL	Johns	PTE	/876	SEAHAM HARBOUR	NEWCASTLE	13/1/19	COMMISSIONED 27/11/17 DLI, ATT WILTSHIRE REGT(1st BN). AGE 26 WOUNDED SPINE AT SERRE.
TURNBULL	Jos H	PTE	/1285	GOSFORTH	SOUTH SHIELDS		TO 11th, 19th BNS, CLASS Z RESERVE.
TURNBULL	Rich	LCPL	/871	CORBRIDGE	DURHAM CITY 25/9/14	KR para 392 12/1/18	
TURNER	Les D	PTE	/398	SACRISTON		1/7/16 THIEPVAL MEM	AGE 24 BORN HEATON LNER CLERK OPERATING DEPOT NEWCASTLE
TWEDDELL	Wm	PTE	/1726	BISHOP AUCKLAND	SOUTH SHIELDS	28/9/17 ROCLINCOURT MIL CEM	AGE 31
TWEDDLE	Wm	PTE	/625		DURHAM CITY 25/9/14	24/3/19	TO 18th BN, CLASS Z RESERVE.
VART	Paul	LCPL	/188	SADBERGE	21/9/14	29/4/19	TO 20th, 15th, 20th, 52nd BNS.
VASEY	Wm O	PTE	/400		21/8/14		TO DEPOT.
VICKERS	Arth	LCPL	/401	SPENNYMOOR			STUDENT BEDE COLLEGE 1907
VOCKNICH	ThosR	PTE	/981	NORTH SHIELDS	SOUTH SHIELDS		LCPL AGE 23 LNER FREIGHT SHUNTER TYNEDOCK
WAGGOTT	David	PTE	/205				TO CLASS Z RESERVE.
WAKE	Wm H	PTE	/899				TO LABOUR CORPS, CLASS Z RESERVE. LAB CORPS No 32259
WAKEFIELD	Edmd	SGT	/1289	SEAHAM		25/1/19	TO CLASS Z RESERVE.
WAKEFIELD	Thos	LCPL	/1288	SILKSWORTH	SUNDERLAND	19/7/18 PLOEGSTEERT MEM	BORN SEAHAM HARBOUR AGE 31.

Surname	Forename	Rank	No.	Residence	Enlistment	Casualty / Date	Notes
WALKER	Cla H	PTE	/404	WEST HARTLEPOOL			TO 7 OFFICER CADET BN, COMMISSIONED 24/9/18. LCPL
WALKER	Fred	PTE	/200				TO CLASS Z RESERVE.
WALKER	FredT	PTE	/647	GOSFORTH	DURHAM CITY 25/9/14	16/1/19	COMMISSIONED.
WALKER	Herbt	PTE	/1089	YORK	YORK	1/7/16 THIEPVAL MEM	
WALKER	Levi	PTE	/935			20/1/19	TO CLASS Z RESERVE.
WALKER	Normn	PTE	/1667	PALLION	SUNDERLAND	2/10/16 BRONFAY FARM MIL CEM	TO 20th BN. BORN SILKSWORTH AGE 24
WALKER	Wm	PTE	/885	RYHOPE	SUNDERLAND	1/7/16 THIEPVAL MEM	TO 19th BN. CLASS Z RESERVE.
WALKER	Wm	CSM	/1610	SALFORD			DID NOT SERVE OVERSEAS.
WALKER	Wm E	PTE	/1756		12/8/15		COMMISSIONED 17/12/17.
WALL	John	PTE	/900			KR para 392 18/4/16	TO 3rd BN. AGE 30
WALL	John	PTE	/409	FERRYHILL	19/9/14	KR para 392 19/10/17	TO 13th BN. CPL AGE 38
WALLACE	Fredk	PTE	/1339	STOCKTON	30/1/15	KR para 392 13/7/18	DIS 15/2/19 DIED 1/9/20 OXBRIDGE LANE C ATT 31st DIV ASSISTANT PROVOST MARSHALL, 18th, CLASS Z RES. DIED OF PNEUMONIA
WALLACE	Percy	PTE	/1364	HAVERTON HILL		10/3/19	TO CLASS Z RESERVE.
WALLER	ArthA	LCPL	/201	DURHAM CITY			TO CLASS Z RESERVE.
WALTERS	James	LCPL	/193	WEST HARTLEPOOL	STOCKTON	3/3/17 VARRENNES MIL CEM	TO 14th, 18th BNS. AGE 28
WALTON	Issac	LCPL	/648	DARLINGTON	DURHAM CITY 25/9/14	KR para 392 16/11/17	ATT 3rd ENTRENCHING BN, 18th, 13th, 13th BNS, CLASS Z RES.
WALTON	James	PTE	/1488	DARLINGTON		3/5/17 ARRAS MEM	TO HDL
WALTON	John	PTE	/1765	BISHOP AUCKLAND	COCKEN HALL	16/1/19	TO CLASS Z RESERVE.
WALTON	Robt	PTE	/1207	WEST HARTLEPOOL			TO 15th BN.
WALTON	Valt	SGT	/866				
WANDLESS	J	PTE	/1335	WEST HARTLEPOOL	2/11/14	1/7/16 THIEPVAL MEM	
WARD	Alf	PTE	/403			VDH 26/8/16	TO DEPOT.
WARD	Geo	PTE	/896			9/3/19	TO CLASS Z RESERVE.
WARD	Jas	PTE	/1256	ROOKHOPE		13/1/19	TO 18th, ATT R ENGINEERS(257 TUN COY), 18th BN, CLASS Z RES.
WARD	JohnG	PTE	/1340	SHINEY ROW		18/2/19	COMMISSIONED 30/11/18. SGT
WARD	JohnM	PTE	/644	WEST HARTLEPOOL		19/2/19	ATT 93rd LIGHT TRENCH MORTAR BATTERY. TO 3rd BN. CLASS Z RES
WARD	Wilf	PTE	/1287	WESTGATE		15/2/19	TO CLASS Z RESERVE.
WARD	Wm	LCPL	/1022		DURHAM CITY 25/9/14	KR para 392 25/10/18	TO CLASS Z RESERVE. WOII CSM
WARNOCK	John	PTE	/1444			KR para 392 3/6/19	TO CLASS Z RESERVE.
WARWICK	Issac	CPL	/190		18/9/14		TO ARMY RESERVE CLASS W.
WARWICK	Jacqu	SGT	/189		21/9/14	22/8/17 TYNE COT MEM	STUDENT BEDE COLLEGE 1904, HOSP ALNWICK 1916
WATERHOUSE	Jos	PTE	/1072	SPENNYMOOR	SPENNYMOOR		ATT 3rd ENTRENCHING BN, 18th BN, CLASS Z RESERVE.
WATERS	Jos	PTE	/204	DURHAM CITY	DURHAM CITY 25/9/14	KR para 392 27/1/19	TO 10th BN. BORN WHITWORTH
WATKIN	Wilf	SGT	/638			KR para 392 18/12/17	COMMISSIONED.
WATKIN	Wm	PTE	/646		3/2/15	KR para 392 1/9/17	
WATSON	Alex	PTE	/1380	DARLINGTON	18/9/14		DID NOT SERVE OVERSEAS.
WATSON	James	PTE	/902				DID NOT SERVE OVERSEAS.
WATSON	John	LCPL	/207			19/4/19	TO ARMY RESERVE CLASS W. AGE 21. 2nd SOUTHERN GEN HOSP BRISTOL 8/7/16
WATSON	Wm	PTE	/405				TO CLASS Z RESERVE.
WATSON	Wm A	PTE	/639	DURHAM CITY	DURHAM CITY 25/9/14	17/5/17 ARRAS MEM	COMMISSIONED 7/11/15.
WATT	Alf	CPL	/197	DARLINGTON	DARLINGTON 18/9/14		TO 20th BN PRIOR TO EMBARKATION.
WATT	Wm W	PTE	/887	WEST HARTLEPOOL		KR para 392 8/11/18	TO 15th, 18th BNS. AGE 28. LIVING 19 KENSINGTON TERRACE DARLINGTON 1914
WEAR	Arth	SGT	/122			23/2/19	
WEARMOUTH	Fred	PTE	/417	WOLSINGHAM			COMMISSIONED YORK & LANCASTER REGT.
WEARMOUTH	JohnR	PTE	/1090			KR para 392 28/1/19	TO CLASS Z RESERVE. ACPL
WEARS	Robt	PTE	/1086	WEST HARTLEPOOL		22/2/19	
WEATHERALL	Robt	PTE	/907			19/3/19	TO WEST YORKS REGT(1/6th 15/17th BNS) ATT EAST LANCS(11th) TO 18DLI, CLASS Z RESERVE. W YORKS No 43643
WEATHERLEY	Wm J	PTE	/402			29/1/19	
WEAVER	ThosA	PTE	/210	DARLINGTON	DARLINGTON	1/8/16 LONGUENESSE SOUVENIR CEM	TO CLASS Z RESERVE. STUDENT BEDE COLLEGE 1908

Surname	Forename	Rank	No	Birthplace	Enlisted	Casualty / Discharge	Notes
WEBB	Chas	PTE	/208	WOODFORD NORFOLK	DARLINGTON 18/9/14	KR para 392 4/2/16	TO 21st BN. AGE 22, TO MIL HOSP FOVANT CAMP TUBERCULOSIS, 6', 147Lbs
WEBB	Stan	PTE	/209			9/3/19	TO CLASS Z RESERVE.
WEBSTER	Robt	PTE	/888	WEST HARTLEPOOL		1/7/16 THIEPVAL MEM	TO 18th, 10th(OCT 16), 19th, 10th BNS, CLASS Z RES IN 4 SECTION 13 PLATOON
WEIGHELL	Herbt	PTE	/963	SOUTHWICK	SUNDERLAND		
WELFORD	Chas	PTE	/630		DURHAM CITY 25/9/14		COMMISSIONED 14/4/15.
WELTON	Geo	PTE	/1010	WEST HARTLEPOOL			
WEST	Fred	CQMS	/903	HIGH MOORSLEY	HOUGHTON LE SPRING	KR para 392 30/1/19	TO CLASS Z RESERVE.
WESTGARTH	Thos	PTE	/1316	COUNDON		7/6/19	ATT 3rd ENTRENCHING BN, 18th BN. IN VI PLTN.AGE 22
WESTON	Thos	PTE	/1404	SUNDERLAND	SUNDERLAND	20/1/19	TO CLASS Z RESERVE.
WETHERELL	Walt	PTE	/934	BRANCEPETH	DURHAM CITY 25/9/14	12/7/16 BISHOPWEARMOUTH CEM	
WHARF	Walt	PTE	/653	RIPON	18/9/14		ATT 3rd ENTRENCHING BN, 18th BN, CLASS Z RESERVE.
WHARTON	James	LSGT	/410	WEST HARTLEPOOL		WOUNDS 25/4/17	TO MACHINE GUN CORPS MGC No 22773 COMM ASC 2nd Lt
WHEELWRIGHT	Robt	PTE	/908	WEST HARTLEPOOL	WEST HARTLEPOOL	KR para 392 28/1/19	TO DEPOT. LOST RIGHT ARM IN SHELL EXPLOSION
WHITE	Alf	LCPL	/889			16/8/16 LE TOURET MIL CEM	AGE 18.
WHITE	Alf A	PTE	/1020	WEST HARTLEPOOL	10/5/15	KR para 392 11/2/19	DID NOT SERVE OVERSEAS.
WHITEHEAD	John	SGT	/512	MIDDLESBROUGH		16/2/19	TO CLASS Z RESERVE. CQMS
WHITFIELD	Geo	SGT	/416	DURHAM CITY	DURHAM CITY 25/9/14	KR para 392 23/1/17	TO DEPOT. AGE 31
WHITFIELD	Jos	PTE	/645	WITTON PARK	DURHAM CITY	19/7/18 AVAL WOOD MIL CEM	BORN FERRYHILL
WHITTAKER	Norm	SGT	/1021		10/5/15	KR para 392 27/10/16	TO 15th BN, DEPOT. AGE 24
WHITTON	Rich	PTE	/1524	CHILTON		17/1/19	TO CLASS Z RESERVE.
WICK	Wm	PTE	/206	BROWNEY COLLIERY	DURHAM CITY 25/9/14	KR para 392 2/4/19	AGE 39.
WIGGINS	Geo D	PTE	/649	SEAHAM HARBOUR			COMMISSIONED 17/12/17.
WILKINSON	Alf	PTE	/1089	FERRYHILL VILLAGE	DURHAM CITY 2/10/14	1/3/17 GOMMECOURT BRIT CEM No 2	BORN WEST CORNFORTH.
WILKINSON	Ben	PTE	/936			13/6/19	TO CLASS Z RESERVE.
WILKINSON	Geo A	PTE	/418	FERRYHILL STATION	DURHAM CITY 25/9/14	KR para 392 6/12/17	TO ARMY RESERVE CLASS W. AGE 33
WILKINSON	JohnG	CPL	/652	CROOK	4/1/15	KR para 392 3/7/19	TO 20th BN, CHILTON MOOR HOSP 4/15
WILKINSON	Jos	CPL	/1153				TO CLASS Z RESERVE.
WILKINSON	Jos	PTE	/890			KR para 392 24/4/18	TO 18th, 15th, 1/9th BNS, CLASS Z RESERVE.
WILKINSON	Ray H	PTE	/1375		21/9/14	21/3/19	TO ARMY RESERVE CLASS P. AGE 29.STUDENT BEDE COLLEGE 1910
WILKINSON	Wm	PTE	/1070				TO CLASS Z RESERVE.
WILLAN	Walk	PTE	/419	DURHAM CITY			TO 15th, 20th, 15th, 12th BNS, CLASS Z RESERVE. CPL
WILLIAMS	Fred	PTE	/1310			18/2/19	TO CLASS Z RESERVE.
WILLIAMS	James	PTE	/534	FENCEHOUSES			
WILLIAMS	John	PTE	/1209	BLACKHALL COLLIERY	FERRYHILL	29/7/16 ABBEVILLE COM CEM	AGE 27, BORN MIDDLE RAINTON. BROTHER RSM OF 21st BN.
WILLIAMS	John	PTE	/635	SOUTH CHURCH		3/7/16 DOULLENS COM CEM EXT No 1	BORN BINCHESTER AGE 22.
WILLIAMS	JohnA	PTE	/1327	MIDDLE RAINTON			COMMISSIONED 29/1/18.
WILLIAMS	JohnH	PTE	/411	CHILTON	DURHAM CITY 25/9/14	1/7/16 THIEPVAL MEM	
WILLIAMS	Monty	PTE	/1208	WEST RAINTON	2/10/14	22/2/19	BAND HUT
WILLIAMS	Thos	PTE	/1129	WEST HARTLEPOOL	WEST HARTLEPOOL	1/7/16 THIEPVAL MEM	BORN BINCHESTER.
WILLSON	Wm	PTE	/650	DURHAM CITY	DURHAM CITY 25/9/14	28/7/16 MERVILLE COM CEM	TO LABOUR CORPS, CLASS Z RESERVE. LAB CORPS No 214402
WILLSON	Robt	PTE	/1290	DURHAM CITY		30/9/18 STRAND MIL CEM	AGE 26
WILSON	Abt	PTE	/909				AGE 25.
WILSON	EdwdR	LCPL	/637	PENSHAW	COCKEN HALL		CPL.AGE 23, DURHAM CITY CRICKET CLUB.
WILSON	Geo	CPL	/633	SUNDERLAND			TO 2nd, 2nd BN, CLASS Z RESERVE.
WILSON	Geo W	PTE	/1244	PELTON FELL	DURHAM CITY 25/9/14	18/9/16 THIEPVAL MEM	TO 14th BN.
WILSON	Jhn J	PTE	/1453			DIS 24/4/19 DIED 28/11/20 BISHOPWEARMO	TO CLASS Z RESERVE.BORN NEWCASTLE
WILSON	JohnH	PTE	/937			KR para 392 16/11/17	TO ARMY RESERVE CLASS W. AGE 22
WILSON	JohnR	PTE	/641			KR para 392	ATT 3rd ENTRENCHING BN, 18th, 20th BNS.
WILSON	Robt	PTE	/1181	DURHAM CITY	DURHAM CITY 25/9/14		COMMISSIONED 13/3/15.
WILSON	Steph	RQMS	/651	BISHOP AUCKLAND	DURHAM CITY 25/9/14		COMMISSIONED.
WILSON	Tom	RQMS	/632	DURHAM CITY	DURHAM CITY 25/9/14	3/5/17 ARRAS MEM	
WILSON	Wm	CPL	/1303	COCKERTON		26/6/17 ETAPLES MIL CEM	TO 20th BN PRIOR TO EMBARKATION. AGE 32

Surname	Name	Rank	No.	Place	Place	Date	Notes
WILSON	Wm A	PTE	/1245	SHEFFIELD	WEST HARTLEPOOL	1/7/16 THIEPVAL MEM	TO LABOUR CORPS. LAB CORPS No 343793. AGE 40
WILSON	Wm H	CPL	/194	STOCKTON	STOCKTON	3/6/18 FOREST TOWN(ST ALBANS)CH YD	BORN LIVERPOOL AGE 23. NOK RIVERSDALE TERRACE 1920'S
WILSON	Wm W	LSGT	/914	SUNDERLAND	SUNDERLAND	1/7/16 THIEPVAL MEM	TO CLASS Z RESERVE.
WINN	Rolnd	SGT	/198			13/4/19	
WISE	John	PTE	/1247	DURHAM CITY	DURHAM CITY	28/7/16 ST VAAST POST MIL CEM	AGE 24, REPORT OF BURIAL BY CofE PADRE IN DA.
WISE	Syd	PTE	/202			18/4/19	TO 2nd BN, CLASS Z RESERVE.
WITHAM	Hald	PTE	/1071	MOSTON LANCS	MIDDLESBROUGH	14/7/16 MOSTON ST MARY'S CHYD	
WOOD	AbtE	PTE	/948			27/3/19	ATT "L" SPECIAL COY RE, 18th BN, CLASS Z RESERVE.
WOOD	Andw	CPL	/913	SELKIRK	SUNDERLAND	1/7/16 THIEPVAL MEM	
WOOD	Geo	LCPL	/1599		8/6/15	KR para 392 3/1/17	TO 15th BN. AGE 27
WOOD	Robt	PTE	/539				TO 11th BN, CLASS Z RESERVE.
WOODHOUSE	John	PTE	/191				
WOODWARD	Alf	LCPL	/1246	FERRYHILL	WEST HARTLEPOOL	KR para 392	
WOODWARD	Thos	PTE	/628	DURHAM CITY	DURHAM CITY 25/9/14	3/3/17 GOMMECOURT BRIT CEM No 2	
WOOLARD	Andw	PTE	/634	BROWNEY COLLIERY	DURHAM CITY 25/9/14	5/7/16 ST MARIE CEM	
WRAGG	Geo	PTE	/1725	SEDGEFIELD			
WRAY	Alf	PTE	/1466	DARLINGTON	9/4/15	KR para 392 6/6/17	TO CLASS Z RESERVE.
WRAY	Chas	PTE	/1760	BEDALE	DARLINGTON	18/9/16 THIEPVAL MEM	TO ARMY RESERVE CLASS P. AGE 29
WRAY	Robt	PTE	/1097			KR para 392 6/2/19	TO 14th BN.
WRENCH	JohnG	CPL	/407	BISHOP AUCKLAND	BISHOP AUCKLAND	16/6/17 BAILLEUL RD EAST CEM	ATT WEST YORKSHIRE REGT(1/6th BN), 18th BN. AGE 24
WRENCH	Thos	PTE	/408	BISHOP AUCKLAND	BISHOP AUCKLAND	28/9/17 ROCLINCOURT MIL CEM	AGE 28
WRIGHT	Alb B	SGT	/901	WEST HARTLEPOOL		20/3/19	TO CLASS Z RESERVE.
WRIGHT	Geo	PTE	/904	WEST HARTLEPOOL		22/3/19	TO CLASS Z RESERVE.
WRIGHT	Stan	PTE	/905	WEST HARTLEPOOL		4/3/19	ATT 93rd LIGHT TRENCH MORTAR BATTERY, CLASS Z RESERVE.
WYLD	Sam R	SGT	/1383	WITTON GILBERT	DURHAM CITY 25/9/14		COMMISSIONED 27/11/17. TO 22nd(B COY) BN. FROM BRADFORD.
YARKER	H T	LCPL	/654	SHERBURN HILL			
YORK	Ralph	PTE	/211		7/9/14	7/2/19	TO 19th, 2nd BNS, CLASS Z RESERVE.
YORKE	James	PTE	/211			KR para 392 11/9/17	TO 4th BN. AGE 24
YOUNG	BertW	SGT	/915	NEW BRANCEPETH			COMMISSIONED 14/4/18.
YOUNG	Robt	SGT	/1517	BYKER	WEST HARTLEPOOL	24/7/17 BYKER & HEATON CEM	TO 14th BN, CLASS Z RESERVE. LEFT BACK FOR SUNDERLAND AFC 1919 - 1925. AGE 38
YOUNG	Wm G	PTE	/1033	NEW HERRINGTON	25/9/14	27/6/19	TO CLASS Z RESERVE. CQMS
YOUNGER	Thos	PTE	/420				

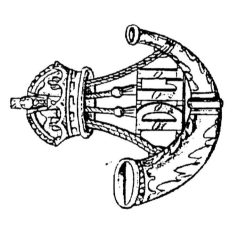

ALPHABETICAL NOMINAL ROLL OF ORIGINAL OTHER RANKS

19th (Service) Battalion Durham Light Infantry (2nd County) (Bantams) 1915 – 1919

NAME	INITIALS	RANK	NUMBER	TOWN_VILL	DATE & PLACE_ENL	CAUSE & DATE DIS DIED & BURIED	TRANSFER
ABRAM	JohnW	CPL	382	FERRYHILL			TO LABOUR CORPS, LAB CORPS No 112575
ADAMS	John	SIG	1179	BLACKHILL			TO CLASS Z RESERVE.
ADAMS	Edwd	PTE	1207	BLACKHILL	2/6/15	KR para 392 15/10/17	TO ARMY RESERVE CLASS W.
ADAMSON	Harry	PTE	675				TO LABOUR CORPS, LAB CORPS No 116712
ADAMSON	Wm	PTE	8	WEST HARTLEPOOL	WEST HARTLEPOOL	14/10/18 TYNE COT MEM	ATT NOTTS & DERBY REGT(15th BN), TO 19th BN. AGE 24
AIRSON	Paul	SGT	1321	BIRTLEY			TO CLASS Z RESERVE.
ALDERSON	Matt	PTE	291				TO LABOUR CORPS, LAB CORPS No 112569
ALDRIDGE	JohnH	PTE	678			18/7/16 THIEPVAL MEM	
ALLEN	Henry	PTE	1270	SUNDERLAND			TO LABOUR CORPS, LAB CORPS No 619751
ALLEN	Wm	PTE	1550	DARLINGTON			TO 2nd BN. BORN TUDHOE AGE 18
ALLEN	Wm	CPL	1028	HEBBURN COLLIERY	JARROW	11/8/16 HAMEL BRIT CEM	TO LABOUR CORPS, LAB CORPS No 116710
ALLISON	Geo F	PTE	1389				
ALSTON	Walt	LCPL	123			KR para 392	
ANDERSON	Alex	PTE	630	BLACKBURN LANCS	BLACKBURN	20/4/17 VANDENCOURT BRIT CEM	AGE 27.
ANDERSON	H M	PTE	221	JARROW	SUNDERLAND	13/9/16 HARBARCQ COM CEM	TO MACHINE GUN CORPS(106th MG COY), CLASS Z RESERVE.
ANDERSON	James	PTE	1282			16/7/19	
ANNISON	JohnT	PTE	170	EASINGTON LANE	HOUGHTON LE SPRING WASHINGTON 29/2/15	KR para 392	ATT 35 DIV HQ, TO 185 LAB COY, B BN TANK CORPS, LAB CORPS BASE DEPOT, 22nd BN, 19th BN. CLASS Z RESERVE
APPLEBY	Geo	LCPL	439	FATFIELD		13/5/16 MERVILLE COM CEM	BORN FERRYHILL, AGE 25
APPLETON	Robt	PTE	339			10/9/16 FABOURG D'AMIENS	5'2" AGE 28 YRS 10 MNTH MINER Z COY
ARCHBOLD	RobtT	PTE	1339				TO DEPOT.
ARCHER	Fred	PTE	1559		12/6/15	WOUNDS 7/2/17	DID NOT SERVE OVERSEAS.
ARCHER	ThosG	PTE	1567		10/8/15	KR para 392 24/3/16	TO LABOUR CORPS, LAB CORPS No 116664
ARMOUR	James	SGT	188				TO LABOUR CORPS, LAB CORPS No 112658
ARMSTRONG	Chas	PTE	169			KR para 392 7/8/17	AGE 24.
ARMSTRONG	Chas	PTE	1523		27/2/15		TO CLASS Z RESERVE.
ARMSTRONG	Femwk	PTE	1387	DAWDON	SEAHAM HARBOUR	31/3/18 ARRAS MEM	TO 20th, 19th, 19th BNS. BORN MONKWEARMOUTH
ARMSTRONG	John	LCPL	438	CASTLE EDEN	1/3/15	KR para 392 6/12/17	TO 23rd,19th BNS, ATT PB BN, 35 IBD, ORDNANCE DEPOT ETAPLES MINER AGE 29,5'0",FRESH,GREY EYES,BROWN HAIR.ARMY RES W
ARMSTRONG	Jos S	PTE	1196				TO 10th, 19th BNS, CLASS Z RESERVE.
ARMSTRONG	Rob	PTE	1403	SUNDERLAND	SUNDERLAND	8/10/16 FAUBOURG D'AMIENS	AGE 20
ARMSTRONG	Rob J	PTE	799	SPENNYMOOR	SPENNYMOOR	24/8/16 THIEPVAL MEM	
ARMSTRONG	Thos	CQMS	197				TO CLASS Z RESERVE.
ARMSTRONG	Wm	PTE	641				TO LABOUR CORPS, LAB CORPS No 111961
ATKINS	Augst	PTE	1562	MIDDLESTONE MOOR	SPENNYMOOR	24/8/18 VIS-EN-ARTOIS MEM	TO MIDDLESEX REGT(1/7th BN). AGE 25, BORN SHILDON, MDSX REGT No G/44796
ATKINSON	Edwd	PTE	370				TO LABOUR CORPS, LAB CORPS No 112662
ATKINSON	Geo	PTE	227				TO CLASS Z RESERVE
ATKINSON	John	PTE	685	GATESHEAD			TO CLASS Z RESERVE.
ATKINSON	Steph	PTE	628		8/3/15	SICK 17/8/15	DID NOT SERVE OVERSEAS.
ATKINSON	ThosW	PTE	86				TO LABOUR CORPS, LAB CORPS No 111839
AUSTIN	D	CSM	1102				TO CLASS Z RESERVE.
AUTY	Frank	PTE	533				TO LABOUR CORPS(No 9 LAB GROUP HQ) LAB CORPS No 121961
BAINBRIDGE	John	PTE	423		8/3/15	KR para 392	
BAINBRIDGE	Wm	PTE	440			SICK 17/8/15	DID NOT SERVE OVERSEAS.
BAINBRIDGE	Wm	PTE	599		22/3/15	RHEUMATISM 28/1/19	AGE 34 DID NOT SERVE OVERSEAS.
BAINS	Geo W	PTE	892		11/3/15	KR para 392 6/3/19	AGE 41.
BAINS	Wm	ASGT	1303	SOUTH SHIELDS	SOUTH SHIELDS	14/10/18 DADIZEELE NEW BRIT	TO 15th, 19th BNS.
BAKER	Tim	PTE	56	SOUTH SHIELDS	SOUTH SHIELDS	11/10/16 AVESNES LE COMTE	AGE 30.
BALDWIN	John	PTE	1621		9/10/15	KR para 392 17/9/18	TO 20th, 20th BNS. AGE 24

Surname	Forename	Rank	No	Birthplace	Enlisted	Fate / Cemetery	Remarks
BARKER	Jos	PTE	230	HESLEDEN			TO LABOUR CORPS(117 LAB COY). LAB CORPS No 112664
BARNES	Geo	PTE	935				TO LABOUR CORPS. LAB CORPS No 116820
BARRAS	Abt	PTE	1511	SOUTH SHIELDS	COCKEN HALL 2/8/15	MEDICALLY UNFIT 11/1/18	TO DEPOT, COMMAND DEPOT RIPON, RAMC(5th & 7th TRG BNS). 2 SHOSP ABBEVILLE, MANCHESTER HOSP 11/9/16, RAMC No 133693
BARTON	Richm	PTE	146	MEDOMSLEY			TO LABOUR CORPS(298, 196 COYS),19th BN, ATT RE,19th BN LAB CORPS No 124496, CLASS Z RESERVE
BATES	Math	PTE	1420			KR para 392	AGE 23 DID NOT SERVE OVERSEAS.
BATES	Thos	PTE	1375		23/6/15	AMBLYOPIA 29/1/19	TO LABOUR CORPS, R ENGINEERS, DURHAM LI. FGCM
BATTY	Wm	LCPL	298				TO 1/6th BN, CLASS Z RESERVE.
BATTY	JohnR	CPL	229		16/3/15		TO 3rd BN. AGE 30
BEATTIE	Benj	PTE	820	FENCEHOUSES		KR para 392 22/4/19	TO CLASS Z RESERVE.
BEATTIE	Hugh	PTE	642				TO 2nd BN, ATT 174 TUN COY RE, 2nd BN. BORN SOUTH SHIELDS AGE 30
BEAUMONT	Thos	PTE	1376	BYKER	NEWCASTLE 1/3/15	28/6/17 LOOS MEM	TO DEPOT. DISCHARGED KR para 392. AGE 24
BEDLINGTON	Thos	PTE	287	NEW LAMBTON	SUNDERLAND 8/3/15	22/2/17 BURIED 13/11/17 ALL SAINTS PENS	BORN SOUTH SHIELDS
BELL	Abt	PTE	195	HORDEN COLLIERY		25/7/17 TINCOURT NEW BRIT	TO 1/7th BN. AGE 22
BELL	Abt	PTE	659			KR para 392 14/3/18	TO LABOUR CORPS. LAB CORPS No 111936
BELL	Edw M	PTE	65				TO LABOUR CORPS, 19th BN. STILL SERVING 15/3/20.
BELL	JohnG	PTE	1067				TO 14th BN, CLASS Z RESERVE.
BELL	Jonth	PTE	375				TO LABOUR CORPS. LAB CORPS No 116670
BELL	RobtG	PTE	959				BORN GATESHEAD
BELL	Wm	LCPL	589	HEBBURN NEW TOWN	JARROW 14/5/15	18/7/16 DIVE COPSE CEM	TO 3rd BN. AGE 23
BELL	Wm	PTE	1094			KR para 392 22/4/18	TO 13th, ATT 203 FLD COY RE, 19th BN, CLASS Z RESERVE.
BELL	Wm	PTE	1252				TO LABOUR CORPS, LAB CORPS No 116669
BELLAMY	JohnW	PTE	1039				TO CLASS Z RESERVE.
BENNETT	Jos H	COMS	39	WEST HARTLEPOOL		24/4/17 AIX NOULETTE COM CEM	TO LABOUR CORPS. LAB CORPS No 112577
BENTHAM	Matt	PTE	62				AGE 28
BERRY	Wm	PTE	201	SOUTHWICK	SOUTHWICK		MENTIONED IN COMS PROUD'S NOTEBOOK.
BESTFORD	Wilk	PTE	441	WEST AUCKLAND	BISHOP AUCKLAND	19/8/17 TEMPLEUX LE GUERARD	TO 23rd,19th BNS,17 ASC LAB COY,LABOUR CORPS(187, 365 COYS) LAB CORPS No 111917, AWOL 19/5-26/5/15,DESERTS 12/6-23/7/15
BEWICK	Geo	PTE	897	SUNDERLAND	SUNDERLAND 21/3/15	KR para 392 11/3/19	TO SCOTTISH RIFLES. SCOT RIF No 241815
BEWICKE		PTE	925	FENCEHOUSES			TO 3rd BN, CLASS Z RESERVE.
BEWICKE	Benj	PTE	13	GATESHEAD			ATT NOTTS & DERBY REGT(15th BN), TO 19th BN.
BIBBY	Thos	PTE	325	RYHOPE	SUNDERLAND 9/3/15	23/8/16 GUILLEMONT ROAD CEM	TO ARMY RESERVE CLASS P. AGE 21
BLACK	Ernst	SGT	646			KR para 392 3/4/17	TO LABOUR CORPS. LAB CORPS No 116666
BLACKBURN	Wm	CPL	605				ATT 35 IBD, TO 19th, 10th, 2nd, 15th BNS, CLASS Z RESERVE.
BLACKLOCK	Jos	LCPL	988				TO 18th, 14th, 18th BNS, CLASS Z RESERVE.
BLAKEMAN	Geo	PTE	1074				TO 20th, 3rd BNS. AGE 22
BLAKEY	NichT	PTE	290		1/3/15	KR para 392 6/5/18	TO LABOUR CORPS(134 DLI LAB COY). LAB CORPS No 403869,BOILER MAKER AGE 26
BLAND	HendJ	PTE	878	SUNDERLAND	WEST HARTLEPOOL 21/3/15	31/10/18 DUNHALLOW ADS CEM	TO LABOUR CORPS(188 LAB COY, LAB BUREAU POPERINGHE, 185 COY) LAB CORPS No 112578.MINER AGE 36,107 F AMB 27/12/16 SCABIES
BLAND	Henry	PTE	32	LEADGATE	15/3/15	6/3/19.	TO 19th, 10th, 1/6th BNS.
BLAND	Les	PTE	1570			KR para 392	TO LABOUR CORPS. LAB CORPS No 111964
BLENKINSOPP	Robt	PTE	81				ATT 173 & 12 FLD COYS RE, W YORKS(1/6th) 14th BN. AGE 34 BORN SACRISTON
BLOOMFIELD	Edwd	PTE	122	DURHAM CITY	DURHAM	20/11/17 CAMBRAI MEM	TO LABOUR CORPS. LAB CORPS No 112074
BODDY	Arth	PTE	315	FYLANDS			DID NOT SERVE OVERSEAS.
BOLAN	Geo	PTE	446		27/2/15	SICK 21/7/15	TO 2nd BN, ATT 1st ARMY ARTY SCHOOL, No 5 GRU, 18th, 2nd BNS CLASS Z RES
BONE	Robt	PTE	822				TO 19th, 19th BN, CLASS Z RESERVE.
BOOTH	Wm	PTE	1181				TO 29th BN, CLASS Z RESERVE.
BOULTON	Harry	PTE	64				TO CLASS Z RESERVE.
BOWDITCH	JohnH	PTE	104				
BOWIE	Jas F	PTE	1565	HENDON	SUNDERLAND	19/7/16 BERNAFRAY WOOD BRIT	

Surname	Forename	Rank	No.	Residence	Enlisted	Fate / Memorial	Notes
BOWMAN	Thos	PTE	228				TO CLASS Z RESERVE
BOYD	James	PTE	576				TO 23rd BN. DID NOT SERVE OVERSEAS
BOYNTON	Thos	PTE	1535				TO LABOUR CORPS. LAB CORPS No 112663
BRANTON	Frank	PTE	445				TO LABOUR CORPS. LAB CORPS No 116667
BRIGGS	Geo	PTE	408	TEAMS	7/3/15	SICK 7/2/16	TO 14th BN. AGE 22. BORN BILLQUAY
BROOKS	Geo	PTE	699	SUNDERLAND	SUNDERLAND	22/4/17 LOOS MEM	TO ROYAL ENGINEERS(33rd LT RAILWAY OP COY). RE No 251928
BROTHWICK	Wm	SGT	979	WEST HARTLEPOOL	SUNDERLAND	21/10/17 RENINGHELST NEW MIL	TO 19th, 10th, 11th, 19th BNS. CLASS Z RESERVE.
BROWELL	Robt	LSGT	893		22/3/15	KR para 392 15/2/18	TO 3rd BN. AGE 35
BROWN	G	PTE	823			3/2/17 BISHOPWEARMOUTH CEM	
BROWN	Geo A	PTE		MIDDLESBROUGH		19/10/17 POELCAPELLE BRIT CEM	TO MACHINE GUN CORPS(106th MG COY). MGC No 25213
BROWN	Geo H	SGT	1273	GATESHEAD		25/7/16 THIEPVAL MEM	
BROWN	John	SGT	934				TO CLASS Z RESERVE.
BROWN	Matt	PTE	304				TO LABOUR CORPS. LAB CORPS No 112666
BROWN	Wm	PTE	657			KR para 392	TO LABOUR CORPS. LAB CORPS No 116668
BROWNLESS	Alex	PTE	1612				
BRUCE	FredL	SGT	386	STANHOPE	11/3/15	KR para 392 17/9/17	TO 2nd BN, CLASS Z RESERVE.
BRUCE	Robt	PTE	5	WEST HARTLEPOOL	4/8/15	KR para 392 5/12/18	TO CLASS Z RESERVE.
BUCKLEY	John	PTE	902				TO 3rd BN. AGE 23
BUNTON	Robt	PTE	1518				TO 28th BN. AGE 30
BURNIP	Thos	PTE	1540	TUDHOE COLLIERY			TO 20th, 20th BN, CLASS Z RESERVE.
BURNS	Peter	PTE	125	DURHAM CITY			TO LABOUR CORPS(195 LAB COY). LAB CORPS No 116672
BURTON	JohnT	SGT	959	SOUTH SHIELDS	SOUTH SHIELDS	25/7/16 THIEPVAL MEM	TO 18th, 19th, 51st BNS, CLASS Z RESERVE.
BUSSEY	Ben	CPL	309	DARLINGTON	5/3/15	KR para 392	
BUTLER	James	PTE	310			KR para 392 30/9/18	AGE 40.
BYRNE	Wm	PTE	557			23/4/18 BOUZINCOURT COM CEM	ATT 176 TUN COY RE, ATT MACHINE GUN CORPS. BORN SOUTHWICK
CAIRNS	Geo W	PTE	1138	PELTON	SUNDERLAND 27/2/15	KR para 392 16/11/17	TO ARMY RESERVE CLASS W. AGE 30
CAIRNS	Thos	PTE	454	SEAHAM HARBOUR	27/2/15		TO 14th, 2nd BNS, CLASS Z RESERVE.
CALLANDER	NichT	PTE	135		BARNARD CASTLE 27/2/15	18/7/16 THIEPVAL MEM	AGE 20 BORN SUNDERLAND.
CALVERT	JohnT	LCPL	1046		27/2/15	KR para 392 12/2/18	TO ARMY RESERVE CLASS W. AGE 24
CAMERON	David	CPL	1494	JARROW	15/3/15		TO CLASS Z RESERVE. LSGT
CAMERON	Henry	PTE	101				TO 3rd BN. RIVET HEATER AGE 20.5"1" DESERTED 10/6/16 SOUTH SHIELDS
CAMPBELL	E	PTE	633		GATESHEAD	27/8/17 ST PATRICK'S CEM	TO 11th, 18th, 14th BNS. SHOWN IN WGR AS 18th BN
CAMPBELL	Henry	PTE		SUNDERLAND	15/3/15		TO CLASS Z RESERVE.
CAMPBELL	Jack	PTE	1604	NEWCASTLE	2/2/15	KR para 392 14/6/18	TO DEPOT. AGE 23
CAMPBELL	Rich	PTE	1527	TUDHOE	25/6/15	KR para 392 1/5/17	TO ARMY RESERVE CLASS P. AGE 24
CAMSEY	Wm F	LCPL	425		FERRYHILL	12/4/17 THIEPVAL MEM	
CARMEDY	Steve	LCPL	1187				TO CLASS Z RESERVE.
CARNEY	John	CPL	455	SPENNYMOOR			TO LABOUR CORPS. LAB CORPS No 116721
CARR	Thos	PTE	1525	LOW SPENNYMOOR	29/2/17	KR para 392 2/5/17	TO 11th, 19th BNS, CLASS Z RESERVE.
CARRICK	Wm	PTE	762		JARROW 26/6/15	24/8/16 THIEPVAL MEM	TO CLASS Z RESERVE
CAVANAGH	Thos	PTE	759		4/8/15	KR para 392 15/2/18	TO ARMY RESERVE CLASS P. AGE 25
CHALLINOR	Isaac	CPL	238				
CHAMBERS	Thos	PTE	71			KR para 392 29/5/18	TO 20th, 10th BNS, DEPOT. AGE 22
CHANDLER	Gowan	PTE	729	JARROW			TO 18th BN. CLASS Z RESERVE.
CHAPLIN	Henry	PTE	1209				TO LABOUR CORPS. LAB CORPS No 111969
CHAPMAN	Fredk	PTE	688				
CHAPMAN	James	PTE	399				TO CLASS Z RESERVE.
CHAPMAN	Jos	SGT	1522			10/7/19	TO 12th, 19th BNS, CLASS Z RESERVE. CSGT. DISCHARGED AT RIPON
CHARLTON	Andrw	PTE	1048		SUNDERLAND 1/3/15	26/11/16 FAUBOURG DE AMIENS	AGE 27 BORN FELLING
CHARLTON	Phil	PTE	393	SHOTTON COLLIERY	JARROW	25/11/17 MARCOING COM CEM	TO 18th, 14th BNS. BORN WEST STANLEY
CHARLTON	Thos	PTE	341	JARROW	DURHAM	KR para 392 15/6/16	
CHAYTOR	Chas	PTE	124 / 965	LANGLEY PARK	29/3/15		

Surname	Forename	Rank	No. / Birthplace	Enlisted	Discharge / Death	Remarks
CHICK	Lawr	PTE	682 SUNDERLAND	SUNDERLAND	30/7/16 THIEPVAL MEM	TO 18th BN, ATT 6th DIV RE, 2nd BN, 18th BN, CLASS Z RESERVE
CHILD	Harld	PTE	1033			TO 18th, 15th BNS, CLASS Z RESERVE.
CHRISTAL	James	PTE	241			TO 4th BN, ATT ARMY SERVICE CORPS. AGE 24
CLAPPERTON	Hen J	PTE	240	27/2/15	KR para 392 20/3/18	TO LABOUR CORPS. LAB CORPS No 112659
CLARK	James	CPL	412			TO 20th BN. AGE 33
CLARK	Jos	PTE	802	15/3/15	KR para 392 22/4/19	TO DEPOT. AGE 28
CLEAUGHAN	Henry	PTE	131	27/2/15	31/8/19 WEST RAINTON CH YARD	TO LABOUR CORPS. LAB CORPS No 116718
CLOSE	James	PTE	694			ATT 3rd ARMY SCHOOL, TO 19th BN, CLASS Z RESERVE.
COATES	JohnA	PTE	436			TO ARMY RESERVE CLASS P. AGE 22
COCKBURN	Waltr	PTE	1413 NEWCASTLE	3/7/15	KR para 392 22/6/18	ATT 185 TUN COY RE, TO 11th, 19th, 15th BNS. 3 RAILWAY COTTAGES BONDGATE IN AVL.
COGLAN	Geo	PTE	374 BISHOP AUCKLAND	BISHOP AUKLAND 15/4/15	24/10/18 VIS-EN-ARTOIS MEM	ATT ARMY ORDNANCE CORPS.
COGLAN	Wm	PTE	994	15/4/15	KR para 392 28/1/19	TO ARMY RESERVE CLASS W. AGE 21
COMB	Alex	PTE	347	1/3/15	KR para 392 13/11/17	TO 12th, 15th BNS. AGE 23
CONLEY	JohnG	PTE	900	22/3/15	KR para 392 25/4/19	TO MACHINE GUN CORPS(106th MG COY), MGC No 25216. AGE 27
CONNER	JohnW	PTE	155 WEST HARTLEPOOL	WEST HARTLEPOOL 20/5/15	5/5/17 NESLE COM CEM	TO 19th BN. AGE 25
COOK	John	PTE	1149		KR para 392 23/4/19	ATT 106 LIGHT TRENCH MORTAR BTY. AGE 19
COOK	RichH	PTE	841 MONKWEARMOUTH	SUNDERLAND 7/3/15	1/5/17 MARTEVILLE COM CEM	TO 18th BN, ARMY RESERVE CLASS P. AGE 27
CORCORAN	Thos	PTE	610	11/3/15	KR para 392 2/4/19	TO 11th, 19th BNS. AGE 35
CORK	John	PTE	701 CHESTER LE STREET	WEST HARTLEPOOL	17/10/17 HARTLEPOOL HART RD	AGE 20.
CORKER	Jos	PTE	43 WEST HARTLEPOOL	WEST HARTLEPOOL 27/2/15	22/2/19 BURIED 28/12/19 WITTON GILBERT	TO 19th BN, ARMY RESERVE CLASS P. AGE 31
COSGROVE	John	PTE	129 WITTON GILBERT	26/5/15	KR para 392 2/8/16	TO DEPOT. AGE 37
COSTELLO	Thos	PTE	1386	27/2/15	KR para 392 10/4/17	TO 10th BN, ARMY RESERVE CLASS P. AGE 42
COSTELLO	Com	PTE	237		26/4/18 HOOGE CRATER CEM	TO 2nd BN. AGE 26
COULT	Thos	PTE	1566 DARLINGTON	DARLINGTON 31/5/15	KR para 392 14/4/16	AGE 20. DID NOT SERVE OVERSEAS
COUSINS	Benj	PTE	1247	CROOK 11/5/15	DEBILITY 28/1/19	TO 3rd BN(No 6 COY), AGE 46 DID NOT SERVE OVERSEAS
COUSINS	John	PTE	828 SHINCLIFFE	CROOK 16/3/15	WOUNDS 11/4/17	TO 17th BN. MINER AGE 19,5'2". DESERTED 28/12/15 RUGELEY CAMP
COWAN	M	PTE	527	3/3/15	KR para 392 14/4/16	TO DEPOT.
COWIE	Jas M	PTE	1243 LANGLEY PARK	LANGLEY PARK 26/3/15		TO CLASS Z RESERVE.
COXON	Robt	PTE	488			DID NOT SERVE OVERSEAS.
CRAFT	Alf	PTE	342			TO 15th BN. CLASS Z RESERVE.
CRAGGS	Geo	PTE	559			TO CLASS Z RESERVE.
CRAIG	JohnT	PTE	1192 GLASGOW	GLASGOW	9/12/16 WANQUETIN COM CEM	AGE 20
CRAIK	Sam	PTE	825		KR para 392	TO LABOUR CORPS. LAB CORPS No 112667
CRANMER	Jonth	PTE	1452			TO 18th BN, CLASS Z RESERVE.
CROMAR	Chas	PTE	1010			TO CLASS Z RESERVE
CROMPTON	John	PTE	236 BURNOPFIELD	BURNOPFIELD		TO CLASS Z RESERVE.
CRUICKSHANKS	Jas W	PTE	558 SUNDERLAND	SUNDERLAND	19/7/16 THIEPVAL MEM	AGE 27 MASTER AT HARTLEPOOL RC SCHOOL, PLAYED FOR BEARPARK FC
CUMMINGS	Robt	PTE	19 BEARPARK	WEST HARTLEPOOL 11/5/15	20/7/16 LA NEUVILLE BRIT CEM	TO ARMY RESERVE CLASS P. AGE 20
CUNNINGHAM	Steph	CSM	1044		KR para 392 10/4/17	TO LABOUR CORPS(957 LAB COY), LAB CORPS No 111877. AGE 47
CURRY	Harry	PTE	199 SUNDERLAND	SUNDERLAND	19/7/16 THIEPVAL MEM	TO 22nd, 19th BNS, CLASS Z RESERVE.
CURRY	JohmC	PTE	676 GATESHEAD	SUNDERLAND	29/9/19 BISHOPWEARMOUTH	BORN MURTON
CURTIS	John	LSGT	432		29/1/16 TIDWORTH MIL CEM	TO 10th, 10th BN.
CURTIS	Jos S	CPL	716 SEAHAM	SUNDERLAND	23/6/17 TYNE COT MEM	TO QOR WEST KENT REGT(6th BN). QORWKENT No G/31882
CURTIS	Jos T	PTE	723 MURTON	NEWCASTLE	21/9/18 UNICORN CEM	AGE 38.
CURTIS	Thos	PTE	561 NEWCASTLE	NEWCASTLE	1/4/16 RUE PETTILLON MIL	TO 21st,23rd, 19th BNS,ASC(236 COY), LAB CORPS(188 COY) LAB CORPS No 112580.MINER AGE 19.NOK RESIDENT MANCHESTER
DAGLISH	Wm	PTE	918 GATESHEAD			
DALE	Wm	PTE	1398 SOUTH HETTON	HOUGHTON LE SPRING 30/6	2/4/18	
DARWIN	Rich	PTE	819	15/3/15	KR para 392 29/12/17	AGE 34
DAVEY	AlexW	PTE	606	8/3/15	SICK 26/2/17	TO DEPOT. ON MR AS DESERTED

Surname	Forename	Rank	No.	Place	Enlisted	Casualty / KR	Notes
DAVIDSON	Marti	PTE	1159		5/3/15	KR para 392	TO 2nd, 18th, 1/9th BNS, CLASS Z RESERVE. MINER AGE 20, FGCM NOV 1916
DAVIES	Arth	PTE	625	GATESHEAD			TO CLASS Z RESERVE.
DAVIES	James	PTE	859		29/3/15	KR para 392 12/9/18	AGE 38.
DAVIES	Thos	PTE	962		27/2/15	KR para 392 31/3/19	TO ARMY RESERVE CLASS P. AGE 35
DAVIS	Geo	CPL	182	HETTON LE HOLE			TO LABOUR CORPS. LAB CORPS No 112581
DAVIS	Geo	PTE	1127				TO LABOUR CORPS(742 EMP COY).
DAVIS	Geo	PTE	1582	LANGLEY MOOR			TO ARMY RESERVE CLASS P. AGE 19
DAVISON	Geo B	LSGT	1176	SUNDERLAND	18/8/15	KR para 392 1/12/16	20/10/17 TYNE COT MEM
DAVISON	Rob A	PTE	883	NEW WASHINGTON	GATESHEAD	25/7/16 THIEPVAL MEM	BORN DURHAM
DEAN	Edwd	PTE	791	SUNDERLAND	GATESHEAD		TO 3rd BN. DID NOT SERVE OVERSEAS
DEANS	Wm	PTE	299		SUNDERLAND 15/3/15	SICK 23/8/16	TO CLASS Z RESERVE.
DENNEY	Harld	PTE	401	OLD PENSHAW	1/3/15		
DENNEY	Syd	PTE	1600		23/8/15		DID NOT SERVE OVERSEAS.
DENTON	John	CPL	191	SHIELDFIELD		11/2/18 ALL SAINTS NEWCASTLE	TO LABOUR CORPS(365 EMP COY). LAB CORPS No 111874, AGE 23
DEVLIN	Mich	PTE	1328	DALTON LE DALE	1/3/15	25/7/16 THIEPVAL MEM	DID NOT SERVE OVERSEAS.
DICKSON	Robt	PTE	460	SEAHAM HARBOUR		KR para 392 14/4/16	TO 19th, 2nd, 20th, 12th, 12th, CLASS Z RES 5CCS 15/7/16, 4 CAN GEN HOSP
DINSDALE	Edwd	PTE	1533	SUNDERLAND	4/8/15	GSW 18/2/19	TO 14th BN, DEPOT. AGE 38
DITCHFIELD	Jos	CPL	245		27/2/15	KR para 392 26/12/17	TO DEPOT.
DIXON	Geo	CPL	1419		5/7/15	WOUNDS 1/5/17	
DIXON	Hugh	CPL	735	SUNDERLAND	13/3/15	13/5/16 ST VAAST POST MIL	DID NOT SERVE OVERSEAS.
DIXON	Jas W	PTE	1400			SICK 17/8/15	TO DEPOT. AGE 25
DIXON	Jos	LSGT	831	SUNDERLAND	30/6/15	KR para 392 22/12/17	AGE 18.
DOBBS	Thos	PTE		MONKWEARMOUTH		19/7/16 LA NEUVILLE BRIT CEM	TO 11th, 19th, 18th BNS, CLASS Z RESERVE.
DOCHERTY	Jos C	PTE	360	BLAYDON	SUNDERLAND	21/9/17 LIJSSENTHOEK MIL CEM	TO 13th BN.
DODD	Edwd	PTE	1595	WEST HARTLEPOOL		KR para 392 4/4/19	TO 19th BN. STILL SERVING 1920. SGT
DODD	John	CPL	141	GATESHEAD / BARNARD CASTLE		KR para 392 14/1/18	RAILWAYMAN AGE 31
DODDS	Matth	PTE	244	DUNSTON	12/7/15	KR para 392 6/3/19	TO 2nd BN. SGT AGE 33
DODDS	Wm	PTE	1616		27/2/15	18/7/16 THIEPVAL MEM	AGE 25
DONALD	Wm	PTE	956		30/8/15		TO 14th BN. AGE 34
DONKIN	Fred	PTE	248		27/3/15		DID NOT SERVE OVERSEAS.
DONKIN	Thos L	PTE		SUNDERLAND		19/7/16 LA NEUVILLE BRIT CEM	ATT 185 TUN COY RE. 19th, 14th, 18th, 19th BNS, CLASS Z RESERVE. MINER AGE 35, FGCM NOV 1916
DOWSEY	Henry	PTE	1429		6/7/15		AGE 39
DREYER	Rownt	LCPL	503	SUNDERLAND			TO 20th, 18th BNS, CLASS Z RESERVE.
DUIGNAN	John	PTE	132				TO CLASS Z RESERVE.
DUNN	Alex	PTE	1409				TO LABOUR CORPS. LAB CORPS No 112668
DUNN	Geo	PTE	1082				FGCM NOV 1916 STILL SERVING 10 YEARS PENAL SERVITUDE 1920.
DUNN	Jos S	PTE	89		28/2/15	KR para 392 20/2/19	TO ARMY RESERVE CLASS P. AGE 32
DUNN	Rich	CPL	684		10/3/15	SICK 6/11/15	TO 21st BN. DID NOT SERVE OVERSEAS
DUNN	RobtD	PTE	860			KR para 392	TO CLASS Z RESERVE.
DUNN	Walt	PTE	1585				
DUNNELL	Wm H	PTE					TO 20th,14th BNS, LABOUR CORPS, R FUSILIERS, SERVING 20/3/20 LAB CORPS No 412877, R FUS No 102746
EAGLE	John	PTE	1333				MENTIONED IN CQMS PROUD'S NOTEBOOK.
EAMES	JohnJ	PTE	250	WALLSEND			ATT WEST YORKSHIRE REGT(1/6th BN), 19th BN. BORN WILLINGTON ON TYNE
EDMUNDSON	Geo	PTE	332				TO LABOUR CORPS. LAB CORPS No 112609
EDGAR	John	PTE	1380		GATESHEAD	3/9/16 ARRAS MEM	TO WEST YORKSHIRE REGT. W YORKS No 63657
ELLIOTT	JohnE	PTE	1037	FELLING	SUNDERLAND	3/9/16 ARRAS MEM	ATT WEST YORKSHIRE REGT(1/6th BN), 19th BN.
ELLIOTT	JohnW	PTE	189	HETTON LE HOLE		SICK 10/3/17	TO DEPOT.
ELLIOTT	Thos	PTE	278		27/2/15	KR para 392	
ELSINOR		PTE					
EMBLETON	Alf	PTE	18				TO 1/6th BN, CLASS Z RESERVE.

Surname	Forenames	Rank	No. / Residence	Enlisted	Death	Notes
EMBLETON	Robt	PTE	134 LUDWORTH	27/2/15	KR para 392 16/11/17	TO ARMY RESERVE CLASS W. AGE 38.HOSP ABERDEEN 8/16,STRETCHER BEARER
EMMERSON	Robt	PTE	960			TO 2nd, 12th, 10th, 15th, 1/8th BN, CLASS Z RESERVE.
ENDERBERG	James	CPL	1418	6/7/15	KR para 392 4/10/17	TO DEPOT. AGE 34
ENGLISH	Alf G	PTE	873 RYHOPE	SUNDERLAND	14/10/18 DADIZELE NE BRIT CEM	BORN NORMANBY YORKS.
EVANS	Chas	PTE	369			DESERTED STILL AWOL 11/1220.
EWART	James	PTE	940			TO LABOUR CORPS. LAB CORPS No 112669
FAGHY	Geo E	LCPL	176			TO CLASS Z RESERVE.
FAWCETT	Jos G	PTE	1352 SOUTH SHIELDS		10/11/18 HARTON CEM	TO LABOUR CORPS. LAB CORPS No 111721, AGE 23
FENNY	Arth	SGT	140 CHESTER LE STREET			TO CLASS Z RESERVE.
FENTON	Edwd	PTE	464 CROOK			TO CLASS Z RESERVE.
FERRIDAY	Robt	PTE	770			TO LABOUR CORPS. LAB CORPS No 116723.
FINCH	Edwd	PTE	1446			TO LABOUR CORPS. LAB CORPS No 112670
FINLEY	D R	ASGT	1214			TO LABOUR CORPS(109 LAB COY). LAB CORPS No 382253
FISHER	Abt	PTE	251 SUNDERLAND	SUNDERLAND	10/7/19 RYHOPE ROAD CEM	AGE 29.
FOORD	Humph	PTE	1047 SOUTH SHIELDS	10/2/15	18/7/16 THIEPVAL MEM	TO LABOUR CORPS, ROYAL DEFENSE CORPS. CHIMNEY SWEEP. FGCM NOV 16
FORREST	D	PTE	633		20/7/17 VILLERS FAUCON CEM	ATT 173 TUN COY RE, 19th BN.
FOSTER	Geo	SGT	1347 MOSLEY DURHAM	DURHAM	22/8/17 BARD COTTAGE CEM	STOPPED SGT STONES AT POLICE BATTLE POST.
FOSTER	Robt	PTE	136	27/2/15	KR para 392 20/2/19	TO 11th BN.
FOSTER	Thos	SGT	214		KR para 392	DID NOT SERVE OVERSEAS. TO CLASS Z RESERVE.
FOX	Wm Hy	PTE	465	27/2/15	KR para 392 27/1/19	TO LABOUR CORPS. LAB CORPS No 111953
FRADGLEY	Elija	PTE	536		KR para 392 31/1/17	DID NOT SERVE OVERSEAS.
FRASER	Wm	CPL	207			TO LABOUR CORPS. LAB CORPS No 116615
FROST	Thos	PTE	1385	25/6/15		TO CLASS Z RESERVE.
FUTERS	John	PTE	127 LANGLEY MOOR			TO ARMY ORDNANCE CORPS(NUMBER O36656). LABOURER AGE 19,51".
GALILEE	Wm	LCPL	466			DESERTED 8/8/15 AT FENCEHOUSES
GALLAGHER	John R	PTE	1410 HEBBURN	NORTH SHIELDS 27/7/15		TO 4th TRG RES BN, 51st BN NORTHBLD FUS. CLASS Z RESERVE,
GARBUTT	Harld	SGT	24			TO 14th, 18th BNS, ARMY RESERVE CLASS W. AGE 30
GARDINER	Thos	PTE	916			TO CLASS Z RESERVE. FGCM NOV 16
GARRITTY	Thos A	PTE	380		KR para 392 8/11/17	TO 20th, 19th BNS, CLASS Z RESERVE.
GARSIDE	John	PTE	1575	23/3/15		TO 22nd, 14th, 11th BNS, CLASS Z RESERVE.
GIBBINS	Thos	PTE	777			TO LABOUR CORPS. LAB CORPS No 116724, FGCM NOV 16
GIGGENS	Geo W	PTE	1274			TO LABOUR CORPS. LAB CORPS No 112661
GILMORE	Reg	SGT	592		KR para 392 26/7/18	TO 15th BN. AGE 21
GLANCEY	James	PTE	1574 DARLINGTON	13/8/15		MINER, SHOT BY FGCM
GOGGINS	Peter	LCPL	158 SOUTH MOOR	1/3/15	18/1/17 ST POL COM CEM	DID NOT SERVE OVERSEAS.
GOLDEN	James	LCPL	1068	12/5/15	KR para 392 17/8/15	ATT LABOUR CORPS, TO 19th BN, CLASS Z RESERVE.
GOLDSBOROUGH		LCPL	289			TO CLASS Z RESERVE.
GOODCHILD	Thos	PTE	754	SOUTH SHIELDS	15/11/16 LANCHESTER	TO DEPOT.
GORSE	Winsk	PTE	45 BOLDON			TO 11th, 19th, 13th, 19th BNS, CLASS Z RESERVE.
GOWLAND	Fred	PTE	1563			TO 10th, 22nd, 12th, 2nd BNS, CLASS Z RESERVE.
GRAHAM	Edwd	PTE	1271			TO 12th, 1/8th BNS. BORN HEIGHINGTON AGE 19
GRAHAM	Rich	PTE	1354 KIRK MERRINGTON	FERRYHILL / WEST HARTLEPOOL 31/5/15	13/4/18 PLOEGSTEERT MEM	MINER AGE 32, 50". DESERTED 9/8/15 AT FENCEHOUSES.
GRAHAM	Robt	PTE	1224	8/3/15	KR para 392 15/10/17	TO DEPOT. AGE 24
GRAINGER	Edwd	CPL	601		KR para 392	TO 20th BN.
GRAINGER	Jos	PTE	600 SUNDERLAND	DURHAM	25/3/17 THIEPVAL MEM	
GRANT	David	PTE	1317 WATERHOUSES	26/7/15	KR para 392 17/9/17	BORN SUNNISIDE.
GRAY	Anthy	PTE	1480			TO DEPOT. AGE 30
GRAY	Robt	PTE	46 SOUTH SHIELDS	SOUTH SHIELDS	25/2/18 RIDGE WOOD CEM	
GRAY	Thos	PTE	1298 TRINITY HARTLEPOOL	WEST HARTLEPOOL	23/8/16 THIEPVAL MEM	
GRAY	Wm R	PTE	968		KR para 392	TO LABOUR CORPS, ROYAL FUSILIERS(36th BN). LAB C No 116725.RFUS No G/62650, IN COMS PROUD'S NOTEBOOK

Surname	Forename	Rank	No	Town	Enlisted	Died / Memorial	Notes
GREAVES	Harry	PTE	233	SOUTH HETTON	HOUGHTON LE SPRING	9/6/16 LE TOURET MIL CEM	TO LABOUR CORPS, EAST YORKSHIRE REGT, LAB C No 116678, E YORKS No 42669. FGCM NOV 16
GREEN	Jas	PTE	1293	HETTON LE HOLE	HOUGHTON LE SPRING	24/8/16 THIEPVAL MEM	BORN HASWELL AGE 20
GREEN	John	PTE	1490	DARLINGTON		8/11/16 FAUBOURG D'AMIENS	BORN EASINGTON
GREEN	JohnW	PTE	281	LANCHESTER			ATT 176 TUN COY RE. TO 20th(A COY), 2nd BNS, CLASS Z RESERVE 139 FLD AMB 19/11/16 EVAC 41 DRS PUO AGE 29
GREEN	ThosG	SGT	95	MONKWEARMOUTH		25/2/19 MEREKNOLLS CEM S/LND	ATT GUARDS DIV 8/2/16 - 15/2/16. BORN DEPTFORD AGE 28
GREEN	Jos	PTE	1323				TO LABOUR CORPS LAB CORPS No 112671. TO CLASS 2 RESERVE.
GREENFIELD	Normn	CPL	1026				TO LABOUR CORPS(49 LAB COY). LAB CORPS No 116678
GREENWOOD	Arth	PTE	838	SPENNYMOOR	SPENNYMOOR	27/5/18 VIGNACOURT BRIT CEM	ATT 185 TUN COY RE, TO 11th, 19th BNS, CLASS Z RESERVE.
GREENWOOD	Jos	PTE	645	CROOK			TO 19th, 18th, 12th, 15th, 1/5th BNS. BORN BIRTLEY AGE 36
GRICE	H	PTE	1000	BIRTLEY			DID NOT SERVE OVERSEAS.
GRICE	Henry	PTE	1099	CHESTER LE STREET	NEWCASTLE 5/6/15	21/7/18 SOISSONS MEM; KR para 392 17/7/15	
GRINDLE	J	PTE	1301				TO LABOUR CORPS(187 LAB COY). LAB CORPS No 111948,AGE 28.5'1".DESERTED 26/7/15 LEAMSIDE
GRUMMETT	Wm	SGT	1278	SUNDERLAND	SUNDERLAND 2/6/15	5/12/18 BISHOPWEARMOUTH CEM	TO 13th BN.
GURKIN	James	PTE	871	GATESHEAD	FERRYHILL	7/6/17 RAILWAY DUGOUTS CEM	TO 15th, 20th, 19th BNS, CLASS Z RESERVE.
GUY	Henry	CPL	469	NETTLESWORTH			TO CLASS 2 RESERVE.
HALL	James	PTE	1079				TO CLASS 2 RESERVE.
HALL	John	PTE	172	HETTON LE HOLE	HOUGHTON LE SPRING 3/3/15	25/7/16 THIEPVAL MEM; KR para 392 25/3/19	TO 11th, 2nd BNS. AGE 20
HALL	JohnJ	PTE	470				TO 20th, 10th, 1/7th BNS, CLASS Z RESERVE.
HALL	Peter	PTE	778		HOUGHTON LE SPRING	16/11/16 LIJSSENTHOEK MIL CEM	TO 20th BN. BORN SHILDON
HALLIDAY	Thos	PTE	1238	FENCEHOUSES	SOUTH SHIELDS	18/7/16 DIVE COPSE BRIT CEM	AGE 33.LNER SHEETMAN TYNEDOCK SHEDS DESERTED 27/12/16, STILL AWOL 15/3/20.
HAMILTON	Rich	PTE	471	SOUTH SHIELDS			TO CLASS 2 RESERVE.
HAMILTON	Alex	PTE	1095				
HARDING	Chas	CPL	257	STANLEY			TO LABOUR CORPS. LAB CORPS No 111368.POS IN POST B 25/26 NOV 1916
HARDING	Arth	PTE	206	SUNDERLAND	SUNDERLAND	19/7/16 THIEPVAL MEM	
HARDING	Jos	PTE	1191				TO 3rd BN. AGE 34
HARGREAVES	James	LCPL	219		27/2/15	KR para 392 31/1/18	TO 20th,1/9th BNS, CLASS Z RESERVE.
HARLE	Wm	PTE	336	TURSDALE			TO LONDON REGT(1/5th BN). LONDON No 45264
HARPER	Thos	PTE	6	WEST HARTLEPOOL	WEST HARTLEPOOL	1/9/18 ST SEVER CEM ROUEN	AGE 27
HARPER	Wm	PTE	685	SPENNYMOOR			TO 22nd, 18th BNS, CLASS Z RESERVE.
HARRIS	WmH	PTE	1590	CROOK	BISHOP AUCKLAND	4/11/16 FAUBOURG D'AMIENS	TO 2nd, 19th BNS, CLASS Z RESERVE. PLATOON STOREMAN
HARRISON	Mark	PTE	830	RYHOPE			TO 20th BN, CLASS Z RESERVE.
HASWELL	Abt	PTE	1471				AGE 22.
HASWELL	Wm	PTE	562	SOUTH SHIELDS	SOUTH SHIELDS	26/7/16 ETAPLES MIL CEM	TO 20th BN
HATTON	James	PTE	937	FELLING	NEWCASTLE	31/7/17 MENIN GATE MEM	TO CLASS Z RESERVE.
HAWKE	Wm	SGT	55				TO 20th, 10th, 18th, 20th BNS, CLASS Z RESERVE.
HAYS	AbtE	PTE	911	SHINEY ROW			ATT WEST YORKSHIRE REGT(1/6th BN), 19th BN. AGE 23
HAZARD	Len J	PTE	1371	SUNDERLAND	SUNDERLAND	10/8/16 BISHOPWEARMOUTH CEM; KR para 392	
HEAD	Jos	PTE	259				TO 3rd BN. AGE 31
HEATH	Wm	PTE	311		1/3/15		TO CLASS Z RESERVE.
HEDLEY	John	PTE	824				
HENDERSON	Fred	CPL	1190	BARNARD CASTLE	BARNARD CASTLE	27/2/17 THIEPVAL MEM	
HENDERSON	JohnW	PTE	1571	JARROW	JARROW	31/8/16 ABBEVILLE COM CEM	
HENDERSON	Jos S	PTE					
HERON	Wm	PTE	574	NORTH SHIELDS	SOUTH SHIELDS	19/7/16 THIEPVAL MEM	AGE 18
HESLOP	Jos B	PTE	174	WEST RAINTON			ATT 185 TUN COY RE, TO 11th, 19th BNS, CLASS Z RESERVE. CPL
HEWISON	Chris	PTE	150				TO 1/8th BN, CLASS Z RESERVE.
HEWITT	Steph	PTE	910				TO 15th, 1/8th BNS, CLASS Z RESERVE.
HEWITT	Abt	PTE	258	GATESHEAD			TO CLASS Z RESERVE.
HEWITT	B B	PTE	884				FGCM NOV 16.

Surname	Forename	Rank	No	Place	Date	Cemetery/Memorial/Discharge	Notes
HILL	John	PTE	58		27/2/15	WOUNDS 21/3/17	TO DEPOT.
HILLS	Geo	PTE	1388		26/6/15	KR para 392 18/3/18	AGE 34
HOCKWORTH	Edwd	PTE	255				ATT 251 TUN COY RE, TO 22nd, 19th BNS, CLASS Z RESERVE.
HODGSON	Harry	PTE	473	SUNDERLAND	19/5/15	30/11/15 TIDWORTH MIL CEM	AGE 19
HODGSON	Steph	PTE	1137	SUNDERLAND		KR para 392 19/11/17	TO DEPOT. AGE 32
HODSON	Wm H	LCPL	1542	SHOTTON COLLIERY		4/11/17 ST SEVER CEM ROUEN	BORN MANCHESTER
HOEY	John	PTE	840				TO ROYAL ARMY SERVICE CORPS.
HOGG	MichJ	SGT	371				TO LABOUR CORPS. LAB CORPS No 116727
HOGG	James	PTE	1304	SOUTH SHIELDS		24/8/16 THIEPVAL MEM	
HOGG	Matt	PTE	639				TO LABOUR CORPS. LAB CORPS No 116730
HOGG	Wm	PTE	1412	WALKER / NEWCASTLE		18/7/16 THIEPVAL MEM	TO LABOUR CORPS. LAB CORPS No 111974. MINER 21/3/16 59 FA, 19/3/16 2 LNDN CCS
HOLDER	Edwd	PTE	1406	SUNDERLAND			TO ROYAL AIR FORCE. RAF No 409824
HOLLINGSBURY	Alf	WOII	989	DARLINGTON			INVOLVED IN FGCM OF LSGT STONES
HOLROYD		PTE	198				TO 11th BN, CLASS Z RESERVE.
HOOPER	Thos	PTE					
HOPE	Fred	PTE	1086	FENCEHOUSES	30/6/15	7/8/17 YPRES RESEVOIR CEM	TO LABOUR CORPS(195 LAB COY), LAB CORPS No 116731, BORN LANGLEY MOOR
HOPE	James	PTE	1618	EASINGTON		KR para 392 26/2/19	TO 20th, 3rd(No 3 COY) BNS, ARMY RESERVE CLASS P. AGE 24
HOPE	NormS	PTE	271	CONSETT	11/5/15	KR para 392 17/8/15	ATT 902 AE COY LABOUR CORPS, TO 20th, 19th BNS, CLASS Z RES
HOPE	Robt	PTE	1031				DID NOT SERVE OVERSEAS.
HOPKINSON	E	LCPL	1311				MENTIONED IN CQMS PROUD'S NOTEBOOK. FGCM NOV 16.
HOPPER	GeoH	LSGT	1168	SUNDERLAND		29/3/18 POZIERES MEM	TO 2nd BN, PB BN DLI, HQ 3rd ARMY, INF SCHOOL, 19th BN. AGE 23 BORN WEST RAINTON
HORN	Leond	PTE	472				TO 19th, 11th BNS, CLASS Z RESERVE.
HORNSBY	John	PTE	731	HERRINGTON	13/3/15	KR para 392 18/12/17	TO 19th, 4th BNS. AGE 23
HUDDER	Chas	PTE	231				TO LABOUR CORPS, LAB CORPS No 111950
HUDSON	Thos	PTE	538				TO CLASS Z RESERVE.
HUDSPETH	Thos	LCPL	758	NEWCASTLE			ATT ROYAL FUS(36th BN), 195 LAB COY, TO 22nd, 18th BNS Z RES. R FUS No G/62649, LAB CORPS No 116732
HUGHES	AndwB	PTE	766				TO LABOUR CORPS(195 LAB COY), LAB CORPS No 116729
HUGHES	John	CPL	474	CHESTERFIELD / STANLEY	8/3/15	18/7/16 THIEPVAL MEM	ATT NOTTS & DERBY REGT(15th BN), 19th, ATT 185 TUN COY RE, 11th, 19th BNS, CLASS Z RESERVE
HUGHES	JosH	PTE	1244	SPENNYMOOR		KR para 392 24/3/16	DID NOT SERVE OVERSEAS.
HUGHES	Wm	PTE	591				TO CLASS Z RESERVE.
HUGHES	Wm	CPL	1081	GATESHEAD			TO 2nd, 18th, 15th BNS, CLASS Z RESERVE.
HULL	Well	PTE	1506				TO 2nd BN. AGE 19
HUMBLE	Norm	PTE	1036	PALLION / SUNDERLAND		16/9/16 THIEPVAL MEM	ATT 176 TUN COY RE, 19th BN. BORN SHERRIFF HILL
HUMPHRIES	John	LCPL	724	BRANDON COLLIERY / DURHAM		20/11/17 TYNE COT MEM	TO LABOUR CORPS(122 LAB COY), LAB CORPS No 425674
HUMPHRIES	Sid	PTE	1129	DARLINGTON			TO LABOUR CORPS(185 LAB COY), LAB CORPS No 112585
HUNT	James	PTE	126	ESH WINNING			IN POST WITH HOPKINSON & HARDING 21/11/16 TAKEN POW
HUNT	John	PTE	537				DESERTED
HUNTLEY		PTE					
HUTCHINSON	Edwd	PTE	1607	SUNDERLAND / DURHAM		24/10/17 TYNE COT MEM	TO 11th, 19th BNS, CLASS Z RESERVE.
HUTCHINSON	JohnW	PTE	1316	SOUTH SHIELDS		25/7/16 THIEPVAL MEM	TO CLASS Z RESERVE.
HUTCHINSON	Norm	CQMS	308	DARLINGTON		19/7/16 THIEPVAL MEM	BORN JARROW
HUTCHISON	John	PTE	1519	WEST HARTLEPOOL / COCKEN HALL	8/6/15		TO 15th, 2nd BNS, ATT 18th LIGHT TRENCH MORTAR BTY, CLASS Z. AGE 18, CofE
IDLE	Rich	LCPL	1332				TO LABOUR CORPS. LAB CORPS No 111937
ILEY	JohnW	PTE	798	FERRYHILL		KR para 392 7/5/19	TO 18th, 20th, 19th BNS. AGE 24
IMESON	Chas	PTE	977		16/3/15		
INGOE	JohnE	PTE	1370	SOUTH SHIELDS		18/7/16 DANZIG ALLEY CEM	AGE 19

Surname	Forename	Rank	No. & Enlistment	Place	Cause / Memorial	Remarks
JACKSON	Ernst	CSM	200 SUNDERLAND	SOUTH SHIELDS	24/7/16 THIEPVAL MEM	
JACKSON	James	PTE	52 SOUTH SHIELDS	10/5/15	KR para 392 9/1/18	TO CLASS Z RESERVE.
JACKSON	Jos	PTE	1038			TO 20th BN. DEPOT. AGE 24
JACKSON	Sam	PTE	108 SHERBURN	DURHAM	18/7/16 LA NEUVILLE BRIT CEM	BORN STATION TOWN AGE 21,
JAMES	Emmrs	LCPL	948 WATERHOUSES	WEST HARTLEPOOL	20/11/17 DUNHALLOW ADS CEM	BORN NEW HERRINGTON AGE 37.
JANE	Elija	PTE	779 OLD PENSHAW	HOUGHTON LE SPRING	20/8/17 VILLERS FAUCON CEM	
JAQUES	JohnW	PTE	130 HUNWICK			TO LABOUR CORPS(188 LAB COY). LAB CORPS No 112673
JARRETT	James	PTE	1489			TO 12th, 20th, 20th BNS, CLASS Z RESERVE.
JEFFERSON	Arth	SGT	1264			TO CLASS Z RESERVE.
JENKINS	Geo	PTE	145			TO LABOUR CORPS. LAB CORPS No 111927
JENNINGS	Alex	PTE	1500			TO ROYAL ENGINEERS, DLI(2nd BN), LABOUR CORPS, DLI(19th BN). RE No 128158. LAB CORPS No 376188
JOBLING	Fred	PTE	794 MONKWEARMOUTH	SUNDERLAND	8/10/17 POPERINGHE NEW MIL	TO 14th, 2nd, 20th BNS, PB BN(19th CORPS). AGE 19
JOBLING	Thos	PTE	478	2/3/15	WOUNDS 2/3/15	ATT WEST YORKSHIRE REGT(1/6th BN), DEPOT.
JOBLINS	JohnW	PTE	636		KR para 392 21/3/17	TO 18th BN, CLASS Z RESERVE.
JOHANNESSEN	CarlO	SGT	1343 WEST HARTLEPOOL	15/3/15		TO CLASS Z RESERVE. BROTHER ARTH GNR A/46 BDE RFA
JOHNSON	Benj	PTE	815 HULL	SUNDERLAND 23/7/15	KR para 392 26/11/17	TO 20th BN, DEPOT. AGE 27. 139 FLD AMB 12/7/16 SCABIES TO DUTY
JOHNSON	Chas	PTE	1478 HULL	9/3/15		LABOURER AGE 22,5'2". DESERTED 26/7/15 LEAMSIDE.
JOHNSON	Geo	PTE	1139		KR para 392 6/12/19	TO LABOUR CORPS(195 LAB COY). 19th BN, CLASS Z RESERVE.
JOHNSON	James	PTE	650 COUNDON	DURHAM		TO 19th BN, ATT WEST YORKS REGT(1/6th BN),TO 15th BN DLI.
JOHNSON	John	LCPL	1248 SACRISTON		18/4/18 TYNE COT MEM	TO 15th BN.
JOHNSON	JohnA	SGT	370 EASINGTON	SUNDERLAND		TO LABOUR CORPS(195 LAB COY). LAB CORPS No 116733
JOHNSON	Jos S	CPL	477 SUNDERLAND	28/2/15	24/7/16 BRONFAY FARM MIL CEM	TO ARMY RESERVE CLASS P. AGE 33
JOHNSON	ThosR	PTE	98		KR para 392 26/2/19	TO CLASS Z RESERVE.
JOHNSTON	JohnT	PTE	171 HETTON LE HOLE		KR para 392	TO 19th, 12th, 12th BNS, CLASS Z RESERVE.
JORDAN	Wm	PTE	668 LEADGATE	17/3/15		TO ARMY RESERVE CLASS W. AGE 29
JOSE	James	LCPL	923 BISHOP AUCKLAND		KR para 392 22/5/17	TO 13th, 19th, 22nd, 10th, 11th BNS, CLASS Z RESERVE.
KEARNEY	Thos	PTE	828		19/12/19 NEWBURN CEM	BORN SUNDERLAND
KEENAN	JohnW	PTE	738			TO YORK & LANCASTER REGT(9th BN). Y&L No 39869 AGE 34
KEENLYSIDE	Robt	LCPL	1404 ASHINGTON	SUNDERLAND	15/9/16 FAUBOURG D'AMIENS	TO LABOUR CORPS. LAB CORPS No 116685
KELL	Anthy	LCPL	774 BLEGGETT NTHBLD	SUNDERLAND	25/7/16 THIEPVAL MEM	BORN SHINEY ROW
KELLY	Alex	PTE	806 NORTH SHIELDS		18/10/17 TYNE COT MEM	TO 3rd BN. BORN BENWELL
KELLY	Peter	PTE	4			TO 11th, 19th BNS, DEPOT. AGE 34
KEMP	John	PTE	183 HETTON LE HOLE	HOUGHTON LE SPRING	19/7/16 THIEPVAL MEM	TO DEPOT.
KEMP	Matt	PTE	121 QUEBEC Co DURHAM	DURHAM	14/3/16 LA GORGUE COM CEM	TO 19th, 18th, 19th, 1/7th BNS, CLASS Z RESERVE. MINER AGE 22 CofE
KENNYFORD	Jas W	PTE	479 HAMSTERLEY COLLIERY	GATESHEAD	11/2/16 ST JOHNS CHOPWELL	
KEYS	Edwd	PTE	113	27/2/15	KR para 392 10/4/18	
KIDDELL	Walt	PTE	1493	27/7/15	WOUNDS 3/2/17	
KILPATRICK	John	PTE	595	1/3/15		
KING	Mich	PTE	279 CONSETT	6/3/15	KR para 392 16/11/17	
KIRTLEY	James	PTE	644		18/7/16 THIEPVAL MEM	
KITCHING	Alf	PTE	1434 YORK	EASINGWOLD 5/7/15		AGE 19, 5'1" FARM SERVANT DESERTED EN ROUTE 5/7/15
LAMB	John	PTE	1299 SUNDERLAND	SUNDERLAND 4/6/15		HAWKER AGE 21, 5'0". DESERTED 19/6/15 LEAMSIDE
LAMBERT	Geo	PTE	1382		KR para 392 22/4/19	TO LABOUR CORPS. LAB CORPS No 111933
LAMBERT	Rob P	PTE	803 PELTON FELL	15/3/15		TO 19th BN. AGE 38
LANE	JohnG	PTE	1075 SUNDERLAND	SUNDERLAND	11/5/16 ST VAAST POST MIL C	
LARMAR	Edwd	PTE	643 MIDDLE RAINTON			TO 10th, 11th BNS, CLASS Z RESERVE.
LAVERICK	G W	PTE	263 SUNDERLAND			AGE 34
LAVERICK	Peter	PTE	324		16/11/20 BISHOPWEARMOUTH CEM	ATT ROYAL FUS(36th BN), 195 LAB COY, TO 19th BN, CLASS Z RES
LAWLOR	John	SGT	805 WALLSEND	WALLSEND	24/8/16 DIVE COPSE CEM	AGE 27
LAWS	Thos	PTE	745			ATT 185 TUN COY RE. RE BASE DEPOT. 74 FLD AMB RAMC, 19th BN, CLASS Z RES
LAWSON	Jos	PTE	1614	30/8/15	WOUNDS 10/4/17	TO DEPOT.

Surname	Forename	Rank	Number / Place	Residence / Date	Death / Memorial	Remarks
LAWTON	John	PTE	261	22/3/15	KR para 392 15/6/15	TO 12th BN, CLASS Z RESERVE.
LAWTON	Sam	PTE	891			AGE 36 DID NOT SERVE OVERSEAS.
LAZENBY	Wm	PTE	402			TO LABOUR CORPS. LAB CORPS No 116738
LEDGER	Ernst	SGT	696			ATT ROYAL FUS, ATT 35 DIV HQ, TO 19th BN, CLASS Z RES, AWOII
LEE	Darcy	PTE	40 HARTLEPOOL	WEST HARTLEPOOL	19/10/17 TYNE COT MEM	TO MACHINE GUN CORPS(106th MG COY), MGC No 25214, AGE 27
LEE	Jos	PTE	282		KR para 392	TO LABOUR CORPS. LAB CORPS No 112603
LEE	Jos	PTE	563			TO 19th, 20th, BNS, CLASS Z RESERVE. LCPL
LEIGHTON	Wm	PTE	116 LANGLEY MOOR			ATT 19th ORDNANCE DEPOT, PB BN, 24 GEN HOSP, 14 CORPS HQ, 62 FLD AMB RAMC, CLASS Z RESERVE
LEIGHTON	Wm	PTE	1194			ATT ASC(17 LAB COY)TO LABOUR CORPS(187 LAB COY). LAB CORPS No 111923.106FA,37CCS, AGE 40 IN 1919
LEONARD	JohnC	PTE	260 GATESHEAD	GATESHEAD 27/2/15	18/7/16 DELVILLE WOOD CEM	TO LABOUR CORPS. LAB CORPS No 116689
LEWIS	Frs P	PTE	730 ST HILDAS HARTLEPOOL	WEST HARTLEPOOL		DEAD ON MR.
LIDDELL	Thos	LCPL	483			TO LABOUR CORPS. LAB CORPS No 111926.BORN DURHAM SON IN NAVY
LIDLE	Wm	PTE	69			TO CLASS Z RESERVE. LCPL
LIDSTER	Wm	PTE	938 SUNDERLAND	SUNDERLAND	21/7/17 VLAMERTINGHE NEW MIL	TO LABOUR CORPS. LAB CORPS No 111947
LITTLEFAIR	John	PTE	1189 BARNARD CASTLE			TO 20th BN. BORN FELLING, AGE 34
LIVINGSTONE	Arth	PTE	1134	SUNDERLAND	1/10/16 THIEPVAL MEM	TO CLASS Z RESERVE
LOFTUS	Peter	PTE	1115 WHEATLEY HILL	17/3/15	FRAC SKULL 30/8/16	TO DEPOT.
LONGSTAFF	Chris	PTE	72			LSGT.
LONGSTAFF	JohnG	CPL	837		KR para 392	TO 2nd, 19th BNS, CLASS Z RESERVE.
LONGWORTH	Thos	CPL	739			TO DEPOT.
LOWE	Matt	PTE	1253			TO LABOUR CORPS(187 LAB COY). LAB CORPS No 111848.MINER AGE 19, 5'1". ALIAS WM ROBINSON
LOWERY	Edwd	PTE	690	10/3/15	KR para 392 6/4/17	TO LABOUR CORPS, R ENGINEERS, LANCASHIRE FUSILIERS. FGCM NOV 16, L/C No 112132, RE No 308709, LANC FUS No 46449
LOWTHER	Wm	PTE	608 WHEATLEY HILL	WEST HARTLEPOOL 8/3/15		TO LABOUR CORPS. LAB CORPS No 116736.GROCERS AST AGE 19,4 SCOTTISH GHOSP 1918
LUMLEY	John G	PTE	950			AGE 27.
LUNDY	Simon	PTE	1234 NEWCASTLE	NEWCASTLE 26/5/15	RT LEG AMPUTATED 22/7/18	AGE 23 BORN GATESHEAD
LYES	Robt	PTE	1408 PELTON	1/7/15	KR para 392 23/4/19	ATT ASC(17 LAB COY)TO LABOUR CORPS(187,365 LAB COYS) W RES. LAB COR No 111940..106FA,37CCS,29GHOSP,35IBD,7CONVD,18GHOS
LYNCH	Henry	PTE	1132 CARLISLE	GATESHEAD	26/11/16 FAUBOURG D'AMIENS	TO 3rd BN. AGE 34
LYNCH	James	PTE	1373 WALLSEND	NEWCASTLE 22/6/15	GSW CHEST 20/3/18	TO 20th, 12th, 20th BNS, CLASS Z RESERVE.
LYNCH	Wm	PTE	180 HETTON LE HOLE	27/2/15	KR para 392 21/7/17	AGE 21,MENTIONED IN COMS PROUD'S NOTEBOOK
LYONS	Hard	PTE	931			ATT 185 TUN COY RE, TO 11th, 19th, 20th, 15th BNS. BORN CHESTER LE STREET, AGE 38
LYTH	Henry	PTE	20 WEST HARTLEPOOL	WEST HARTLEPOOL	25/8/17 TEMPLEUX LE GUERARD	TO 18th BN, CLASS Z RESERVE.
MADDISON	Thos	PTE	598 OLD PENSHAW	SHINEY ROW	7/11/18 DOURLERS CEM EXT	TO 1/7th BN, CLASS Z RESERVE.
MAKEPEACE	John	PTE	487 HOUGHTON LE SPRING			FGCM NOV 16
MALLETT	James	PTE	876			TO 15th BN.
MANN	J G	PTE				DID NOT SERVE OVERSEAS.
MAPSTONE	Edwin	PTE	100 SUNDERLAND	SUNDERLAND	2/10/17 TYNE COT MEM	TO 28th BN.
MARGIOTTE	Luigi	PTE	1501 RIPON	BISHOP AUCKLAND 23/3/15	19/10/16 FAUBOURG D'AMIENS	TO 15th BN. AGE 21
MARSDEN	Henry	PTE	919		KR para 392 17/8/15	TO 3rd BN. AGE 40
MARSHALL	Wm W	PTE	GATESHEAD			
MARTIN	John	PTE	181 HOUGHTON LE SPRING	HOUGHTON LE SPRING 14/8/15	6/8/17 BUCQUOY ROAD CEM	TO LABOUR CORPS. LAB CORPS No 116821
MATHER	Robt	PTE	1526		KR para 392 6/5/18	ATT 185 & 176 TUN COYS RE, TO 11th BN, CLASS Z RESERVE.
MATHEWSON	Geo T	SGT	579			TO CLASS Z RESERVE.
MATTHEW	John	PTE	185			BORN BROOMSIDE AGE 32
MATTHEWS	Norm	PTE	654 HUTTON HENRY	WEST HARTLEPOOL	27/10/17 DOZINGHEM MIL CEM	TO 14th BN AGE 20. IN SDGW AS 12/1002
MATTHEWS	Robt	PTE	1589 HAZELRIGG		17/8/17 DUNKIRK TOWN CEM	
McANENY	Geo	PTE	1002 SUNDERLAND	SUNDERLAND		

Surname	First	Rank	No	Place	Enlisted	Casualty	Notes
McARDLE	Geo	PTE	1268	SUNDERLAND	1/6/15		TO 3rd BN. MINER AGE 25,5'1". DESERTED 1/8/15 LEAMSIDE.3/2/16 SHIELDS
McCALLUM	John	PTE		GATESHEAD	SOUTH SHIELDS 1/9/15		HORSE DRIVER AGE 22.5'0". DESERTED 1/9/15 SOUTH SHIELDS
McCAULEY	Rich	CPL	1431				TO CLASS Z RESERVE.
McCLOUD	JohnW	PTE	1283				TO LABOUR CORPS. LAB CORPS No 112587
McCONE	Matt	PTE	786		16/3/15		TO DEPOT.
McCONVEY	Arth	PTE	147				TO CLASS 2 RESERVE.
McCOURT	Wm	PTE	287	WASHINGTON			TO CLASS 2 RESERVE.
McDONALD	John	LCPL	420	SUNDERLAND		18/1/17 ST POL COM CEM	LABOURER AGE 28.SENTENCED TO BE SHOT BY FGCM.
McDONALD	Walt	PTE	581				TO LABOUR CORPS. LAB CORPS No 116741
McDONNELL	H	PTE	1174	SOUTH SHIELDS			TO 12th, 12th BN. CLASS Z RESERVE.
McGAHAN		PTE	493				ATT 185 TUN COY RE, TO 11th, 19th, 18th BNS, CLASS Z RESERVE
McGAW	Geo	PTE	266		6/6/15	KR para 392 9/11/17	TO 3rd BN. AGE 30
McGIN	Wm	PTE	1312				TO LABOUR CORPS. LAB CORPS No 117686
McGRAW	Thos	SGT	68				TO LABOUR CORPS. LAB CORPS No 116739
McKENZIE	John	PTE	1150		21/5/15	KR para 392 10/6/16	DID NOT SERVE OVERSEAS.
McMAHON	John	PTE	674	HENDON		14/5/16 PHILOSOPHE BRIT CEM	TO 14th BN. AGE 21
MERLIN	Alf	PTE	11	WEST HARTLEPOOL		27/5/18 ST ERME COM CEM	TO 12th, 20th, 17th BNS. AGE 19
METCALF	JohnW	PTE	847		16/3/15	KR para 392 11/5/18	TO 20th BN. AGE 22
METCALFE	Harr	PTE	391		1/3/15	SICK 21/7/15	DID NOT SERVE OVERSEAS.
MIDDLEMISS		PTE	1543	MIDDRIDGE			ATT 104 LIGHT TRENCH MORTAR BATTERY. CLASS Z RESERVE.
MILBURN	Geo R	PTE	295	HAMSTERLEY COLLIERY			TO LONDON REGT(1/5th BN). LONDON REGT No 45304. RENUMBERED 307251
MILBURN	Jos	PTE	274				TO LABOUR CORPS, ROYAL FUSILIERS, ROYAL ENGINEERS. LAB CORPS No 116740. R FUS No G/62630. RE No 362224
MILLER	Geo B	LSGT	428	WHEATBOTTOM	2/3/15	25/7/16 THIEPVAL MEM	DID NOT SERVE OVERSEAS.
MILLER	Thos	PTE	431			KR para 392 17/8/15	CPL.
MILLER	Willo	PTE	3	WEST HARTLEPOOL			TO 13th, 18th BNS, CLASS Z RESERVE.
MILLETT	John	PTE	958				
MILLINGTON	Sam	PTE	1468	BILSTON STAFFS	2/3/15	17/7/16 CORBIE COM CEM	TO DEPOT.
MILLS	James	PTE	489		2/3/15	WOUNDS 14/6/17	BORN HEDLEY HILL
MILLS	James	PTE	494	BRANDON COLLIERY	DURHAM	18/7/16 THIEPVAL MEM	DEAD ON MR.
MILLS	Robt	PTE	1016				TO DEPOT.
MINCOFF	Harry	PTE	640		9/3/15	WOUNDS 26/3/17	
MITCHELL	ChasW	PTE	626	GATESHEAD			TO LABOUR CORPS. LAB CORPS No 112640
MITCHELL	Geo	PTE	781				
MOFFITT	James	PTE	961	GATESHEAD		1/8/16 ST SEVER CEM ROUEN	TO ARMY RESERVE CLASS P. LCPL, AGE 25
MOLE	ThosP	PTE	857		22/2/15	KR para 392 31/10/16	TO MACHINE GUN CORPS(106th MG COY), MGC No 25215, AGE 32
MONCRIEFF	John	PTE	51	SOUTH SHIELDS		23/10/17 DOZINGHEM MIL CEM	TO 12th BN. ATT ARMY SERVICE CORPS, CLASS Z RESERVE.
MONTAGUE	Andrw	PTE	686				TO 10th, 22nd BNS. ALSO AT 12 COATSWORTH ROAD.SPELT MOODY
MOODIE	Geo F	SGT	929	GATESHEAD	25/3/15	KR para 392 29/1/19	ATT 188 LAB COY, TO 22nd, 18th, 18th BNS, CLASS Z RESERVE.
MOORE	James	PTE	492				TO ARMY RESERVE CLASS W. AGE 30
MOORE	Syd C	PTE	1423	FENCEHOUSES	6/7/15	KR para 392 18/10/17	TO 19th BN. CLASS Z RESERVE.
MORDUE	Wm	PTE	105				TO DEPOT.
MORGAN	James	PTE	975		29/3/15	SICK 21/12/16	
MORGAN	John	PTE	1259				
MORRIS	JohnT	PTE	1508				TO LABOUR CORPS. LAB CORPS No 116692
MORTON	Robin	PTE	491	DEWSBURY	STANLEY	25/11/16 FAUBOURG D'AMIENS	
MOTT	Robt	PTE	1337	HARTLEPOOL	WEST HARTLEPOOL 11/6/15	13/2/18 MENDINGHEM MIL CEM	SHIP PLATER AGE 24,5'3".DESERTED 23/7/15 FENCEHOUSES.
MOULD	Thos	PTE	404	WASHINGTON	WASHINGTON	25/7/16 THIEPVAL MEM	
MUDD	David	PTE	720	DURHAM	WEST HARTLEPOOL		
MULLOY	John	PTE	1465	CONSETT	CONSETT 19/7/15		LABOURER AGE 32,5'2", DESERTED 31/7/15 FENCEHOUSES.
MULVANA	Arth	CQMS	1331	WEST HARTLEPOOL	15/3/15	WOUNDS. 10/2/17	TO CLASS Z RESERVE.
MULVEY	James	PTE	785		SUNDERLAND	12/9/16 FAUBOURG D'AMIENS	TO DEPOT.
MUNRO	Henry	PTE	1186	SUNDERLAND			

Surname	Forename	Rank	No. / Birthplace	Residence	Date	Death / KR	Notes
MURGATROYD	Jas W	PTE	827 MIDDLESBROUGH	MIDDLESBROUGH		24/8/16 DIVE COPSE CEM	BORN SHIPLEY YORKS AGE 35. TO 15th, 19th BN.
MURKIN	Alf	PTE	264			KR para 392	TO DEPOT.
MURPHY	Wm H	PTE	1151		21/5/15	WOUNDS 8/8/17	
NALLS	Chris	PTE	523 SOUTH SHIELDS			KR para 392	AGE 23.
NAPIER	Jas W	SGT	422 SOUTH SHIELDS			28/11/16 WANQUETIN COM CEM	ATT 185 TUN COY RE, TO 11th, 19th BNS, CLASS Z RESERVE. AGE 33 DIED OF GAS POISONING
NAYLOR	John	PTE	742 WEST CORNFORTH			1/4/19 WEST CORNFORTH	
NEAL	JohnW	PTE	497 LEADGATE				TO CLASS Z RESERVE.
NEALE	Jas W	PTE	947				
NELSON	Robt	PTE	622 GATESHEAD			3/11/18 GATESHEAD EAST CEM	TO 20th, 19th, 14th, 11th BNS, CLASS Z RESERVE.
NESBITT	James	PTE	1364 SEAHAM				TO 20th BN, STILL SERVING 20/3/20.
NESHAM	Benj	PTE	1318				
NEWBY	Jos	PTE	430 SUNDERLAND	SUNDERLAND		29/7/16 MEREKNOLLS CEM S/LAND	AGE 21.
NEWBY	Wm	PTE	1286		1/6/15	KR para 392 24/6/17	TO 12th, 12th BN. AGE 22
NEWCOMBE	Henry	PTE	1240		29/5/15	KR para 392 6/2/19	
NEWCOMBE	Thos	PTE	1578 WILLINGTON			KR para 392	TO DEPOT. LABOURER AGE 21, 5'1", DESERTED 27/10/16 NEWCASTLE
NEWTON	Andw	PTE	1560 SUNDERLAND	SUNDERLAND 10/8/15			
NEWTON	G	PTE	109 DARLINGTON				
NEWTON	Geo	PTE	110 DARLINGTON				
NEWTON	Jos	PTE	1456		3/6/15	KR para 392 12/11/17	TO 14th, 19th, 15th BNS, CLASS Z RESERVE.
NEWTON	Thos	PTE	1295				TO ARMY RESERVE CLASS W. AGE 42, DID NOT SERVE OVERSEAS
NICHOL	Wm	PTE	1235				ATT 19th ORDNANCE DEPOT, LABOUR CORPS, 19th BN, CLASS Z RES. LAB CORP No 446210
NICHOLSON	Geo	PTE	152		27/2/15	KR para 392 14/11/17	TO ARMY RESERVE CLASS W. AGE 40
NICHOLSON	Robt	PTE	554				TO 10th, LABOUR CORPS, 15th BN, CLASS Z RESERVE.
NICHOLSON	RobtH	PTE	496				TO 10th, 22nd, 19th, 1/7th BNS, CLASS Z RESERVE. ON MR AS /497
NIMMO	Jas H	LSGT	495 WEST CORNFORTH		2/3/15	KR para 392 3/1/17	TO ARMY RESERVE CLASS P. AGE 28
NIXON	Thos	PTE	813				TO CLASS Z RESERVE.
OAKES	Herbt	PTE	44		25/2/15	KR para 392 12/2/19	DID NOT SERVE OVERSEAS.
OATES	Thos	PTE	499		2/3/15	KR para 392 13/1/19	TO 11th, 18th, 11th BNS. AGE 28
OATES	Walt	PTE	725		3/3/15	22/10/16 FAUBOURG D'AMIENS	AGE 19
O'HARA	James	PTE	1605	SUNDERLAND		KR para 392 3/5/18	AGE 23
OLDKNOW	James	PTE	286		24/8/15	KR para 392 23/4/19	TO 11th, 19th BNS, ARMY RESERVE CLASS P. AGE 28. FGCM NOV 1916
OLIVER	James	PTE	345 SOUTHWICK		1/3/15	SICK 6/12/16	TO DEPOT.
ONEILL	Frncs	PTE	395 LEAMSIDE	SEAHAM HARBOUR		11/5/16 ST PATRICKS CEM LOOS	ATT 173 TUN COY RE.
OWEN	Jas A	PTE	1118				TO 13th, 13th, 12th BNS, CLASS Z RESERVE.
OWENS	James	PTE	215				TO LABOUR CORPS. LAB CORPS No 112589
PALIN	ThosF	PTE	895				TO 18th, 19th BNS, CLASS Z RESERVE.
PALMER	Thos	PTE	1424				TO LABOUR CORPS. LAB CORPS No 111943
PARK	Franc	CPL	1103				TO 20th, 12th, 12th BNS, CLASS Z RESERVE.
PARRY	Sam	PTE	63				TO 19th BN, CLASS Z RESERVE. SGT
PATTERSON	Sam	PTE	619 CRAGHEAD		8/3/15	KR para 392 3/1/17	TO ARMY RESERVE CLASS P. AGE 38
PATTISON	Alf E	PTE	586			KR para 392	
PATTISON	John	PTE	571			KR para 392	TO 15th BN, CLASS Z RESERVE.
PEACOCK	JohnR	SGT	1296 WEST HARTLEPOOL	DEAF HILL		28/7/17 MENIN GATE MEM	TO CLASS Z RESERVE. BROTHERS 2nd E YORKS, 74 SIG COY RE.
PEARCE	FredW	PTE	1285 WINGATE				TO 12th, 20th BNS.
PEARSON	Geo	PTE	808 CHESTER LE STREET				TO 20th, 2nd BNS, CLASS Z RESERVE.
PEAT	Rob B	PTE	294				TO 19th BN, CLASS Z RESERVE.
PENNELL	Jos	PTE	1022 FULWELL			KR para 392 11/7/17	ATT 35 DIV HQ, ARMY HQ PORTUGESE DIV, 13 CORPS HQ, Z RESERVE
PENNELL	John	PTE	1080				TO DEPOT. LCPL AGE 26
PERKS	Jos	PTE	985				TO CLASS Z RESERVE.
PERRY	Frank	SGT	689 TYNE DOCK	NORTH SHIELDS	13/5/15	13/7/17 ST SEVER CEM ROUEN	BORN TYNEMOUTH

Surname	Initials	Rank	No. / Town	Cemetery / Memorial	Enlisted	Date / KR	Notes
PETCH	Abd	PTE	103				TO LABOUR CORPS, LAB CORPS No 111914
PHELPS	Edwin	PTE	435 HULL				DESERTED EN ROUTE TO W HARTLEPOOL 14/5/15, SEAMAN COMMISSIONED 29/5/17.
PHILIPS	Hny	PTE			NEWCASTLE 14/5/15	KR para 392	DID NOT SERVE OVERSEAS
PHILIPS	Stan	SGT	1622				TO 28th BN.
PICKERING	J O	PTE	1391		28/6/15	KR para 392 28/7/16	TO CLASS Z RESERVE. SERVED IN BN BAND
PIKE	CyR D	PTE	285 GATESHEAD				TO CLASS Z RESERVE. WITNESS AT THE FGCM OF SGT STONES
PINE	Wm H	CPL	66 SOUTH SHIELDS				
PINKNEY	John	PTE	362 EASINGTON				
POOLEY	Geo	PTE	312		1/3/15	KR para 392 24/3/16	TO LABOUR CORPS, LAB CORPS No 111932
POPE	JohnT	PTE	765				
PORTER	John	PTE	OLD PENSHAW				TO DEPOT, 19th BN. LABOURER AGE 21,5'1", DESERTED 27/10/16 NEWCASTLE
POTTER	Geo W	PTE	330 SOUTH SHIELDS	15/9/18 BELGIAN BATTERY CRNR	SOUTH SHIELDS 1/3/15		TO 2nd, 11th 18th BNS.
POTTS	Geo	PTE	1350 SUNDERLAND	10/5/17 DUISANS BRIT CEM	SUNDERLAND		TO 20th, 14th, 22nd BNS, CLASS Z RESERVE.
POTTS	Robt	PTE	203				FGCM NOV 16
POTTS	W	PTE					TO 13th BN.
POUNDER	Thos	SGT	9 WEST HARTLEPOOL	5/10/18 BEAUREVOIR BRIT CEM	CHESTER LE STREET		TO 19th BN. ON MR AS DEAD
POWELL	Wm	SGT	348 LEAMSIDE	26/6/16 CORBIE COM CEM	SUNDERLAND		TO LABOUR CORPS(940 LAB COY), 19th BN, CLASS Z RESERVE. LAB CORPS No 442649
PRATER	Arth	PTE	1360 SILKSWORTH				TO LABOUR CORPS, LAB CORPS No 112677
PREECE	John	PTE	999				TO 13th BN, CLASS Z RESERVE.
PRIESTMAN	David	PTE	812				TO CLASS Z RESERVE. BORN 1892. PROMOTED RQMS 4/12/17
PRINGLE	John	PTE	192				TO LABOUR CORPS, LAB CORPS No 116743. FGCM NOV 16
PROCTOR	Harry	PTE	417				TO CLASS Z RESERVE. MENTIONED IN CQMS PROUD'S NOTEBOOK
PROUD	JohnC	RQMS	649 WEST HARTLEPOOL		10/3/15		TO 14th, 2nd, 1/7th BNS, CLASS Z RESERVE.
PROUDFOOT	Hubert	PTE	30				TO CLASS Z RESERVE.
PURVIS	Wm	PTE	658 WREKENTON			30/5/19	TO 21st,23rd, 19th BNS, LABOUR CORPS(188, 185 LAB COYS), LAB CORP No 112680.WAS 20743 CHESHIRE REGT DISCHARGED15/3/15
PYBUS	Thom	LCPL	500				TO 15th BN. DESERTED 10/12/18
QUAYLE	John	PTE	373				TO 13th, 20th, 20th BNS, CLASS Z RESERVE.
QUEENAN	John	PTE	906 SOUTH SHIELDS		JARROW 28/3/15	29/3/19	TO DEPOT.
QUINN	Chas	PTE	289		27/2/15	KR para 392 11/2/18	TO 1st BN, CLASS Z RESERVE. WAR MEDAL ONLY, SERVED OVERSEAS ONLY IN INDIA
RAGAN	Wm D	PTE	398				
RAGG	Ralph	PTE	936				
READER	Chas	PTE	364		1/3/15	WOUNDS 17/2/17	TO 2nd, 18th(A COY) BNS.
REED	Thos	PTE	782	24/8/16 THIEPVAL MEM	NEWCASTLE		TO ROYAL ENGINEERS
RENFORTH	Robt	CPL	1032 NEWCASTLE	19/7/16 THIEPVAL MEM	SUNDERLAND		TO 2nd, 20th BNS.
RENNEY	ThosB	PTE	383 SUNDERLAND	18/5/17 ARRAS MEM	SUNDERLAND		LABOURER AGE 19,5'2", DESERTED 11/6/15 FENCEHOUSES.
RENNEY	Wm	PTE	751 SUNDERLAND				
RICE	John	PTE	411 BIRTLEY				
RICE	Pat	PTE	144 WORKINGTON	16/9/16 THIEPVAL MEM	GATESHEAD		TO MACHINE GUN CORPS, MGC No 136380.
RICH	Chas	PTE	1212 SUNDERLAND	19/5/16 ST VAAST POST MIL	SUNDERLAND 27/5/15		BORN SOUTH SHIELDS
RICHARDSON	Geo S	PTE	1416 SUNDERLAND				ATT ARMY SERVICE CORPS(236 COY), 19th BN, CLASS Z RESERVE.
RICHARDSON	J W	PTE	880	10/10/16 FAUBOURG D'AMIENS	HOUGHTON LE SPRING		TO 23rd BN. DID NOT SERVE OVERSEAS
RICHARDSON	ThosP	SGT	418 HETTON LE HOLE				TO CLASS Z RESERVE.
RIDDLE	Arth	PTE	1603 CHESTER LE STREET	SICK 27/2/16	2/3/15		TO LABOUR CORPS, LAB CORPS No 28206
RILEY	JohnG	PTE	504				MINER AGE 20,FGCM NOV 16 AWARDED PENAL SERVITUDE.
RISPIN	Geo	SGT	381				TO DEPOT.
RITCHIE	N	PTE	741 FENCEHOUSES				TO 2nd BN.
RITCHIE	T	PTE	505				TO CLASS Z RESERVE.
ROACH	Wm J	PTE	1390	SICK 8/5/16	3/3/15		
ROBERTS	Wm	PTE	1433 NORWICH	8/6/17 CHOCQUES MIL CEM	28/6/15		
ROBINSON	Geo L	PTE	787 SEAHAM		EASINGWOLD YORKS		

Surname	Forename	Rank	No	Town	Enlisted	Died / Discharged	Notes
ROBINSON	Henry	PTE	1290		2/6/15	KR para 392 31/10/17	TO ARMY RESERVE CLASS W. AGE 25
ROBINSON	Jas H	PTE	718	SUNDERLAND	SUNDERLAND	23/8/16 THIEPVAL MEM	
ROBINSON	John	LCPL	502	TRIMDON COLLIERY	FERRYHILL	24/8/16 THIEPVAL MEM	
ROBINSON	Thos	PTE	1204	SUNDERLAND	SUNDERLAND	27/5/18 SOISSONS MEM	TO 10th, 22nd BN. AGE 24
ROBINSON	Wm B	PTE	88				TO 19th, 19th, 7th BNS, CLASS Z RESERVE.
ROBSON	Alf H	PTE	50	SOUTH SHIELDS	27/2/15	22/8/16 BURIED 26/12/17 WESTOE CEM	TO 23rd BN. DID NOT SERVE OVERSEAS
ROBSON	Dan	PTE	565			11/2/22	STILL SERVING 15/3/20.
ROBSON	Ralph	PTE	790	SUNDERLAND	WEST HARTLEPOOL 15/3/15 SICK 26/4/15		RIVET HEATER, AGE 19, 5'0",115lbs, DID NOT SERVE OVERSEAS
ROCHESTER	Thos	PTE	797		27/2/15	KR para 392 28/7/16	TO DEPOT. AGE 20
ROGERS	Geo H	PTE	708	NORMANTON	SUNDERLAND	25/11/16 FAUBOURG D'AMIENS	TO ROYAL IRISH RIFLES. R I RIFLES No 40076
ROONEY	T	LCPL	508	MURTON COLLIERY			TO CLASS Z RESERVE.
ROSSI	Louis	PTE	727		2/3/15		TO LABOUR CORPS. LAB CORPS No 111958
ROWAN	Frank	PTE	433	SUNDERLAND			TO CLASS Z RESERVE.
ROWE	Rich	LCPL	377				TO CLASS Z RESERVE. FGCM NOV 1916
RUMLEY	Robt	PTE	137	BRANDON			TO 4th BN.
RUMNEY	Jos R	PTE	340	NEW BRANCEPETH			TO 26th BN, CLASS Z RESERVE.
RUSSELL	Arth	LCPL	1130	DURHAM CITY	GATESHEAD	19/7/18 PLOEGSTEERT MEM	TO 18th BN(A COY). AGE 23
RUSSELL	JohnR	PTE	1205	NEWCASTLE			TO 10th BN. DESERTED
RUTLEY	Right	PTE	550		28/2/15		TO DEPOT.
RUTLEY	Wm	PTE	73		SUNDERLAND	WOUNDS 27/3/17	TO CLASS Z RESERVE.
RUTTER	Peter	PTE	722	MURTON		19/7/16 THIEPVAL MEM	
RYAN	Lowes	PTE	852				TO LABOUR CORPS. LAB CORPS No 111955
SALMON	RobtH	PTE	400		STANLEY	23/10/17 ARTILLERY WOOD CEM	TO 20th, 1/9th(C COY) BNS, CLASS Z RESERVE. RES SHERBURN HILL 1916
SANDERS	Wm Ed	PTE	618	TANFIELD LEA			TO 20th BN.
SCOLLEN	Sam	ASGT	128	EASINGTON COLLIERY			TO CLASS Z RESERVE.
SCOTT	David	PTE	868	SOUTH SHIELDS	SOUTH SHIELDS	21/10/18 OUTRIJVE CHYD	TO LABOUR CORPS. LAB CORPS No 116702
SCOTT	Geo G	ASGT	1237				TO 19th BN.
SCRATCHARD	Harld	PTE	1447		10/5/15	KR para 392 29/3/19	TO 2nd, 2nd, 13th BNS, STILL SERVING 15/3/20.
SCRUBY	Sid	PTE	1018				TO LABOUR CORPS. LAB CORPS No 112650
SEYMOUR	Arth	PTE	921	SOUTH MOOR	STANLEY	18/7/16 THIEPVAL MEM	MENTIONED IN CQMS PROUD'S NOTEBOOK.
SHAW	James	PTE	1226				TO 20th, 15th BNS, CLASS Z RESERVE.
SHEPHERD	Norrn	PTE	1587		13/5/15		TO CLASS Z RESERVE.
SHEPHERD	Jos	PTE	354				AGE 21
SHIEL	Chris	PTE	984			KR para 392 4/3/18	TO LABOUR CORPS(720 LAB COY), LAB CORPS No 112649
SHIELDS	Owen	PTE	1087		WEST HARTLEPOOL	30/5/17 HEUDICOURT BRIT CEM	
SHONE	Frank	PTE	761	HARTLEPOOL			
SHORT	Geo	PTE	1445	DARLINGTON	SOUTH SHIELDS	2/4/16 RUE PETILLON MIL CEM	TO DEPOT. AGE 26, MINER
SIMPSON	Jas	PTE	54	JARROW	8/7/15	KR para 392 28/2/17	TO 20th BN(B COY).
SIMPSON	Jos	PTE	1432				TO 19th BN. CLASS Z RESERVE. 3rd NORTHERN GEN HOSP SHEFFIELD 8/7/16
SIMPSON	Wm	PTE	963	BILLQUAY		16/9/16 THIEPVAL MEM	TO 15th BN. CLASS Z RESERVE.
SINCLAIR	Jos	PTE	70		9/2/15		
SKIMMINGS	Normn	CPL	957				
SKINNER	Wm	PTE	689				
SLATER	J G	PTE	1415		9/2/15	KR para 392 15/6/16	DID NOT SERVE OVERSEAS.
SLOAN	J	PTE			3/7/15	KR para 392 29/10/15	BN TWEEDMOUTH AGE 19.5'2". FAIR BLUE, WESLEYAN, ELECTRICIAN.
SMEDLEY	Andrw	PTE	1216	NEWCASTLE	GATESHEAD 27/5/15	16/4/16 ST VAAST POST MIL	TO ARMY RESERVE CLASS W. AGE 40
SMITH	Anthy	PTE	47		27/2/15	KR para 392 8/7/18	AGE 41
SMITH	Anthy	PTE	760		15/3/15	KR para 392 15/10/16	TO 18th BN, CLASS Z RESERVE.
SMITH	Geo W	PTE	736		13/3/15	KR para 392 3/4/19	TO LABOUR CORPS. LAB CORPS No 116747
SMITH	Harry	LSGT	292				
SMITH	Hertt	PTE	306				
SMITH	JohnH	LCPL	817	CROOK		19/10/18 HARLEBEKE NEW BRIT	ATT 185 TUN COY RE, TO 11th, 19th BNS. AGE 22

Surname	Forename	Rank	No.	Birthplace	Enlisted	Fate / Memorial	Notes
SMITH	JohnH	PTE	1160	GATESHEAD	NEWCASTLE 1/6/15		TO CLASS Z RESERVE.
SMITH	Peter	PTE	1260	ALSTON			TO 3rd BN. LABOURER AGE 40,5'2". DESERTED 15/11/15 TIDWORTH.
SMITH	Rich	PTE	1061				
SMITH	Rich	LSGT	1566	NEW SEAHAM	SEAHAM HARBOUR	KR para 392	TO 22nd, 19th BNS. BORN STARGATE RYTON
SMITH	Sam	PTE	1462	DEPTFORD		25/3/18 POZIERES MEM	TO 22nd, 20th BNS. AGE 20
SMITH	Steph	PTE	945	CROOK		23/9/17 HOOGE CRATER CEM	TO LABOUR CORPS(185 LAB COY), LAB CORPS No 112647
SMITH	Syd	PTE	613	HIGH SPEN			
SMITH	Wilf	PTE	512	SUNDERLAND	SUNDERLAND	6/5/17 THIEPVAL MEM	AGE 29.
SNAITH	Geo	SGT	75	SUNDERLAND	SUNDERLAND	20/4/18 DOULLENS MIL CEM	TO 1/6th BN, CLASS Z RESERVE. IN Z COY
SNAITH	JohnT	PTE	275	CORNSAY COLLIERY			TO DEPOT.
SNOWBALL	Wm	PTE	1249			WOUNDS 11/5/17	TO LABOUR CORPS. LAB CORPS No 111962
SNOWDON	JohnT	PTE	1062	SUNDERLAND	31/5/15		TO LABOUR CORPS, 19th BN, CLASS Z RESERVE. LAB CORPS No 111424
SNOWDON	John	PTE	1448		SUNDERLAND	3/12/17 VLAMERTINGHE NEW MIL	TO CLASS Z RESERVE.
SPARK	Ernst	PTE	1050				TO LABOUR CORPS(717 LAB COY). IN POST WITH McDONALD & RITCHIE 25/11/1? LAB CORPS No 111631
SPENCE	Cuthb	PTE	190	NEWCASTLE	SUNDERLAND		STILL SERVING FEB 1920.
SPENCER	Rich	PTE	1428			11/11/16 FAUBOURG D'AMIENS	AGE 23
SPOURS	Thos	PTE	877	FULWELL			TO 18th, 19th BNS, CLASS Z RESERVE.
STAFF	James	SGT	1430				TO TRAINING RESERVE BN. TRG RES No TR5/8604
STAINES	G	PTE	1436	STANLEY	NEWCASTLE	22/10/16 FAUBOURG D'AMIENS	BORN CRAGHEAD
STAINES	JohnP	PTE	272	OXHILL	3/3/15	KR para 392 14/11/17	AGE 28.
STAVELEY	Matth	CPL	202				TO LABOUR CORPS. LAB CORPS No 116745
STEPHENSON	Fred	CPL	53		27/2/15	KR para 392 29/11/18	TO 4th BN. AGE 21
STEPHENSON	Geo	CPL	1006	SUNDERLAND	SUNDERLAND 5/3/15	24/8/16 THIEPVAL MEM	TO 18th, 1/9th, 11th, 19th BNS. AGE 22
STEPHENSON	Jos	LCPL	584		JARROW 2/3/15	KR para 392 3/8/18	BORN WALDRIDGE FELL
STEPHENSON	Wm	PTE	1548	CHESTER LE STREET		19/7/16 THIEPVAL MEM	TO DEPOT.
STERLING	James	PTE	367			KR para 392 23/11/16	IN POST A 25/26 NOV 1916
STEVENS	Harry	CPL					TO 20th BN, CLASS Z RESERVE.
STEVENSON	James	PTE	818	SEAHAM HARBOUR			TO CLASS Z RESERVE.
STEWART	James	PTE	1521		SEAHAM HARBOUR	25/7/16 THIEPVAL MEM	
STEWART	Pat	PTE	637		NEWCASTLE 29/6/15	Z RES 30/3/19	TO DEPOT, 19th BN, ASC(21 LAB COY),LABOUR CORPS(188 LAB COY) LAB CORP No 112595. CARTMAN AGE 23 5'1", LC BASE D 28/9/17
STIDSON	Fred	PTE				KR para 392 6/6/18	
STOBBS	John	PTE	1395	NEWCASTLE	27/2/15	22/9/16 ETAPLES MIL CEM	AGE 21
STOKER	RobtE	PTE	175		NEWCASTLE	18/1/17 ST POL COM CEM	BORN BRADFORD AGE 29.
STOKOE	Fred	LSGT	1458	BYKER		25/7/16 THIEPVAL MEM	SENTENCED TO BE SHOT BY FGCM.
STONES	Jos W	PTE	647	CROOK	SUNDERLAND 29/5/15	KR para 392 29/10/15	AGE 22.
STOREY	Isaac	PTE	1227	EASINGTON LANE			DID NOT SERVE OVERSEAS.
STOTHARD	James	PTE	358				FGCM
SURTEES	T	PTE	821				
SWEENEY	John	PTE	1001		10/3/15		TO LABOUR CORPS. LAB CORPS No 116748
SWIFT	Thos	PTE	964	OLD PENSHAW		GSW 8/8/16	TO 4th BN.
SWINHOE	John	PTE	887	SOUTHWICK			TO LABOUR CORPS, 13th, 13th BN, CLASS Z RESERVE. LAB CORPS No 112594
SYDNEY	A	PTE	85		SUNDERLAND	23/8/16 THIEPVAL MEM	
TATE	JohnT	SGT	1055				DEAD ON MR.
TAYLOR	ChasL	PTE					TO LABOUR CORPS. LAB CORPS No 111366
TAYLOR	Dobsn	PTE	1422	SUNDERLAND	SUNDERLAND 5/7/15		TO LABOUR CORPS(LAB CORPS No 42033). RIVET HEATER AGE 20, 5'2". DESERTED 5/8/15 COCKEN HALL
TAYLOR	E	PTE	162	TYNEMOUTH	NORTH SHIELDS	13/5/16 ST VAAST POST MIL	TO LABOUR CORPS. LAB CORPS No 111915
TAYLOR	James	PTE	515				TO CLASS Z RESERVE.
TAYLOR	James	PTE	889				TO CLASS Z RESERVE.
TAYLOR	Matt	BNDSN	1097	WEST HARTLEPOOL			

Surname	Forename	Rank	No.	Place	Enlisted/Res.	Discharge/Death	Notes
TAYLOR	Ralph	PTE	575	BRANDON	1/3/15	KR para 392 25/1/19	TO CLASS Z RESERVE.
TAYLOR	Wm	PTE	379		SHINY ROW	27/5/18 TINCOURT NEW BRIT	DID NOT SERVE OVERSEAS.
TAYLOR	Jos	PTE	634		10/6/15	KR para 392 12/7/18	TO CLASS Z RESERVE.
TEASDALE	Thos	SGT	549	NEW HERRINGTON			TO LABOUR CORPS. LAB CORPS No 573284
TEMPERLEY	Thos	PTE	1326			KR para 392	TO 14th BN, DEPOT, AGE 29
TEMPLE	Thos	PTE	10	WEST HARTLEPOOL			TO LABOUR CORPS. LAB CORPS No 112073
THIRLWALL	Wm U	PTE	856		WEST HARTLEPOOL	22/7/16 CARNOY MIL CEM	ATT 19th ORDNANCE DEPOT.
THOMAS	Frank	PTE	2	GLAMORGAN	GATESHEAD	3/6/16 LE TOURET MIL CEM	BORN BRADFORD.
THOMPSON	Fred	PTE	1340	THORNBURY YORKS			TO CLASS Z RESERVE.
THOMPSON	Fred	PTE	303	DAWDON			TO 20th, 16th, 19th BNS. CLASS Z RESERVE.
THOMPSON	John	PTE	971		26/8/15	KR para 392 8/12/17	TO ARMY RESERVE CLASS W. CPL AGE 30
THOMPSON	JohnW	PTE	1609		NORTH SHIELDS	28/12/15 TIDWORTH MIL CEM	BORN TYNEMOUTH. AGE 21 ACCIDENTALLY KILLED.
THOMPSON	M	CPL	870	NORTH SHIELDS	WEST HARTLEPOOL 15/5/15		MINER AGE 21,5'3". DESERTED 15/8/15 COCKEN HALL
THOMPSON	R	PTE	405	SUNDERLAND			DID NOT SERVE OVERSEAS.
THOMPSON	Robt	PTE	1085	SUNDERLAND	27/2/15	KR para 392 17/8/15	TO ROYAL DEFENCE CORPS. RDC No 76433
THOMPSON	Robt	PTE	157				TO 3rd BN. LABOURER AGE 20,5'0". DESERTED 18/11/18 SOUTH SHIELDS
THOMPSON	W	PTE	972		SUNDERLAND 8/5/15	KR para 392	ATT DETAILS BN DLI, CLASS Z RESERVE.
THOMSON	Wm C	SGT	1007	SUNDERLAND			MENTIONED IN CQMS PROUD'S NOTEBOOK
THORNLEY	Geo	PTE	1193		24/6/15	KR para 392 31/1/19	TO 18th BN. AGE 21
TILLBURY		PTE	1276				TO LABOUR CORPS. LAB CORPS No 116704
TIMNEY	Thos	PTE	1384				TO LABOUR CORPS(187 LAB COY). LAB CORPS No 111941
TODD	Nich	PTE	1538				BORN GATESHEAD
TODD	Robt	PTE	151	FIR TREE			ATTACHED MACHINE GUN CORPS, DETAILS BN DLI. CLASS Z RESERVE.
TODD	Wm	PTE	276	BIRTLEY	GATESHEAD	24/7/16 THIEPVAL MEM	TO 19th, 20th, BNS, CLASS Z RESERVE.
TOSHACK	James	SGT	552				TO 10th, 22nd. BNS. AGE 23
TRAINER	Franc	PTE	29	WEST HARTLEPOOL	25/5/15	KR para 392 6/3/19	TO CLASS Z RESERVE.
TRAYNOR	JohnW	PTE	1173	JARROW			TO 3rd BN. DID NOT SERVE OVERSEAS
TROTTER	John	PTE	1113		5/3/15	SICK 6/12/16	TO 20th, 19th BNS, CLASS Z RESERVE.
TUDOR	James	PTE	585				TO ARMY RESERVE CLASS P. AGE 29
TULIP	Ladas	PTE	671	SEAHAM	7/6/15	KR para 392 2/4/17	BORN HARRATON AGE 29
TULIP	Thos	PTE	1309	FENCEHOUSES	HOUGHTON LE SPRING	18/7/16 DIVE COPSE BRIT CEM	TO PB BN DLI(BASE), CLASS Z RESERVE.
TULLY	JohnT	PTE	551	FENCEHOUSES			TO LABOUR CORPS. LAB CORPS No 111916
TUNNICLIFFE	John	PTE	793				TO CLASS Z RESERVE.
TURLEY	Thos	PTE	832				TO 11th BN, CLASS Z RESERVE.
TURNBULL	Jos	CPL	743		WEST HARTLEPOOL	21/10/17 NINE ELMS POPERINGHE	TO 10th BN, BASE DETAILS, ATT 17 CORPS HQ. SHOWN AS DEAD ON MR??
TURNBULL	Robt A	PTE	715		1/3/15	KR para 392 31/7/19	TO LABOUR CORPS. LAB CORPS No 111966
TURNER	Geo	PTE	1083	WEST HARTLEPOOL			TO 15th BN. COMMORATED IN ROYE NEW BRIT CEM. AGE 21
TURNER	John J	PTE	1241	GATESHEAD	GATESHEAD	22/3/18 MARCHELEPOT BRIT CEM	TO 12th, 15th, 1/7th BNS, CLASS Z RESERVE. MEMBER PRIMITIVE METHODIST CHOIR
VARDY	James	PTE	1441	CHILTON	27/2/15	KR para 392 19/1/18	TO LABOUR CORPS. LAB CORPS No 112596
VERNEY	Robt	PTE	363				TO DEPOT. AGE 26
WADE	Henry	LCPL	518				ATT TRENCH MORTAR SCHOOL, 19th, ATT 106 LTMB, 19th, 15th BNS Z RES
WAINWRIGHT	Rich	PTE	1528				MENTIONED IN CQMS PROUD'S NOTEBOOK STILL SERVING 15/3/20.
WAINWRIGHT		PTE					TO 1/8th BN, CLASS Z RESERVE.
WAITE	John	PTE	1165				TO LABOUR CORPS. LAB CORPS No 111968
WAKE	John	PTE	317				TO 2nd, 19th BNS. AGE 23
WALKER	Ern B	PTE	586				TO LABOUR CORPS. LAB CORPS No 116709
WALKER	John	PTE	1564	STANLEY	11/8/15	KR para 392 6/12/18	
WALKER	ThosN	PTE	212		24/5/15	KR para 392 31/1/18	TO DEPOT. AGE 29
WALKER	Wm	PTE	1155				

Surname	Forename	Rank	No.	Place 1	Place 2	Date / Memorial	Notes
WALLACE	John	LCPL	27	WEST HARTLEPOOL			TO 22nd BN, CLASS Z RESERVE.
WALLACE	Wm	PTE	631				TO LABOUR CORPS. LAB CORPS No 116751
WALLIS	Robt	SGT	178	NEWBOTTLE			
WARD	Chas	SGT	1512	LANGLEY PARK	3/8/15	KR para 392	TO 12th BN. AGE 27
WARD	Jas	PTE	1359	OLD PENSHAW	SHINEY ROW	KR para 392 4/7/18	TO 2nd BN. AGE 23
WARD	John	PTE	522		1/3/15	21/3/18 ARRAS MEM	DID NOT SERVE OVERSEAS.
WARD	Pat	PTE	1561		10/8/15	KR para 392 17/8/15	DID NOT SERVE OVERSEAS.
WATERS	Chris	PTE	1529	SUNDERLAND	SUNDERLAND	KR para 392 8/9/16	AGE 22.
WATKINS	ThosW	PTE	17	WEST HARTLEPOOL		23/10/17 TYNE COT MEM	DESERTED.
WATSON	Herbt	PTE	1294	HORDEN	SEAHAM HARBOUR	19/7/16 SERRE ROAD No 2 CEM	BORN SUNDERLAND AGE 20.
WATSON	JohnE	SGT	111	PLAWSWORTH	DURHAM	12/9/17 BRANDHOEK NEW MIL	TO LABOUR CORPS. LAB CORPS No 111871.DLI No ON MR 41
WATSON	Ralph	PTE	796	GATESHEAD	NEWCASTLE	22/10/16 FAUBOURG D'AMIENS	
WATSON	Wm	PTE	97				ATT 106 & 104 LIGHT TRENCH MORTAR BATTERY'S, CLASS Z RES. TO 14th, 11th 1/5th BNS, ATT LOYAL REGT(9th BN), CLASS Z RES ATT 5th ENTRENCHING BN 1918
WATT	JohnW	PTE	424	BRANDON			
WAUGH	Geo H	PTE	756	HARTLEPOOL	WEST HARTLEPOOL	19/7/16 THIEPVAL MEM	TO LABOUR CORPS. LAB CORPS No 111954
WAUGH	Geoff	PTE	160				AGE 23.
WAYSON	Geo K	PTE	1483	NEWFIELD	BISHOP AUCKLAND	31/7/17 MENIN GATE MEM	TO 20th BN.
WEATHERLEY	James	PTE	567				TO LABOUR CORPS. LAB CORPS No 111946
WEBSTER	Reg H	SIG	858	GATESHEAD			
WEETMAN	ThosB	PTE	394				TO LABOUR CORPS. LAB CORPS No 116819
WEIGHTMAN	Leon	PTE	1580				COMMISSIONED 3/8/15.
WEIGHTMAN	Thos	PTE	1027				TO 20th, 15th BNS, CLASS Z RESERVE.
WENNINGTON	Alf E	CPL	1221	DARLINGTON	DARLINGTON	13/9/16 FAUBOURG D'AMIENS	
WHITE	Geo P	CPL	337	SPENNYMOOR	SPENNYMOOR	23/6/16 THIEPVAL MEM	AGE 23.
WHITE	JohnT	PTE	783		15/3/15	KR para 392 3/4/19	AGE 21.
WHITE	Pat	PTE	1320		8/6/15	KR para 392 26/10/17	ATT GUARDS DIV 8/2/16 - 15/2/16. TO CLASS Z RESERVE. CQMS
WHITE	Wm	SGT	41	WEST HARTLEPOOL	SUNDERLAND 18/5/15	20/7/16 CORBIE COM CEM	TO 3rd BN. MINER AGE 28,5'2". DESERTED 5/2/16 SOUTH SHIELDS
WHITEHEAD	Alf	SGT	1119	DARLINGTON	SUNDERLAND	DEFECTIVE SIGHT 22/1/19	AGE 21
WHITEHEAD	Thos	PTE	1421	SUNDERLAND	24/2/15	13/8/15 MASHAM YORKS	TO ARMY RESERVE CLASS W. AGE 31 DID NOT SERVE OVERSEAS
WHITEHOUSE	A E	PTE	38		SUNDERLAND		AGE 40. BORN PRESTON LANCS.
WHITESIDE	JohnW	PTE	1291	SUNDERLAND			ATT 104 LIGHT TRENCH MORTAR BTY.
WIGGINTON	Geo	PTE	982	TUDHOE			TO LABOUR CORPS. LAB CORPS No 116752
WIGHAM	Allan	SGT	164	FULWELL	SUNDERLAND 7/3/15	18/7/16 THIEPVAL MEM	TO DEPOT.
WILBY	Ernst	PTE	594			WOUNDS 14/5/17	ATT 35 DIV HQ, 185 LAB COY, HQ TANK CORPS,RE DUMP, LAB CORPS 185, 188 LAB COYS, 19th DLI, CLASS Z RESERVE
WILDE	Jas R	PTE	1017	WASHINGTON			ATT 232 EMP COY, 35 DIV SALVAGE COY, CLASS Z RESERVE.
WILDEN	Dan	PTE	397	WASHINGTON	17/5/15	MYALGIA 28/1/19	AGE 36 DID NOT SERVE OVERSEAS.
WILKINSON	JohnC	CPL	1126		23/3/15	GASTRITIS 28/1/19	AGE 43 DID NOT SERVE OVERSEAS.
WILKINSON	Thos	PTE	901		27/2/15	KR para 392 1/4/19	TO 19th, 15th BNS, ARMY RESERVE CLASS P. AGE 39
WILLIAMS	Edwd	PTE	521	SOUTH CHURCH	1/6/15	KR para 392 10/9/17	TO DEPOT. AGE 23
WILLIS	Augus	LCPL	1285				TO CLASS Z RESERVE.
WILLMORE	Alf	SGT	313				TO LABOUR CORPS. LAB CORPS No 112599
WILSON	Adam	SGT	1030				TO LABOUR CORPS. LAB CORPS No 111938
WILSON	Geo H	PTE	784				TO LABOUR CORPS. LAB CORPS No 111924
WILSON	James	PTE	392		GATESHEAD 3/8/15		TO DEPOT. AGE 25, 5'1", DESERTED 4/2/16 IN HUDDERSFIELD RENUMBERED 10965
WILSON	James	PTE	1509	GATESHEAD			FGCM
WILSON	Jos	PTE	520				
WILSON	P	PTE	1071		11/5/15	KR para 392 31/10/16	DID NOT SERVE OVERSEAS.
WILSON	Ralph	PTE	187	HETTON LE HOLE	HOUGHTON LE SPRING	11/5/16 ST PATRICKS CEM LOOS	AGE 41.
WILSON	Robt	PTE	1063	PENTONVILLE	SUNDERLAND	18/7/16 DIVE COPSE BRIT CEM	

Surname	Name	Rank	No.	Place	Born/Place 2	Date/Memorial	Notes
WILSON	RobtW	SGT	519	HAMSTERLEY COLLIERY	CONSETT	23/8/16 THIEPVAL MEM	TO LABOUR CORPS. LAB CORPS No 112113
WILSON	Thos	PTE	283	SUNDERLAND		MISCONDUCT 20/12/15	BORN BYKER
WILSON	Thos	LCPL	1065	DURHAM		10/6/16 LE TOURET MIL CEM	TO 3rd BN LABOURER AGE 43
WILSON	Wm	SGT	353	GATESHEAD			CPL
WILSON	Wm	PTE	833	GATESHEAD			TO CLASS Z RESERVE.
WINDLE	John	PTE	357		1/3/15		TO DEPOT. AGE 38
WINN	Thos	PTE	352		1/3/15	KR para 392 11/3/17	TO ARMY RESERVE CLASS W. AGE 36
WOOD	Robt	PTE	616		8/3/15	KR para 392 21/11/17	DID NOT SERVE OVERSEAS
WOOD	Roger	PTE	1365			KR para 392 27/1/19	TO 12th, 10th, 1/7th BNS, CLASS Z RESERVE.
WOOD	Wm	PTE	142				TO CLASS Z RESERVE.
WORMWALD	FredG	LSGT	555	WEST HARTLEPOOL	WEST HARTLEPOOL	18/7/16 DELVILLE WOOD CEM	BORN CASTLEFORD AGE 18.
WORTHY	Jas P	PTE	1289	HASWELL COLLIERY	HOUGHTON LE SPRING	11/10/16 HARBARCQ COM CEM	BORN PENSHAW AGE 21.
WORTHY	Tim	PTE	677		8/3/15	KR para 392 6/3/19	TO ARMY RESERVE CLASS P. AGE 39
WRIGHT	Lawr	PTE	1267	NEW BRANCEPETH	DURHAM	18/7/16 THIEPVAL MEM	BORN GLASGOW.
WRIGHTSON	Wm	CSM	419	NEWBOTTLE	2/3/15	KR para 392 1/4/19	ATT GUARDS DIV 8/2/16 - 15/2/16,TO 3rd BN, ARMY RES CLASS P. AGE 30
YOUNG	Wm	CPL	869				TO 18th BN, CLASS Z RESERVE.
YULE	Robt	SGT	1005	DURHAM CITY	WEST HARTLEPOOL	17/7/16 PERONNE RD CEM	BANDMASTER, SGT STRETCHER BEARER. AGE 42.
YULE	Wm P	CPL	898	FULWELL	NEWCASTLE	7/11/18 DOURLERS COM CEM EXT	TO 188 LAB COY, 22nd, 18th, 15th BNS. LAB CORPS No 112626, BORN MONKWEARMOUTH AGE 27

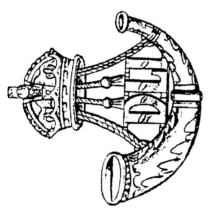

ALPHABETICAL NOMINAL ROLL OF ORIGINAL OTHER RANKS

22nd (Service) Battalion Durham Light Infantry (3rd County)(Pioneer)

1915 – 1919

NAME	INITIAL	RANK	NUMBER	TOWN_VILL	DATE & PLCACE ENL	DATE & CAUSE, DIS, DIED BURIED	TRANSFER NEW NUMBER DESERTED ETC
ADAMSON	Jos	PTE	/1048	EGGLESTONE	7/12/15	KR para 392 17/9/18	AGE 30.
ADDISON	John	PTE	/956	DARLINGTON			TO 1/7th, 1/6th BNS, CLASS Z RESERVE.
ALDERSON	James	PTE	/870	BISHOP AUCKLAND	DARLINGTON	19/6/18 DUEVILLE COM CEM ITALY	ATT 14th CORPS HQ. BORN BARNARD CASTLE AGE 23
ALDERSON	Perci	PTE	/779	DURHAM CITY	BISHOP AUCKLAND	23/10/16 THIEPVAL MEM	TO DEPOT. AGE 26
ALDERSON	Herbt	PTE	/879		7/12/15	KR para 392 18/12/17	TO CLASS Z RESERVE.
ALLAN	Edwd	PTE	/932				TO 1/5th, 20th BNS, CLASS Z RESERVE.
ALLEN	ThosF	PTE	/380	DAWDON			ATT ROYAL ENGINEERS, 22nd, 13th, 22nd, 11th, 22nd, Z RESERVE
ALMOND	Edwd	PTE	/798	WEST HARTLEPOOL			TO 1/7th BN, CLASS Z RESERVE.
ALNWICK	Harrl	PTE	/681	SEAHAM HARBOUR	SEAHAM HARBOUR	30/8/17 STRAND MIL CEM	AGE 28
ANDERSON	Geo W	PTE	/852	HETTON LE HOLE	HOUGHTON LE SPRING	19/9/17 HETTON LE HOLE CEM	AGE 22 BORN EPPLETON.
ANDERSON	Thos	PTE	/1050	HERRINGTON	HOUGHTON LE SPRING		ATT 180 TUN COY RE.
ANDERSON	Hubt	CPL	/704				TO CLASS Z RESERVE.
ANNANNDALE	AlexH	CSGT	/4				TO CLASS Z RESERVE.
APPLEBY	Jos	PTE	/844				TO 1/9th BN. DESERTED 16/11/18, STILL AWOL MARCH 1920
ARCHBOLD	Camm	PTE	/696	ROKER	SUNDERLAND	3/7/18 PLOEGSTEERT MEM	ATT 257 TUN COY RE, TO 18th BN. AGE 25
ARCHBOLD	T	PTE	/770	HETTON-LE-HOLE	SUNDERLAND	26/3/18 PARGNY BRIT CEM	TO 14th, 2nd BNS, CLASS Z RESERVE.
ARCHER	Wm	PTE	/91	HEBBURN COLLIERY		20/5/18 HEBBURN CEM	AGE 23.
ARMOUR	Thos	PTE	/465	COUNDON			TO ARMY RESERVE CLASS P. AGE 23
ARMSTRONG	Emmer	PTE	/340				TO 1/7th BN, CLASS Z RESERVE.
ARMSTRONG	Fred	LCPL	/669	ESH WINNING	6/12/15	KR para 392 2/4/19	TO 1/7th BN, CLASS Z RESERVE.
ARMSTRONG	Arth	LCPL	/1051	WEST HARTLEPOOL			ATT 180 TUN COY RE, 22nd BN.
ARNISON	Chris	LCPL	/318				TO 1/7th BN, CLASS Z RESERVE.
ASPEL	Wilf	PTE	/356		19/11/15	KR para 392 24/10/17	TO 14th, 2nd, 7th BNS, CLASS Z RESERVE.
ASPINALL	Colin	PTE	/825				AGE 17
ATKINSON	Jos	PTE	/119				ATT 170 COY RE, 22nd BN, COMMISSION DLI 25/2/17.
ATKINSON	Gord	PTE	/319				BORN EMBLETON NTHBLD AGE 21
ATKINSON	James	SGT	/523	WEST HARTLEPOOL	WEST HARTLEPOOL	23/10/16 BANCOURT BRIT CEM	AGE 26
AYTON	Wm H	PTE	/67			27/5/18 SOISSONS MEM	ATT 170 TUN COY RE, 22nd BN. BORN DARLASTON STAFFS
BACKHOUSE	Geo H	PTE	/733	COXHOE	DURHAM	5/3/17 FINS NEW BRIT CEM	ATT 8th DIV RE. 22nd, 19th BNS, CLASS Z RESERVE.
BACKHOUSE	Sam	SGT	/399	MIDDLESBOROUGH	DARLINGTON		MINER AGE 20 5'5", DESERTED 12/2/16 WEST HARTLEPOOL
BAGGOTT	John	PTE	/1040	WASHINGTON STATION	HOUGHTON LE SPRING	26/3/18 POZIERES MEM	AGE 21.
BAILEY	Wm	PTE					TO DEPOT.
BAILEY	John	PTE	/743		11/12/15 WEST HARTLEPOOL		ATT 8th DIV RE, 22nd BN. LNER PULLEY REPAIRER DARLINGTON
BAINBRIDGE	John	PTE	/82	WITTON GILBERT	BISHOP AUCKLAND	11/11/16 THIEPVAL MEM	AGE 24.
BAINBRIDGE	RobtH	PTE	/207	TOW LAW	2/11/15	SICK 7/6/17	TO CLASS Z RESERVE.
BANKS	Horac	PTE	/320	WEST HARTLEPOOL	DARLINGTON	22/11/16 STRANTON CEM HARTLEPOOL	AGE 37
BARKHOUSE	Fred	PTE	/753	HETTON LYONS	8/12/15	KR para 392 14/12/18	ATT 180 TUN COY RE. AGE 29
BARNETT	Nathn	PTE	/194	WEST HARTLEPOOL			ATT 180 TUN COY RE, 22nd, 2nd, 20th, 22nd, 1/7th BNS, Z RES
BAXTER	Alex	LCPL	/27	SUNDERLAND	GATESHEAD	22/7/16 CAMBRIN CH YD EXT	ATT 3rd CORPS SANITARY SEC. 22nd, 1/7th BNS, CLASS Z RESERVE
BAXTER	Alex	PTE	/987	DAWDON	SUNDERLAND	18/8/17 TYNE COT MEM	TO 1/7th BN, CLASS Z RESERVE.
BAXTER	Jos	PTE	/400	WEST HARTLEPOOL			TO CLASS Z RESERVE.
BEACH	John	PTE	/422				TO CLASS Z RESERVE.
BECK	JohnT	LCPL	/285	WEST HARTLEPOOL			TO 14th, 18th BNS, CLASS Z RESERVE.
BEDDOW	Ernst	PTE	/100				TO 14th, 19th BNS, CLASS Z RESERVE.
BEDFORD	Alf	PTE	/288				TO 15th, 14th 19th BNS, CLASS Z RESERVE.
BELL	JohnT	PTE	/19				
BELL	Rob H	PTE	/20				
BELL	Jas	PTE	/121				
BELL	Vick	PTE	/365	WEARHEAD	BISHOP AUCKLAND	1/6/18 DAINVILLE BRIT CEM	TO RIFLE BRIGADE(1/5th BN LONDON REGT). RIFLE BDE No 45383 AGE 34

NAME	INITIAL	RANK	NUMBER	TOWN_VILL	DATE & PLACE ENL	DATE & CAUSE_DIS, DIED BURIED	TRANSFER NEW NUMBER DESERTED ETC
BELL	JohnW	LCPL	/713				TO 1/7th, 26th BNS, CLASS Z RESERVE.
BELL	Raisb	CPL	/769	MORTON GRANGE			TO 22nd, 1/7th BNS.
BENNETT	Wm K	RQMS	/12				TO 1/7th, 20th, 1/7th BNS, CLASS Z RESERVE.
BENSON	Fred	SGT	/466				ATT 8th DIV RE, 22nd BN, CLASS Z RESERVE.
BIERMAN	Jos	PTE	/916				ATT 8th DIV RE, 22nd, 1/7th BNS, CLASS Z RESERVE.
BILLAM	Wm	PTE	/957	JARROW			TO 20th, 14th, 22nd BNS, CLASS Z RESERVE.
BINKS	Geo E	PTE	/457	KIRKBY STEPHEN	FERRYHILL	26/3/18 POZIERES MEM	ATT 8th DIV RE, 22nd BN, CLASS Z RESERVE. LNER LENGTHMAN FERRYHILL STATION
BIRD		SGT	/341				ATT 8th DIV RE, 22nd BN, CLASS Z RESERVE. FORMERLY 9728 1st NTHBLD FUS, FORMER SERVICE RESTORED
BIRLINSON	Wm M	PTE	/855			KR para 392	
BLACKBURN	JohnW	SGT	/11	HETTON LE HOLE			TO 1/7th BN, CLASS Z RESERVE.
BLACKBURN	Alf E	PTE	/322		15/11/15	KR para 392 13/10/17	TO DEPOT. AGE 25
BLACKETT	Robt	SGT	/699				TO 1/7th BN, CLASS Z RESERVE.
BLADES	Wm	PTE	/754	STANHOPE			TO 20th, 10th, 22nd, 19th, 1/7th BNS, CLASS Z RESERVE.
BLAND	JohnT	PTE	/988	TUDHOE	10/12/15	KR para 392 22/4/19	AGE 31.
BLENCH	RichW	PTE	/199				TO 1/7th BN, CLASS Z RESERVE.
BLENCH	John	PTE	/450				ATT 8th DIV RE.ARMY SERVICE CORPS(No 2 AHTD),1/9th BN,Z RES
BLENKINSOPP	Wm	PTE	/745	HETTON LE HOLE			
BLYTH	Wm	PTE	/649				TO CLASS Z RESERVE.
BOLAM	Geo	PTE	/366				TO 11th, 22nd, 1/9th BNS, CLASS Z RESERVE.
BOLLANDS	RobtW	PTE	/200	NEW SHILDON	DARLINGTON	31/3/18 ST SEVER CEM EXT ROUEN	AGE 28.LNER LABOURER SHILDON LOCO SHEDS.
BOLTON	JohnW	CPL	/436	WEST HARTLEPOOL	WEST HARTLEPOOL	30/7/16 CAMBRIN CH YD EXT	AGE 33
BOND	ThosG	PTE	/958				TO 12th, 14th BNS, CLASS Z RESERVE.
BONHAM	Frank	SGT	/515				TO 1/7th BN, CLASS Z RESERVE.
BONSALL	Reg	SGT	/342	CHESTER LE STREET	18/11/15	KR para 392 14/11/18	TO DEPOT. AGE 30
BOOTH	Wm	PTE	/291	WEST HARTLEPOOL			ATT 170 TUN COY RE, 22nd BN, CLASS Z RESERVE.
BOTTOMLEY	Harry	PTE	/804				TO 11th BN, CLASS Z RESERVE.
BOWER	Gord	LCPL	/1044	SOUTH SHIELDS	SOUTH SHIELDS	23/10/16 BIENVILLERS MIL CEM	AGE 28 BORN LEEDS INSTRUCTOR WITH DURHAM COUNTY COUNCIL
BOWMAN	Oliv	SGT	/304				ATT 180 TUN COY RE, 22nd BN, COMMISSIONED 31/7/17.
BOYD	John	PTE	/690		18/11/15	KR para 392 12/7/16	
BOYLAN	Vinc	PTE	/212	DARLINGTON	DARLINGTON	6/7/17 BELGIAN BATTERY CORNER CEM	BORN DARLINGTON.
BRABINER	Wm	LCPL	/147	WEST HARTLEPOOL			TO CLASS Z RESERVE.
BRANDON	Thos	PTE	/945	OLD SPENNYMOOR	SPENNYMOOR	4/3/17 THIEPVAL MEM	
BRASS	Steph	LCPL	/771	HETTON LE HOLE			TO 1/7th BN, CLASS Z RESERVE.
BREWSTER	Wm	PTE	/1031	CHILTON			TO CLASS Z RESERVE.
BRIGGS	Robt	PTE	/382	CASTLE EDEN	22/11/15 SUNDERLAND	KR para 392 9/5/17	ATT 180 TUN COY RE, 22nd BN, ARMY RESERVE CLASS P. LABOURER AGE 23 5'6". DESERTED 20/4/16 SCOTTC
BROADHEAD	Edwd	SGT	/238	WEST HARTLEPOOL			ATT 180 TUN COY RE, 22nd, 2nd, 1/7th BNS, CLASS Z RESERVE
BROPHEY	Rich	PTE	/383	WEST HARTLEPOOL			TO CLASS Z RESERVE
BROTTON	Wm D	SGT	/72	DARLINGTON			TO CLASS Z RESERVE. MISSING MARCH 1918
BROWN	Thos	PTE	/323	JARROW	JARROW	25/6/17 BELGIAN BATTERY CORNER CEM	
BROWN	Jos	LCPL	/367	WILLINGTON	BISHOP AUCKLAND	30/1/17 YPRES RESERVOIR CEM	BORN BYERS GREEN AGE 29
BROWN	Jos	LCPL	/368	CROOK	CROOK	26/3/18 POZIERES MEM	ATT 180 TUN COY RE, 22nd BN. CPL AGE 24
BROWN	StanI	SGT	/490	IVESTON	SUNDERLAND	24/11/16 GUARDS CEM LESBOEUFS	BORN SUNDERLAND
BROWN	JohnG	PTE	/861	SUNDERLAND	SUNDERLAND	25/11/16 GROVETOWN CEM	ATT 8th DIV RE, 22nd BN. AGE 28
BROWN	Jos	PTE	/467		6/12/15	KR para 392 8/4/18	TO 4th BN. AGE 35
BROWN	Robt	PTE	/808		11/12/15	KR para 392 11/10/16	TO DEPOT. AGE 21
BROWN	Jos E	PTE	/1053	EVENWOOD	8/12/15	KR para 392	TO 18th, 4th BNS. AGE 31
BUCHAN	WaltT	PTE	/477	WEST HARTLEPOOL	WEST HARTLEPOOL	20/7/16 CAMBRIN CH YD EXT	
BULMER	Walt	PTE	/1055	TUDHOE VILLAGE	FERRYHILL	14/11/16 GUARDS CEM LESBOEUFS	ATT 253 TUN COY RE, 22nd BN. BORN SEATON CAREW
BULTITUDE	Ernst	PTE	/934		8/12/15	SICK 20/7/17	TO DEPOT.

INITIAL	RANK	NUMBER	TOWN_VILL	DATE & PLACE ENL	DATE & CAUSE_DIS, DIED BURIED	TRANSFER NEW NUMBER DESERTED ETC
Normn	SGT	/714	WOLSINGHAM	BISHOP AUCKLAND	14/11/16 AIF BURIAL GROUND FLERS	
Thos	PTE	/284				
Geo	PTE	/58				
Wm T	PTE	/317		16/11/15	KR para 392 10/2/19	
F	PTE	/487	SUNDERLAND	25/11/15 GATESHEAD		
Ernst	PTE	/1112	SILKSWORTH			TO CLASS Z RESERVE.
Sam	PTE	/1059	SHERBURN			AGE 34.
Nich	LCPL	/298	BYERS GREEN			TO CLASS Z RESERVE.
Ernst	PTE	/352	DARLINGTON			TO 22nd, 22nd BN.
Geo	SGT	/324	MIDDLE HERRINGTON			LABOURER AGE 23 5'4", DESERTED 12/5/16 SCOTTON CAMP.
Lance	PTE	/881		7/12/15	KR para 392 21/2/19	To 18th BN, YORK & LANCASTER REGT(10th BN), 22nd BN, Z RES, YORK & LANCASTER No 33055
Chas	PTE	/458	WEST HARTLEPOOL			To 14th, 22nd, 2nd, 22nd, 11th BNS, CLASS Z RESERVE.
RichA	PTE	/1128	WEST HARTLEPOOL			TO 1/7th BN. DEAD ON MR
Ralph	PTE	/265	EBBW VALE	8/11/15 SPENNYMOOR		ATT ARMY SERVICE CORPS(No 2 AHTD), 11th BN, CLASS Z RESERVE.
Thos	PTE	/259		26/10/15	KR para 392 19/6/17	AGE 26.
John	PTE	/92	COCKFIELD			TO 11th BN, CLASS Z RESERVE.
Normn	PTE	/929		DARLINGTON	26/10/16 GROVETOWN CEM	TO 1/7th BN, CLASS Z RESERVE.
Arth	PTE	/423				MINER AGE 31 5'2", DESERTED 15/4/16 SCOTTON CAMP.
Jos W	PTE	/877	HETTON LE HOLE	HOUGHTON LE SPRING	4/3/17 FINS NEW BRIT CEM	TO ARMY RESERVE CLASS P. AGE 20
Robt	CPL	/198				BORN NORTH SHIELDS AGE 30 TEACHER AT COCKFIELD SCHOOL
Alf	LCPL	/47				TO 1/7th BN, CLASS Z RESERVE.
Thos	PTE	/857	LANGLEY MOOR	DURHAM	31/3/18 POZIERES MEM	BORN EASINGTON LANE.
Vic	PTE	/725	COCKFIELD	COCKFIELD	26/3/18 PARGNY BRIT CEM	ATT 253 TUN COY RE. 22nd, 1/7th BNS, CLASS Z RESERVE.
Geo	PTE	/776	SPENNYMOOR			TO CLASS Z RESERVE.
Wm	PTE	/7				AGE 27 BORN BRANDON.
Chas	PTE	/701	SHOTTON COLLIERY	WEST HARTLEPOOL	26/3/18 POZIERES MEM	AGE 24, IN 1 PLTN.
Matt	LCPL	/923				TO 19th, 1/7th BNS, CLASS Z RESERVE.
Fred	PTE	/863				TO CLASS Z RESERVE.
Rich	CQMS	/237				BORN THORNLEY.
JohnW	PTE	/499				TO CLASS Z RESERVE.
Robt	PTE	/193	WEST AUCKLAND	4/11/15 WEST HARTLEPOOL		TO 1/7th BN, CLASS Z RESERVE.
Isaac	PTE	/369				ATT 170 TUN COY RE, 22nd BN, COMMISSION 1/4/17.
John	CPL	/139	GATESHEAD	1/1/15	KR para 392 26/11/18	TO 1/7th BN, CLASS Z RESERVE.
Jas R	PTE	/883			KR para 392.	TO CLASS Z RESERVE. MINER AGE 25 5'5", DESERTED 4/11/16 FRANCE
Jas R	PTE	/803		7/12/15	KR para 392 9/8/17	TO 1/9th, 1/7th BNS, CLASS Z RESERVE.
Jos	PTE	/1113				AGE 23.
Dan	PTE	/24				ATT 8th DIV HQ, 1/7th BN, ATT 8th DIV HQ, 26th BN, ATT DETAILS BN, 8th DIV HQ, 1/9th BN, CLASS Z RESERVE.
Wm	PTE	/279	LANCHESTER	GATESHEAD	10/3/17 THIEPVAL MEM	TO 1/7th BN, CLASS Z RESERVE.
Robt	PTE	/363	HEBBURN		KR para 392	ATT 270 TUN COY RE, 22nd BN.
FredT	PTE	/1057				TO 1/7th BN, CLASS Z RESERVE.
Wm	PTE	/433	DARLINGTON			ATT ROYAL ENGINEERS, 22nd BN, CLASS Z RESERVE. CPL
James	PTE	/872				ATT ARMY SERVICE CORPS(No 2 AHTD), 11th BN, CLASS Z RESERVE.
John	PTE	/949	SEDGEFIELD			ATT ARMY SERVICE CORPS(No 2 AHTD), 1/7th BN, CLASS Z RESERVE.
Jas H	SGT	/667		9/12/15	KR para 392 10/1/19	AGE 29.
R	PTE	/876				TO CLASS Z RESERVE.
Wm	CPL	/434	HURWORTH			ATT LEWIS GUN SCHOOL, 22nd, 1/7th BNS, CLASS Z RESERVE.
JohnA	PTE	/830	DURHAM CITY			ATT 8th DIV RE, 211 DIV EMP COY, 1/7th BN, CLASS Z RESERVE. L/CPL
Jas W	PTE	/1058				TO 19th, 15th, 22nd BNS, CLASS Z RESERVE.
Wm	PTE	/680	FERRYHILL	7/12/15	SHELL WOUND 16/7/17	TO DEPOT.

NAME	INITIAL	RANK	NUMBER	TOWN_VILL	DATE & PLCACE ENL	DATE & CAUSE_DIS, DIED BURIED	TRANSFER NEW NUMBER DESERTED ETC
CRAWFORD	John	PTE	/260	DARLINGTON			ATT 180 TUN COY RE, 1/7th, 18th BNS, CLASS Z RESERVE.
CRISP	Percy	CPL	/882				TO CLASS Z RESERVE.
CRISP	Robt	PTE	/962	WHITBURN			TO 19th BN, CLASS Z RESERVE.
CRUDEN	John	LCPL	/39				TO 1/7th BN, CLASS Z RESERVE.
CULLEN	Jas R	CPL	/1118	NEWCASTLE	SEAHAM HARBOUR	23/10/16 THIEPVAL MEM	BORN FULHAM AGE 25.
CUMISKY	Pat	PTE	/1045				TO 1/7th BN, CLASS Z RESERVE.
CUMMINS	Geo W	CSGT	/503				COMMISSIONED 28/5/18
CURRAN	Edwd	PTE	/388	SUNDERLAND	22/11/15 SUNDERLAND		LABOURER AGE 26 5'10". DESERTED 20/4/16 SCOTTON CAMP.
DALTON	Wm G	PTE	/417	CROOK	BISHOP AUCKLAND	26/3/18 POZIERES MEM	ATT 180 TUN COY RE, 22nd BN. ACPL AGE 23
DANBY	Thos	CSGT	/2	WEST HARTLEPOOL			ATT ROYAL ENGINEERS, CLASS Z RESERVE.
DARLOW	Jack	CPL	/222	HETTON LE HOLE			BORN BRIGHTON.
DAVEY	Ernst	PTE	/1042	SUNDERLAND		23/10/16 THIEPVAL MEM	TO 13th, 22nd BNS.
DAVIDSON	John	PTE	/386	WEST HARTLEPOOL		26/3/18 POZIERES MEM	ATT ARMY SERVICE CORPS, 11th BN. CLASS Z RESERVE.
DAVIDSON	John	PTE	/717				TO 19th BN, CLASS Z RESERVE.
DAVIDSON	JohnW	PTE	/1060				ATT ARMY SERVICE CORPS(No 2 AHTD), 1/9th BN, CLASS Z RESERVE
DAVISON	Henry	PTE	/95				TO 18th BN, CLASS Z RESERVE.
DAVISON	Robt	CPL	/682				TO CLASS Z RESERVE.
DAVISON	Wm	PTE	/782	NEWTON CAP B AUCKLAND			TO CLASS Z RESERVE.
DAVISON	Robt	PTE	/1036				TO 18th BN, ATT SCHOOL OF FARRIERS, 93 COY MGC, 18th BN, Z RES
DAWSON	Arth	PTE	/732	SUNDERLAND	SUNDERLAND	2/3/17 FINS NEW BRIT CEM	ATT 8th DIV BAND, 211 DIV EMP COY, 1/7th BN, CLASS Z RESERVE
DAWSON	Geo	PTE	/1039				TO 13th, 1/9th BNS.
DENNIS	J	PTE	/1110	BRISTOL	WEST HARTLEPOOL	15/9/17 ST MARTIN CALVAIRE BRIT CEM	TO 12th, 22nd, 11th, 22nd BNS, CLASS Z RESERVE. IN 7 PLATOON
DEWELL	Arth	PTE	/339	CROOK			COMMISSIONED ROYAL ENGINEERS 20/4/17.
DITCHBURN	David	SGT	/1043				TO CLASS Z RESERVE.
DIXON	Thos	PTE	/804	FISHBURN		26/3/18 POZIERES MEM	TO 14th BN. BORN SUNDERLAND
DOBSON	John	PTE	/719	RYHOPE	SUNDERLAND	KR para 392	TO 1/7th BN.
DOBSON	Robt	PTE	/1041				
DOBSON	Wm T	PTE	/878	HETTON LYONS			
DODD	John	PTE	/130	SWALWELL	GATESHEAD	18/12/16 ABBEVILLE COM CEM	BORN BRAMPTON CUMBERLAND
DODDS	James	PTE	/885	COUNDON	CROOK	28/10/16 THIEPVAL MEM	
DODDS	Jos	PTE	/1061	DURHAM CITY	DURHAM	26/3/18 PARGNY BRIT CEM	ATT 180 TUN COY RE, 22nd BN. AGE 31
DODDS	Edwd	SGT	/325	HEBBURN			ATT ROYAL ENGINEERS, 1/7th BN. CLASS Z RESERVE.
DOIDGE	John	PTE	/406	DARLINGTON	DARLINGTON		ATT 180 TUN COY RE, 22nd, 10th, 11th, 2nd, 1/7th BNS, Z RES
DORR	Geo W	PTE	/950	DARLINGTON		16/2/18 YPRES RESERVOIR CEM	TO 20th, 22nd BN. BORN NORTON AGE 22
DORR	Chas	PTE	/850				
DOUGLAS	Percy	CSM	/56	CROFT	25/10/15	KR para 392 9/5/17	TO DEPOT. AGE 41
DOVASTON	Roland	PTE	/225	WEST HARTLEPOOL	WEST HARTLEPOOL	18/3/16 NORTH CEM WEST HARTLEPOOL	
DOVASTON	Jas	SGT	/25	GATESHEAD			TO 1/7th BN, CLASS Z RESERVE.
DOVE	RobtW	PTE	/163	PRESTON N SHIELDS			ATT 170 TUN COY RE, 22nd BN. BORN GATESHEAD
DOVING	John	PTE	/344		FELLING	27/3/18 POZIERES MEM	
DOYLE	Thos	PTE	/716		29/11/15	KR para 392 14/6/19	
DUFFY	Edwd	PTE	/185		2/11/15	KR para 392 22/9/16	
DUNN	Wm E	PTE	/747	DAWDON			TO 1/6th, 1/6th, 11th BNS, CLASS Z RESERVE.
DYER	Walt	PTE	/1111	WEST HARTLEPOOL	WEST HARTLEPOOL	24/10/16 CARNOY MIL CEM	ATT 8th DIV RE, 22nd BN. AGE 19.
EASEY	Harry	PTE	/253	WEST HARTLEPOOL	10/11/15	21/9/17 DIED 1/7/18 HARTLEPOOL	TO DEPOT. AGE 38
EASTER	Jos	PTE	/1062				TO 20th BN, CLASS Z RESERVE.
EBDON	Wm	CPL	/351	WOLSINGHAM			TO CLASS Z RESERVE.
EDDY	John	PTE	/833		3/12/15	KR para 392 3/9/17	TO DEPOT. AGE 26
EDES	AlbtE	PTE	/749	NEWCASTLE	7/12/15 JARROW		TO 20th, 22nd BNS, CLASS Z RESERVE. ORDER CLERK AGE 24 5'7". DESERTED 20/4/16

NAME	INITIAL	RANK	NUMBER	TOWN_VILL	DATE & PLACE ENL	DATE & CAUSE, DIS, DIED BURIED	TRANSFER NEW NUMBER DESERTED ETC
EDINGTON	Wm	PTE	/964		15/11/15	KR para 392 15/2/18	TO 3rd BN. AGE 28
EDMUNDSEN	Robt	PTE	/ 666				TO 1/7th BN. CLASS Z RESERVE.
EDWARDS	John	CSM	/ 40				TO 11th, 2nd BNS. STILL SERVING 1920.
ELDER	Jos	PTE	/648	WEST HARTLEPOOL		4/3/17 FINS NEW BRIT CEM	AGE 23
ELLIOTT	Robt	PTE	/774				ATT CRE 8th DIV. 22nd BN. CLASS Z RESERVE.
ELLISON	John	PTE	/1126		8/12/12	KR para 392 7/5/17	TO DEPOT. AGE 25
ELLIS	Cuthb	PTE	/930	DARLINGTON	DARLINGTON	26/3/18 POZIERES MEM	ATT 170 TUN COY RE. 22nd, 15th BNS. BORN TYNE DOCK AGE 29
ELMS	Robt	PTE	/ 294				TO 1/7th BN. CLASS Z RESERVE.
ELMS	ChasW	PTE	/ 295				ATT 253 TUN COY RE. 22nd BN. CLASS Z RESERVE.
EMMERSON	Thos	PTE	/ 71	FROSTERLEY	BISHOP AUCKLAND	2/10/17 PROWSE POINT MIL CEM	
EMMERSON	Wm	PTE	/ 887	WEST CORNFORTH	FERRYHILL	28/7/16 BETHUNE TOWN CEM	AGE 25.
ENGLISH	Edwd	PTE	/152	WEARHEAD	BISHOP AUCKLAND	11/11/16 CABARET ROUGE BRIT CEM	AGE 23.
ENGLISH	John	PTE	/ 842				ATT ARMY SERVICE CORPS(No 2 AHTD). 1/9th BN. CLASS Z RESERVE
ENGLISH	Lance	LSGT	/1119				ATT 253 TUN COY RE. 22nd BN. CLASS Z RESERVE.
EVANS	Wm	PTE	/726				TO CLASS Z RESERVE.
FAIRBAIRN	Robt	RQMS	/218				TO 1/7th BN. CLASS Z RESERVE.
FALDON	Fred	PTE	/418	DUNSTON	20/11/15	KR para 392 20/6/19	ATT 180 TUN COY RE. 22nd BN. LCPL.
FARMAN	Geo	PTE	/175		1/11/15	SICK 21/6/16	DID NOT SERVE OVERSEAS.
FAWCETT	Thos	PTE	/889	HEBBURN	15/11/15	KR para 392 4/9/19	ATT 253 TUN COY RE. 1/7th BN. CLASS Z RESERVE.
FAWCUS	John	PTE	/326		8/12/15	KR para 392 8/11/18	ATT 170 TUN COY RE. 22nd BN.
FELL	Geo G	PTE	/817				TO 3rd BN. AGE 27
FELL	W	PTE	/ 85				TO 3 CCS 25/6/16. SYN KNEE TO CONV DEPOT 26/6/16.
FENWICK	Jas H	PTE	/809	SOUTH SHIELDS	SOUTH SHIELDS	26/3/18 BELLACOURT MIL CEM	ATT CRE 8th DIV. 22nd 18th BNS. AGE 24
FENWICK	Geo	PTE	/992		10/12/15	KR para 392 19/12/17	TO DEPOT. AGE 31
FIDDES	John	CQMS	/438	WEST HARTLEPOOL			ATT 8th DIV RE.TO 3rd BN. CLASS Z RESERVE. COMS
FINK	Frank	PTE	/955				ATT 8th DIV COOKERY SCHOOL. ARMY SERVICE CORPS(No 2 AHTD). 1/7th BN. CLASS
FINLEY	JohnT	PTE	/186				ATT 253 TUN COY RE. 22nd, 20th, 10th, 1/7th, 1/9th BNS. Z RE
FINNITY	Geo	PTE	/1027	SEAHAM HARBOUR	SEAHAM HARBOUR	20/6/17 DICKEBUSCH NEW MIL CEM	TO PB BN. 22nd, 1/7th, 2/6th, 18th BNS. CLASS Z RESERVE.
FLATT	Geo S	PTE	/468	SEAHAM	20/11/15	KR para 392 12/7/17	BROTHER KIA 1st TYNESIDE IRISH
FLATT	John	PTE	/ 384		5/11/15	KR para 392 4/12/17	TO DEPOT. AGE 29
FLEETHAM	Chris	PTE	/ 246				TO 3rd BN. AGE 21
FLEWKER	Bem	PTE	/1140				TO 13th, 22nd. 1/7th BNS. CLASS Z RESERVE.
FLORENCE	Andrw	PTE	/ 232				TO 1/7th BN. CLASS Z RESERVE.
FLYNN	Aust	PTE	/ 368	CROOK			
FORSTER	Walt	CSM	/ 1				COMMISSIONED Lt & QM 11/5/17.
FOSTER	JohnA	PTE	/125	DARLINGTON			TO CLASS Z RESERVE. PRISONER OF WAR
FOXALL	John	PTE	/168	WEST HARTLEPOOL			TO CLASS Z RESERVE.
FRANCIS	Timth	PTE	/720	THORNLEY	10/12/15 BISHOP AUCKLAND		LABOURER AGE 19 5'2". DESERTED 1/3/16 HARTLEPOOL.
FRANKLIN	Rob	PTE	/ 46				TO 1/7th, 11th. BNS. CLASS Z RESERVE.
FRANKS	Wm	PTE	/ 362				TO 11th BN. CLASS Z RESERVE.
FRAZER	Stan	PTE	/759				TO 18th BN. CLASS Z RESERVE.
FRIAR	ThosW	CPL	/871	NEWCASTLE	HOUGHTON LE SPRING	23/10/16 THIEPVAL MEM	AGE 27 GOODS CLERK WASHINGTON STATION
GAIR	John	PTE	/1066	SHOTTON COLLIERY	WEST HARTLEPOOL	23/10/16 THIEPVAL MEM	ATT 170 TUN COY RE. 22nd BN. BORN WINDY KNOOK
GALLEN	Robt	PTE	/1149		15/1/16	KR para 392 15/4/18	TO 2nd. 18th BNS. AGE 21
GARDNER	Alf J	SGT	/691	WEST HARTLEPOOL			TO 1/7th BN. CLASS Z RESERVE.
GAUDIE	Irvne	SGT	/742				ATT 8th DIV SCHOOL. TO 22nd BN. CLASS Z RESERVE.
GAYTHORPE	Robt	PTE	/1065				ATT ARMY SERVICE CORPS(No 2 AHTD). 1/9th BN. CLASS Z RESERVE
GEGGIE	Dan	CPL	/965				COMMISSIONED 31/7/17
GERALDIE	Ralph	PTE	/765	WEST HARTLEPOOL			TO 18th, CLASS Z RESERVE.
GERALDIE	Antol	PTE	/953	SUNDERLAND	WEST HARTLEPOOL	2/2/17 RAILWAY DUGOUTS BURIAL GRC	TO 12th BN.

NAME	INITIAL:	RANK	NUMBER	TOWN_VILL	DATE & PLCACE ENL	DATE & CAUSE_DIS, DIED BURIED	TRANSFER NEW NUMBER DESERTED ETC
GIBBON	Thos	PTE	/469	COUNDON		KR para 392	TO CLASS Z RESERVE.
GIBBON	Geo H	SGT	/828	STAINDROP			TO 1/7th BN. CLASS Z RESERVE.
GIBBON	John	LCPL	/928	ROWLANDS GILL			BORN WORKINGTON
GIBSON	RobtJ	PTE	/141		GATESHEAD	11/11/16 THIEPVAL MEM	TO 1/7th BN. CLASS Z RESERVE.
GIBSON	Geo	CPL	/703				TO 3rd BN. AGE 25
GILBEY	Rich	CPL	/694		7/12/15	KR para 392 20/8/18	
GILROY	Wm	PTE	/591			KR para 392	
GILROY	Wm	PTE	/491		13/12/15	KR para 392 1/5/17	
GLEASON	Frank	SGT	/890	HEBBURN NEWTOWN			
GLENDINNING	Wm	PTE	/407	COXHOE	DEAF HILL	4/3/17 THIEPVAL MEM	ATT 253 TUN COY RE, 22nd BN. CLASS Z RESERVE.
GLENTON	Abt	PTE	/834	GILESGATE			ATT 180 TUN COY RE, 22nd BN. BORN CORNFORTH AGE 21
GOULDSBROUGH	John	PTE	/188	SHILDON	BISHOP AUCKLAND	9/1/17 THIEPVAL MEM	ATT 8th DIV RE, 1/7th BN, CLASS Z RESERVE. BORN BILDERSHAW Co DURHAM.LNER LABOURER SHILDON LOCO SHEDS
GOUNDRY	John	PTE	/183				ATT 253 TUN COY RE, 22nd BN, CLASS Z RESERVE. AGE 21.
GRAHAM	Sydh	PTE	/146		1/11/15	KR para 392 13/11/17	TO 11th BN. CLASS Z RESERVE.
GRAHAM	Wm	PTE	/1017				
GRAYSON	Wm	PTE	/858	SHERBURN STATION	DURHAM	10/3/17 SHERBURN ST MARYS CH YARD SICK 9/6/16	AGE 26
GRAYSON	RobtW	LCPL	/35		19/10/15		DID NOT SERVE OVERSEAS.
GREEN	Walt	CPL	/401	WEST HARTLEPOOL		10/4/17 BRAY MIL CEM	ATT 180 TUN COY RE, 22nd BN. LNER TICKETER WEST HARTLEPOOL AGE 25.
GREEN	Jos	PTE	/248	PELTON	WEST HARTLEPOOL	9/11/15	BROTHERS KOYLI & RFA.
GREEN	Geo	LCPL	/435		CROOK	KR para 392 25/7/18	ATT 211 DIV EMP COY. 8th DIV HQ.TO 1/7th BN, CLASS Z RESERVE
GREENBANK	Fred	CPL	/891	CROOK		26/3/18 POZIERES MEM	ATT 253 TUN COY RE, 22nd BN.BORN HEMLINGTON AGE 26
GREGG	Edwd	PTE	/831	SACRISTON		KR para 392	
GREGGS	Geo	PTE	/90		26/10/15	KR para 392 20/2/19	TO ARMY RESERVE CLASS P. AGE 23
GRINT	Fred	PTE	/181	WEST CORNFORTH	FERRYHILL	26/3/18 FOUQUESCOURT BRIT CEM	IN 1 PLATOON
GRUNDY	Dan	CPL	/18				ATT ROYAL ENGINEERS, 22nd BN, CLASS Z RESERVE.
HALES	Jas E	CQMS	/236				TO 19th BN.
HALEY	Dan	PTE	/1130				
HALL	Geo	PTE	/393		22/11/15	KR para 392 17/9/17	
HALL	Chas	PTE	/73		23/10/15	KR para 392 29/3/16	TO DEPOT. AGE 21
HANBY	Chris	PTE	/1069		10/12/15	KR para 392 28/12/17	DID NOT SERVE OVERSEAS.
HANDLEY	Seth	LCPL	/180	CHILTON	8/4/15	KR para 392 20/7/18	ATT 180 TUN COY RE, 22nd BN. DEPOT. AGE 23
HANDLEY	Harry	PTE	/182	CHILTON	1/11/15	KR para 392 31/3/19	AGE 25.
HANDYSIDE	Edwd	PTE	/327	HEBBURN COLLIERY			TO ARMY RESERVE CLASS P. AGE 33
HARDING	Wm	LCPL	/966				TO 1/7th BN, CLASS Z RESERVE. COMMISSIONED 28/5/18.
HARDY	Fredk	PTE	/201	DARLINGTON	DARLINGTON	29/12/15 DARLINGTON WEST CEM	
HARDY	Andrw	PTE	/308				AGE 37 BORN SADBERGE.
HARE	Thos	PTE	/1120			KR para 392	TO 1/7th BN, CLASS Z RESERVE.
HARPER	Olaf	PTE	/521		8/1/16	KR para 392 26/3/18	TO 15th, 1/5th BNS. AGE 21
HARRISON	John	PTE	/34	EPPLEBY YORKS			TO 11th BN. CLASS Z RESERVE.
HARRISON	Thos	PTE	/360		DARLINGTON	27/3/18 ARRAS MEM	TO EAST YORKS REGT(11th BN).
HARRISON	Jos	PTE	/459	WEST HARTLEPOOL		KR para 392	
HARRISON	Ralph	PTE	/810		7/12/15	KR para 392 22/4/18	ATT ARMY SERVICE CORPS(No 2 AHTD). 1/9th BN, CLASS Z RESERVE.
HARRISON	Geo	PTE	/865		2/11/15 DARLINGTON		ATT 8th DIV RE, 22nd BN, CLASS Z RESERVE.
HARRISON	John	PTE	/538	TOTTENHAM	WEST HARTLEPOOL		DID NOT SERVE OVERSEAS.
HARWOOD	Sid	PTE	/208	WEST HARTLEPOOL		28/3/18 ST SEVER CEM EXT ROUEN	SHOEMAKER AGE 38 5'3", DESERTED 2/4/16 SCOTTON CAMP.
HARWOOD	Geo	PTE	/472	WOLSINGHAM	BISHOP AUKLAND	26/3/18 PARGNY BRIT CEM	LCPL AGE 24.
HAWKINS	JohnG	PTE	/364				ATT 180 TUN COY RE, 22nd BN. AGE 29
HENDERSON	Jos	PTE	/439				TO CLASS Z RESERVE.

NAME	INITIAL	RANK	NUMBER	TOWN_VILL	DATE & PLACE ENL	DATE & CAUSE_DIS, DIED BURIED	TRANSFER NEW NUMBER DESERTED ETC
HENDERSON	Henry	PTE	/772	WEST HERRINGTON			TO 1/9th BN, CLASS Z RESERVE.
HENDERSON	Syd	CPL	/1070				TO CLASS Z RESERVE.
HENDRICK	Jos	PTE	/859	LANGLEY MOOR			TO 18th BN.
HIGGINS	James	SGT	/54	WEST HARTLEPOOL	DURHAM	20/7/18 LE QUESNOY COM CEM	TO LABOUR CORPS(837 AE COY), LAB CORPS No 446397
HILDRETH	Percy	SGT	/97		23/1/15	KR para 392 20/2/19	TO 19th, 22nd BNS, ARMY RESERVE CLASS P. AGE 25
HILDRETH	Wm	PTE	/240				TO 22nd, 11th BNS, CLASS Z RESERVE.
HILDRETH	Geo W	PTE	/513				TO CLASS Z RESERVE.
HILL	Edwin	PTE	/782				TO 1/7th BN, CLASS Z RESERVE.
HILL	JohnJ	PTE	/1071				TO CLASS Z RESERVE.
HILL	Geo W	LSGT	/74				TO 1/7th BN, CLASS Z RESERVE.
HILLS	JohnE	PTE	/1067		23/10/15	KR para 392 6/5/18	TO 3rd BN. AGE 28
HILLS	JohnG	PTE	/41				ATT 180 TUN COY RE, 22nd, 1/7th BNS, CLASS Z RESERVE.
HODGSON	Wm	CPL	/87	CLEADON VILLAGE	SUNDERLAND	22/3/18 ARRAS MEM	TO 2nd BN. BORN SCARBOROUGH
HOLDEN	JohnT	PTE	/748				TO 1/7th BN, CLASS Z RESERVE.
HOLLAND	Wm	PTE	/1025	NEWFIELD			TO CLASS Z RESERVE.
HOLMES	Thos W	PTE	/522	GATESHEAD			TO LABOUR CORPS LAB CORPS No 513042.
HOLMES	Wm A	PTE	/1010	WHEATLEY HILL			ATT 8th DIV RE, 22nd BN, CLASS Z RESERVE.
HOOD	Fred	PTE	/761	DURHAM CITY			TO 10th, 22nd, 2nd, 11th BNS, CLASS Z RESERVE.
HOOK	Geo	PTE	/66		25/10/15		TO 2nd, 11th BNS, CLASS Z RESERVE. BROTHER KIA 15 DLI
HOPPER	Wm	PTE	/345	WINDLESTONE		KR para 392 28/11/17	TO 3rd BN. AGE 22
HOPPER	John	PTE	/289	STRANTON	FERRYHILL	23/10/16 THIEPVAL MEM	BORN SPENNYMOOR.
HOPPS	JohnF	LCPL	/370	WASHINGTON	WEST HARTLEPOOL	23/10/16 THIEPVAL MEM	
HOPPS	Robt	PTE	/133			KR para 392	ATT 180 TUN COY RE, 22nd BN.
HORNER	JohnR	PTE	/478	WEST HARTLEPOOL	11/12/15 DURHAM		TO 20th, 22nd BNS, CLASS Z RESERVE.
HORNER	Jos	PTE	/647	DURHAM CITY	SUNDERLAND	26/3/18 POZIERES MEM	LABOURER AGE 22 5'6". DESERTED 13/4/16 SCOTTON CAMP.
HOSKINS	Chas	PTE	/764	WEST HARTLEPOOL			TO CLASS Z RESERVE.
HOWE	ThosR	PTE	/354		3/12/15		TO CLASS Z RESERVE. AWOll
HOWELLS	Jos	SGT	/452			KR para 392 5/4/18	TO 12th BN. AGE 28
HUDSON	James	PTE	/829	CARLISLE	DURHAM		TO 11th BN, CLASS Z RESERVE.
HUDSON	Claud	PTE	/786	TYNE DOCK	SOUTH SHIELDS		TO 1/7th BN, CLASS Z RESERVE.
HUGALL	Wm	PTE	/266		10/12/15	264/4/18 POZIERES MEM	ATT 180 TUN COY RE, 22nd BN. AGE 31 BORN MAIDSTONE LNER TUBE BRUSHER TYNEDOCK LOCO SHEDS
HUGGON	James	PTE	/1068		BARNARD CASTLE	28/10/16 BENAFRAY WOOD BRIT CEM	TO 3rd BN. AGE 28
HUGHES	Bert	PTE	/894			KR para 392 13/2/18	
HUGHES	Jos P	PTE	/371			14/11/16 AIF BURIAL GROUND FLERS	
HULL	John	PTE	/241	STARTFORTH		KR para 392	
HUMBLE	Chas	CPL	/102			16/6/17 DICKEBUSCH NEW MIL EXT	BORN QUARRINGTON HILL. AGE 25.
HUNTER	Henry	PTE	/993	HOUGHALL DURHAM	DURHAM	20/6/17 MENIN ROAD SOUTH MIL CEM	ATT 180 TUN COY RE, 22nd BN.
HUNTER	Thos	PTE	/228	GATESHEAD	SOUTH SHIELDS	KR para 392	
HUNTER	Geo	SGT	/223				STILL SERVING 1921.
HUTCHINSON	Harld	SGT	/1013				TO 11th BN, CLASS Z RESERVE.
HUTCHINSON	Wm	PTE	/895				TO 18th, 22nd BN. AGE 29
HYLAND	Steph	PTE	/357	ROSS Co MAYO	JARROW	29/5/18 VAILLY BRIT CEM	ATT 180 TUN COY RE, 22nd BN.
IMESON	Ralph	LCPL	/402	NORTON ON TEES	WEST HARTLEPOOL	26/3/18 POZIERES MEM	TO DEPOT. AGE 36
IRWIN	John	PTE	/408		24/11/15	KR para 392 28/11/17	ATT 180 TUN COY RE, 22nd, 18th, 22nd BNS. BORN CORNFORTH AGE 25. IN VIII PLATOON B COY
ISETON	Abt	PTE	/527	COXHOE	DEAF HILL	27/5/18 SOISSONS MEM	ATT 8th DIV RE, 22nd BN, CLASS Z RESERVE.
JACKSON	Geo	CPL	/372		22/11/15	KR para 392 19/11/18	TO 3rd BN. AGE 31
JACKSON	Edwin	CPL	/419				ATT 180 TUN COY RE, 22nd, 1/7th BNS, CLASS Z RESERVE.
JACKSON	Jos	PTE	/1037				TO 1/7th BN, ATT DETAILS BN, CLASS Z RESERVE.
JACKSON	Geo	PTE	/135				
JAMEISON	JohnW	PTE		ROWLANDS GILL	GATESHEAD	27/3/18 ST SEVER CEM EXT ROUEN	BORN WINLATON AGE 22

NAME	INITIAL	RANK	NUMBER	TOWN_VILL	DATE & PLACE ENL	DATE & CAUSE DIS, DIED BURIED	TRANSFER NEW NUMBER DESERTED ETC
JAMES	Frank	LCPL	/806	SPENNYMOOR	FERRYHILL	31/7/17 RAILWAY DUGOUTS CEM	BORN TYNEMOUTH. SPECIAL MEMORIAL IN CEM.
JAMES	Frank	PTE	/332	WEST HARTLEPOOL			TO 1/7th BN, CLASS Z RESERVE.
JAMES	Edwd	PTE	/896	OAKENSHAW			TO 20th BN, CLASS Z RESERVE.
JAMESON	Wm H	PTE	/164				TO CLASS Z RESERVE.
JAMIESON	JohnC	PTE	/57	WEST HARTLEPOOL			ATT ROYAL ENGINEERS, 22nd BN, CLASS Z RESERVE
JAYE	Jos	PTE	/315	WEST AUCKLAND	SPENNYMOOR 13/11/15	KR para 392 12/2/19	TO 1/7th BN. HORSEMAN AGE 31 5'5". DESERTED 20/4/16 SCOTTON CAMP
JAYE	Robt	PTE	/750	WEST AUCKLAND	9/12/15	GSW 15/8/17	TO DEPOT.
JENNINGS	Wm	PTE	/103	SPENNYMOOR			TO CLASS Z RESERVE.
JOBLING	Reg D	CPL	/646	BLAYDON	BLAYDON		AGE 25.
JOBLING	Fred	PTE	/768			28/3/18 PARGNY BRIT CEM	TO 1/7th BN. DEAD ON MR
JOBSON	Walt	PTE	/933	USHAW MOOR	DURHAM		BORN HEATON. AGE 27.
JOHNSON	JohnW	PTE	/373	BLACKHILL	CONSETT	12/9/16 VERMELLES BRIT CEM	AGE 23.
JOHNSON	Abrah	PTE	/122	CROOK		30/5/17 BENFIELDSIDE CEM	TO 11th BN, CLASS Z RESERVE.
JOHNSON	Thos	PTE	/337				TO 1/7th BN, CLASS Z RESERVE.
JOHNSON	Fred	PTE	/967				TO 20th BN, CLASS Z RESERVE.
JOHNSON	Chas	PTE	/994				TO 1/7th BN, CLASS Z RESERVE.
JOHNSON	FredG	PTE	/1073		5/2/15	KR para 392 25/4/19	AGE 23
JOHNSON	ChasE	PTE	/449	BISHOP AUCKLAND			ATT 8th DIV RE, 1/7th BN, CLASS Z RESERVE.
JOICE	Ray	PTE	/1132	MIDDLETON IN TEESDALE	WEST HARTLEPOOL		TO 2nd BN. BORN EVERTON
JONES	Tom	SGT	/254	SPENNYMOOR	BISHOP AUCKLAND	22/10/18 VADENCOURT BRIT CEM	ATT "A" SIGNAL COY RE, 22nd BN. BORN DALTON LE DALE
JONES	James	LCPL	/1009			4/12/17 VLAMERTINGHE NEW MIL CEM	
JONES	Peter	PTE	/297			KR para 392	
JONES	Edwd	PTE	/410				ATT 180 TUN COY RE, 22nd BN, CLASS Z RESERVE.
KAYSER	Albt	PTE	/728	KIRK MERRINGTON	3/1/15	KR para 392 18/9/17	TO 3rd BN. AGE 27
KELL	Hall	LCPL	/1008		FERRYHILL	28/3/18 POZIERES MEM	BORN BRANDON.
KELLY	JohnG	PTE	/243				TO CLASS Z RESERVE.
KEMP	Alf	PTE	/479	CROOK	BISHOP AUCKLAND	12/11/16 PERONNE RD CEM MARICOURT	ATT 180 TUN COY RE, 22nd BN. AGE 31. 57" MED BUILD. DESERTED 29/6/17 FRANCE
KENNY	Thos	PTE	/391		22/11/15	KR para 392 16/5/18	ATT 13th, 12th BNS, CLASS Z RESERVE. LABOURER AGE 36 5'4". DESERTED 13/4/16 SCOTTON CAMP
KIDD	Jas H	PTE	/166		WEST HARTLEPOOL 2/11/15		ATT 8th DIV RE, 22nd BN. AGE 22
KIRKHAM	Fred	PTE	/425	SEAHAM HARBOUR		28/6/18 SARRALBE MIL CEM	TO 12th BN.
KNOWLES	Wm	PTE	/969	TRIMDON	SEAHAM HARBOUR	12/7/17 AEROPLANE CEM	TO CLASS Z RESERVE.
KYDD	ChasA	CPL	/276				TO 1/7th BN, CLASS Z RESERVE.
LACK	Jos	PTE	/31	WEST HARTLEPOOL			AGE 42 BORN SUNDERLAND
LAIDLER	Robt	PTE	/914	WEST HARTLEPOOL	WEST HARTLEPOOL	30/7/16 CAMBRIN CH YD EXT	
LAMB	RobtW	PTE	/112			KR para 392	
LAMBERT	Jerrni	PTE	/528	BILLY ROW	CROOK	28/3/18 POZIERES MEM	BORN CROOK AGE 39.
LAMBERT	Jos	LCPL	/329	PELTON FELL	JARROW	13/10/17 PONT D'ACHELLES MIL CEM	ATT 170 TUN COY RE, 2nd, 22nd BN.
LAMBERT	Ernst	LCPL	/799				TO 1/7th BN, CLASS Z RESERVE.
LAUDER	Fred	SIG	/426	WEST HARTLEPOOL			TO CLASS Z RESERVE.
LAWRENSON	JohnW	PTE	/970	SOUTH SHIELDS	SOUTH SHIELDS 11/12/15		LABOURER AGE 28 5'4". DESERTED 19/12/15 & 1/3/16, HARTLEPOOL
LAWSON	Robt	PTE	/519	TRIMDON GRANGE	FERRYHILL	24/7/17 PERTH CEM CHINA WALL	BORN SUNDERLAND.
LAWSON	James	LSGT	/875	HETTON LE HOLE	HOUGHTON LE SPRING	13/3/17 FINS NEW BRIT CEM	AGE 28. TRAINEE TEACHER AT SUNDERLAND DAY TRG COLLEGE.
LAYBOURN	Jos	LCPL	/86				TO 20th BN, CLASS Z RESERVE.
LAYFIELD	Jos	PTE	/221	HETTON LE HOLE			TO 14th, 11th BNS, CLASS Z RESERVE.
LAZENBY	Norrn	PTE	/206		2/11/15	KR para 392 6/2/18	TO DEPOT. AGE 23
LECK	Benj	PTE	/746	SEAHAM			
LEE	Wm	PTE	/1074	DAWDON			TO 19th, 22nd, 1/7th, 3rd BNS, CLASS Z RESERVE.
LEEMING	ChasR	SGT	/113				TO CLASS Z RESERVE.
LEEMING	JohnE	PTE	/114				TO 1/7th BN, CLASS Z RESERVE.

INITIAL	RANK	NUMBER	TOWN_VILL	DATE & PLACE ENL	DATE & CAUSE_DIS, DIED BURIED	TRANSFER NEW NUMBER DESERTED ETC
Arth	PTE	/506	DARLINGTON	DARLINGTON 2/12/15	21/3/18 ARRAS MEM	LABOURER AGE 35 5'6". DESERTED 8/4/16 SCOTTON CAMP.
Thos	PTE	/995	TYNE DOCK			ATT 180 TUN COY RE, 22nd, 2nd BNS. AGE 29
Perci	CPL	/1007				TO 19th, 13th BNS. CLASS Z RESERVE.
John	CPL	/59				TO 1/7th BN. CLASS Z RESERVE.
Geo W	PTE	/272	WEST HARTLEPOOL	WEST HARTLEPOOL	SOISSONS MEM	AGE 21
Geo W	PTE	/1034	LOW SPENNYMOOR			ATT 8th DIV RE, CLASS Z RESERVE.
James	PTE	/22		11/10/15	KR para 392 20/2/19	TO ARMY RESERVE CLASS P. AGE 43
Geo H	PTE	/346	NEW SHILDON	BISHOP AUCKLAND	4/3/17 FINS NEW BRIT CEM	LNER WAGON REPAIRER SHILDON WORKS
Gilbt	PTE	/670	WEST AUCKLAND			TO 2nd, 1/9th BNS. CLASS Z RESERVE.
RobtW	PTE	/971		11/12/15	KR para 392 6/5/18	TO 20th BN. AGE 29
Henry	CPL	/1029	SUNDERLAND	SUNDERLAND	6/4/18 ST SEVER CEM EXT ROUEN	
Geo F	CSM	/217	DARLINGTON			TO CLASS Z RESERVE.
Geo C	PTE	/355	WEST HARTLEPOOL			TO 1/7th BN, CLASS Z RESERVE.
Edwd	PTE	/101	BROWNEY COLLIERY			TO 2nd, 11th BNS, CLASS Z RESERVE.
JohnW	PTE	/215	DARLINGTON	DARLINGTON	20/6/17 DICKEBUSCH NEW MIL EXT	AGE 35.
John	PTE	/512		1/12/15	KR para 392 9/11/17	TO DEPOT. AGE 38
JohnG	PTE	/897				TO 11th, 22nd BNS, CLASS Z RESERVE.
John	PTE	/313		15/11/15	KR para 392 24/1/18	TO 1/7th BN, CLASS Z RESERVE.
Herbt	CPL	/1012	STANHOPE	STANHOPE		TO CLASS Z RESERVE.
JohnE	PTE	/757	DURHAM CITY	DURHAM CITY		BORN HASWELL.
Thos	PTE	/841	PHILADELPHIA	HOUGHTON LE SPRING	26/6/18 HAM BRIT CEM	ATT ARMY SERVICE CORPS, 11th BN, CLASS Z RESERVE.
JohnJ	PTE	/301	ST JOHNS CHAPEL			TO 1/7th BN, CLASS Z RESERVE.
Henry	PTE	/997				
Norm	PTE	/758	LOW SPENNYMOOR			BORN ABERDEEN AGE 28
James	PTE	/1016	GLASGOW	WEST HARTLEPOOL	27/5/18 SOISSONS MEM	TO 4th BN. AGE 21
JohnL	PTE	/952		16/11/15	KR para 392 8/4/18	TO 12th BN.
Thos	PTE	/453			KR para 392	TO 1/7th, 1/9th BNS. CLASS Z RESERVE. SHIPS FIREMAN AGE 21 5'4". DESERTED 17/4/16 CATTERICK
James	PTE	/737	WILLINGTON QUAY	SUNDERLAND 18/1/16		TO 1/7th BN. CLASS Z RESERVE.
Geo	SIG	/778	ELDON LANE			TO 1/7th BN. CLASS Z RESERVE.
Ernst	PTE	/731				ATT 180 TUN COY RE, 22nd BN. BORN NORTH SHIELDS AGE 36 LNER CRANE MAN WEST HARTLEPOOL
JohnR	SGT	/411	WEST HARTLEPOOL	WEST HARTLEPOOL	28/11/17 NINE ELMS BRIT CEM	
Chas	PTE	/10	STOCKTON ON TEES	WEST HARTLEPOOL	27/5/18 SOISSONS MEM	ATT 8th DIV RE, 22nd BN, CLASS Z RESERVE.
JohnH	PTE	/847				TO 22nd, 1/7th BNS, CLASS Z RESERVE.
AlbtE	CPL	/492				
John	PTE	/946		10/12/15	KR para 392 15/2/18	TO 1/6th BN. DIED WHILST A POW
Chas	PTE	/689	SUNDERLAND		21/7/18 HAMBURG CEM	
ThosW	CSM	/3	SILKSWORTH	WEST HARTLEPOOL	26/3/18 POZIERES MEM	TO CLASS Z RESERVE.
Hugh	PTE	/755				ATT ARMY SERVICE CORPS(No 2 AHTD), 11th BN, CLASS Z RESERVE.
John	LCPL	/789		9/12/15	SICK 9/11/17	ATT 253 TUN COY RE, 22nd, 4th BNS. AGE 29
Wm	PTE	/1075		11/12/15	KR para 392 5/9/17	TO DEPOT. AGE 30
Wm	PTE	/1047	SUNDERLAND	SUNDERLAND	26/3/18 POZIERES MEM	AGE 27.
ChasF	LCPL	/790	WEST HARTLEPOOL			ATT 8th DIV RE, 22nd BN, CLASS Z RESERVE.
Ben	PTE	/480	CROOK	12/12/15	KR para 392 7/4/19	TO 10th, 1/5th, 15th BNS
Jos W	PTE	/832				TO 13th, 1/5th, 13TH BNS, CLASS Z RESERVE.
Wm	PTE	/972				ATT 8th DIV RE, 22nd BN. BORN SOUTH SHIELDS
Octav	PTE	/1077	TYNE DOCK	TYNE DOCK	4/9/17 HARTON CEM	TO 18th BN. CLASS Z RESERVE.
Robt	PTE	/1137	BLACKHALL COLLIERY	SOUTH SHIELDS		ATT 8th DIV RE, 22nd BN. BORN SOUTH SHIELDS
JohnR	PTE	/394	FERRYHILL			ATT 180 TUN COY RE, 19th, 11th, 19th, 22nd, 1/7th BNS, Z RES
Rich	CPL	/947				TO 20th BN, CLASS Z RESERVE.

NAME	INITIALS	RANK	NUMBER	TOWN, VILL	DATE & PLACE ENL	DATE & CAUSE, DIS, DIED BURIED	TRANSFER NEW NUMBER DESERTED ETC
MOFFATT	ThosW	CPL	/427	CARLISLE	CARLISLE	24/11/16 GUARDS CEM LESBOEUFS	ATT 170 TUN COY RE, 22nd BN.
MONTGOMERY	Hugh	PTE	/286	WEST HARTLEPOOL	WEST HARTLEPOOL	16/7/16 BETHUNE TOWN CEM	BORN PORT GLASGOW.LNER CARPENTER ENG DEPT WHARTLEPOOL
MOORE	ChasV	PTE	/127	DARLINGTON	DARLINGTON	9/1/17 THIEPVAL MEM	AGE 19
MOORE	F	PTE	/131	DARLINGTON			
MOORE	Wm	PTE	/205				TO CLASS Z RESERVE.
MOORE	Ernst	PTE	/822		11/12/15	KR para 392 17/6/18	TO DEPOT. AGE 26
MOORES	Fred	LCPL	/1147	ECCLES LANCS	SALFORD	27/5/18 SOISSONS MEM	
MORDAIN	John	PTE	/998				ATT LEWIS GUN SCHOOL, 22nd BN, CLASS Z RESERVE.
MORGAN	Edmd	PTE	/741	LITTLETOWN			TO 1/7th BN, CLASS Z RESERVE. BN HQ. ALSO IN AVL 15 SOUTH VIEW USHAW MOOR
MORLEY	James	PTE	/444	CARLISLE	CARLISLE 30/11/15		HOLDER UP AGE 40 5'2". DESERTED 24/4/16
MORRELL	Chas	PTE	/791		9/12/15	SICK 21/2/17	TO DEPOT.
MORRIGAN	Wm	PTE	/30	WEST HARTLEPOOL			STILL SERVING 1920.
MORTON	Walt	PTE	/792	DARLINGTON	11/12/15	KR para 392 19/6/18	AGE 27.
MOUNSEY	Fred	PTE	/202	DARLINGTON			TO 1/7th BN, CLASS Z RESERVE.
MUDD	Arth	PTE	/709				TO 11th BN, CLASS Z RESERVE.
MULLER	Sam	PTE	/481	BARNARD CASTLE			TO 1/7th BN, CLASS Z RESERVE.
MULLIGAN	Andrw	PTE	/526	NEWCASTLE	SPENNYMOOR	23/10/16 THIEPVAL MEM	BORN LIVERPOOL
MUNROE	John	PTE	/999	TYNE DOCK	SOUTH SHIELDS	4/3/17 THIEPVAL MEM	ATT 180 TUN COY RE, 22nd BN.
MUSE	ThosD	PTE	/851		6/12/15	KR para 392 13/2/18	TO DEPOT. AGE 26
NAISBITT	Wm	PTE	/99	HOUGHTON LE SPRING			TO CLASS Z RESERVE.
NEAL	Wm	PTE	/973				TO 1/7th BN, CLASS Z RESERVE.
NELSON	Fred	SGT	/32		16/10/15	KR para 392 28/12/17	TO ARMY RESERVE CLASS W.
NELSON	Geo	PTE	/1079		24/11/15	KR para 392 10/4/17	TO ARMY RESERVE CLASS P. AGE 30
NEWBY	Franc	PTE	/296		13/11/15	WOUNDS 7/3/17	TO 1/9th BN, DEPOT.
NOBLE	Abt	PTE	/898	WEST HARTLEPOOL	WEST HARTLEPOOL	19/8/17 BRANDHOEK NEW MIL CEM No AGE 26.	
NORMAN	Syd	CPL	/801				TO CLASS Z RESERVE.
NORTON	Raymd	PTE	/697	GRANGETOWN	SUNDERLAND	2/3/18 YPRES RESERVOIR CEM	AGE 25.
ODGERS	Wm A	PTE	/525				ATT 8th DIV RE, 22nd, 18th BNS, CLASS Z RESERVE.
OGLE	Robt	PTE	/1060	SOUTH SHIELDS	SOUTH SHIELDS	24/10/17 ST STEPHENS SOUTH SHIELD AGE 30.	
OKEY	Sam	PTE	/128				TO 20th BN, STILL SERVING 1920.
OLIVER	James	LCPL	/739		10/12/15	KR para 392 15/10/19	
O'NEILL	Thos	SGT	/493	JARROW	JARROW	26/3/18 POZIERES MEM	
ORANGE	Jos T	PTE	/1081	BEDLINGTON	SOUTH SHIELDS	26/3/18 PARGNY BRIT CEM	AGE 21.
ORD	James	PTE	/179				ATT 253 TUN COY RE, 22nd BN, CLASS Z RESERVE.
OTTWELL	Geo H	PTE	/1082	SUNDERLAND	SOUTH SHIELDS	16/8/17 TYNE COT MEM	ATT 180 TUN COY RE, 22nd BN.
PALLISTER	Geo	PTE	/915				ATT ARMY SERVICE CORPS LAB COY, 18th, 1/7th BNS, CLASS Z RES
PARK	E N	PTE	/1083				AGE 32.IN 2 PLTN.
PARKER	Reg J	PTE	/374	SOUTHMOOR		11/4/19 RYHOPE ROAD CEM	
PARKER	Chas	CPL	/374				TO 1/7th BN, CLASS Z RESERVE.
PARKER	John	PTE	/395	MIDDLETON IN TEESDALE DURHAM 22/11/15			ATT 180 TUN COY RE, 22nd, 1/7th BN, CLASS Z RESERVE. MINER AGE 23 5'6". DESERTED 20/4/15 SCOTTON CAI
PARKIN	Jos W	PTE	/309		15/11/15	KR para 392 25/7/19	
PATTEN	Edwd	PTE	/900	WEST HARTLEPOOL	WEST HARTLEPOOL	24/9/16 DERNANCOURT COM CEM EXT	TO 12th BN (B COY) AGE 24 BORN CAMBRIDGE.
PATTISON	Robt	PTE	/1087	SOUTH SHIELDS	SOUTH SHIELDS	16/6/17 ARRAS MEM	TO NORTHUMBERLAND FUSILIERS(13th BN). NORTHBLD FUS No 46479
PAYLOR	Jos	PTE	/974	WILLINGTON	WILLINGTON	9/1/17 THIEPVAL MEM	
PAYNE	JohnE	PTE	/447	SPENNYMOOR	WEST HARTLEPOOL	13/8/16 VERMELLES BRIT CEM	AGE 20.
PEARSON	Wilf	PTE	/793				ATT 8th DIV RE, CLASS Z RESERVE.
PEART	Frank	PTE	/150	ST JOHNS CHAPEL			TO 1/7th BN, CLASS Z RESERVE.
PEART	Henry	PTE	/267	STANHOPE			TO 1/7th BN, CLASS Z RESERVE.
PEART	Emms	PTE	/307	WEARHEAD	13/11/15	KR para 392 3/12/18	AGE 22.

NAME	INITIAL	RANK	NUMBER	TOWN_VILL	DATE & PLACE ENL	DATE & CAUSE_DIS, DIED BURIED	TRANSFER NEW NUMBER DESERTED ETC
PEDELTY	Jos	PTE	/1085	CROOK			TO 19th, 22nd BNS, CLASS Z RESERVE.
PIGGIN	Jos	PTE	/331		15/11/15	KR para 392 26/2/19	ATT 180 TUN COY RE, 22nd BN, ARMY RESERVE CLASS P. AGE 23
PLACE	Thos	PTE	/535	HETTON LE HOLE	HOUGHTON LE SPRING	27/3/18 POZIERES MEM	
PLACE	Ernst	PTE	/976				TO ROYAL DEFENCE CORPS. RDC No 66289, IN FRANCE 16/6/16-12/11/16
PLANT	Frank	PTE	/8	HORDON COLLIERY			TO 12th, 22nd BNS, CLASS Z RESERVE.
PLATER	FredJ	PTE	/169	SOUTH SHIELDS	WEST HARTLEPOOL2/11/15		MINER AGE 19 5'3", DESERTED 24/4/16 SCOTTON CAMP.
PLOWS	Jos	PTE	/311	NEW SEAHAM	SEAHAM HARBOUR	24/10/16 THIEPVAL MEM	TO 12th, 22nd, 19th BNS. BORN SUNDERLAND
PORTER	John	PTE	/767	PENSHAW	SUNDERLAND	15/9/18 TYNE COT MEM	TO CLASS Z RESERVE.
PORTEUS	John	PTE	/1084				AGE 27.
PRESTON	Chas	PTE	/213	DARLINGTON	DARLINGTON	24/12/15 DARLINGTON WEST CEM	STILL SERVING 1921.
PRINCE	Peter	LSGT	/292				ATT ARMY SERVICE CORPS, 22nd, 1/7th BNS, CLASS Z RESERVE. TRANSPORT SECTION
PRINGLE	Jas	LCPL	/375	GATESHEAD			TO 2nd, 13th, 1/9th BNS, CLASS Z RESERVE.
PROBERT	Wm J	PTE	/1086	DAWDON			TO CLASS Z RESERVE.
QUEENAN	Fred	PTE	/718				ATT CRE 8th DIV, DIV CONVALECENT COY, 22nd BN. AGE 23
RAINE	Arth	PTE	/868	SUNDERLAND	DARLINGTON	31/3/18 MOREUIL COM CEM	TO 1/7th BN. CLASS Z RESERVE.
RAINE	JonthP	PTE	/376	WILLINGTON			ATT 170 TUN COY RE. AGE 27
RAINE	John	PTE	/943		10/12/15	KR para 392 6/4/18	TO CLASS Z RESERVE.
RAMSHAW	Marm	LCPL	/1068				TO 1/7th BN, CLASS Z RESERVE.
RANSOME		PTE	/154				TO 11th BN, CLASS Z RESERVE.
RANSON	Wm	PTE	/184				TO ARMY RESERVE CLASS W. AGE 22. DID NOT SERVE OVERSEAS
RATCLIFFE	John	PTE	/1088		10/11/15	KR para 392 30/5/17	TO CLASS Z RESERVE. PRISONER OF WAR
READDIE	Thos	PTE	/281	GATESHEAD			
REDPATH	JohnP	CPL	/134	BISHOP AUCKLAND	BISHOP AUCKLAND	28/10/16 THIEPVAL MEM	TO 1/7th BN, CLASS Z RESERVE.
REEVES	Frank	COMS	/412	CARLISLE			SHOWN AS DEAD ON MR? MISTAKE
RICHARDS	Henry	PTE	/28				TO CLASS Z RESERVE. AGE 24
RICHARDSON	Thos	PTE	/51	RYTON WOODSIDE		15/3/19 HOUGHTON LE SPRING	TO CLASS Z RESERVE. ALSO AT 58 MILTON ROAD WEST HARTLEPOOL AVL
RICHARDSON	Arth	PTE	/530	HOUGHTON LE SPRING			AGE 25
RICHARDSON	Chas	PTE	/89	TOW LAW			ATT 8th DIV RE, 18th, 14th, 1/5th BNS.
RICHARDSON	John	PTE	/944	CROOK	BISHOP AUCKLAND	10/11/16 ST SEVER CEM EXT ROUEN	TO 10th, 15th BNS. DESERTED 12/4/18
RICHARDSON	Jos	PTE	/763	DURHAM CITY		KR para 392	ATT 8th DIV RE, 18th, 14th, 1/5th BNS.
RICHARDSON	ThosW	PTE	/826	DAWDON			TO 1/7th BN, ATT 8th DIV HQ, 22nd CORPS HQ, CLASS Z RESERVE.
RICHARDSON	WaltH	PTE	/977	HOUGHTON LE SPRING			ATT 180 TUN COY RE, 22nd, 19th, 22nd BNS, CLASS Z RESERVE.
RICHARDSON	Amb	PTE	/1090	STAINDROP	BISHOP AUCKLAND 28/12/15		AGE 31 5'9", DESERTED 16/4/16 CATTERICK
RICHARDSON	Wm	PTE	/508	HETTON LE HOLE	HOUGHTON LE SPRING	20/6/17 DICKEBUSCH NEW MIL EXT	ATT 180 TUN COY RE, 22nd BN, AGE 28.LNER GOODS CLERK LEAMSIDE STATION
RIDLEY	JohnH	LCPL	/1089				TO 2nd, 22nd, 2nd BNS, ATT ASC(No 2 AHTD), 11th BN, CLASS Z.
RISING	Chas	PTE	/978	DURHAM CITY			TO 20th, 1/6th BN, CLASS Z RESERVE.
RITCHIE	Geo F	PTE	/348		22/10/15	KR para 392 25/9/17	TO DEPOT. AGE 26
ROBERTS	Thos	PTE	/48	BISHOP AUCKLAND	14/1/16	KR para 392 24/12/18	TO 18th, 19th, 10th, 1/7th, 3rd BNS. AGE 26
ROBERTS	Cyril	PTE	/677				TO CLASS Z RESERVE.
ROBINSON	Walt	PTE	/336				TO 11th, 22nd BNS, CLASS Z RESERVE.
ROBINSON	EdwdJ	CPL	/665				TO 1/7th BN, CLASS Z RESERVE.
ROBINSON	Robt	PTE	/698				TO CLASS Z RESERVE.
ROBINSON	Arth	PTE	/734				TO CLASS Z RESERVE.
ROBINSON	John	PTE	/807	FERRYHILL	11/12/15	KR para 392 1/10/18	TO 14th, 19th BNS. AGE 33
ROBINSON	Jos	PTE	/1001	USWORTH	20/12/97	SICK 17/6/16	DID NOT SERVE OVERSEAS.
ROBINSON	Cyril	PTE	/497		3/1/15	KR para 392 20/7/16	
ROBSON	Thos	PTE	/190	NEWBOTTLE	HOUGHTON LE SPRING 10/12/1	21/2/19	TO CLASS Z RESERVE. AGE 23, 5'6", 136LBS. LCPL
ROBSON	Thos	PTE	/773	KILLINGWORTH	GATESHEAD	23/10/16 BANCOURT MIL CEM	AGE 32
ROBSON	MattJ	PTE	/278				

INITIAL	RANK	NUMBER	TOWN_VILL	DATE & PLCACE ENL	DATE & CAUSE, DIS, DIED BURIED	TRANSFER NEW NUMBER DESERTED ETC
JohnW	PTE	736	DARLINGTON	22/12/15	KR para 392 23/11/17	TO DEPOT. AGE 26
Wm A	PTE	937	THORNLEY COLLIERY			ATT ARMY SERVICE CORPS(No 2 AHTD). 1/7th BN, CLASS Z RESERVE
Thos	PTE	532	WEST HARTLEPOOL			TO ROYAL ENGINEERS, WEST RIDING REGT, LABOUR CORPS BORN 1870. SERVED WITH 117 & 41 LAB COYS
Jas E	SGT	116	WEST HARTLEPOOL	17/1/16		TO 15th, 22nd BNS, CLASS Z RESERVE.
RichH	PTE	117	WEST HARTLEPOOL			TO 1/7th BN, CLASS Z RESERVE.
Henry	PTE	404	SOUTH SHIELDS	SUNDERLAND 23/11/15		LABOURER AGE 21 57". DESERTED 20/4/16.
JohnC	PTE	211				TO CLASS Z RESERVE.
James	PTE	925		8/12/15	KR para 392 29/3/19	TO 3rd BN. AGE 25
Sid	SGT	1133	HORDEN	WEST HARTLEPOOL	23/10/16 BANCOURT MIL CEM	BORN BATTERSEA, NOK 150 CHATSWORTH ROAD CHESTERFIELD.
Matt	PTE	441	RYHOPE	SUNDERLAND	26/3/18 MOREUIL COM CEM	ATT 8th DIV RE, 22nd BN.
Jas S	PTE	176				TO 20th, 1/7th BNS, CLASS Z RESERVE.
Wm	PTE	483	WEST HARTLEPOOL			ATT 8th DIV RE, TO 12th BN. DEAD ON MR
John	PTE	252	PRUDHOE	CHESTER LE STREET	23/10/16 THIEPVAL MEM	
Norm	SGT	151	ST JOHNS CHAPEL	28/10/15	KR para 392 23/12/18	AGE 22.
JohnW	SGT	173	HEBBURN		KR para 392	
Robt	PTE	901	SPENNYMOOOR	SPENNYMOOR	26/3/18 POZIERES MEM	IN IIi PLTN. AGE 28 BORN TUDHOE GRANGE.
Alex	CPL	38		19/10/15	KR para 392 19/2/19	TO 22nd BN.
Abt	PTE	926				ATT 180 TUN COY RE, CLASS Z RESERVE.
Thos	PTE	442	CASTLE EDEN	WEST HARTLEPOOL	27/5/18 SOISSONS MEM	BORN BRAWBY YORKS AGE 40.
Arth	SGT	1095				TO CLASS Z RESERVE.
Jas W	PTE	1142	EASINGTON COLLIERY			TO CLASS Z RESERVE. PRISONER OF WAR
Hugh	PTE	197	SOUTH SHIELDS	SOUTH SHIELDS	19/9/17 PROWSE POINT MIL CEM	TO 19th, 22nd BNS.
Wm	PTE	159	COATHAM MUNDEVILLE	DARLINGTON	27/5/18 SOISSONS MEM	TO 20th, 22nd BNS. BORN AYCLIFFE AGE 26
Wm	LCPL	738				COMMISSIONED 1/4/17
John	LCPL	413				TO CLASS Z RESERVE.
Walt	PTE	428				AGE 23.
Geo H	PTE	683	SUNDERLAND	SUNDERLAND	20/7/16 CAMBRIN CH YD EXT	STILL SERVING 9/3/20.
Jas	PTE	903	OLD PENSHAW			TO DEPOT. AGE 24
Geo	PTE	700	BIRMINGHAM	10/12/15	KR para 392 11/9/17	ATT 253 TUN COY RE, 22nd, 1/7th BNS, CLASS Z RESERVE.
Alf	PTE	938	MIDDLETON IN TEESDALE		27/4/18 POZIERES MEM	AGE 32
Peter	LSGT	195	WEST HARTLEPOOL	SOUTH SHIELDS	26/3/18 PARGNY BRIT CEM	TO 1/7th BN, ATT 2nd CANADIAN TRAMWAY COY, CLASS Z RESERVE.
Edwd	LCPL	1092	TYNE DOCK			TO DEPOT.
Wm	PTE	979	PENSHAW	9/12/15	GSW HEAD 24/11/16	STILL SERVING MARCH 1920. ALSO REG AT 89 VICTORIA ROAD
Abt	PTE	904	DARLINGTON			AGE 19 BORN PHILADELPHIA(USA OR COUNTY DURHAM??)
Geo	PTE	668	JARROW	JARROW	10/7/16 CAMBRIN CH YD EXT	
John	PTE	174	WEST HARTLEPOOL			COMMISSIONED 16/6/17.
WaltC	PTE	864				
Wm J	CPL	751	HIGH FELLING	22/10/15	KR para 392 6/12/18	AGE 37.
Geo W	LCPL	50		18/11/15	SICK 26/3/17	TO DEPOT.
And	PTE	1134	SUNNISIDE CROOK			TO 1/7th, 2/6th BNS, CLASS Z RESERVE. LCPL
Wm H	PTE	679	CROOK	CROOK	27/7/16 CAMBRIN CH YD EXT	AGE 24
Frank	PTE	902	HARTON			TO CLASS Z RESERVE.
David	PTE	250				TO 1/7th BN, CLASS Z RESERVE.
JohnJ	PTE	273				
Abt	PTE	353	WEST HARTLEPOOL		KR para 392	
Jack	PTE	414				TO 1/7th BN, CLASS Z RESERVE.
Herbt	PTE	692				TO 1/7th BN, CLASS Z RESERVE.
Percy	PTE	794			KR para 392	
Wm J	LCPL	795				TO 11th, 22nd, 1/7th BNS, CLASS Z RESERVE.

INITIAL	RANK	NUMBER	TOWN_VILL	DATE & PLCACE ENL	DATE & CAUSE_DIS, DIED BURIED	TRANSFER NEW NUMBER DESERTED ETC
Wm D	PTE	/846	SHINEY ROW	8/12/15	WOUNDS 21/5/17	TO 18th, 11th BN, CLASS Z RESERVE.
Jos B	PTE	/872				TO DEPOT.
Jas H	PTE	/980				TO 12th, 10th, 14th BNS, CLASS Z RESERVE.
Wm	PTE	/1022		10/12/15	KR para 392 21/11/17	TO CLASS Z RESERVE.
ThosC	PTE	/1023		7/12/15	KR para 392 12/6/17	TO DEPOT. AGE 30
JohnF	PTE	/860				TO ARMY RESERVE CLASS P.
Percy	SGT	/963				ATT 170 TC RE,35IBD, LAB CORPS(881 LAB COY),R DEFENCE CORPS. LAB CORPS No 409090. RDC No 90924
Thos	PTE	/421	WEST HARTLEPOOL	WEST HARTLEPOOL		FORMERLY 22117 HUSSARS AGE 23.
Syd G	CPL	/471	FULWELL		23/10/16 GUARDS CEM LESBOEUFS	TO 13th OFFICER CADET BN. COMMISSIONED 25/6/18.
Percy	PTE	/888	WEST HARTLEPOOL	WEST HARTLEPOOL		TO 1/7th, 1/9th, 1/7th BNS, CLASS Z RESERVE.
John	PTE	/1099		4/12/15	KR para 392 26/7/17	TO DEPOT. AGE 33
RobtG	PTE	/429				TO 1/7th BN, CLASS Z RESERVE.
Waltn	SGT	/330	LAMBTON			TO 3rd BN, CLASS Z RESERVE.
James	PTE	/705	HEBBURN	HEBBURN	13/3/17 FINS NEW BRIT CEM	ATT 170 TUN COY RE, 22nd BN.
Syd	PTE	/1145				TO 14th, 22nd BNS, CLASS Z RESERVE.
Henry	PTE	/224	HARRATON			TO 1/7th BN, CLASS Z RESERVE.
Wm	CPL	/96				ATT 253 TUN COY RE, 22nd BN, CLASS Z RESERVE.
Rich	PTE	/1002	KIMBLESWORTH	DURHAM	4/3/17 SAILLY SAILLISEL	ATT 180 TUN COY RE, 22nd BN. AGE 21
Geo A	SGT	/270				TO 18th, ATT 257 TUN COY RE, 22nd, 1/7th BNS, CLASS Z RESERV
ArthL	SGT	/377	HOWDEN LE WEAR			
Ralph	PTE	/941	TOW LAW	BISHOP AUCKLAND	23/10/16 THIEPVAL MEM	BORN WOLSINGHAM AGE 26.
RobtL	SGT	/377	HOWDEN LE WEAR			TO 1/7th BN, CLASS Z RESERVE.
John	PTE	/462				TO 15th BN, CLASS Z RESERVE.
Geo	SGT	/921		9/2/16	KR para 392 30/9/19	ATT 170 TUN COY RE.
John	PTE	/488	SOUTHWICK	SUNDERLAND	26/3/18 PARGNY BRIT CEM	TO 1/7th BN, CLASS Z RESERVE.
Wm	PTE	/1021				TO CLASS Z RESERVE.
Alex	PTE	/1003	JARROW			ATT 180 TUN COY RE, 22nd BN, CLASS Z RESERVE.
James	PTE	/1004	BYERS GREEN			TO CLASS Z RESERVE. AWOI
RobtH	CSM	/312				TO CLASS Z RESERVE.
Lambt	PTE	/784				TO 1/7th BN, CLASS Z RESERVE.
Thos	SGT	/683		24/11/15	KR para 392 12/11/17	TO ARMY RESERVE CLASS W. AGE 29
Abt	PTE	/1093				ATT 8th DIV RE.ARMY SERVICE CORPS(No 2 AHTD);1/7th BN.Z RES
John	PTE	/144		SUNDERLAND	28/11/15 NORTH CEM WEST HARTLEPOOL	TO 10th, 1/7th BN, CLASS Z RESERVE.
Geo W	PTE	/378	SEAHAM HARBOUR			TO 1/7th BN, CLASS Z RESERVE.
Alf	PTE	/906				STEWART IN AVL.
JohnT	SGT	/275		GATESHEAD	26/4/18 POZIERES MEM	TO CLASS Z RESERVE.
JohnS	PTE	/454	USWORTH			TO ARMY RESERVE CLASS P. AGE 23
James	PTE	/1122				ATT CRE 8th DIV, 22nd BN, CLASS Z RESERVE.
John	PTE	/255		9/11/15	KR para 392 31/3/19	TO 1/7th BN, CLASS Z RESERVE.
RobtW	PTE	/214	BLACKWELL			TO 1/7th BN, CLASS Z RESERVE.
Robt	PTE	/1020	THORNLEY			TO CLASS Z RESERVE. LCPL
James	PTE	/1102				TO ROYAL DEFENCE CORPS. IN FRANCE 17/6/16-29/3/18. RDC No 93215
Fred	PTE	/505	THROSTON			BORN BRANDON AGE 31.
Steph	PTE	/45				
Arth	PTE	/1103	CROXDALE	DURHAM	25/12/16 ETAPLES MIL CEM	AGE 29.
Geo B	CPL	/379	HOWDEN LE WEAR			
Abt	PTE	/1035	SKELTON	FERRYHILL	30/7/16 CAMBRIN CH YD EXT	AGE 27. IN III PLTN
Emst	PTE	/685	SEAHAM HARBOUR	SEAHAM HARBOUR	27/5/18 SOISONNS MEM	
Vic	SGT	/349				ATT 170 TUN COY RE, 22nd BN, COMMISSION BORDER REGT 28/5/18

NAME	INITIAL	RANK	NUMBER	TOWN_VILL	DATE & PLACE ENL	DATE & CAUSE_DIS, DIED BURIED	TRANSFER NEW NUMBER DESERTED ETC
TAYLOR	Thos	PTE	/819	DURHAM CITY	WEST HARTLEPOOL	26/3/18 POZIERES MEM	ATT 8th DIV RE, 22nd, 1/7th BNS, CLASS Z RESERVE.
TEECE	Wm	PTE	/192	NORTH ORMESBY	WEST HARTLEPOOL	14/11/16 AIF BURIAL GROUND FLERS	AGE 29.
TEMPLE	H	PTE	/268	WEST HARTLEPOOL	9/12/15	WOUNDS 30/4/17	TO DEPOT.
THEW	Luke	PTE	/673				ATT 8th DIV ASC, TO 20th, 19th, 15th BNS, CLASS Z RESERVE.
THIRKETTLE	Geo	PTE	/727				TO RIFLE BRIGADE(1/5th BN LONDON REGT). RIFLE BDE No 45292. AGE 23
THOMPSON	Fredk	PTE	/210	GATESHEAD		15/6/18 AUBIGNY COM CEM EXT	ATT 8th DIV RE, 11th BN, CLASS Z RESERVE.
THOMPSON	Wm	PTE	/840		15/2/16		TO DEPOT. AGE 24
THOMPSON	Thos	LCPL	/913			KR para 392 20/8/17	TO 1/7th BN, CLASS Z RESERVE.
THOMPSON	John	LCPL	/1104				
THOMSON	James	PTE	/820			KR para 392	
TINDALE	Wm Ed	PTE	/204	RAVENSWORTH	JARROW	29/10/16 THIEPVAL MEM	AGE 21.
TINKLER	Henry	PTE	/908		9/12/15	KR para 392 22/2/18	ATT 8th DIV RE, 22nd BN, CLASS Z RESERVE
TINLIN	JohnR	PTE	/524	SEAHAM			TO 1/7th BN, CLASS Z RESERVE.
TODD	John	PTE	/118	WEST HARTLEPOOL			TO 20th, 22nd, 1/7th BNS, CLASS Z RESERVE.
TONES	John	PTE	/922	WEST HARTLEPOOL	9/12/15	KR para 392 16/11/17	ATT 170 TUN COY RE. LCPL. AGE 27
TRIBBECK	Chas	PTE	/124		10/11/15	KR para 392 15/12/17	TO DEPOT. AGE 35
TROTTER	Ernst	LCPL	/430	DURHAM CITY			TO 1/7th BN, CLASS Z RESERVE. CPL
TURNBULL	Harry	SGT	/15	CHESTER LE STREET	HOUGHTON LE SPRING	4/3/17 HEM FARM MIL CEM	BORN WINDSOR AGE 27
TURNBULL	Wm S	CPL	/53	NEWBOTTLE	23/10/15	KR para 392 19/10/17	AGE 43.
TURNBULL	Thos	PTE	/302	SUNDERLAND	SUNDERLAND	26/3/18 POZIERES MEM	
TURNBULL	Hugh	PTE	/229	WEST HARTLEPOOL			ATT 170 TUN COY RE, 1/7th BN, CLASS Z RESERVE.
TURNER	Fred	PTE	/172			KR para 392 26/2/19	TO ARMY RESERVE CLASS P. AGE 23
TURNER	Alex	PTE	/796				TO CLASS Z RESERVE.
TWEEDALE	Arth	PTE	/1025				TO CLASS Z RESERVE.
TYSON	John	SGT	/431	SUNDERLAND	SUNDERLAND	26/4/18 POZIERES MEM	ATT 8th DIV RE, CLASS Z RESERVE. AGE 29
UMPELBY	Thos	PTE	/850				TO 13th, 1/9th BNS, CLASS Z RESERVE.
URCH	Henry	PTE	/856		4/12/15	KR para 392 22/2/18	AGE 29
URQUHART	ThosH	LCPL	/797				TO 18th, 22nd BNS, CLASS Z RESERVE.
USHER	Chas	PTE	/816	CHILTON			TO 12th BN, CLASS Z RESERVE.
USHER	Matt	PTE	/75		25/10/15	KR para 392 31/1/17	TO DEPOT. AGE 26
VARLEY	Percy	PTE	/981				TO CLASS Z RESERVE.
VASEY	Fred	PTE	/160	SACRISTON	1/11/15	SICK 23/6/16	TO 16th BN. DID NOT SERVE OVERSEAS
VOWELL	David	PTE	/775	SHINY ROW	SUNDERLAND	23/10/16 THIEPVAL MEM	AGE 23
WADE	John	LCPL	/752	DARLINGTON	11/12/15	KR para 392 11/3/19	AGE 26 PRISONER OF WAR. LIVING 10 DANESBURY TERRACE??
WAGGOTT	JohnA	PTE	/910	CHESTER LE STREET	DURHAM	26/3/18 POZIERES MEM	TO CLASS Z RESERVE.
WALKER	Henry	PTE	/446	WEST HARTLEPOOL			ATT NOTTS & DERBY REGT(3rd BN), CLASS Z RESERVE.
WALKINGTON	John	PTE	/911	CROOK	CROOK	20/2/18 YPRES RESERVOIR CEM	BORN BISHOP WILTON YORKS.
WALLACE	James	PTE	/49				TO 1/7th BN, CLASS Z RESERVE.
WALLINGER	Herbt	PTE	/800	DARLINGTON	3/12/15	KR para 392 11/3/19	TO 3rd BN. AGE 28
WALLS	James	PTE	/1105	SUNDERLAND	SUNDERLAND	24/10/16 BENAFRAY WOOD BRIT CEM	AGE 28
WALSH	Thos	LCPL	/158	SOUTH SHIELDS	SOUTH SHIELDS	28/10/16 THIEPVAL MEM	
WALTON	Stan	CPL	/827				COMMISSIONED 31/1/17.
WANLESS	James	PTE	/105		26/10/15	KR para 392 29/10/17	AGE 40.
WARD	Jim	PTE	/145	WEST HARTLEPOOL	WEST HARTLEPOOL	4/3/17 HEM FARM MIL CEM	AGE 19
WARD	Thos	PTE	/94	TOW LAW	BISHOP AUCKLAND	11/11/16 GUARDS CEM LESBOEUFS	AGE 23
WARD	Arth	PTE	/264				ATT ROYAL ENGINEERS, 1/7th BN, CLASS Z RESERVE.
WARD	Geo H	PTE	/463				TO CLASS Z RESERVE.
WATSON	Ernst	CPL	/940				TO 20th BN, CLASS Z RESERVE.